READINGS IN

D0205229

Adult Development and Aging

K. Warner Schaie
The Pennsylvania State University

James Geiwitz

LITTLE, BROWN AND COMPANY

Boston   Toronto

Library of Congress Catalog Card No. 81-86377

ISBN 0-316-772720

9 8 7 6 5 4 3 2 1

MV

Published simultaneously in Canada
by Little, Brown & Company (Canada) Limited

Printed in the United States of America

Readings in
Adult Development
and Aging

Preface

The purpose of a college textbook cannot and should not be merely to arouse interest and provide entertainment under the guise of scientific communication. It should introduce students to the type and range of inquiry current in the field. In creating this book of readings as well as our textbook, *Adult Development and Aging,* we have drawn from the substantial body of literature available in our field of study. We offer this collection of articles and excerpted chapters as a representation of the scholarly inquiry and as a convenient source of relevant and stimulating readings for courses in adult development and for practitioners who work in the adulthood field. Although the selections in this volume are keyed to the suggested readings in our textbook, this book can be used as a core text for a course or as an adjunct to other adult development books.

We have attempted in both our textbook and this book of readings to integrate the processes inherent in development with the natural progression of events across adult life. The sequencing of the contents of this book reflects this integration. After the opening section—background, theoretical issues, and methodology—follows a series of topical sections. Each focuses on a particular issue, such as careers or intellectual development across the years of adulthood. Interspersed with the topics are three episodic sections looking at the main segments of adult life. The readings within both the topical and episodic sections highlight key questions that researchers consider and feature the salient work being done in our field.

Each major section in this book is preceded by a brief introduction summarizing the key issues and indicating why a selection was chosen. In general, we have tried to choose an overview essay that might be assigned prior to lecture coverage, a relevant research article, and where possible an integrative review essay to deepen understanding. At the end of each section we provide suggestions for one or more additional readings that because of their length or complexity were not included here.

We have tried to augment the usefulness of this book of readings by listing major handbook and journal resources that students might use in preparing term papers or other class projects. This list appears at the end of the book.

The choice of readings in this collection is obviously influenced by the point of view of the editors. We have nevertheless attempted to present a balanced selection of relevant readings in an interdisciplinary framework. We hope students and instructors will enjoy these readings as much as we enjoyed assembling them.

Our thanks are due to Pat Hollander, who provided the technical support for assembling the readings and obtained the necessary permissions, and to our wives, Sherry Willis and Bobbie Klatzky, who patiently supported us in the work that led to this volume and the related textbook.

K. Warner Schaie
James Geiwitz

Contents

Readings in
Adult Development
and Aging

Historical Background, Theoretical Issues, and Methodology

The scientific study of adult development and aging has surprisingly recent origins. One reason is that, in the past, people simply assumed the adult years to be a time of stability, especially in one's career, family life, and personality. Another reason is that, in the past, there were very few elderly citizens, so that aging was a less noticeable societal issue.

The first selection in this section sets the stage by reviewing the characteristics of today's elderly and by projecting what the elderly will look like in the coming decade. The article is an adaptation of an invited address given by the first editor (*K. Warner Schaie*) to an annual meeting of the American Society of Hospital Social Work Directors. It consequently emphasizes those characteristics of the elderly which make them a special concern of health care and human services professionals.

Theories of adult development attempt to explain changes with age and also differences in such changes between individuals or groups. The second selection, by *Paul B. Baltes*, links the historical background of lifespan developmental psychology to theoretical issues and the development of subject–matter–appropriate research methodologies. The first issue discussed in depth is the need to reconceptualize the biological growth models traditionally used to describe child development in order to extend the concept of development into adulthood. Next, Baltes considers different influences on development, introducing the concepts of normative influences, normative age-graded influences, and normative history-graded influences. He then shows how ontogenetic and cultural influences can jointly effect development, and finally, briefly suggests the need for research methods appropriate to the special needs of the developmental sciences.

One of the key distinctions in research methodology for studies of adult development is between *cross-sectional* and *longitudinal* designs. Cross-sectional designs compare several age groups (*cohorts*) at the same time and yield data on *age differences*. Longitudinal designs compare members of the same cohort at different times and therefore yield *age differences*. It is also possible to compare two groups of persons of the same age to determine whether or not behavior at a given age remains constant over time, a design called *time-lag*. *K. Warner Schaie* tries to clear up the confusion between these data-gathering strategies, which will frequently be mentioned in many of the selections to follow. He also calls attention to how these designs relate to alternate models of aging.

Additional Suggested Readings

Baltes, P. B., Reese, H. W., & Nesselroade, J. R. *Life-span developmental psychology: Introduction to research methods.* Belmont, Calif.: Wadsworth, 1977.

   A thorough treatment of research designs and problems for studies of developmental problems, not typically found in standard psychological statistics or research design volumes. Written by researchers active in psychological research on adults.

Bengtson, V. L., Kasschau, P. L., & Ragan, P. K. The impact of social structure on aging individuals. In J. E. Birren & K. W. Schaie (eds.), *Handbook of the psychology of aging.* New York: Van Nostrand Reinhold, 1977, pp. 328–353.

   Provides a social-psychological background for our understanding of adult development by discussing issues such as the social definition of time and aging, group variations in patterns of aging, and the effect of social change.

Riegel, K. F. History of psychological gerontology. In J. E. Birren & K. W. Schaie (eds.), *Handbook of the psychology of aging.* New York: Van Nostrand Reinhold, 1977, pp. 70–102.

   A scholarly account of the Anglo-American, Continental European, and dialectic approaches to the study of psychological development in adulthood.

America's Elderly in the Coming Decade

K. WARNER SCHAIE

The elderly are described as a population of concern to health care and human services professionals. The current situation of the elderly population is summarized in terms of their demographic and selected psychological characteristics. Projections are made with respect to the characteristics of the elderly population in the next decade. Implications for the planning of professional services for the future elderly are discussed with regard to stereotypes about old age, health education, transition from the world of work and extending the health care system into the community.

Introduction

The topic covered in this presentation concerns what I believe to be one of the central issues of our time, and one which has preoccupied my professional activities over the past quarter century. I speak to you from the background of a basic scientist who has tried to understand the facts of human psychological aging both in the laboratory and in field research. I also speak to you as a research administrator who has administered programs of rather applied intervention and evaluation research and who has had to keep in mind societal priorities and available resources. Last but not least I speak to you as an educator most broadly defined, concerned with the training of professionals, as well as with the translation of our knowledge base for the use of professionals, and for the development of policy positions. My presentation will cover three main topics: First, I shall review the current situation of the elderly population. In this context I will re-

mind you that this situation is obviously in flux, and that the elderly of the future will be somewhat different and have somewhat different needs than those you encounter today. Secondly, I will attempt some cautious projections of needs of the elderly in the next decade, emphasizing consequences of demographic and epidemiological changes. Finally, I will try to offer some suggestions as to the services which must be planned by professional groups concerned with the well-being of the elderly to meet the projected needs.

The needs of populations at risk such as those most likely seen by welfare agencies or in hospitals are often very different from those of persons of the same age who are at a level of physiological well-being and stability. Nevertheless, we must begin by considering some broad population characteristics, and discuss what we can expect for the typical older person, before we can deal with specific aspects caused by the added stress of physiological disease or psychopathology.

Source: Adapted from Schaie, K. W. America's elderly in the coming decade. Invited address to the annual meeting of the American Society of Hospital Social Work Directors, Denver, Colorado, August 1980.

The Elderly as a Population of Concern to Professionals

Researchers and practitioners in the human services fields at the beginning of the development of their professions focused primarily upon the early stages of life, only slowly shifting their concern from infancy and childhood on towards adolescence, and then to the period of family establishment. What came beyond was largely ignored, and for good reasons. Consider that in the year 1900 only 28 percent of America's population, just slightly above one fourth, had passed the 35th year of age, and no more than a trivial 3 percent had reached or exceeded the magical age of 65, which is often thought of in our culture as the threshold of old age (Knox, 1977). But by contrast, today, in 1980, 45 percent of our population has passed age 35, and 11 percent are 65 years of age or above. Over the same period of time, average life expectancy in the United States has improved from an average of 51.1 years to 76.4 years for women, and from an average of 48.2 years to 68.7 years for men. I wonder how many of you are aware of the little published fact that the U.S. census in 1970 identified about 110,600 Americans who had reached the age of 100 years or above?

In the past, surviving into old age was a relatively rare phenomenon and one often restricted only to the most hardy and environmentally favored, indeed that rare breed of person that very likely would require little professional attention throughout their life. Moreover, early professional opinion held that when older persons suffered severe disease or psychopathology, successful intervention was likely to be difficult, and with postintervention life expectancy suspected to be brief, often not deemed worthy of the professional's efforts and energy. To be quite frank, many professionals still hold the stereotype of the "old crock" who should be humored and gotten

rid of as quickly as possible because successful treatment outcome is not thought to be likely. Also many old persons are found to be highly suspicious of the health-related human services professions. As a consequence we find that mutually aversive stereotypes have interfered with the quality provision of services to the elderly in the public sector, while apprehension as to the oldsters' lack of economic resources may often have inappropriately deterred referral within the context of private practice.

Obviously these stereotypes require revision when we examine the factual situation of today's elderly. On the one hand they remain one of our critical under-served population sub-groups, but on the other, those among the elderly who need massive services are probably, as will become clearer as we proceed, a relatively small proportion of the total group. Typically they are those who are in double or triple jeopardy: With an increasingly fragile physiology, these are the individuals who because of poverty and/or other disadvantages have likely been at risk as well when they were younger. What then are some of the salient characteristics of today's elderly?

During the past two decades there has been a knowledge explosion in the developmental sciences concerned with human age changes (cf. Binstock & Shanas, 1976; Birren & Schaie, 1977; Birren & Sloane, 1980; Busse & Blazer, 1980; Finch & Hayflick, 1977). Much of the material which has been gathered suggests that old age is likely to be experienced by most persons in developed societies. However, it suggests also that our knowledge based on the behavior of young adults cannot be generalized to the elderly with impunity because there are many normative as well as individualized age changes and because there are marked generational differences. Further, it is clear that old age for most need not be and is not likely to be a disastrous experience, particularly if there is an increasing emphasis on primary prevention and prompt intervention when personal catastrophes do appear imminent. To provide adequate professional services, however, it is necessary to be aware of some of the normative physiological and behavioral changes that do occur as people move from middle to old age, and from early old age to the fragile and often dependent period of the eighties and nineties.

The Current Situation of the Elderly Population

I will now briefly review some of the facts about the current elderly as gleaned from recent statistics and research. I will begin with some gross demographic facts, and then proceed to discuss some salient physiological and psychological characteristics of the typical elderly.

How many people are we talking about? The 1970 census indicated that there were roughly 20 million persons 65 or older; of these about 8 million were over 75. We must differentiate immediately by sex, for as we know because of differential life expectancies there are more older women than men. For the total group, there were approximately 58 percent women and 42 percent men, or a ratio of approximately 10 women to 7 men. For the group over 75 the sex ratio was even less favorable; i.e., there were 61 percent women and 39 percent men, or a ratio of about 10 women to 6 men. Where do the elderly live? According to the 1970 census, 73 percent live in urban and 27 percent in rural areas. However, within the urban setting the aged are over-represented in small towns and the inner city, while they are underrepresented in suburbia. In rural areas they are often concentrated in small farming communities.

Although the typical living arrangement in the United States for most persons is to live with one or more relatives, typically within the nuclear family setting, this is an arrangement which due to loss of spouse,

distance and often the desire to maintain independence, is far from true for today's elderly. In the age range from 45 to 54 only 7 percent of the men and 8 percent of the women live by themselves. This figure rises for the young-old, those between 65 and 74, to 12 percent for the men and 36 percent for the women. For the old-old, past 75, these figures are 21 percent and 48 percent respectively.

What about the economic status of the elderly? It is certainly not the most affluent, but it has improved markedly. In 1959 as many as 35 percent of the elderly were considered to be below the poverty line. In 1976 that percentage has been reduced to 15 percent. Of course, these are overall figures. Those in double jeopardy for being old and black, for example, improved also but much less so. In 1959 62 percent of the black elderly were below the poverty line; this number had been cut substantially by 1976, but still amounted to 35 percent of that group.

What about the general status of health of the older population? Obviously the probability of physiological and psychological pathology much increases as we get older. It is well known that there is increased incidence of hospitalization and utilization of health services by the elderly. What might come as somewhat of a surprise though, are the data upon the effect of illness. For the aged, these data relate particularly to the incidence and effects of chronic diseases. Now if we take the overall figures, matters seem quite grim. While only about 20 percent of individuals under age 17 have one or more chronic conditions, for those over 65 years the figure is a whopping 81 percent. But matters look far less calamitous if we consider the impact of chronic conditions. When we consider a person's major activities to include such matters as the ability to work, to keep house or to engage in educational activities, we find that only 26 percent of the elderly are limited in amount or kind of major activity and only 16 percent are unable to carry on major activities of daily living. That, however, is still a formidable proportion and up from about 2 percent for the general population. Nevertheless, if we wish to accent the positive we must note the reverse side of the coin, namely that 84 percent or more than four out of every five elderly are capable of engaging in the major activities of daily living.

Since I am not a physician or biological scientist, I will refrain from describing physiological aspects of old age in detail. Instead, I would like to alert you, quite selectively, to some important physiological changes that do impact upon the behavior and adaptive capabilities of today's elderly. These include changes in sensory and perceptual capacity, changes in energy level and the impact of cardiovascular disease on behavior.

As we all know both visual and auditory acuity declines with age. Most elderly individuals do compensate to a great extent by means of eyeglasses for changes in vision, and a lesser number by means of hearing aids for decreasing sensitivity of the auditory apparatus. What is often forgotten is that compensation for visual or auditory acuity does not necessarily compensate for other aspects of sensory and perceptual loss. Older persons have reduced peripheral vision, their color discrimination is reduced, accommodation takes a longer period of time, and the older eye is more sensitive to glare. These problems, even though some compensation by appropriate environmental engineering is possible, create safety hazards, reduce mobility at night, and are likely to induce fatigue sooner than for the young. Similarly, hearing loss has byproducts such as increased difficulty in discriminating speech sounds, and distinguishing signals from noise. There is interference with optimal communication, often to the extent of inducing paranoid ideations. Another age change of consequence is the slowing of

perceptual speed. The older person requires more scanning time to digest information, usually requires more built-in redundancy in new information to be sure it will be properly encoded and retained, and as a result we often cannot take for granted that instructions and information have actually penetrated into the older nervous system, under conditions optimal for younger individuals.

Without doubt, one of the first cues of the onset of consequential physiological aging is the subjective and objective experience of lowered energy level. Although this may often be due to adopting a non-optimal sedentary or low-activity life style and may be reversible through appropriate programs of fitness maintenance, it is nevertheless true that perceived low energy will negatively affect such diverse behaviors as the initiation of sexual activity, participation in intellectually stimulating and physically invigorating activities, or the development and replacement of friendship or interest patterns.

Of importance also is the high probability of moderate disturbances of the circulatory system with increasing age. There is a close interaction of the cardiac system and the brain in controlling voluntary behavior. Even small changes in efficient blood-flow and cardiac output may therefore affect behavioral competency. Indeed, formal evidence is beginning to amass that at least some of the cognitive deficit thought to be inevitable in old age may be directly linkable to specific cardiovascular problems.

What about directly observable changes in behavioral competence in today's elderly? Here we must immediately raise the important distinction between age-related decline and obsolescence due to tremendous changes in the requirements to cope successfully with an ever more complicated technological society. Once again we must distinguish between the young-old (to about age 75) and the old-old. The former show relatively little decline from previous levels of functioning, but they compare unfavorably with more recently born persons, because, on average, they have had less education, poorer nutritional levels, and less favorable environments than has been true for more recent generations. Because of the sensory and other physiological changes discussed earlier, however, psychological variables do show decline in the old-old. Nevertheless, these changes within persons are quite modest until the high eighties are reached.

But what about the popular stereotype, that senility will catch up with us if we get but old enough? The epidemiological data suggest that this stereotype is simply false. The best data so far estimate that only 6 to 8 percent of those over 65 suffer from organic mental disorders; however, this figure increases to 20 percent for those over 80 (Kay, 1972), once again suggesting that the major ravages of aging appear rather late. But even for the old-old only 1 in 5 currently is clearly demented. Because of severe diagnostic problems in distinguishing between depression and the organic disorders, these figures may even be an overstatement. It is depression, particularly reactive depression, and alcoholism which are conditions of growing concern, as we find larger and larger groups of individuals retiring from active participation in society to a condition of rolelessness and concomitant drop in self-esteem as well as a deterioration of the persons' life-long defenses against anxiety in the face of radically altered conditions of living, and frequently loss of loved ones and social support networks.

To summarize then, today's older population consists largely of individuals who on average are not poor, are in reasonable health, are heavily concentrated in the inner city and rural communities and will live longer than previous generations. We distinguished between the young-old, who except for being mostly retired and having experienced modest decline in physiological

and psychological capabilities, are really not that different from the middle aged, and the old-old, who have on average suffered significant decline and among whom we find the larger proportion of individuals requiring professional services.

The Elderly in the Next Decade

Planning services for future generations of children is often difficult because we have no good handle on future fertility rates or the characteristics of generations of children as yet unborn. The gerontologist has the advantage that all of his future clients are already in existence, albeit now at different life stages. Thus barring unforeseen wars and natural catastrophes it is currently possible to estimate fairly accurately how many people will reach age 65, for example, at any given time through the year 2045. We know therefore that by 1990 the number of people above age 65 in the United States will have increased by another 5 million to just under 30 million persons, and their proportion in the population will have risen another percentage point, to approximately 12 percent of the total. Important particularly for this group, however, is the fact that the gain will be disproportionately made up of the old-old, those requiring more services. On the other hand, we also know that those reaching the conventional limits of old age during the next decade will be a somewhat different population from today's elderly. The new group reaching old age will be the first generation of elderly born past World War I. This means that they will be better educated, in general, having received better early health care than the preceding generation, and that there will be a much smaller proportion that is foreign born.

While the typical older person today has had a grade school education or less, during the next decade we will see that average level rise to at least some high school education.

Today's typical older person has been a blue collar or semi-skilled worker, or has spent much of his or her early life in farming occupations. Because of shifting technology, a far greater number of persons now retiring have been involved in high technology and/or white collar occupations. Many more women now reaching old age will have held a job, frequently having returned to the world of work after their children left home, and the group of persons with retirement-related problems will no longer be predominantly male.

Not only will the elderly of the next decade be better educated, but they will also have greater economic resources, and what is of concern to professionals, much higher expectations of the quality of life—and of professional services—to be experienced in old age. These expectations may indeed be, and here is a potential source of future social conflict, far in excess of what is readily available at the present stage of our knowledge and of service facilities, or what is within the economic resources of our society. As a consequence, we may expect increasing difficulties for the social security, Medicare, and private pension systems. Maintaining inflation-adjusted current benefit levels might require greater contributions by those in the work force than can be sustained by the implicit contract between the generations. Keep in mind that the benefits for the older generation must always be financed by the younger generations. Agonizing choices may therefore lie ahead for us—including those which may lead to inter-generational conflict—unless we recognize the economic realities imposed by the changing demography. If retirement benefits cannot be maintained at current levels, this would likely result in a shift from ever earlier retirement to longer work lives. The changes in laws concerned with mandatory retirement—in California, Maine or for federal civil servants there is now none, and in the rest of the nation it has recently been lifted to age 70—will become translated into changing retirement practices in the next decade. While a longer work life may be economically and psychologically beneficial for many older persons, such changes may also entail additional health risks and occupational safety hazards as yet hard to surmise.

Another consequence of a more energetic and better educated group of the young-old is likely to be their increasing militancy and participation in the political process, as witnessed by the increasing importance of groups such as the Gray Panthers, the American Association of Retired Persons and others. But in the professional service sector we may also expect to see older persons who will be less docile, who will demand full participation in the treatment planning process, and who will become increasingly litigious. Physicians will have to be much more careful in maintaining their patient relations, and ancilliary health personnel, particularly those concerned with making decisions for admission or refusal of treatment programs, or of milieu interventions, will become increasingly liable to legitimate questioning as well as harassment by means of malpractice suits.

A further change of concern to professionals serving the elderly is the changing structure of the family network which can be called upon to support older persons in need. Note that the increasing trend to smaller families has the corresponding result that in old age the number of older sick persons with one or more younger healthy siblings will decrease, a problem of particular concern to older women who must expect to outlive their spouses. This problem is, of course, particularly severe for older persons without children. But what is true for all is that the increasing length of life and the deferral of significant dependency upon others into very old age must mean that the children caring for their aged parents may themselves be aged at that point where maximum effort for care is required. Indeed, four generation families are becoming more frequent and five generation families are no longer unknown. And with ever smaller families, the future means that the middle-aged will have to work hard to finance the raising of their children and the support of the retired, while the young-old may frequently spend a significant portion of what should be a very enjoyable and rewarding period in caring for their fragile old-old parents!

As I indicated earlier, past generations of elderly have been somewhat suspicious of professional service resources, and in the welfare sector have often been reluctant to take full advantage of services they are entitled to because of the mistaken notions that such use would involve accepting charity or admitting to personal incompetence. I would predict a radical change in these attitudes for the next cohort of elderly. This change will mean increasing pressures for service. And this pressure will be felt most strongly in the mental health and ancillary health professions sectors. Especially on both coasts, we will have a group of older people who during midlife learned the acceptability of receiving professional counseling and/or psychotherapy. Thus we can expect during the next decade that there will be an increasing demand for mental health and other supportive services, not just to deal with catastrophes but to assist with the relatively minor neuroses and discomforts which accompany changing life status and life roles.

To summarize, the elderly of the nineteen-eighties will increase in number, particularly in the old-old category. The new young-old will be healthier, better educated, more resourceful, but also more demanding. They will require a new response from the health care system, in that they will be more sophisticated and more demanding consumers, and in particular they will be more likely to use mental health and other supportive health services.

How Should Professionals Plan to Meet the Needs of the Elderly in the Coming Decade?

I believe that the facts about the elderly as they hold today and the manner in which they will change in the coming decade suggest a clear challenge to the practice and training of professionals in the health and health-related disciplines. To understand the directions in which we need to proceed, we must emphasize at least dramatic changes in the provision of services for the elderly. The first is the fact that the population at highest risk has become the very old; the young-old requiring institutional care will not differ markedly from similar patients in mid-life. The second change is that health care for the chronically ill (a large portion of the elderly requiring services) is moving from institutions into the community. Our first response when faced with dependent elderly clients will now typically be to attempt provision of services in their home rather than immediate institutionalization. And the third change is the increasing sophistication and energy of the community-dwelling elderly who demand inclusion and primary roles in their own care.

The response to these changes in my judgment makes substantial demands upon health professionals as educators, both of themselves and of their client population. An extensive effort at primary prevention is needed here if only to conserve the resources that could be spent upon inappropriate care. All of these efforts must be based on the understanding that working with older individuals must begin in late middle age, when some of the transitions begin, unsuccessful resolutions of which result in dysfunction requiring professional services in later life. This effort as I see it must occur in at least three areas: Education of the media and the public services sector; health education; and support of the transition from the world of work.

Stereotypes About Old Age

Many of the disabilities of early old age are directly related to stereotypes about aging which become self-fulfilling prophecies. Health professionals tend to deal primarily with the small proportion of elderly who are truly disabled and disadvantaged. To be able to distinguish aging and other non-age related conditions it is important to provide opportunities for health professionals to obtain experience with the 95% of the elderly population who are not institutionalized, to recognize that most elderly can be and are active participants in our society. At the same time it is important to convey a proper understanding to health professionals regarding the modest sensory deficits as well as interpersonal problems related to life-role changes which may lead to an all too frequent somatization of psychological concerns. The bottom line must simply be to inculcate the attitude that elderly clients should be valued as much as the young and that they deserve high quality service and attention.

Health Education

An increasingly successful job is being done to convince the general public that dietary, smoking and drinking behaviors must be controlled in mid-life to assure physical fitness in old age. This effort must be continued with increased vigor, to enlist the elderly themselves in the prevention of disabling conditions. Unfortunately we have been far less successful in preventive education in the mental health area. And here it is where a sustained effort will be required to

reduce health facility utilization by the elderly. The effort must begin by urging older individuals to monitor their own sensory changes and to seek out services to provide adequate compensation by the regular fitting and modification of eyeglasses and hearing aids, as well as suitable modification of their living environments to maximize good vision and audition. It is important further to teach older individuals how to manage stress and conserve their personal energy. And the public must be sold on the reality that mental health problems in later life are as important and worth treating as at younger ages. The formal educational system must be enlisted to offer ways for older persons to reduce their realistic feelings of bewilderment and obsolescence in a world full of "Future Shock." Educational and community resources allocated to maintaining the meaning and quality of life for the elderly may be quite cheap when compared to the health care costs likely to arise when psychological and spiritual well-being are neglected.

Transition from the World of Work

Many of the problems of the young-old result from an inadequately handled transition from the full involvement with the world of work to an enforced leisure role. Since retirement in the future will become a complex negotiated process, it is likely that the health care system will have to become more directly involved in diagnostic appraisal leading to the retirement decision as well as to coping with the problems arising upon retirement. It is likely that social workers and psychologists will bear the brunt of these new demands, but all sectors of the health care and health-related professions will need to become heavily involved with preretirement counseling and post-retirement support systems, both within industrial settings and in the community.

Extending the Health Care System into the Community

Our emphasis on primary prevention should not overshadow the fact that many old persons face physiological crises as well as the fact that increasingly fragile organisms require increased maintenance and support. With older persons, we must be alert that the problem coming to professional attention will typically be the tip of the iceberg. Most physiological problems require change in life-styles or environmental support, and most behavioral problems have physical concomitants. During the next decade we need to provide better integrated systems for community care, including programmed sequences from totally independent to more or less dependent existence through a variety of intermediate settings. Such systems of care and support must be buttressed by adequate diagnostic assessment facilities geared to comprehensive care. Many of these supportive services are not within the scope of economics of individual hospitals or small communities, and regional development and planning will be necessary.

Some Final Comments

It has been the purpose of this presentation to outline some of the characteristics of today's elderly, to state what is known and make some surmises about those whom society will think of as the new generation of elderly in the decade to come and to speculate how health professionals might prepare for what is becoming a problem of ever increasing magnitude. Some of the challenges I have outlined are indeed formidable. I will end with the observation that the quality of life in developed nations can readily be sensed from the manner in which we facilitate the transition from middle to old age and insure that the life of older persons will have a minimum of stress and involve the preservation of maximal personal freedom and opportunities. It is the responsibility of all segments of our society to attend to this matter, but a special opportunity for professionals in the health care and personal services fields who can make a large contribution to ensure that our society will pass this test.

References

Binstock, R. H., & Shanas, E. *Handbook of aging and the social sciences.* New York: Van Nostrand Reinhold, 1976.

Birren, J. E., & Schaie, K. W. *Handbook of the psychology of aging.* New York: Van Nostrand Reinhold, 1977.

Birren, J. E., & Sloane, R. B. *Handbook of mental health and aging.* Englewood Cliffs, N. J.: Prentice-Hall, 1980.

Busse, E. W., & Blazer, D. G. *Handbook of geriatric psychiatry.* New York: Van Nostrand Reinhold, 1980.

Finch, C. E., & Hayflick, L. *Handbook of the biology of aging.* New York: Van Nostrand Reinhold, 1980.

Kay, D. K. W. Epidemiological aspects of organic brain disease in the aged. In C. M. Gaitz (ed.), *Aging and the brain.* New York: Plenum, 1972.

Knox, A. B. *Adult development and learning.* San Francisco: Jossey-Bass, 1977.

Life-Span Developmental Psychology: Some Converging Observations on History and Theory

PAUL B. BALTES

Observations are offered on the confluence of history, theory, and method of life-span developmental psychology. Contrary to most current beliefs, it is shown that throughout the history of developmental psychology, beginning in the late eighteenth century, a life-span approach to the study of behavioral development has been espoused repeatedly though in an insular fashion. Life-span developmental psychology stretches the boundaries of any developmental orientation because of its primary concern with long-term processes. Therefore, a life-span approach is apt to accentuate, amplify, and articulate important theoretical and methodological issues and principles beyond the level of clarity suggested in age-specific developmental specialties, such as child development or gerontology. Examples are used to illustrate the enduring significance of several theoretical and methodological themes. These themes include (a) the reformulation of the concept of development to encompass models other than only biological growth models, (b) the expansion of the substantive scope of developmental constructs, (c) the linkage of ontogenetic and biocultural change in an interactive and contextual framework, and (d) the formulation of appropriate development-specific methodologies. It is argued that life-span researchers should continue to focus on explicating the methodological and theoretical uniqueness and challenge of the developmental orientation expressed in these themes. Continual awareness of and concern for these themes will not only increase the general impact of a life-span orientation but also promote more significant research endeavors.

Introduction

It is often observed that the field of life-span developmental psychology has emerged during the 1960s and 1970s. There is a tremendous outpouring of life-span work both in psychology and in neighboring disciplines, such as sociology (e.g., Brim & Wheeler, 1966; Clausen, 1972; Elder, 1975; Hill & Mattessich, 1979; Hill & Rodgers, 1964; Riley, 1976, 1978; Riley, Johnson, & Foner, 1972; Rosenmayr, 1978; Van Dusen & Sheldon, 1976). However, this recent growth of life-span research has been pre-

Source: Abridged with slight changes from Baltes, P. B. Life-span developmental psychology: Some converging observations on history and theory. In P. B. Baltes & O. G. Brim, Jr. (eds.), *Life-span development and behavior* (Vol. 2). New York: Academic Press, 1979, pp. 255–279. Copyright 1979 by Academic Press, Inc. Reprinted by permission.

ceded by a lengthy historical gestation of life-span developmental ideas. The field of adult development and aging has played a pivotal role in this development, most likely because aging is easily conceptualized as an outcome of life history. Eminent psychological gerontologists, such as Pressey, Kuhlen, Havighurst, Shock, Birren, Neugarten, Riegel, Thomae, and Schaie, all, at one point or another, have argued for and contributed to the advancement of life-span developmental conceptions. A review article by Baltes, Reese and Lipsitt (1980) provides a lengthier summary of the historical and theoretical perspectives associated with the emergence of a life-span approach.

The explosion of life-span work in psychology is evident in numerous types of publications. Following the early twentieth century work of scholars such as Hollingworth, Pressey and Charlotte Buehler, post World War II contributions were made by Bayley (1963), Birren (1964), Bühler and Massarik (1968), Erikson (1959), Havighurst (1948), Neugarten (1969) and the volumes resulting from the West Virginia Conferences (e.g., Baltes & Schaie, 1973a; Datan & Ginsberg, 1975; Datan & Reese, 1977; Goulet & Baltes, 1970; Nesselroade & Reese, 1973). . . .

There are also several handbooks on human development and aging that exhibit a life-span framework. The first was a German handbook of developmental psychology edited in 1959 by Thomae; the second was a handbook on socialization edited in 1969 by Goslin. Moreover, life-span perspectives are evident in the recently published handbooks on aging (Binstock & Shanas, 1976; Birren & Schaie, 1977) in which close to 10 chapters pay explicit tribute to a life-span conception of sociological and psychological aging. . . .

A number of neglected questions need to be addressed, however. For example, is the explosion in the quantity of life-span work paralleled by an increasing insight into its historical, theoretical, and methodological foundations? To what degree is this surge of life-span thinking reflected in a change in actual empirical developmental work, data interpretation, and theoretical conception? Moreover, are there any reasons to believe that this recent outpouring is more than a short-lived fad and that we are not dealing with mere rhetoric rather than with a cogent theoretical argument and framework?

The primary goal of this chapter is to place the recent surgence of a life-span orientation into a historical perspective by specifying some of its theoretical and methodological underpinnings and by articulating some recurrent themes that may serve as guides in the current period of quantitative explosion in life-span work. A life-span orientation is surprisingly old in the history of developmental psychology, particularly in Europe. In fact, it will be argued that there are a number of theoretical and methodological themes which have been identified repeatedly throughout the history of life-span work. These themes may help to explicate and amplify the special role of a developmental approach to the study of behavior and to place in perspective current endeavors in life-span work.

Notes on the History of Life-Span Developmental Psychology

Early Precursors: Tetens, Carus, Quetelet

A number of reviews on historical facets of developmental psychology (Birren, 1961a, 1961b; Charles, 1970; Groffmann, 1970; Hofstätter, 1938; Munnichs, 1966; Reinert, 1976, 1979; Riegel, 1977) are available. Together, they provide much insight into the origins of life-span developmental psychology. Let me, however, begin my notes on the history of life-span developmental psychology by quoting from the Preface to a textbook of developmental psychology:

> The author . . . has for many successive years conducted a course in developmental psychology. . . . With the remarkable progress in psychology during those years, two things have happened. The older volumes on genetic psychology have become inadequate. . . . The more recent volumes have been devoted to rather narrow sections of human growth, such as "preschool age," "adolescence," and "senescence." (p. *vi*)

The author continues:

> But the general student is interested in the whole career of human life, not merely in its infancy and school days. (p. *vii*)

These statements reflect the search for life-span coverage and are very representative of what many authors of current developmental psychology textbooks maintain. The fact is, however, that these quotations are 50 years old! They are found in the Preface to a forgotten, but excellent textbook by H. L. Hollingworth (1927) titled *Mental Growth and Decline: A Survey of Developmental Psychology*.

The quotations from Hollingworth (1927) illustrate an important though often overlooked historical fact. The emergence of life-span developmental psychology is seen as a recent event; this is not true. On the contrary, a life-span view of behavioral development has origins that antedate the emergence of any age-specific developmental speciality, such as child psychology. A strong life-span emphasis in the formative stages of developmental psychology is due largely to a group of European scholars. Review articles by Hofstätter (1938), Groffmann (1970), and particularly a recent *tour de force* historical review by Reinert (1976, 1979) have provided massive evidence. These authors have identified at least three

major developmental-psychological works of the eighteenth and nineteenth centuries advocating an explicit life-span orientation toward the study of human development. These are publications by Tetens in 1777, F.A. Carus in 1808, and Quetelet in 1835 (1838 in German; 1842 in English). Indeed, a careful examination of these heralds of developmental psychology is most educational and humbling. Their works exemplify both depth and scope in theory and methodology rarely witnessed in the early stages of a field. It is unfortunate that they did not have much impact on subsequent developments.

Twentieth-Century Precursors

In the first decades of the twentieth century occasional contributions to an understanding of all stages of the human life-span appeared, including the establishment of the field of gerontology (Hall, 1922; see Birren, 1961a, 1961b; Riegel, 1977, for reviews of the history of gerontology). Gerontology is particularly prone to suggest a life-span conception because of its concern with life processes which lead to aging. However, with one notable exception (Sanford, 1902), it was not until the late 1920s and 1930s that a concerted effort to develop an integrative view of life-span development was again attempted. The exception is a largely unknown review article by Edmund Clark Sanford published in 1902 in the *American Journal of Psychology* with the title "Mental Growth and Decline." In this article, Sanford treats development as a continuous process from birth to death, applying this view of development to "the course of mental development from the first beginnings of mind . . . at birth . . . to old age" (p. 426).

In the third and fourth decades of the 20th Century, there are three books which mark the reappearance of a life-span conception: Hollingworth (1927), Charlotte Bühler (1933), and the coauthored volume by Pressey, Janney, and Kuhlen in 1939. The

1927 text by Hollingworth, although the earliest of the three, is perhaps the least known. Each of these books is inherently life-span developmental in that the authors do not simply present an accumulation of age-specific information (infancy, childhood, adolescence, etc.) but attempt to articulate life-span developmental processes. It is interesting that, although these three books were published within a dozen years of each other, they exhibit more or less complete independence in citation and practically no reference to their 19th Century precursors (Charlotte Bühler makes a reference to F. A. Carus in a footnote). This is particularly surprising in the case of the Pressey *et al.* book which did not acknowledge the 1927 American text by Hollingworth while acknowledging Charlotte Bühler's 1933 German work.

In any case, each of these books is unique and quite remarkable in conception and in-depth treatment of life-span developmental events and processes. Similar to Quetelet's early 1835 work, the Hollingworth (1927) and Pressey, Janney, and Kuhlen (1939) books especially present a basic conception of human development that is empirical, process oriented, multidimensional, multidirectional, contextual, and clearly cognizant of the impact of social change and ecological contingencies. For example, Hollingworth (1927, p. 326) presents a chart that summarizes the complexity of life-span development in a format which is standing the test of modern times. Furthermore, Pressey's and his co-workers' rich exposition of the macro- and microlevel "conditions and circumstances of life," embeddedness of human development in a changing culture, and concern with the real-life behaviors represent a powerful forerunner of what is now termed an ecological (Bronfenbrenner, 1977), dialectical (Riegel, 1976a, 1976b), and external-validity (Hultsch & Hickey, 1977) orientation. Pressey's and his co-workers' empirical data

may lack precision. However, their basic theoretical orientation is amazingly similar to what the current trends in developmental psychology appear to be: a movement toward models of development which are nonpersonological, contextualistic, and multilinear.

The fact that practically all the historical marker publications dealing with a life-span orientation (Hollingworth, Pressey *et al.*, Quetelet) present a very explicit concern with what are now seen as contemporary trends (e.g., contextualism, social-evolutionary change, and development-specific methodology) is a noteworthy situation in my view. This is especially remarkable because the cross-references in these works are so few. It indicates that the involvement of current life-span researchers in such themes as cohort effects, social change, and other macro-level features might be intrinsic to a life-span orientation rather than a reflection of the personal interest of the individual researchers. In fact, it is this hitherto unrecognized historical continuity in ideas and issues which is the focus of the remainder of this chapter.

Recurrent Themes in Life-Span Developmental Theory

What are some of the current themes in life-span developmental theory and research that exhibit historical continuity? Moreover, what are some of the reasons why I judge the recurrence of these themes to be significant for an evaluation of their theoretical power? Four themes are discussed as illustrative examples.

It will become evident that each of the themes covered has achieved a high degree of articulation and resolution primarily because studying human development from a life-span perspective stretches the conceptual boundaries of the developmental approach (Baltes, Reese & Lipsitt, 1980; Baltes & Schaie, 1973b). Life-span processes extend over long time periods, involve explanatory mechanisms requiring an explicit concern for distal and cumulative causation (historical paradigms), and accentuate the continuity–discontinuity dimension for both the description and explanation of behavior. These extreme conditions of life-span research are apt to exemplify and magnify the basic rationale and foundation of developmental psychology.

Reformulating the Concept of Development

Most writers identifying the key features of life-span developmental research . . . emphasize that the traditional concept of development needs expansion or modification when applied to life-span change. Typically, it is argued that the developmental "growth" concept borrowed from biology, while useful for some purposes, has some features that are inappropriate or too restrictive for the study of ontogenetic change in a life-span framework.

Definition of Development Let me illustrate this argument in greater detail. Traditionally, conceptions of developmental change (e.g., Harris, 1957; Lerner, 1976; Wohlwill, 1973) have focused on a definition of development as behavioral change manifesting characteristics of: (a) sequentiality, (b) unidirectionality, (c) an end state, (d) irreversibility, (e) qualitative-structural transformation, and (f) universality. This definitional position has much conceptual strength and good support from biological approaches to child development, especially maturational–personological ones. Research on life-span development in a variety of areas, most notably cognitive and social development, however, has resulted in the conclusion that such a conception of development is unduly restrictive (Baltes & Willis, 1977, 1978).

During the recent decades in the United States, dissatisfaction with the aforementioned definition of development was probably first expressed in Havighurst's (1948) concept of developmental tasks and the contention of several gerontologists (see also Benedict, 1938; Birren, 1964; Neugarten, 1969) that there is much discontinuity between child development and the remainder of the life span. Similarly, in the extensive German literature on life-span development after World War II (for reviews, see Löwe, 1977; Thomae, 1959, 1979), it has been consistently argued that "one-factor" (biological) and unidimensional (growth–decline) conceptions of life-span development are inappropriate. On the contrary, German writers have espoused a position that includes multidimensionality, multidirectionality, and discontinuity as key features of any theory of human development through the life span.

Figures 1A and B are taken from Baltes and Willis (1978). They illustrate such a view of development that is more complex than those represented in simple cumulative and unidirectional conceptions. Figure 1A (upper part) depicts the notion that interindividual variability in behavior increases as life-span change evolves. Furthermore, the lower part of Figure 1A suggests that life-span changes can be rather diverse in nature: Multidimensionality and multidirectionality of behavior-change processes are frequent outcomes.

Figure 1B further portrays the complexity of life-span development. Besides the notions of large interindividual differences, multidimensionality, and multidirectionality (Figure 1A), possible discontinuity due to life-course grading (Neugarten, 1969) is graphically shown in Figure 1B. Behavior-change processes in life-span development do not always extend across the entire life span nor are they always outcomes of continuous influences and processes. Thus, behavior-change processes can differ in terms of onset, duration, and termination

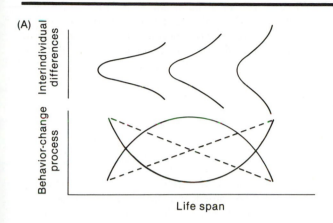

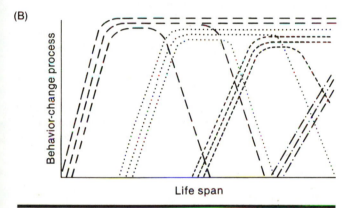

FIGURE 1

Selective examples of life-span developmental processes. Figure
1A illustrates multidimensionality, multidirectionality, and age-
correlated increases in interindividual variability. Figure 1B
summarizes notions of life-course grading and discontinuity.
Developmental functions (behavior-change processes) differ in
terms of onset, duration, and termination when charted in the
framework of the life course; moreover, they involve both quantitative and qualitative aspects of change (see also Baltes, Cornelius, & Nesselroade, 1979). (From Baltes & Willis, 1978)

when charted in the framework of the life
course. Moreover, as illustrated in
Havighurst's (1948) formulation of developmental tasks, novel behavior-change
processes can emerge at many points in the
life span, including old age.

Explanation of Development   This expansion or modification of a monolithic concept of development is important not only in
answering the descriptive question: What
does development look like? It also applies to
its explanatory counterpart: Where does

development come from? Again, Quetelet, already in 1835, and surely Pressey *et al.* in 1939, adopted a multicausal position and enumerated a large list of potential determinants of life-span change. Only some of the determinants, moreover, are usefully related to simple cumulative age-associated factors and mechanisms. Similarly, they espoused interactive-contextual rather than personological modes of explanation.

In the current scene, similar expansive views in regard to developmental explanations can be noted. For example, Hultsch and Plemons (1979) have reviewed the concept of "significant life events" as an organizing explanatory principle for adult-developmental change; Bengtson and Black (1973) and Riley (1976) have used structural features of intergenerational and age–cohort relations as explanatory principles for ontogenetic change: and Reese (1976) and Kohlberg (1973) have argued that in the areas of memory and moral judgment, respectively, explanatory discontinuity is predominant. Different modes of develop-

mental explanation (e.g., mechanistic versus organismic and maturational versus environmental) become attractive to account for developmental changes at different segments of the life span.

Figure 2, modified from Baltes, Cornelius, and Nesselroade (1979, in press; see also Baltes & Willis, 1978), summarizes a multicausal and interactive view that appears to be necessary to account for the complexity of life-span development. Three major sets of antecedent factors influencing individual development involve normative age-graded, normative history-graded, and non-normative life events. The three sets of influences interact in the production of developmental change processes.

Normative age-graded influences refer to biological and environmental determinants exhibiting a high correlation with chronological age. They are the ones usually considered in traditional developmental psychology. Examples of such age-graded influences include biological maturation and socialization when it is viewed as con-

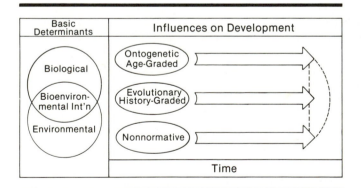

FIGURE 2
The interaction of three systems of influences regulates the nature of life-span development: ontogenetic (age-graded), evolutionary (history-graded), and nonnormative. Further explanation of the figure is contained in Baltes, Cornelius, and Nesselroade (1979) and Baltes and Willis (1978). (Modified from Baltes *et al.*, 1979)

sisting of the acquisition of a series of normative age-correlated roles or competencies.

Normative history-graded influences consist of fairly general events or event patterns experienced by a given cultural unit in connection with biosocial change, for example, as evidenced by cohort effects (Baltes, Cornelius, & Nesselroade, 1978). As was true for normative age-graded influences, history-graded influences can involve both environmental and biological characteristics.

Nonnormative influences on life-span development, finally, refer to environmental and biological determinants which, while significant in their effect on individual life histories, are not general. They do not occur for everyone or necessarily in easily discernible and invariant sequences or patterns. Events and event patterns related to occupational careers (unemployment), family life (divorce, death of a significant other), or health (serious sickness) are examples.

Figure 2 suggests that these three sets of influences interact with each other. The arrows to the right also indicate that they accumulate in their effects and may change over time. It is also important to recognize that there is a convergence between the complexity of life-span development depicted in Figure 1 and the multicausal system of influences postulated in Figure 2. This results because diversity and discontinuity in influences (in terms of content, sequencing, duration, patterning, etc.) are prerequisites for diversity in developmental outcomes.

Furthermore, it might be useful to speculate about the relative significance of age-graded, history-graded, and nonnormative influences on development at varying points in the life span or on a given behavior-change process. For instance, one could hypothesize that age-graded influences are primarily important in child development and perhaps in advanced aging, whereas history-graded and nonnor-

mative influences become the dominant influence systems in early and middle adulthood. Such a *differential life profile* of the relative magnitude of the influence systems would explain why much work in child development has been focused on age-graded influences, whereas the reverse has been true for recent work in adult development (see also Hultsch & Plemons, 1979).

A biological growth concept of development, predominant in the early stages of the field, is being recognized increasingly as a special case, or subclass of a larger class of developmental phenomena. Moreover, in accord with the basic position espoused by historical proponents of a life-span approach, simple personological and cumulative forms of description and explanation are judged to be of restricted value. While the trend toward complex, multilinear, and multivariate models of development is likely to be useful, it is necessary to be aware, however, of potential dangers that may result from overgeneralizing this trend. For example, it would be unwise to let this expansion of the concept of development evolve into a total lack of specificity, i.e., of equating any behavioral change with developmental change. Indeed, it will be important to specify some minimum definitional criteria or boundaries so that the uniqueness of a developmental orientation is not lost in toto.

Expanding the Scope of Developmental Constructs

The expansion of the concept of development is paralleled by an expansion in substantive developmental constructs. A life-span approach is apt to draw attention to new classes of developmental behavior. Again, historical forerunners, such as Quetelet (1835) and Pressey *et al.* (1939), had already proposed a much larger array of substantive areas to be the province of developmental psychology than is evidenced in the territory claimed by contemporary standard textbooks. In Pressey's and his coworkers' 1939 text, for example, such areas as work, occupation, leisure, and family life were given much more prominent consideration than a topical review of developmental psychology (especially of the child developmental ilk) of recent decades would indicate.

The expansion of classes of developmental behavior suggested by life-span research follows in principle two directions. One is to expand a specific construct to include life-span perspectives; the other is to delineate classes of behavior that workers in age-specific fields, such as child development, would easily overlook.

Let me use attachment as an example of the first strategy, where the expansion in scope of a construct is likely to occur when conceptualized in a life-span framework. As discussed recently by Lerner and Ryff (1978; see also Hartup & Lempers, 1973), attachment behaviors do not occur only in early life in the context of parent–child relations, but attachments may be developed at many occasions in the life span, such as in the formation and transformation of adolescent and adult friendships; occupational settings; family systems such as marriage, divorce, or remarriage and the death of spouses and friends. . . . Attachment behaviors are likely to undergo many transformations across the life span involving not only acquisition but aspects of maintenance, dissolution, and transfer. Similar expansive perspectives may be applied to other constructs such as achievement motivation, love, self-concept, or the development of life ideologies. . . .

The second strategy of identifying novel developmental classes of behavior suggested by a life-span perspective is most easily evident in classical research on the nature of life biographies or life histories (Bühler, 1933; Dollard, 1949), but also in examples from research in adult development and aging. In life-history research, Elder (1977, 1979) has provided recently a comprehensive and insightful review of the need for temporal constructs aimed at delineating the social course of lives.

Linking Ontogenetic and Biocultural Change

Another theme emerging both from a historical review and the current scene is that individuals change in a changing biocultural context. Research on cohort effects and intergenerational relations are examples. This theme implies that the study of development must deal with at least two streams of interactive changing systems: the individual and society broadly defined, or ontogeny and biocultural evolution (e.g., Elder, 1975; Neugarten & Datan, 1973; Riegel, 1976a, 1976b; Riley, 1976). The focus on age-graded and history-graded influences in Figure 2 already has indicated a concern with linking individual and biosocial change. Again, it is the extreme conditions of a life-span developmental perspective that accentuate this theme. When long-term processes are the focal concern, the assumption of an invariant biocultural or ecological context is not generally a fruitful one.

The role of historical change in the study of individual development can take several forms and may vary according to conceptual beliefs in a given research area. Baltes, Cornelius, and Nesselroade (1978), for example, suggest four distinct conceptual treatments of cohort effects on behavioral development. They argue that the cohort variable or cohort variance can be seen as (a) error, (b) momentary disturbance, (c) a dimension of quantitative generalization, or (d) a theoretical process variable similar to a process view of chronological age. None of these strategies is true or false. A life-span approach, however, because of its extension in both individual and historical time

(Neugarten & Datan, 1973), makes it less likely that a history-irrelevant or error-type approach would be a viable option. . . .

It is again impressive to see how our historical forerunners have forcefully tackled this issue. Quetelet in 1835, for example, discussed extensively the roles of evolutionary change and historical periods as modifiers of specific age-developmental functions. Similarly, he provided a lengthy discussion of conditions under which it would be possible to discern in a changing world what he called "general developmental laws." General developmental laws, as defined by Quetelet (1835), transcend the perturbations created by period-specific effects. Quetelet's view on general developmental laws, incidentally, is similar to Wohlwill's (1973) conceptualization of developmental functions. The same is true for Quetelet's successors in the history of life-span developmental psychology, such as Hollingworth and Pressey.

In short, there is an impressive continuity evident in life-span writings on the relationship between individual and biocultural change. An understanding of current discussions about the meaning and import of cohort effects is greatly aided by a historical perspective. For example, it helps to separate important arguments regarding developmental theory from relatively trivial questions concerning the empirical magnitude of cohort effects (Horn & Donaldson, 1976). Paraphrasing Anastasi's (1958) classical paper on the nature–nurture issue, the central question is not "How much cohort variance?" but rather "*How* do historical and ontogenetic factors interact in codetermining individual development?"

Advancing Development-Adequate Methodology

The fourth theme in the history as well as the current scenario of life-span developmental psychology deals with the need for method-

ologies that are specifically designed for the analysis of ontogenetic change.

As an illustration, Hayne Reese, John Nesselroade, and the author (Baltes, Reese & Nesselroade, 1977) recently have attempted to summarize development-specific research methods. The general conclusion was that many of the methods produced by general psychology in its methodological arsenal are ill suited to the study of . developmental change. In fact, existing methods often result in a situation where the phenomenon of development is either ruled out on an a priori methodological basis or only captured in an inadequate manner due to a lack of development-sensitive methodology. This situation has resulted because the traditional focus in psychological research methodology has been oriented toward such features as optimal prediction (rather than representation of change), stability (rather than change), and interindividual differences (rather than patterns of intraindividual change).

Again, because of the radicalism in the developmental formulation of a life-span approach, this perspective highlights the inappropriateness of existing methodologies. For example, if one acknowledges that change is pervasive, that individuals live in a changing biocultural context, that the explanation of long-term processes is apt to involve complex historical paradigms, and that long-term processes are likely candidates for explanatory discontinuity rather than simple cumulative causal explanations, then the search for new methodologies becomes a critical task. The need for new development-specific methodologies is amplified to such a degree by life-span thinking that it cannot be avoided.

In our historical review an immediate concern for development-specific methodologies was expressed by practically all our precursors. Thus, it is not surprising that the search for development-appropriate methodology continues among current researchers with life-span interests. For instance, in addition to methodological discussions on cohort-sequential methodology, there are efforts by life-span oriented researchers to advance models aimed at assessing developmental changes in measurement validity (Schaie, 1978), consider external validity as a research dimension not only as equal in significance to internal validity but also as a contextual component intrinsic to any developmental explanation (Hultsch & Hickey, 1978), and to advance the use of structural equation models in identifying long-term causal chains (Kohn & Schooler, 1977; Labouvie, 1974; Rogosa, 1979). In my judgment, there is a logic to life-span thinking in each of these cases which pushes the formulation of development-specific methodology beyond a level of articulation that is likely to be accomplished by any age-specific developmental specialty, such as child development or gerontology. In other words, the fact that many life-span researchers are interested in theoretical and methodological issues is not accidental. Rather, it reflects the stimulation resulting from the conceptual extremities inherent in life-span conceptions. Moreover, the conceptual extremity required by life-span questions requires the formulation of new methodologies that will likely advance the state of developmental design generally.

References

Anastasi, A. Heredity, environment, and the question "How," *Psychological Review,* 1958, 65, 197–208.

Baltes, P. B., Cornelius, S. W., & Nesselroade, J. R. Cohort effects in behavioral development: Theoretical and methodological perspectives. In W. A. Collins (Ed.), *Minnesota symposium on child psychology* (Vol. 11). Hillsdale, N.J.: Erlbaum, 1978.

Baltes, P. B., Cornelius, S. W., & Nesselroade, J. R. Cohort effects in developmental psychology. In J. R. Nesselroade & P. B. Baltes (Eds.), *Longitudinal research in the behavioral sciences: Design and analysis.* New York: Academic Press, 1979.

Baltes, P. B., Reese, H. W., & Lipsitt, L. P. Life-span developmental psychology. *Annual Review of Psychology,* 1980, 31, 65–110.

Baltes, P. B., Reese, H. W., & Nesselroade, J. R. *Life-span developmental psychology: Introduction to research methods.* Monterey: Brooks/Cole, 1977.

Baltes, P. B., & Schaie, K. W. (Eds). *Life-span developmental psychology: Personality and socialization.* New York: Academic Press, 1973. (a)

Baltes, P. B., & Schaie, K. W. On life-span developmental research paradigms: Retrospects and prospects. In P. B. Baltes & K. W. Schaie (Eds.), *Life-span developmental psychology: Personality and socialization.* New York: Academic Press, 1973. (b)

Baltes, P. B., & Schaie, K. W. On the plasticity of intelligence in adulthood and old age: Where Horn and Donaldson fail. *American Psychologist,* 1976, 31, 720–725.

Baltes, P. B., & Willis, S. L. Toward psychological theories of aging and development. In J. E. Birren & K. W. Schaie (Eds.), *Handbook of the psychology of aging.* New York: Van Nostrand-Reinhold, 1977.

Baltes, P. B., & Willis, S. L. Life-span developmental psychology, cognition, and social policy. In M. W. Riley (Ed.), *Aging from birth to death.* Washington, D. C.: American Association for the Advancement of Science, 1978.

Bayley, N. The life-span as a frame of reference in psychological research. *Vita Humana,* 1963, 6, 125–139.

Benedict, R. Continuities and discontinuities in cultural conditioning. *Psychiatry,* 1938, 1, 161–167.

Bengtson, V. L., & Black, K. D. Intergenerational relations in socialization. In P. B. Baltes & K. W. Schaie (Eds.), *Life-span developmental psychology: Personality and socialization.* New York: Academic Press, 1973.

Binstock, R., & E. Shanas (Eds.), *Handbook of aging and the social sciences.* New York: Van Nostrand-Reinhold, 1976.

Birren, J. E. A brief history of the psychology of aging. Part I. *Gerontologist,* 1961, 1, 69–77. (a)

Birren, J. E. A brief history of the psychology of aging. Part II. *Gerontologist,* 1961, 1, 127–134. (b)

Birren, J. E. (Ed.). *Relations of development and aging.* Springfield: Thomas, 1964.

Birren, J. E., & Schaie, K. W. (Eds.). *Handbook of the psychology of aging.* New York: Van Nostrand Reinhold, 1977.

Brim, O. G., Jr., & Wheeler, S. *Socialization after childhood: Two essays.* New York: John Wiley, 1966.

Bronfenbrenner, U. Toward an experimental ecology of human development. *American Psychologist,* 1977, 32, 513–531.

Bühler, C. *Der menschliche Lebenslauf als psychologisches Problem.* Leipzig: Hirzel, 1933.

Bühler, C., & Massarik, F. (Eds.). *The course of human life.* New York: Springer, 1968.

Carus, F. A. *Psychologie. Zweiter Theil: Specialpsychologie.* Leipzig: Barth & Kummer, 1808.

Charles, D. C. Historical antecedents of life-span developmental psychology. In L. R. Goulet & P. B. Baltes (Eds.), *Life-span developmental psychology: Research and theory.* New York: Academic Press, 1970.

Clausen, J. A. The life course of individuals. In M. W. Riley, et al. (Eds.), *A sociology of age stratification.* New York: Russell Sage Foundation, 1972.

Datan, N., & Ginsberg, L. H. (Eds.). *Life-span developmental psychology: Normative life crises.* New York: Academic Press, 1975.

Datan, N., & Reese, H. W. (Eds.). *Life-span developmental psychology: Dialectical perspectives on experimental research.* New York: Academic Press, 1977.

Dollard, J. *Criteria for the life history.* New York: Peter Smith, 1949.

Elder, G. H., Jr. Age-differentiation in life course perspective. *Annual Review of Sociology,* 1975, 1, 165–190.

Elder, G. H., Jr. Family history and the life course. *Journal of Family History,* 1977, 2, in press.

Elder, G. H. Historical change in life patterns and personality. In P. B. Baltes & O. G. Brim, Jr. (Eds.), *Life-span development and behavior* (Vol. 2). New York: Academic Press, 1979.

Erikson, E. H. Identity and the life cycle: Selected papers. *Psychological Issues,* 1959, 1, 50–100.

Gergen, K. J. Stability, change, and chance in understanding human development. In N. Datan & H. W. Reese (Eds.), *Life-span developmental psychology: Dialectical perspectives on experimental research.* New York: Academic Press, 1977.

Goslin, D. A. (Ed.). *Handbook of socialization theory and research.* Chicago: Rand McNally, 1969.

Goulet, L. R., & Baltes, P. B. (Eds.). *Life-span developmental psychology: Research and theory.* New York: Academic Press, 1970.

Groffmann, K. J. Life-span developmental psychology in Europe. In L. R. Goulet & P. B. Baltes (Eds.), *Life-span developmental psychology: Research and theory.* New York: Academic Press, 1970.

Hall, G. S. *Senescence: The last half of life.* New York: Appleton, 1922.

Harris, D. B. Problems in formulating a scientific concept of development. In D. B. Harris (Ed.), *The concept of development.* Minneapolis: University of Minnesota Press, 1957.

Hartup, W. W., & Lempers, J. A problem in life-span development: The interactional analysis of family attachments. In P. B. Baltes & K. W. Schaie (Eds.), *Life-span developmental psychology: Personality and socialization.* New York: Academic Press, 1973.

Havighurst, R. J. *Developmental tasks and education.* New York: David McKay, 1948.

Hill, R., & Mattessich, P. Family development theory and life-span development. In P. B. Baltes & O. G. Brim, Jr. (Eds.), *Life-span development and behavior* (Vol. 2). New York: Academic Press, 1979.

Hill, R., & Rodgers, R. H. The developmental approach. In H. T. Christiansen (Ed.), *Handbook of marriage and the family.* Chicago: Rand McNally, 1964.

Hofstätter, P. R. Tatsachen und Probleme einer Psychologie des Lebenslaufes. *Zeitschrift für Angewandte Psychologie,* 1938, 53, 273–333.

Hollingworth, H. L. *Mental growth and decline: A survey of developmental psychology.* New York: Appleton, 1927.

Horn, J. L., & Donaldson, G. On the myth of intellectual decline in adulthood. *American Psychologist,* 1976, 31, 701–719.

Hultsch, D. F., & Hickey, T. External validity in the study of human development: A dialectical perspective. *Human Development,* 1978, 21, 76–91.

Hultsch, D. F., & Plemons, J. K. Life events and life-span development. In P. B. Baltes & O. G. Brim, Jr. (Eds.), *Life-span development and behavior* (Vol. 2). New York: Academic Press, 1979.

Huston-Stein, A., & Baltes, P. B. Theory and method in life-span developmental psychology: Implications for child development. In H. W. Reese (Ed.), *Advances in child development and behavior* (Vol. 11). New York: Academic Press, 1976.

Kohlberg, L. Continuities in childhood and adult moral development revisited. In P. B. Baltes & K. W. Schaie (Eds.), *Life-span developmental psychology: Personality and socialization.* New York: Academic Press, 1973.

Kohn, M. S., & Schooler, C. *The reciprocal effects of the substantive complexity of work and intellectual flexibility: A longitudinal assessment.* Unpublished manuscript, National Institute of Mental Health, Washington, D. C., 1977.

Labouvie, E. W. Developmental causal structures of organism-environment interactions. *Human Development,* 1974, 17, 444–452.

Löwe, H. *Einführung in die Lernpsychologie des Erwachsenenalters.* Berlin: VEB Deutscher Verlag der Wissenschaften, 1977.

Munnichs, J. M. A. A short history of psychogerontology. *Human Development,* 1966, 9, 230–245.

Neugarten, B. L. Continuities and discontinuities of psychological issues into adult life. *Human Development,* 1969, 12, 121–130.

Neugarten, B. L., & Datan, N. Sociological perspectives on the life cycle. In P. B. Baltes & K. W. Schaie (Eds.), *Life-span developmental psychology: Personality and socialization.* New York: Academic Press, 1973.

Pressey, S. L., Janney, J. E., & Kuhlen, R. G. *Life: A psychological survey.* New York: Harper, 1939.

Quetelet, A. *Sur l'homme et le développement de ses facultés.* Paris: Bachelier, 1835.

Quetelet, A. *Über den Menschen und die Entwicklung seiner Fähigkeiten.* Stuttgart: Schweizerbart's Verlagshandlung, 1838.

Quetelet, A. *A treatise on man and the development of his faculties.* Edinburgh: William and Robert Chambers, 1842.

Reese, H. W. The development of memory: Life-span perspectives. In H. W. Reese (Ed.), *Advances in child development and behavior* (Vol. 11). New York: Academic Press, 1976.

Reinert, G. Grundzüge einer Geschichte der Human-Entwicklungspsychologie. In H. Balmer (Ed.), *Die europäische Tradition: Tendenzen, Schulen, Entwicklungslinien.* Vol. 1 of: *Die Psychologie des 20. Jahrhunderts.* Zürich: Kindler, 1976.

Reinert, G. Prolegomena to a history of life-span developmental psychology. In P. B. Baltes & O. G. Brim, Jr. (Eds.), *Life-span development and behavior* (Vol. 2). New York: Academic Press, 1979.

Riegel, K. F. *Psychology of development and history.* New York: Plenum, 1976. (a)

Riegel, K. F. The dialectics of human development. *American Psychologist,* 1976, 31, 689–700. (b)

Riegel, K. F. History of psychological gerontology. In J. E. Birren & K. W. Schaie (Eds.), *Handbook of the psychology of aging.* New York: Van Nostrand-Reinhold, 1977.

（Life-Span Developmental Psychology 25）

Riley, M. W. Age strata in social systems. In R. Binstock & E. Shanas (Eds.), *Handbook of aging and the social sciences.* New York: Van Nostrand-Reinhold, 1976.

Riley, M. W., Johnson, M., & Foner, A. *Aging and society* (Vol. 3). New York: Russell Sage, 1972.

Rogosa, D. Causal models in longitudinal research. In J. R. Nesselroade & P. B. Baltes (Eds.), *Longitudinal research in the study of behavior and development: Design and analysis.* New York: Academic Press, 1979.

Rosenmayr, L. (Ed.). *Die menschlichen Lebensalter.* München: Piper, 1978.

Sanford, E. C. Mental growth and decay. *American Journal of Psychology,* 1902, 13, 426–449.

Schaie, K. W. External validity in the assessment of intellectual performance in adulthood. *Journal of Gerontology,* 1978, 33, 695–701.

Tetens, J. N. *Philosophische Versuche über die menschliche Natur und ihre Entwicklung.* Leipzig: Weidmanns Erben und Reich, 1777.

Thomae, H. (Ed.). *Entwicklungspsychologie.* Göttingen: Hogrefe, 1959.

Thomae, H. The concept of development and life-span developmental psychology. In P. B. Baltes & O. G. Brim (Eds.), *Life-span development and behavior* (Vol. 2). New York: Academic Press, 1979.

Van Dusen, R. A., & Sheldon, E. B. The changing status of American women: A life cycle perspective. *American Psychologist,* 1976, 31, 106–116.

Wohlwill, J. F. *The study of behavioral development.* New York: Academic Press, 1973.

Age Changes and Age Differences

K. WARNER SCHAIE

Almost as soon as objective measures were defined which could be used to index intellectual abilities and other cognitive functions, researchers began to express interest in individual differences on such measures. One of the most persistent of such interests has been the investigation of developmental changes in cognitive behavior. Most treatments covering age changes in cognitive behavior have closely followed the prevalent approaches in the description of developmental theories. Although great attention has always been paid to early development, and maturation during childhood and adolescence is fully described, very little is said about the further development of intelligence and other cognitive variables during adulthood or senescence. In fact, the concern with age changes in cognitive behavior during adulthood did not come to be of serious interest to psychologists until it became clear that the I.Q. concept used in age scales was inapplicable for the measurement of intelligence in adults. As a consequence of the work of Wechsler (1944) in developing special measures for the description of the intelligence of adults but also due to the earlier descriptive works of Jones and Conrad (1933) with the Army Alpha and that of the Stanford group working with Miles (1933), it soon became clear that somewhat different conceptual models would be required for the proper understanding of adult cognitive development.

It will be noted that emphasis has been placed upon the term "age changes." The literature on the psychological studies of aging has long been haunted by a grand confusion between the terms "age change" and "age difference." This confusion has beclouded the results of studies involving age as a principal variable and has loaded the textbook literature with contradictory findings and what will be shown to be spurious age gradients. This presentation intends to clarify in detail the relationship between age changes and age differences and to show why past methodologies for the study of age-related changes have been inadequate.

Much of the literature on aging and cognitive behavior has been concerned with describing how older individuals differ from their younger peers at a given point in time. Such a descriptive attempt is quite worthwhile and is necessary in the standardization of measurements. This approach, however, is restricted to a description of the very real differences between organisms of various lengths of life experience at a given point in time. Unless some very strong assumptions are made, these attempts beg the issue and fail to produce relevant experiments on the question of how the behavior of the organism changes over age. This is a strong statement, and it is not made rashly since it clearly questions much of the work in the current literature. But it is required since we find ourselves increasingly puzzled about the results of our own and others' studies of age differences. Let us be explicit in clarify-

Source: Schaie, K. W. Age changes and age differences. *The Gerontologist,* 1967, 7, 128–132. Copyright 1967 by the Gerontological Society. Reprinted by permission.

ing the basis of our concerns and in tracing the resulting implications for the interpretation of much of the data in the developmental literature.

A general model has been developed which shows how the previously used methods of developmental analysis are simply special cases which require frequently untenable assumptions. This model has been described elsewhere in more detail (Schaie, 1965). At this time, however, it would be useful to state the most important characteristics of a general model required for the explanation of aging phenomena as they pertain to the relationship between age changes and age differences.

Let us begin then by clearly distinguishing between the concepts of age change and age difference. Before we can do so effectively, we must also introduce some new concepts and redefine various familiar concepts. The concept of *age* is, of course, central to our discussion. It needs to be carefully delineated, however, and whenever used will be taken to denote the age of the organism at the time of occurrence of whatever response is to be measured. Even more precisely, age will refer to the number of time-units elapsed between the entrance into the environment (birth) of the organism and the point in time at which the response is recorded.

In addition, it is necessary to introduce two concepts which are relatively unfamiliar in their relevance to developmental study. The first of these concepts is the term *cohort*. This term has frequently been used in population and genetic researches and is useful for our purpose. The term implies the total population of organisms born at the same point or interval in time. Restrictions as to the nature of the population and the latitude in defining the interval in time designated as being common to a given cohort or generation must be determined by the special assumptions appropriate to any given investigation.

The second concept to be introduced is

that of *time of measurement*. It will take on special significance for us as it denotes that state of the environment within which a given set of data were obtained. In any study of aging it is incumbent upon the investigator to take pains to index precisely the temporal point at which his measurements occur. Such concern is most pertinent since changes in the state of the environment may contribute to the effects noted in an aging study.

With these definitions in mind let us now examine Figure 1 which will help us in understanding the distinction between age changes and age differences. Figure 1 contains a set of six independent random samples, three of which have a common age, three of which have been given some measure of cognitive behavior at the same point in time, and three of which have been drawn from the same cohort; i.e., whose date of birth is identical. If we compare the performance of samples 1, 2, and 3 we are concerned with *age differences*. Discrepancies in the mean scores obtained by the samples may be due to the difference in age for samples measured at the same point in time. But note that an equally parsimonious interpretation would attribute such discrepancies to the differences in previous life experiences of the three different cohorts (generations) represented by these samples.

If, on the other hand, comparisons were made between scores for samples 3, 5, and 6, we are concerned with *age changes*. Here the performance of the same cohort or generation is measured at three different points in time. Discrepancies between the mean scores for the three samples may represent age changes, or they may represent environmental treatment effects which are quite independent of the age of the organism under investigation. The two comparisons made represent, of course, examples of the traditional cross-sectional and longitudinal methods and illustrate the confounds resulting therefrom.

Lest it be thought that there is no way to

Time of Birth (Cohort)		Sample 3	Sample 5	Sample 6
	1910	Age 45	Age 50	Age 55
		$A_1C_3T_1$	$A_2C_3T_2$	$A_3C_3T_3$
	1905	Sample 2	Sample 4	
		Age 50	Age 55	
		$A_2C_2T_1$	$A_3C_2T_2$	
	1900	Sample 1		
		Age 55		
		$A_3C_1T_1$		
Time of Testing		1955	1960	1965

A—Age level at time of testing.
C—Cohort level being examined.
T—Number of test in series.

FIGURE 1
Example of a set of samples permitting all comparisons deducible from the general developmental model.

separate the effects of cohort and time differences from that of aging, we shall now consider a further set of differences which may be called *time lag*. If we compare samples 1, 4, and 6, it may be noted that the resulting differences will be independent of the organism's age, but can be attributed either to differences among generations or to differences in environmental treatment effects or both.

Any definitive study of age changes or age differences must recognize the three components of maturational change, cohort differences, and environmental effects as components of developmental change; otherwise, as in the past, we shall continue to confuse age changes with age differences and both with time lag. Hence, it may be argued that studies of age differences can bear upon the topic of age changes only in the special case where there are no differences in genetically or environmentally determined ability levels among generations and where there are no effects due to differential environmental impact. It follows, therefore, that findings of significant age dif-

ferences will bear no necessary relationship to maturational deficit, nor does the absence of age differences guarantee that no maturational changes have indeed occurred.

As a further complication, it is now necessary to add the notion that differences in the direction of change for the confounded developmental components may lead to a suppression or an exaggeration of actual age differences or changes. As an example, let us suppose that perceptual speed declines at the rate of one half sigma over a five-year interval. Let us suppose further that the average level of perceptual speed for successive five-year cohorts declines by one-half sigma also. Such decrement may be due to systematic changes in experience or to some unexplained genetic drift. Whatever their cause, if these suppositions were true, then a cross-sectional study would find no age differences whatsoever because the maturational decrement would be completely concealed by the loss of ability due to some unfavorable changes in successive generations.

As another example, let us suppose that

there is no maturational age decrement but that there is systematic improvement in the species. In such a case successive cohorts would do better than earlier ones, and cross-sectional studies would show spurious decrement curves, very much like those reported in the literature for many intelligence tests.

One of the most confusing facets of aging studies therefore is the fact that experimental data may reveal or fail to reveal a number of different combinations of underlying phenomena. Yet the understanding of the proper conceptual model which applies to a given set of data is essential before generalizations can be drawn. Let us illustrate the problem by considering some of the alternative models that might explain the behavior most typically represented in the literature on developmental change. Reference here is made to cross-sectional gradients such as those reported by Wechsler (1944) or by Jones and Conrad (1933). These gradients typically record a steep increment in childhood with an adult plateau and steep decrement thereafter.

When we address ourselves to the question of what developmental changes are represented by such data, we face relatively little difficulty in determining whether maturational changes are contained in the age differences noted during childhood and adolescence. Our own children provide us with at least anecdotal evidence of the longitudinal nature of such change. Whether this portion of the developmental curve, however, is a straight line or a positive asymptotic curve is still in doubt. Also, it should be remembered that even if we agree upon the validity of evidence for maturational changes, we must still consider that such changes will be overestimated by cross-sectional data if there are positive cohort differences and/or negative environmental experience effects. Similarly, maturational growth will be underestimated in the event of cohort decrement or the effect of positive environmental influences.

For the adult and old-age portions of the developmental span, matters are much more complicated. While we can readily accept the fact of psychological maturational growth during childhood, similar evidence of maturational decline on psychological variables by means of longitudinal study remains to be demonstrated. As a consequence, we also must at least entertain models which would account for age differences in the absence of maturational age changes.

The detailed analysis of the general developmental model (Schaie & Strother, 1964) shows that it is possible to differentiate as many as 729 models to account for developmental change if one considers the direction and slope as well as the three components involved in developmental change gradients. Of the many possible models, three will be considered now which seem to be high probability alternatives for the classical textbook age-gradients. Our three examples are models which not only would fit these textbook gradients but would furthermore predict that the cross-sectional data depicted by the gradients could not possibly be replicated by longitudinal studies.

The first of these models might be called an "improvement of the species" model. It holds that the form of the maturational gradient underlying the typical representatives of the textbook gradients is positive asymptotic; i.e., that there is systematic increment in performance during childhood, slowing down during early adulthood, and that there is no further maturational change after maturity. The model further holds that the cohort gradient, or the differences between generations, should also be positive asymptotic.

Successive generations are deemed to show improved performance for some unspecified genetic or prior experience reason, but it is also assumed that improvement has reached a plateau for recent generations. The effect of the environment is furthermore assumed to be constant or positive asymptotic also. When these components are combined they are seen to provide a cross-sectional age gradient which shows steady increment during childhood, a plateau in midlife, and accelerating decrement in old age.

The same model, however, when applied to longitudinal data will predict steady increment during childhood, but slight improvement in midlife, and no decrement thereafter. The only reason the cross-sectional gradient will show decrement is that the younger generations start out at a higher level of ability and thus in the cross-sectional study the older samples will show lower performance. Of course, this means no more than that the older samples started out at a lower level of ability even though they showed no decrement over their life-span.

A second no less plausible alternative to account for the textbook age gradients might be called the "environmental compensation" model. This model also specifies a concave maturational gradient with increment in youth and decrement in old age, much as the cross-sectional gradient. In addition, however, this alternative calls for a positive environmental experience gradient. Here the effect of an environmental experience increases systematically due to a progressively more favorable environment. The effects of cohort differences in this model are assumed to be neutral or positive asymptotic.

If the second model were correct, then our prediction of longitudinal age changes would result in a gradient with steep increment in childhood but no decrement thereafter, since maturational changes would be systematically compensated for by a favorable environment. Since the environmental component of change over time is not measured in the cross-sectional study, assessment would be made only of the maturational decrement yielding information on the state of a population sample of different ages at a given point of time. But it would provide misleading information as to what is going to happen to the behavior of this population sample as time passes.

Third, let us propose a more extreme alternative which we might label the "great society" model.[1] This model specifies a positive asymptotic maturational gradient; i.e., increment during childhood and a plateau thereafter. The model further specifies a positive asymptotic cohort gradient; i.e., successively smaller increments in performance for successive generations. Finally the model specifies increasingly favorable environmental impact. The reason for calling this alternative the "great society" model should be readily apparent. The model implies (a) that maturity is an irreversible condition of the organism, (b) that the rapid development of our people is reaching the plateau of a mature society, and (c) that any further advance would now be a function of continually enriching the environment for us all. Note that the cross-sectional study of groups of different age at this time in our history will still conform to the textbook cross-sectional gradients. Their longitudinal replication, however, would result in a gradient which would be steep during childhood, which would level off during adulthood, but which would show continued growth until the demise of the organism.

Obviously, it is still possible that the straightforward decrement model might hold equally well for the classical gradients. The information we have on longitudinal studies such as those of Owens (1953) and Bayley and Oden (1955) and the more recent sequential studies by Schaie and Strother (1968a; 1968b) let it appear that any one of the above alternatives may be a more plausible one.

It is hoped that the examples just given have alerted the reader to some of the flaws in the traditional designs used for the studies

---

[1] In more recent literature this model has been referred to as an "adult stability" model (Ed. note).

of aging phenomena. Caution is in order at this time lest the premature conclusion be reached that the increase in sophistication of our methods has indeed led to a better understanding of how and why organisms age. Thus far it seems just as likely that all which has been investigated refers to differences among generations and thus in a changing society to differences which may be as transient as any phase of that society. Only when we have been successful in differentiating between age changes and age differences can we hope therefore that the exciting advances and methods in the more appropriate studies now in progress will truly assist us in understanding the nature of the aging process.

Summary

The concepts of age change and age difference were differentiated by introducing a three-dimensional model for the study of developmental change involving the notions of differences in maturational level (age), differences among generations (cohorts), and differential environmental impact (time of measurement). It was shown that age differences as measured by cross-sectional methods confound age and cohort differences while age changes as measured by the longitudinal method confound age and time of measurement differences. Conceptual unconfounding permits specification of alternate models for the prediction of age changes from age differences and resolution of the meaning of discrepancies in the findings yielded by cross-sectional and longitudinal studies. Examples of alternative models for aging phenomena were provided.

References

Bayley, N., and M. H. Oden: The maintainance of intellectual ability in gifted adults. *J. Geront.*, 10: 91–107, 1955.

Jones, H. E., and H. S. Conrad. The growth and decline of intelligence: a study of a homogenous group between the ages of ten and sixty. *Genet. Psychol. Monogr.*, 13: 223–298, 1933.

Miles, W. R.: Age and human ability. *Psychol. Rev.*, 40: 99–123, 1933.

Owens, W. A.: Age and mental abilities; a longitudinal study. *Genet. Psychol. Monogr.*, 48: 3–54, 1953.

Schaie, K. W.: A general model for the study of developmental problems. *Psychol. Bull.*, 64: 92–107, 1965.

Schaie, K. W., and C. R. Strother: Models for the prediction of age changes in cognitive behavior. Unpubl. mimeo. paper, West Virginia Univ. Also abstract in *Gerontologist*, 4: 14, 1964.

Schaie, K. W., and C. R. Strother: A cross-sequential study of age changes in cognitive behavior. *Psychol. Bull.*, 70: 671–680, 1968. (a)

Schaie, K. W., and C. R. Strother: The effects of time and cohort differences on the interpretation of age changes in cognitive behavior. *Multivar. Beh. Res.*, 3: 259–294, 1968. (b)

Wechsler, D.: *The measurement of adult intelligence.* Williams & Wilkins, Baltimore, 1944.

SECTION **2**

Families

PEOPLE WHO NEED PEOPLE

A family can be viewed as a system of interdependent relationships in which each member depends on others for some needs and fills some needs for the others. For example, most families engage in a division of labor, in which commonly even the youngest and oldest family members participate. A family typically begins with a marriage of young people. The particular interdependencies on which marriages are based are sexual, emotional, and familial (that is, the desire to provide a context for having children). These needs lead to the establishment of the nuclear family consisting of parents and their children. But the nuclear family is part of an extended family system—grandparents, aunts, uncles, cousins, and eventually nieces, nephews, and grandchildren.

It is often said that the nuclear family is isolated from their kin (the extended family) in today's world. This myth is based on the belief that extended families were common in earlier eras of American life and on the belief that nuclear families of today have little contact with kin. Our first selection by *Rudy Ray Seward* casts some doubt on the extent to which the extended family was ever common in our country. It illustrates the need of collaboration between historians and social scientists to avoid the possibility that the social scientist constructs explanatory models that are not founded in historical reality. He concludes that even though the colonial family was larger than the present average family, this structure was remarkably similar to that prevailing in contemporary America.

Families are an important agent for children's socialization—the transmission of values and traditions from one generation to the next. This transmission is accomplished in many ways: by direct teaching and by example or modeling, to name just two. Parents have the responsibility to provide guidance for their children, which often results in ''generation-gap'' conflicts. An in-depth review of research on issues related to this generation gap is provided in the selection by *Vern L. Bengtson*. It appears that children tend to accept their parents' influence in important moral and social values, but peers may have more influence on superficial values involving tastes in dress and music (which perhaps define the identity of a generation). As children grow older, a type of bilateral negotiation develops, as each generation champions the values and behaviors it has found important and useful. Parents sometimes learn from their children as much as children learn from their more experienced parents. Although older people, as grandparents, perceive the greatest generation gap, it is also true that they frequently conclude that the gap occurs primarily outside of their family; they feel that within their own family there are far more similarities than differences.

Older persons in our society may become more dependent in limited respects, but typically the relationship between adult children and aging parents becomes more mature: one adult interacting with another, with bonds of affection and duty. Nevertheless, one of the major social myths about aging is the widely held belief that in contemporary American society old people are alienated from their children. *Ethel Shanas* in our third selection analyzes this proposition in depth and shows it to be generally false. She also considers in detail the proposition that because of the existence of large human service bureaucracies families are no longer important as caregivers for older people, and shows that the facts are to the contrary.

Additional Suggested Readings

Skolnick, A. *The intimate environment.* 2nd ed. Boston: Little, Brown, 1978.
A very readable account of the establishment of men-women relationships—their care, maintenance, and problems within the context of marriage.

Sussman, M. B. The family life of old people. In R. H. Binstock & E. Shanas (eds.), *Handbook of aging and the social sciences.* New York: Van Nostrand Reinhold, 1977, pp. 218–43.
Families are defined and an authoritative account is presented on kin networks; intergenerational transfers and relationships of families and their elders are also discussed.

The Colonial Family in America: Toward a Socio-Historical Restoration of Its Structure

RUDY RAY SEWARD

During the last two decades there have many advocates for interdisciplinary work between the fields of history and sociology. Despite favorable arguments (listing the advantages of collaboration) and the founding of committees and journals (aimed at aiding or initiating cooperation) a number of writers have noted the aloofness of both fields and the lack of any real commitment to interdisciplinary work. But with an increasing interest in the study of family history over the last decade by both historians and sociologists there does seem to be an opportunity, and to some degree a necessity, for an interdisciplinary effort between these two fields. The focus here is upon one area of family history that has recently received much attention. from both fields—the colonial American family. Both disciplines are involved in a restoration of the colonial family which, in the process, is providing the beginnings of an interdisciplinary effort. The presentation of the results produced up to this point and the problems arising in the restoration process are reviewed with the expectation of stimulating further comparable research and collaboration. A growing knowledge and appreciation of the works, concepts, and techniques of both fields should enable meaningful efforts in the future between the two disciplines. The result will be, for this particular area of study, a more precise image and better understanding of the colonial family system. This should eventually lead to a clearer understanding of familial change and societal change, in general.

When exploring past social phenomena of interest, we only too often find an absence of any quantitative information upon which to base analysis that may lead to understanding. Whether we are concerned with family structures, the process of industrialization, or population structure and trends, the "facts" we find are based primarily upon a collection of impressions from various literary sources. These "facts" are supported by "statistical" evidence which is, more often than not, the result of the conjectures (or based upon an observation of a limited number of phenomena) by the authors of these literary sources. When discussing colonial America, for example,

Source: Abridged from Seward, R. R. The colonial family in America: Toward a socio-historical restoration of its structure. *Journal of Marriage and the Family,* 1973, 35, 58–70. Copyright 1973 by the National Council on Family Relations. Reprinted by permission.

one cannot deny the extensive use of the observations and comments of such prominent writers as Franklin, Sewall, Jefferson, and others in forming an image of the various aspects of colonial America.

The focus of this paper will be upon the restoration of the colonial or preindustrial family in America that is presently taking place to portray the colonial family in a more quantitative and precise manner.

This paper will look at one area of sociohistorical study—the colonial American family—to assess to what extent collaboration does or does not exist. Full collaboration has certainly not been obtained but it appears at least to be initiated and growing. There are not yet any joint efforts, but there is a growing awareness and appreciation of interdisciplinary work.

Traditional View of the Colonial Family

The traditional view of the colonial family is being challenged by historians and sociologists. Their challenges are aiding in the restoration of the colonial family, resulting in a new image of the family which contrasts sharply with what Goode (1963:6-7) terms "the classical family of Western nostalgia." The evidence for a majority of the aspects presented by the nostalgic traditional view is derived largely from "verbal data" such as diaries, sermons, novels, and other literary sources. In 1919 Arthur W. Calhoun published a social history of the American family which primarily used these literary sources, particularly those written by leading contemporaries for the colonial period. His work, for many years, has been considered the most comprehensive description of the colonial family (cf. Edwards, 1969:12). The characteristics of the colonial family as described by Calhoun that have been the focus of recent studies are as follows:

1. The colonial family was viewed as being "extended" rather than "nuclear," the implication being that a number of generations of kin, a number of siblings and their spouses were all a part of the family unit.

2. The number of children per family was large, and when combined with the "extended" nature of the family, the total unit had a very large size. According to Calhoun (1919:87), "Large families were the rule. Families of ten to twelve children were common. Families of from twenty to twenty-five children were not rare enough to call forth expression of wonder."

3. Marriage occurred at a very early age in the colonial family. Although child marriages were not permitted, Calhoun (1919:67) states that women usually married by age sixteen or under and men by age twenty or under.

4. The mortality rate for infants was particularly high (Calhoun, 1919:89).

The preceding aspects of the colonial family are those which have been under close scrutiny in the last decade. These familial aspects will be of primary interest in this paper although others will be mentioned.

Data for Restoration

Kinship Structure

The assumption that the colonial family was "extended" has come under much attack despite its widespread support. In addition to the views of Calhoun, Greenfield (1967:312) observes it is "generally viewed in sociological theory" that the "small nuclear family found in Western Europe and the United States" is the "consequence of the urban-industrial revolution." Furthermore the "extended" family was the expected form that preceded the urban-industrial revolution (for a typical example of this argument, see Ogburn and Nimkoff, 1950:469-473). Greenfield (1967), through an excellent use of comparative and historical techniques, challenges this assumed relationship between the family and the urban-industrial revolution and even suggests the reverse: the small nuclear family might possibly have helped produce industrialization.

Greenfield makes the important suggestion (1967:322) that the "small nuclear family was brought to the United States from Great Britain by its earliest settlers." He bases this on Arensberg's contention (1955:1149) that "the 'nuclear' or 'democratic' family . . . came with [the] Yankees from England." But there is also additional support for this contention. In his study of the aristocracy between 1558 and 1641, Stone (1967:269) notes there is a lack of evidence that the "sixteenth century household had taken the form of an extended family." There appeared, in fact, to be little "encouragement for younger sons to remain home, and daughters were almost invariably married off at an early age" (Stone, 1967:269). Laslett and Harrison (1963: 167), in their study of Clayworth and Cogenhoe during the last quarter of the seventeenth century, found that the family was not extended, because in most cases the "household did not ordinarily contain more generations than two, [and] . . . living with in-laws or relatives was on the whole not to be expected. . . . Most important is the rule that it was unusual, very unusual, to find two married couples within the same family group." Laslett (1969) in a later work expanded the geographical coverage of these conclusions. He supports the contention that the family form brought to the new world by the English settlers was "nuclear" in nature rather than "extended." Thus if the extended family was typical in the colonies, it must have been because of indigenous elements in the new world.

But based upon recent work completed, the "nuclear" family was also typical in the American colonies in contrast to the stereotype. A number of studies completed since 1965 of the colonial family conclude that the extended structure was the exception rather than the rule. Demos (1965:279) notes that in the Plymouth colony "there were not extended families at all, in the sense of 'under the same roof'."[1] Using family wills as a source, Demos (1965:279) observes "that married brothers and sisters never lived together in the same house" and that "as soon as a young man becomes betrothed, plans were made for the building, or purchase, of his own house." In his study of Dedham, Massachusetts, between 1636 and 1736, Lockridge (1966:343) observes that "80 per cent of adult, married men had their own house . . . [hence there was] not extensive doubling-up of two families in one house . . . [and] it was most unusual for married fathers with married sons to live together in an extended family group."

In his study of the seventeenth century family structure in Andover, Massachusetts, Greven (1966:254–255) describes what he termed a *"modified extended family*—defined as a kinship group of two or more generations living within a single community in which the dependence of the children upon their parents continues after the children have married and are living under a separate roof." Greven's findings are not, however, at odds with the previous findings. What he terms the *modified extended family* refers to the family of interaction, and to be consistent with the other works, we must use as a basis for the family unit the family of residence (see footnote 1 above). If we apply the latter definition to Greven's families the difference in structure disap-

[1] The distinction between an "extended" versus a "nuclear" family unit is determined by membership in the family of residence or the group of persons who are related by blood, marriage, or adoption who share the same dwelling unit. The importance of the interpersonal relationships between all kin whether in the same dwelling unit or not—the family of interaction—cannot yet be dealt with in quantitative terms.

pears. This distinction made, the family structure as described by Greven is, in fact, nuclear, as the families in the works previously cited.

In a later study by Demos (1968:44) of colonial Bristol, Rhode Island, he supports the predominance of the ''nuclear'' family by observing that ''married adults normally lived with their own children and *apart* from all other relatives.'' Together, these works provide evidence based upon quantitative data to challenge the contention of the predominance in the colonial period of the ''extended'' family.

Family Size

Another contention under close scrutiny is that the number of children per family was quite large. The assumption of a large number of children, together with the presumption of the ''extended'' nature of the colonial family, accounts for the widespread image of large colonial family units. In reference to this, there are two aspects to be considered: the number of children per family and the overall family size.

First, let us examine the number of children per family in the colonial period. It is true that colonial families, on the average, had more children than families of the present day. However, the difference between these two periods has been much exaggerated and certainly the difference is much less than indicated by Calhoun. Indeed, if we look at Demos' statistics (1968) there appears to be little variance in the average number of children from the present figure. Demos (1968:45) reports the mean number of children per family in colonial Bristol for 1689 as 3.27 and the median as 3.04. Only two families of those surveyed by Demos had more than seven children. If the mean reported by Demos—3.27—is compared to the mean reported by the United States Cen-

sus Bureau (1963:1,465) for 1960—which is 1.72—the difference—1.55—is much less than might be presumed. Regardless of whether this figure is considered a significant difference, the figures presented by Demos (1968) certainly challenge the image of the typical colonial family having a large number of children.

However, there are discrepancies between the figures reported for number of children per colonial family in various works which should be noted. In an earlier work Demos (1965:270) reports for the Plymouth colony ''an average of seven to eight children per family who actually grew to adulthood.'' If the children who died before the age of 21 are included in Demos' sample, the average is raised to between eight and nine children. In a recent work dealing only with eighteenth century Quakers, Wells (1971:74–75) reports the average number of children per family as 5.69. Other figures reported include the following: Greven (1966:238) for Andover, Massachusetts, reports an average of 8.5 children per family, with 7.2 children in these families reaching the age of 21 years; Lockridge (1966:330) for Dedham, Massachusetts, reports an average of 4.64 children for each family; Higgs and Stettler (1970:286–287) for 10 different New England towns report an average of 7 children per family; Norton (1971:444) for Ipswich, Massachusetts, reports a mean number of 4.3 children per family where ''the date of the end of union is known'' and a mean of 6.4 children for those families that were ''technically complete'';[2] and Smith (1972:177) for Hingham, Massachusetts, presents a mean number of 6.53 children per family—the overall mean for six marriage cohorts that cover a period from 1641 to 1800—but there are significant

---

[2] In this instance completed families are those in which the wife remains married at least until the age of 45 or in which the union lasts at least 27 years (Norton, 1971:443).

variations from this average, especially the 1691–1715 cohort which had the lowest mean of 4.61 children per family. Hence, even if we accept the highest reported averages, the stereotype is challenged. Still there exists a wide discrepancy between the various figures reported that must be explored.

One explanation for the discrepancy might be that the various figures reported are unique for the particular town or area studied. Thus, just as it is impossible to describe accurately colonial life based only upon observations by Ben Franklin and others, it is also impossible to generalize and relate from the findings of one town in colonial America to an entire area or era. In an attempt to control for this problem, Higgs and Stettler (1970) collected data from a number of different towns. They observe that differences between towns do exist that must be realized and expected. Higgs and Stettler (1970:289), for example, note the average number of children per family varied from "a low of 5.19 in Malden to a high of 7.76 in Brookfield." The difference—2.57—between the average number of children, presented in their study, is still much smaller than the difference—5.23—between figures reported by Greven (1966) and Demos (1968) as previously noted. Geographical differences in sampling then may be a partial explanation for this discrepancy but does not suffice as a complete explanation.

Another factor that accounts for part of the discrepancy is a decline during the colonial period in complete fertility. Smith (1972:177–179) notes a decline in eighteenth century completed fertility, as compared to the seventeenth century, with the lowest rate recorded by those women marrying at the beginning of the eighteenth century (1691:1715). As Smith suggests, this is a pattern not unique to Hingham and is, to some degree, supported by the rates presented by the other studies—the higher means, in

most cases, come from studies of seventeenth century populations and the lower means, usually, come from studies of eighteenth century populations. This decline in completed fertility is a factor in the discrepancy and a factor that must be explored further but there is a simpler explanation for the wide differences reported.

A larger proportion of the difference can be explained in another way. The main reason for the widespread range of figures presented above is the use of varying operational definitions determining the number of children per family. The biggest difference results from the use of different time perspectives by observers of the colonial family unit. Currently the United States Census Bureau (1963:xxiv) reports the number of children per family as only those children residing in a household—family of residence—at the time of enumeration. Thus children who have left home, died, or are yet to be born are not counted. Plus, included in the calculation of the average number of children per family are childless couples, including newly married and elderly couples, who were usually not included in colonial studies' figures. This represents a cross-sectional view of the family and its characteristics. With only one exception (Demos, 1968), all of the studies reported above with regard to number of children per family take a longitudinal perspective.

Utilization of the longitudinal perspective means observing the completed family when noting the number of children in each family. The completed family includes: a man with his wife and any children born into their union. Although this has been the most common operational definition of the family used to determine the number of children and family size, there are some unique qualifications used by some of the researchers that should be noted. In his earlier study, for example, Demos (1965:270) used only "families in which both parents lived at least to age 50, or else if one parent died, the other quickly remarried." In their study, Higgs and Stettler (1970:284) included only families for which continuous residence in the same town was recorded throughout the entire childbearing period. Also note the difference—2.1—between families that were "technically complete" and those families where the date the union ended was known, as reported by Norton (1971:444). But even the latter and lower mean—4.1—is overstated, as compared to contemporary figures, because it is still based upon a longitudinal perspective and because of restrictions on the sample (Norton, 1971:443).

It becomes obvious that the number of children per family derived from an operational definition, based upon the completed family, gives us a much larger number than the cross-sectional perspective. This is not only the case for the colonial era but also for the United States today. Plus, with the use of additional limitations, like those used by Demos (1965), Higgs and Stettler (1970), and Norton (1971), a representative sample cannot be obtained from the areas being studied. Higgs and Stettler (1970:284 and 288) admit that their estimates of the number of children and family size are overstated. Certainly overstatement must occur in all those other works using a similar type of operational definition. Yet, because of the uneven recording of the data, the qualification of using only those families for which complete data exist seems to be necessary. In addition to overstatement resulting from sample qualifications, smaller, mobile families were less likely to generate the necessary birth, death, and marriage registrations in subsequent years which would assure inclusion in the sample. The fact that these small, mobile families had a lower probability of being included in a sample supports the contention that samples dealing only with completed families—using the longitudinal perspec-

tive—are unrepresentative and their figures overstated.

The only colonial data comparable to contemporary census data are provided by Demos' (1968) figures, based upon a census taken of colonial Bristol in 1689, which indicates the least variance between the contemporary and colonial figures (for figures see above). Although differences would still be expected, if we could derive comparable data—cross-sectional in nature—from the other colonial studies the average number of children per family would be reduced significantly. The conclusion must be that the number of children per family has been much exaggerated and that the actual number of children per family is not too different from the present figures.

In regard to overall family size it seems reasonably clear that the size of the colonial American family was much smaller than presumed. First, we noted the restricted nature—only two generations—for the family of residence in regard to generational make up. Second, the actual number of children in the colonial family unit at any given time appears to have been smaller than previously presumed. Thus, the exaggerated figures presented for family size—assuming the U.S. Census' present definition of family size—appears to have resulted from most authors using completed families and usually only a portion of these families to determine overall family size.

An additional element which produced an exaggerated family size was the presence of nonrelatives in the family's household who were counted as family members. An extreme example is presented by Demos (1965:285) using the household of Samuel Fuller. At Fuller's death in 1633, there were nine people in his household; five of these were not family members. In addition to his wife, son, and a nephew; there were two servants, a ward, and two "additional children." The "additional children" had been sent from other families to the Fuller household for education. The inclusion of wards, servants, boarders, resident employees, and others as part of the overall family size existed in preindustrial England, as well, as noted by Laslett and Harrison (1963:167–169) and Laslett (1965a:589). [It is noteworthy that the practice of counting all household members as members of the same family of residence, regardless of their relationship to one another, was continued by the United States Census Bureau (1949:18) until 1930.]

Considering only studies of colonial families where the exaggeration factors are controlled or eliminated, the family size appears to have been relatively small indeed. Lockridge (1966:343) derives from lists of houses, counting only parents and children, an average family size of six for Dedham, a little under six for Medfield, and less than five for Salem. In colonial Bristol, where Demos (1968:45) also eliminated all servants and counted only parents and children, the average family size was 5.304. If we compare these figures with the average family size for the United States (Bureau of Census, 1963:465) in 1960—3.65—the difference ranges from 2.35 to less than 1.34 persons per family. By these standards, clearly, the presumed large family did not exist in the majority of cases.

Age at Marriage

The ages presented by Calhoun appear to be completely erroneous based upon a consensus of the recent works surveyed. Not only is the colonial marriage age much higher than stated by Calhoun, but the ages for both men and women are higher than those of the present day. Demos (1965:275) reports for the Plymouth colony that the average age at first marriage for men dropped from 27.0 to 24.6 years and for women it increased from 20.6 to 22.3 years. This included people born

before 1600 and those born by 1700 which were divided into 25-year groups based upon year of birth. Norton (1971:445) found in Ipswich a similar pattern in regard to age at first marriage and, in fact, very similar ages but the similar age levels occurred approximately half a century later than in the Plymouth colony. Lockridge (1966:331) reports for Dedham from 1640 to 1690 the average age at first marriage for men was 25.5 years and for women 22.5, and Greven (1966:240) observes for Andover almost identical results. In Hingham, although the overall trend is the same, the highest ages at first marriage for both sex increased initially and reached their highest level at the turn of the century (1691–1715) before declining (Smith, 1972:177). For colonial Bristol, Demos (1968:55) reports the lowest ages at first marriage of all the colonial studies yet cited. For those couples in colonial Bristol who married before 1750, the men had an average age of 23.9 and the women had an average age of 20.5 and, for those couples who married after 1750, the men had an average age of 24.3 and the women's average age was 21.1. Higgs and Stettler (1970:285) report ages remarkably similar to those reported by Demos for Bristol.

Comparability of the above figures with current data is problematical because age at marriage is reported by the United States Census Bureau in terms of medians, not means or averages—the statistics reported by most colonial family studies with the exception of Demos' (1968) study of colonial Bristol in which he reports both the mean and the median age. His data are presented along with other colonial data and more current data in Table 1.

The ages Demos presents from his 1968 study are remarkably similar to ages presented for the contemporary figures. Utilizing this data, in addition to the ages reported by other works, age at first marriage was not extremely early, as contended

TABLE 1
Age at First Marriage: Figures from Colonial Studies and the U. S. Census Bureau[a]

Time of Marriage	Age of Men		Age of Women	
1600's	Mean	Median	Mean	Median
Before 1624[b] (Plymouth)	27.0		20.6	
1640–1690[c] (Dedham)	25.5		22.5	
Before 1691[d] (Hingham)	27.4		22.0	
1700's				
1691–1715[d] (Hingham)	28.4		24.7	
Before 1750[e] (Bristol)	23.9	22.4	20.5	20.3
After 1750[e] (Bristol)	24.3	23.8	21.1	20.8
1800's				
1890[f] (U.S.)		26.1		22.0
1900's				
1930[f] (U.S.)		24.3		21.3
1966[f] (U.S.)		22.8		20.5

[a] Data for the 1600's and the 1700's have been selected from a number of recent studies dealing with families residing in colonial communities.
[b] Source: Demos (1965:275)
[c] Source: Lockridge (1966:333)
[d] Source: Smith (1972:177)
[e] Source: Demos (1968:55)
[f] Source: Smigel and Seiden (1968:15–16)

by Calhoun, but similar to current figures and sometimes higher.

Considering the discrepancies between the ages reported by the various colonial family studies, we should first note that the lower ages presented by Demos' (1968) and Higgs and Stettler (1970:285) contrast with the higher ages reported by Lockridge (1966), Greven (1966), and Demos (1965). The difference appears to be related to the century in which the births of the individuals in the sample occurred. The latter group, with the higher marriage ages for men and women, used samples of individuals born in the seventeenth century; while the former group, with lower marriage ages, used individuals born in the eighteenth century. The data presented by Norton (1971:445) and Smith (1972:177), who present figures

for both centuries, support these trends—for men the average age at first marriage was higher in the seventeenth century and declined in the eighteenth century and for women the average age was initially lower in the seventeenth century, increased around the end of the seventeenth century and the beginning of the eighteenth century, declined somewhat during the middle of the eighteenth century, and increased slightly toward the end of the eighteenth century. Further there appears to be a return to a higher age for both sexes in the nineteenth century, as represented by the 1890 data in Table 1, that is similar to the higher ages for those individuals born in the seventeenth century. Although the former figure is a median and the latter a mean, at this point there is little basis to suppose a much greater difference would result if the statistics were the same.

A tentative fluctuation pattern for age at marriage emerges. Age at first marriage was quite high in the seventeenth century colonies but dropped to a lower level during the eighteenth century; the latter age level was remarkably similar to a level obtained during the present century. Then during the nineteenth century there occurred a marriage age remarkably similar to the high levels reported for the colonial seventeenth century.

Focusing on the colonial period there are a number of factors that have been cited as determining age-levels at marriage. The high ages for men and the low ages for women at first marriage during the first decades of settlement in the seventeenth century have been attributed to a severely imbalanced sex ratio (Henretta, 1971:387; Smith, 1972:176) as suggested by Moller's (1945:113–153) study of passengers on ships coming to New England. But as Norton (1971:445–446) has noted, the Puritans emphasized from the beginning that Massachusetts—where the majority of the communities studied and cited here are located—must be colonized by family units rather than single men. For Ipswich an excess of males only occurred for a brief period after it was founded. Norton suggests that economic considerations, particularly the demand for male labor, were important in determining age-levels at marriage. In the eighteenth century the role of certain "external pressures"—limited geographical expansion, military threat from the Indians and French, inheritance systems, migration, and overcrowded towns—upon marital age patterns has been emphasized (cf. Henretta, 1971:389–391; Smith, 1972: 176–180). As with the tentative fluctuation pattern in marital age-levels described above, data on the marital age patterns for the colonial period and, in particular, an

understanding of the factors determining these patterns, are fragmentary, although they do provide researchers with a basis for further investigation.

A later age at marriage for colonial women, as these studies appear to indicate, has implications for the birth rate and ultimately family size. A later age at marriage for women is a form of family limitation (cf. Wrigley, 1966a:82–109) which reduces the birth rate because the number of birth potential years is shortened. Smith (1972:178) notes that 43.3 per cent of the decline in completed marital fertility for his 1691–1715 marriage cohort can be accounted for by an increase in female age at marriage.

Infant Mortality Rate

It has been assumed by Calhoun and others that the infant mortality rate was quite high. However, based upon certain preceding challenges of the stereotypic view of the colonial family, there is some support—even without data—that a view of high infant mortality rate should be altered. If the number of children per family (completed families) is less than expected, the majority of children born must survive to maintain a family unit that will survive from generation to generation. Furthermore, the fact that marriage was occurring at a much later age than assumed reduces the number of children that can be born. These two factors would seem to indicate the probability of a lower infant mortality rate than previously assumed.

The infant mortality rates reported by the various works are quite low but each author notes the tentative nature of these findings. Demos (1965:271) observes the rate of infant mortality for Plymouth to have been "relatively low" with only one child in five dying before the age of 21. Demos notes that the exact date of death frequently cannot be established so it is more accurate to speak of infant and child mortality together. This would apply to the other works, as well. Potter (1965:656, 658–660), in a recalculation of data from New Jersey for the latter part of the eighteenth century, found ''an astonishingly low infant mortality rate.'' Greven (1966:237) found in Andover that only 15.7 per cent of the children whose births were ascertained died before the age of 21. Norton (1971:442) for Ipswich found ''strikingly low'' infant and child mortality rates even after correcting for underrecording.

One major problem that particularly plagues infant mortality data for the colonial period is underrecording. As Lockridge (1966:329) observes, it is ''known that stillborn infants and infants who died within two or three days of birth were not recorded.'' Norton (1971:439–443) estimated that 33 per cent of all infant deaths were not registered. Yet even after correcting for underrecording, applying estimates and techniques proscribed by Henry et al., and using family reconstitution[3] to check upon the level of mortality derived from aggregative analysis, the mortality rates for Ipswich were quite low. Thus, most recent works note a lower infant mortality rate than previously presumed, but the data are limited to approximate levels of infant mortality.

One explanation that has received some support argues that elements in the colonial environment reduced the probability of a high infant mortality rate. Potter (1965:663) and Klingaman (1971:555) describe the food supply for the colonies as generally adequate and increasingly abundant. In his review of mortality rates for Dedham and

Watertown, Lockridge (1966:336) notes that these towns went through a century of life ''substantially'' free of disasters which could have cut deeply into the ranks of the population. This is in sharp contrast to the demographic crises experienced in similar European villages for the same period. Noting the lack of disease and hunger in these towns, Lockridge (1966:337) believes it is ''quite possible that the new land had substantial gifts to offer and freedom to bestow other than the freedom from Anglican persecutions.'' Norton (1971:449–450) suggests that the most important cause in reduced mortality was the apparent marked decrease in death resulting from infectious disease. This appears to be the result of a number of factors related to the environmental conditions of the colonists—there were fewer sources of infection (all had to be imported), a decreased rate of spread of infection (sparse population), and greater survival chances once the infection was contracted. Furthermore, as these conditions changed the mortality rates increased. These elements helped to sustain the health of childbearing-age women and improved the survival chances of infants; thus keeping infant mortality rates down.

Discussion

The foregoing briefly surveys the work being done on the structural characteristics of the colonial family as previously outlined. These studies provide an important step toward the goal of a restoration of the colonial family system but the scope of these works is limited and further efforts are required. As Greven (1967:443) has observed, the fullest development of ''early American history . . . cannot focus exclusively upon the accumulation of data from vital records, nor should it be mesmerized by the prospects of quantification.'' Other sources of a quantitative nature and ''verbal data'' are essen-

[3] In using family reconstitution to calculate mortality rates, only the mortality of married adults and, usually, only those children that remain in the family of residence can be studied.

tial to add the necessary dimensions to further inquiries concerning the family and communities. A move to add the necessary dimensions is observed by Saveth (1969: 326–327) in his discussion of Bailyn's concept and technique of "family style."

Before the last two decades, our image of the colonial family had been based primarily upon the reports of a restricted set of "verbal data." With the development of new techniques and an expanding interest, this earlier image is being revised by quantitative and documented facts. Before complete restoration can occur one final step is necessary. This step involves the better understanding of the complex interrelationships between patterns of demographic characteristics—family size, birth rates, geographical mobility, health conditions—and family patterns which cannot be quantified—authority pattern, sex role definitions, power relationships, *etc.* Dealing with the interrelationships between various demographic characteristics and their effect upon colonial population growth, Smith (1972) provides an excellent basis and example for further work in this direction. Once this final step is obtained, many family observers anticipate that located within the family will be "the basic determinants of historical change" (Saveth, 1969:326).

There are some limitations, which indicate the direction of further study, that should be mentioned in regard to the status of the restoration of the colonial American family. Although dealing with the general subject of the colonial family, the majority of data thus far reported are limited to families located in New England. Hence, it is necessary to provide data on familial variables for the Middle and Southern colonies, especially in light of the substantial demographic differences that existed, which have important implications for the colonial family (*cf.* Potter, 1965). Of course, there are differences to be expected among the

families located in the New England colonies. Even the communities which have been studied thus far vary significantly. Certainly there are different factors affecting the family in a coastal settlement like Ipswich, which depended primarily upon maritime industries, than in an agricultural community like Plymouth. In addition, there are virtually no data available for families residing in frontier settlements, although indications are that major differences existed there (Laslett, 1970:85–86). Further study is necessary upon other factors which played a role in the familial behavior of the colonial American population. Some of this work has begun but further efforts are necessary both on the more obvious variables, such as migration (*cf.* Potter, 1965; Norton, 1971: 433–436; Smith, 1972:174), landholding customs (Henretta, 1971:389–391), age distribution, sex ratio, and some of the less visible variables, such as family limitation and relative age of husband in relation to wife's fertility (Smith, 1972:180–182). The work that remains to be done seems almost limitless, yet the work already completed plus an apparent increasing interest should result in a better understanding of the colonial family and its surrounding physical and social environment.

Most sociologists working in the colonial family area have been concerned with rediscovering behavior patterns that are supposedly unique to industrialized societies. Concern has been less directly with restoration of the colonial family and more with challenging the presumed influences of industrialization and urbanization upon the familial institution. Works of this nature make important contributions to the restoration process by establishing the stability or change of various family patterns since the colonial period. In addition a number of sociologists are attempting to determine what factors have brought about the changes in family patterns that have occurred. In a recent review of sociologists' work in this area, Adams (1971:75) notes the increasing precision with which the colonial family can be described. Further, he observes that only a few changes in the family "can be directly related to the industrial revolution."

An example of the "sociologists' approach" is offered by Furstenberg's (1966:337) analysis of the written accounts by foreign travelers in the United States. According to his findings there are striking similarities to the contemporary American family in regard to the system of mate selection, parent-child relations, and the marital relationship in the preindustrial American family. Similarly, Lantz et al. (1968: 424–425), using content analysis of colonial magazines, observed the prevalence of the romantic love complex and the importance placed upon personal happiness as a motive in mate choice. Both of these patterns are contrary to the commonly postulated patterns for a preindustrial society. It is noteworthy that both of these examples provide data derived primarily from "verbal data," not empirical data. Like the more quantitative work already presented, this approach also contributes to the restoration of the colonial family and the establishment of essential base lines. Through the establishment of these base lines, we can differentiate the dimension and the extent of change. This will lead not only to a refining of our understanding of the relationship between industrialization and the family, but also to a better understanding of total societal change.

In summary, resulting from all the works surveyed, a new, more realistic, image of the colonial family has emerged. In short, the colonial family appears to be structurally similar in many ways to the present family in the United States. Colonial families were predominantly restricted or nuclear units which, at any given point in time, were similar in size to present family units. Although the completed colonial family was larger than the contemporary family, the difference is not as large as previously assumed. Infant mortality did not play the role in affecting family size as commonly assumed. Furthermore, there is mounting evidence that certain behavioral patterns that were presumed unique to the contemporary family existed in the colonial family system. Thus, there appear to be more similarities than differences between these two family systems. It is surprising, but accurate, that this is a recent perspective in regard to family study. This is primarily due to an overemphasis in the past upon the phenomenon of change. This overemphasis has led to the neglect of what has remained permanent in the American family structure. In support, Aries (1962:9) observes that the "historical differences [in the family] are of little importance in comparison with the huge mass of what remains unchanged." Important changes have occurred but the focus must be upon exactly what has changed and the factors which have brought about this change.

This process of restoration is by no means complete; much work remains to be done. Although the emphasis in this paper has been upon the structural similarity between the colonial and the contemporary family system, there are important differences. Changes, occurring in the patterns of premarital sexual behavior and norms, husband and wife roles, and divorce laws, have been widely accepted by family observers (cf. Adams, 1971:64–75). A major difficulty is that patterns of this nature lend themselves less to quantification. This becomes even more of a problem because most of the data concerning these patterns can no longer be obtained, and in many cases the data were not initially recorded in the colonial era. The work must continue on these patterns, however, despite the difficulties to provide a full account of what has changed and to what extent since the colonial family.

Summary

It has been the attempt of this paper to survey the present status of the restoration of the colonial family which is being conducted primarily by historians and sociologists. In the past, interdisciplinary efforts have been encouraged but infrequently carried out. In the study of the colonial American family it must be concluded that, in the past, both disciplines have gone their own directions. But a growing knowledge and appreciation by each discipline of the work in both fields is evident in recent publications (Saveth, 1969; Gordon and Bernstein, 1970; Anderson, 1971). An additional aim of this paper is to add to this growing knowledge and appreciation of the works, concepts, and techniques of both disciplines. The final expectation is that this growing knowledge and appreciation will result in a meaningful collaboration in the future. The success of this collaboration will act as an example to other scholars.

References

Adams, Bert N.
  1971   The American Family: A Sociological Interpretation. Chicago:Markham Publishing Company.

Anderson, Michael
  1971   Family Structure in Nineteenth Century Lancashire. New York:Cambridge University Press.

Arensberg, Conrad M.
  1955   "American communities." American Anthropologist 57 (December):1143–1162.

Aries, Philippe
  1962   Centuries of Childhood. New York: Alfred Knopf.

Calhoun, Arthur W.
  1919   A Social History of the American Family: From Colonial Times to the Present. 3 Volumes. Cleveland, Ohio:Arthur H. Clark.

Committee on Historiography
  1954   The Social Sciences in Historical Study. Bulletin 64. New York:Social Science Research Council.

Demos, John
  1965   "Notes on life in Plymouth Colony." William and Mary Quarterly, Third Series 22 (April):264–286.

  1968   "Families in Colonial Bristol, Rhode Island: an exercise in historical demography." William and Mary Quarterly, Third Series 25. (October):40–57.

Edwards, John (ed.)
  1969   The Family and Change. New York:Alfred A. Knopf.

Eversley, D. E. C.
  1966   "Exploitation of Anglican parish registers by aggregative analysis." Pp. 44–95 in E. A. Wrigley (ed.), An Introduction to English Historical Demography from the Sixteenth to Nineteenth Century. New York: Basic Books.

Furstenberg, Frank F., Jr.
  1966   "Industrialization and the American family: a look backward." American Sociological Review 31 (June):326–337.

Glass, D. V.
  1965   "Introduction." Pp. 1–20 in D. V. Glass and D. E. C. Eversley (eds.), Population in History: Essays in Historical Demography. Chicago: Aldine Publishing Company.

Goode, William J.
  1963   World Revolution and Family Patterns. New York:The Free Press.

Gordon, Michael and M. Charles Bernstein
  1970   "Mate choice and domestic life in the nineteenth-century marriage manual." Journal of Marriage and the Family 32 (November):665–674.

Greenfield, Sidney M.
1961   "Industrialization and the family in sociological theory." American Journal of Sociology 67 (November):312–322.

Greven, Philip J., Jr.
1966   "Family structure in the seventeenth century Andover, Massachusetts." William and Mary Quarterly, 3rd Series 23 (April):234–256.

1967   "Historical demography and colonial America." William and Mary Quarterly, Third Series 24 (July):438–454.

Hareven, Tamara K.
1971   "The history of the family as an interdisciplinary field." The Journal of Interdisciplinary History 2 (Autumn): 399–414.

Henretta, James A.
1971   "The morphology of New England society in the colonial period." The Journal of Interdisciplinary History 2 (Autumn):379–398.

Henry, Louis
1968   "Historical demography." Daedalus 97 (Spring):385–396.

Higgs, Robert and H. Louis Stettler, III
1970   "Colonial New England demography: a sampling approach." William and Mary Quarterly, Third Series 27 (April):282–293.

Hollingworth, Thomas H.
1969   Historical Demography. Ithaca, New York:Cornell University Press.

Klingaman, David
1971   "Food surpluses and deficits in the American colonies, 1768–1772." The Journal of Economic History 31 (September):553–569.

Lantz, Herman, Raymond Schmitt, Margaret Britton, and Eloise Snyder
1968   "Pre-industrial patterns in the colonial family in America." American Sociological Review 33 (June):413–426.

Laslett, Peter
1965a   "The history of population and social structure." International Social Science Journal 27 (August):582–594.

1965b   The World We Lost. New York: Charles Scribner's and Sons.

1969   "Size and structure of the household in England over three centuries." Population Studies 23 (July):199–224.

1970   "The comparative history of household and family." Journal of Social History 4 (Fall):75–87.

Laslett, Peter and John Harrison
1963   "Clayworth and Cogenhoe." Pp. 157–184 in H. E. Bell and R. L. Ollard (eds.), Historical Essays 1600–1750: Presented to David Ogg. London: Adam and Charles Black.

Lockridge, Kenneth A.
1966   "The population of Dedham, Massachusetts, 1636–1736." Economic History Review, Second Series 19 (August): 318–344.

Moller, Herbert
1945   "Sex composition and correlated culture patterns of colonial America." William and Mary Quarterly, Third Series 2 (October):113–153.

Norton, Susan L.
1971   "Population growth in colonial America: a study of Ipswich, Massachusetts." Population Studies 25 (November):433–452.

Ogburn, W. F. and Meyer F. Nimkoff
1950   Sociology. Boston:Houghton Mifflin.

Potter, J.
1965   "The growth of population in America, 1700–1860." Pp. 631–688 in D. V. Glass and D. E. C. Eversley (eds.), Population in History: Essays in Historical Demography. Chicago: Aldine.

Saveth, Edwards N.
1969   "The problems of American family history." American Quarterly 21 (Summer):311–329.

Smelser, Neil
1967   "Sociological history: the industrial revolution and the British working-class family." Journal of Social History 1 (Fall):17–35.

1968   Essays in Sociological Explanation. Englewood Cliffs, New Jersey: Prentice-Hall.

Smigel, E. O. and R. Seiden
1968   "The decline and fall of the double standard." The Annals 376 (March): 6–17.

Smith, Daniel S.
1972   "The demographic history of colonial New England." The Journal of Economic History 32 (March): 165–184.

Stone, Lawrence
1967   The Crisis of the Aristocracy, 1558–1641. New York:Oxford.

United States: Bureau of the Census
1949   Historical Statistics of the United States 1789–1945. Washington, D.C.:United States Government Printing Office.

1963   United States Population: 1960: Detailed Characteristics United States Summary. Final Report PC(1)-1D. Washington, D.C.:United States Government Printing Office.

Vinovskis, Marie A.
1971   "The 1789 life table of Edward Wigglesworth." The Journal of Economic History 31 (September):570–590.

Wrigley, E. Anthony
1966a   "Family limitation in pre-industrial England." Economic History Review, Second Series 19 (April):82–109.

1966b   "Family reconstitution." Pp. 96–159 in E. A. Wrigley (ed.), An Introduction to English Historical Demography from the Sixteenth to Nineteenth Century. New York:Basic Books.

Research Across the Generation Gap

VERN L. BENGTSON

The problem of generations is as old as mankind's earliest writings and as contemporary as this morning's newspaper. The succession of one generation by another involves an inevitable tension between change and continuity, reflected in the lives of individuals and of social groups as they move through time.

Although the "generation gap" is neither new nor unprecedented it may appear to be both—judged by contemporary mass media accounts of intergenerational relations. The purpose of this chapter is to present a brief overview of some current research perspectives on contrasts and similarities between contemporaneous generations. My focus is on a neglected link in the succession of generations: relations between middle-aged children and their aging parents in today's society.

To dissect the contemporary "generation gap" rationally and scientifically is not all that easy. For one thing, the current sociological literature concerning intergenerational relations and aging is underdeveloped, compared to other arenas of family life. To date there have been relatively few studies on which to base generalizations concerning the place of aged family members in current American society. Professionals and social scientists often find themselves dealing with a welter of myth and misinformation concerning contemporary family life, perpetuated by the mass media. We hear much about the "troubled American family" and about the neglect and isolation of older family members. As Ethel Shanas (1979) has pointed out, such alarm is misplaced. Yet the research basis on which we can attach such myths is only now beginning to receive attention.

Second, there has been until recently a lack of adequate conceptual tools to examine the multifaceted interactional dimensions represented in the contemporary American family. We have heard much in the past decade concerning a "generation gap" which is evident within families and between age groups. Take any current political issue; for example, Proposition 13 and limitations in the use of property taxes to finance social services. If Grandpa advocates the passage of such legislation and his 19 year-old granddaughter is vehemently against it, does this constitute a "generation gap," and if so, what are the underlying causes of such differences? Is this an example of increasing conservatism that comes with old age as a "normal" and "inevitable" part of life course changes, or can the contrast be traced to events specific to cohorts which came of age during contrasting points of sociopolitical history? Only recently has it become clear that generational differences reflect complex configurations of time and social structure, and that the "generation gap" may be more apparent than real—depending on the conceptual lenses through

Source: Adapted from Bengtson, V. L. Research perspectives on intergenerational interaction. In P. Ragan (ed.), *Aging parents*. Los Angeles, Calif.: University of Southern California Press, 1979, pp. 41–68. Reprinted by permission.

which such differences are viewed (Schaie, 1965; Bengtson, 1971; Bengtson & Cutler, 1976).

A third problem is over-generalization. Common sense tells us that no two families are alike. Yet in our comments about the American family we tend to ignore the diversity between subgroups in our society at the very time more and more families are asking practitioners for specific solutions to specific problems in family life. Many of these problems involve intergenerational negotiation (Hill, Foote, Aldous, Carlson, & MacDonald, 1970; Rosenfeld, 1979 & 1980; Shanas, 1979; Shanas & Streib, 1965; Sussman, 1976; Treas, 1975). Practitioners and scholars must appreciate diversity, just as they must recognize common patterns that emerge from available studies.

With these three problems as background, I want to examine four issues in family structure and interaction patterns between generations from the standpoint of contemporary research. The first issue concerns conceptual problems in intergenerational relations; the second, differences across generational boundaries; the third, problems in family relations which are particularly acute in families where an aged individual is undergoing some of the normal transitions of aging; finally, processes in resolving these problems within families.

Conceptual Tools in Dissecting the "Generation Gap"

Conceptual clarity is my first concern as we attempt to dissect the various elements of the so-called "generation gap." Individuals, families, and age groups are social entities moving through time; they exhibit attributes of both change and continuity when compared at different points in historical time. When we attempt to unravel the causes of such change and continuity, we must begin with an historical perspective (Elder, 1974).

The social movements exhibited in America of the 1960–1970 period provide a most useful example. During this decade Americans became concerned about the prospect of social and political cleavages between age groups which appeared to be pulling society apart—the "generation gap." Four social movements appeared during this protest-filled decade. First, in 1960 the Civil Rights Movement emerged with predominantly young Whites and Blacks marching together, culminating in bloody confrontations which troubled an entire nation. Next, in 1964 the Free Speech Movement began; college youth questioned the legitimacy of their elders' total control over educational governance. Then, by 1966 the Viet Nam protest movement had begun a momentum which drove one president from power and shook traditional views concerning American foreign policy. Most colleges during 1968–1970 experienced some form of organized protest on the part of youth questioning the moral and legal basis for an undeclared war directed by their elders; most families probably experienced the disquieting effects of intergenerational confrontation about the war. The fourth set of issues and events which can be termed a social movement was the emergence of the "counter-culture." Groups of youth began espousing values and behaviors which ran counter to the ethos of productivity, cleanliness, and capitalism that appeared to characterize their parents' generation. Long hair, second- and third-hand clothes, recreational use of drugs and sex, communal living—all these reflected an emerging lifestyle in clear contrast to middle-class, middle-aged conventions of the 1960's. Margaret Mead (1970) suggested that these youth were "immigrants in time" moving into a new cultural system and reversing prior mechanisms of socialization. Whereas in human society prior to this time children had learned from their parents, the pace of social and technological innovation has accelerated to such a pace that, according to Mead, soon children will have to teach their parents how to survive, what is good or valuable, what is bad or maladaptive. Or, as Edgar Friedenberg (1969) summarized this view, "Young people today aren't rebelling against their parents: they are *abandoning* them."

Ten years later such pronouncements now appear almost quaint; on today's quiet college campuses there are few reminders that the Sixties' clash between generations were so pervasive and portentous. Age groups do not seem to oppose each other; rather, as in the 1950's, all age groups today appear vaguely concerned about inflation, taxes, and jobs. Perhaps the pendulum swing is exactly the point: that both change and continuity are exhibited by individuals, families, and age groups at different points in historical time.

How can one account for such contrasts? What are the causes of differences—and similarities—between generations? Three concepts may be useful in examining the change and continuity in intergenerational comparisons: cohort effect, lineage effect, and period effect (see Bengtson & Cutler, 1976, for a more comprehensive discussion). Although all three effects are interrelated, each provides a slightly different perspective for viewing aging and social change.

The *cohort effect,* or in the language of mass media, the "cohort gap," refers to real or apparent differences between individuals born at different points in historical time. In 1978 persons born in 1940 compared with those born in 1920 will have a very different set of life-cycle concerns as well as life experiences. First, because they were born in different points in time, they will be at different points in the life cycle—at different stages psychologically, physiologically, and sociologically. Second, because they were

born at different points in time, they will also have experienced sociopolitical events differently, as those events were encountered at different stages of life span development. The war in Viet Nam, to give one example, was undoubtedly experienced quite differently by most twenty-year-olds compared to their forty-year-old parents. There are good reasons for the existence of contrasts between individuals born at different points in time, either on the basis of maturation or cohort experience. There is, in short, good reason for a cohort-level generation gap.

The *lineage effect,* or "lineage gap," refers to real or perceived differences between generations within families. The family may be viewed as a system of social organization in which there are a series of statuses defined by ranked descent. Fathers and mothers, sons and daughters, grandchildren, and great-grandchildren form successive links in an unending succession of biological and social generations. This particular conceptual tool was used by the very first historians to put in order events of history: Old Testament periods are set off by lineage; time of a particular event was frequently set by reference to the life span of a particular ancestor in the lineage chain.

Are there inevitable differences between generations by virtue of differential status as parent or child? Most of modern psychology assumes, following the insight of Freud, that indeed an inevitable and useful rebellion occurs as young children wish, first of all, to become their parents, and secondly, to take over many of the attributes of their parents. Although the Freudian model has not been universally accepted, the theme of generational conflict within families appears frequently throughout literature. One thinks, for example, of the aged King Lear at the beginning of Shakespeare's play—an embittered king seeing his wishes disrespected, and crying "Oh, the infamy that is to be a parent!"—his words indeed reflect a lineage gap.

Similarly, the third concept, the *period effect,* is useful to look at attitudes at a given point in time and compare them with attitudes of another time. Examining relationships between generations or between groups within society, it is likewise instructive to compare similarities as well as differences. Throughout philosophical literature one reads the laments of older generations concerning the young. Plato's observations about the young being undisciplined, unmotivated, and taking drugs is often repeated today as solace for those of us in the middle generation who may find that our own children's lack of industry fails to meet our ideals. It may be that the so-called generation gap is really not much more serious even in today's fast-changing society than it was a hundred years ago. It may be that there is an inevitable "period gap."

As Treas (1975) has suggested, there are historical differences in demography, and therefore differences in contact within families, compared with the last century. There are differences simply in the number of individuals per generation within a given family. You can ask yourself about the amount of contact between successive generations in your family. My mother and I are in contact every week. She was in contact with her mother only the three or four times a year when she could visit on the Nebraska farm. In turn, my grandmother never saw her grandmother after she immigrated to this country at the age of eleven; and my great-grandmother never saw her mother, who died in childbirth. Much more contact takes place between generations today than at any other time in American history simply because of advances in telecommunications and other technological innovations that make such contact possible. Whether the quality of contact has changed as much as the quantity, I do not know. I do know in reading 19th century American novels built around the theme of disaffection between generations, the conflict was usually re-

solved by the younger generation moving west to the frontier and having no further contact with the older generation.

In short, when we look at intergenerational interaction and the differences which appear between generations, it is necessary to distinguish among three conceptual causes. Each effect—cohort, lineage, and period—may create natural and inevitable differences in attitudes, values, and behaviors of the individuals involved in the drama of intergenerational interaction. But each also can be seen as effecting some degree of continuity. Maturational changes can be expected to bring children closer to their parents' orientations as they mature in adulthood; lineage effects involve transmission between generations and therefore greater similarity; period effects involve all contemporaneous generations experiencing similar socio-historical events and adapting to them in parallel, if not in series. For generations are social units moving through time, exhibiting both change and continuity.

Differences Between Generations, Real and Perceived

I have suggested that, in theory, comparisons between age groups reflect both continuity and contrast as one considers the effects of cohort, lineage, and historical period on behaviors and orientations. The question remains: how different are contemporary generations? What does contemporary research indicate concerning contrasts between youth, their middle-aged parents, and their aging grandparents?

A pervasive perception in today's society is that there are significant differences between age groups today—that there is a serious and profound "generation gap" in contemporary culture. We hear this in a variety of ways: stereotypes concerning youthful rebellion and geriatric conser-

54 Vern L. Bengtson

vatism, dismay about the declining importance of the American family, discussions about the "sexual revolution" which today appears less concerned with physical sexuality than with male-female sex roles.

Two decades of research concerning the generation gap have produced a mixture of generalizations about contrasts and similarities (Troll & Bengtson, 1978). Generational differences appear in some areas but not in others; sometimes they seem pronounced, sometimes trivial. I would like to illustrate with some findings from a large-scale survey conducted during the past six years at the University of Southern California. These case studies amplify some of the causes, similarities, and differences. The survey data come from 2,044 individuals who are members of three-generation families. These families were contacted through the membership list of a large Southern California health care plan, and consisted of at least one grandparent, one or more middle-aged children, and the grandchildren between the ages of 16 and 26 (see Bengtson, 1975, for a more complete description of this sample).

One area we investigated involved value orientations. We asked the members of the, three generations to rank in order of importance 16 items reflecting various goals or orientations. The results are displayed in Figure 1.

By comparing answers from grandparents, parents, and youth for each item, one sees clear contrasts between generations. "Achievement," for example, was ranked highest by the middle-aged parents, significantly lower by youth, and lower still by grandparents. "Personal freedom" was ranked very high by youth, but two scale-points lower by the grandparents—a pattern seen also in "skill" and "exciting life."

But while there are value differences between generations reflected in these data, there are also similarities; and what is most interesting is that many of the differences run counter to usual expectations. The three

generations show rather similar rankings on items such as "respect" and "possessions" as well as "service to mankind." Some contrasts are surprising. On the item "a world at peace" we expected the highest ranking to be given by the youngest generation; after all, it was the youth who appeared to be in the forefront of peace demonstrations in the 1960's. But of the three groups it was the grandparents who ranked this value highest. Similar patterns appeared on "service to mankind" and "equality of mankind" —valued highest by the grandparents, next by the grandchildren, third by the parents. These scores on humanistic values suggest that some stereotypes about generational differences in orientations are inaccurate. Not only are there similarities in value rankings, but the differences that exist run counter to many expectations.

In another analysis of these data (Bengtson, 1975), value orientations were examined in terms of cohort vs. lineage effects. Here it was found that there were strong lineage (within-family socialization) effects despite cohort differences. Through three generations, value similarities could be traced which suggest the strength of lineage continuity in orientations.

The *perception* of generational differences may be more important than actual contrasts in orientations and behavior. Data from the University of Southern California survey suggest that there is a strong tendency to believe that generational differences exist, but that the perception of such differences varies across generational boundaries in both cohort and lineage terms. In this section of the study respondents were asked to rate the "closeness" of the relationship between members of various generational groupings depicted in two social contexts: the "broader society" (cohort) and "your own family" (lineage). (see Tables 1A and 1B.)

The results of this analysis indicate three things. First, the "cohort gap" perceived

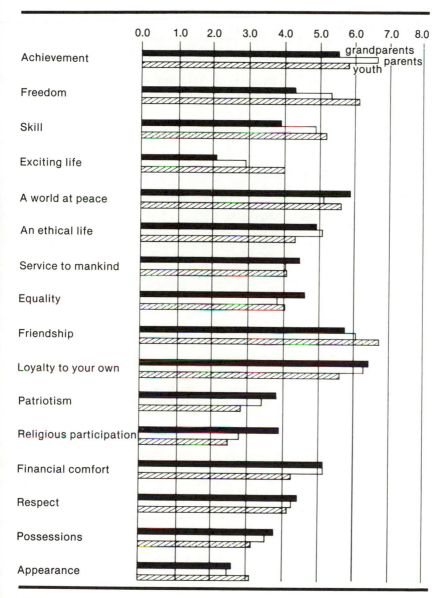

FIGURE 1
Mean of each value ranking, by generation.

between generations in the broader society is considerably larger than the "lineage gap" perceived within the respondents' own families. Second, the age of the *perceiver* makes some difference in the degree to which a "gap" is seen: the youngest age group (youth, age 16–26) perceives the least closeness, particularly at the family level. At

TABLE 1A
Mean Perception of "Cohort Gap" by Generation of Respondent[a]

	Referent						
	Between G3–G2		Between G3–G1		Between G2–G1		Total by generation of respondent
Respondent	x̄	s.d.	x̄	s.d.	x̄	s.d.	x̄
G1	3.62	1.37	3.90	1.63	3.00	1.31	3.51
G2	3.20	1.12	4.25	1.31	2.81	1.11	3.42
G3	3.28	1.35	4.42	1.44	2.95	1.19	3.55
Total by generation of referent	3.38	1.29	4.17	1.48	2.92	1.21	3.49

[a] "Some people say there is a 'generation gap' between age groups in American society today. How much of a 'gap' do you think there is between the following groups?" (The groups referred to are the column headings in this table.) Subjects gave responses on a six-point scale from "no gap whatsoever" (scored 1) to "very great gap" (scored 6).

TABLE 1B
Mean Perceptions of the "Lineage Gap" by Generation of Respondent[b]

	Referent						
	Between G3–G2		Between G3–G1		Between G2–G1		Total by generation of respondent
Respondent	x̄	s.d.	x̄	s.d.	x̄	s.d.	x̄
G1	2.19	1.24	2.06	1.23	1.81	1.19	2.02
G2	2.35	1.04	3.62	1.53	2.72	1.28	2.89
G3	2.96	1.34	3.75	1.62	2.70	1.23	3.14
Total by generation of referent	2.46	1.24	3.07	1.65	2.38	1.30	2.64

[b] "In your family, how great is the 'gap' between the three generations, in your opinion?"

Source: Bengtson, 1971.

the cohort level, the old and the young attribute similar levels of distance. Grandparents see the greatest amount of closeness within the family. Third, the age of the *referent* constitutes an important difference: a greater "gap" is perceived between the youth and the elderly than between the other generational dyads mentioned.

The general conclusion, then, is that the nature of cross-generation perceptions varies according to several factors, primary of which is the context of the generational grouping (family vs. broader society). For the older family members this contrast is particularly pronounced. Respondents seem to be saying, "Yes, there *is* a generation gap—but not in *my* family."

Why are there such differences in generational perceptions, and why are differences focused on when there is evidence of intergenerational similarity? Cohort, lineage, and period effects combine to give each member of the generational chain a different perception of the meaning of generational contrasts and similarities. Each family member has a contrasting "generational stake" or investment in the other generation which colors his or her perception of the other and of the relationship (Bengtson & Kuypers, 1971).

Each individual in the family is a changing entity, developing as an individual; so too the relationship among family members must change. A family in which there is an adolescent is enmeshed in working out compromises between separateness and connectedness. As Erik Erikson has noted, the major psychological issues in adolescence involve a thrust toward identity, a selfhood separate from one's parents, and intimacy, especially with others outside the family. This sets up an inevitable confrontation between desires for separateness in identity and intimacy on the one hand, and the fact of residence within the parental family with its authority patterns on the other. At the other end of the life cycle the same issues of autonomy and dependency are encountered: when a 70-year-old father, independent all his life, self-sufficient, and autonomous, is stricken with ill health, the balance of family dynamics must change, for the older person has moved into a different stage of life.

What I am suggesting is that differences between generations—and especially the perception of those differences—are colored by developmental agendas, the negotiation of which causes apparent differences to be highlighted and brought into consciousness by normal crises which involve transformations in autonomy or dependency.

Added to developmental changes is another contrast between cohorts: differences in life history. A case study (incidentally, from my own family) illustrates this. When Grandpa Engstrom died in 1976 he was 106 years old; his life suggests many ways in which perceptions and contrasts between generations are tied to history. Born in rural Sweden in 1869, he emigrated to Minnesota, worked as a day laborer and then as a chauffeur, and finally borrowed enough money to become a cement contractor in Seattle. After a series of minor fortunes and minor failures he "retired" following a heart attack in 1933, and shortly thereafter moved in with his daughter. He lived 43 years in retirement—42 years in the household of his child, 46 years without his spouse. His life spanned a century of technological innovations, a biography of crises and triumphs, a legacy of five generations. His death was the occasion to reflect on an enormous degree of continuity and change represented in one lifetime, in one family. When Engstrom was born, the midwife came in the snows of the January Swedish winter and delivered him. When he struck out for a new land, he never did see his brothers and sisters again; he saw his father only once. There was little contact between Engstrom and the rest of his own family after he immigrated to America. The kinds of experiences that shaped his life made him the conservative, independent person that he was. Not until his 93rd birthday did he accept Medicare and Social Security, so strong were his values of individualism and so abhorrent was the notion of being supported by "charity."

Within other families the contrast of historical change or of developmental agenda may not be quite so dramatic as this particular example, but in any family there are differences that are inevitable. So to the popular question of whether there is a serious generation gap in American society I would answer, "Yes, differences are perceived between generations; yes, some *actual* differences can be cited. But the differences are not what we think they are, and some of the differences are normal consequences of developmental or historical events."

Problems Between Generations

Every family has its problems. Many of them involve interaction between generations. Frequently the problems are related to actual lineage or to period differences, real or imagined. From the University of Southern California study of generations questionnaire and from ethnographic interviews I have conducted over the past four or five years, I find four separate but related problems which families mention again and again in describing dealing with interaction between generations. Many are related to developmental and historical contrasts between cohorts (see Bengtson & Treas, 1980).

Role Transition

The first problem can be several issues of role transition. By that I simply mean the changing roles and expectations that go along with growing up and growing old. As Linda George (1980) has documented, these role transitions are often accompanied by psycho-social stress. Grandpa Engstrom, as I suggested, retired in 1929 at the age of 60 because he had a stroke. He lived for 46 years in retirement. He had to make an adjustment to the fact that in his eyes he was no longer a productive member of society. His family too had to adjust to his no longer working; and some of the adjustments had to do with economic differences. More than that, however, their adjustments reflected roles and expectations that are indicative of growing up and growing old.

Many of the middle-aged women in our sample reported that the last child's leaving home, whether for marriage, college, or employment, was either the source of great rejoicing on the part of Mom and Dad (a new freedom for a second honeymoon, traveling, new money to spend on themselves) or the source of a period of depression which neither parent understood. Most parents have a high degree of investment in the lives and the fortunes of those unpredictable individuals who bear their names. That role transition can require considerable adaptation on the part of both generations of family members. What I see increasingly in the lives of 70- and 80-year-old people is the sorrow they feel at seeing their children or grandchildren split up, or at witnessing the death of children or grandchildren—a tragic role reversal, the elderly outliving their children. In Barbara Myerhoff's 1976 Academy Award-winning documentary on aged Jews in Venice, *Number Our Days,* one of the most poignant moments is an interview with an 87-year-old woman, a survivor of Nazi persecution, the Holocaust in Poland, who came to this new land, raised four children, and outlived every one of them (Myerhoff, 1976). I find that increasingly common. It didn't occur 30 years ago, or 60 years ago, because individuals usually did not survive into the sixth, seventh, or eighth decade. Little has been written about this role transition—perhaps the most tragic one can see.

Very little has been written about the role transition of widowhood or widowerhood. An exception is *Widowhood in an American City* by Helena Lopata (1973), which describes a study of the adjustment of several hundred Chicago-area widows to the loss of spouse.

There are inevitable role transitions in a family, and those transitions are involved in what may be the number one problem of the normal family: coping with intergenerational relations over the years. The changing circumstances of family members and their changing roles create different expectations on the part of both children and parents. I can't expect Dad to be what he was ten years ago; I certainly can't expect my son to act the same way he did ten years ago. A common complaint of parents, as they look down the generational boundaries, is that they wish their children would take more responsibility. At the other end of the life cycle, interestingly, the 70- to 75-year-old parent often wishes his or her child would take *less* responsibility for him.

Autonomy and Dependency

The second major problem I find in talking about family issues concerns autonomy and dependency. Issues of autonomy and dependency are fundamental in negotiations that must be carried out within every family on a day-to-day, year-to-year, decade-to-decade basis. The adolescent is concerned primarily with autonomy: "I want to be my own person." Parents, if able to put it into words, probably wish for their child's autonomy, but not at the expense of infringement—pushing parental limits, flaunting an oppositional life style, being insensitive.

At the other end of the life cycle one sees the same issue of autonomy as a problem in family relations. How often are elderly, dependent—but sensitive—parents treated with condescension by their middle-aged children? There is a childishness frequently attributed to dependent elderly parents which must be galling for them. In hospitals it is common to see conferences of children and grandchildren: "What are we going to do with Grandpa?" Frequently, Grandpa is not unaware of those discussions, and the result has to be, on his part, a feeling of tremendous dependency, loss of control, and loss of autonomy. Many of our nursing homes epitomize an institutionalization of inappropriate dependency. Putting the aged in a category where they receive custodial care must still recognize that old age reflects survivorship and a lifetime of experience

and coping. Too many of us look at the dependency and ignore the autonomy.

I have argued that much of the drama of intergenerational relations concerns issues of autonomy on the one hand and dependency on the other. Of course, one is always partly autonomous and partly dependent throughout life. The challenge within the family is to allow relevant, realistic, and equitable balance between dependency and autonomy as individuals change with the passage of time. The balance changes throughout life, and always requires a normal interval of negotiation as the individuals concerned adapt to changes in autonomy.

Equitable Exchange

A third problem concerns issues of allocating a just balance of giving and receiving between generations. Grandpa Engstrom lived with his daughter from 1935 to 1975—forty years. One of his major concerns involved maintaining equity in the face of that dependency: what could he be doing? He tried to solve this in a number of ways—by being the gardener, by being the dishwasher, and by being the cook. Grandpa insisted on doing the gardening long after heart attacks and cataracts had made it inappropriate for him to do so. During Christmas Day 1974, when he was 105, he fell off a ladder while trying to clean out the gutter. Thereafter everybody in the family pleaded with Grandpa to quit trying to do the gardening. They pleaded with Grandpa to quit doing the dishes, because he kept chipping them. The electric dishwasher was intended to preserve whatever china was left. Nobody dared to plead with Grandpa to quit cooking the breakfast, because he was up earlier than anyone else. The point is that Grandpa *had* to make a contribution.

Many issues in generational relations focus around a just and equitable exchange between generations. "My parents have done so much for me; what can I do for them? Can I send them money? I know they need it. No, they won't take it; it's a blow to their pride. What can I do? Can I send them tickets to come down and visit me? That's O.K.'' I know of one family in which the issue of a just exchange between generations was satisfied very nicely by two tickets to the Super Bowl which the father treasured as something he would remember to the end of his life. The same issue, of course, is even more poignant in the lives of senior citizens: ''What can I give my kids? What can I give my grandkids? What can I do for them?'' The intensity of generational investment is real in the lives of most individuals (Hill, Foote, Aldous, Carlson, & Macdonald, 1970; Shanas, Townsend, Wedderburn, Friis, Milhøj, & Stehouwer, 1968).

A specific focus of equitable intergenerational exchange is the issue of legacies: inheritances both economic and social. Jeffrey Rosenfeld (1979) has noted that the study of inheritance — and disinheritance — allows some fascinating insights into contemporary social organization of family life. It is of interest to me how much effort elderly individuals give to their testamentary dispossessions in an attempt to provide a just and equitable distribution of tangible resources. Undoubtedly the most dramatic are cases in which the wills provide for disinheritance of children.

Rosenfeld's analysis found that 3.5 percent of wills probated in Nassau County, New York, between 1973 and 1978 involved parent-child disinheritance. Examination of probated wills, which are part of public record and which can be read as freely as any other public document, suggests three patterns (Rosenfeld, 1980). The first Rosenfeld terms ''benevolent disinheritance,'' reflecting the feeling that other people needed the money more than did the children. A second category, ''disinheritance by default,'' occurred when parents had no idea where their children could be reached. Most of the parents in this category had been living as

''social isolates'' or had been receiving long-term nursing care at the time they wrote the will. Almost half the cases fell in a third category, ''vindictive disinheritance.'' Here the parent carefully spelled out long-standing differences, parental displeasure with the children's way of life, or accusations that the children had been disrespectful. Cases of vindictive disinheritance generally involved small estates. Most often parents who disinherit were older than those who did not. Rosenfeld notes that the increasing opportunities for elderly people to develop new social involvements, as well as their added longevity, may indicate a continued decline in old social constraints — including the implied obligation of leaving everything to the children.

Equally interesting are non-economic legacies — a memorial, a testament of the right way to live. Frequently, these are explicit, sometimes they are dramatic. One of my best friends, a Mormon, recalls his grandfather's last will and testament. Nine children and 11 grandchildren were crowded into his hospital room. He asked them to hold hands and pray, entreating God and his Holy Spirit to provide guidance to those family members and keep them in the faith and in the Book of Wisdom. That was the principal legacy of a man who had an estate of perhaps $12,000 to divide among nine children. His legacy was a spiritual tradition, a way of life which he wanted for his children and his children's children. The most valuable exchange, then, may be a key to a way of life the older family member has found to be important.

Continuity vs. Disruption

A fourth and related problem concerns continuity in the family vs. disruption of that continuity. I find that with advancing years the continuity of a family identity, a family tradition, or a family legacy often assumes increasing importance. That is not to sug-

gest that it is not important for young people. As a matter of fact, one of the unre-
searched topics in my field concerns the
pride which young adults have in the accomplishments (and even more than that,
the very being, the very existence) of their
parents and especially their grandparents. A
highly-regarded ancestor is one of the things
which students often cite as we talk about the
importance of family in sociology courses.
Characteristics of their grandparents or
great-grandparents indicate continuity, and
are an important theme throughout the
generations.

There are some very serious threats or
disruptions to that continuity in contemporary American society. I'd like to mention
four of these.

1. Geographic mobility. The first is
geographic mobility. We live in a very
mobile society in which the average
Californian moves once every four years.
The average Midwestern family moves once
every seven years. Geographic mobility is a
part of our culture, and that can represent a
potential disruption to the issue of man's
continuity.

2. Divorce. A second and even more
dramatic disruption is divorce. I observe
many grandparents who have a child who is
married and who from a first marriage has
three children, from a second marriage two
children; some go on to a third marriage and
another child. These may all be regarded as
grandchildren. Equally interesting are the
ties that remain with the daughters-in-law or
the sons-in-law who no longer are spouses of
offspring. Much continuity is maintained,
and this calls for some rather delicate
negotiation in terms of family get-togethers,
birthdays, funerals, and weddings. Maintaining family continuity between the
generations appears important to many of
the elderly parents and grandparents. From
the standpoint of the grandchild where there
has been a divorce, such continuity may be a

source of comfort and security. The kids that
I talk to coming from families in which there
has been remarriage can sort out the grandparents, and "It's O.K."; they have relationships with each of them. Probably the
children find one or two grandparents more
significant, and these may or may not be
from the direct-bond relationship. But the
relationship between grandchildren and
grandparents is very important in maintaining stability when the husband and the wife
split up. Though this has not often been
discussed in contemporary American society, it does represent an important aspect of
continuity in the face of potential family
disruption.

3. Change in life-style. A third problem
in continuity vs. disruption concerns
changes in life-style. Often youth present
their families with a conversion to a new
religion, to a political cause, to vegetarian-
ism, or to new sexual modalities. I know of
several cases in which there has been a conversion experience, and the son or daughter
has come home with gospel tracts to save the
souls of all the elder family members. I know
other instances of what is commonly called
"backsliding," in which, after all the grades
of Sunday School, Johnny's gone away to
college and lost his faith; he comes home
smoking "pot" and quoting D. H. Lawrence. Such changes in life-style do occur.
They represent a threat in the continuity of
the family — an issue to be dealt with and
negotiated.

4. Death. As Victor Marshall (1980) has
so persuasively noted, although the death of
a family member always is the source of an
immediate and observable disruption, it frequently is the occasion also for a reaffirma-
tion of family continuity. Funerals, in my
experience, are occasions for people who
perhaps have gotten together relatively infrequently within the last few years to come
together, not only to mourn the loss of the
departed, but also to knit up the shredded

fabric of disrupted families that death has caused. Wakes in Irish and Mexican families are the occasion for family members to tell stories about the departed. This is also true in Swedish families. When my father died, I remember sitting there in the mortuary in Minnesota with all the brothers and sisters and probably 20 of my 34 cousins. . . . Long into the night we told stories about my father. I wish I had recorded that evening. There was a theme going through most of the stories — not just, ''Here was a man who was good and important; he's gone, and let's treasure his memory,'' but also, ''Here we are, part of a family — a family which lives on and which carries on some of the same traditions that this man stood for in his life.''

Processes

What are the processes that occur between generations within families in solving some of these problems? Two issues seem to summarize successful intergenerational interaction. First, I want to emphasize the issue of negotiation. We don't usually think of families as an arena of negotiation. The term ''negotiation'' brings the image of Ford Motor management and a group of labor union leaders locked together hammering out a contract which eventually nobody is really happy with and nobody terribly dissatisfied with. The same things happen every day in families, but the negotiations are not quite as direct as they are between Ford Motor Company and the United Auto Workers. Negotiations are inevitable in families. As each individual family member acts out his or her own developmental agenda, negotiation is inevitable. It is also continuous, happening all the time. And it is bilateral: negotiations not only involve the parent influencing the child, but also the child influencing the parent. There is a bilateral negotiation in the family which is easily overlooked, especially in the so-called ''golden years'' among senior citizens. Just

because Grandpa has had a stroke doesn't mean he is no longer a person who should be accorded dignity and autonomy and some sense of control over what happens to him. This inevitable, continuous, and bilateral negotiation is rooted in the passage of time. It is also rooted in the process of aging. As we grow up and grow old, the relationships that we have within the family change.

Thus, the process of solving family problems involves negotiations, and those negotiations occur whether we are aware of them or not. Much of family relations is not explicit and not as honest as negotiations between the lawyers from the labor unions and the lawyers from the manufacturers. But control is exercised in the family in a variety of subtle ways. Wives control their husbands, husbands control their wives, in many ways that are nonverbal. I think we must recognize that negotiation is part of the family process of every normal, well-functioning family in contemporary society.

The second point I would like to make is that much of the natural process in families involves conflict. As humans interact, conflict is normal, inevitable, and universal. It does not necessarily have to be destructive. One of the myths that we carry with us in American society, especially in Northern European ethnic traditions, is that conflict within the family is bad; it is indicative of bad manners, if not serious disruption.

Barbara Myerhoff (1977) in her study of Jews of Venice notes that expression of conflict is one of the most creative aspects of the daily lives of these elderly individuals. Bickering, negotiating, teasing, nagging in this particular subculture from rural Eastern Europe are indications, not only of affection, but also an affirmation of simply being *alive*.

Perhaps in mainstream American culture we expect families to be conflict-free. I don't know why we have that tradition. Certainly any reading of the Old Testament would suggest to us that if there is one theme running through every family, it is conflict.

Think of poor King David and the problems that he had with his lineal descendants. Think of Jacob and his sons; the words of Moses the preacher dictate that one should honor one's father and mother—you don't, however, necessarily have to like them. Probably some of the healthiest families I have seen are families in which there can be and are explicit statements of disagreement. This represents conflict, and yet there is a sense of love that allows autonomy. It allows differences of expression. Certainly, I am not saying the higher the degree of conflict, the better the relations between generations within a family. What I am pointing out is that conflict is a normal part of the continuous negotiation that must occur in families, as we grow up and grow old. Acknowledgement of inevitable differences, and adequate negotiation of conflict, are two keys to understanding successful intergenerational interaction.

Conclusion

Contrasts between generations are inevitable, universal, perhaps even desirable—reflecting as they do the tension between change and continuity rooted in the passage of time. What I have suggested is that any reasoned discussion of the "generation gap" must consider four issues indicated by contemporary research on intergenerational relations.

First, it is important to maintain conceptual clarity in the often emotional arena of intergenerational relations. We must distinguish between effects of cohort, lineage, and historical period as each contribute to observable differences between generations. And we should acknowledge that each effect also creates its own degree of intergenerational continuity.

Second, the available research literature documents differences between generations. But frequently the contrasts are not as large as one might expect from mass media accounts; sometimes the differences run counter to popular expectations, as with grandparents displaying higher "humanistic" value orientations than grandchildren. Often the differences are more perceived than actual, though they are experienced as very real.

Third, problems of intergenerational relations reflect the contrasting psychosocial agendas of family members born into different cohorts and experiencing different developmental issues. Four issues may be universal as families attempt to confront change: role transition, autonomy-dependency, equitable exchange, continuity-disruption. These issues surface at each stage in a family's career; they are as salient for old age as for adolescence.

Fourth, the process of successful intergenerational relations involves the negotiation of differences. In the face of inevitable change, the negotiation of transitions, autonomy, exchanges, and continuity becomes a necessary part of every family agenda. Often conflict is inevitable. How these conflicts are acknowledged and resolved is perhaps the central issue in understanding our own intergenerational relations.

References

Bengtson, V. L., Inter-age differences in perception and the generation gap. *Gerontologist,* 1971, 11(2), 85–90.

Bengtson, V. L. Generation and family effects in value socialization. *American Sociological Review,* 1975, 40, 358–371.

Bengtson, V. L., and Cutler, N. Generations and intergenerational relations: Perspectives on age groups and social change. In R. Binstock & E. Shanas (Eds.), *Handbook of aging and the social sciences.* New York: Van Nostrand Reinhold, 1976.

Bengtson, V. L., & Kupers, J. A. Generational difference and the developmental stake. *Aging and Human Development,* 1971, 2, 249–259.

Bengtson, V. L. & Treas, J. Intergenerational relations and mental health. In R. B. Sloan and J. E. Birren (Eds.), *Handbook of mental health and aging.* New York: Prentice-Hall, 1980.

Dowd, J. *Stratification and aging.* Monterey, Calif.: Brooks-Cole, 1980.

Elder, G. *Children of the Great Depression.* Chicago: University of Chicago Press, 1974.

Friedenberg, E. Current patterns of generational conflict. *Journal of Social Issues,* 1969, 25 (2), 21–38.

George, L. K. *Role transitions in later life.* Monterey, Calif.: Brooks-Cole, 1980.

Hagestad, G. O. Problems and promises in the social psychology of intergenerational relations. In R. Fogel, E. Hatfield, S. Kiesler, & J. March, (Eds.), *Stability and change in the family,* 1980.

Hagestad, G. O. Patterns of communication and influence between grandparents and granchildren in a changing society. Paper presented at the 9th World Congress of Sociology, Uppsala, Sweden, 1978.

Hess, B. B., and Waring, J. M. Parent and child in later life: Rethinking the relationship. Pp. 241–273 in R. M. Lerner & G. B. Spanier (Eds.), *Child influences on marital and family interaction.* New York: Academic Press, 1978.

Hill, R., Foote, N., Aldous, J., Carlson, R., & Macdonald, R. *Family development in three generations.* Cambridge, Mass.: Schenkman, 1970.

Lopata, H. *Widowhood in an American city.* Cambridge, Mass.: Schenkman, 1973.

Marshall, V. *Last chapters: A sociology of aging and dying.* Monterey, Calif.: Brooks-Cole, 1980.

Mead, M. *Culture and commitment: A study of the generation gap.* New York: Longmans, 1970.

Myerhoff, B. *Number our days.* Los Angeles: Public Television for Los Angeles (KCET), 1976.

Myerhoff, B. A symbol perfected in death: Continuity and ritual in the life of an elderly Jew. In B. Myerhoff & A. Simic (Eds.), *Life's career—aging: Cultural variations in growing old.* Beverly Hills, Calif.: Sage Publications, 1977.

Rosenfeld, J. P. *Legacy of aging: Inheritance and disinheritance in social perspective,* Ablex Publishing, 1979.

Rosenfeld, J. P. Benevolent disinheritance: The kindest cut. *Psychology Today,* 13 (12), 1980.

Schaie, K. W. A general model for the study of developmental problems. *Psychological Bulletin,* 1965, 64, 92–107.

Shanas, E., Townsend, P., Wedderburn, D., Friis, H., Milhøj, P., & Stehouwer, J. *Old people in three industrial societies.* New York: Atherton, 1968.

Shanas, E., & Streib, G. *Social structure and the family: Generational relations.* Englewood Cliffs, N.J.: Prentice-Hall, 1965.

Sussman, M. B. The family life of old people. In R. Binstock & E. Shanas (Eds.), *Handbook of aging and the social sciences.* New York: Van Nostrand Reinhold, 1976.

Treas, J. Aging and the family. In D. Woodruff & J. Birren (Eds.), *Aging: Scientific perspectives and social issues.* New York: Van Nostrand Reinhold, 1975.

Troll, L. E. The family in later life: A decade review. *Journal of Marriage and the Family,* 1970, 33, 263–290.

Troll, L., & Bengtson, V. L. Generations in the family. In W. Burr, R. Hill, I. Reiss, & I. Nye (Eds.), *Handbook of contemporary family theory.* New York: The Free Press, 1978.

Social Myth as Hypothesis: The Case of the Family Relations of Old People

ETHEL SHANAS

Every society has its own social myths. Such myths are those collective beliefs which everyone within a given society knows to be "right," and which everyone accepts as "true." Because everyone, or almost everyone, believes in them, social myths act as a cohesive force within a society. They may be described as a glue which holds societies together. However, such myths or beliefs may also serve to obstruct both thought and action by encouraging people to accept as fact that which may really be fiction.

The Myth of Alienation

This paper deals with a social myth — the widely-held belief that in contemporary American society old people are alienated from their families, particularly from their children. All sorts of theories have been proposed to justify this myth, including those theories which stress the values of the nuclear family in industrial society. Proceeding from the assumption that this myth is "true" there has also been a special emphasis on programs to meet the needs of the alienated aged, who, in keeping with the myth, are assumed to be the majority of the aged.

Evidence to support the belief that the aged are alienated from their families, par-

ticularly children, is sparse, however. Much of it is comprised of illustrative case studies of individuals known to the adherent of the alienation myth. The strongest evidence that can be mustered to support the myth is the fact that many old people in the U. S. live apart from their children. Some old people, with or without children, even have the temerity to live alone. The assumption that old persons who live alone or apart from their children are neglected by their children and relatives is implicit in the alienation myth. Why young persons who live alone are not regarded as alienated from their parents and relatives is an interesting if peripheral question.

The myth that old people are alienated from their families and children has guided much of social gerontological research about the elderly for the last 30 years. The myth and its multiple ramifications are reminiscent of the Hydra, the monster of Greek mythology slain by Hercules. The Hydra had nine heads. These heads were unique in that each time one was cut off, it was replaced by two others. In the same way, each time evidence has been presented that old people are not alienated from their families, new adherents of the myth rise up, not only among the mass media and the writers for the popular press, but also among research investigators and even among old people

Source: Shanas, E. Social myth as hypothesis: The case of the family relations of old people. Reprinted by permission of *The Gerontologist,* Vol. 19, No. 3 (1979).

themselves. Many old people when describing their active involvement with their children and grandchildren will say "But, of course, my family is different." The extent to which old people have internalized the alienation myth may be further illustrated with a finding from a national survey. Those old people who were most likely to agree with the statement "Children don't care anything about their parents except for what they can get out of them" turned out to be the persons who had no children.

The theme of this paper is adopted from a statement of Thomas Huxley who described as the great tragedy of science "the slaying of a beautiful hypothesis by an ugly fact." The beautiful hypotheses to be discussed here are the various corollaries of the belief that old people are rejected by their families. The ugly facts are that these hypotheses have been demonstrated to be in error. In contemporary American society, old people are not rejected by their families nor are they alienated from their children. Further, where old people have no children, a principle of family substitution seems to operate and brothers, sisters, nephews and nieces often fulfill the roles and assume the obligations of children. The truly isolated old person, despite his or her prominence in the media, is a rarity in the United States.

Some Acknowledgements

I propose to present the evidence that I have collected over the last 25 years that destroys the "beautiful hypotheses." Before I do so, however, I should like to acknowledge those persons who influenced me in my search for "ugly facts." These include Robert J. Havighurst and the late Ernest W. Burgess with whom I began my career in aging research some 30 years ago; the late Clyde W. Hart, one-time director of the National Opinion Research Center at the University of Chicago and Selma F. Monsky of that center, now of the University of California,

who urged me to investigate the spatial distribution of older parents and their adult children; Bernice L. Neugarten, my long-time colleague at the University of Chicago; and Wilma Donahue and Clark Tibbitts who for a quarter of a century gathered together at the University of Michigan persons interested in aging and the aged and encouraged each of us in our professional growth and enthusiasms. I have been influenced in my view of society and of how people, young or old, are incorporated into social groups and act together by the teacher in my first course in Sociology and subsequently, a life-long friend, Herbert Blumer, now Professor Emeritus of Sociology at the University of California at Berkeley.

Almost a score of years ago, I demonstrated, at least to my own satisfaction, that old people in the U.S. were not rejected by their families nor alienated from their children. Because the alienation of old people from their families was often considered to be a concomitant of industrialization, I sought verification of these U.S. findings in other industrialized societies. I wanted to know whether old people in the U.S. were unique in their involvement with family and kin helping networks, or whether similar phenomena were to be found in other industrialized countries. European colleagues in both the highly industrialized and less developed countries sharpened and clarified my thinking on these topics. I am particularly indebted to Peter Townsend, Dorothy Wedderburn and Amelia I. Harris in Britain, and to Henning Friis, Poul Milhøj and the late Jan Stehouwer in Denmark.

Most of all, in the search for facts I owe a debt to those thousands of older men and women and the members of their families who answered my questions and told me and my associates about their lives. It is from older people themselves, living both in the community and in institutions, that I learned what the family life of old people in the U. S. is really like.

Definitions

Old age, like other social phenomena, can only be studied by asking pertinent questions, testing observed reality against theoretical constructs, and by modifying or even discarding these constructs for others should they prove inadequate in explaining observed behavior. Before one can ask pertinent questions, however, one needs to define one's terms. I shall therefore begin this discussion of my empirical findings about old people and their families with a definition of the family and a discussion of the function of the family. In contemporary U. S. many definitions of the family are possible. Since World War II a variety of family forms and life styles have emerged which, as Marvin Sussman has said, "if not legitimized are at least tolerated" (1976). These variant family forms, however, have been more popular with the young than with the old, and seem to have been embraced by only a small proportion of older people in this country. For most older people, the family is that group of individuals to whom they are related by blood or marriage and this is the definition which I have adopted. This definition of the family implies that the family includes more than the individual's immediate family, that is, spouse, children, and perhaps siblings. The family may include those persons somewhat distantly related by blood or marriage, such as cousins of various degree or in-laws, all of whom may be perceived as family members. Further, for any one person the family network is not static. It may expand to include even more distant relatives as a need arises for information, services, or help from these relatives.

Nothing in this definition of the family as a kin network implies that a family must live under the same roof. Those living together under the same roof may or may not be a family as here defined. They comprise a household. While households of unrelated old people who act as though they were related family members are becoming more common, only a tiny fraction of the elderly live in such arrangements.

Peter Laslett in his work on family and household makes a strong case for distinguishing family, that is, perceived kin, from household, that is, co-residents (1972). Much of the rhetorical murkiness which surrounds discussions of old people and their children stems from a confusion of family as here defined, and household. In these discussions there also seems to be an underlying belief that somehow several generations living under the same roof makes for happiness for older household members, and that the separation of the generations into separate households makes for unhappiness on the part of the older generation. I forbear from further comment on this topic except to quote from a 23-year-old female respondent in a national survey whose parents and parents-in-law were all living. When asked about living arrangements for older people she said: "I don't approve of sharing a kitchen with anyone, old or young" (Shanas, 1962).

The Functions of Families Today

In our society, most families are no longer economic units. Further, human service systems, organized into powerful bureaucracies, provide education for family members, care for the sick and frail, and even offer professional emotional support to individuals if necessary (Shanas & Sussman, 1977). The 20th century indeed can be described as the age of the social worker. What then does the contemporary family do? It is still the family, that group of individuals related by blood or marriage, that is the first resource of both its older and younger members for emotional and social support, crisis intervention, and bureaucratic linkages.

Moreover, I would argue that the one place in contemporary life where the individual may be "himself" or "herself" is within the family. The complex nature of contemporary urbanized society results in individuals, whether children or adults, living segmented roles within different life sectors. The busy executive is quite different from the scout leader, the ardent sportsman from the community volunteer. Yet, these roles may all be facets of the life of the same person. It is in the family that the basic "persona," not the segmented social image, can show itself. The family as a refuge and private place for its adult members may perhaps be more important now than earlier in its history.

Talcott Parsons, the American sociologist, is perhaps the best-known exponent of the theory that the nuclear family, husband, wife, and their offspring, is the most functional type of family in contemporary society. Social researchers, following Parsons, have stressed that the primary function of this nuclear family is the socialization of the child. Many scholars seem less acquainted with another Parsonian dictum, a response perhaps to those scores of anthropological and sociological studies which demonstrate the existence and operation of family kin networks. Professor Parsons has also stated: "The family can thus be seen to have two primary functions, not one. On the one hand it is the primary agent of socialization for the child, while on the other it is the primary basis of security for the normal adult" (1965).

The findings on family relationships given in this paper are a validation of Professor Parsons' belief that the family is the primary basis of security for adults in later life. The data come from nationwide probability surveys of noninstitutionalized persons aged 65 and over, commonly defined as older people. These surveys made in 1957, 1962, and 1975 may be thought of as snapshots of the aged population in the community at three points in time and over a period of 20 years. In surveys such as these there are no volunteer subjects. Every eligible person has a predetermined chance of being selected. Not every eligible person is located, however, and some small proportion of those located cannot be interviewed. The probability design is such, however, that for practical purposes the chances are about 19 out of 20 that the true proportion of any variable will be within the range of estimate reported here, plus and minus one standard deviation.

The surveys report the situation of the noninstitutionalized elderly living in the community. In 1975, at the time of the latest survey, about 94 to 95% of all persons over 65 were community residents (Siegel, 1976). That 5 or 6% of the elderly in institutions, whether in homes for the well or the sick aged, differ in demographic characteristics from the community elderly. On the average, institutional residents are older than persons living in the community. About one of every eight persons over 80 years of age now lives in an institution. Old people in institutions are three times as likely as the community elderly to have never married, and are twice as likely to be widowed. Those persons without close family, the never married and the very old widowed, are more likely than other persons to seek residence in a home for the aged or to be institutionalized when they are ill.

The Alienation Myth Revisited

To this stage I have given a definition of the family, discussed the functions of the family, and indicated the scope of the populations studied. I want now to return to the alienation myth, the belief that older people are alienated from their families, and to consider some of the hypotheses which derive from it. These are: (1) Because of the geographic mobility of the population of the U. S. most old people who have children live at great distances from their children; (2) Because of the alienation of old people from their children, most older parents rarely see their children; (3) Because of the predominance of the nuclear family in the U. S., most old people rarely see their siblings or other relatives; and (4) Because of the existence and availability of large human service bureaucracies, families are no longer important as a source of care for older people.

These hypotheses all seem reasonable. Everyone knows that Americans move all the time, everyone knows at least one old person whose children all live at the other end of the continent, and everyone knows of a sick old person whose adult children are trying to find a residence for him, or, more usually, her. Despite what everyone knows, each of the above hypotheses has been disproved. In the U. S. most old people with children live close to at least one of their children and see at least one child often. Most old people see their siblings and relatives often, and old people, when either bedfast or housebound because of ill health, are twice as likely to be living at home as to be resident in an institution.

About four of every five noninstitutionalized persons over 65 in the U. S. have living children. The proportion of old people with living children is unchanged over the last 20 years. The proportion of old people with children who live in the same household with one of these children has declined, however, from 36% in 1957 to 18% in 1975. At the same time that the proportion of parents and children living in the same household has declined, there has been a rise in the proportion of old people living within ten minutes distance of a child. As a result, the proportion of old people with children who either live with one of their children or within ten minutes distance of a child has remained fairly constant over 20 years: 59% in 1957, 61% in 1962, and 52% in 1975. The findings indicate that while old people no longer live in the same household with a child they

now live next door, down the street, or a few blocks away. Older people and their children both place a value on separate households. Many old people say they want to be independent. Their children in turn stress a desire for privacy. As the economic situation of old people and their children has improved over the last 20 years, it has become possible to implement the desire for independence and privacy of both generations.

Old people who live alone are commonly considered a particularly isolated group among the elderly. Among all old people who live alone, however, half of those with children are within ten minutes distance of a child (Shanas, 1962; Shanas et al., 1968). Many of these persons stress that they and their children share "intimacy at a distance" (Rosenmayr & Köckeis, 1963). It is the childless elderly living alone who are the vulnerable elderly but even they, as we shall see, call upon family resources.

Whether old people in the future increasingly will live at greater distances from their children cannot be answered from the data from the years 1957 to 1975. What these data do show is that despite the geographic mobility of the population of the U. S. older people who have children live close to at least one of these children. In 1975, three of every four persons with children either lived in the same household as a child or within a half hour's distance of a child. The first hypothesis, that because of the geographic mobility of the population of the U. S. most old people who have children live at great distances from their children, must therefore be rejected.

Living near adult children is no guarantee that the older parent will see his or her children. In 1975, however, 53% of persons with children, including those with a child in the same household, saw one of their children the day they were interviewed or the day before that. The proportion of the older parents who saw at least one child during the week before they were interviewed has remained stable over roughly 20 years: 83% in 1957, 77% in 1975. Perhaps even more important, the proportion of older parents who have not seen at least one of their children for a month or more has remained stable over the 20 year period, at about one in ten. What of old people with children who live alone? About half of these persons had seen at least one child the day they were interviewed or the day before that, and three of every four had seen at least one child during the week before they were interviewed. There has been no decrease in visiting between parents and at least one of their children from the first survey to the last.

Again, the data do not answer all the questions that might be raised about the relationships between older parents and their adult children. We do not know whether these meetings between parents and children are brief or lengthy, friendly and warm, or acrimonious and hostile. Every family is a separate constellation of interacting persons. The visits between some parents and their children may be unpleasant for both generations. On the other hand, some parents and their children may find joy and comfort in knowing that each generation is well and functioning. What the data do show is that older parents see adult children often. The second hypothesis, that because of the alienation of older parents from their children, most older parents rarely see their children, must also be rejected.

Even though most older people live close to and see at least one of their children often they still may have lost touch with their brothers and sisters or other relatives. The data show otherwise. David Schneider, the anthropologist, in discussing the family life of old people, speaks of the "hour glass effect" in the American kin system. Persons have many contacts with siblings and other relatives in their youth, these contacts shrink in young adulthood and middle life, and increase in later life.

Brothers and sisters, in particular, become important to the older person. The proportion of old persons with siblings was the same in both 1962 and 1975, about eight of every ten. Even when those persons over 75 years of age are considered separately from those under 75, seven of every ten still report surviving brothers and sisters. In 1975 one-third of all old persons with living brothers and sisters saw at least one of these during the week before they were interviewed, and more than half of old people with brothers and sisters saw at least one of these during the month before they were interviewed.

Widowed persons and old persons who have never married are especially dependent on their brothers and sisters. For many widowed persons, siblings assume some of the responsibilities of a now deceased husband or wife. Many persons who have never married live in the same household with a sibling. While about one-third of all persons with siblings had seen a brother or sister the previous week, three-fourths of these who had never married saw a brother or sister during that time.

Old people not only visit with and are visited by siblings, they also visit with other relatives who are not among their direct descendants. In 1975, about three of every ten older persons said that they had seen some relative, who was neither a brother nor a sister, a child nor a grandchild, during the previous week. For the childless elderly this relative often is a niece or nephew who assumes the responsibilities of a child.

The data confirm the findings of many other studies of family and kin in the U. S. The dominant family form for old people in the U. S. is the modified extended family. This family includes not only members of the old person's immediate family and relatives of his own generation such as siblings, it also includes nephews, nieces, and other relatives by blood or marriage. The hypothesis that because of the predominance of the nuclear family in the U. S. older people rarely see their siblings or other relatives is contradicted by the evidence and must be rejected.

Finally, what of that hypothesis that postulates that because of the existence of large human service bureaucracies, families are no longer important as a source of care for older people? Data from a variety of studies are available to test this hypothesis. Because the health system, of all contemporary bureaucracies, probably impinges most directly on the life of the elderly and their families, I shall discuss some relevant findings about families and the health care of the elderly.

In the 1962 national survey, 2% of the elderly in the community were reported as totally bedfast at home and 6% were reported as housebound. These persons were being taken care of by family members, with some minor assistance from public health nurses and other home aides. That 8% of the elderly bedfast and housebound at home was about twice the proportion of old people in institutions of all kinds whether these were institutions for the well or the sick aged.

Health insurance for the aged, Medicare, became operational in 1966. Medicare, Title XVIII of the Social Security Act, and a companion program of medical assistance, Medicaid, Title XIX, together provide payments for long-term care of the elderly in such health institutions as chronic disease hospitals, extended care facilities, and skilled nursing facilities. Many persons expected that the passage of this legislation would result in a great increase in the number and proportion of the elderly in long-term institutions. Indeed, one of the arguments used by opponents of this legislation was that it would destroy the will of the family to take care of its sick aged.

The 1975 survey, however, indicates no marked change from 1962 in the proportion of the elderly bedfast and housebound at home. Neither is there a marked change in the proportion of the elderly in institutions. In 1975, nine years after Medicare, about 3% of the elderly were bedfast at home and about 7% were housebound. That 10% of old people bedfast and housebound at home, just as in 1962, was almost twice the proportion of old people in institutions of all kinds. There is some indication in both these surveys, however, that the greatly impaired aged are more likely to be in institutions and the less impaired are more likely still to be at home.

Family help in providing long-term care for the elderly persists despite the alternative sources of care available in 1975 which were not available in 1962. Rosenmayr has made an interesting comment on why family help patterns may tend to continue despite the presence of such alternative help sources. ''Public action to give support to the elderly has the innate danger to classify them as marginal. It is the dialectics of institutionally organized help to a certain group that this group becomes conscious of a certain bereavement; whereas individual and informal help and assistance based on intimacy may avoid this type of consequence . . .'' (1975). It is the alienation of the elderly that the family wants to avoid by providing health care at home.

The circumstances that bring the elderly to institutions have been carefully studied. The United States General Accounting Office in a study in Cleveland, Ohio, focusing on the costs of care concluded that ''The importance of family and friends is evidenced by the fact that greatly or extremely impaired elderly who live with their spouses and children generally are not institutionalized, whereas those who live alone usually are'' (Laurie, 1978). Incidentally, our own research indicates that ill health on the part of the parent is often a cause of older parents and adult children living together.

Elaine Brody, among others, has pointed out that clinical evidence reinforces gerontological research findings that adult children do not "dump" old parents into institutions. In this connection she says: "Studies of the paths leading to institutional care have shown that placing an elderly relative is the last, rather than the first, resort of families. In general, they have exhausted all other alternatives, endured severe personal, social and economic stress in the process, and made the final decision with the utmost reluctance" (1977).

The hypothesis that because of the existence of large human service bureaucracies families are no longer important as a source of care for the elderly, like the other hypotheses derived from the alienation myth, must also be rejected.

In this paper I have presented evidence to show that the belief that old people are alienated from their families, particularly their children, is a myth, not a truism. I now wish to comment on some of the kinds of research and the kind of social policy that should follow the abandonment of this myth.

Research and Policy in the Wake of the Slain Myth

We need more studies of those family forms in which some old people live which differ from the norm. While the number of persons in such arrangements is small now they will undoubtedly increase in the future. We especially need to know what services these pseudo-families can and cannot perform for their members and what supports they need to function effectively. We need research on the special situation of the childless elderly. If the birth rate continues to drop, some 35 years from now we will have a large proportion of old people who have no children or

only one child. We should now investigate how childless old persons establish helping relationships with child substitutes among their available pool of kinfolk and among their friends. If we knew how these arrangements develop we would be able both to better assist the present elderly and to establish guidelines for the future.

I would also like to suggest a research topic that might be more difficult to implement. A question that concerns me is why we Americans who are interacting with our older relatives in a helping way persist in believing that we are neglecting our elderly. Why do we continue to berate ourselves while each of us is saying "But my family is different?"

In the area of social policy every effort should be made to assist families to maintain viable relationships with their older members. This means that services should be made available to old people irrespective of whether they live alone or with others. Sometimes, good family relationships are dependent on such services. Further, human service systems and their personnel must cease to behave as though the families of the elderly were enemies of the system. There is a need for an increased sensitivity to both older people and their families and for a willingness to listen on the part of such systems and their functionaries (Shanas & Sussman, 1977).

In conclusion, this paper has been designed to underscore one of my beliefs. My work has been a search for facts, for I believe that if social research and social policy in aging are to be more than exercises in futility they must be based on the facts about older people and their families, and not upon myths, however seductive.

References

Brody, E. *Long-term care for older people.* Human Sciences Press, New York, 1977.

Laslett, P. (Ed.). *Household and family in past time.*

Cambridge Univ. Press, Cambridge, England, 1972.

Laurie, W. F. Employing the Duke OARS

methodology in cost comparisons: Home services and institutionalization. *Center reports on advances in research* 2, Duke Univ. Ctr. for the Study of Aging and Human Development, Durham, NC, 1978.

Parsons, T. The normal American family. In S. Farber, P. Mustacchi & R. H. Wilson (Eds.), *Man and civilization: The family's search for survival.* New York, 1965.

Rosenmayr, L., & Köckeis, E. Propositions for a sociological theory of aging and the family. *International Social Science Journal,* 1963, 15, 410–426.

Rosenmayr, L. The many faces of the family. Paper presented at a meeting of the Int. Assoc. of Gerontology, Jerusalem, Israel, 1975.

Shanas, E. *The health of older people: A social survey.* Harvard Univ. Press, Cambridge, MA, 1962.

Shanas, E., & Sussman, M. B. Family and bureaucracy: Comparative analyses and problematics. In E. Shanas and M. B. Sussman (Eds.), *Family, bureaucracy and the elderly.* Duke Univ. Press, Durham, NC, 1977.

Shanas, E., Townsend, P., Wedderburn, D., Friis, H., Milhøj, P., & Stehouwer, J. *Old people in three industrial societies.* Atherton and Routledge Kegan Paul, New York and London, 1968.

Siegel, J. Demographic aspects of aging and the older population of the U. S. *Current population reports: Special studies.* USGPO, Series P-23, No. 59, Washington, DC, 1976.

Sussman, M. The family life of old people. In E. Shanas & R. H. Binstock (Eds.), *Handbook of aging and the social sciences,* Van Nostrand Reinhold, New York, 1976.

3

Careers

A career is a life-long pattern of work. One usually chooses the first job in young adulthood, in a process not unlike choosing a mate. Family influences on career choice are both direct, with parents encouraging certain occupations and discouraging others, and indirect, through the effect of the family on personality. Vocational values, for both college and noncollege youth, have changed since the 1960s; although young people still believe in hard work and material success, they also view American business with considerable cynicism, and they desire jobs that are challenging and fulfilling. Since few jobs offer such opportunities, especially for noncollege youth, the outcome may be increasing frustration and dissatisfaction.

Women are working outside the home in increasing numbers, even during the most common childbearing years, between the ages of twenty-five and thirty-four. They are encountering discrimination, a lack of female mentors, and other conditions that often leave them underpaid and undervalued, even though much progress has occurred during the past decade. In our first selection *Studs Terkel* narrates the story of a middle-aged woman who works in a luggage factory. It provides a vivid portrayal of the career experience (or lack thereof) of a working-class woman.

In occupations more likely to be chosen by college-trained persons, the individual must establish himself, once the occupation has been chosen. Not only is it necessary to "learn the ropes," but it helps to acquire a *mentor,* a more experienced senior worker or professional who serves as teacher, sponsor, guide, and model. That the choice of an appropriate mentor may be crucial for career advancement has long been suspected. In an empirical study *Elyse Goldstein* examines the productivity of persons who received the Ph.D. in psychology, who had either male or female mentors. She finds that productivity is enhanced by having a same-sex mentor and possibly inhibited in the case of cross-sex role models. She concludes that it appears that more ambitious graduate students tend to seek same-sex advisors.

Following the establishment and development of a career, retirement occurs for most people in the sixties. In spite of changes in the laws regarding retirement, it still seems that for most workers retirement is not voluntary. Many workers would prefer to continue working, not necessarily because they enjoy work, but because they need or want the income and fringe benefits, because of inflation, or because they value the social network closely connected with their jobs. Contrary to popular belief, however, retirement does not commonly lead to a decline in physical and mental health or to an early death. Personality variables play a role in one's reaction to retirement, with well-adjusted and well-defended personalities best able to handle it.

Robert C. Atchley provides a thoughtful analysis of the problems of adjustment to loss of job at retirement. He points out that the individual's reaction will much depend on how important the job was in the individual's hierarchy of personal goals. If the job was high in the hierarchy, then upon retirement there may be a need to seek either another job or other substitute activities. If no such solution is possible, the individual may show withdrawal behavior and have adjustment difficulties. On the other hand, if the job was not important in the first place, then retirement may involve no serious threat to personal goals, and thus require little effort for postretirement adjustment.

Additional Suggested Readings

Levinson, D. J. *The season of a man's life.* New York: Knopf, 1978.
  A literate treatment of the personal and career development of professional men, with particular emphasis on the phenomenon of the midlife crisis.

Van Dusen, R. A., & Sheldon, E. B. The changing status of American women. *American Psychologist,* 1976, 31, 106–116.
  A review of the effects of the increased participation of women in the work force, as well as remaining obstacles and psychological costs in the transition from the traditional role model.

Interview with Grace Clements

STUDS TERKEL

She is a sparrow of a woman in her mid-forties. She has eighteen grandchildren. "I got my family the easy way. I married my family." She has worked in factories for the past twenty-five years: "A punch press operator, oven unloader, sander, did riveting, stapling, light assembly . . ." She has been with one company for twenty-one years, ARMCO Corporation.

During the last four years, she has worked in the luggage division of one of the corporation's subsidiaries. In the same factory are made snowmobile parts, windshield defrosters, tilt caps, sewer tiles, and black paper speakers for radios and TV sets.

"We're about twelve women that work in our area, one for each tank. We're about one-third Puerto Rican and Mexican, maybe a quarter black, and the rest of us are white. We have women of all ages, from eighteen to sixty-six, married, single, with families, without families.

"We have to punch in before seven. We're at our tank approximately one to two minutes before seven to take over from the girl who's leaving. The tanks run twenty-four hours a day."

The tank I work at is six-foot deep, eight-foot square. In it is pulp, made of ground wood, ground glass, fiberglass, a mixture of chemicals and water. It comes up through a copper screen felter as a form, shaped like the luggage you buy in the store.

In forty seconds you have to take the wet felt out of the felter, put the blanket on — a rubber sheeting — to draw out the excess moisture, wait two, three seconds, take the blanket off, pick the wet felt up, balance it on your shoulder — there is no way of holding it without it tearing all to pieces, it is wet and will collapse — reach over, get the hose, spray the inside of this copper screen to keep it from plugging, turn around, walk to the hot dry die behind you, take the hot piece off with your opposite hand, set it on the floor — this wet thing is still balanced on my shoulder — put the wet piece on the dry die, push this button that lets the dry press down, inspect the piece we just took off, the hot piece, stack it, and count it — when you get a stack of ten, you push it over and start another stack of ten — then go back and put our blanket on the wet piece coming up from the tank . . . and start all over. Forty seconds. We also have to weigh every third piece in that time. It has to be within so many grams. We are constantly standing and moving. If you talk during working, you get a reprimand, because it is easy to make a reject if you're talking.

A thirty-inch luggage weighs up to fifteen pounds wet. The hot piece weighs between three to four pounds. The big luggage you'll

Source: From *Working: People Talk About What They Do All Day and How They Feel About What They Do* by Studs Terkel. Copyright © 1972, 1974 by Studs Terkel. Reprinted by permission of Pantheon Books, a Division of Random House, Inc. and Wildwood House Limited.

maybe process only four hundred. On the smaller luggage, you'll run maybe 800, sometimes 850 a day. All day long is the same thing over and over. That's about ten steps every forty seconds about 800 times a day.

We work eight straight hours, with two ten-minute breaks and one twenty-minute break for lunch. If you want to use the washroom, you have to do that in that time. By the time you leave your tank, you go to the washroom, freshen up a bit, go into the recreation room, it makes it very difficult to finish a small lunch and be back in the tank in twenty minutes. So you don't really have too much time for conversation. Many of our women take a half a sandwich or some of them don't even take anything. I'm a big eater. I carry a lunch box, fruit, a half a sandwich, a little cup of cottage cheese or salad. I find it very difficult to complete my lunch in the length of time.

You cannot at any time leave the tank. The pieces in the die will burn while you're gone. If you're real, real, real sick and in urgent need, you do shut it off. You turn on the trouble light and wait for the tool man to come and take your place. But they'll take you to a nurse and check it out.

The job I'm doing is easier than the punch presses I used to run. It's still not as fast as the punch press, where you're putting out anywhere to five hundred pieces an hour. Whereas here you can have a couple of seconds to rest in. I mean *seconds*. (Laughs.) You have about two seconds to wait while the blanket is on the felt drawing the moisture out. You can stand and relax those two seconds — three seconds at most. You wish you didn't have to work in a factory. When it's all you know what to do, that's what you do.

I guess my scars are pretty well healed by now, because I've been off on medical leave for two, three months. Ordinarily I usually have two, three burn spots. It's real hot, and if it touches you for a second, it'll burn your arm. Most of the girls carry scars all the time.

We've had two or three serious accidents in the last year and a half. One happened about two weeks ago to a woman on the hydraulic lift. The cast-iron extension deteriorated with age and cracked and the die dropped. It broke her whole hand. She lost two fingers and had plastic surgery to cover the burn. The dry die runs anywhere from 385 degrees to 425.

We have wooden platforms where we can walk on. Some of the tanks have no-skid strips to keep you from slipping, 'cause the floor gets wet. The hose we wash the felter with will sometimes have leaks and will spray back on you. Sometimes the tanks will overflow. You can slip and fall. And slipping on oil. The hydraulic presses leak every once in a while. We've had a number of accidents. I currently have a workman's comp suit going. I came up under an electric switch box with my elbow and injured the bone and muscle where it fastens together. I couldn't use it.

I have arthritis in the joints of some of my fingers. Your hands handling hot pieces perspire and you end up with rheumatism or arthritis in your fingers. Naturally in your shoulder, balancing that wet piece. You've got the heat, you've got the moisture because there's steam coming out. You have the possibility of being burnt with steam when the hot die hits that wet felt. You're just engulfed in a cloud of steam every forty seconds.

It's very noisy. If the tool man comes to talk to you, the noise is great enough you have to almost shout to make yourself heard. There's the hissing of the steam, there's the compressed air, a lot of pressure — it's gotta lift that fifteen pounds and break it loose from that copper screen. I've lost a certain percentage of my hearing already. I can't hear the phone in the yard. The family can.

In the summertime, the temperature

ranges anywhere from 100 to 150 degrees at our work station. I've taken thermometers and checked it out. You've got three open presses behind you. There's nothing between you and that heat but an asbestos sheet. They've recently put in air conditioning in the recreation room. There's been quite a little discussion between the union and the company on this. They carry the air conditioning too low for the people on the presses. Our temperature will be up to 140, and to go into an air-conditioned recreation room that might be set at 72 — 'cause the office force is happy and content with it — people on the presses almost faint when they go back. We really suffer.

I'm chairman of the grievance committee.[1] We have quite a few grievances. Sometimes we don't have the support we should have from our people. Sometimes the company is obstinate. For the most part, many of our grievances are won.

Where most people get off at three, I get off at two o'clock. I have an hour to investigate grievances, to work on them, to write them up, to just in general check working conditions. I'm also the editor of the union paper. I do all my own work. I cut stencils, I write the articles, copy the pictures. I'm not a very good freehand artist (laughs), so I copy them. I usually do that in the union office before I go home and make supper. It takes about five hours to do a paper. Two nights.

(Laughs.) I daydream while I'm working. Your mind gets so it automatically picks out the flaws. I plan my paper and what I'm going to have for supper and what we're gonna do for the weekend. My husband and I have a sixteen-foot boat. We spend a lot of weekends and evenings on the river. And I try to figure out how I'm gonna feed twenty, twenty-five people for dinner on Saturday. And how to solve a grievance . . .

They can't keep the men on the tanks. We've never been able to keep a man over a week. They say it's too monotonous. I think women adjust to monotony better than men do. Because their minds are used to doing two things at once, where a man usually can do one thing at a time. A woman is used to listening to a child tell her something while she's doing something else. She might be making a cake while the child is asking her a question. She can answer that child and continue to put that cake together. It's the same way on the tanks. You get to be automatic in what you're doing and your mind is doing something else.

I was one of the organizers here (laughs) when the union came in. I was as anti-union in the beginning as I am union now. Coming from a small farming community in Wisconsin, I didn't know what a union was all about. I didn't understand the labor movement at all. In school you're shown the bad side of it.

Before the union came in, all I did was do my eight hours, collect my paycheck, and go home, did my housework, took care of my daughter, and went back to work. I had no outside interests. You just lived to live. Since I became active in the union, I've become active in politics, in the community, in legislative problems. I've been to Washington on one or two trips. I've been to Springfield. That has given me more of an incentive for life.

I see the others, I'm sad. They just come to work, do their work, go home, take care of their home, and come back to work. Their conversation is strictly about their family and meals. They live each day for itself and that's about it.

My whole attitude on the job has changed since the union came in. Now I would like to be a union counselor or work for the OEO. I work with humans as grievance committee chairman. They come to you angry, they come to you hurt, they come to you puzzled. You have to make life easier for them.

[1] It is a local of the UAW.

"I tried to get my children to finish vocational school. One of the girls works for a vending machine company, serving hot lunches. She makes good. One of the daughters does waitress work. One of the girls has gone into factory work. One of the boys is in a factory. He would like to work up to maintenance. One girl married and doesn't do any work at all. My husband is a custodian in a factory. He likes his work as a janitor. There's no pushing him.

This summer I've been quite ill and they've been fussin' about me. (Laughs.) Monday and Tuesday my two daughters and I made over sixty quarts of peaches, made six batches of jam. On Wednesday we made five batches of wild grape jelly. We like to try new recipes. I like to see something different on the table every night. I enjoy baking my own bread and coffee cake. I bake everything I carry in our lunch."

I attended a conference of the Governor's Commission on the Status of Women. Another lady went with me. We were both union officers. Most of the women there were either teachers or nurses or in a professional field. When they found out we were from labor, their attitude was cold. You felt like a little piece of scum. They acted like they were very much better than we were, just because we worked in a factory. I felt that, without us, they'd be in a heck of a shape. (Laughs.) They wouldn't have anything without us. How could we employ teachers if it wasn't for the factory workers to manufacture the books? And briefcases, that's luggage. (Laughs.)

I can understand how the black and the Spanish-speaking people feel. Even as a farmer's daughter, because we were just hard-working poor farmers, you were looked down upon by many people. Then to go into factory work, it's the same thing. You're looked down upon. You can even feel it in a store, if you're in work clothes. The difference between being in work clothes going into a nice department store and going in your dress clothes. It is two entirely different feelings. People won't treat you the same at all.

I hope I don't work many more years. I'm tired. I'd like to stay home and keep house. We're in hopes my husband would get himself a small hamburger place and a place near the lake where I can have a little garden and raise my flowers that I love to raise . . .

Effect of Same-Sex and Cross-Sex Role Models on the Subsequent Academic Productivity of Scholars

ELYSE GOLDSTEIN

The author of this article measured the academic productivity of four groups: male PhDs who had male dissertation advisors, female PhDs who had female advisors, male PhDs who had female advisors, and female PhDs who had male advisors. As predicted, scholars in the two same-sex conditions published significantly more research than did scholars in the two cross-sex conditions ($p < .001$). The article discusses possible advantages or facilitation effects of providing individuals with same-sex role models, as well as factors that may inhibit professional advancement in the case of cross-sex role models.

The impact of adult role models on the child's development and socialization has been discussed by both social-learning theorists (Bandura, 1969) and Freudian theorists (Blum, 1953). There is, however, a lack of literature documenting the existence of role-modeling phenomena in adults. The shortage of female role models in many professions has triggered some nonexperimental papers emphasizing the importance of female models. Arguments for female role models have emphasized the importance of women's identification with female models, the significance of information provided by the model's behavior, and positive incentive through illustrative success. According to Angrist and Almquist (1975), successful women academicians, in writing their biographies, emphasize the dominant role that older female role models played in their own academic development. Walum (quoted by Douvan, 1976) found that 25 married female PhDs all had strong identifications with some female model. Douvan (1976) stated that the presence of effective role models helps "the young intellectual woman to concretize her own role conception, invest her aspirations with greater reality, and perhaps offer her some useful clues about ordering her spheres of action" (p. 5).

In the corresponding male role-model situation, "illustrative success" was not emphasized, probably for two reasons: (1) Men often witness the success of other males, and (2) it is culturally perceived as "in-role" behavior for the male to succeed professionally. For males, the benefits reaped from same-sex role models were seen to stem from

Source: Goldstein, E. Effect of same-sex and cross-sex role models on the subsequent academic productivity of scholars. *American Psychologist,* 1979, 34, 407–410. Copyright 1979 by the American Psychological Association. Reprinted by permission.

the ability of the male role model to identify with his protegé. Epstein (1970), in discussing the sponsor–protegé system (the mechanism by which apprentices are often assimilated into the professional domain), suggested that male sponsors more readily identify other males as their eventual successors. They might therefore bestow the male protegé with greater responsibility, make him aware of the informal values, attitudes, and expectations necessary for success, help pave the way for his acceptance by others, and provide feedback to strengthen the protegé's image of himself as a competent professional (White, 1970).

Research on inhibitory factors in the case of cross-sex role models has primarily focused on the male-sponsor/female-protegée relationship because the reverse situation occurs less frequently. Epstein suggested that jealousy stemming from the male sponsor's and the female protegée's other role partners (e.g., wife, husband) may inhibit the relationship. A male sponsor may be reluctant to sponsor a woman professionally because he may not see her as someone who will carry on his ideas, or he may believe that women's family commitments may interfere with professional ones, that women may not be compatible with male colleagues, or that females are financially less dependent on career-oriented jobs than men are (Epstein, 1970; Lewin & Duchan, 1971; White, 1970).

Teghtsoonian (1974) examined the representation of male and female psychologists on the editorial boards of professional journals and found that women were not represented as often as one might predict from their numbers as authors; after controlling for APA division membership, women had publication records similar to those of men. Her data did not suggest, however, how such bias in editor selection operated. She offered as possible reasons the inhibitory factors discussed by Epstein, Lewin and Duchan, and White.

The present research was directed toward testing whether there were differences in the academic productivity of four groups: male and female scholars who had same-sex and cross-sex role models. Academic productivity, the dependent variable, was measured by the quantity of research published by these groups for a period of four years after subjects' PhDs had been awarded. The method of using publication rate as an indicator of academic competency, achievement, and productivity had been used by Teghtsoonian (1974). It was hypothesized that the two same-sex role-model groups would be academically more productive than the cross-sex role-model groups. Thus, an interaction effect between sex of academic advisor and sex of scholar was expected. No main effects were expected.

Method

Subjects

All subjects were adult males and females who were recipients of doctoral degrees in psychology from three universities, City University of New York, The New School for Social Research, and New York University, during the years 1965–1973. Subjects were classified according to their own sex and the sex of their advisor and were assigned to one of four conditions: male PhDs who had female advisors $(n = 26)$, female PhDs who had male advisors $(n = 30)$, female PhDs who had female advisors $(n = 25)$, and male PhDs who had male advisors $(n = 29)$. The total numbers of subjects from which each respective group was randomly selected were as follows: $N = 35$, $N = 155$, $N = 31$, $N = 260$. The total N of 110 subjects in this sample had an equal number of male and female PhDs. The ns for the subjects from the three schools were 36, 34, and 40, respectively.

In 1978 the mean ages of advisors for the four groups were as follows: 49.5 for female advisors of males, 52.1 for male advisors of females, 52.5 for female advisors of females, and 51.9 for male advisors of males. The percentages of ages that were unobtainable for advisors in these four respective groups were as follows: 6%, 9%, 8%, and 9%. At the time they received their degrees, the mean ages of PhDs in the four groups were as follows: male PhD/female advisor, 34.1; female PhD/male advisor, 34.4; female PhD/female advisor, 35.1; male PhD/male advisor, 33.9. The percentages of ages that were unobtainable for these four respective groups were as follows: 10%, 11%, 7%, 8%.

Scholars obtained their PhDs in experimental, clinical, social, personality, developmental, physiological, environmental, community, and industrial psychology. The membership of scholars in these fields was organized according to the following classification: experimental, clinical, social/personality, or other. The breakdown for the four groups was as follows: male scholars/female advisors — 12 experimental, 7 clinical, 7 social/personality; female scholars/male advisors — 6 experimental, 9 clinical, 10 social/personality, 5 other; female scholars/female advisors — 6 experimental, 5 clinical, 9 social/personality, 5 other; male scholars/male advisors — 7 experimental, 7 clinical, 8 social/personality, 7 other.

Procedure

The name and the date of degree conferred for each individual subject was obtained. After classification of individuals into the four groups, subjects were randomly selected from the larger population by use of a random number table. The initial classification of graduates into four groups was made in order to ensure a large enough sample size for each of the four conditions.

A revised list of subjects with only the name and the date of degree conferred was comprised. The advisor's name was deleted. In this manner, the experimenter was unaware of the exact experimental condition of a subject, although a knowledge of sex of subject was unavoidable. *Psychological Abstracts* was then consulted for each subject individually for a time period of four years after the degree was conferred.

Tabulations were then made for frequency of publication per subject, each article being counted as one, regardless of whether the subject was sole author, first or second author in a coauthorship, or third author. An analysis of variance was performed on these data to determine the difference in publication rates among the four groups. The publications of these four groups were then broken down into three mutually exclusive categories: sole author, first author, or second and third author. Tabulations were also made for the number of publications that were dissertation offshoots. A publication was considered a dissertation offshoot in two cases: (1) if it was listed in *Psychological Abstracts* as such or (2) if the title of the publication coincided with the title of the dissertation.

Results

Table 1 presents the mean numbers of publications of scholars within the four groups during the 4-year period after being awarded their doctoral degrees. As hypothesized, the analysis of variance revealed no significant main effects but a significant Sex of Advisor × Sex of Scholar interaction, $F(1, 106) = 20,960$, $p < .001$. Post hoc Scheffé comparisons were made on all six possible comparisons.

From the total of 139 articles published by the entire group, 110 articles (79%) were published by subjects in the same-sex role-model conditions and 29 articles (21%) were published by subjects in the cross-sex role-model conditions.

Of the 16 articles published by males who

TABLE 1

Mean Number of Publications as a Function of Sex of Scholar and Sex of Advisor, for the 4–year Post–PhD Period

	Advisor	
Scholar	Male	Female
Male	2.069_a	$.615_b$
Female	$.433_b$	2.000_a

Note. Means with different subscripts are significantly different at $p < .05$, using the Scheffé procedure.

had female advisors, 10 articles (63%) were of sole authorship, 4 articles (25%) were first authored, and 2 articles (12%) were second and third authored. Of the 13 articles published by females who had male advisors, 5 articles (38%) were of sole authorship, 4 articles (31%) were first authored, and 4 articles (31%) were second and third authored. Of the 50 articles published by females who had female advisors, 22 articles (44%) were of sole authorship, 14 articles (28%) were first authored, and 14 articles (28%) were second and third authored. Of the 60 articles published by males who had male advisors, 26 articles (43%) were of sole authorship, 13 articles (22%) were first authored, and 21 articles (35%) were second and third authored.

Forty-four percent of the articles published by males who had female advisors were dissertation offshoots; 46% of the publications produced by females who had male advisors were dissertation offshoots; 34% of the publications by females who had female advisors were dissertation offshoots; 58% of the publications produced by males who had male advisors were dissertation offshoots.

Discussion

These results must be interpreted cautiously. A causal relationship between scholar/advisor sex and academic productivity cannot be inferred. We have no way of knowing whether male and female subjects in same-sex groups would have performed even more successfully had they had opposite-sex advisors. Furthermore, even if we were to find that role modeling is responsible for this effect, we would then have to specify more clearly how this process operates. Since role modeling is difficult to verify empirically, perhaps a reformulation, consisting of isolating the separate contributions of the advisor, the scholar, and interpersonal variables, would be useful. The importance of rapport, for example, is an interpersonal factor that needs to be explored; the same is true for similarity of cognitive style between scholar and advisor. Examining job recommendations made by advisors for same-sex and opposite-sex students might inform us of the possible favoring of one sex over the other. Scholars' expectations of their relationship with their advisors should be examined. To what extent does sex of advisor influence students' choices of advisors? What factors lead a person to choose a same-sex or an opposite-sex advisor?

It is not implausible that the results obtained were due to self-selection: More ambitious or intelligent males and females seek out same-sex advisors. In this study, males and females who had female advisors were sampled from a relatively small population. This probably reflects the fact that there was a smaller percentage of female advisors available to students. However, we might also ask whether fewer or only certain students choose to work with female advisors (e.g., nonambitious males and ambitious females). But even if self-selection was operating, then we are left with another unanswered question: Why would the more ambitious or successful students choose same-sex advisors?

The last finding that deserves comment concerns the publication styles of the four groups. The distribution of authorship data showed a substantial amount of sole authorship and first authorship for the four groups, as well as a trend for more sole authorship than first authorship. Although the difference between the percentage of sole authors and that of first authors appeared to be greatest in the male scholar/female advisor group, it may be difficult to interpret this in light of the small number of publications for both cross-sex groups. Future research should investigate trends in authorship style among the four groups.

Of the two productive same-sex groups, male scholars published a greater percentage of dissertation offshoots than females did (58% vs. 34%). Thus it might be that these males were not necessarily more productive per se but sought to make the most of what they had done and used better strategies. This might necessitate the investigation of publications of scholars for more years than the 4-year post-PhD period in which dissertation offshoots are common.

The replication of this study for several time periods might be useful in documenting historical trends. Also, replication in different geographic areas would certainly enhance the generalizability of the results.

References

Angrist, S. S., & Almquist, E. M. *Careers and contingencies: How college women juggle with gender.* Port Washington, N.Y.: University Press of Cambridge/Dunellen, 1975.

Bandura, A. Social-learning theory of identificatory processes. In D. A. Goslin (Ed.), *Handbook of socialization theory and research.* Chicago: Rand McNally, 1969.

Blum, G. S. *Psychoanalytic theories of personality.* New York: McGraw-Hill, 1953.

Douvan, E. The role of models in women's professional development. *Psychology of Women Quarterly,* Fall 1976, pp. 5–19.

Epstein, C. F. Encountering the male establishment: Sex-status limits on women's careers in the professions. *American Journal of Sociology,* 1970, 75, 965–982.

Lewin, A. Y., & Duchan, L. Women in academia. *Science,* 1971, 173, 892–895.

Teghtsoonian, M. Distribution by sex of authors and editors of psychological journals, 1970–1972. *American Psychologist,* 1974, 29, 262–269.

White, M. S. Psychological and social barriers to women in science. *Science,* 1970, 170, 413–416.

Adjustment to Loss of Job at Retirement

ROBERT C. ATCHLEY

This paper presents an approach to adjustment to the loss of job at retirement which attempts to integrate earlier approaches by focusing on the impact of retirement on the individual's hierarchy of personal goals. If the job is high in that hierarchy and yet unachieved, then the individual can be expected to seek another job or a job substitute. If this is unsuccessful, then the hierarchy of personal goals must be reorganized. If the individual is broadly engaged, the hierarchy can be consolidated. If he or she is narrowly engaged, then alternate roles must be sought. If the search is successful, a new hierarchy emerges. If not, the individual must withdraw. If the job is not high in the hierarchy to begin with, then no serious change in personal goals accompanies retirement.

How do people adjust to retirement? This is an area in which there has been a fair amount of systematic research as well as a good deal of theorizing.

Apparently most people respond favorably to life in retirement. In our study of retired teachers and telephone company employees [1], not quite 30 per cent felt that they would never get used to retirement. Harris [2] found that 33 per cent of his sample viewed retirement as less than satisfactory. Streib and Schneider [3] found that about 10 per cent of their sample rejected retirement by taking another job, and these people tended to be high on a scale of job deprivation, a measure of the extent to which they missed their jobs. The percentage encountering difficulty retiring is higher among women, among those with low incomes, and among those with poor health [3,4].

Among those who encounter difficulty adjusting to retirement, financial problems head the list (40 per cent), followed by health problems (28 per cent), missing one's job (22 per cent), and death of spouse (10 per cent) [5]. Retirement *per se* is directly responsible for only two of these sources of difficulty: missing one's job and financial problems. Health problems are almost always a cause rather than a consequence of retirement [3]. And certainly retirement is only rarely directly related to the death of one's spouse.

Of the approximately 30 per cent of retired people who encountered difficulty adjusting to retirement, about 7 per cent had difficulty due to missing their jobs, and about 12 per cent had financial difficulties. The other 11 per cent or so had difficulties which created problems for them but which were basically unrelated to retirement [2].

Source: Atchley, R. C. Adjustment to loss of job at retirement. *International Journal of Aging and Human Development,* 1975, 6, 17–27. Copyright 1975 by Baywood Publishing Co. Reprinted by permission.

Theory is a necessary element in the development of knowledge. Theory serves to identify gaps in knowledge and as a guide for organizing research. With regard to adjustment to retirement, theories are needed to describe and explain (1) adjustment to changes in income and (2) adjustment to no longer having job responsibilities.

As yet no theory concerning how people adjust to income decline has been developed. What is needed is descriptive data on the phases of adjustment and on the strategies that are employed. A decision model would probably be useful. However, at this point the basic descriptive data necessary to begin to develop such a theory have not been assembled.

More attention has been given to the problem of adjusting to the loss of one's job. Several theories of adjustment have emerged, each of which has a different emphasis.

Activity theory assumes that the job means different things to different people and that to adjust successfully to the loss of one's job, one must find a substitute for whatever personal goal the job was used to achieve. The most often quoted proponents of this theory are Friedmann and Havighurst [6] and Miller [7]. Friedmann and Havighurst approach the matter in terms of substitute activities, and Miller carried it one step further to include substitute activities which serve as new sources of identity. The assumption here is that the individual will seek and find a work substitute. In a test of this theory, however, Shanas [8] found it to be of very limited utility when applied to American society. In my own research, activity theory has fit the behavior of only a tiny proportion of retired people [9].

Continuity theory assumes that, whenever possible, the individual will cope with retirement by increasing the time spent in roles he already plays rather than by finding new roles to play [10]. This assumption is based on the finding that older people tend to stick with tried and true ways rather than to experiment, and on the assumption that most retired people want their life in retirement to be as much like their preretirement life as possible. However, continuity theory allows for a gradual reduction in overall activity. Obviously, these basic assumptions do not fit *all* retired people, although they may fit the majority.

Disengagement theory [11–13] holds that retirement is a necessary manifestation of the mutual withdrawal of society and the older individual from one another as a consequence of the increased prospect of biological failure in the individual organism. This theory has been criticized for making the rejection of older people by society seem "natural" and, therefore, right. However, the fact of the matter is that many people *do* want to withdraw from full-time jobs and welcome the opportunity to do so. Streib and Schneider [3] refined disengagement theory to apply more directly to the realities of retirement. *Differential disengagement* is the term they use to reflect the idea that disengagement can occur at different rates for different roles. And they do not contend that disengagement is irreversible. They hold that by removing the necessity for energy-sapping labor on a job, retirement may free the individual with declining energy to increase his level of engagement in other spheres of life. Such increases in involvement do in fact occur [1].

Thus, both continuity theory and the theory of differential disengagement attempt to explain why people do not adjust to retirement as activity theory would lead us to expect.

Hazardous as it may be, I would like to offer another approach to understanding adjustment to the loss of job which accompanies retirement. It is to some extent speculative, but I think it is also based on the facts as we now know them. It also synthesizes the major elements of the three theories mentioned above. In sum, the central processes of adjustment are held to be *internal compromise* and *interpersonal negotiations.* While these two elements interact quite strongly in real situations, for analytical purposes I shall treat them separately.

When a person retires, a new role is taken on and an old one relinquished, at least to a degree. The extent to which this triggers a need for a new adjustment on the part of the individual depends on how the job role fits into his pattern of adjustment prior to retirement.

It is probably safe to say that retirement represents a certain amount of disruption in the lives of just about everyone who retires. But why is this disruption so much more serious for some than for others? The answer to this is to be found by examining the relationship between the amount of change introduced by retirement and the capacity of the individual to deal with change routinely.

When people can deal with a substantial amount of change in a more or less routine fashion, we call them flexible. We also tend to think of changes as *serious* only if they exceed the magnitude which can be dealt with routinely by the individual. People who have difficulty adjusting to retirement can be people with a low level of tolerance for any change (inflexible). They can also be people who are confronted with especially serious change. Obviously, the degree to which any change is serious depends on how adaptable the individual is. Thus, among those who have difficulty adjusting to retirement, we would expect to find a group of rigid, inflexible people for whom even small changes in the status quo are seen as serious. We would also expect to find a group of reasonably flexible people who are having to adjust to what seems *to them* a high magnitude of change.

A second important variable is the individual's hierarchy of personal goals. Everyone has personal goals—important results which, if achieved, give the individual a strong sense of personal worth or satisfaction. These goals are of several types.

Some of them involve learning to respond to life in a particular manner—the development of certain personal qualities, such as honesty, ambition, cheerfulness, kindness, and so on, which can be exhibited in most situations and in most roles. Other personal goals are materialistic and involve achieving ownership of particular property such as land, house, stereo, car, etc. Still other personal goals involve successfully playing certain roles. Thus, a person's desire to succeed as a parent, a job-holder, an artist, or any number of other roles can be viewed also in relation to this hierarchy of personal goals.

These various types of goals differ a great deal in terms of their transferability and their capacities as enduring sources of satisfaction. Materialistic goals seem to be the most transitory. After material goals are achieved, they seem to have the capacity to turn to ashes in the mouth of the achiever. This process of disillusionment can take some time, however, and many people have materialistic goals they never achieve. Thus, while this type of goal may have certain drawbacks, it is a common type of goal in American society. And to the extent that lowered income in retirement interferes with materialistic goals not yet achieved, retirement can trigger adjustment problems.

Personal goals that are related to success in various roles are less concrete than materialistic goals. The object of materialistic goals is obvious, but the criteria for successful role playing can be illusory indeed. While this means that the individual often cannot be sure whether he has or has not been a success as a role player it also means that he is much more free to decide for himself. Also, the fruits of successful role playing can be savored long after the success is achieved. In fact, often such successes literally improve with distance from achievement as the negative aspects are forgotten and only the positive ones remain in one's memories.

Goals related to personal qualities are at

the same time more difficult to *achieve* and also less vulnerable to changing circumstances. It may be difficult to *become* a cheerful person, but if one is a cheerful person, this characteristic tends to carry over to all kinds of situations. Thus, if one is, and wants to be, friendly, kind, neat, moral, and self-assured, these achievements are valued in any situation. On the other hand, it is difficult, although not impossible, to learn to be self-confident if one is not already disposed in that direction.

An individual's personal goals are organized into a hierarchy which indicates the individual's priorities for achieving them. This hierarchy reflects the *relative* importance of particular personal goals. The hierarchy and the personal goals that comprise it constantly change as goals are added or dropped and as success or failure alters priorities. Personal goals come from three major sources: goals we are taught and are expected to hold as personal goals; personal goals which are held by others we seek to emulate; and personal goals which grow out of our own experiences and knowledge about ourselves and our capabilities. Any or all three sources in various combinations may contribute to motivation toward a given personal goal.

The hierarchy of personal goals is influenced by a number of factors. The norms concerning which goals are appropriate for receiving top priority are important. Sex and age norms are particularly pertinent. Males run into trouble if they attempt to take on full-time child rearing as a top priority personal goal. Likewise, females run into trouble if they want to be auto mechanics. More subtly, there are also sex differences in the priority that various personal qualities such as aggressiveness or emotionality are expected to be given in the individual's hierarchy of personal goals.

Norms also exist concerning the hierarchy most appropriate at various ages. As a child, the individual finds that such goals as learn-

ing manners, developing various personal qualities such as trustworthiness, and gaining the skills necessary to be an adult are the main types of personal goals which are held out to him by society as important. There is a conspicuous absence of matters such as marriage, parenthood, or career at the top of the child's working, day-to-day structure. On the other hand, a twenty-eight-year-old man preoccupied with learning to play jacks (the kind you play with a ball, not playing cards) would be considered weird indeed, for we would expect him to have mastered the skills involved much earlier. Thus, an important aspect of many personal goals is that once they are achieved they can be given a lower priority, although they may remain important.

An important dimension of the norms concerning the individual's hierarchy of personal goals involves what is supposed to happen in retirement. The norms demand that upon retirement, the job is no longer eligible to occupy a top spot in the hierarchy of personal goals, and factors such as managing one's own affairs and maintaining an independent household are moved up on the list of expected priorities. And this is becoming increasingly true.

But the norms about the hierarchy of personal goals often tell the individual more about what he cannot do than about what he can do, and the individual usually still has plenty of choices even within the bounds of what is allowable for a given sex at a given stage in the life cycle. Much of the task of matching the individual's capabilities and interests with the options that are available as personal goals is left up to the individual. Family, school, friends, bosses, and co-workers exert influence along the line to be sure, but in the final analysis, the individual must make his own internal compromises *if* he is to become a self-sufficient adult. Of course, some people never make it this far and remain creatures of the demands placed on them in the situation of the moment.

For our purposes, the most important compromises involve the top priority *roles* in the hierarchy. The individual starts off in adolescence with a tentative hierarchy. To the extent that he can gain experience through school, summer jobs or other means concerning how workable the tentative hierarchy of roles is, the individual can gradually move toward stabilizing the hierarchy, particularly the top-priority roles. This sort of stability is important at this stage because it gives the budding adult the security of a firm sense of purpose—of knowing where he is going. Of course, achieving this sort of stability may take some time and may be quite painful in the process. Some people never achieve it, others may achieve stability early and stick with the same hierarchy their entire lives, others may experience several stable hierarchies over their lifetime and still others may gravitate in and out of a feeling of stability.

Such stability in the hierarchy of personal goals may be achieved in two ways. The hierarchy may be positively reinforced, become satisfying, meet with success, and, therefore, attract the individual's commitment. Or the hierarchy may produce results that are neither bad enough to cause it to be abandoned nor good enough to attract the individual's commitment, but at the same time the hierarchy may have been used long enough to have become a habit. For people who are *committed* to a hierarchy with the job at or near the top, retirement is more difficult than for people for whom the job is a prime consideration only out of habit. Of course, retirement is but one of many changes that *can* destroy the stability of one's hierarchy of personal goals. Whether retirement *does* destroy this stability depends on where the job role fits into this hierarchy.

For people who stress personal qualities, the job may be quite far down on the list. Materialistic people may consider the job more important, to the extent that it governs ability to achieve materialistic goals. Even among people who judge their successes primarily in terms of role performance, however, the job may not be a primary source of satisfaction.

Figure 1 shows a schematic diagram of how retirement affects the hierarchy of personal goals. It shows the points at which internal compromise becomes necessary as a mechanism of adjustment to retirement. Retirement obviously introduces a change. The crucial question, however, is whether retirement is a *consequential* change, a change that is important enough to necessitate a reorganization in the upper reaches of the individual's hierarchy of personal goals. If not, then retirement produces no change in the criteria the individual uses to select from among the behavioral alternatives available to him. People who strive mainly to develop personal qualities are particularly likely to find themselves in the latter situation. People for whom roles other than the job are more paramount could also fit into this particular category. The same may be true for people who have given the job a top priority but who also have achieved their ambitions regarding the job.

For many people, however, retirement does involve some amount of reorganization in their hierarchy of personal goals. If the job is *very* high on the list of personal goals, and yet unachieved, the individual can be expected to try to replace it with a substitute job. Ability to accomplish this is directly related to the degree to which the necessary personal and environmental prerequisites are present. First, the individual must be physically able to take up a new job. He must also have or be able to get job skills that are salable in the job market. He must also have other personal qualities such as self-confidence and drive which are necessary to getting out to seek a new job.[1] But most important, there must be job opportunities. If all of

---

[1] This factor was suggested by Helena Lopata.

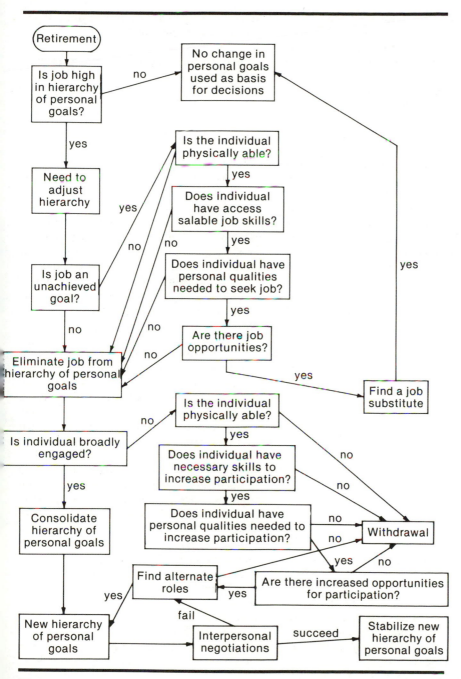

Figure 1
Effect of retirement on personal goals.

these conditions can be satisfied, then the individual can find a substitute job which allows him to retain his hierarchy of personal goals intact. This is the model of activity theory. Of course, this is usually a temporary response since retirement becomes a necessity for virtually everyone who lives long enough.

If any one of the prerequisites for finding a substitute job cannot be satisfied, then the individual will be unable to find one and must reorganize his hierarchy of personal goals. If the job is not very high in the hierarchy, but high enough to cause a need for reorganization, then the individual proceeds directly with reorganizing his hierarchy of personal goals and does not try to find a substitute job. The reorganization will simply take the form of consolidating the remaining roles within the hierarchy of personal goals. Suppose a person's hierarchy of personal goals looked like this, with the most important at the top:

Being a decent, moral person
Being a "good" husband
Having a comfortable, well-furnished
    home
Being a "good" golfer
Being a "good" neighbor
Being a "successful" insurance salesman
Keeping a lid on my temper
Improving myself through reading
Being a dutiful son-in-law to my wife's
    mother

Obviously, retirement need make little change in the essential hierarchy. None of the top items would be disturbed by retirement although reduced income might interfere with house and golf. In this case, there is really no need to search about for new alternatives. There are many there already. This is essentially the model used in continuity theory.

If, on the other hand, the individual is

narrowly engaged [12], his hierarchy of personal goals might look like this:

Being a successful corporation president
.

.

.

Being a "good" husband

The dotted line is there to indicate distance and also to indicate that a large number of personal goals, both qualitative and materialistic, are tied to success on the job. For this type of individual, retirement takes out not only the job but several other goals as well. And it leaves very little. In this situation, the individual was involved in the job to the exclusion of everything else, and as a result must find alternatives to replace the job in his hierarchy of personal goals. The extent to which this task can be accomplished depends again on the individual's having the necessary physical energy, skills, personal qualities and opportunities. Failure to satisfy any of these prerequisites will necessarily result in withdrawal. This is the model of disengagement theory. Success gives the individual the materials with which to forge new hierarchy of personal goals. This is the model of activity theory. The theory of differential disengagement leads us also to expect that the individual will often undergo a net decline in activity even if the hierarchy of goals is successfully reorganized.

The process involved in developing or changing the hierarchy of personal goals is, of course, decision-making, and the expression *internal compromise* is used to describe this decision-making process in order to indicate that its outcome is far from determinate. The process whereby people reorganize their criteria for decision-making, though it may exist, is one we know precious little about.

An important aspect of all this is just where the retired role (as opposed to the job role) fits into this hierarchy. Some people may resist including successful retirement in their hierarchy of personal goals at all. Still others may put it at the bottom. Increasingly, however, playing the role of retired person seems to be taking a high position in the hierarchy and, therefore, can be expected to play a part in the reorganization of the hierarchy. Research is needed to establish just where the retirement role fits into the structure of personal goals and under what circumstances its rank may vary.

Interpersonal negotiations is a process which articulates the individual's goals and aspirations with those of the people he interacts with. It is through this process that the world outside the individual can influence development of and change in his hierarchy of personal goals. When we say that we "know" a person, one of the things we "know" is his hierarchy of personal goals. When this hierarchy changes, the individual indicates to others, through the decisions he makes or through his actions, that a change has taken place. I use the term negotiation here because often the individual runs into resistance in getting others who are important to him to accept his new hierarchy of personal goals. And at this point, the results of internal compromise and feedback from significant others enter into a dialectic.

Unfortunately, while the interpersonal negotiation process is no doubt important to the development of a stable hierarchy of personal goals in retirement, the research evidence provides few clues as to how this process works and how retirement and job roles are dealt with in the process.

This illustrates the importance of basic descriptive research to the theory-building enterprise, for while sufficient facts were present to allow a fairly explicit theory of internal compromise to be developed, no such facts were available with respect to interpersonal negotiations. Theory and research must be developed hand-in-hand. And endeavors which become overbalanced in either direction tend to be less useful than a balanced progression.

Summary

Not quite a third of the retired population encounters difficulty in adjusting to retirement. Adjusting to reduced income is by far the most frequently encountered reason for difficulty in adjustment (40 per cent) among those who have difficulty. Missing one's job accounts for about 22 per cent of the adjustment difficulties. The remaining 38 per cent is accounted for by factors such as death of spouse or declining health which are directly related to retirement adjustment only in that they influence the situation in which retirement adjustment must be carried out. This suggests that certain situational prerequisites are often necessary to a good adjustment.

From a positive point of view, it seems safe to say that adjustment to retirement is greatly enhanced by sufficient income, the ability to gracefully give up one's job, and good health. In addition, adjustment seems to be smoothest when situational changes other than loss of job are at a minimum. Another way of viewing this is to say, assuming that one's fantasy concerning the retirement role is based on reality, that factors which upset the ability of the retirer to live out his retirement ambitions hinder his ability to adjust to retirement smoothly.

People who have difficulty adjusting to retirement tend to be those who are either very inflexible in the face of change or faced with substantial change or both. The prime things about retirement that must be adjusted to are loss of income and loss of job. We know very little about how people adjust to loss of income.

A theory of how people adjust to a loss of

job at retirement was presented which attempts to integrate existing theories by means of the impact of retirement on the individual's hierarchy of personal goals. If the job is high in that hierarchy and yet unachieved, then the individual can be expected to seek another job. If a job substitute cannot be found, then the hierarchy of personal goals must be reorganized. If the individual is broadly engaged, then he must search for alternate roles. If he is successful, he then develops a new hierarchy of personal goals. If not, he withdraws. Of course, if the job is not high in the hierarchy to begin with it requires no serious change in the personal goals used as the basis for everyday decisions.

References

1. Cottrell, Fred and Atchley, Robert C. *Women in Retirement: A Preliminary Report,* Oxford, Ohio: Scripps Foundation for Research in Population Problems, 1969.

2. Harris, Louis. "Pleasant Retirement Expected." *Washington Post,* November 28, 1965.

3. Streib, Gordon F. and Schneider, Clement J. *Retirement in American Society.* Ithaca, N.Y. Cornell University Press, 1971.

4. Heidbreder, Elizabeth M. "Factors in Retirement Adjustment: White Collar/Blue Collar Experience." *Industrial Gerontology,* 1972, 12, pp. 69–79.

5. Riley, Matilda W. and Foner, Anne E. *Aging & Society: Volume I., An Inventory of Research Findings.* New York: Russell Sage Foundation, 1968.

6. Friedmann, Eugene and Havighurst, Robert J. (eds.). *The Meaning of Work and Retirement.* Chicago: University of Chicago Press, 1954.

7. Miller, Stephen J. The social dilemma of the aging leisure participant. In Arnold M. Rose and Warren A. Petersen (eds.), *Older People and Their Social World.* Philadelphia: F. A. Davis, 1965, pp. 77–92.

8. Shanas, Ethel. Adjustment to retirement: Substitution or accommodation? In Frances M. Carp (ed.), *Retirement.* New York: Behavioral Publications, 1972, pp. 219–244.

9. Atchley, Robert C. "Retirement and leisure participation: Continuity or Crisis? *Gerontologist,* " 1971, 11, 1 (part I), pp. 13–17.

10. Atchley, Robert C. *The Social Forces in Later Life: An Introduction to Social Gerontology.* Belmont, California: Wadsworth, 1972.

11. Cumming, Elaine and Henry, William E. *Growing Old: The Process of Disengagement.* New York: Basic Books, 1961.

12. Cumming, Elaine. New thoughts on the theory of disengagement. In Robert Kastenbaum (ed.), *New Thoughts on Old Age.* New York: Springer, 1964.

13. Henry, William E. The theory of intrinsic disengagement. In P. From Hansen (ed.), *Age with a Future.* Copenhagen: Munksgaard, 1965.

Personality Development

THE LIFELONG SEARCH FOR IDENTITY

Personality is the dynamic organization within individuals of those biosocial systems (traits, habits, values) which determine their unique adjustment to the world around them. Although the basic attributes of personality tend to be determined quite early in life, environmental circumstances may affect further development dramatically. For example, Carl Jung, in theorizing about the adult years, hypothesized that people tend to become more introverted as they age and that men and women become more similar, men becoming more feminine and women becoming more masculine. Whether such developments are characteristic of the entire human species, or whether they are quite culture-specific is the topic of our first selection by *David Gutmann.* He reviews cross-cultural studies of aging from many diverse cultures — Middle Eastern, African, native American, and Israeli, as well as modern American urban subcultures. His provocative themes include the age-grading of male and female passivity, the age-grading of female dominance, age-sex roles and the parental imperative, preliterate gerontology, and the integration of nature and social nurture in the later part of life.

In the individual-differences approach to personality development one compares test scores at different ages to determine stability or change. Stability is indicated by no differences in average trait scores, which suggest no general age trend, and by high correlation between scores at different ages, suggesting little shift in the rank order of individuals. Of course, correlations can be computed only if the same individuals are involved at different ages, that is, if the study is longitudinal. Fortunately, several such studies have been reported in recent years and reports from two studies using different types of personality inventories have been included here.

In the first study, by *K. Warner Schaie* and *Iris A. Parham,* theoretical positions for and against a stability model of adult personality are discussed. Results are reported for as a sequential study of nineteen personality factors, most of which fit into the Cattell personality trait framework (usually measured by the 16 PF), conducted over a seven-year period for persons ranging in age from twenty-two to eighty-four years. In this study stability across age is found to be the rule, although there are many substantial differences between successive generation groups. The article also presents a typology of personality traits that explains the different developmental trends obtained for various personality factors.

In the second study *Diana S. Woodruff* and *James E. Birren* examine the results of a follow-up study with the California Test of Personality. Persons who took the test as adolescents in 1944 were asked, twenty-five years later, to answer the inventory as they thought they would have in middle age and also as they thought they would have as adolescents. Interestingly enough, objective age changes were small, but the participants of the study thought that they had changed when actually they had not. Again, objective cohort differences were found to be more important than age changes.

It appears then that individuals tend to place themselves in environments, including marriages and careers, that promote the stability of personalities. Nevertheless, humans are characterized by exceptional adaptability, and the potential for change is significant. Thus successive generations adapt their personalities to different methods of childrearing, persons change some personality attributes in response to salient historical events, and individuals adapt to nonnormative events, resulting in dramatic changes in their interpersonal and physical environment.

Additional Suggested Readings

Vaillant, G. E. *Adaptation to life.* Boston: Little, Brown, 1977.
   A readable account of midlife adaptation from a psychoanalytic point of view. Perhaps somewhat biased toward overgeneralization from data observed in upper-middle-class, highly educated persons.

Neugarten, B. L. Personality and aging. In J. E. Birren and K. W. Schaie (eds.), *Handbook of the psychology of aging.* New York: Van Nostrand Reinhold, 1977, pp. 626–49.
   Review of the research literature covering theories of adult change, time and the life-span; age-related change in personality and recent theoretical formulation of the adult development of personality.

The Cross-Cultural Perspective: Notes Toward a Comparative Psychology of Aging

DAVID GUTMANN

Introduction: Methods, Shortcomings, and Possibilities of Cross-Cultural Studies

The comparative psychology of aging is a field that lacks concepts, methods, and investigators. Indeed, the useful literature is mainly produced by ethnographers and sociologists, by those with, at best, incidental interest in the psychology of aging. Where these investigators have considered the psychological condition of aging populations, they have — in line with their theoretical interests — treated these states as the dependent outcomes of externally imposed sociocultural conditions. Paradoxically, the few psychologists who have attempted cross-cultural studies usually join the anthropologists and sociologists in derogating the independent status of psychological variables. Thus we find almost no comparative studies — those conducted by the same investigator(s) using the same tools and theoretical conceptions across cultures — of the sort required to either test or generate a developmental, ''species'' conception of aging psychology.

Certainly, geriatric psychologists have abundant reasons for avoiding the discomforts, methodological pitfalls and dubious rewards of cross-cultural research. Neugarten and Bengtson (1968) discuss these in detail. Along with the formidable problem of creating constructs and instruments that have cross-cultural validity, there is also the hard task of obtaining truly equivalent data from a variety of cultural settings, particularly when the investigators represent different social backgrounds and scientific traditions. Also noted is the problem of defining comparable samples, plus the difficulty of making interpretations which will be meaningful in the context of each society. Overtly similar behaviors noted in different cultures can have markedly different functions relative to their setting, just as seemingly different behaviors can have similar functions, across cultures. Furthermore, the difficulties of cross-cultural research are compounded by the drawbacks inherent in the study of later life *per se:* the lack of well-developed research methods and sophisticated conceptions in this field.

While acknowledging these limitations, Neugarten and Bengtson argue that cross-cultural studies are a necessary corrective to the cultural blindspots of theory builders; that they pay off in greater generality of findings, and in greater richness of conceptions. Though deficient on the side of theory testing, such research still provides a unique means for developing hypotheses and for identifying powerful variables whose effects can be rigorously tested in single cultures, or

Source: Abridged from Gutmann, D. The cross-cultural perspective: Notes toward a comparative psychology of aging. In J. E. Birren & K. W. Schaie (eds.), *Handbook of the psychology of aging.* New York: Van Nostrand Reinhold, 1977, pp. 303–326. Reprinted by permission.

in those controlled settings where these same variables *could not have been initially identified.* Cross-cultural, comparative studies help to generate explanatory frameworks which illuminate hitherto unobserved regularities and relationships at the local level.

The cross-cultural approach is particularly important in establishing a developmental psychology of aging: such studies vary, and thus control for social or extrinsic contributions to the aging process and any residual transcultural regularities can be logically referred to intrinsic, or developmental forces. Thus, the developmental armatures of aging personality—if these exist — can be identified through (preferably longitudinal) studies of aging populations across disparate cultural settings.

. . . This chapter will largely focus on data sources from those simple societies which provide evidence of psychological genotypes in aging personality. We will also consider the general transformations, the phenotypic outcomes of such genotypes under the impact of modernization and urbanization. In addition, we will use cross-cultural, cross-national, cross-ethnic and rural urban comparisons in order to shed light on important questions in gerontological psychology: persistence and change in adult personality, the universality and adaptive value of disengagement, psychological coordinates of longevity; the religiosity of later life. . . .

We start by reviewing age-grade prescriptions from agrarian, preliterate societies. Such systems are age-qualified recipes for proper social behavior, but in such usually gerontocratic societies these prescriptions may be crafted by the aged to their own specifications. . . . Thus, by reviewing the conditions of social nurture, we may pinpoint some underlying conditions of human nature, some psychological universals that characterize the latter half of the human life cycle.

The Age Grading of Male Passivity

Asian Systems

Mead (1967) reports that younger Chinese men are expected to be achievement-oriented and aggressive, whereas older men are expected to be relaxed, meditative, and "noble." Similarly, Yap (1962) reports that elderly Chinese are expected to abstain from meat and sex, and to practice self-cultivation, worship and meditation. In exchange for this "moral work," they will receive food and shelter. Rustom (1961) reports that four major stages of life are recognized by Burmese villagers: until puberty the task of the individual is to respect parents and elders and to acquire their wisdom. The next, or "virgin" age is centered around the search for a spouse. During the third stage, the young husband's duty is to acquire property, to "give, show, teach," and to provide. Parents are expected to remain economically active until all their children have been married. In the fourth stage, the older Burman leaves mundane tasks to younger family members and devotes himself to religious activities, to merit-acquiring deeds and to meditation. . . . Along similar lines, Cowgill (1968) notes that, despite a continuing deference to the Thai aged, the real leadership is in the hands of the middle-aged. Following their abdication, many older Thai men will enter the priesthood.

The Hindu *Asrama,* or life cycle, has four major stages: the student, the married householder, the "forest" state, and finally *Sanyasa,* involving the complete renunciation of worldly attachments. Steed (1957) elicited somewhat similar views of the Indian life cycle in a Gujurat village. Younger men are expected to be impetuous and driven by a need to succeed; maturity brings a more peaceful nature, followed by a return of peevish anger and egocentricity in old age.

Thus, the Oriental versions of the life cycle cluster towards a consensus. Young men are expected to push and sweat for success in the pragmatic world; but in later life they are expected to shift their concern to the next world, and to their relationship with God.

Middle Eastern and African Societies

The belief that younger men should fulfill the productive style of their culture while old men should contemplate the productive powers of God is not limited to Asian societies. Thus, Gutmann (1974) notes a similar pattern among elderly Druze, a Levantine sect defined by religious beliefs which are held secret even from younger Druze. After his initiation into the religious society, the outward behavior and the inner life of the older Druze are devoted to the service of Allah: he shaves his head, adopts special garb, gives up tobacco, devotes much time to prayers, and dwells on God's mercy, while forgetting his own past grossness and stupidities.

Sub-Saharan tribes institutionalize, within rigid age-set and age-grade systems, some equivalent conceptions. Thus, Spencer (1965) found that Samburu males are divided into age-sets, composed of peers who move together through the sequential age grades which define their rights, their duties and even their attitudes. The most important distinction is cut between the *Moran,* the age-set of young unmarried warriors, flamboyant predators of other men's herds and wives, and the moderate, responsible "bourgeois" householder. The *Moran* are kept in line by the elders of the most advanced age grades, who cannot match them in physical strength, but who can deploy potent curses against them.

Spencer discovers that these patterns are repeated wherever polygamy gives older

men a monopoly over younger wives. Thus, among the Groote Eylandt of Australia, the young men are secluded from the mainstream of social life, their energy and aggression is directed outwards towards prey and enemy, and if they challenge the political and sexual prerogatives of their seniors, the older men will retaliate against them with sorcery.

Prins (1953) finds the age-sets of the Kikuyu (Kenya) moving through the same cycle of age-graded transitions: the younger men are organized into warrior societies and their form of "production" is to steal from the enemy. In their turn, the elder's age grade deals with the possibly disastrous consequences of any breach of *tabu*. The younger men deal with the threats from enemy power, while the older men deal with threats from supernatural power.

Amerindian Age Grading

Kardiner and Linton (1945) found an equivalent age-grading pattern among the Comanche, horse soldiers of the American Southwest. While young men initiate war parties, two roads are open to the older ex-warrior: he can either become the "Peace Chief," or the "bad old man," who substitutes sorcery for the lost prowess of the warrior. In either case, the older Comanche has the task of controlling external power: he either restrains the warriors, or he matches their innate strength with power "borrowed" from totemic sponsors.

In sum, there appears to be a certain unanimity among the prescriptions for the various age grades maintained by quite disparate cultures: young men are expected, through their *own* energies, to wrest resource and power from physical nature, from enemy or from both; older men are expected, through rituals or through postures of accommodation, to coax power — whether for good or malign purposes

— from the supernaturals. In each society, the age-graded expectations for appropriate behavior operate as rules and norms to which all proper men must conform; but the thematic solidarity across separate sets of rules suggests that age-grading systems are responsive to trans-cultural universals, some *intrinsic* sequences of which are independent of the cultural institutions that they shape.

The Informal Age-Grading of Male Passivity

Asian Studies

The relatively sparse ethnographic evidence concerning the informal and personally expressive behavior of aging men tends to replicate the tentative findings developed by our review of the more formal age-grading structures, and suggests that men tend to age psychologically along an activity-passivity continuum. Thus, Quain (1948) observed that Fijian men bestow increasing time and affection on the women of their household and on their gardens as they age. They become more "domesticated," less interested in the company and affairs of men, and their productive efforts shrink to the household garden.

Murdock (1935) demonstrates that, in simple societies, any domestic task is usually defined as "women's work." Accordingly, this "tend your own garden" attitude of the elder Fijian suggests that, as part of their burgeoning passivity, they take on interests hitherto reserved for women. This "feminization" of older men can go forward even without social approval — Simmons (1945) notes that an aged Arawak warrior who cooked was insultingly referred to as "an old woman."

Amerindian and Meso-American Studies

The androgyny of old men shows up in a different culture area, encompassing Mexico and the American Southwest. Powers (1877) writes: "When a Pomo Indian becomes too infirm to serve any longer as a warrior or hunter, he is henceforth condemned to the life of a menial and scullion. He is compelled to assist the squaws in all their labors. . . . These superannuated warriors are under the woman's control as much as children and are obliged to obey their commands implicitly." Simmons (1945) found that older Hopi men, unable to go to the fields, would knit, card wool, or make sandals at home. Cornshelling was woman's work, but old Hopi men would routinely do it.

Southwards, in Yucatan, Press (1967) observed that older Mayan men turn to Catholicism, typically the woman's religion, giving it priority over the native Mayan religion which is more pragmatic and instrumental, oriented to the cultivation of the productive earth, rather than a pure soul. In the same village, this author (Gutmann, 1966) found corresponding feminine identifications in the Thematic Apperception Test responses given by the older men.

Independently administered psychological tests produce further evidence of an intersexual shift in another sector of Mexico. Thus, Lewis (1951), describing the results of Rorschach tests administered in Tepoztlan, a Mexican village, reports that men are "likely to be more exuberant than women, but also more anxious and insecure. As they grow older they lose their dominant position and the older adults appear disturbed, impulsive and anxious. They seem to be losing the grip on society that the older women are taking over."

Similarly, Butler (1963) was impressed by the use of denial as an ego defense among the older Maya of the Guatemalan Highlands. Again, denial is a primitive defense which protects an essentially passive position: security is preserved by illusory rather than practical means.

Using the Kluckhohn and Strodtbeck values scale in the urban sector of South

America, Webber, Coombs, and Hollingsworth (1974) found that older community leaders in three Colombian cities were more apt than younger leaders to favor harmony with nature over mastery of nature; past time over present time; "being" over "doing"; and collateral (familistic) over individualistic relationships. While these results could reflect secular trends, the experimental design supports a developmental interpretation: the leaders of the most traditional city showed as strong an association between older age and "passive mastery" values as that found among the leaders of the more modern cities. If cohort effects alone accounted for the age variance, then we would expect the age differences to be most marked among the leaders of the rapidly modernizing cities, and weakest in traditionalist Popoyán, where young and old alike have been socialized towards similar values.

Israeli and Western Studies

In sum, older men, whether traditional-urban or rural-preliterate, move towards values, interests and activities which are no longer stereotypically masculine. Confirmatory evidence comes from students of the inner and social life of Israelis, a sophisticated, Westernized people. Thus, Abarbanel (1972) found that younger Israeli farmers were more achievement-oriented than their fathers, a difference which led to friction over the management of the family farm. Again, this conflict could reflect an age rather than a cohort effect: the cautious fathers were once the pioneering generation of Israel.

Furthermore, in Israel — as in Fiji — Talmon-Garber (1962) has noted the upwelling of domestic interests, though among the pioneer *kibbutzniks* this development makes for psychic trouble rather than tranquility. However, Wershow (1969), who restudied Talmon-Garber's original sample, found that in the eight years between

Talmon-Garber's work and his restudy, the aging *kibbutzniks* had presumably completed the transfer of power to the young and were more tolerant of their own placid, domesticated life. Another Israeli, Shanan (1968), carried out an important interethnic, inter-generational study of aging psychology. His Jerusalem sample, consisting of Sephardic and Ashkenazi Jews subdivided as to sex and level of education, was tested with questionnaire and projective instruments. His data analyses indicate that older men, regardless of ethnic background or education, show reduced future orientation, as well as a decline in "active coping."

Studies of aging European populations generate further evidence of the older male's need to give priority to community over agency: Havighurst (1960) finds that German men — like aging *Yucatecos* — spend more time in church than do women of equivalent age, a reversal of the usual sex differences in that country. Studying the themes of German adult life, Thomae (1962) finds that younger white collar workers look to their jobs for change, contact and satisfying activity, whereas men fifty and over chiefly desire job security. Thomae's German findings are confirmed by Bergler (1961). This placid work orientation is also noted by Heron and Chown (1962): English supervisors and foremen prefer older workers, who cooperate with management, over younger employees, who "work for themselves."

Studies in U.S. Subcultures

Turning to inter-ethnic and interracial studies within the United States, Youmans, Grigsby, and King (1969) found that both older blacks and whites in rural Florida share a heightened interest in "familistic" values. The same later life tug towards familism may reactivate earlier ties to the family of orientation: an inter-ethnic study conducted by Clark and Anderson (1967) in

San Francisco showed that strong sibling ties reappear in later life, following the thinning out of membership in the family of procreation.

The older males' drift towards the passive stance has been noted in older middle class, American men by Lipman (1962) who found that elderly retirees take pleasure in domestic activities; by Giambra (1973) who found that daydreams regarding heroic action or personal advancement decline steadily with age; by DeGrazia (1961), who found that gardening becomes the favored activity of the older American male; and by Lovald (1962) who found that older skid row residents are less likely than their younger companions to get in trouble with the police.

Psychotherapy with American patients also leads to formulations consistent with those independently derived from the transcultural study of normal aging. Thus, Wolff (1959) refers to a return of infantile demands in old age, such that the older male patient will seek support from parental surrogates. The upwelling of infantile demands, and the falling off of competitive drives both contribute to later life feelings of inferiority. Senescent neurosis and psychosis are organized around metaphors of denial: the manic escape into confabulated happiness and/or the regression to infantilism, where the end is denied in the fantasy of a new beginning. Other psychiatrists — Meerloo (1955), Zinberg and Kaufman (1963), Berezin (1963) — all stress the aging American's withdrawal from active engagement with the world in favor of more cerebral, introversive and arbitrarily defended positions.

Towards a Species Psychology of Masculine Aging

These first soundings on a species psychology of aging are based on a *potpourri* of studies, undertaken by different investigators, using different sites. This motley collection underlines the need for more orderly and truly comparative research. One such attempt has been made by this author, who has kept investigator, methods, hypotheses and analytic frameworks fairly constant across disparate cultures. The overall aim has been to establish, through application of the comparative method, some basis for a developmental psychology of aging (see Gutmann, 1966, 1967, 1969, 1971 a and b, 1974). The program has involved intensive interviewing and projective testing of younger (aged 35–54) and older (aged 55 and over) men — and some women — of traditional and usually preliterate societies: the lowland and highland Maya of Mexico, the Navajo, and the Druze of Israel, including the Golan Heights. These societies differ from each other in ethnic composition, the content of culture, and their physical environment. They are alike in that they are composed of isolated marginal agriculturalists who hold to their traditional ways. Thus, those cultural values and practices that might influence individual personality tend to remain constant across the generations. Accordingly, if standard psychological differences appear between the younger and older individuals of such static societies, the age variation may be imputed to intrinsic (developmental) rather than extrinsic social variations. . . .

In sum, we see traces of an autonomous current in human development that urges men in their younger and middle years towards competitiveness, agency and independence, and in later life towards some reversal of these priorities: familism takes priority over agency; a receptive stance, particularly in regard to women, tends to replace independence; passive affiliation with supernatural power tends to replace the control and deployment of individual strength.

The Age Grading
of Female Dominance

The available trans-cultural evidence suggests that women may reverse the order of male aging: where adult men start from active mastery and move towards passive mastery, women start from passive mastery — characterized by dependence on and deference to the husband — but move in later life to active mastery. Across cultures and with age they seem to become more domineering, more agentic, and less willing to trade submission for security.

We cannot (as we could with men) study the "masculinization" of the older woman by reviewing the content of formal age-grading systems. Though these exist for women, their content is rarely studied or reported. However, looking across cultures at actual behavior, we do find mid and late life "women's liberation," even where this development is not given formal recognition. Again, we will start with the data from Asian societies, and end by considering our own Western culture.

Asian Studies

Yap (1962) reports that when a woman heads the Chinese equivalent of a retirement home, she is addressed as a male patriarch; and when the aging husband retires from the management of the family, he concedes control to his wife and oldest son. Apparently, older Chinese women are less likely than Chinese men to move to a contemplative old age. Similarly, Okada (1962) finds that the old widow has great power in the traditional Japanese family: as in China, she runs the family jointly with the oldest son.

This oriental matriarchy may have psychological coordinates. Tachibana (1962) finds that Japanese men are more extroversive than women until age 60 when a marked decline in these terms puts their scores below

the female mean, which rises steadily across age groups. The extroversion of the older Japanese woman may be the result of, or the precondition for matriarchy: in either case it implies a greater interest in the nature and management of external affairs. This Japanese arrangement is replicated in Burma: Rustom (1961) finds that the Burmese widow becomes the head of the household and is responsible for family affairs as long as she remains interested.

DeBeauvoir (1972) cites further evidence of this Oriental pattern: sex differences disappear with age. The older Balinese woman can occupy hitherto exclusively patriarchal slots, and govern entire households. Among the neighboring Samoans, "a group of older women may say things that no one else would dare to say."

From the Hindu sector, Rowe (1961) reports that older village women may attain the status of *malikin* and control family affairs. Despite *de jure* patriarchy, Harlan (1964) discovers that the older man's status in the Indian family is finally upheld by his wife, who ensures that his edicts are obeyed.

Similar developments occur in Highland, Muslim India. Pehrson reports (personal communication) that the Baluchi, a nomadic group of the Northwest frontier, are strongly patriarchal. Yet in later life the chief — while retaining nominal control — gives over the management of the tribe's daily affairs to his wife and older son, and spends his time in discourse with the priests.

The Older African Woman

The older woman's domestic rule, particularly in league with her oldest son, is not restricted to Asia. Spencer (1965) reports that older Samburu women acquire status through alliance with their *Moran* sons against the fathers. Indeed, throughout Africa older women are bonded to younger men, either as allies or as antagonists. Nadel

(1952) tells us that the Nupe recognize two kinds of supernatural power. Bad power is exercised by domineering older women — who also engage in trade. Men use good power to combat witchcraft; but the older women use deadly power to attack younger men. This variation suggests that older women may enact their "rebirth" as a man either through alliances with virile young males and/or direct competition with them. This rebirth may be explicitly recognized: Goody (1962) finds that only post-menopausal women, who have "become men" are allowed to wash corpses. Social authority, he adds, is generally vested in men, or in those elderly Lodagaa women who are most like men.

The Older Meso-American and Amerindian Woman

In the Americas, the trend holds: Kardiner and Linton (1945) report that among the warrior tribes of the Southwest, matrons were called "manly hearted women." Levy (1967) notes an Amerindian pattern of giving post-menopausal women greater sexual freedom and the right to participate in ritual and healing practices. Mexican Americans also concede social power to older women, despite the official *machismo* of Chicano culture. Thus, Leonard (1967) finds that the *Chicana* is very important in the home; and this importance increases as she ages.

The Older Woman in Western European Society

Evidence for the "matriarchy of later life" comes from societies closer in values and organization to our own. Cesa-Bianchi (1962) reports that female residents of Italian old age homes do more institutional work than older male residents, that they have more intellectual efficiency and autonomy, and that they are more ex-

trapunitive, with a greater tendency to externalize blame for subjective trouble.

Studies of U. S. suicide rates (DeGrazia, 1961) confirm that men are more likely than women to commit suicide at any age, and that the male lead increases steadily over successive age groups. Psychoanalytic doctrine holds that suicide represents a deployment of murderous aggression against the self, and away from its original target in the outer world. If so, then older U. S. men — like the Japanese men studied by Tachibana and the Italians studied by Cesa-Bianchi — are more apt to manage their rage introversively, even to the point of self-murder, while older U. S. women take the extroversive position, and turn their aggression against others.

The superior vigor of older women is captured in Townsend's (1957) description of English old people on an outing: "The women clearly had more bounce." Objective findings suggest that English "bounce" and longevity go hand in hand. Kleemeier (1960) states that elderly English women are less likely to die in mental hospitals than their male age peers.

The Aging Woman in American Ethnic Subcultures

Turning to comparative U. S. studies, Clark and Anderson (1967) find that, across San Francisco ethnic groups, old women are more likely than old men to describe themselves in positive terms and show a higher degree of social participation. Contrasting black and white elderly, Rubenstein (1971) finds that single women score higher on a measure of morale than do solitary men. Such findings suggest a greater autonomy, a greater ability to live off one's own psychic resources among older women, regardless of race.

Studies of American middle class women suggest that the sex-role reversals noted in other societies appear in this country as well:

thus, Kuhlen (1964) finds less evidence of need affiliation among older American women than in their male age-peers; Kerckoff (1966) notes a later life "reversal," in that older husbands show a greater sensitivity to human relationships than their wives, who are interested in practical affairs; and Lowenthal, Thurnher and Chiriboga (1975) observe that middle-aged women become more dominant in the family, even as the husbands become more self-indulgent, move into the filial niche that has been vacated by their grown children, and look to interpersonal rather than inner resources for remedy. Consistent with these shifts towards the normal unisex of later life, Cameron (1967) and Kelly (1955) find increasing "masculinity" in middle-aged women. And at the more subjective level, Brenneis (1975) finds in the dreams of older women a striking increase in robust, active representations of the dreamer.

Finally, Kaufman (1940), a psychoanalyst, notes the emergence of the "reverse Oedipus" in older women, where the son is related to as though he were a father, and the daughter related to as though she were the mother. This syndrome could be the clinical echo of the overt mother-son alliance against the father-husband that has been noted in the trans-cultural materials.

Age-Sex Roles and the Parental Imperative

This author (Gutmann, 1975) has proposed a tentative schema, based on a concept of parenthood, to explain shifts in male and female sex roles that shape the trans-cultural data. The sharp sex role distinctions of early parenthood are presumably based on the vital needs of the young for physical and emotional security. These requirements are a formidable stimulus to younger parents, causing each sex to surrender to the other the qualities that would interfere with the provision of their special mode of security. Male providers of physical security give up the dependency needs that would interfere with their courage and endurance; these they live out through identification with their wives and children. By the same token, women, the providers of emotional security, give up the aggression that could alienate their male providers or that could damage a vulnerable and needful child. Each sex lives out, through the other, those aspects of their nature that could interfere with adequate performance in their parental role, and that could therefore be lethal to their children.

But as children take over the responsibility of their own security, the chronic sense of parental emergency phases out, and both sexes can afford to live out the potentials that they once had to relinquish in the service of their parental task. Men recapture the "femininity" that was previously repressed in the service of productive instrumentality; and women generally become more domineering and independent. In effect, "masculine" and "feminine" qualities are distributed not only by sex but by life period. Men are not forever "masculine"; rather, they can be defined as the sex that shows "masculine" traits before the so-called "feminine" pattern. The reverse is true for women.

Preliterate Gerontocracy: The Old Man as Hero

However, despite the older man's inner migration away from aggressive forms of authority, in preliterate societies his official powers increase. Simmon's (1945) review of 71 distinct tribes shows that chieftainship by old men is nearly universal at this level of social development.

But, while "some degree of prestige for the aged seems to be practically universal in all known societies," Simmons has also identified ecological and social factors associated with wide variations in gerontocracy. Thus, extremes of climate appear to

reduce gerontocracy, as does imperma-
nency of residence. Conversely, male gerontocracy increases as society becomes more
stable and more complex. In organized folk
settings, the usefulness and prestige of the
aged depends on their wisdom, their experience, their acquired property rights,
and their ritual powers.

Implicitly, Simmons accuses the preliterate aged of sharp practice: they declare the
best foods off limits to the young; they hold
onto their property; they marry off their
children to their own advantage; and in
many societies they have acquired a
monopoly over the youngest, most attractive women. . . .

In effect, the anthropologist's explanation
of primitive gerontocracy is very much a
young man's explanation: old men are powerful because they control more of the symbolic and material goods that the young man
is least likely to have and is most likely to
want. To the anthropologist, the old man is
only a young man who has had time to
become successful in terms of those achievement criteria that he shares with his sons and
with the culture in general. But our foregoing review shows that old men do not invariably share younger men's definitions of
success, problem or remedy. And while they
value prestige, they may conceive of it and
move towards it in ways that would not occur to the young.

The Old Man as "Power Broker"

Possibly then, there is not only an age shift in
the sheer amount of status, but also some orderly change in the bases for status ascrip-
tion, such that older tribesmen acquire
power via routes unavailable even to rich
young men. To clarify this point, we must
digress to consider preliterate conceptions of
power. In the folk mind, the *mana* which sustains the pragmatic world has its ultimate origin in supernatural, extra-communal
sources — in the spirits of ancestral dead, in

the mythic past, in totemic animals, in enemy, and in the gods. The particular power
sources vary culturally, but wherever this
world view holds, anointed figures are required to live on the interface between the
mundane and supernatural worlds, so as to
"attract" the benevolent aspect of supernatural power, and make it available to the
community and its ecosystem. The human
metaphors of *mana* are those residents of the
pragmatic community who "extend" beyond it, and represent the various extraordinary domains within it. Here, quite apart
from his wealth, is the crux of the aged traditionalist's social power. Unlike the young,
who are bonded through action to the immediate world, the aged merge and blend
with the domains of *mana*.

In some cultures the aged blend with the
revered, deified figures of the ancestors; and
they were born in the semi-mythic past,
another storehouse of power. Thus, Durkheim noted that old people are the only
witnesses to the acts of the holy ancestors —
therefore, they are unique intermediaries
between the present and the past. Shelton
(1965) finds that the revered tribal elders of
the Nigerian Ibo are closest to the
spiritualized forefathers, who are closest to
the gods. Here again, the aged merge with
the mythic time when the people emerged
from the sacred into the banal world; thus,
they carry the power that moved events in
those special times.

Senescent *mana* is not confined to the older
man's body, but dominates a *tabu* zone
around him. Cowgill (1968) reports that
younger Thai crouch before aged men in
order to avoid the *tabu* power which surrounds the elder's head. This elder power is
strong enough to harm even its possessor.
According to Hurlbert, (1962) the Hare Indians of northwest Canada believe that a
medicine man's power will increase with age
to the point where it blinds him.

But the final paradox of the gerontocrat's
power is that it stems as much from weakness

as from the particular wisdom or skills that he may have acquired over time. Precisely *because* of their frailty, the aged are moving into the country of the dead; they take on some of the fearsome aura of the corpse that they will soon become. Furthermore, in old age, a strong spirit is revealed in its own terms, no longer masked by the vitality of a young body. Thus, besides intersecting the mythic past, the aged overlap the spirit world which they will soon enter; and as they blend with that world they acquire its essential physiognomy and powers. Accordingly, Mead (1967) found the Balinese life-cycle to be circular: both the child and the grandsire are at the "highest point" of life because each is closest to the other world.

By the same token, older men gain status *because* of the very passivity that becomes prominent in their psychic life. Róheim (1930) cites much data from preliterate societies which shows that the power broker typically exhibits abasive and even masochistic behavior. Across cultures, the gods mainly give power to those men who approach them submissively, even in the guise of women. Thus, in the religious community it is the older men, cleansed of sex and aggression, humble in bearing (and not the Promethean young men), who can draw good influences from the gods without offending them. In the folk mind, the power bringer must be a metaphor of the power that he would attract. Accordingly, the "maternal" old man becomes a vessel for nutritive "good power," while the angry old woman becomes a vessel for bad supernatural power, and is suspected of witchcraft. The folk mind transforms the older traditionalist's passivity — in urban cultures the badge of his psychic weakness — into the very pivot of his social strength.

Furthermore, just as they utilize his passivity, traditional societies can also articulate into executive capacities the older man's quotient of magical mastery, an ego stage founded on the (developmentally) primitive belief that the universe and its powers are coerced by symbolic, metaphoric forms of control. In a secular society, magical mastery mainly takes the form of aberrant and psychotic acts; but in the religious and traditional society, magical mastery as a personal style is readily assimilated to a conventionalized symbol and ritual system, through which important events are presumably regulated.

The Integration of Nature and Social Nurture in Later Life

A trans-cultural overview demonstrates that no single perspective can account for the forms and variations of geriatric prestige and security in the preliterate society. Environmental features play some part, as does the advantage that accrues to the aged in static societies; but the consequences of these factors for the older person's power and well-being are clearly mediated by an independent constraint — the nature and level of affectional bonds, of object relations, in a particular society. Thus, old men can control property and rituals even in societies where envy is a dominant *motif,* but they will be in constant danger — the rich old shaman will be accused of being a sorcerer as well as a healer, and in times of plague or famine his life will be at risk. He will be feared and respected for his powers, but also hated for the malice that presumably went into their acquisition.

Finally, to account for phenotypic variations in aging psychology we must consider the *interactions* among important variables, for example, the developmental potentials of later life and the cultural *value* setting in which they emerge. Thus, Clark (1967) reminds us that aging should be studied in those contexts where the values that the aged are *naturally* prone to adopt are already the core values of the society. Thus, where social norms and values interface with the affiliative and "magical" potentials released by the older man's withdrawal from the instrumental-productive life, then new personal configurations are possible, registered in renewed ego identity, and in forms of social prestige unavailable to the young. Conversely, where cultures devalue the "passive" male potentials, these are more likely to emerge as the basis of mid-life crisis or psychosomatic illness. By the same token, the revived, uncloseted aggression of the older woman can lead either to her stigmatization as the witch, or to her elevation as the *Malikin,* again depending on the culture's attitude towards female aggression.

The importance of this coordination between developmental "givens" and the value consensus which "receives" them is highlighted by the work of Hsu (1951), who found that the aged were *particularly* revered in traditional China, a society based on mutual cooperation and *dependence* among family members. Wolff (1959) supports him with clinical evidence: Chinese patients with chronic brain syndrome (CBS) rarely show the psychotic reactions that often accompany CBS in our society.

Another fortunate nature-nurture matching is found by Shelton (1965) among the Nsukka Ibo, an African society which emphasizes both achievement and interpersonal skills. In effect, the Ibo male has two lives: first as an instrumental leader, later as a socio-emotional leader — and Ibo culture encourages each mode in its proper, developmentally ordained season. (Arth (1968) contradicts Shelton. The Ibo, he claims, are not dual valued, but unilaterally favor achievement. Accordingly, the young high achievers are ambivalent towards the elders, whose achievement days are over.)

Another optimal personal-social matching is revealed in Leonard's (1967) observations of the Mexican-American elderly, whose subculture elevates the principles of passive mastery to an ethic, and there is no celebration of work *per se.* Accordingly, old age is honored as a time to rest and to dole out accumulated wisdom. Thus, older *Chicanos* — unlike their Anglo age peers — feel no compunction about receiving help from their children.

This "interactionist" perspective may shed new light on the long standing debate in the gerontological literature on the religious predilections of the aged. The trans-cultural reviews suggest that the aged are not innately "religious" but that they develop potentials which are best sponsored — translated into executive capacities — in a religious atmosphere. Thus, Abarbanel (1972) analyzed the relationship between the prestige of old persons and their control over cultural resources in 62 cultures. His preliminary findings are that older people replace their decreased involvement in economic production with increased involvement in the form of "moral production" represented by religion. Again, the sources of phenotypic behavior are not finally founded either in nature or nurture, but in some dynamic, constantly shifting interplay between them.

Rural and Urban Aging

Rural-urban transformations, within "advanced" societies, have consequences similar to those observed when traditional societies modernize. Reviewing the effects of modernization *within* Western society, Burgess (1960) states that the "roleless role" of the aged reflects shifts from home to family production; from rural to urban residence; from the extended to the conjugal family; from small to large organizational structures; and the marked increase in leisure time.

Burgess' generalizations are borne out by Aldrich (1974) who found that rural-urban differences were more powerful than cultural differences in determining family attitudes in Portugal and Brazil. While rural subjects maintained "traditional, familistic and intergenerational deferential patterns," respect for elders decreased with education and in the urban milieux of both societies.

At the heart of Western Europe, Kooy (1962) observes the same effect. The urban-proximal regions of Holland provide less status to the aged than do the urban-remote enclaves, where the extended family predominates. Similarly, Baumert (1962) finds more multigenerational, coresidential families in farming areas of Germany, and less exclusion of rural elders. Likewise, Havighurst (1960) concludes that older rural people of Western Europe have less need for institutionalized ego supports since family and work already provide these.

The U.S. findings replicate those from Western Europe. Jackson (1970) reports that black aged in the rural south will turn first to their families, even in time of illness. This pattern is reversed in the southern city where the older black is more likely to turn to the hospital or to the church for remedy.

Perhaps, in keeping with their "familism," and out of a wish to sponsor their own "reengagement," older men — even those reared in the city — are apt to migrate away from urban settings and back to the countryside, the ecology of the extended family. This author has observed a "return to the blanket" among older men of the Amerindian, Mexican Indian and Druze groups. By the same token, Chevry (1962) notes a tendency among Frenchmen aged 65 and over to migrate to rural areas. It is mainly the younger men who vacate the French countryside for the cities.

The urban milieu provides such skimpy emotional support that Rosow (1962) warns against scattering the aged throughout urban neighborhoods, where psyche-groups are not composed of cross-generational kin, but of age-peers. Paradoxically, in industrialized neighborhoods with a "normal" age-distribution, the aged tend — because of their infirmity and fear — to be walled off from each other and cannot form their own peer communities. Thus, contrary to much conventional wisdom, Rosow favors pooling

older people in retirement communities which are more apt to provide the "raw materials" of a significant group life.

The Matriarchy of the Cities

Urbanization and industrialization may have different effects with respect to disengagement in each sex. Generally, we find that the patriarchal organization of the folk-traditional or rural society is very vulnerable to even glancing contact with modern ways. But the unofficial matriarchy that has been noted even in some folk societies may survive the transition to modern ways. Generally, cities are settled by young refugees liberated from the stifling control exercised in the small community by old men, religious leaders and omnipresent extended family. The city represents among other things the outcome of a revolution against male gerontocracy. Not surprisingly then, as the patriarch declines in the city, hitherto disadvantaged groups, including women, may find their freedom there.

This matriarchy of the cities becomes more apparent as we compare various socio-emotional arrangements along the rural-urban continua of the West. Thus, Sheldon (1960) discovers that the increase in life expectancy brought about by modernization is most impressive in the case of women. Also, Kooy (1962) discovers that, *save in rural areas,* older Dutch women outnumber older Dutch men. Likewise Chevry (1962) reports that the proportion of aged men, *particularly widowers,* increases in step with the agricultural character of the French municipality.

Rural life may be more lethal for women and less lethal for men because of the hard physical labor and continuous child-bearing that are borne by the peasant wife. But Youmans' (1967) work suggests that sex differences in mortality have more to do with the unequal distribution of love, rather than labor, along rural-urban continua. Reviewing patterns of association in the Western world, he concludes that men are likely to be

110 David Gutmann

the recipients of emotional supplies in rural areas, and that this pattern is reversed in the cities. Jackson's (1971) comparisons of rural and urban American blacks also suggest a correlation between later life survival and familial bonds. Again, rural black men outlive women; and the urban shift towards superior female longevity is accompanied by a corresponding shift in the patterning of affectional ties. In the city, these are strongest between mothers and daughters; and this close bond pays off in the form of greater direct assistance to the aging black mother at all social class levels.

Other theorists, commenting on aging in Western nations, make equivalent points. Burgess (1960) notes that the matrilocal extended family can function in stable working class neighborhoods as the urban equivalent of the patriarchal extended family of the countryside. The urban family is based on strong bonds between grandmothers, mothers and daughters. In the city, Burgess says, "men have friends; women have relatives." . . .

The decline of patriarchy has usually been linked to the older male's loss of control over urban financial, cognitive and ritual resources. The city is a young man's terrain, and old men (except tycoons and successful politicians) presumably lose prestige because they lose access to urban power. However, we now find that urban matriarchy is founded on women's superior capacity for intimacy, rather than acquisition. Again, the students of the social life — perhaps out of masculine bias — seem to have downplayed intimacy in favor of power as a determinant of the reduced status, morale and viability of urban men.

Passive Mastery in Urban Males

While cutting older men off from the emotional resources of the community, urban living may also release other, contrasurvival masculine tendencies. Scattered findings suggest that the urban decline in patriarchy may be linked to the more passive-dependent bent of the city man of any age, in contrast to his country cousin. Thus, Kreps (1968) reports that after age 65, 70 percent of male residents of agricultural countries are still employed as against only 38 percent for men of industrialized countries. Since these figures may reflect the urban retirement norm, a more meaningful comparison deals with the uses of leisure. Thus, Youmans (1967) finds that the tendency to "sit and think" increases with age, in Kentucky, more markedly for urban than for rural men.

Religious leanings are a possible expression of dependent yearnings; and Jackson (1970) found that urban blacks are more likely than their rural age peers to turn to the church for remedy in later life. The passive propensities of urban men also appear at the more "appetitive" level of personality. This author (Gutmann, 1971b) found that oral-incorporative tendencies increased in his Navajo and Druze male samples as a function of age, but also as a function of the closeness to cities. Empirical evidence from both groups confirms the orality score as a register of passive-dependency; and this trait increases dramatically in the urban-proximal sectors of two very different cultures.

Aging and the Mind of the City

In order to understand the concomitant variation between social life and individual psychology, researchers have neglected rural-urban or folk-urban comparisons in favor of intercultural comparisons. However, the admittedly minimal evidence supports this generalization: urbanization within cultures seems to replicate the psychological effects of aging across cultures. On the one hand, it appears to sponsor masculine passivity and early mortality; on the other hand, it increases the authority and freedom of older women and the young. Cities may be founded by bold young emigrés, masculine rebels against patriarchy; but their urban descendants, particularly in later life, appear less self-reliant than their rural counterparts.

Like the folk society, the city is more than a characteristic arrangement of social and economic institutions. It is also the habitat for mental and affective dispositions strikingly different from those found in the small, tradition-directed community. No writers have systematically considered the relationship between aging and urban forms of mentation. . . .

The emergence of the modern, urban individual seems to have crucial consequences for the aged. The city-sponsored boundaries that define the self not only separate individuals but also sexes, races, ethnic groups, and generations. The "generation gap" that is strikingly absent in the village and folk society bisects the heart of the nuclear and modified-extended family in the city. These divisions are sharpened by narcissism. In the city, the sense of familiarity does not proceed along the lines of natural, transgenerational groupings — clan, family, or neighborhood—but is organized along egocentric principles. Urban individuals mainly confer the sense of community, of "we-ness," on those who share with them the most concrete and visible tokens of sex, age, skin color or sexual preference. The politics of the city become the politics of narcissism: Youth Liberation, Women's Liberation, Black Liberation, or Gay Liberation. . . .

Predictably then, our urban alienation has reached the point where — judging from the increase in child abuse — even babies are often at risk from their own parents. Thus, it is not surprising that the aged should also be major casualties of urbanization. The aged are always in danger of becoming the *other,* of being regarded — like strangers everywhere — with a mixture of awe and revulsion. In the preliterate mind, which conceives the human community englobed in sacred power, the awe of the aged predominates. But in urban societies, where power is secularized, where heroes or rarefied spirits are not required to man some sacred perimeter of the community, revulsion takes precedence over awe. The narcissistic *ethos* of the city, which asserts that "nothing strange is human," further crystallizes the tendency to put the aged in this potentially lethal position of the "other." Stripped of the magical powers that ratify their strangeness, or — particularly in the case of men — of the affectional bonds that minimize it, the urban aged tend to be dehumanized, and are increasingly ignored, (or worse, sentimentalized) and warehoused in retirement homes, nursing homes or back wards. "Disengagement" may be the most recent term that we have invested to excuse and disguise this process.

References

Abarbanel, J. 1972. Aging, family phase, and intergenerational relations in an Israeli farming cooperative. Paper presented at the December, 1972 meetings of the American Gerontological Society, San Juan, Puerto Rico.

Aldrich, D. 1974. Familism and the prestige of the aged in two societies. Paper presented at the October, 1974 meetings of the American Gerontological Society, Portland, Oregon.

Arth, M. 1968. Ideals and behavior. A comment on Ibo respect patterns. *Gerontologist,* 8, 242–244.

Baumert, G. 1962. Changes in the family and the position of older person in Germany. *In,* C. Tibbetts and W. Donahue (eds.), *Social and Psychological Aspects of Aging: Aging Around the World,* pp. 415–425. New York: Columbia University Press.

Berezin, M. 1963. Some intra-psychic aspects of aging. *In,* N. Zinberg (ed.), *Normal Psychology of the Aging Process,* pp. 93–117. New York: International Universities Press.

Bergler, R. 1961. Beiträge Zur Psychologie Des Erwachsenen Alters. *Bibliotheca Vita Humana.* Basel: Karger.

Brenneis, C. B. 1975. Developmental aspects of aging in women. *Arch. Gen. Psychiat.,* 32, 429–435.

Burgess, E. 1960. Aging in western culture. *In,* E. Burgess (ed.), *Aging in Western Societies,* pp. 3–28. Chicago: University of Chicago Press.

Butler, R. 1963. Some observations on culture and personality in aging. *Social Work,* 8, 79–84.

Cameron, P. 1967. Introversion and egocentricity among the aged. *J. Gerontol.,* 22, 465–468.

Cesa-Bianchi, M. 1962. A further contribution to the study of adjustment in old age. *In,* C. Tibbetts and W. Donahue (eds.), *Social and Psychological Aspects of Aging: Aging Around the World,* pp. 623–627. New York: Columbia University Press.

Chevry, G. 1962. One aspect of the problem of older persons: housing conditions. *In,* C. Tibbetts and W. Donahue (eds.), *Social and Psychological Aspects of Aging: Aging Around the World,* pp. 98–110. New York: Columbia University Press.

Clark, M. 1967. The anthropology of aging: a new area for studies of culture and personality. *Gerontologist,* 7, 55–64.

Clark, M., and Anderson, B. 1967. *Culture and Aging: An Anthropological Study of Older Americans.* Springfield, Illinois: Charles C. Thomas.

Cowgill, D. 1968. The social life of the aging in Thailand. *Gerontologist,* 8, 159–163.

Cowgill, D. 1971. A theoretical framework for consideration of data on aging. Paper delivered at meetings for the Society for Applied Anthropology, Miami, Florida, April, 1971.

DeBeauvoir, S. 1972. *The Coming of Age.* New York: J. P. Putnam's Sons.

DeGrazia, S. 1961. The uses of time. *In,* R. Kleemeier (ed.), *Aging and Leisure,* pp. 113–154. New York: Oxford University Press.

Giambra, L. 1973. Daydreaming in males from seventeen to seventy-seven: a preliminary report. *Proceedings of the 81st Annual Convention of the American Psychological Association, Montreal, Canada,* 8, 769–770.

Goody, J. 1962. *Death, Property and the Ancestors.* Stanford: Stanford University Press.

Gutmann, D. 1966. Mayan aging: a comparative TAT study. *Psychiatry,* 29, 246–259.

Gutmann, D. 1967. On cross-cultural studies as a naturalistic approach in psychology. *Hum. Develop.,* 10, 187–198.

Gutmann, D. 1969. The country of old men: cross-cultural studies in the psychology of later life. *In, Occasional Papers in Gerontology, No. 5.* Ann Arbor: Institute of Gerontology, University of Michigan-Wayne State University.

Gutmann, D. 1971a. Navajo dependency and illness. *In,* E. Palmore (ed.), *Prediction of Life Span.* Lexington: Heath.

Gutmann, D. 1971b. The hunger of old men. *TransAction,* 9, 55–66.

Gutmann, D. 1974. Alternatives to disengagement: aging among the highland Druze. *In,* R. LeVine (ed.), *Culture and Personality: Contemporary Readings,* pp. 232–245. Chicago: Aldine.

Gutmann, D. 1975. Parenthood: key to the comparative psychology of the life cycle? *In,* N. Datan and L. Ginsberg (eds.), *Life Span Developmental Psychology,* pp. 167–184. New York: Academic Press.

Harlan, W. 1964. Social status of the aged in three Indian villages. *Vita Humana,* 7, 239–252.

Havighurst, R. 1960. Life beyond family and work. *In,* E. Burgess (ed.), *Aging in Western Societies,* pp. 299–353. Chicago: University of Chicago Press.

Heron, A., and Chown, S. 1962. Semi-skilled and over forty. *In,* C. Tibbitts and W. Donahue (eds.), *Social and Psychological Aspects of Aging: Aging Around the World,* pp. 195–207. New York: Columbia University Press.

Hsu, F. 1951. *The Challenge of the American Dream: The Chinese in the U. S.* Belmont: Wadsworth.

Hurlbert, J. 1962. *Age as a Factor in the Social Organization of the Hare Indians of Fort Good Hope, Northwest Territories.* Ottawa, Ontario, Canada: Northern Co-ordination and Research Centre, Department of Northern Affairs and National Resources.

Jackson, J. 1970. Aged Negroes: their cultural departures from statistical stereotypes and rural-urban differences. *Gerontologist,* 10, 140–145.

Jackson, J. 1971. Sex and social class variations in black aged parent-adult child relationships. *Aging and Human Development,* 2, 96–107.

Kardiner, A., and Linton, R. 1945. *The Psychological Frontiers of Society.* New York: Columbia University Press.

Kaufman, M. 1940. Old age and aging: the psychoanalytic point of view. *Am. J. Orthopsychiat.,* 10, 73–79.

Kelly, E. L. 1955. Consistency of the adult personality. *American Psychologist,* 10, 659–681.

Kerckoff, A. 1966. Family patterns and morale. *In,* I. Simpson and J. McKinney (eds.), *Social Aspects of Aging,* pp. 173–192. Durham: Duke University Press.

Kleemeier, R. 1960. The mental health of the aging. *In,* E. Burgess (ed.), *Aging in Western Societies,* pp. 203–270. Chicago: University of Chicago Press.

Kooy, G. 1962. The aged in the rural Netherlands. *In,* C. Tibbitts and W. Donahue (eds.), *Social and Psychological Aspects of Aging: Aging Around the World,* pp. 501–509. New York: Columbia University Press.

Kreps, J. 1968. Comparative studies of work and retirement. *In,* E. Shanas and J. Madge (eds.), *Methodological Problems in Cross National Studies in Aging,* pp. 75–99. Basel: Karger.

Kuhlen, R. 1964. Developmental changes in motivation during the adult years. *In,* J. Birren (ed.), *Relations of Development to Aging,* pp. 209–246. Springfield, Illinois: Charles C. Thomas.

Leonard, O. 1967. The older Spanish-speaking people of the Southwest. *In,* E. Youmans (ed.), *The Older Rural Americans,* pp. 239–261. Lexington: University of Kentucky Press.

Levy, J. 1967. The older American Indian. *In,* E. Youmans (ed.), *The Older Rural Americans,* pp. 231–238. Lexington: University of Kentucky Press.

Lewis, O. 1951. *Life in a Mexican Village: Tepoztlan Restudied.* Urbana: University of Illinois Press.

Lipman, J. 1962. Role concepts of couples in retirement. *In,* C. Tibbitts and W. Donahue (eds.), *Social and Psychological Aspects of Aging: Aging Around the World,* pp. 475–485. New York: Columbia University Press.

Lovald, K. 1962. The social life of the aged on skid row. *In,* C. Tibbitts and W. Donahue (eds.), *Social and Psychological Aspects of Aging: Aging Around the World,* pp. 510–517. New York: Columbia University Press.

Lowenthal, M., Thurnher, M., and Chiriboga, D. 1975. *Four Stages of Life.* San Francisco: Jossey-Bass.

Mead, M. 1967. Ethnological aspects of aging. *Psychosomatics,* 8 (supp.), 33–37.

Meerloo, J. 1955. Psychotherapy with older people. *Geriatrics,* 10, 583–590.

Murdock, G. 1935. Comparative data on the division of labor by sex. *Soc. Forces,* 15, 551–553.

Nadel, S. 1952. Witchcraft in four African societies: an essay in comparison. *Am. Anthropologist,* 54, 18–29.

Neugarten, B., and Bengtson, V. 1968. Cross-national studies of adulthood and aging. *In,* E. Shanas and J. Madge (eds.), *Methodological Problems in Cross-National Studies of Aging,* pp. 18–36. Basel: Karger.

Powers, S. 1877. Tribes of California. *In, Contributions to North American Ethnology, Vol. III.* Washington, D.C.: Department of the Interior.

Press, I. 1967. Maya aging: cross-cultural projective techniques and the dilemma of interpretation. *Psychiatry,* 30, 197–202.

Prins, A. 1953. *East African Age-Class Systems.* Groningen: Walters.

Quain, B. 1948. *Fijian Village.* Chicago: University of Chicago Press.

Róheim, G. 1930. *Animism, Magic and the Divine King.* London: Kegan-Paul.

Rosow, I. 1962. Retirement housing and social integration. *In,* C. Tibbitts and W. Donahue (eds.), *Social and Psychological Aspects of Aging: Aging Around the World,* pp. 327–340. New York: Columbia University Press.

Rowe, W. 1961. The middle and later years in Indian society. *In,* R. Kleemeier (ed.), *Aging and Leisure,* pp. 104–112. New York: Oxford University Press.

Rubenstein, D. 1971. An examination of social participation found among a national sample of black and white elderly. *Aging and Human Development*, 2, 172–188.

Rustom, C. 1961. The aging Burman. *In,* R. Kleemeier (ed.), *Aging and Leisure*, pp. 100–103. New York: Oxford University Press.

Shanan, J. 1968. *Psychological Changes During the Middle Years-Vol. I.* (In Hebrew). Jerusalem: Gons and Grafica.

Sheldon, H. 1960. The changing demographic profile. *In,* C. Tibbitts (ed.), *Handbook of Social Gerontology*, pp. 27–61. Chicago: University of Chicago Press.

Shelton, A. 1965. Ibo aging and eldership: notes for gerontologists and others. *Gerontologist*, 5, 20–23.

Simmons, L. 1945. *The Role of the Aged in Primitive Society*. New Haven: Yale University Press.

Spencer, P. 1965. *The Samburu: a Study of Gerontocracy in a Nomadic Tribe*. Berkeley: University of California.

Steed, G. 1957. Notes on an approach to personality formation in a Hindu village in Gujarat. *In,* M. Marriott (ed.), *Village India*, pp. 102–144. Chicago: University of Chicago Press.

Tachibana, K. 1962. A study of introversion-extraversion in the aged. *In,* C. Tibbitts and W. Donahue (eds.), *Social and Psychological Aspects of Aging: Aging Around the World*, pp. 655–656. New York: Columbia University Press.

Talmon-Garber, Y. 1962. Aging in collective settlements in Israel. *In,* C. Tibbitts and W. Donahue (eds.), *Social and Psychological Aspects of Aging: Aging Around the World*, pp. 426–441. New York: Columbia University Press.

Thomae, H. 1962. Thematic analysis of aging. *In,* C. Tibbitts and W. Donahue (eds.), *Social and Psychological Aspects of Aging: Aging Around the World*, pp. 657–663. New York: Columbia University Press.

Townsend, P. 1957. *The Family Life of Old People*. Glencoe: The Free Press.

Webber, I, Coombs, D, and Hollingsworth, J. 1974. Variations in value orientations by age in a developing society. *J. Gerontol.*, 29, 676–683.

Wershow, H. 1969. Aging in the Israeli Kibbutz. *Gerontologist*, 9, 300–304.

Wolff, K. 1959. *The Biological, Sociological and Psychological Aspects of Aging*. Springfield, Illinois: Charles C. Thomas.

Yap, P. 1962. Aging in under-developed Asian countries. *In,* C. Tibbitts and W. Donahue (eds.), *Social and Psychological Aspects of Aging: Aging Around the World*, pp. 442–453. New York: Columbia University Press.

Youmans, E. 1967. Disengagement among older rural and urban men. *In,* E. Youmans (ed.), *The Older Rural Americans*, pp. 97–116. Lexington: University of Kentucky Press.

Youmans, E., Grigsby, S., and King, M. 1969. Social change, generation, and race. *Rural Sociology*, 34, 305–312.

Zinberg, N., and Kaufman, I. 1963. Cultural and personality factors associated with aging: an introduction. *In, Normal Psychology of the Aging Process*, pp. 17–71. New York: International Universities Press.

Stability of Adult Personality Traits: Fact or Fable?

K. WARNER SCHAIE AND IRIS A. PARHAM

Theoretical positions for and against a stability model for adult personality traits are examined. Results of a sequential study of 19 personality factors over a 7-year period and with participants ranging in age from 22 to 84 years suggest that stability within generations appears to be the rule, albeit combined with many differences between successive population cohorts and subject to transient secular trends. A typology of 13 possible models is offered to account for the different developmental trends observed for the various personality factors.

One of the more curious developments in the history of the psychology of aging has been that most investigators have generally assumed the validity of an age decrement model for learning, the intellectual functions, and psychomotor behaviors, but have contrariwise assumed that personality traits and attitudes remain stable over the adult life course. Over the past two decades the first author and his associates have worked to demolish the general consensus on a decrement model for the intellectual processes (cf. Baltes & Schaie, 1974; Schaie, 1973, 1974; Schaie & Gribbin, 1975). In the past, we were able to demonstrate that much of the apparent age decrement was an artifact of data collected from cross-sectional studies comparing cohorts with differing base levels of ability.

It occurs to us now that the assumed stability of adult personality traits (e.g., Reichard, Livson, & Peterson, 1962) might be equally artifactual, involving fortuitous combinations of generational differences in the expression of personality traits and attitudes, with secular trends and ontogenetic trends operating in opposing directions. Further, just as it has been profitable to hypothesize different age trends for crystallized and fluid intelligence abilities, there may well be personality and attitudinal constructs that are overdetermined by species-specific ontogenetic transformation, which should show true age patterns, as opposed to culturally determined traits, which might be subject to secular change but are not affected by ontogenetic events as such. It is the purpose of this paper to summarize briefly some of the related theoretical and methodological issues and then to examine the results of sequential analyses of a set of 19 personality and attitudinal factors that we have recently abstracted from our long-term studies with participants ranging in age from 22 to 84

Source: Schaie, K. W., & Parham, I. A. Stability of adult personality: Fact or fable? *Journal of Personality and Social Psychology,* 1976, 34, 146–158. Copyright 1976 by the American Psychological Association. Reprinted by permission.

years for the 7-year time period from 1963 to 1970.

Theoretical Basis of the Stability Model

To no one's surprise, the origin of the stability model of adult personality may well be attributed to the neglect of adult development by personality theorists. That is, the early dominance of psychoanalytic thought among child psychologists led to the notion that basic personality traits are indeed established in the first few years of life and that only modifications of such early traits occur during adulthood. Individual differences here are attributed to fixations at earlier stages, and actual reversals are seen as special cases on the regression mechanism. Similarly, life-span models that involve growth, maturity, and decline in cognitive functions nevertheless do not postulate a decline in personality traits; consequently, they portray adulthood as a period during which earlier achieved behavior change becomes stabilized rather than being subjected to further significant modification (Kohlberg, 1969; Kuhlen, 1959). Other writers see early life experiences as oriented toward developing traits that may have importance in later life, but that are affected by biobehavioral events that may not be developmental in nature. Such writers argue for individual change, but they also present evidence for a continuity model of personality (Livson, 1973; Mischel, 1971; Neugarten, 1966, 1969).

Further analysis of the stability model suggests that there may actually be a diversity of genotypic models that would account for the phenotype of adult stability. The first possibility would be a strictly hereditarian one. It would hold simply that individual differences in personality are genetically determined (and thus that certain traits may indeed show systematic differences between sexes, races, or other heritable classifica-

tions). Further, if this model were appropriate, we would have no reason to postulate either ontogenetic change or generation differences. A second model would argue that there is a critical period early in life that determines the formation of personality traits and/or attitudes and that the pattern then formed will persist throughout life. The first two models could be distinguished only if there were cultural changes in child-rearing practices that would result in the detection of cohort differences, provided no ontogenetic or transitory secular trends prevailed.

A third model would postulate systematic generational changes in child-rearing practices whose impact we might fail to detect in adulthood because of the presence of opposing ontogenetic trends. For example, there might be a tendency for people to become less aggressive with increasing age; this trend might not be detected if changes in child-rearing practices led to successive population cohorts showing lower aggressiveness. A fourth model would be quite compatible with social learning theory (Ahammer, 1973) in prescribing that individual differences in personality traits at any age are specific responses to individual environmental programs. Such differences, when averaged over populations, should in general lead to a finding of stability in the adult personality, since age differences would be detectable only for those traits or attitudes that are significantly affected by societal stereotypes regarding the age appropriateness of certain role expressions (cf. Neugarten & Datan, 1973).

Only the first two alternatives above are true stability models; the third is merely phenotypically stable, and the fourth may or may not be a stability model, depending upon whether stimulus situations follow an ontogenetic sequence or occur without reference to the age status of the organism. Our own studies thus far seem to suggest, interestingly enough, that the fourth model (which is really a pseudostability model) may be the most plausible with respect to personality (cf. Schaie & Parham, 1974). But in any event it would be desirable to differentiate the alternative assumptions for the stability model, and in particular to differentiate between intergenerational shifts and transitory secular trends that seem to affect members of all adult cohorts over limited periods of time. We will return to this matter later when we turn to appropriate research paradigms.

Adult Differentiation Models

Although most theoretical models seem to argue for stability of adult personality traits, there is at least some evidence from cross-sectional studies (Chown, 1968; Neugarten, 1973; Schaie & Marquette, 1972) that adult age differences can be observed on many personality variables. However, such differences may also be a function of a number of different combinations of developmental events. Certain dynamic models (cf. Erikson, 1964; Kohlberg, 1973), which imply that adult differentiation occurs as a function of successive transformations to more advanced stages, would also seem to require corollary changes in the structure of personality. None of these models, however, requires that such transformations occur according to an ontogenetically determined timetable. Indeed, Erikson's schematic of the eight stages of development, each of which requires successful mastery of the preceding stage, permits a total of 15 personality types, but there is no necessary prescription as to the incidence of each type at any given life age.

It might be argued that any model of aging that involves the concept of stages or differentiation may imply an ontogenetic pattern, which places such stages, whether mandated by the biological matrix or the social context, at a specific chronological age. Thus disengagement (Cumming & Henry,

1961) may occur only in old age (whether for some or all individuals) or the onset of profound rigidity in response style may occur in midlife (Schaie, 1962). But, alternately, such phenomena may also be the direct consequence of societal expectations that may change at different historical points in time for all individuals or may be transformed gradually as a function of successive cohort membership. In the latter case we might observe disengagement shift to different life stages: Have we not seen the "disengagement" of the young in the decade of the 1960s? We might also note shifts in the occurrence of peak levels on various traits and attitudes which at first glance appear as most curious if we try to force the data into a matrix requiring linear developmental phenomena that disregard the nonlinear transformations so characteristic of sociocultural change (e.g., Schaie & Parham, 1974).

It is the interaction of changes in the sociocultural matrix with the biologically determined attributes of the life course that is so puzzling both to the developmentally oriented student of individual differences and to the social psychologist who is impressed solely by changes in the social matrix. Neither stability nor a series of regular transformations (e.g., changes in level or quality) seems to fit the data at hand. As always in situations such as these, the truth would seem to lie somewhere in between, but where it lies precisely may be difficult to ascertain.

Three Types of Personality Traits

For the purpose of studying changes in traits and attitudes over the life span, it may be well to distinguish three different kinds of traits. In our further discussion we will refer to the three groups of variables identified below as biostable, acculturated, and biocultural traits. First there is a class of *biostable* traits, behavior that may be genetically determined or constrained (or in any event, shaped) by environmental influences that occur early in life, perhaps during a critical imprinting period. The most noteworthy attribute of these traits is that they show systematic sex differences at all age levels, but few if any age differences, whether examined by cross-sectional or longitudinal measures. A second set of *acculturated* traits appears, conversely, to be overdetermined by environmental events occurring at different stages in the individual's life as well as being subject to rather rapid modification by sociocultural change. Such traits generally show no systematic sex differences and have puzzling age difference patterns that can frequently be resolved into generational shifts and/or secular trend components by sequential analysis.

A much more infrequently occurring type is the *biocultural* trait, which in cross-sectional studies shows an Age × Sex interaction. This kind of variable would seem to reflect ontogenetic trends whose expression is modified either by generational shifts or by sociocultural events affecting all age levels in a similar fashion. We first encountered this trichotomy in a study in which we compared 50 retired college graduates with a mean age of 76 years with a group of graduate students matched for field of study on the Edwards Preference Schedule (Schaie & Strother, 1968). There was no opportunity at that time to trace this observation further, but we are now convinced that an orderly description of the adult development of personality requires notation of groups of variables with different life courses.

Some Methodological Issues

It may be apparent from the above discussion that there is disagreement in theory and interpretation of facts. Much of this disagreement, we think, just as was true in the field of intellectual changes with age, may be attributed to the common mistake of using results gained from cross-sectional studies as

evidence for or against the stability model of personality. Moreover, undue inferences are often based on rather unique samples subjected to single-cohort longitudinal study (e.g., Kelly, 1955; Livson, 1973). A detailed account of the methodological issues that have recently been set forth in detail elsewhere (Schaie, 1973, 1974, 1977; Schaie & Gribbin, 1975) will not be given here. Instead, we will simply (a) indicate some of the design requirements that we think need to be adhered to in order to obtain interpretable data and then (b) describe the results of collecting data following these prescriptions.

Comparability of data   If one is concerned with adult development over a long time period, then the issue arises whether personality structure remains constant. This matter can be handled most elegantly by constructing separate instruments for each differentiable cohort and then engaging in boundary studies and cross-instrument factor matching. Cattell (1965) has attempted such an approach with limited success with children. We doubt, however, whether this procedure is realistic with adults, although it should perhaps be attempted by constructing different instruments, perhaps one for each age decade. A more limited approach would be to identify a master universe of self-report items or descriptors to be factored separately for different ages and cohorts. Again, this is an undertaking that should be attempted, but remains to be done. A third approach, and one that we have taken, is to administer a manageable set of carefully selected items to a population stratified by age over the major portion of the adult life span, and most importantly, to sample each age level for at least two different cohorts. The latter constraint is important to minimize the impact of transient secular events in overdetermining individual differences variance.

Control for experimental artifacts   One of the important concerns in personality investigations using self-report material is that completion of a questionnaire may actually serve to formulate individuals' attitudes about themselves and the behaviors to be indexed. It is consequently necessary in designing a developmental study of personality both to look at repeated measures taken from the same individuals and to compare independent random samples taken from the same cohorts over the time interval during which the repeated measurement sample has been followed.

Sequential designs   In order to unconfound the sources of variance that might be mistaken for adult personality change (or stability), it will be necessary to assess two or more cohorts at a minimum of two measurement points (cross-sequential method). In addition, we will want to assess individuals at two or more age levels at a minimum of two measurement points (time-sequential method). The first scheme is most appropriate if we assume the validity of the stability model and therefore wish to differentiate between generational trends and current sociocultural events. The second scheme must be used if we have reason to believe that there are indeed age-related developmental trends for some of the variables under study. A reasonable procedure (cf. Schaie & Parham, 1974) is to begin with an application of the cross-sequential method to a repeated-measurement sample, to check resulting data by looking at a comparable independent random sample, and finally to apply the time-sequential method to the latter sample to see whether changes in F ratios require questioning of the stability assumption.

Method

The literature does not contain work that will satisfy the above design criteria with the exception of a study by Woodruff and Birren (1972) limited to a single cohort over a 26-year period. Our own studies of cognitive

behavior, however, contained material that upon proper reanalysis could meet our requirements at least in substantial part and thus shed some light on the questions raised. Throughout our study we have used a 75-item questionnaire (Schaie & Parham, 1975) that contains 22 subtle and 9 obvious rigidity items as well as 44 social responsibility items. As is true with any questionnaire, this pool of items was selected not because it represented pure measures of rigidity or social responsibility, but simply because the test items showed high saturation on relevant scales. Obviously each item contains additional variance, and what we have done here is sort out this additional variance as a first stab at the sequential study of personality. Our basis of analysis consists of approximately 2,500 questionnaires collected during 1963 and 1970 on subjects ranging in age from 21 to 84 years of age, approximately equally distributed by sex and age.

We began by factoring the intercorrelations among the 75 items by the conventional principal axes method. Examination of eigenvalues by Kaiser's criterion and Cattell's scree method led to the acceptance of 19 non-error factors. These factors were then rotated by means of the oblimin procedure to maximum simple structure. Careful analysis of item content of the resulting factors and comparison with existing taxonomies (Cattell, 1957) suggested that we were able to identify personality scales (albeit of shorter length and possibly lower reliability) that estimate 13 of the personality factors identified by the Sixteen Personality Factor Questionnaire (16 PF): affectothymia (A +), excitability (D +), dominance (E +), superego (G +), threctia (H −), premsia (I +), coasthenia (J +), protension (L +), praxernia (M −), untroubled adequacy (O −), conservatism of temperament (Q1 −), group dependency (Q2 −), and self-sentiment (Q3 −). In contrast to the balanced nature of the 16 PF scales, however, our scales typically represent only one end of the trait continuum described by a given factor (cf. Cattell, Eber, & Tatsuoka, 1970). In addition, we have identified six attitudinal scales that we labeled flexibility, honesty, financial support of society, humanitarian concern, community involvement, and interest in science.

We next computed factor scores on all 19 scales for our samples tested for the first time in 1963 and 1970 and for the repeated measurements obtained for the 1963 sample in 1970. We consequently have two cross-sectional samples of subjects arranged in eight 7-year age intervals, the youngest group ranging in age from 22 to 28 and the oldest from 71 to 77 years. In addition we have short-term longitudinal data for eight cohorts over the 7-year period, the youngest cohort being followed from mean age 25 to 32 and the oldest cohort from mean age 74 to 81. For hypothesis testing purposes we combined these data into three analyses: a cross-sequential repeated measurement analysis to test the stability model with respect to cohort differences, sex differences and sociocultural change ($n = 410$); a cross-sequential analysis with independent samples to test whether results obtained in the first analysis would be maintained when the effects of retesting are eliminated ($n = 1,556$); and a time-sequential analysis with independent samples, conducted to test the assumption of the stability model and to differentiate ontogenetic changes from sociocultural change ($n = 1,610$).

Results

Repeated Measurement Cross-Sequential Analysis

Cohort differences significant at or beyond the 1% level of confidence were found for nine of the personality factors and four of the attitude factors. Successive cohorts were found to be more outgoing, less excitable, more coasthenic (internally restrained),

with higher protension (jealous suspiciousness), greater superego strength, lower praxernia (practical down-to-earth mindedness), increased conservatism, increased group dependency, and increased self-sentiment. Successive cohorts also reported themselves to be more honest, more interested in science, and to have more interest in community involvement and less interest in humanitarian concerns (see Table 1).

Three personality factors and two attitudinal factors showed significant time trends from 1963 to 1970. There was a drop in excitability and protension, with an increase in praxernia. There was also a decline in positive interest in financial support of society and in universal political concern.

Sex differences significant at or beyond the 5% level of confidence occurred on six of the thirteen personality factors and on two of the six attitude factors. Men received higher scores than women on affectothymia (outgoing participation), threctia (threat reactivity), coasthenia, praxernia, untroubled adequacy, honesty, and interest in science. Women scored higher than men on group dependency.

Cohort × Time of Measurement interactions occurred only for community involvement and humanitarian concern. For the former there appeared to be little change over time for the older and middle cohorts, with increased involvement by the youngest cohort. In the case of humanitarian concern there was a marked drop by the oldest cohort, with a lesser decline by the middle and younger cohorts. A significant triple interaction suggested a particularly noteworthy lessening of humanitarian concern by the oldest female cohorts.

These results offer strong support for the stability model, since ontogenetic trends in the cross-sequential analysis, if any, should appear as spurious time-of-measurement effects. Because there are unlikely to be ontogenetic trends for the attitudinal factors the results for which seem so clearly in tune

TABLE 1
Repeated Measurement Cross-Sequential Analysis of Variance:
Significant F Ratios

Factor		Cohort	Time	Sex
A	+ Affectothymia	3.35[b]		4.13[a]
D	+ Excitability	4.16[b]	8.01[b]	
E	+ Dominance			
G	+ Superego strength	2.89[b]		
H	− Threctia			16.48[b]
I	+ Premsia			
J	+ Coasthenia	3.38[b]		6.24[a]
L	+ Protension	11.60[b]	5.99[a]	
M	− Praxernia	4.07[b]	5.26[a]	9.66[b]
O	− Untroubled adequacy			15.28[b]
Q1	− Conservatism of temperament	9.34[b]		
Q2	− Group dependency	2.40[b]		20.04[b]
Q3	− Low self-sentiment	2.70[b]		
Honesty		2.81[b]		20.99[b]
Interest in science		3.72[b]		70.09[b]
Flexibility				
Financial support of society			10.39[b]	
Humanitarian concern		3.34[b]	7.39[b]	
Community involvement		6.48[b]		

Note. Degrees of freedom: cohort (7, 394); time (1, 394); sex (1, 394). The Cohort × Time interaction was significant for flexibility ($F = 2.08$, $p < .05$), humanitarian concern ($F = 2.82$, $p < .01$), and community involvement ($F = 2.64$, $p < .01$). The triple interaction of Cohort × Sex × Time was significant for humanitarian concern at $p < .01$ ($F = 2.16$).
[a] $p < .05$.
[b] $p < .01$.

with our expectations for this historical epoch, we are left with the possibility of ontogenetic trends for excitability, protension, and praxernia. But before we address ourselves to a further check, we must next consider the issue of possible confounding of results in the longitudinal sample by the impact of repeated measurement affecting attitude formation and self-description of personality traits. The proper avenue of inquiry here is the comparison of within-cohort changes based on independent samples.

Independent Samples Cross-Sequential Analysis

Cohort differences significant at or beyond the 1% level of confidence were replicated for all factors for which such differences appeared in the repeated measurement study. Successive cohorts were also found to be more group dependent and to express more flexible attitudes. Significant time-of-measurement effects were also replicated, and additional effects were detected at the

1% level of confidence for an increase in dominance and a decrease in untroubled adequacy. (Note that suggestive effects significant at the 5% level further appeared for increased conservatism, group dependency, and flexibility, and an increase in honesty.)

All sex differences detected in the repeated measurement study were replicated, and in addition differences significant at or beyond the 1% level of confidence occurred, with women showing higher excitability and men greater community involvement. On the other hand, none of the interactions reported for the repeated measurement data could be replicated at the 1% level of confidence (see Table 2).

Independent Samples Time-Sequential Analysis

It was noted earlier that the component of sociocultural change identified in the cross-sequential ANOVA, if our assumption of the stability of personality through adulthood does not hold, could be confounded

TABLE 2

Independent Samples Cross-Sequential Analysis of Variance: Significant F Ratios

Factor	Cohort	Time	Sex
A + Affectothymia	21.02^b	4.60_a	
D + Excitability	13.21^b	8.17^b	6.46^b
E + Dominance		8.44^b	
G + Superego strength	18.85^b		
H − Threctia	7.35^b		468.24^b
I + Premsia			6.18^b
J + Coasthenia	3.94^b		27.48^b
L + Protension	32.14^b	4.70^a	
M − Praxernia	7.49^b	12.78^b	28.42^b
O − Untroubled adequacy	2.45^a	6.40^b	37.96^b
Q1 − Conservatism of temperament	60.26^b	3.93^a	
Q2 − Group dependency	7.62^b	4.26^a	19.81^b
Q3 − Low self-sentiment	14.18^b	8.17^b	5.61^a
Honesty	7.23^b	5.23^a	48.54^b
Interest in science	9.65^b		155.05^b
Flexibility	10.87^b	4.23^a	
Financial support of science		6.78^b	
Humanitarian concern	17.69^b	9.04^b	
Community involvement	22.71^b		6.75^b

Note. Degrees of freedom: cohort (7, 1,524); time (1, 1,524); sex (1, 1,524). The Cohort × Time interaction was significant for flexibility ($F = 2.59, p < .05$). The Cohort × Sex interaction was significant for affectothymia and threctia (both $Fs = 2.16, p < .05$).
[a] $p < .05$.
[b] $p < .01$.

with maturational change occurring over the 7-year period under investigation. This question can be approached with our data base by reorganizing the data into an Age × Time of Measurement design and applying a time-sequential ANOVA. This alternative design differentiates age levels and sociocultural change while confounding cohort effects.

It should be noted that the 7-year aging effect for the time period monitored would appear in the cross-sequential analysis in the main effect for time of measurement rather than in the cohort level effect, which covers a span of 56 years. By the same token, the generational confound in the time-sequential analysis would be located in the main effect for aging covering the 56-year span rather than in the 7-year time-of-measurement effect. Consequently, those time-of-measurement effects that remain significant can now be attributed unambiguously to sociocultural change, while those that disappear must be attributed to maturational factors. Likewise, F ratios for age levels that are equivalent or lower than the comparable ratios for cohorts in the cross-sequential analysis will still need to be interpreted as generation differences. In those instances where the F ratio is increased markedly and where the above-mentioned changes in the time-of-measurement effect have been noted, we will have to consider revision of our stability assumption. In addition, where a time-of-measurement effect now appears, even though it did not show in the cross-sequential analysis, it must be considered a confound for cohort differences, rather than evidence for sociocultural change, which would otherwise appear in both analyses (see Table 3).

The evidence from the time-sequential analysis is quite clear: Within the domain of factors identified in our study, we can with confidence support the stability model for all variables, with the exception of excitability and humanitarian concern, both of which increase with age (Table 4 provides mean scores by age group for these factors). In addition to the sociocultural trends apparent for individuals at all ages already identified in the cross-sequential analysis, we now find additional time trends significant at or beyond the 1% level of confidence for increased conservatism and group dependency.

Cohort Personality Profiles

Our analysis also allows us to describe characteristic profiles for each of the eight cohorts studied (see Table 5). Cohort 1 (mean birth year 1889), for example, was found to be the least outgoing, most excitable, highest in praxernia, and lowest in self-sentiment. Notably, this cohort is most willing to accept responsibility for the financial support of society and consistent with this shows the highest humanitarian concern.

Cohort 2 (mean birth year 1896) is quite similar to Cohort 1 in terms of high praxernia and low self-sentiment. Cohort 2 has its highest mean score on untroubled adequacy; that is, members of this cohort perceive themselves to be more self-assured, placid, or complacent.

Cohort 3 (mean birth year 1903) was also high in untroubled adequacy (similar to Cohort 2) and next highest only to Cohort 1 in financial support of society. Cohorts 3 and 4 (birth year 1910) are quite similar in their high scores on dominance. In fact, the latter cohort has the highest mean score for all groups sampled on the dominance factor.

Cohort 5 (mean birth year 1917) scored highest on threctia (threat reactivity) and premsia (tendermindedness). This cohort also has a high interest in science, second only to the youngest cohort. Note that Cohorts 4 and 5 fall into a special group in regard to the importance of certain personality factors, for example, tendermindedness, threat reactivity, and dominance,

TABLE 3
Independent Samples Time-Sequential Analysis of Variance:
Significant F Ratios

	Factor	Age	Time	Sex
A	+ Affectothymia	17.15[b]	19.74[b]	
D	+ Excitability	17.58[b]		5.64[a]
E	+ Dominance		11.29[b]	
G	+ Superego strength	17.36[b]		
H	− Threctia	8.21[b]		469.78[b]
I	+ Premsia	2.26[a]	3.97[a]	4.75[a]
J	+ Coasthenia	3.81[b]	6.57[b]	28.21[b]
L	+ Protension	22.81[b]	31.86[b]	
M	− Praxernia	8.74[b]	14.13[b]	26.95[b]
O	− Untroubled adequacy	2.47[a]	12.10[b]	35.89[b]
Q1	− Conservatism of temperament	54.10[b]	45.91[b]	
Q2	− Group dependency	6.83[b]	8.24[b]	20.17[b]
Q3	− Low self-sentiment	13.53[b]	6.99[b]	5.21[a]
	Honesty	12.08[b]		53.99[b]
	Interest in science	7.39[b]	4.63[a]	147.45[b]
	Flexibility	10.82[b]	12.44[b]	
	Financial support of society		5.77[a]	
	Humanitarian concern	14.11[b]		
	Community involvement	25.43[b]	27.12[b]	8.89[b]

Note. Degrees of freedom: age (7, 1,578); Time (1, 1,578); sex (1, 1,578). The Age × Time interaction was significant ($p < .05$) for interest in science ($F = 2.08$), universal political concern ($F = 2.06$), and community involvement ($F = 2.03$). Age × Sex was significant for superego strength ($F = 2.15$, $p < .05$), and Age × Sex × Time was significant for threctia ($F = 2.49$, $p < .05$).
[a] $p < .05$.
[b] $p < .01$.

TABLE 4
Means for Factors Showing Significant Age Trends

	Age							
	(22–28)	(29–35)	(36–42)	(43–49)	(50–56)	(57–63)	(64–70)	(71–77)
D + Excitability								
Males	45.69	47.23	48.30	49.18	48.86	51.07	51.59	52.86
Females	43.01	48.96	50.38	50.49	50.28	51.13	52.46	52.11
Humanitarian concern	49.85	48.83	47.48	48.87	50.02	50.85	52.77	54.77

TABLE 5

Mean Scores of Personality Factors by Cohorts

Factor	C8 1938	C7 1931	C6 1924	C5 1917	C4 1910	C3 1903	C2 1896	C1 1889
A + Affectothymia	48.79	48.63	48.45	49.23	49.84	52.24	54.15	56.00
D + Excitability	46.41	49.08	49.18	50.19	49.97	51.42	51.97	53.19
E + Dominance	49.81	49.51	50.07	49.58	50.10	49.96	49.58	48.67
G + Superego	51.32	51.25	52.22	50.98	50.26	48.59	46.36	45.77
H − Threctia	51.55	50.04	50.27	51.25	49.98	49.88	47.80	48.32
I + Premsia	49.45	50.13	50.98	50.43	50.01	49.91	48.92	49.97
J + Coasthenia	50.98	50.42	51.08	50.27	49.37	49.49	48.97	48.06
L + Protension	51.67	51.41	51.80	50.96	49.47	47.57	46.67	44.22
M − Praxernia	50.99	50.16	48.81	48.77	49.78	50.21	51.49	52.24
O − Untroubled adequacy	49.55	49.34	49.00	50.79	50.24	50.69	51.14	50.48
Q1 − Conservatism of temperament	52.96	52.44	52.66	51.97	49.06	46.41	44.39	42.22
Q2 − Group dependency	52.18	50.69	50.69	49.41	49.41	48.14	48.06	47.37
Q3 − Low self-sentiment	47.19	49.28	48.97	49.03	50.37	52.12	53.25	53.67
Honesty	52.73	50.89	51.06	50.26	49.71	49.71	47.89	49.50
Interest in science	51.80	49.98	50.59	51.34	49.98	48.52	46.68	46.31
Flexibility	53.17	51.04	51.08	49.53	49.19	47.45	47.80	49.92
Financial support of society	49.76	50.46	49.64	50.07	50.26	50.90	50.14	51.18
Humanitarian concern	48.17	48.68	47.64	49.18	50.24	51.98	53.66	55.31
Community involvement	52.74	50.98	51.96	50.16	49.50	47.79	46.41	45.86

Note. C8 = Cohort 8 (whose mean birth year is 1938), and so on for C7–C1.

which may reflect the pressures of middle age such as anticipated retirement, menopausal change, and reduced physical vigor.

Cohort 6 (mean birth year 1924) resembles Cohorts 7 and 8 in being high on protension (jealous suspiciousness). Cohort 6 resembles Cohorts 3 and 4 in being high on dominance. Another instance of continuity between the cohorts involves Cohorts 5 and 6, who are comparably high on premsia. Cohort 6 is comparably high with Cohorts 7 and 8 on superego strength, in marked contrast to the low scores for Cohorts 1, 2, and 3 on this factor. A similar pattern is found for coasthenia (internal restraint).

Cohort 7 (mean birth year 1931) is high on financial support of society and, again, resembles Cohorts 6 and 8 in being high on protension. The youngest cohort, Cohort 8 (mean birth 1936) is highest on conservatism of temperament, group dependency, flexibility, interest in science, honesty, and community involvement.

There is remarkable similarity and continuity between adjacent cohorts on these personality factors; nevertheless, a clear break may be noted between the three oldest cohorts and the younger cohorts on protension, superego, and coasthenia. The cohort groupings found for these personality factors are quite similar to groupings previously noted for intelligence data (Schaie & Labouvie-Vief, 1974).

Discussion

The results of our study point to the tremendous complexity of the task of describing the adult life course of personality traits. We find it necessary therefore to reexamine the trifold model suggested earlier and to present a revision that will do more justice to the data. In terms of our earlier analysis it would seem that of the factors included in our sequential study, 9 are of the biostable, 6 or 7 of the acculturated, and only 1 or 2 of the biocultural variety. It is clear, however, that the trifold typology is far too simple, since it

was formulated on the basis of cross-sectional data and consequently glosses over the full complexity of developmental phenomena. On the basis of the present analysis it is possible to describe at least 13 subtypes, examples for 9 of which may be given from our own data. These subtypes are derived by identifying the possible combinations of the joint occurrence or absence of sex differences, ontogenetic change or cohort differences, and sociocultural change.

Biostable Traits

These are traits that because of genetic or early environmental influences show sex differences that are reliably maintained throughout the adult life course. Although cross-sectional studies may show age differences, these are found by sequential analysis to be cohort differences or sociocultural change. Four subtypes may be identified:

1. *Stable sex differences only.* Such traits would appear to be overdetermined by genetic variance probably located on the sex chromosome. The only trait qualifying for this model in our study is that of premsia (tendermindedness). Even here we must vacillate, since that factor was significant at the 5% level of confidence also for time and age (see Table 3), suggesting that upon replication it might well be assigned to the biocultural traits. Indeed, it does not seem too likely that we could find personality traits that would fit the purely inherited trait category without ambiguity.

2. *Time-of-measurement differences only.* These traits would also appear to be overdetermined by genetic variance, but are modified in their expression by transient sociocultural changes. In our analysis this type was represented by untroubled adequacy, which showed a decrease over the period we monitored (see Figure 1).

3. *Cohort differences only.* These are stable traits not subject to transient environmental

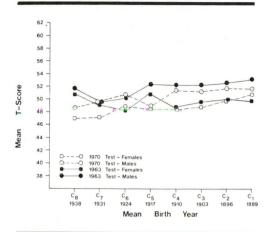

FIGURE 1
Untroubled adequacy.

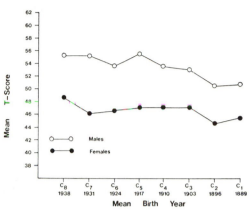

FIGURE 2
Threctia.

influences, but ones in which different patterns in early training or socialization produce significant generational differences. It is likely that many traits developed via early socialization follow this pattern. In our study those falling into this category were threat reactivity, coasthenia, expressed honesty, interest in science, and community involvement (see Figure 2).

4. *Time-of-measurement and cohort differences.* Some age-related traits develop in response to early socialization and appear to be subject both to cohort differences in such socialization practices and to transient socio-cultural impact. In our study these include praxernia and group dependency, both of which showed a time-of-measurement effect in the cross-sequential and time-sequential analyses, as well as no noteworthy difference between the two analyses in F ratios for age and cohort (see Figure 3).

Acculturated Traits

These traits show no sex differences, but cross-sectional studies typically identify age differences. It is assumed here that these are either culturally prescribed and age-related

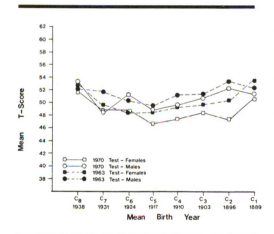

FIGURE 3
Praxernia.

patterns, or that upon longitudinal inquiry, suspected age differences are identified as either cohort or transient secular trends. Six different patterns are possible for this type of trait.

5. *Age changes only.* Such traits reflect social roles that might be determined by uni-

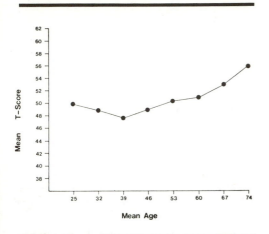

FIGURE 4
Humanitarian concern.

versals underlying a stage model of develop-ment and that would be rather impermeable to cohort differences or secular trends. Identification of such traits changing in the appropriate direction would, incidentally, be required as support for disengagement theory. In our study the only such trait was humanitarian concern, which to the prob-able chagrin of supporters of disengagement theory showed increase rather than decrease with age (see Figure 4).

6. *Age changes and cohort differences.* Traits here would be mediated by stage changes in universally determined life role, which in turn are modified by shifts in early socializa-tion practices. Lacking the data for a cohort-sequential analysis, we had to infer that our data did not contain such traits. Examina-tion of relative F ratios, however, suggests that affectothymia, protension, and low self-sentiment could conceivably fit this pattern instead of the cohort-differences-only pat-tern to which the present study assigns them (see Subtype 8).

7. *Age changes and time-of-measurement dif-ferences.* Such traits would also be mediated by universally determined life roles and

would be impermeable to early socialization practices, but would be subject to transient influence at all ages. Frankly, it is difficult to imagine such a trait, and we did not identify any fitting this pattern in our study.

8. *Cohort differences only.* These traits are not subject to ontogenetic change but in-stead are ones in which the specific pattern of early socialization might mediate the par-ticular trait expression as an adult. This pat-tern held for affectothymia, superego strength, protension, and low self-sentiment (see Figure 5).

9. *Time-of-measurement   differences   only.* Such traits are non-age-related, apparently independent of early socialization practices, but subject to transient modification by so-ciocultural change at all ages. Dominance and financial support of society fit this pat-tern, with the time-of-measurement effect remaining significant in both the cross-se-quential and time-sequential analyses (see Figure 6).

10. *Cohort differences and time-of-measure-ment differences.* Non-age-related traits that are modified by specific patterns of early so-cialization as well as by transient socio-

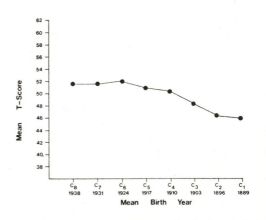

FIGURE 5
Superego.

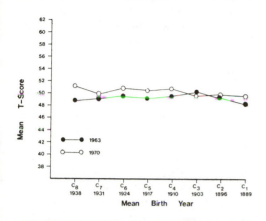

FIGURE 6
Dominance.

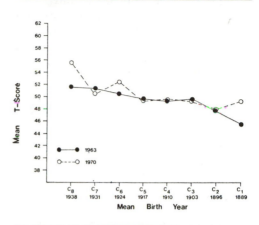

FIGURE 7
Flexibility.

cultural change affecting all ages belong in this subtype. Note that the F ratios for cohort in the cohort-sequential analysis show little difference from the F ratios for age in the time-sequential analysis; there is also an increase in the time-of-measurement effect in the time-sequential analysis. Our study identified the flexibility factor as falling into this group (see Figure 7).

Biocultural Traits

These traits, which appear to be overdetermined by genetic variance and consequently show significant sex differences, are also subject to modification in their expression because of universally experienced life stage expectancies. Moreover, some of these traits may be affected by early socialization experiences or sociocultural change. Three subtypes are possible:

11. *Age changes only.* These traits have clear ontogenetic "programs" and appear to be impermeable to cohort differences or sociocultural change affecting all ages. Our only example of this type was excitability, which increased with age, with the time-of-

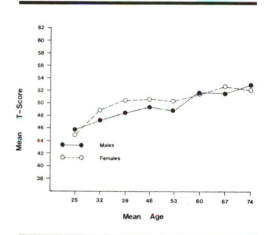

FIGURE 8
Excitability.

measurement effect appearing in the cross-sequential analysis (see Figure 8). Although probably a rare type, a wider sampling of personality traits would no doubt identify several others (e.g., surgency).

12. *Age changes and cohort differences.* Modification of cohort level through early

experience would here be required. Although our design makes it difficult to detect such traits (lacking a cohort-sequential analysis), it is unlikely that such traits exist.

13. *Age changes and time-of-measurement differences.* Here we would expect modification of the ontogenetic "program" for all ages due to specific environmental interventions. We did not identify any such trait at the 1% level of confidence, but we could have so classified premsia had we accepted the 5% level of confidence.

Conclusions

The methodological approach used here, that is, the application of sequential designs, has previously been successfully employed in assessing intellectual changes as a function of age. In the intellectual domain (cf. Schaie, 1974) it has been demonstrated that the universal decrement model for cognitive processes is not the most useful. The decrement model had been supported primarily by artifactual data from cross-sectional studies that had compared cohorts with differing base levels of ability. The present paper now demonstrates the utility of applying the same methodology to the area of personality trait development with age. We have shown that stability of personality traits is the rule rather than the exception, but that such stability, nevertheless cannot be attributed to lack of change after adolescence, as most traditional personality theorists might believe. Rather, in the 19 personality traits studied here much change was observed. The change, however, is a function of specific early socialization experiences, commonly shared generation-specific environ-

mental impact, and particular sociocultural transitions that may affect individuals at all ages. For those variables that are overdetermined by biological constraints or early socialization there seems indeed to be life-long stability. It is only the unusual trait of excitability (biocultural) that shows clear ontogenetic "programs" and appears to be unaffected by cohort differences or sociocultural change. This trait exhibited increment with age.

The conceptualization suggested here allows a more sophisticated examination of the development of personality traits. Within the three major types of personality trait that were suggested on the basis of cross-sectional studies of personality (biostable, acculturated, and biocultural), further breakdowns into subtypes of personality traits are now possible. These subtypes have been derived by identifying all possible combinations of the joint occurrence or absence of sex differences, ontogenetic change, cohort differences, and sociocultural change. Thus, for example, the trait of expressed honesty can now be identified as a biocultural trait that is not subject to transient environmental influences, but is affected by cohort differences produced by different patterns of early training or socialization. Determination of the specific developmental status of a given personality trait can move our understanding beyond the level of simple categorization.

It may then become possible to conduct more precise analyses on the developmental course of different types of personality traits as well as to determine the points, whether in childhood or adulthood, where intervention may or may not be practicable.

References

Ahammer, I. M. Social learning theory as a framework for the study of adult personality development. In P. B. Baltes & K. W. Schaie (Eds.), *Life-span developmental psychology: Personality and socialization.* New York: Academic Press, 1973.

Baltes, P. B., & Schaie, K. W. Aging and the IQ: The myth of twilight years. *Personality Today,* March 1974, pp. 35–38; 40.

Cattell, R. B. *Personality and motivation structure and measurement.* New York: World Book, 1957.

Cattell, R. B. *The scientific study of personality.* Baltimore: Penguin Books, 1965.

Cattell, R. B., Eber, H. W., & Tatsuoka, M. M. *Handbook for the Sixteen Personality Factor Questionnaire (16PF).* Champaign, Ill.: Institute for Personality and Ability Testing, 1970.

Chown, S. M. Personality and aging. In K. W. Schaie (Ed.), *Theory and methods of research on aging.* Morgantown: West Virginia University, 1968.

Cumming, E., & Henry, W. E. *Growing old.* New York: Basic Books, 1961.

Erikson, E. H. *Insight and responsibility.* New York: Norton, 1964.

Kelly, E. L. Consistency of the adult personality. *American Psychologist,* 1955, 10, 659–681.

Kohlberg, L. Stage and sequence: The cognitive-developmental approach to socialization. In D. A. Goslin (Ed.), *Handbook of socialization theory and research.* Chicago: Rand-McNally, 1969.

Kohlberg, L. Continuities in childhood and adult moral development revisited. In P. B. Baltes & K. W. Schaie (Eds.), *Life-span developmental psychology: Personality and socialization.* New York: Academic Press, 1973.

Kuhlen, R. G. Aging and life-adjustment. In J. E. Birren (Ed.), *Handbook of aging and the individual.* Chicago: University of Chicago Press, 1959.

Livson, N. Developmental dimensions of personality: A life-span formulation. In P. B. Baltes & K. W. Schaie (Eds.), *Life-span developmental psychology: Personality and socialization.* New York: Academic Press, 1973.

Mischel, W. *Introduction to personality.* New York: Holt, Rinehart & Winston, 1971.

Neugarten, B. L. Adult personality: A developmental view. *Human Development,* 1966, 9, 61–73.

Neugarten, B. L. Continuities and discontinuities of psychological issues into adult life. *Human Development,* 1969, 12, 121–130.

Neugarten, B. L. Personality change in late life: A developmental perspective. In C. Eisdorfer & M. P. Lawton (Eds.), *The psychology of adult development and aging.* Washington: American Psychological Association, 1973.

Neugarten, B. L., & Datan, N. Sociological perspectives on the life cycle. In P. B. Baltes & K. W. Schaie (Eds.), *Life-span developmental psychology: Personality and socialization.* New York: Academic Press, 1973.

Reichard, S., Livson, F., & Peterson, P. *Aging and personality.* New York: Wiley, 1962.

Schaie, K. W. A field-theory approach to age changes in cognitive behavior. *Vita Humana,* 1962, 5, 129–141.

Schaie, K. W. Methodological problems in descriptive developmental research on adulthood and old age. In J. R. Nesselroade & H. W. Reese (Eds.), *Life-span developmental psychology: Methodological issues.* New York: Academic Press, 1973.

Schaie, K. W. Translations in gerontology — from lab to life: Intellectual functions. *American Psychologist,* 1974, 29, 802–807.

Schaie, K. W. Quasi-experimental designs in the psychology of aging. In J. E. Birren & K. W. Schaie (Eds.), *Handbook of the psychology of aging.* New York: Reinhold-Van Nostrand, 1977.

Schaie, K. W., & Gribbin, K. Adult development and aging. *Annual Review of Psychology,* 1975, 26, 65–96.

Schaie, K. W., & Labouvie-Vief, G. Generational versus ontogenetic components of change in adult cognitive behavior: A fourteen-year cross-sequential study. *Developmental Psychology,* 1974, 10, 305–320.

Schaie, K. W., & Marquette, B. W. Personality in maturity and old age. In R. M. Dreger (Ed.), *Multivariate personality research. Contributions to the understanding of personality in honor of Raymond B. Cattell.* Baton Rouge, La.: Claitor, 1972.

Schaie, K. W., & Parham, I. A. Social responsibility in adulthood: Ontogenetic and sociocultural change. *Journal of Personality and Social Psychology,* 1974, 30, 483–492.

Schaie, K. W., & Parham, I. A. *Manual for the Test of Behavioral Rigidity* (2nd rev. ed.). Palo Alto, Calif.: Consulting Psychologists Press, 1975.

Schaie, K. W., & Strother, C. R. Cognitive and personality variables in college graduates of advanced age. In G. A. Talland (Ed.), *Human aging and behavior: Recent advances in research and theory.* New York: Academic Press, 1968.

Woodruff, D. S., & Birren, J. E. Age changes and cohort differences in personality. *Developmental Psychology,* 1972, 6, 252–259.

Age Changes and Cohort Differences in Personality

DIANA S. WOODRUFF and JAMES E. BIRREN

To examine ontogenetic and generational change in personality, longitudinal and cross-sectional comparisons were made with the personality test scores of three cohort groups. Adolescents tested in 1944 on the California Test of Personality were retested 25 years later when they were middle-aged adults. These subjects were asked to answer the inventory a second time as they thought they had answered it in 1944. Contemporary high school and college students also answered the California Test of Personality. Longitudinal comparisons indicated that objective age changes in personality were small but subjective age changes were large. Differences in personality test scores for the various cohorts were statistically significant suggesting that objective cohort differences in personality were great. These results confirmed in the domain of personality what previous investigations demonstrated in the area of cognition. Objective cohort differences were much greater than objective age changes from adolescence to middle age.

Although personality inventories are one of the most reliable and valid measures of personality available to psychologists, few lifespan studies reporting personality test scores are described in the literature. Unfortunately, all of these studies which have been reported are based on simple cross-sectional or longitudinal designs. Little attempt has been made to heed the methodological suggestions of Schaie (1965, 1967) or Baltes (1968) to distinguish between age differences and age changes and to use sequential strategies in order to separate ontogenetic from generational change components. Designs with controls for cohort differences or with replications over several

cohort groups have not been used in this area. Consequently, the personality literature contains apparent discrepancies concerning the magnitude of age changes in personality test scores.

For example, in a longitudinal study of Bernreuter Personality Inventory scores, Kelly (1955) found small age changes in personality over a 19-year span. Kelly concluded that in the cohort group he studied, results were in favor of consistency rather than change in personality from adolescence to middle age. Cross-sectional studies presented a different picture. A large number of cross-sectional studies on inventories such as the Minnesota Multiphasic

Personality Inventory (Brozek, 1955; Calden & Hokanson, 1959; Hardyck, 1964; Postema & Schell, 1967), the Guilford-Zimmerman Temperament Schedule (Bendig, 1960), and the Maudsley Personality Inventory (Eysenck & Eysenck, 1969; Gutman, 1966) indicated that fairly substantial age differences in personality existed. Thus, while the results of a longitudinal study suggested that age changes in personality were small, data from cross-sectional studies were interpreted to indicate that age differences in personality were substantial. None of the authors of these studies attempted to discuss the relative magnitude of the effects of age and cohort.

Schaie (1965) pointed out that longitudinal studies measure maturational changes while cross-sectional studies assess generational differences as well as maturational changes. Since the longitudinal data of Kelly suggested that age changes in personality were small, much of the variance observed in cross-sectional studies of personality may have resulted from cohort differences. Indeed, in the light of recent studies (Schaie, 1970; Schaie & Strother, 1968) on the relative impact of age and cohort on adult development in intelligence, such an interpretation is rather likely. Unfortunately, age and cohort were hopelessly confounded in cross-sectional studies on personality, and it was impossible to separate the relative contributions of the effects of age and cohort.

The present article represents an attempt to clarify this issue using one specific personality inventory. Direct comparisons were made of the effects of age and cohort on scores on the California Test of Personality. On the basis of the longitudinal data in the literature, it was hypothesized that age changes in personality would be small. Results from cross-sectional studies led to the second hypothesis that cohort differences in personality would be greater than age changes over the age range of 19.5–44.5 years.

Method

Design

A follow-up study was undertaken in a research design similar to that used by Owens (1966) for the investigation of ontogenetic changes in mental abilities. The original data were collected in the fall semester of 1944 by Morris Kimber who tested 485 undergraduates at the University of Southern California. Kimber (1947) was interested in the amount of insight college students had in a personality inventory. He asked students to answer the California Test of Personality by describing themselves (*self* condition) and by describing a well-adjusted contemporary (*insight* condition). Data from the self condition were used in the present study. Data from the insight condition were reported previously (Woodruff & Birren, 1971).

Participants from the original study were contacted and retested in the fall semester of 1969 permitting longitudinal comparisons of the test-retest data over a 25-year span. In addition to describing themselves, follow-up subjects were asked to answer the California Test of Personality as they thought they had answered it in 1944. This testing condition was referred to as the *retrospection* condition.

To provide data for cohort comparisons, a group of University of Southern California students were tested in the fall semester of 1969 on the California Test of Personality. They took the California Test of Personality in the self and insight conditions. Due to increased public awareness of psychological test and issues in the years between 1944 and 1969, it was hypothesized that adolescents in 1969 would be more sophisticated in their ability to take a personality inventory and hence score higher in adjustment than adolescents tested in 1944. This hypothesis led to the inclusion of a third group to determine if there was a trend to greater test-taking sophistication at younger ages with succeeding cohorts. A group of high school students was also tested in the self and insight conditions on the California Test of Personality, and it was hypothesized that high school students in 1969 would score similarly to college students in 1944 while college students in 1969 would score higher in level of adjustment than both groups.

Subjects

The majority of Kimber's subjects were white, upper-middle-class college students. As would be expected of a college sample, the group was of above-average intelligence. Mean Army Alpha Examination scores were 161.8 and 149.5 for men and women, respectively. Follow-up subjects were traced via the University of Southern California alumni files, and addresses were found for 143 of the original sample. A large majority of the subjects resided in suburban and urban areas. All of these subjects were contacted by mail, and 85 participated in the study. Fifty-four of the 85 participants completed both the self and retrospection conditions. Comparisons of the 1944 scores of participants and nonparticipants in the follow-up study indicated that the 1969 participants were representative of the original 1944 sample. The subjects' mean age was 19.5 at the time Kimber tested them in 1944. Their mean age was 44.5 at retest. This group is referred to as the 1924 cohort.

The 1969 college-age sample was comprised of 34 male and female volunteers. A total of 145 randomly selected undergraduates at the University of Southern California were mailed letters of introduction, and 34 returned usable data. Inasmuch as these subjects were selected from the same university as the follow-up sample, it was assumed that the groups would be comparable on variables such as intelligence and social class. This assumption seemed to be valid in the case of social class as college-age subjects reported a median annual family income similar to the family income reported

by the 1924 cohort. Intelligence test scores were not available for this group. The mean age of the college group was 19.6. This group is called the 1948 cohort.

The California Test of Personality was administered to 43 high school students from two local high schools. Students were selected only if they planned to attend a 4-year university. This precaution was taken in an attempt to equate the high school sample to the college and adult samples on variables such as social class and intelligence. The mean age of the high school students was 16.2. This group is referred to as the 1953 cohort.

Measuring Instrument

The California Test of Personality consists of a series of five questionnaires for successive age levels purporting to measure a number of components of personal and social adjustment. The test includes 180 items divided into 12 subtests. Since the 1942 edition of the California Test of Personality was out of print when the follow-up study was undertaken, the authors obtained permission from the California Testing Bureau to duplicate that edition of the test.

Answer forms were modified to include instructions comparable to those which Kimber gave orally in 1944. A detailed description of the instruction conditions and scoring procedure was presented in a previous paper (Woodruff & Birren, 1971).

Packets containing the California Test of Personality, a background information questionnaire, an appropriate answer form, an explanatory letter, and a stamped return envelope were mailed to all adult and college participants. The same material was presented to the high school group by the first author or by an assistant.

Results

Mean California Test of Personality scores and standard deviations for the three cohort

TABLE 1

Mean California Test of Personality Scores and Standard Deviations for Three Cohort Groups in all Testing Conditions

Condition	Cohort								
	1924			1948			1953		
	N	M	SD	N	M	SD	N	M	SD
Self, 1969									
Men	35	155.9	16.2	17	137.2	14.5	15	137.7	15.4
Women	19	150.6	17.4	17	135.9	20.7	28	135.4	16.4
Self, 1944									
Men	35	150.9	16.8		—			—	
Women	19	152.7	15.3		—			—	
Retrospection, 1969									
Men	35	143.1	25.4		—			—	
Women	19	137.0	22.0		—			—	

groups in all testing conditions are presented in Table 1. Since it had been impossible to test all groups in all conditions, separate comparisons were made within the 1924 cohort and between the three cohort groups.

Within-Cohort Comparisons

Longitudinal comparisons of the mean personality test scores of the cohort of 1924 were made with a 2 × 2 analysis of variance comparing the effects of age and sex. Scores achieved in the self condition by men and women in 1944 were compared to self scores achieved in 1969. The method of unweighted means (Winer, 1962) was used to correct for unequal group size in this comparison and in all analysis of variance comparisons where group size was unequal. The effects of age and sex were not significant (Fs = .31 and .46, respectively), and there was no significant interaction effect (F = 1.91). These results indicated that personality test scores remained stable for both men and women over a 25-year period. Hence, there were no significant age changes in mean personality test scores.

A 2 × 2 analysis of variance comparing the effects of time of testing and sex was used to compare retrospection scores with the actual scores achieved in 1944. The effect of time was significant (F = 4.09, df = 1/52, $p < .05$), and there were no significant sex or Sex × Time interaction effects (Fs = .14 and .45, respectively). Adults scored significantly lower when they described themselves as students than they had actually scored when they were students 25 years previously. They projected a negative picture of themselves back in time. Graphically depicted in Figure 1 are the two within-cohort comparisons.

Between-Cohort Comparisons

To compare the effect of cohort and sex on the California Test of Personality scores, two 3 × 2 analysis of variance tests were made. In the first test, the scores achieved in the self condition in 1944 by men and women in the 1924 cohort were compared to the self set scores of the cohorts of 1948 and 1953. Hence, time of testing was confounded, and age was held relatively constant for all cohort groups as they were all in their late teens. The effect of cohort was

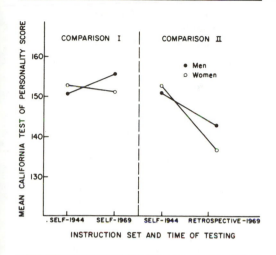

FIGURE 1
California Test of Personality scores in 1944 and 1969 for the 1924 cohort in the self and retrospection conditions.

significant   (F = 11.95,   df = 2/125, p < .001), and there was also a significant Sex × Cohort interaction (F = 4279.47, df = 2/125, p < .001).

In the second cohort comparison, time of testing was held constant while age was varied. Scores achieved in 1969 on the self set by the 1924 cohort were compared to self set scores of the cohorts of 1948 and 1953. Again, the effect of cohort was significant (F = 15.87,   df = 2/125,   p < .001), and there was a significant interaction between the effects of cohort and sex (F = 4842.93, df = 2/125, p = < .001).

Because a number of post hoc comparisons were made, the conservative alpha level or error rate experimentwise was adopted. Scheffé's multiple-comparison method was used for all post hoc comparisons (Myers, 1966). Post hoc comparisons of the cohort effect indicated that the cohort of 1924 scored significantly higher than the combined mean score for the cohorts of 1948 and 1953. This comparison was significant whether the 1924 cohort was

tested at age 19.5 (F = 10.98, df = 2/128, p < .001) or at age 44.5 (F = 16.10, df = 2/128, p < .001). Post hoc comparisons of the scores of the cohorts of 1948 and 1953 indicated that the scores were not significantly different (F = .00).

The retrospection condition scores of the 1924 cohort were compared to the self condition scores of the cohorts of 1948 and 1953 in a 3 × 2 analysis of variance testing the effects of cohort and sex. The effect of cohort was significant (F = 5.72, df = 2/125, p < .01), and there were significant sex and Sex × Cohort interaction effects (F = 11.54, df = 1/125, p < .001; F = 2682.27, df = 2/125, p < .001, respectively). Hence, adults describing themselves as students had mean scores which were significantly higher than the mean scores of contemporary students. Women's scores were significantly lower than the scores of men, and there was a greater difference between the scores of men and women in the 1924 cohort than between scores of men and women in the cohorts of 1948 and 1953. The three between-cohort comparisons are presented in Figure 2.

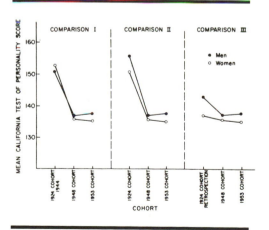

FIGURE 2
California Test of Personality scores for three cohorts in 1944 and 1969 on the self condition and for one cohort in the retrospection condition.

Discussion

Objective Age Changes

The hypotheses that age changes in personality would be slight and that they would be smaller than cohort differences were supported. Thus, the present data support for the domain of personality what recent research (Nesselroade, Schaie, & Baltes, 1972; Schaie & Strother, 1968) had demonstrated for the area of cognitive development.

Longitudinal comparisons indicated that men and women described themselves in the present study almost exactly as they had described themselves in 1944. These results suggest that for the 1924 cohort there is consistency rather than change in personality over a 25-year span between ages 19.5 and 44.5 years.

Objective Cohort Differences

There were obvious differences in the manner in which the cohort of 1924 and the cohorts of 1948 and 1953 answered the California Test of Personality regardless of the age at which the 1924 cohort answered the test. The scores of students in 1944 and students in 1969 differed from 12 to 18 points, and members of the 1924 cohort always scored higher in self and social adjustment than did members of the 1948 and 1953 cohort groups.

The 1942 edition of the California Test of Personality was used throughout the study, so the inventory was standardized on a cohort population similar to the 1924 cohort group. This fact might account for some of the discrepancies between cohort groups, but the item content of the current edition of the California Test of Personality has been only slightly modified, and revised standard scores remain much the same as the standard scores of earlier editions. Thus, either the California Test of Personality has not

been sufficiently revised to be consistent with current adolescent standards of adjustment, or adolescents in 1969 are less well adjusted than adolescents in earlier cohort groups.

The hypothesis that adolescents in 1969 would be more sophisticated in their ability to take a personality test was not supported. Cohort differences in personality test scores were so great that they obscured any improvement in adjustment score that might have been attributed to increases in test-taking sophistication.

The large difference in personality test scores seems to represent a genuine cohort difference which might be reflected in what is popularly called the "generation gap." Behavioral differences between cohorts have been a topic of concern for centuries, and contemporary literature about cohort differences stresses the inevitable and perhaps adaptive nature of the differences (Bengston, 1969). Unique socio-historical forces impinge on the members of each generation when they are in different stages of development. Generations of individuals mature in different eras, so these groups experience various social institutions differently. Mannheim (1952) suggested that the experience of coming to age in a different era produces a psychological "set" or imprint which may permanently characterize the attitudes of a cohort. Bengtson (1969) contended that in a rapidly changing society the effect of coming to age in a different era is adaptive as it leads to discontinuities in generations which allow a new cohort to face new problems with new solutions.

Subjective Similarities and Differences

There was some evidence in the data from the present study that there may be more than one component contributing to the generation gap. In addition to the objective cohort differences in personality test scores, there was also the suggestion of a subjective component of the generation gap within one cohort. In the retrospection condition, adults projected a relatively negative picture of themselves as adolescents. In retrospect they thought that their adolescent level of adjustment was much lower than it actually had been. Adults seemed to subjectively experience a discontinuity between their adolescent and adult personality which did not exist objectively.

Riegel (1971) suggested that the flow of psychological (subjective) time may be altogether different from the flow of chronological (objective) time. Data from the present study adds to a mounting body of evidence (e.g., Ahammer & Baltes, 1972) which indicates that Riegel's statement is accurate. Moreover, it has been suggested that perceived rather than actual age differences are of the greatest significance in determining interage and intergenerational behavior (Ahammer, 1970; Bengtson & Kuypers, 1971; Thomae, 1970). Ahammer and Baltes (1972) found that subjective personality differences between cohorts were greater than objective differences. Data from the present study corroborate the results of Ahammer and Baltes (1972) inasmuch as subjective personality differences were greater than objective differences within the 1924 cohort.

Several interpretations for the discrepancy between subjective and objective personality differences are plausible. On the one hand, individuals may like to consider themselves better adjusted in the present than they were when they were younger. Members of the 1924 cohort may have projected a negative picture of themselves as adolescents to indicate that they had matured and become better adjusted with time.

If this interpretation is accurate, adults would also consider themselves to be better adjusted than contemporary adolescents. Hence, they might be less willing to accept the fact that adolescents were capable of making responsible decisions. In this man-

ner the subjective discontinuity between adolescent and adult personality may serve to magnify the objective personality differences existing between cohorts.

An equally plausible explanation for the subjective discontinuity in adults' personality test scores involves the fact that adults and adolescents tested in 1969 scored similarly when describing their respective adolescent personalities. Although adults' mean retrospection score was significantly higher than contemporary adolescents' self description, the adult's mean retrospection score was more similar to contemporary adolescents' mean self score than to the mean self score adults achieved when they were adolescents. Item analysis was undertaken to clarify the nature of the similarities and differences between subjective and objective personality descriptions of the two cohorts. The proportion of subjects answering each of the 180 items on the California Test of Personality correctly was computed for the cohort groups in the various conditions, and separate analyses were made for men and women. Proportions of subjects in each group who correctly answered each of the 180 California Test of Personality items were compared with a t test for proportions (McNemar, 1955). Since 180 comparisons were made, a corrected t score for the .05 level of confidence was used.

Item comparisons revealed the fact that there were fewer differences between the retrospection instruction condition of the 1924 cohort and the way in which the cohort of 1948 described themselves than between the 1924 cohort's retrospection score and the way these same subjects had described themselves in 1944 when they were students. Hence, although there were significant differences between the mean scores of the 1924 cohort's retrospection condition and the 1948 and 1953 cohorts' self scores, item analysis indicated that the adults' retrospection answers were more like the answers of contemporary adolescents than like the answers the adults had given when they were adolescents in 1944. Members of the 1924 cohort subjectively described their adolescent personalities in a manner similar to the objective self description of contemporary adolescents.

This result may be an indication that at a given period in history there are prevailing stereotypes characterizing individuals of various age groups. There may be a concept of adolescence in 1969 of which both adults and adolescents are aware, and this contemporary concept of adolescence is altogether different from the way in which adolescents described themselves in 1944. Seventy-six percent of the subjects in the follow-up group had children of high school or college age, so the adults may have described their children when they tried to describe themselves as adolescents. Perhaps since they were familiar with the attitudes of contemporary adolescents, their current experience with adolescent attitudes influenced their description of themselves as they had been as adolescents. Hence, adults may have identified with contemporary adolescents when they tried to describe themselves in retrospect. In this interpretation, generational discontinuity is minimized as adults may have accepted and incorporated into their own subjective personalities the traits of succeeding cohorts.

In the present study, comparisons of subjective and objective personality descriptions between cohorts clarify some issues while raising others. There is clear evidence for large objective personality differences between cohorts, but the nature of subjective personality similarities and differences between and within cohorts cannot be resolved with the present data. Hopefully, the current enthusiasm for the phenomenological approach which places emphasis on subjective experience (e.g., Adshead, Kerschner, & Sparks, 1970; Ahammer & Baltes, 1972; Riegel, 1971; Thomae, 1970)

will stimulate research clarifying the unresolved issues raised in this study.

Age versus Cohort Effects

Taken as a whole, the results of this study confirm what has been suggested by the discrepancy between cross-sectional and longitudinal literature on personality test scores. The slight differences which occur in personality test scores for the same individuals over long periods of time indicate that objective age changes in personality are small from adolescence to middle age. Larger age differences resulting from cross-sectional studies suggest that objective cohort differences in personality may be great. Data from the present study extend the concern with cohort differences from the area of intelligence (Nesselroade, Schaie, & Baltes, 1971; Schaie & Strother, 1968) to the domain of personality.

The results of this study suggest new strategies for future developmental research in the area of personality. Future research concerned with the ontogenetic and generational components of personality can employ the more sophisticated personality inventories developed in recent years, and the use of multivariate sequential strategies proposed by Baltes and Nesselroade (1970) would be most appropriate for this area. Evidence has also been presented which suggests that it is useful to observe subjective as well as objective reports of personality. Another research strategy is to reanalyze existing data in time-lag designs and compare scores achieved by different cohorts on the same personality inventories. Such a study is currently in the planning stage. The authors intend to extend the present study by comparing California Test of Personality scores achieved by cohorts of adolescents in the various decades between 1944 and 1969.

It has become apparent that separating the effects of age changes and cohort differences in personality can add new dimensions to the existing body of developmental literature on personality. The present data suggest that it is only when these two sources of variance are confounded that a confusing picture ensues.

References

Adshead, F. L., Kerschner, P. A., & Sparks, P. M. Phenomenology and gerontology. *Gerontologist,* 1970, 10, 1970. (Abstract)

Ahammer, I. M. Alternative strategies for the investigation of age differences. Paper presented at the regional meeting of the Southeastern Conference of the Society for Research in Child Development, Athens, Georgia, 1970.

Ahammer, I. M., & Baltes, P. B. Objective versus perceived age differences in personality: How do adolescents, adults, and older people view themselves and each other. *Journal of Gerontology,* 1972, 27, 46–51.

Baltes, P. B. Longitudinal and cross-sectional sequences in the study of age and generation effects. *Human Development,* 1968, 11, 145–171.

Baltes, P. B., & Nesselroade, J. R. Multivariate longitudinal and cross-sectional sequences for analyzing ontogenetic and generational change: A methodological note. *Developmental Psychology,* 1970, 2, 163–168.

Bendig, A. W. Age differences in the interscale factor structure of the Guilford-Zimmerman Temperament Survey. *Journal of Consulting Psychology,* 1960, 24, 134–138.

Bengtson, V. L. The "generation gap": Differences by generation and by sex in perception of parent-child relations. Paper presented at the annual meeting of the Pacific Sociological Association, Seattle, Washington, April 1969.

Bengtson, V. L., & Kuypers, J. A. Generational differences: Perception, reality and the developmental stake. *Aging and Human Development,* 1971, 2, in press.

Brozek, J. Personality changes with age: An item analysis of the MMPI. *Journal of Gerontology,* 1955, 10, 194–206.

Calden, G., & Hokanson, J. E. The influence of age on MMPI responses. *Journal of Clinical Psychology,* 1959, 15, 194–195.

Eysenck, S. B. J., & Eysenck, H. J. Scores on three personality variables as a function of age, sex and social class. *British Journal of Social and Clinical Psychology,* 1969, 8, 69–76.

Gutman, G. M. A note on the MPI: Age and sex differences in extraversion and neuroticism in a Canadian sample. *British Journal of Social and Clinical Psychology,* 1966, 5, 128–129.

Hardyck, C. D. Sex differences in personality changes with age. *Journal of Gerontology,* 1964, 19, 78–82.

Kelly, E. L. Consistency of the adult personality. *American Psychologist,* 1955, 10, 659–681.

Kimber, J. A. M. The insight of college students into the items of a personality test. *Educational and Psychological Measurement,* 1947, 7, 411–420.

Mannheim, K. *Essays on the sociology of knowledge.* London: Routledge & Kegan Paul, 1952.

McNemar, Q. *Psychological statistics.* New York: Wiley, 1955.

Myers, J. J. *Fundamentals of experimental design.* Boston: Allyn & Bacon, 1966.

Nesselroade, J. R., Schaie, K. W., & Baltes, P. B. Ontogenetic and generational components of structural and quantitative change in adult cognitive behavior. *Journal of Gerontology,* 1972, 27, 222–228.

Owens, W. A., Jr. Age and mental abilities. *Journal of Educational Psychology,* 1966, 57, 311–325.

Postema, L. J., & Schell, R. E. Aging and psychopathology: Some MMPI evidence for seemingly greater neurotic behavior among older people. *Journal of Clinical Psychology,* 1967, 23, 140–143.

Riegel, K. F. Time and change in the development of the individual and society. Unpublished manuscript, University of Michigan, 1971.

Schaie, K. W. A general model for the study of

developmental problems. *Psychological Bulletin,* 1965, 64, 92–107.

Schaie, K. W. Age changes and age differences. *Gerontologist,* 1967, 7, 128–132.

Schaie, K. W. A reinterpretation of age-related changes in cognitive structure and functioning. In L. R. Goulet & P. B. Baltes (Eds.), *Lifespan developmental psychology: Research and theory.* New York: Academic Press, 1970.

Schaie, K. W., & Strother, C. R. The effect of time and cohort differences on the interpretation of age changes in cognitive behavior.

Multivariate Behavioral Research, 1968, 3, 259–294.

Thomae, H. Theory of aging and cognitive theory of personality. *Human Development,* 1970, 13, 1–16.

Winer, B. J. *Statistical principles in experimental design.* New York: McGraw-Hill, 1962.

Woodruff, D. S., & Birren, J. E. Age and personality: A twenty-five year follow-up. Unpublished manuscript, University of Southern California, 1971.

Young Adulthood

INDEPENDENCE VERSUS INTIMACY

Young adulthood ranges from approximately eighteen to thirty-five or forty years of age. It is a period characterized by the developmental tasks of starting a career, choosing a mate, starting a family, and settling down. Personal identity is an important issue, as young adults struggle to establish themselves as independent entities, separate from their families. Their need for independence, however, must be balanced with the need for intimacy. These two powerful needs, of course, are to some extent contradictory and often in conflict with one another.

Young adults, expanding their personal space to include an intimate other, also face the task of defining their relationship with the larger community. Their participation in community affairs depends to some extent upon the orderliness of their career. Young adults also expand their time perspectives; they plan or preview their further life, particularly in the areas of career, family life, and social responsibilities. In the first selection *Robert C. Atchley* analyzes the life course, age grading, and age-linked demands for decision making as social mechanisms that serve as major influences in charting the adult life course. Atchley suggests that most individuals have expectations as to the point in their life when many crucial life changes are likely to occur. Age grading is seen as a process that controls the individual's access to many roles, groups, and social situations as well as forming attitude values and beliefs. Age-linked decision demands motivate the individual and others in decision-making roles to impose structure on what might otherwise lead to contradictions between age-linked opportunities, age norms, and personal expectations.

One of the major tasks of young adulthood is the establishment of intimacy. Intimacy, like identity, is not easily defined. Romantic love has been studied as a combination of physiological arousal plus an intellectual affection. Other researchers view love as a sort of attachment bond, much like that between parent and infant. Some psychologists have constructed self-report instruments that permit the scientific investigation of love relationships. A study by *Margaret Neiswender Reedy, James E. Birren,* and *K. Warner Schaie* uses Q technique, in which people sort statements into categories ranging from most to least characteristic of themselves. The study investigated six components of a love relationship: emotional therapy, respect, help and play behaviors, communication, sexual intimacy, and loyalty. Differences in the salient characteristics of intimate love relationships during young adulthood, middle age, and old age are also reported.

Additional Reading Suggestions

Dennis, W. Creative productivity between the ages of 20 and 80 years. *Journal of Gerontology,* 1966, 21, 1–8.
  A succinct survey of the empirical literature on creative output of scholars, scientists, and professionals in many fields of endeavours.

Rubin, Z. *Liking and loving.* New York: Holt, Rinehart & Winston, 1973.
  An account of the many variables that affect interpersonal attraction, and on the processes that lead to the establishment of personal bonds resulting in a new family unit.

The Life Course, Age Grading, and Age-Linked Demands for Decision Making

ROBERT C. ATCHLEY

Life-span developmental psychology intersects with sociology at the point where social systems, whether they be small groups or nations, deal with the biological and social maturation and aging of their individual members. The basic premise of this paper is that age is an important variable that cuts across all areas of social life, and that it does so primarily through three social mechanisms: the life course, the system of age grading, and age-linked demands for decision making.

This paper treats the life course, age grading, and age-linked demands for decisions as highly interrelated social forces operating in the development of human beings. The life course is portrayed as a crude road map with quite a few alternative routes for getting through life's various stages. The existence of the life course provides a conception of successive changes in the structure of an individual's life and an expectation that these changes will occur. Age grading is portrayed as a process that combines with sex to control the individual's access to various groups, roles, aspects of culture (including norms, attitudes, values, beliefs, and skills), social situations, and social processes. Decision demands provide the individual, and those who care about him or her, with motivation for imposing structure on what otherwise would be a chaotic system of sometimes contradictory age norms and age-linked opportunities. Decision demands are a prime normative mechanism for providing the movement that translates the static age grading system into the life course and ultimately into the biography of an individual.

This paper represents a preliminary excursion into poorly charted territory. It contains many speculations intended to promote thinking and spark research in new directions. It is necessarily short on well-documented answers to the issues it raises. At the same time, it seeks to provide a more complex approach to the sociology of the life span than has been available to developmental researchers in the past.

The Life Course

The life course is a heuristic and conceptual tool through which sociologists attempt to relate social structure and process to the life spans and unique biographies of individuals. Several terms can be used in place of "life course." For example, Cain (1964) lists "life cycle," "life span," and "stages of

Source: Abridged from Atchley, R. C. The life course, age grading, and age-linked demands for decision making. In N. Datan & L. Ginsberg (eds.), *Life-span developmental psychology: Normative life crises.* New York: Academic Press, 1975, pp. 261–278. Reprinted with permission.

life'' as roughly synonymous. I have chosen ''life course'' because I feel that it best serves to differentiate between social time, through which society structures the life span of individuals, and biographical time, which deals with the individual's experiencing of his own life span.

Just as a cohort of individuals becomes progressively more differentiated throughout its life span, the life course represents an increasingly more complex maze of age-linked alternatives. At the early stages of the life course, there is a great deal of age determinism. Gradually, however, it becomes more and more difficult to predict an individual's place in society mainly from knowledge of age. The life course is rather like a successively bigger equation made up of a series of *contingent* probabilities; that is, the older a person gets, the more tomorrow's alternatives are contingent on yesterday's selections. However, toward the end of the life span, there is a reduction in the number of variant life courses due to the impact of the symptoms of old age.

As Clausen (1972) has pointed out, individuals do not select at random from among contingencies. Personal resources such as intelligence, appearance, strength, health, temperament, and initiative have an important bearing on what come to be defined as realistic alternatives. The guidance, support, and outright help that is available from others are other important variables that influence choices, even within the constraints of the age grading system. Likewise, whether age-linked opportunities are open or closed is related to such factors as sex, ethnicity, race, social class, and personal contacts (Clausen, 1972, p. 463). This is another reason why there are many alternative versions of the life course.

Yet with all of the latitude represented by the various alternative life courses, there are general, consensual age standards that comprise a sort of master timetable to which detailed alternatives may, and often must,

be tied. Neugarten, Moore, and Lowe (1965, p. 711) put it well:

> There exists what might be called a prescriptive timetable for the ordering of major life events: a time in the life span when men and women are expected to marry, a time to raise children, a time to retire. This normative pattern is adhered to, more or less consistently, by most persons in the society.

In the sense it is used here, time refers to stages of life. Stages of life are most often identified in terms of major events. But stages of life also exist in several dimensions. Figure 1 portrays several dimensions of the life course with *approximate* relationships of various sequential stages with chronological age. There are wide fluctuations around any given point on any given dimension. Yet the existence of future stages tied to age on given dimensions exerts a pull that results in more consistency than might otherwise be expected (Neugarten & Datan, 1973).

The life course is thus a convenient device for conceptualizing the sequential aspects of social structure through which individuals pass in the process of social maturation and aging. At the same time, it is also clear that a detailed appreciation of the life course requires more than a linear, structural approach. Accordingly, the next two sections of this paper deal with age grading, which provides a detailed view of structure, and age-linked demands for decision making, which provide insight into the dynamic processes that motivate people to tie themselves to age-related aspects of social structure.

Age Grading

Age grading is one of the several social mechanisms through which individuals find out what they can expect to be *allowed* to do and to be, as well as what they will be *required* to do and to be. Age grading systematically links the age of individuals to a large and

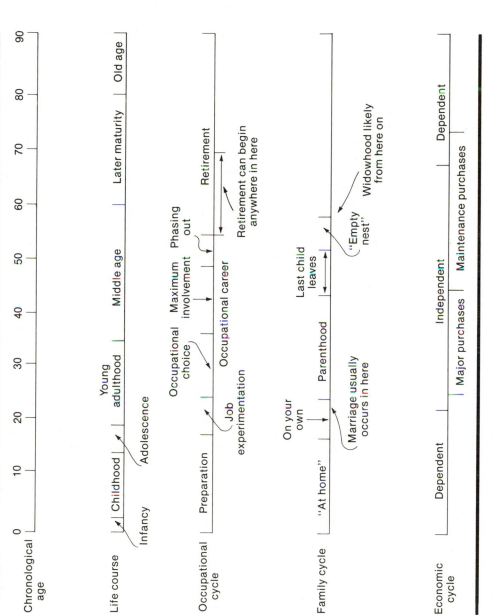

FIGURE 1

Relationships among age, life cycle, occupational cycle, and family cycle. (These relationships fluctuate widely for specific individuals and for various social categories such as ethnic groups or social classes.)

various body of norms in the individual's culture or subculture.

Sources of Age Norms

Many age norms are handed down through tradition. However, other norms result from a negotiation process. Cain (1974) has pointed out, for example, that the age of 65 for retirement under social security resulted from negotiations within Congress, and not from a tradition established by Bismarck, as has been widely assumed. Still other norms arise out of the fact that even without tradition or conflict-resolution processes, customs may evolve from modal behavior patterns. Among American working-class young people, for instance, marriage customarily follows soon after graduation from high school. As a result, age at first marriage is less variable for the working class than for the middle class, in which there are several options concerning when job preparation is complete and whether it should be completed before marriage occurs.

Regardless of whether age norms grow primarily out of tradition, negotiated agreement, or modal behavior patterns, standing behind these norms is a series of assumptions concerning biological and social development and aging. Many of the age norms that people confront are based on assumptions, often uninformed, concerning what people of a given chronological age are *capable* of doing — not just what they *ought* to do but what they *can* do. For example, Americans seldom try to teach children to play the violin at age 4 because it is assumed that they cannot do it and will only be frustrated by the experience. But the Japanese have had widespread success with teaching violin to very young children. On the other hand, very few 4 year olds are strong enough to lay cement blocks, and in this case proscriptive age norms seem to make more sense. Thus, what often appear on the surface to be norms based on

natural biological limits are often in fact arbitrary social norms based on untested biological or psychological assumptions. Conceptions of social maturation (often called "getting the necessary experience") are also used to justify age norms. It seems justifiable that a child of 3 not be able to vote. But for his 15 year old sibling, the question is not so clear-cut. On both the physical and social dimensions, then, there are natural limits concerning what people can do. Part of the job of setting arbitrary limits is often related to the cost of error, sometimes simply presumed, sometimes discovered through experience.

Age norms thus sometimes rest on actual social and physical limits. But often age norms are only arbitrarily related to relevant aspects of maturation or aging. The greater the disparity between actual functioning and the level of functioning implied by the age norms, the more likely it is that the individual will feel that age norms make invidious, unjust distinctions among people.

At the beginning of the life span, the limits are overwhelmingly natural, biological, and maturational. As soon as children begin to move around, however, they quickly encounter both natural and arbitrary limits centered around social maturation. Throughout childhood there is a mixture of these various types of limits. However, as the individual moves through childhood and into adolescence, there is a sharp reduction of the natural, biological limits and natural, social limits, but the arbitrary social limits diminish more slowly. In early adulthood, all three types of limits are at their lowest point. Of course, individuals are not necessarily free of all types of norms at this stage, they are simply freer of *age* norms. From there, however, aging causes physical limits to begin to reappear. After young adulthood there is also a resurgence of social limits, both natural and arbitrary (Clausen, 1972). Aging brings natural social limits to the extent that with rapid cultural change it is difficult for older cohorts to know enough about the language and culture of younger cohorts to be able to continue to play the role of young adult. More important, however, is the fact that the dictum to act one's age, an arbitrary social limit, will not allow people to play roles too "youthful" for their age. This restriction grows stronger during the latter two-thirds of the life span. It is probably stronger for women than men because standards for women are more closely tied to chronological age (Atchley & George, 1973).

Criteria for Applying Age Norms

How age is defined and applied to persons varies along several dimensions. *Social age* is calculated from several reference points — birth, entry into a given position or situation, or stage in the life course. *Individual age* is assessed in terms of appearance and/or level of functioning. In addition, there are important sex differences in the applicability of these various dimensions of age.

Chronological age is the easiest kind of social time to study. The arbitrary nature of calendar time means that chronological age is easy to compute, and rules associated with specific chronological ages are the most explicit of age norms. Likewise, norms governing tenure — the length of time an individual has held a position (not to be confused with academic tenure) — the length of time an individual has held a position (not to be confused with academic tenure) — tend to be tied to calendar time and are therefore easier to observe. Rules based on life stages tend to be more difficult to study, primarily because multiple contingencies are often employed as criteria. For example, it is easy to define the point at which a person becomes ineligible to be a member of the PTA by simply using the exit of his or her children from the school as a criterion. It is more difficult to predict the point at which the individual can form a socially approved marriage, because there are several alternative combinations of life-stage characteristics that can qualify a person for marriage.

With regard to chronological and tenure age norms, sex has less impact on the application of the norms than on whether the person has access to the groups, roles, or situations in which these norms are applied. Sexually segregated groups develop standards that do not apply outside the group. Even when men and women *do* participate in the same groups, their roles within the groups may differ in terms of the application of age norms. Sex differences in certain age norms result from the effects of childbearing and child-rearing on the woman's career. How much this will change in the future we cannot be sure, but there is a tendency toward less sex differentiation in family roles, and this will probably have an effect on the sexual dual standard in age norms.

Physical appearance and level of functioning are important criteria for assigning age norms, but again there is little research on these dimensions. Among children, appearance is an often-used basis for making judgments as to which age standards should be applied. Big, strong-appearing children are allowed more independence than children of the same chronological age who are small and frail in appearance. Gray hair and wrinkled skin cause people to be categorized as "old." To the extent that it exists, the sexual dual standard (Sontag, 1972) makes appearance a more important criterion for women than for men across the entire life span, although people do not necessarily occupy the same position on the scale of attractive physical appearance at the various stages of their lives.

Level of physical functioning is also an important consideration in assigning age norms. Chronologically old people who are gray and wrinkled but still physically spry arouse no particular interest on the tennis court, but a frail older person certainly would. Again there is a fairly well-developed sexual dual standard, particularly during and after adolescence. Men are expected to exhibit a high degree of physical strength and agility and they are expected to exhibit a certain amount of sexual prowess. In these terms, men very often encounter teasing and labeling related to aging in their 30s. Men also often self-assign themselves to an age grade in order to commit themselves to a lower level of physical performance. This is a surprisingly effective social mechanism for "copping out."

The Focus of Age Norms

Individuals, social structure, social processes, phases of involvement with social structure, and combinations of these are influenced by age norms. This is an issue separate from assigning norms to particular people. It deals with the focus of the norms.

Age norms concerning the person deal mainly with expected appearance and behavioral demeanor (as opposed to specific, instrumental action). That one should dress properly for one's age and behave in a manner appropriate for one's age are examples.

Age norms governing social structure include norms linking age with various groups, roles, social situations, and subcultures. To date, sociologists have been concerned primarily with age-related roles, with little attention to other attributes of social structure (Riley *et al.*, 1972; Cain, 1964). However, roles are usually attached to specific positions within specific groups. For example, one has to be 11 years old and male to join a Boy Scout troop, but within a given troop, roles are allocated on the basis of tenure and performance, and a discussion of a young man's role as a Boy Scout would be incomplete without reference to the rules of the specific group. Age norms for social structure are assigned by all of the various mechanisms. Age norms also apply to unstructured situations. For instance, in a bar with a youth-oriented live rock band, a 40

year old may be exposed to sanctions from younger patrons simply on the basis of his or her appearance. That person is simply not eligible to be in that specific situation. Age norms are also related to access to various subcultures through the effect of age norms on access to age-segregated settings. For example, teenagers develop language that is uniquely theirs and cannot be mastered by nonteenagers simply because of the age-segregated interactional basis of teenage slang.

People approach, enter, master, and often relinquish their relationships to structural niches in society. Accordingly, age norms related to structure can be differentiated into those that apply to preparation, entry, incumbency, and exit. Most structural elements have age-related entry criteria, but age norms are only sporadically related to the other phases — approach, maturity, aging, or withdrawal — as they apply to particular structural elements. In addition, different assignment criteria are used to allocate people to various age-linked phases, even for a given structural element.

Goals of Age Norms

Age norms can demand that people do or be something or not do or be something. They can also allow people to do certain things, but not require any specific thing. Age norms can also demand that certain choices be made. That is, age norms can prescribe and proscribe specific behavior or relations of the individual to specific structural elements, but they can also delineate a field of permitted behaviors and structural niches. Age norms can also demand that choices be made from this field. More will be said about these factors later.

Application of Age Norms

Age norms can be formal or informal in terms of how sanctions are applied. At the one end of the continuum, laws are more or less rigid, universalistic age norms. Age regulations may also be formal and universalistic, as in the case of mandatory retirement rules. Unwritten laws, or mores, may be informal but they carry a great deal of weight. For example, there is no law against a 40 year old woman's dating a 20-year-old man, but powerful informal sanctions may be brought to bear in such cases. Folkways and mores tend to be consensual, but they may be translated into laws.

Many times age norms are applied to the individual by the individual. This may be simply an accurate view of conformity. But in a changing world, it is also possible for individuals to apply stricter standards to themselves than would be applied by the community at large. Of course, age norms can be and are applied to the individual by others, as in the case of the minimum legal age to vote.

Age Grading and Human Development Research

There are several ways that research can explore the effect of age norms on human development. It is obvious that, given the extreme complexity of age grading, more attention needs to be paid to interaction among the various dimensions of age norms. Legal age norms tend to be arbitrary, direct, externally sanctioned, chronological, and based on community of societal standards. Most other age norms can exhibit a very large array of combinations of dimensions. It is particularly important to see how the various assignment criteria interact with the object of the age norm. For example, which objects — persons, social structure, phase of development, or social processes — are most often associated with chronological age?

Another useful task would be to evaluate the scientific validity of various justifications for age norms which are based on assumptions about human development. It would

also be useful to examine the age norms implicit in the work of psychologists such as Piaget, Jung, Erikson, and Buhler. It may well be that their formulations need reconsideration in the light of social change. It is also important to know something about the part group reinforcement plays in the dynamics to age norms as personal standards. It might be particularly interesting to see how age norms affect the presentation of self (Goffman, 1959).

Age-Related Demands for Decision Making

Externally, the complex of age norms is tied to the life course by the assignment process, the process through which groups apply age norms to persons. But what about internal processes? How do age norms become translated into significant symbols for the individual? People come to understand what age norms are through socialization, but age norms become salient through interaction and demands for decision making.

Age norms that deal with personal qualities such as appearance or manner of acting become salient when individuals become aware, through interaction with other persons, that particular age norms are being applied to them. Age norms that deal with social structure become salient in a variety of ways. They may be externally imposed, as with formal age norms, or selected by the individual from within a socially defined field of eligibles. This section of the paper deals with age-linked decision-making demands as a normatively dictated mechanism for the internal organization of age norms and the articulation of age norms with the life course.

Decision demands are norms tied to the life course which set intervals — zones of decision — within which selections must be made from an age-linked field of possible structural niches. For example, following the completion of preparatory education, young adults usually enter a period of job experimentation. The field of possibilities expands dramatically immediately following graduation (certification) and continues to expand while the individual gains job experience. But after a time there is an increasing expectation that the individual will find a position of employment into which he will settle, and during this period, the field of jobs for which he is eligible may slowly contract. Contraction also occurs as a result of career choices by others in the cohort. For many jobs, career tracks are difficult to begin after 45. For others, it is difficult to break in after age 35. Clausen (1972) points out that people who make job career decisions relatively late have more orderly careers. This suggests that they simply forgo the job experimentation that usually accompanies entry into a career track. Even within the dimensions of job careers, various occupations and work places differ with respect to the size of the age interval within which career selections must be made.

Age-related zones of decision exist with regard to careers in education, the family, employment, residence, retirement, voluntary associations, friendships, leisure pursuits, and in other areas. Although they are often somewhat flexible, the deadlines associated with zones of decision provide motivation for individuals to organize their thoughts and to negotiate an acceptable choice with significant others. Scholars often accept deadlines as a means of pushing themselves into organizing their thoughts and coming to grips with an intellectual issue. Age-related decision deadlines operate in much the same fashion.

The foregoing implies a very active part for the individual in the process of decision making. However, individuals vary a great deal in the extent to which they make their own decisions. Some important dimensions of this include the individual's self-esteem and self-confidence, the support received from others, and age norms themselves.

Prior to young adulthood, people are expected to be involved in decisions about their own life courses, but in cases of conflict to defer to those in charge, usually parents. Women are likely to be expected to be deferent longer than men are, and often marriage simply shifts responsibility for decisions about the woman's life from one man (her father) to another (her husband.) This may be changing, but it affected the life courses of those cohorts of women currently in their later years. Likewise, one family may encourage younger members to make their own decisions while others impose fairly specific age-related roles on their members. Older adults are often discouraged by their families from assuming a self-confident attitude about making their own independent decisions. Again, *decisions in response to age-related decision demands remain a variable to be explained in research rather than to be assumed.*

Conclusion

In this chapter I have attempted to show that the life course, age grading, and age-linked decision demands are *problematic* aspects of the sociocultural environment whose effects on human development have yet to be discovered. I have tried to provide some tools for diagnosing and for injecting these factors into human development research. I can only hope that others share with me the sense of excitement concerning the promise this area of sociopsychological research holds for adding to our understanding of human development.

The life course represents a basic, normative ideal to which individual biographies can be related. For example, life graphs (Back & Bourque, 1970) can be used to study both the life course and individual biographies and aspirations. Neugarten *et al.* (1965) have given an example of how age grading can be approached, but more immediate, phenomenological approaches are needed. Finally, age-linked decision demands represent a virtually untapped empirical point at which the social impact on human development could be studied. All of these approaches can enrich our understanding of both human development and the social systems that shape it.

References

Atchley, R. C., & George, L .K. Symptomatic measurement of age. *The Gerontologist,* 1973, 13, 332–336.

Back, K. W., & Bourque, L. B. Life graphs: Aging and cohort effects. *Journal of Gerontology,* 1970, 25, 249–255.

Cain, L. D., Jr. Life course and social structure. In R.E.L. Faris (Ed.), *Handbook of modern sociology.* Chicago: Rand McNally, 1964. Pp. 272–309.

Cain, L. D., Jr. The growing importance of legal age in determining the status of the elderly. *The Gerontologist,* 1974, 14, 167–174.

Clausen, J. A. The life course of individuals. In M. W. Riley, M. Johnson, & A. Foner (Eds.), *Aging and society, volume three: A sociology of age stratification.* New York: Russell Sage Foundation, 1972. Pp. 457–514.

Goffman, E. *The presentation of self in everyday life.* New York: Doubleday, 1959.

Lopata, H. Z. *Widowhood in an American city.* Cambridge, Massachusetts: Schenkman, 1973.

Neugarten, B. L., & Datan, N. Sociological perspectives on the life cycle. In P. B. Baltes & K. W. Schaie (Eds.), *Life-span developmental psychology: Personality and socialization.* New York: Academic Press, 1973. Pp. 53–69.

Neugarten, B. L., Moore, J. W., & Lowe, J. C. Age norms, age constraints, and adult socialization. *American Journal of Sociology,* 1965, 70, 710–717.

Riley, M. W., Johnson, J., & Foner, A. (Eds.), *Aging and society, volume three: A sociology of age stratification.* New York: Russell Sage Foundation, 1972.

Sontag, S. The double standard of aging. *Saturday Review,* 1972, September 12, 29–38.

Age and Sex Differences in Satisfying Love Relationships across the Adult Life Span

MARGARET NEISWENDER REEDY, JAMES E. BIRREN, and K. WARNER SCHAIE

The purpose of this research was to identify age and sex differences in the major characteristics of satisfying heterosexual love relationships. 102 happily married young, middle-aged, and older couples completed a 108-statement Q-sort of love experiences. Scores were determined for six components of love: Emotional security, Respect, Help and play behaviors, Communication, Sexual intimacy and Loyalty. Statistical analyses showed that older lovers had higher ratings for emotional security and loyalty and lower ratings for sexual intimacy, while young adult lovers had higher ratings for communication. Men were found to have higher ratings for loyalty, while women had higher ratings for emotional security.

Since love and attachment appear to be essential to survival and well-being throughout life (Bowlby, 1969; Harlow, 1971; Kalish and Knudtson, 1976; Lee, 1977; Lowenthal and Haven, 1968; Spitz, 1945), it would seem vitally important to increase our understanding of the nature of successful and satisfying love relationships between men and women across the adult life span. Paradoxically, research suggests that married love relationships which are lasting are not necessarily those which are most satisfying (Hicks and Platt, 1970). Based on the findings of cross-sectional and longitudinal research, marital satisfaction generally shows a progressive decline from the time children are born through middle age and the child-launching years, with an upswing after that (Blood and Wolfe, 1960;

Hicks and Platt, 1970; Pineo, 1961; Rollins and Feldman, 1970).

Although little is known about what keeps love alive and well as lovers grow older together, increasing interest is being expressed in understanding the characteristics and dimensions of attachment across the life span (Antonucci, 1976; Hartup and Lempers, 1973; Kalish and Knudtson, 1976; Knudtson, 1976; Troll and Smith, 1976; Weinraub et al., 1977), and developmental theories of love suggest that there are qualitative changes in the nature of affectional relationships over time (Bissett, 1970; Freud, 1949; Harlow, 1971; Levinger, 1974; Levinger and Snoek, 1972; Maslow, 1954; Orlinsky, 1972; Rosow, 1957; Shostrom, 1972; Winch, 1967).

An examination of the theoretical and em-

Source: Reedy, M. N., Birren, J. E., & Schaie, K. W. Age and sex differences in satisfying love relationships across the adult life span. *Human Development,* 1981, 24, 52–66. Copyright 1981 by S. Karger AG, Basel. Reprinted by permission.

pirical literature on the developmental nature of attachment in adult love relationships suggests two themes. The first theme is that relationships move toward deeper levels of intimacy over time and that the passionate fires of youthful love are somehow transformed into the deeper, more serene and tender love of advanced age (Driscoll et al., 1972; Kerckhoff and Davis, 1962; Levinger, 1974; Levinger and Snoek, 1972; Troll and Smith, 1976; Winch, 1967). In this view, physical attraction, perceived similarity of the loved one, self-disclosure, romance and passion are seen as being important in new relationships, while the more conjugal factors of security, loyalty, and mutual emotional behavioral investment in the relationship are viewed as sustaining love relationships over long periods of time. For example, according to Levinger and Snoek (1972) and Levinger (1974), "mutuality" sustains love relationships over time and exists when partners (a) share knowledge of each other, (b) assume responsibility for each other's satisfaction, and (c) share private norms governing their relationship. Two processes are seen as being important for mutuality to exist: (a) interpersonal discovery and disclosure, and (b) the emotional and behavioral investment that the partners have put into their common bond. This emotional and behavioral investment results in a sense of loyalty or "pair communality," which sustains the relationship over time.

The second theme in the literature on the developmental nature of love relationships comes from family sociologists who have suggested that there are at least two basic marital types: the institutional type and the companionship (Hicks and Platt, 1970). The institutional relationship is tradition-oriented, with loyalty and security being primary elements of the relationship. In the traditional relationship, normative rules for behavior are sex-differentiated along traditional lines. The husband's role is held to be the more instrumental, while the wife's role

is more expressive (Parsons and Bales, 1955). The companionship relationship, by contrast, places greater emphasis on the affective aspects of the relationship, including passion, expressions of love, rapport, communication, and respect. A number of studies (Cuber and Harroff, 1965; Deutscher, 1962, 1964; Feldman, 1964; Pineo, 1961; Rollins and Feldman, 1970) suggest that, over time, tradition may replace companionship as the primary bonding force in love relationships. In his 20-year longitudinal study, Pineo (1961) found that declines in marital satisfaction from youth to middle age were related to declines in companionship, demonstrations of affection and passion, common interests, consensus and communication. Using retrospective data obtained from interviews, Cuber and Harroff (in Broderick, 1971) described a similar shift in the nature of stable love relationships from youth to middle age. Based on her review of the literature, Troll (1971) concluded that marital interaction between older couples is dominated by three themes not present (or present to a much lesser extent) at earlier ages: decrease in passion and intimate conversation and increased concern with health. Consistent with Troll (1971), Deutscher (1962, 1964), Feldman (1964) and Rollins and Feldman (1970) reported that postparental couples experience a new freedom in later life and a different form of interpersonal relationship which is calmer, more objective, more secure, less energetic and less passionate.

In addition to age differences in the characteristics of satisfying relationships, theoretical and empirical literature also indicates that there are important sex differences in the expression of love and sources of satisfaction in love relationships (Harlow, 1971; Hicks and Platt, 1970). Research suggests that marital satisfaction is significantly related to the presence of traditional role expectations and behavior in the marriage, with men being the "instrumental" or "task" specialists and the women being the "socio-emotional" specialists in relationships (Aller, 1962; Cutler and Dyer, 1965; Hicks and Platt, 1970; Luckey, 1960; Rubin, 1970; Stuckert, 1963; Westley and Epstein, 1960).

The purpose of this research was to describe age and sex differences in the characteristics of satisfying love relationships using data obtained from 102 happily married young adult, middle-aged, and older adult couples who described the characteristics of their current love relationships by completing a 108-statement Q-sort of love experiences. Based on the review of the literature, it was hypothesized that (1) passion and communication would be relatively more important to love in young adulthood, while emotional security and loyalty would become relatively more important to love with advancing age, and (2) women would emphasize emotional security, communication and loyalty more in their love relationships, while men would place more emphasis on sexual passion.

Method

Procedure

Couples were nominated to participate in the study by individuals who knew them well and who described them as being (a) happily married, (b) very much in love, and (c) as having a really satisfying love relationship. These nominations were solicited by a letter sent to several hundred people working at the University of Southern California.

Typically, nominated couples were contacted by telephone, the study was described to them, and a time was arranged to meet with the couple. At the appointed time, the first author spent a few minutes getting acquainted and then the procedure for completing the Q-sort of love experiences was explained. To minimize the tendency subjects might have to respond in socially desirable ways, the following information was given to the subjects: (1) the researcher was interested in learning what being in a love relationship was really like to them; (2) there was no right or wrong way to sort the cards on the Q-sort; (3) the researcher believed they knew more about what being in love was like than anyone else, and (4) all information they provided would be kept strictly confidential. Each subject completed the Q-sort at his or her own pace and most people were able to finish within 40 min.

Subjects

A total of 102 married couples, divided equally into three age-groups, young adult, middle-aged adult, and older adult, participated in the study. The mean age of the young adult group (n = 68) was 28.2 years, with the "couple age" (average age of the husband and wife) ranging from 22.5 to 33.3. The mean age of the middle-aged group (n = 68) was 45.4, with the "couple age" ranging from 36.5 to 56.5. For the older adult group (n = 68), the mean age was 64.7 years and the "couple age" ranged from 57.5 to 83.5. For young adults, middle-aged adults and older adults, the mean number of years married was 4.7, 20.5, and 37.4, respectively. 198 of the subjects were white, 6 were black. Subjects were from the middle or upper-middle class and were well-educated. All of the subjects had at least a high-school education, and a majority had some college education.

Subjects in all age-groups were similarly employed in professional occupations or in skilled technical or clerical work. 28% of women were housekeepers and 3% of the sample were students. 17% of the older participants considered themselves presently retired. 36% of the sample identified themselves as Protestant; 19% were Jewish; 15% were Catholic; and 3% had no religious identification.

65% of young adults had no children, whereas only 12 and 9% of the middle-aged and older couples, respectively, were childless. For young, middle-aged and older adults, the mean number of children resulting from the marriage was 0.5, 2.4, and 2.3, respectively. A number of the lovers were in second marriages. 10, 15 and 4% of young, middle and older subjects were once divorced, respectively. 3% of older subjects were once widowed.

A self-rating of current satisfaction with their relationship showed that similar and high degrees of satisfaction (mean of 8.2 on a 10-point scale) was reported by individuals in all age-groups.

Measuring Instrument

A 108-statement Q-sort of love experiences was used as a measure of the relative importance of six different "components of love": Communication, Sexual intimacy, Respect, Help and play behaviors, Emotional security, and Loyalty. Table I describes the content of the six rating categories and gives a sample statement for each. The task for each subject was to rate each statement in terms of how well it described his or her current love relationship. Subjects were given a cardboard display with pockets which were arranged into an 11-category forced-distribution continuum, and were instructed to sort the 108 statement cards into the pockets according to the procedure outlined by Stephenson (1959). The complete set of 108 statements and a detailed description of the procedure for sorting has been described in a previous paper (Reedy, 1977). Briefly, a rating of (0) meant that a statement was not at all characteristic of the subject's current love relationship, while a rating of (10) meant that a statement was very characteristic of the current love relationship. Husbands and wives each completed their own Q-sort independently and men and women were given identical sets of cards to sort, except that pronouns were appropriately different for each sex. Scores for each subject for each of the six components of love categories were computed by taking the means of the ratings for the 18 statements reflecting each category.

The Q-sort used in this study was a

TABLE 1
Description of Categories in the Q-sort of Love Experiences

Component of love	Meaning	Sample statement
Communication	honest communication, self-disclosure, good listener	'He (she) finds it easy to confide in me.'
Sexual intimacy	physical and sexual intimacy, excitement, and/or tenderness	'We try to please each other physically.'
Respect	respect, understanding, patience, tolerance	'We share common goals for our lives.'
Help and play behaviors	common interests, shared activities, helpful, supportive	'We spend a great deal of time together.'
Emotional security	affection, trust, caring, concern, security	'I really feel I can trust him (her).'
Loyalty	commitment to the future of the relationship	'The future is sure to be perfect as long as we are together.'

modified version of an original 144-item Q-sort used in a previous study (Neiswender, 1975; Neiswender-Reedy et al., 1975, 1976). Details of the development and modification of the original card sort have been previously reported (Neiswender, 1975; Reedy, 1977). Briefly, the 144 statements used in the original card sort were selected from an initial set of over 300 statements derived from the theoretical and empirical literature on love and reflected a wide variety of possible experiences people might have in love relationships. The 144 statements selected for use in the initial Q-sort were those which were consistently classified by independent raters as reflecting one of the six possible components of love. For the present research, the Q-sort was modified to (1) reduce the set of statements to a more manageable number; (2) eliminate the statements which were not related to their intended category as judged from inter-item correlations and item-total score correlations, and (3) maintain or improve the internal consistency reliability of the items reflecting each category. The modified Q-sort of love experiences used

with the current sample of 204 subjects showed an overall internal consistency (Schaie and Heiss, 1964) of 0.90 and the internal consistency reliabilities using Cronbach's (1951) coefficient alpha for the six components of love rating categories were as follows: sexual intimacy, 0.83; loyalty, 0.79; communication, 0.69; emotional security, 0.56; respect, 0.55; and help and play behaviors, 0.46.

Packets containing the Q-sort cards, the Q-sort sorting board, a background information questionnaire, a self-rating of current satisfaction with the relationship index, and a set of instructions for completing the Q-sort were given to each subject.

Results

Mean scores and standard deviations for the six components of love categories for the three age-groups and for men and women are presented in Tables 2 and 3. A 3 (Age) × 2 (Sex) multivariate analysis of variance was performed to test for age and sex differences in the characteristics of satisfying love rela-

TABLE 2

Mean Scores and Standard Deviations by Age for Components of Love Ratings

Age-group		Component of love categories					
		emo-tional security	respect	help/play	com-muni-cation	sexual intimacy	loyalty
Young adult	$\overline{X}$	6.04	6.00	4.78	5.41	4.52	3.20
(n = 68)	SD	0.70	0.76	0.64	0.87	0.87	1.01
Middle-aged adult	$\overline{X}$	6.17	5.92	4.83	5.02	4.60	3.47
(n = 68)	SD	0.78	0.67	0.59	0.83	1.08	0.94
Older adult	$\overline{X}$	6.46	5.82	4.89	4.93	4.08	3.78
(n = 68)	SD	0.58	0.64	0.71	0.80	1.15	0.94
All ages		6.22	5.91	4.83	5.12	4.40	3.48
(n = 204)		0.71	0.69	0.65	0.85	1.06	0.99

TABLE 3
Mean Scores and Standard Deviations by Sex for Components of Love Ratings

Sex		Component of love categories					
		emo- tional security	respect	help/ play	com- muni- cation	sexual intimacy	loyalty
Male	$\overline{X}$	5.99	5.88	4.92	5.14	4.41	3.62
(n = 102)	SD	0.66	0.72	0.64	0.88	1.02	1.01
Female	$\overline{X}$	6.45	5.94	4.75	5.11	4.39	3.35
(n = 102)	SD	0.68	0.67	0.65	0.83	1.11	0.96
Both sexes	$\overline{X}$	6.22	5.91	4.84	5.12	4.40	3.48
(n = 204)	SD	0.71	0.69	0.65	0.85	1.06	0.99

tionships. The scores for five of the components of love categories, including communication, sexual intimacy, respect, emotional security and loyalty were used as the dependent variables in the analysis. To deal with the ipsative nature of the Q-sort and the resulting dependency of the nth score on the other ratings, the help and play behaviors category was omitted from the analyses since it was the category with the lowest internal consistency reliability.

The overall tests of significance for age and for sex, using Wilk's criterion (likelihood ratio test) were highly significant ($p < 0.001$). The F values, using Rao's approximation, were 3.58 and 6.15 for age and sex, respectively. Table 4 shows the significant univariate F ratios for the effects of age and sex. The age × sex interaction was not found to be significant.

Age and the Component of Love Ratings

As Table 4 indicates, univariate F tests showed significant age differences ($p < 0.01$) for the emotional security, communication, sexual intimacy and loyalty ratings. Post-hoc comparisons, using Duncan's Multiple Range procedure, showed

TABLE 4
Summary of Analysis of Variance for the Effects of Age and Sex on the Components of Love Ratings: Significant Univariate F-ratios (n = 204)

Effect	Component of love categories			
	emotional security	communication	sexual intimacy	loyalty
Age	7.53**	6.36**	4.83**	6.26**
Sex	25.12**			4.27*

Degrees of freedom, age = (2,198), sex = (1,198), age × sex = (2,198), * $p < 0.05$, ** $p < 0.01$.

that older lovers had significantly higher ratings (p < 0.05) for emotional security and loyalty and significantly lower ratings for sexual intimacy compared to the young adult and middle-aged groups. Also, young adults had a significantly higher rating (p < 0.05) for communication compared to the middle-aged and older groups. The mean scores for each age-group for the six components of love are plotted in Figure 1. In addition to depicting age differences, the figure also points to the similarities between age-groups in the nature of love. The results showed that the rank order of importance of the six components of love was the same for all three age-groups. For all age-groups, emotional security was ranked first, followed by respect, communication, help and play behaviors, sexual intimacy and loyalty.

Sex and the Component of Love Ratings

As Table 4 indicates, univariate F tests showed significant sex differences for emotional security (p < 0.01) and for loyalty (p < 0.05). Post-hoc comparisons, using Duncan's Multiple Range procedure, indicated that women had a significantly higher rating for emotional security (p <

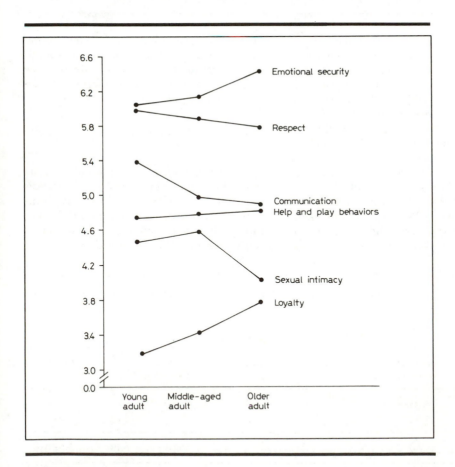

FIGURE 1
Mean scores by age for component of love categories.

0.05), while men rated loyalty significantly more characteristic of love compared to women ($p < 0.05$).

Discussion

Age Differences in the Nature of Satisfying Love Relationships

The findings clearly indicate that the nature of love in satisfying relationships is different at different ages. Both developmental and generational differences explanations for the findings can be proposed. Viewed from a developmental perspective, the results offer support for the first major theme found in the developmental literature on love. The results support the notion that passion and sexual intimacy are relatively more important in early adulthood whereas tender feelings of affection and loyalty are relatively more important to later-life love relationships (Bissett, 1970; Cuber and Harroff, 1965; Freud, 1949; Harlow, 1971; Levinger, 1974; Levinger and Snoek, 1972; Maslow, 1954; Orlinsky, 1972; Rollins and Feldman, 1970; Shostrom, 1972; Rosow, 1957; Winch, 1967). As predicted, older lovers rated emotional security and loyalty as relatively more characteristic of love and sexual intimacy as relatively less characteristic of love compared to the young and middle-aged adult groups. The relatively lower rating for sexual intimacy by older lovers is consistent with other research (Kinsey et al., 1948, 1953; Masters and Johnson, 1968; Neiswender-Reedy, et al., 1975, 1976; Pfeiffer et al., 1969; Troll, 1971; Verwoerdt et al., 1969). General slowing of the nervous system, decreased vigor and energy, lack of novelty in the sexual relationship, illness, the belief that older people "should not" be sexually interested or active, and generational differences in the importance of sex are possible explanations for the reduced importance of sexual intimacy in the relationships of older lovers.

An interesting finding was that sexual intimacy was equally important for young and middle-aged lovers. The implication is that, at least in satisfying relationships, passion maintains its importance in love through middle-age, and only becomes relatively less characteristic of later-life love.

The results indicated that young adult lovers rated communication as relatively more characteristic of their love relationships compared to middle-aged and older lovers. This finding, combined with the finding that emotional security and loyalty were rated as being relatively more characteristic of love in later life, offers support for the second major theme in the literature on the developmental nature of love. The present research suggests that over time satisfying love relationships are less likely to be based on intense companionship and communication and more likely to be based on the history of the relationship, traditions, commitment and loyalty (Cuber and Harroff, 1965; Hicks and Platt, 1970; Rollins and Feldman, 1970). The findings are consistent with the findings of other research that communication and companionship experiences are more characteristic of new relationships (Cuber and Harroff, 1965; Driscoll et al., 1972; Rollins and Feldman, 1970), while loyalty, sacrifice, dependency (Driscoll et al., 1972), conventionality (Troll, 1971), emotional commitment and interdependency (Levinger, 1974; Levinger and Snoek, 1972), and the more traditional, calm, and loyalty-based styles of loving (Cuber and Harroff, 1965) become more characteristic of love in later adulthood.

Finally, the findings of age differences in the importance of communication, loyalty, and emotional security offer a developmental perspective to the concept of "mutuality" proposed by Levinger (1974) and Levinger and Snoek (1972). According to Levinger and Snoek, mutuality in intimate relationships has two aspects: (1) the need for knowledge of the other, which leads to self-disclosure and intimate communication, and (2) pair communality, which involves the sense of interdependency and the development of private norms governing the relationship, and emotional and behavioral commitment. The findings suggest that communication and disclosure are most central to mutuality or attachment early in a relationship, while the sense of pair communality, interdependency, loyalty, security and commitment are primary bonding forces in satisfying relationships which have weathered many years. Whereas communication may be more critical to a sense of attachment, bonding and behavioral control in young relationships, the bonding force in long-standing relationships may come more from the history of the relationship itself, leading to a greater sense of loyalty and security in the relationship.

In addition to these developmental explanations, a generational differences explanation is equally possible. The belief that satisfaction in love means loyalty and being able to depend on one another is likely to be more consistent with the early socialization experiences, attitudes, and beliefs of today's older generation. By contrast, while today's young adult lovers place considerable emphasis on honest communication and self-disclosure in relationships, they are less likely to emphasize loyalty or long-term commitment as essential ingredients in satisfying relationships.

It is also possible that the age differences found reflect the effects of selective sampling, selective survival, and/or selective attrition of couples who become dissatisfied, divorced or widowed over the years. A further difficulty in interpreting the findings is that age is confounded with length of time in the relationship ($r = 0.89$, $p < 0.001$). The result is that it is impossible to know the extent to which it is age or length of time in the relationship which accounts for the differences found between young, middle-aged and older lovers.

Finally, beyond the age differences found, there were remarkable similarities between the generations in the nature of satisfying love relationships. At any age, emotional security was ranked as most important to love, followed by respect, communication, help and play behaviors, sexual intimacy and loyalty. From these results, it is clear that there is considerably more to love than sex and that at any age, emotional security — feelings of concern, caring, trust, comfort and being able to depend on one another — is the most important dimension in the bond of love. The results suggest that a new historical trend in the quality of relationships may be emerging. Whereas in the past decade there was great emphasis on individual freedom and independence in the context of a relationship, this research suggests a possible historical shift toward an increasing emphasis on security, fidelity, trust, and commitment in relationships.

Sex Differences in the Nature of Love

The findings suggest that the nature of love in satisfying relationships is different for men and women. As predicted, women rated emotional security as relatively more characteristic of love compared to men. No support was found for the predictions that women would emphasize communication more than men or that men would emphasize sexual intimacy more. Directly opposite to prediction, men rather than women were found to rate loyalty as more characteristic of their love relationship.

The findings offer some support for the notion that role performance along traditional sex-differentiated lines is important to satisfaction in relationships (Hicks and Platt, 1970). Women's relatively higher ratings for emotional security suggest that women are more dependent on their love relationships for comfort, safety, support and security. This greater involvement of women in the relationship is consistent with the conceptualization of women as "expressive" and "socio-emotional" specialists in relationships (Blood and Wolfe, 1960; Harlow, 1971; Hicks and Platt, 1970; Levinger, 1974; Parsons and Bales, 1955).

The findings of no sex differences for sexual intimacy and communication contradicts other research (Kinsey et al., 1948, 1953; Pfeiffer et al., 1969) and suggests that an important criterion for a satisfying relationship may be the presence of an equal amount of interest and involvement in sexual intimacy and verbal communication by both partners.

Contrary to prediction, men rather than women were found to rate loyalty as being relatively more characteristic of love. The greater loyalty of the male in satisfying relationships is consistent with the notion that an important role for men in satisfying relationships is that of protector, guardian of family, hearth, and home (Harlow, 1971).

In conclusion, given the limitations of the cross-sectional design, the findings of this research offer empirical support for two of the themes which appear in the literature on the developmental nature of attachment and satisfying heterosexual love relationships across the adult life span. First, the results suggest that passion and sexual intimacy are relatively more important to the bond of love in young adulthood, whereas tender feelings of affection and loyalty are relatively more important to attachment between older men and women. Second, the findings also support the notion that, over time, love relationships are less likely to be based on intimate self-disclosure and verbal communication and are more likely to be based on feelings of security, commitment, and loyalty. Beyond the age differences which were found in the characteristics of satisfying love relationships, there were remarkable similarities between the generations in the nature of attachment. From young adulthood to later maturity, emotional security was ranked the most important dimension of love, followed by respect, communication, help and play behaviors, sexual intimacy, and loyalty. Finally, the sex differences found suggest that in satisfying relationships at any age, women emphasize emotional security more, men rate loyalty to the relationship more highly, and both men and women equally emphasize the importance of sexual intimacy and communication.

References

Aller, F. A.: Role of self-concept in student marital adjustment. Family Life Coord. 11: 43–45 (1962.)

Antonucci, T.: Attachment: a life-span concept. Hum. Dev. 19: 135–142 (1976).

Bissett, W. H.: An investigation and synthesis of the literature on love and the creation of a developmental model of love processes; thesis University of Maryland (unpublished, 1970).

Blood, R. D. and Wolfe, D. M.: Husbands and wives: the dynamics of married living (Free Press, Glencoe 1960).

Bowlby, J.: Attachment and loss, vol. 1: Attachment (Hogarth Press, London/Basic Books, New York 1969).

Broderick, C. B.: Beyond the five conceptual frameworks: a decade of development in family theory; in Broderick, A decade of family research and action (National Council on Family Relations, Minneapolis 1971).

Broderick, C. B.: Quoted in the L. A. Times, January 15, 1979.

Burgess, E. W. and Wallin, P.: Engagement and marriage (Lippincott, Chicago 1953).

Cronbach, L. J.: Coefficient alpha and the internal structure of tests. Psychometrika 16: 297–303 (1951).

Cuber, J. F. and Harroff, P. B.: The significant Americans (Appleton-Century, New York 1965).

Cutler, B. R. and Dyer, W. G.: Initial adjustment processes in young married couples. Social Forces 44: 195–201 (1965).

Deutscher, I.: Socialization for post-parental life; in Rose, Human behavior and social process (Houghton-Mifflin, Boston 1962).

Deutscher, I.: The quality of post-parental life. J. Marriage Family 26: 52–60 (1964).

Driscoll, R.; Lipetz, M. E., and Davis, K. E.: Parental interference and romantic love: the Romeo and Juliet effect. J. Pers. Soc. Psychol. 24: 1–10 (1972).

Feldman, H.: Development of the husband-wife relationship. Preliminary report. Cornell Studies of Marital Development (Cornell University, Ithaca 1964).

Freud, S.: Instincts and their vicissitudes; in Jones, The collected papers of Sigmund Freud (Hogarth Press, London 1949).

Harlow, H. F.: Learning to love (Albion, San Francisco 1971).

Hartup, W. and Lempers, J.: A problem in life-span development. The interactional analysis of family attachment; in Baltes and Schaie, Life-span developmental psychology. Personality and socialization (Academic Press, New York 1973).

Hicks, M. W. and Platt, M.: Marital happiness and stability: a review of the research in the sixties. J. Marriage Family 32: 553–573 (1970).

Kalish, R. A. and Knudtson, F. W.: Attachment versus disengagement: a life-span conceptualization. Hum. Dev. 19: 171–181 (1976).

Kerckhoff, A. C. and Davis, K. E.: Value consensus and need complementarity in mate selection. Am. Sociol. Rev. 27: 295–303 (1962).

Kinsey, A. C.; Pomeroy, W. B., and Martin, C. E.: Sexual behavior in the human male (Saunders, Philadelphia 1948).

Kinsey, A. C.; Pomeroy, W. B.; Martin, C. E., and Gebhard, P. H.: Sexual behavior in the human female (Saunders, Philadelphia 1953).

Knudtson, F. W.: Life-span attachment: complexities, questions, considerations. Hum. Dev. 19: 182–196 (1976).

Lee, J. A.: The colors of love (Bantam Books, New York 1977).

Levinger, G.: A three-level approach to attraction: toward an understanding of pair relatedness; in Houston, Foundations of interpersonal attraction (Academic Press, New York 1974).

Levinger, G. and Snoek, J. J.: Attraction in relationship: a new look at interpersonal attraction (General Learning Press, New York 1972).

Lowenthal, M. F. and Haven, C.: Interaction and adaptation: intimacy as a critical variable. Am. social. rev. 33: 20–30 (1968).

Luckey, E. B.: Marital satisfaction and its association with congruence of perception. Marriage Family Living 22: 49–54 (1960).

Maslow, A. H.: Motivation and personality (Harper & Row, New York 1954).

Masters, W. H. and Johnson, V. E.: Human sexual response: the aging female and the aging male; in Neugarten, Middle age and aging (University of Chicago Press, Chicago 1968).

Neiswender, M. E.: Age differences in the experience of love in adult men and women; thesis University of Southern California, Los Angeles (unpublished, 1975).

Neiswender-Reedy, M. E.; Birren, J. E., and Schaie, K. W.: Age and the experience of love in adulthood. Am. Psychol. Ass. Meeting, Chicago 1975.

Neiswender-Reedy, M. E.; Birren, J. E., and Schaie, K. W.: Love in adulthood: beliefs vs. experience. Am. Psychol. Ass. Meeting, Washington 1976.

Orlinsky, D. R.: Love relationships in the life cycle: a developmental interpersonal perspective; in Otto, Love today: a new exploration (Association Press, New York 1972).

Parsons, T. and Bales, R. F.: Family, socialization and interaction process (Free Press, Glencoe 1955).

Pfeiffer, E.; Verwoerdt, A., and Wang, H. S.: The natural history of sexual behavior in a biologically advantaged group of aged individuals. J. Geront. 24: 193–198 (1969).

Pineo, P. C.: Disenchantment in the later years of marriage. Marriage Family Living 23: 3–11 (1961).

Reedy, M. N.: Age and sex differences in personal needs and the nature of love: a study of happily married young, middle-aged and older adult couples; thesis University of Southern California, Los Angeles (unpublished, 1977).

Rollins, R. and Feldman, M.: Marital satisfaction through the life span. J. Marriage Family 32: 20–27 (1970).

Rosow, I.: Issues in the concepts of need complementarity. Sociometry 20: 216–233 (1957).

Rubin, Z.: Measurement of romantic love. J. Pers. soc. Psychol. 16: 265–273 (1970).

Shostrom, E.: The human encounter; in Otto, Love today: a new exploration (Association Press, New York 1972).

Schaie, K. W. and Heiss, R.: Color and personality: a manual for the color pyramid test (Huber, Berne 1964).

Spitz, R. A.: Hospitalism: an inquiry into the genesis of psychiatric conditions in early childhood. Psychoanal. Study Child 1: 53–74 (1945).

Stephenson, W.: The study of behavior (University of Chicago Press, Chicago 1959).

Stuckert, R. P.: Role perception and marital satisfaction: a configurational approach. Marriage Family Living 25: 415–419 (1963).

Troll, L. E.: The family of later life: a decade review. J. Marriage Family 33: 263–290 (1971).

Troll, L. E. and Smith, J.: Attachment through the life span: some questions about dyadic bonds among adults. Hum. Dev. 19: 156–170 (1976).

Verwoerdt, A.; Pfeiffer, E., and Wang, H. S.: The natural behavior in senescence: patterns of sexual activity and interest. Geriatrics 24: 136–154 (1969).

Weinraub, M.; Brooks, J., and Lewis, M.: The social network: a reconsideration of the concept of attachment. Hum. Dev. 20: 31–47 (1977).

Westley, W. A. and Epstein, N. B.: Family structure and emotional health: a case study. Marriage Family Living 22: 25–27 (1960).

Winch, R. F.: Another look at the theory of complementary needs in mate selection. J. Marriage Family 29: 756–762 (1967).

6

Men and Women

For most members of our culture, adult development occurs within the context of the nuclear family, the most important aspect of which is the marriage relationship. But for many of us marriages do not seem to endure the increased span of life. Divorce rates are skyrocketing, to the extent that a marriage today has only an even chance of remaining intact ''until death do them part.'' Attitudes about marriage — from ''wives as property,'' through ''marriage involves love,'' to ''marriage should be a positive experience'' — have changed along with the divorce rate, and this attitude change may in part be causal. The economic liberation of women, however, is probably a more basic cause. The feminist movement in general has contradictory effects on marriage, disrupting it by promoting the independence of women, but at the same time supporting it by allowing a more intimate union based on something more solid than the traditional sex-role stereotypes. Children similarly have twofold effects, on the one hand ''validating'' a marriage by creating a family, on the other increasing the stress on the marriage with increased work loads and reduced intimacies. Divorce is a very stressful experience for most people, affecting both psychological and physical health.

The selection by *Arthur J. Norton* and *Paul C. Glick* focuses on the societal changes in social and economic variables that probably affect divorce rates. They point out that the traditional sources of marriage disruption (young age at marriage, low education, low occupation, and low income) have been changing in a more positive direction, while divorce rates have nevertheless continued to rise. This development is then accounted for by the reduction in negative sanctions for divorced persons as well as the greater ease of obtaining divorces. The authors also make clear that the rising divorce rate should not be seen as an indictment of marriage per se, since remarriage rates have remained high. They finally point out that both marriage and divorce behavior are highly sensitive to major political and economic events.

According to national surveys, over two-thirds of boys and one-half of girls have experienced sexual intercourse by the age of nineteen. Young married people make love on average about three times a week, middle-aged couples about once a week. Barring chronic illness, most elderly couples remain sexually active well into their seventies. There is marked decline of sexual activity after the age of seventy-five, but individuals as old as 100 or more are still capable of expressing love in a physical way.

Changes in sexual attitudes are correlated with changes in sexual activity. Negative attitudes toward sex among the elderly result in jokes about and unfair stereotyping of the "dirty old man" and the postmenopausal woman. Older women often experience vaginal dryness after menopause, but compensatory lubricants are available and effective. The most common reason for an inactive sex life among elderly couples is male impotence, which may have a variety of physical and psychological causes: physical and psychological therapies are generally effective.

Alex Comfort, widely known for his scientific and popular writings on human sexuality, addresses issues relating to sexual behavior in late life in our third selection. He discusses the sexual physiology of later life, surveys statistical data on sexual activity in older persons, counseling on sexual dysfunction and the management of organic impotence. Comfort points out that sexual dysfunction is common at all ages, but that there is no age at which it is too late to restructure one's sexual attitudes, and concludes with the statement that many couples may for the first time have achieved sexual communication and fulfillment in their seventies.

Because of the difference in life expectancy between men and women and because of the tendency for men to marry younger women, it is inevitable that most women will experience widowhood. The disruption of the marriage through death of a spouse is typically accompanied by grief, loneliness, and financial hardship for the female survivor. Nevertheless, it is thought that the economic and social emancipation of women should have generally beneficial effects on the lives future generations of widows, who will have more money of their own and better ideas about how to use it, on their own. *Helena Znaniecki Lopata* in the fourth selection examines some of the societal factors involved in the life-span disruption caused by widowhood. To do so she gives a historical review of the role of widowhood in the life of women, identifies changes in social roles of women in modern societies, and then surveys the social roles in the lives of widows. Both immediate and long-term consequences of widowhood are related to the widow's previous roles in her marriage as a social unit.

Additional Suggested Readings

Bernard, J. *The future of marriage.* New York: Bantam, 1973.
   A classic volume considering the transformations of our attitudes and mores about marriage, and examining the many different scenarios that might characterize the marital arrangements of the future.

Butler, R. N., & Lewis, M. *Sex after sixty: A guide for men and women for their later years.* New York: Harper and Row, 1976.
   A literate treatment of what until recently has been a taboo topic, giving thoughtful attention to the problem of social stereotypes about sexual behavior in later life as well as suggestions on how to deal with them.

Marital Instability in America: Past, Present, and Future

ARTHUR J. NORTON and PAUL C. GLICK

A demographic analysis of trends in marital instability may be made with better factual support if the study features divorce rather than separation. Annual statistics on divorce for the country as a whole are published from vital records, but corresponding statistics on "separation events" are not available. Moreover, the annual statistics on currently separated persons that are published by the Bureau of the Census regularly show a far larger number of women than men reported as separated. In addition, the statistics on separation would be much more meaningful if there were a way of identifying, at a given point in time, the separated persons who would eventually become divorced, those who would become reconciled in their existing marriages, and those who would remain separated. Accordingly, the present discussion focuses attention primarily on probable connections between changes in dissolution of marriage by divorce and concurrent changes in social and economic variables that tend to have an impact on divorce in the United States.

Historical Perspective

Historical trends in American marriage can be traced in terms of patterns of change in vital rates since the early twentieth century. The historical movement of the incidence (or rates) of first marriage, divorce, and remarriage is well documented in the publications of the National Center for Health Statistics (Plateris, 1969; Hetzel and Cappetta, 1971) and in the publications of the U. S. Bureau of the Census (1976, 1977c). Table 1 and Figure 1 show the estimated annual rates of first marriage, divorce, and remarriage in terms of three-year averages for the periods 1921–1923 through 1975–1977. The first marriage rates were calculated with single women under 45 years old as the base, the divorce rates with married women under 45 as the base, and the remarriage rates with widowed and divorced women under 55 as the base. These bases include about 99 percent of all single women who marry, 85 percent of all married women who became divorced, and 80 percent of all women who remarry in a given year.

When observing trends in marital behavior over an extended period of years, rates for women are generally used because they present a more consistent population

Source: Norton, A. J., & Glick, P. C. Marital instability in America: Past, present and future. In G. Levinger & O. C. Moles (eds.), *Divorce and separation: Context, causes, and consequences.* New York: Basic Books, 1979, pp. 6–19. Copyright 1979 by the Society for the Psychological Study of Social Issues. Reprinted by permission.

TABLE 1
Number and Rate of First Marriage, Divorce, and Remarriage: United States, Three-Year Averages, 1921–1977

Period	First Marriage		Divorce		Remarriage	
	Thousands	Rate[a]	Thousands	Rate[b]	Thousands	Rate[c]
1921–23	990	99	158	10	186	98
1924–26	992	95	177	11	200	99
1927–29	1,025	94	201	12	181	84
1930–32	919	81	183	10	138	61
1933–35	1,081	92	196	11	162	69
1936–38	1,183	98	243	13	201	83
1939–41	1,312	106	269	14	254	103
1942–44	1,247	108	360	17	354	139
1945–47	1,540	143	526	24	425	163
1948–50	1,326	134	397	17	360	135
1951–53	1,190	122	388	16	370	136
1954–56	1,182	120	379	15	353	129
1957–59	1,128	112	381	15	359	129
1960–62	1,205	112	407	16	345	119
1963–65	1,311	109	452	17	415	143
1966–68	1,440	107	535	20	511	166
1969–71	1,649	109	702	26	515	152
1972–74	1,662	103	907	32	601	151
1975–77	1,508	85	1,070	37	646	134

[a] First marriages per 1,000 single women 14 to 44 years old.
[b] Divorces per 1,000 married women 14 to 44 years old.
[c] Remarriages per 1,000 widowed and divorced women 14 to 54 years old.
   Source: Glick and Norton, 1977.

base, less affected than rates for men by fluctuations in service in the armed forces. For example, in 1977 there were roughly 8 million veterans who had served in the armed forces during the Vietnam War and who subsequently returned to civilian life. Although many men in the armed forces marry before or during their military service, those who live in barracks or who are stationed overseas are not covered by the Bureau's Current Population Survey.

The trend lines for each of the three measures display similar patterns until the late 1950s. Each shows low points during the economic depression years of the 1930s, followed by a gradual climb that accelerates to peak levels in the immediate post-World War II period, succeeded by declines into the 1950s. The first marriage rate continued its rather steady decline through the 1960s and into the 1970s; it has now reached a low level similar to that shown for the latter years of the Depression. However, both the divorce rate and the remarriage rate turned upward around 1960 and increased dramatically during the ensuing decade; by then, the divorce and remarriage rates were higher than any previously recorded for this country. The rising remarriage rate might reasonably be interpreted as a corollary of

FIGURE 1
Rates of first marriage, divorce, and remarriage for U.S. women:
1921–1977

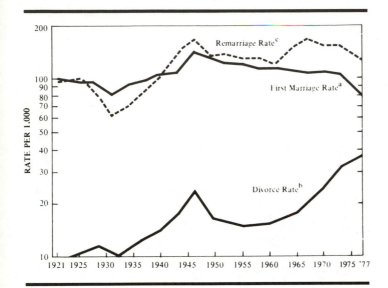

^a First marriages per 1,000 single women 14 to 44 years old.
^b Divorces per 1,000 married women 14 to 44 years old.
^c Remarriages per 1,000 widowed and divorced women 14 to 54 years old.

the rising divorce rate, inasmuch as an estimated four out of every five divorced persons eventually remarry (U. S. Bureau of the Census, 1976). Since 1970, however, the divorce rate has continued its steep upward movement while the remarriage rate has declined sharply.

Another measure of the rise in marital disruption was derived from a special survey on marital history conducted by the Bureau of the Census in June 1975. The assumption was made that the future divorce experience of young women will produce future increments in the percentage divorced that are the same as those for successively older co-

horts of women in the early 1970s. Using this procedure, a projection was made indicating that four out of every ten marriages contracted by women born between 1945 and 1949 would eventually end in divorce, a figure substantially higher than the estimated three out of every ten for women born just a decade earlier (U. S. Bureau of the Census, 1976). However, the decrease in marriage rates and increase in divorce rates cannot continue indefinitely because the pool of divorce eligibles would eventually be used up.

Inspection of the rates in Figure 1 confirms the undeniable connection between the disposition of people to marry, divorce, or remarry and the contingencies of particular time periods. Apparently the Depression of the 1930s caused a downturn in all of these vital rates, whereas the period of relief and release experienced in the immediate post-World War II era gave rise to a temporary but substantial increase in all these rates. The rapid increase in the level of divorce during the 1960s came at a time when divorce laws were being liberalized and when the social structure at large was in a transitory state, a time when basic social institutions, values, and ascribed roles were being questioned and alternatives were being tested. Some have characterized the 1970s as an era of social uncertainty marked by a movement toward individualism which could be partly responsible for the continued increase of the divorce rate and the overall decline of the marriage rate.

Among the variables that have been shown to have an impact on marital stability are age at first marriage and level of education and income. Reports on several studies have demonstrated that divorce after first marriage was inversely related to age at marriage, education, and income considered separately, but without regard to interaction between these variables (Glick and Norton, 1977; U. S. Bureau of the Census, 1977c). Bumpass and Sweet (1972) reported a high correlation between early age at marriage and marital instability among white ever-married women under the age of 45. They also reported that the effect of education on marital disruption is minimal when age at marriage is controlled, but early marriage and low educational attainment are closely correlated among white women (U. S. Bureau of the Census, 1973a).

The results of the 1970 census showed that among persons who first married between 1901 and 1970, the proportion of men who were divorced after their first marriage was more than twice as high for those who married before the age of 20 as for those who

married in their late 20's; it was more than twice as high for women who married before 18 as for those who first married in their early 20's (U. S. Bureau of the Census, 1973a). A substantial proportion of persons who married at a later age had delayed marriage while attending college. Among both men and women who had ever married, the highest proportion who were known to divorce after their first or last marriage (or both) was of those with an incomplete high school education (U. S. Bureau of the Census, 1972).

Similarly, men on the lower rungs of the income ladder in 1970 had a greater proportion known to have been divorced than those with higher incomes. For females, however, the opposite was true; divorced women with a relatively high personal income level tended to delay remarriage or to remain unmarried, whereas those with relatively low incomes tended to remarry within a short time (U. S. Bureau of the Census, 1972).

The median age at first marriage for men and women in the United States was first computed for 1890 when it was 26.1 years for men and 22.0 years for women (U. S. Bureau of the Census, 1977a). There was a fairly constant decline in the ages at which men and women married from the turn of the century to the mid-1950s. The median ages at first marriage for men and women in 1956 were the lowest recorded in the history of the United States — 22.5 years for men and 20.1 for women — and remained at about the same level until the mid-1960s. Since that time, however, the median age at first marriage for both men and women has increased by approximately one year, so that in 1976 the median for men was 23.8 years and that for women 21.3 years.

The increasing tendency during the last decade for men and women to marry at later ages may reflect, in part, the demographic phenomenon referred to as the "marriage squeeze" (Parke and Glick, 1967). This phenomenon depends on the presence of two conditions: (a) a changing level of births, and (b) a traditional differential in the ages at which men and women marry for the first time. In the United States both conditions have been present. Women have traditionally married men a few years older than they are, and the birth rate in this country has been subject to fluctuations that varied from moderate to radical.

The squeeze situation in the mid-1960s arose because more women 18 and 19 years old in 1965 were entering the marriage market than were men 20 and 21 years old in that year; the women were members of large post-World War II birth cohorts, whereas the eligible or targeted men were members of smaller birth cohorts conceived before the end of the war. In addition, the scarcity of young men was intensified by the large increase in the armed forces during the war in Vietnam and the simultaneous acceleration of college enrollment.

Available data suggest that the squeeze was partially resolved by a process whereby many young women in the vanguard of the "baby boom" either postponed marriage as they moved into adulthood or ultimately married men more nearly their own age.

Thus, the marriage squeeze may have been an initial contributor to the establishment of a pattern of delaying marriage, particularly among young women, beyond ages traditionally considered the prime ages for first marriage. The extent of this delay may best be seen by pointing out that in 1960, 28 percent of women 20 to 24 years old were single, but in 1976 the corresponding proportion single had increased to 43 percent (U. S. Bureau of the Census, 1977a).

Concomitant developments associated with this delay in marriage among young adults are far-reaching. Especially among young women, postponement of marriage has occurred along with the pursuit of advanced education or career experience, as a prelude to entering into a family living situation, thus providing women with the basis

for role expansion beyond that of wife and mother. Increasing postponement of first marriage has been a major aspect of the emerging pattern of transitional living arrangements among many young adults after they leave their parental homes, but before they marry conventionally and form their own families.

College enrollment of both men and women increased markedly during the sixteen years from 1960 to 1976, after being fairly stable during the 1950s. For example, 11 percent of all persons 20 to 24 years old in 1960 were enrolled in college as compared to 23 percent in 1976. For men aged 20 to 24, the enrollment rate was more than half again as large in 1976 as in 1960, and for women in their early 20's it more than doubled in those sixteen years (U. S. Bureau of the Census, 1964, 1977b). In addition, there was a sharp upturn in the labor force participation of young women over the last quarter century, a change almost entirely due to the participation rates of young married women. Among women 20 to 24 years old who were married and living with their husbands, about 26 percent were members of the labor force in 1950, as compared to 57 percent in 1975; similarly, for women 25 to 29 years old of the same marital status the comparable increase was from 22 percent in 1950 to 50 percent in 1975.

Most of the socioeconomic indicators discussed here which have been traditionally linked to marital discord (young age at marriage, low education, low occupation, and low income) have been changing in directions that would lessen their impact on marital stability. Why, then, has the level of divorce continued to rise? The current period of adaptation and resocialization regarding the roles of women, particularly as they apply to marriage and family living, will not be passed through easily, especially for those who have deeply entrenched traditional views. In the long run, the broadening of work-and-marriage experience seems likely to encourage women to develop a greater self-perception as players of multiple roles and to result in familial and societal gains; however, the short-term effects may be somewhat disruptive. A married woman — especially one who works in a different establishment from that of her husband — may become economically self-sustaining and, therefore, be more in a position to dissolve a marriage that does not seem viable. Likewise, this circumstance can lessen the economic constraints on men confronted with a potential divorce.

Perhaps more important than this practical consideration is the more theoretical and general impact on marital stability of the need for couples to adjust to a traditional institution (marriage) that is in a state of transition. No longer are the roles of husbands (breadwinners) and wives (homemakers) simply complementary and clearly defined or agreed upon. Marital and familial responsibilities between partners now often overlap; this may generate conflict, which promotes eventual separation. As time goes on, however, expectations regarding marital roles and relationships should become more consistent with "real-world" experiences. In other words, if and when the period of structural transition of the institution of marriage should end, the adjustment to be made by the partners should ideally create less of an emotional strain.

Recent Changes in Divorce

The upsurge of divorce in this country during the last ten years has been stimulated by a growing acceptance of the principle that divorce is a reasonable alternative to an unhappy marriage. While negative sanctions have diminished, so too have the legal and economic constraints of obtaining divorces (see Levinger, 1979). The reform of divorce laws has resulted in the shortening of the required period of residence in the state and the required period of separation.

Moreover, all but a few states have adopted some form of no-fault divorce and most of the other state legislatures are attempting to incorporate this feature into their legal codes.

Whether or not some of the states have what can be termed "true" no-fault divorce is subject to debate. Yet the fact remains that there has been widespread official recognition of the need to overhaul the legal machinery involved in the granting of divorce decrees so that the demands of citizens will be more equitably accommodated. Implicit in most of the administrative changes is a reduction of the economic costs involved in divorce. In addition, the availability of free legal service has enabled many impoverished families to finalize disrupted marriages by divorce.

The elimination of many barriers previously inhibiting divorce has been relatively recent and rapid. Consequently, it seems reasonable to speculate that at least part of the recent increase in the divorce rate may represent an acceleration in the timing of divorces that, under previous conditions, would have been spread over a longer number of years. If this is the case, one might expect the rate of divorce either to eventually decline or at least to level off. In fact, after a decade of steady annual increases during which the divorce rate per 1,000 population doubled (from 2.5 in 1966 to 5.0 in 1976), the rate has begun to level off. Thus, as of February 1978, the twelve-month divorce rate had remained stable at 5.0 for 20 of 23 consecutive months.

At the same time, of course, the argument can be made that the ease with which divorces can now be obtained will likely continue to bring an early termination of many marriages that are near the borderline of viability.

The increased incidence of divorce in this country has occurred at all socioeconomic levels; yet data from the 1970 census (U. S. Bureau of the Census, 1972) for ever-married persons 35 to 44 years old showed the proportion of persons ever-divorced remains clearly the highest for relatively disadvantaged groups. This age group is used for comparative purposes because its members are old enough to have experienced most of their lifetime marriages and divorces and yet are young enough to reflect much of the impact of the recent changes discussed above.

Men 35 to 44 with low incomes and with a low level of educational attainment were more likely to have been divorced than men with higher incomes and educational attainment. Women of this age range with low educational attainment showed the same pattern of greater likelihood of divorce. Also, a higher proportion of women 35 to 44 years old who were in the labor force in 1970 were known to have been divorced than were women of the same age who were not in the labor force — although information is not available to show how many of these women had already entered the labor force well before the time they became divorced. The proportion currently divorced at each survey date is relatively small because this measure disregards the fact that about three-fourths of the women and five-sixths of the men remarry after divorce. Furthermore, the 1970 census shows that 3.8 percent of all ever-married men and 5.0 percent of all ever-married women were currently divorced at the time of the census, but that more than 14 percent of both the men and the women were known to have obtained a divorce. This means that only a small proportion of the adults who had ever experienced a divorce were still divorced at the time of the 1970 census. Nevertheless, revealing comparisons showing the convergence of divorce by social level between 1960 and 1970 can be made by the use of proportions of persons currently divorced.

Between these two dates the proportion divorced among men 35 to 44 years old tended to converge among the educational, occupational, and income groups. As men-

tioned above, men in the upper status groups continue to have a below average proportion divorced (but not remarried). However, the rate of increase in the proportion divorced was more rapid among men in upper as compared to lower status groups between 1960 and 1970 (U. S. Bureau of the Census, 1967, 1972). These results become even more meaningful when one recognizes that the extent of remarriage among the divorced is greater for men at the upper status levels than for men at the lower levels.

Among women 35 to 44 a general trend toward convergence among status levels of the proportion divorced also occurred between 1960 and 1970, but in the opposite direction from that for men. The proportion divorced among all women 35 to 44 went up by nearly one-half during the 1960s; however, among women who were professional workers or who were in the highest income categories (where the proportion divorced for women, unlike men, has been characteristically quite high), the percentage divorced rose by a smaller proportion than among other women. Thus, for upper status women the percentage divorced was converging with that for other women by increasing more slowly than the average, whereas for upper status men the percentage divorced was converging with that for other men by increasing more rapidly than the average.

Data from the June 1975 marital history survey indicate that the trend toward convergence in the proportion divorced among different levels of educational achievement for both men and women has continued through the first half of this decade (U. S. Bureau of the Census, 1977c). In fact, by 1975 the proportion divorced for men with one or more years of college had risen to the level for all other men. However, men and women with four years of college still had the lowest proportions divorced.

The important conclusion that can be drawn from these trends is that the recent increase in divorce has been pervasive with regard to social and economic level, but that socioeconomic differences in divorce are now smaller than they used to be.

Although blacks and whites display generally similar patterns of divorce by social and economic characteristics, the incidence of divorce is uniformly higher for blacks than for whites. In 1975, 25 percent of ever-married black men and women 35 to 44 years old were known to have had a divorce. The comparable figures for white men and women in 1975 were 19 percent and 21 percent, respectively.

A further indication of the higher rate of marital disruption among blacks than among whites is the difference in the proportions of people reporting themselves as separated but not divorced. In 1976, 10 percent of all black men 35 to 44 and 15 percent of all black women 35 to 44 were reported as separated, whereas 2 percent of white men and 4 percent of white women of the same age were separated. Between 1960 and 1976, the proportion separated and the proportion divorced increased among both black and white men and women 35 to 44 years old; however, the rate of increase for each race and sex group was larger for the proportion divorced (Glick and Mills, 1975; U. S. Bureau of the Census, 1977a). This finding brings out the significant fact that decreasing proportions of those with marital problems are leaving them legally unresolved and increasing proportions are resolving them by becoming divorced.

Despite an increasing similarity in the form of marital disruption displayed by the two racial groups, major differences continue to exist. These differences seem to be linked with both the overall level of disruption and the promptness with which divorce and remarriage follow separation. Findings from the 1975 marital history survey showed that although whites and blacks had similar durations of first marriage before divorce, white men and women remarried much

sooner than their black counterparts (U. S. Bureau of the Census, 1976). But even though blacks have a generally higher rate of disruption through marital discord than whites, the estimated rates of disruption for those with racial intermarriages is even greater. Using data from the 1960 and 1970 censuses, Heer (1974) reported ''clearly the black-white marriages are shown to be less stable than racially homogeneous marriages.''

Another characteristic reflecting recent changes in divorce is the presence of children among couples involved in a divorce. The U. S. National Center for Health Statistics reports that an estimated 1,123,000 children were involved in divorces and annulments in 1975, an average of 1.08 children per decree. Although the estimated number of children involved in all divorces has been increasing steadily (logically enough, given the overall increase in divorce), the average per decree has been declining in recent years; in 1964 the average reached a peak of 1.36 children per decree. Perhaps the main reason for the decline is the recent decrease in the birth rate. Other reasons include a slight increase in the proportion childless at divorce, although six out of ten divorces in 1975 were among couples who had children and the estimated interval between marriage and divorce decreased from 7.2 years in 1960 to 7.0 years in 1968, and to 6.5 years in 1975. The estimate of the percentage of divorcing couples who were childless was published by the U. S. National Center for Health Statistics on the basis of data reported for the divorce-registration area (DRA) which in 1975 was composed of 29 participating states, each of which used closely conforming certificates of divorce or annulment and cooperated in testing for completeness and accuracy of divorce registration.

The recently declining fertility rate may have contributed to the rise in the divorce rate. Women with small families are more likely to be in the labor force and, therefore, financially independent of their husbands. And as family size has declined, the proportion of children in the family who are of preschool age has declined. This additional development has tended to free the time of the potential divorcee for work outside the home.

Among other factors which may have influenced the recent rise in divorce are an increase in premarital conceptions and the so-called "incentives" toward family disruption found in the present welfare system. As Davis (1972) points out, premarital conception is conducive to divorce, and an increase in family formation in such circumstances tends to increase the divorce rate. The impact of the welfare system on family and marital disruption is open to debate. Various social scientists have studied this problem and have arrived at conflicting or opposing conclusions (Cutright and Scanzoni, 1973; Honig, 1973; see also Moles, 1979).

Other possible contributors to the rising level of divorce include the prevalence of intergenerational divorce, the effects of intergenerational mobility up and down the socioeconomic ladder, and the problems faced by veterans returning from the war in Vietnam. The returnees are of special interest because they came back from an unpopular war and were sometimes made to feel that they personified the official war policy. This atmosphere must have affected their ability to adjust to traditional life styles.

Since divorcing has always been largely confined to relatively young adults, the lifetime behavior of persons born during the high fertility years that spanned the period between 1947 and the early 1960s will be of major import in this context. As we have pointed out, "the experience of this population subgroup — largely because of its size — is different from that of any other in the age spectrum. During their lives they have faced, and will continue to face, greater

competition for fewer opportunities than their predecessors did or their successors will. They are finding that traditional institutions have not been able to respond effectively to their needs, and their patterns of action have begun to deviate in certain ways from past norms" (Norton and Glick, 1976). Thus, it is clear that their decisions involving marriage, divorce, and living arrangements will have a profound and lasting impact on future lifestyles. As the vanguard of this group has reached adulthood, patterns of change have already become evident. Along with a postponement of first marriage has been an increased tendency to leave parental homes in favor of setting up nonfamily households either as lone individuals or as sharing partners. The latter group includes the often-discussed "living together" couples who have more than doubled in number since 1970 (Glick and Norton, 1977). Whether these developments represent a prelude to entering into more traditionally conventional family living arrangements or herald the beginnings of a new concept of family living is not clear.

Conclusions and Future Perspectives

The variables influencing the marriage and divorce behavior of people in this country are numerous and tend to interact with one another. In general, socioeconomic variables such as education and income which have been regarded as predictor variables have become less discriminating.

Youthful marriage has been found to correlate with a high divorce rate: there is an approximately two-year younger average age at first marriage among those who obtain a divorce before middle age than those whose first marriages remain intact to this age (U.S. Bureau of the Census, 1973a). However, one can only speculate about the future level of age at marriage and its continued usefulness as a short-term predictor of marital stability or instability.

There seems little doubt that a basic transformation of the institution of marriage is underway and that many variables are influencing the direction of the change. This transformation appears to be predicated largely on a restructuring of the roles which men and women play within the traditional boundaries of marriage and family living. Some people can confront this type of change and adapt to it without much difficulty; others find that the process of adjustment is much more difficult and leads ultimately to marital conflict and disruption. Fundamental to the understanding of this change is a comprehension of the redefinition of expectations of individuals involved in a modern marriage.

"More personal fulfillment in marriage," a common current demand, is an elusive idea which can take many forms depending on the individuals involved. It is possible that one of the problems encountered by marriage partners is that many men and women have inadequately defined the happiness they are seeking. This is not an unusual situation in a period of transition. New ideas and values can only gradually replace old or traditional ones. Thus, eventual general recognition and acceptance of a newly established set of rules for marriage may cause expectations to conform to "real-world" conditions. Viewed in this manner, the high rate of divorce can be interpreted as an understandable pursuit of happiness. This does not necessarily mean that people are marrying and subsequently divorcing without care or concern, but rather that there exists a new awareness that a marriage which is subjectively viewed as not viable can be dissolved and — hopefully — replaced by a more nearly viable one. The means to introduce alternatives are ever so much more widely available today than they were 20 years ago. As Davis (1972) puts it, current marriage "is not premised on the condition that wedlock is rigidly determined for the rest of life."

To the extent that the married state — but not necessarily being married only once — is a preferred status, some available indicators may portend a relatively optimistic future for married life. The high divorce rate coupled with a high remarriage rate appears to signal a strong desire for a compatible marriage and family life. In support of this line of reasoning, findings from two separate studies conducted by the Institute for Social Research of the University of Michigan (ISR, 1974) on subjective social indicators (studies of people's perceptions of the quality of life) showed that "marriage and family life are the most satisfying parts of most people's lives and being married is one of the most important determinants of being satisfied with life." Thus, there appears to be a generally high regard for the ideal of being married and living as a family member, but a current inability on the part of growing numbers of couples to achieve and sustain a high level of satisfaction in this sphere without making at least a second attempt.

One might hypothesize that the recent trends away from early age at marriage and the decline in the remarriage rate are indicative of more careful mate selection among those marrying for the first time, as well as among those marrying for a second or subsequent time. Perhaps more persons considering marriage now are influenced by the large number of current marital failures and consequently are making their own decisions in a more serious and cautious manner. At the same time, however, others may be postponing divorce because of the presently uncertain national economic situation. As previously stated, both marriage and divorce behavior appear to be sensitive to major political and economic events. The practical financial constraints imposed by an economy troubled by inflation and recession, coupled with a high unemployment rate, may force individuals contemplating divorce to rethink their positions and possibly to make marital adjustments based on more tolerance of the status quo between themselves and their partners for a longer time, if not permanently.

Speculations regarding the future of marriage and divorce in this country are tenuous; nonetheless, the authors have

called attention to those factors which seem likely to have an impact on marital behavior over the next several years. Additional observations of marital behavior from year to year will surely provide the students of marriage and the family with better explanations of the current situation than anyone can give with confidence today.

References

Bumpass, L., & Sweet, J. Differentials in marital instability: 1970. *American Sociological Review,* 1972, 37, 754–766.

Cutright, P., & Scanzoni, J. Income supplements and the American family. In Joint Economic Committee (Ed.), *The family, poverty, and welfare programs: Factors influencing family instability.* (Studies in Public Welfare, Paper no. 12, part 1). Washington, D.C.: U.S. Government Printing Office, 1973.

Davis, K. *The American family in relation to demographic change.* Report of the U.S. Commission on Population Growth and the American Future, C. F. Westoff & R. Parke, Jr. (Eds.), vol. 1, Demographic and Social Aspects of Population Growth. Washington, D.C.: U.S. Government Printing Office, 1972.

Glick, P. C., & Norton, A. J. Marrying, divorcing, and living together in the U.S. today. *Population Bulletin,* 1977, 32 (5).

Glick, P. C., & Mills, K. M. Black families: marriage patterns and living arrangements. Proceedings of the W. E. B. DuBois Conference on American Blacks, 1975.

Heer, D. M. The prevalence of black-white marriage in the United States, 1960 and 1970. *Journal of Marriage and the Family,* 1974, 36, 246–258.

Hetzel, A. M., & Capetta, M. Marriages: trends and characteristics. National Center for Health Statistics. *Vital and Health Statistics,* Series 21:21. Washington, D.C.: U.S. Government Printing Office, 1971.

Honig, M. The impact of welfare payment levels on family stability. In Joint Economic Committee (Ed.), *The family, poverty and welfare pro-*

grams: Factors influencing family instability. (Studies in Public Welfare, no. 12, part 1). Washington, D.C.: U.S. Government Printing Office, 1973.

Institute for Social Research (ISR). Measuring the quality of life in America. *Newsletter,* 1974, 2 (2), University of Michigan.

Levinger, G. A social psychological perspective on marital dissolution. In G. Levinger & O. C. Moles (Eds.), *Divorce and separation.* New York: Basic Books, 1979.

Moles, O. C. Public welfare payments and marital dissolution: A review of recent studies. In G. Levinger & O. C. Moles (Eds.), *Divorce and separation.* New York: Basic Books, 1979.

Norton, A. J., & Glick, P. C. The changing American household. *Intercom,* 1976, 4 (10), 8–9.

Plateris, A. A. Divorce statistics analysis: United States 1964 and 1965. National Center for Health Statistics. *Vital and Health Statistics,* Series 21:17. Washington, D. C.: U.S. Government Printing Office, 1969.

Parke, R. Jr., & Glick, P. C. Prospective changes in marriage and the family. *Journal of Marriage and the Family,* 1967, 29, 240–256.

U.S. Bureau of the Census. *1960 Census of Population.* School Enrollment. Final Report PC(2)-5A. Washington, D.C.: U.S. Government Printing Office, 1964.

U.S. Bureau of the Census. *1960 Census of Population.* Marital status. Final Report PC(2)-4E. Washington, D.C.: U.S. Government Printing Office, 1967.

U.S. Bureau of the Census. *1970 Census of Population.* Marital status. Final Report PC(2)-4C.

Washington, D.C.: U.S. Government Printing Office, 1972.

U.S. Bureau of the Census. *1970 Census of Population.* Age at first marriage. Final report PC(2)-4D. Washington, D.C.: U.S. Government Printing Office, 1973. (a)

U.S. Bureau of the Census. *1970 Census of Population, vol. 1, part 23—Massachusetts.* Washington, D.C.: U.S. Government Printing Office, 1973. (b)

U.S. Bureau of the Census. *Current Population Reports.* Series P-20:297. Number, timing and duration of marriages and divorces in the United States. Washington, D.C.: U.S. Government Printing Office, 1976.

U.S. Bureau of the Census. *Current Population Reports.* Series P-20-306. Marital status and living arrangements. Washington, D.C.: U.S. Government Printing Office, 1977. (a)

U.S. Bureau of the Census. *Current Population Reports.* Series P-20:309. School enrollment — social and economic characteristics of students. Washington, D.C.: U.S. Government Printing Office, 1977. (b)

U.S. Bureau of the Census. *Current Population Reports.* Series P-20:312. Marriage, divorce, widowhood, and remarriage by family characteristics. Washington, D.C.: U.S. Government Printing Office, 1977. (c)

Sexuality in Later Life

ALEX COMFORT

In our culture many features of individual sexual behavior, and particularly dysfunctional sexual behavior, are sustained by attitudinal and factual misinformation. Many features of "aging" as observed in the same culture are equally examples not of natural change but of role-playing, based on a combination of folklore and prejudice: old people, being "known" to be feeble, ineducable, unintelligent and asexual, are under pressure to assume these attributes as a result of chronological age, although age itself produces no such necessary effects.

In the sexual behaviors of older persons, both streams of misinformation merge, and it is only recently that, as in the case of intelligence and learning-power, the sexual capacities of older people, and their changes with age, have been objectively examined. Asexuality in later life is now known to reflect, as a rule, not loss of capacity but absence of opportunity, particularly in older women, whose sexual capacity changes little with time, but whose social opportunities are culturally and demographically curtailed compared with those of older men.

As in all fields of sexual study, it is the male, moreover, who is so far documented. His sexual "capacity" is marked by, and dependent on, an externally obvious erection, and research has been heavily motivated by male anxiety in this regard. The excess of discussion devoted in this paper to male sexuality represents the distribution of available facts. At least one standard textbook of geriatric medicine omits the discussion of female sexuality altogether, despite the large excess of women over men at higher ages.

The most interesting feature of the changes in human sexual physiology and performance induced by age is that, apart from the programmed termination of fertility at the menopause, the changes are minimal. The folkloristic view of old age as impotent, uninterested in sexuality, and nonfunctional in this regard are the expression of a self-fulfilling prophecy.

Sexual Physiology in Later Life

The slowing of response which is a characteristic feature of many processes in old age affects male sexuality. After the age of 50, purely psychic erection occurs with decreasing frequency: morning erection is retained, but erections during REM sleep become less frequent as age advances. Erec-

Source: Comfort, A. Sexuality in later life. In J. E. Birren & R. B. Sloane (eds.), *Handbook of mental health and aging.* © 1980, pp. 885–892. Reprinted by permission of Prentice-Hall, Inc., Englewood Cliffs, N.J.

tion comes to depend increasingly on direct penile stimulation, and takes longer to induce than in young males. The angle of the erect penis to the abdominal wall becomes greater (90 degrees as against 45 degrees in youth) and the retraction of the testes by the cremaster during orgasm tends to disappear. At the same time, orgasm ceases to occur at every act of intercourse.

These changes are extremely variable in different individuals. They are commonly present by age 60, but show little further advance after that age. Their importance is that while sexually active and unanxious men, accustomed to prolonged sexual play in intercourse, experience them as a gain in control, men whose stereotype of virility depends on hurried erection followed by hurried intercourse may interpret them as loss of function, and the consequent anxiety may induce failure of erection. It can be said with confidence that impotency is never a consequence of chronological age alone. Its increasing frequency with age is due to a variety of causes — the increasing prevalence of diabetes, of which impotency may be the presenting symptom; an increase in incidence of vascular-autonomic insufficiency; the increasing prevalence of conditions such as hypertension and prostatic enlargement, which may lead to problems through the use of medications (notably reserpine and some ganglion blocking agents) of which impotency is a side effect; needlessly radical or negligent surgery; and above all the social expectation of impotence in age, reinforced by loss, ill health or aging of the partner, obesity, increased sensitivity to alcohol, and the increased incidence of depression which may readily be missed. In spite of these factors, objective organic loss of potency verified by penile plethysmography is relatively rare at high ages. What may be seen is an exacerbation of psychosexual problems common to younger males, a loss of interest in sexual activity reflecting loss of competitive self-esteem,

and a welcome excuse to abandon sexual activity in those for whom it has been a source of guilt or anxiety. High-dominance individuals, whose sexual attitudes have always been positive, normally remain both potent and active throughout life. Androgen deficiency does not appear to play any large part in declining sexual function, nor are androgen supplements usually indicated as a remedy for potency problems. Fertility may also persist in males into the tenth decade.

Erectile physiology in males is extremely complex (Weiss, 1972), involving central inhibitory control over a segmental reflex as well as autonomic pathways. At the effector level, blood is diverted into the corpora cavernosa by ''polstern'' in the arteriola walls, and the venous outflow is regulated to maintain circulation in the corpus while keeping the vascular spaces full. It is this complexity which makes the search for a pharmacological or mechanical means of inducing erection extremely difficult, and provides a number of points at which drugs such as ganglion-blocking agents, and diseases of the vessels and nervous pathways, can interfere. What is striking is that the only specifically age-determined change in erectile physiology is the slowing of the general response cycle, combined perhaps with a less perfect regulation of the inflow and outflow of blood in the corpora, since the erection of older males often appears less hard than that in youth, though it is fully adequate. The final preorgasmic hardening of the glans, due to a rise in the venous pressure which precedes the discharge of semen, is also less evident with age.

Of conditions which become more common with age and may impair erection, diabetes is probably the most important. The specific organic interference is probably real, although psychogenic factors are almost invariably present and removal of these can often restore adequate function (Renshaw, 1978). The impairment is believed to be an alteration of vasomotor function rather than an effect of diabetic neuropathy, since diabetes can present an impotence. A similar function loss can occur in simple obesity, but other factors are present — in some cases, diabetes appears to produce not impotence but retrograde ejaculation (Anon, 1967).

It is important to recognize that human sexual function, especially in the male, is *highly idiosyncratic,* both in the interrelation of erectile and ejaculatory functions and in the response of these functions to drugs. Medication which produces impotence in one individual may produce nonejaculation or retrograde ejaculation in another and be without sexual effects in a third, as has been documented in the case of thioridazine (Mellaril®) (Kotin, Wilbert, Verburg, and Soldinger, 1976). Some of these differences may be attributable to different metabolism or accessibility of neurotransmitters, to differences in sympathetic-parasympathetic balance, or to central effects of the drugs; in general, however, idiosyncracy becomes more marked with age. It is likely that drugs similarly affect the incidence and intensity of tumescence, lubrication and orgasm in women. These changes are almost wholly undocumented, reflecting the excessive cultural concentration on male sexual physiology, where it is possible and indeed necessary to observe the outward and visible signs of an inner and spiritual grace.

Increased libido and erectile performance are relatively rare and are equally idiosyncratic effects of medication. While in women androgen administration almost invariably increases libido, some men remain potent and active in the virtual or total absence of testicular androgen; in others androgen may be highly effective in lowering the threshold of excitation, while in yet others it fails to produce any evident result. This simply reflects the fact that there is more than one cause of nonerection, since hypogonadal and so-called ''climacteric'' impotency respond to testosterone better than impotence

that appears to be mainly a learned behavior (Cooper, Ismail, Smith, and Loraine, 1970). The role of androgen in the cycle of male excitation is not known — it is at least as likely that high levels result from, rather than cause, sexual arousal (Kraemer, Becker, Brodie, Doering, Moos, and Hamburg, 1976). The overall but irregular decline in cross-sectional androgen levels with increasing age reported by various authors represents not only endogenous reduction, but also quite probably the reduction in sexual activity imposed by a social ''script'' (Gagnon and Simon, 1973). Where androgen is effective, some of its effects may be due to an increase in general well-being.

It seems probable that while female arousal can be reliably mediated by androgen, the control of male arousal depends on an earlier neurohormone, probably an oligopeptide. Increased libido is consistently seen in males after administration of human chorionic gonadotrophin HCG (Amelar and Dubin, 1977) for infertility. This action probably depends upon follicle stimulating hormone (FSH) or luteinizing hormone (LH) or both, or on a specific peptide as yet unidentified, paralleling the arousal seen in animals of both sexes after intraventricular luteinizing hormone releasing hormone (LHRH) injection. This group of responses is insufficiently investigated to yield present clinical application, but the irregular response to androgen in cases of reduced male libido clearly indicates that other mechanisms are involved. To the extent that libidinal decline is not wholly sociogenic, it may be integrated with the hypothalamic aging ''clock.''

One possibly important factor is the fact that in both sexes fantasy — which in humans is probably the most important single determinant of sexual arousal — is said to decline with age (Cameron and Biber, 1973). Whether the sixfold decline in speed of erection observed between the ages of 20 and 50 is involved with autonomic changes, role-playing, or both, remains to be explored (Solnick and Birren, 1977), but its importance for function is negligible in sexually educated males.

The overriding importance of social roles, social expectation, and socially propagated anxiety, together with the uniqueness of the uses of sexuality made by humans explain why comparative studies, both on age changes and on hormone effects (e.g., in rats), are not only irrelevant but often actively misleading, and have been for the most part omitted from this review. The most relevant primate findings would deal with the interrelation between sexuality and dominance in agonic species — old age has not yet been adequately observed in large hedonic apes — because of the uneasy mixture in humans of sexual components drawn from these two modes ("baboonery" and "chimpanism"). The role of the penis as a dominance signal, and erection as both invitation and dominance display, is clearly critical to the Freudian view of human psychosexual development, which is atypical in that human males are recognized as competitive when they reach walking age, and the dominance releaser is sited in the genitalia themselves, not in the secondary sexual characters (Comfort, 1960). The instability of the human erectile capacity in the face of social stress may in part represent an adaptation which favors the most dominant male, the result brought about in mice by the resorption of fetuses in pregnant females when a less-dominant mate is displaced (Bruce and Parkes, 1961). In humans, it is in the period of middle-age, when status is most threatened, that erectile physiology undergoes the most marked changes, and latent sexual dysfunctions commonly become manifest.

The persistence of sexual function in women has been less fully documented, but the evidence suggests that, excluding fertility, sexual function persists even more effectively in women than in men. There is no evidence that the capacity for orgasm declines at any age, and women are known to have become orgasmic for the first time at ages in excess of 80. Coition may be impaired by vaginal atrophy, lack of lubrication, kraurosis, and pelvic abnormalities such as cystocele and prolapse, but these are remediable conditions. The most common reasons for sexual inactivity in older women are social convention, lack of a partner, or role-playing. There is a clinical impression, unconfirmed by published statistics, that regular intercourse and orgasm are at least as effective as exogenous estrogens in preventing secretory and atrophic changes.

Statistical Studies of Sexual Activity in Older Persons

It has to be remembered that statistical studies of sexuality among the aged include subpopulations of people who are unanxious and sexually active, people who are already anxious, and people who have become dysfunctional at younger ages; few attempts have been made to separate these groups. Sex means very different things to different people — some regard it negatively or are relatively uninterested throughout life, while others appear to think of nothing else. One still encounters couples who have unsuccessfully attempted coitus a few times (lack of success is usually a result of vaginismus) and have remained married but abstinent without ever repeating the attempt or seeking advice. The valuation of sex in society is undergoing rapid change, chiefly in the direction of increased expectation. Some older people will retain the generally anxious or reticent valuation which they learned in their youth, while others, late in life, will be influenced by their culture to recoup experiences they have missed. Yet others, who have always ignored society's reservations, will continue to treat sex with their own valuation. The physician needs to distinguish these, in order to help the second while not impertinently evangelizing the first.

In spite of a high incidence of psychogenic dysfunction at all ages, it appears that older people have always been sexually active but have kept their own counsel. Pearl (1930) recorded nearly 4 percent of males aged 70–79 having intercourse on the average of every third day, and a further 9 percent having it weekly. The figures of Kinsey, Pomeroy, and Martin (1948) indicate a decline in coital frequency with age, but these figures were cross-sectional and unrelated to opportunity or attitude. Finkle, Moyers, Tobenkin, and Karg (1959) questioned 101 men, aged 56 to 86, who were ambulant patients with no complaint likely to affect potency, and found 65 percent under age 69 and 34 percent over 70 "still potent" on their own statement, with two out of five over 80 averaging at least 10 copulations a year. On further inquiry it transpired that some in the sample had never had intercourse. Others, though potentially potent, had no partner. In the over-70 group, the main reasons given for inactivity were "no desire" or "no partner." Of all men over 65, only three gave as a reason "no erection." Newman and Nichols (1960) questioned both sexes aged 60–93 and found 54 percent still active. No significant decline occurred under age 75. Over the age of 75, 25 percent were still active, the decrease being chiefly a result of illness of self or spouse. "Those who rated sexual urges as strongest in youth rated them as moderate in old age: most who described sexual feelings as weak to moderate in youth described themselves as without sexual feelings in old age" (Newman and Nichols, 1960). As in Pearl's study, evidence suggested that early starters of both sexes were late finishers.

Pfeiffer, Verwoerdt, and Wang (1968) at Duke University studied 254 people of both sexes. The median age for stopping "sexual activity" (presumably coitus, not masturbation) was 68 in men (range 49–90) and 60 in women, with a high of 81, the differences being partly attributable to the age differential between spouses. The figures for regular and frequent intercourse were 47 percent between the ages of 60 and 71 and 15 percent age 78 and over. Unlike other studies, this investigation was longitudinal. Over a five-year observation period, 16 percent of propositi reported a falling-off of sexual activity, but 14 percent reported an increase. This study strongly supports the view that what we are seeing is not so much an "age change" as the experience of a mixture of high- and low-activity individuals, in whom those whose sexual "set" is low for physical or attitudinal reasons drop out early, often with recourse to age as an excuse. Social pressure, ill health, lack of a socially acceptable partner, all take some toll among the others, but among the sexually positive and active aging itself abolishes neither the need nor the capacity for intercourse. Masters and Johnson (1970) have confirmed that many aging men who believed themselves impotent could have their condition reversed using the same therapeutic means effective with impotent younger males. A generation with high sexual expectations, exposed to modern attitudes and counseling and devoid of the expectation of decrepitude, will probably score a great deal higher.

Counseling of Sexual Dysfunction in Older Patients

Sexual counseling and therapy depend almost wholly on permission-giving and the correction of false or irrational attitudes towards sexuality. Sexual counseling in the old also involves the correction of false and irrational attitudes toward aging. Apart from the more rigid exclusion of physical and iatrogenic causes of impotency, and the recognition of intercurrent causes such as obesity and alcohol, the therapy of impotence in older men is the same as in younger, and depends on the removal of performance anxiety and the teaching of sexual attitudes which de-emphasize ''sex'' as a purely genital feat rather than an enjoyable interpersonal experience involving all parts of the body.

Sexual problems in later life include those which can occur at any age; those which have been present or latent throughout life and surface in the ''middle-age identity crisis'' as a result of the patient's mistaken belief that age involves automatic asexuality and infirmity; those which result from disease or its treatment; and those which arise — chiefly in women, who outlive men but are socially excluded from sexual appetency in later life — from isolation and lack of a receptive and socially approved partner. Of these, organic causes are the minority. As with other forms of activity, sexual intercourse once abandoned in later life becomes more difficult to resume. The physician needs to be aware of this risk and to avoid prescribing prolonged abstinence. This is especially true during convalescence from cardiac disease. The possibility of desexualization which may arise from the prohibition of intercourse for fear of a heart attack, contributes greatly to depression and demoralization, which is worse for the patient than the trifling exertion involved in gentle intercourse. Coition or masturbation to orgasm can be safely undertaken by any ambulatory patient, and should form a specific part of rehabilitation where inquiry shows sexual activity to have been of concern to the patient. Cardiac death or a stroke occurs more rarely during intercourse, especially marital intercourse, than during sleep. At another level of counseling, the physician will increasingly encounter older patients in good health who require advice and guidance in attempting to achieve greater sexual satisfaction than they experienced in youth, when permission and advice were less readily available. With the end of reproduction, the relational and recreational uses of sex become more, not less, important, and can enrich a period of life which society otherwise penalizes by exclusion from other value-giving activities.

Special geriatric problems are patterned by the changes in physiology already described. The male who attaches value to speed of performance or who regards direct genital stimulation as abnormal will become dysfunctional as a result of normal aging and will require reeducation. Males at all ages seem to fall into two types — those who, when stressed or overtired, run out of potency, and those who in similar circumstances run out of orgasm. The second of these reactions is aggravated by age, and further aggravated by several drugs, including guanethidine, tricyclic antidepressants and monoamine oxidase inhibitors. (Imipramine and phenelzine are effective agents in the treatment of premature ejaculation.) The man who fails to ejaculate vaginally at every act of intercourse can usually do so if masturbation is continued, but if this is done sufficiently often to maintain his previous frequency of orgasm, sensitivity to vaginal friction may be further lowered. Nonejaculation can appear suddenly in the partner of a woman who is undergoing hormone supplementation, as a result of excessive lubrication. This calls for adjustment of the dose of medication given to the woman. Interference with potency, ejaculation, or both is probably the commonest cause of noncompliance in the use of antihypertensives; sexual function is unaltered by thiazides and rarely affected by propranolol. Alcohol and tranquilizers can also derange sexual response more in the old than in the young. One special male problem is *widower's impotency,* occurring when an elderly man remarries after the death of a first wife; this is particularly seen when the first wife had a long terminal illness during which he has abstained from sexual intercourse. This compound of disuse atrophy, unfamiliarity and anxiety over the new partner, and guilt at relief over the death of the invalid responds to the same couple-counseling as does secondary impotence at younger ages. It should be stressed to the "impotent" patient that if he ever gets an erection, on waking, at masturbation, or as demonstrated by penile plethysmography, there is nothing organically wrong with the hydraulics. *Failure to hold erection* is usually the result of haste. The patient should be advised "not to attempt a landing until the nosewheel has locked in the down position"; this may require several minutes of oral or manual stimulation, and the spouse should be instructed in older male physiology.

If penile plethysmography is accompanied by measurement both of the basal and of the coronal penile circumferences, not a few cases of "failure to maintain erection" will be found to represent irregular filling due to an undiagnosed Peyronie's plaque (Karacan, 1978). Erectile difficulty in patients receiving propranolol for long periods should be investigated because of this possibility. *Prostatectomy* when competently performed will almost always result either in retrograde ejaculation or in some alteration of the sensation of climax. Incompetently performed, especially by the perineal route, it can produce impotency by denervation, calling for a prosthetic implant if function is to be restored. In any patient (the majority) where continued potency is an important contributor to self-evaluation, radical prostatectomy should never be rashly undertaken, and loss of potency following the relief of simple prostatic enlargement justifies a malpractice suit, unless (1) an adequate sexual history was taken preoperatively, and (2) careful rehabilitative therapy is initiated after the operation. Lack of these measures may well contribute more to prostatectomy im-

potence than the operative procedure. Patients should be warned to expect absence or reduction of ejaculation.

Although wholesale section of nerves and periurethral damage is responsible for impotency in perineal resection, the 5 percent — 40 percent incidence of impotency after transurethral resections is harder to explain (Finkle and Prian, 1966; Gold and Hotchkiss, 1969; Holgrewe and Valk, 1964). In some cases at least, anxiety over possible injury to potency aggravates the disturbance due to surgery. In other cases, what is described as "impotence" is actually an alteration of orgasmal feeling resulting from partially or wholly retrograde ejaculation. It is interesting that in fracture of the pelvis, urethral injury is the factor correlating most highly with subsequent impotence (King, 1975). Zohar and his coworkers (Zohar, Meiraz, Maoz, and Durst, 1976) found that surgical technique seemed to have little to do with post-prostatectomy impotence, but that in a prospective study it correlated highly with anxiety level, absence of explanation of the surgery, and low satisfaction with life. The problem of psychogenic versus surgically-induced impotence can be resolved by penile plethysmography during sleep, but this should be done both before and after surgery, since some apparently organic impotence predates the operation on which it is blamed.

Management of Organic Impotency

If potency has been irremediably damaged, usually by injudicious surgery, but sometimes also by disease, there are two therapeutic options.

By far, the best strategy is to instruct the patient in techniques of sex which do not involve full erection. Many men fail to realize that not only extragenital orgasm, but penetration, can often be obtained without erection (with the woman in the dorsal knee-chest position, for example, and especially with a multipara).

The choice of surgery depends far more on the patient's psychological investment in erection than on the need to attain orgasm with satisfaction to a partner. This investment is frequently great, and a prosthesis if properly inserted can sometimes abort a depressive illness or a general loss of interest in life. Insertion of a plastic rod prosthesis, which renders the penis permanently rigid, the baculum or os penis in some mammals, can make intercourse possible. The result is often cosmetic rather than truly restorative. In the very old, and in those who have vascular problems compromising healing or predisposing to thrombosis of the corpora, it can produce further problems, and the prosthesis may have to be removed. The Small-Carrion prosthesis (Small and Carrion, 1975) can be removed if function returns or problems arise from migration or buckling (Loeffler, 1977), and involves less surgery than the Furlow inflatable prosthesis where surgery is extensive (Furlow, 1977), with seven out of 36 patients requiring further surgery to correct mechanical problems. Prostheses should not be used as a cover for failure to adopt proper counseling techniques. They are best confined to patients in whom organic interference with erection has been demonstrated by plethysmography and the need for a tangibly stiff penis is paramount, since those prostheses are not without problems.

It should be reiterated that age alone is never a cause of impotency, that the management of impotency at all ages is identical, and that the only relevance of radical measures, such as the insertion of a prosthesis, to sexuality and age lies in the fact that diabetes and surgical assaults on the erectile mechanism increase in frequency at higher ages. At the same time, where potency has been damaged by a demonstrable lesion, age is not a contraindication for the attempt to restore it *secundum artem*. Even the extensive surgery involved in inserting Furlow's prosthesis has been successfully carried out in a man of 77 (Furlow, 1977). In impotence due to multiple sclerosis, the Small-Carrion prosthesis is preferable, since it does not hinder natural erection if the symptom remits (Loeffler, 1977). Penile prostheses cater, however, chiefly to male anxieties; partners have rarely been interviewed.

Androgen therapy has a chequered history in treating secondary impotence. Since androgen levels are rarely depressed in this condition and low androgen levels are not correlated with impotence, any action which exogenous androgens have is likely to result in lowering the threshold of response, or more probably in increasing general well-being. Administration of exogenous androgen has the disadvantage of serving to convince the patient that what is usually a behavioral problem can be cured by pills. If androgens are to be used, mesterolone ("Proviron" Schering) is probably the drug of choice, since it is not read by the hypothalamic sensor as a raised testosterone level, and does not inhibit endogenous hormone production.

The menopause is now known to result from the activity of the hypothalamic "clock," not exhaustion of ova. Cessation of the menses will affect sexual function adversely only in women for whom infertility is perceived as a loss of womanhood or of permission to experience sexual pleasure. In many women it marks a period of resexualization untroubled by anxiety over conception. The so-called "male menopause" is an inaccurate name for the middle-aged identity crisis general in our culture, which may affect sexual self-image but does not represent any radical change in endocrine patterns. It now seems proper to reject the cosmetic use of estrogens in menopausal women. Their value in the prophylaxis of osteoporosis is less than that of diet and exercise, and they should be reserved for the treatment of circumclimacteric symptoms such as hot flashes and given for a limited period only. When indicated for atrophic genital changes, topical application should be tried. Prolonged use of oral contraceptives can mask the menopause. Cessation of ovulation should never be assumed to have occurred, as unwanted pregnancy can occur in the fifth decade. On withdrawing the oral contraceptive for a test period, other birth-control means should be adopted if the spouse is fertile. In elderly women removal of pelvic impediments to coitus (caruncles, prolapsed viscera, injuries to the pelvic floor, stress incontinence) and decent and judicious cosmetic surgery can strikingly improve the sexual pleasure of both partners.

Summary

Human sexual response is normally lifelong unless compromised by ill health, anxiety, or social expectation. The role of the geriatrician is to foster the sexual response as a supportive and enriching part of continued experience without impertinent proselytizing. Patients require to be reassured against their own false expectations, the hostility of society, including children and potential heirs, and the officious interference or prudery of some health personnel. Old persons in institutions should enjoy so far as is possible the same freedom of sexual choice which adults enjoy in society at large, and should not be considered senile, or sedated, in response to the sexual anxieties of the staff.

Where a partner is not available, either temporarily or in general, masturbation has the same function which it has at all ages, that is, a relief of sexual tension, an enjoyable experience, and a means of maintaining function. Explicit discussion of its use with older patients may relieve anxiety caused by earlier prohibitions.

As with the disabled, group discussion among elderly couples and among the elderly in communal living situations is a valuable means of ventilating sexual anxieties and needs which they may otherwise lack the social permission to express. This discussion may be greatly valued, especially by those who have all their lives lacked the opportunity for rational dialogue on sexual subjects. It has to be remembered that sexual dysfunction is very common at all ages, resulting from culture-based anxiety, and that there is no age at which it is too late to restructure attitudes in this regard. There are many couples in their 70s who have for the first time achieved communication and fulfillment which had previously been denied them.

References

Amelar, R. D., and Dubin, L. 1977. Human chorionic gonadotrophin therapy in male infertility. *J. Amer. Med. Assn.*, 237, 2423.

Anon (editorial). 1967. Retrograde ejaculation in diabetes. *J. Amer. Med. Assn.*, 199, 661–662.

Bruce, H. M., and Parkes, A. S. 1961. An olfactory block to implantation in mice. *J. Reproduct. Fertil.*, 2, 195–196.

Cameron, P., and Biber, H. 1973. Sexual thought throughout the lifespan. *Gerontologist*, 13, 144–147.

Comfort, A. 1960. Darwin and Freud. *Lancet, ii*, 107–111.

Cooper, A. J., Ismail, A. A. A., Smith, C. G., and Loraine, J. A. 1970. Androgen function in psychogenic and constitutional types of impotence. *Brit. Med. J.*, 3, 17–20.

Finkle, A. L., Moyers, T. G., Tobenkin, M. I., and Karg, S. J. 1959. Sexual potency in aging males. I. Frequency of coitus among clinic patients. *J. Amer. Med. Assn.*, 170, 1391–1393.

Finkle, A. L., and Prian, D. V. 1966. Sexual potency in elderly men before and after prostatectomy. *J. Amer. Med. Assn.*, 196, 139.

Furlow, W. L. 1977. Surgical management of impotence using the inflatable penile prosthesis. *Mayo Clinic Proc.*, 51, 325–332.

Gagnon, J. H., and Simon, W. 1973. *Sexual Conduct.* Chicago: Aldine Press.

Gold, B. M., and Hotchkiss, R. S. 1969. Sexual potency following simple prostatectomy. *N. Y. State J. Med.*, 69, 2987.

Holgrewe, H. L., and Valk, W. L. 1964. Late results of transurethral prostatectomy. *J. Urol.*, 92, 51–57.

Karacan, I. 1978. Advances in the diagnosis of erectile impotence. *Med. Aspects Human Sexual.*, 12 (5), 85–104.

King, J. 1975. Impotence after fracture of the pelvis. *J. Bone Joint Surg.*, 57A, 1107–1109.

Kinsey, A. C., Pomeroy, W. B., and Martin, C. E. 1948. *Sexual Behavior in the Human Male.* Philadelphia/London: W. B. Saunders.

Kotin, J., Wilbert, D. E., Verburg, D., and Soldinger, S. M. 1976. Thioridazine and sexual function. *Amer. J. Psychiat.*, 133, 82–85.

Kraemer, H. C., Becker, H. B., Brodie, H. K. H., Doering, C. H., Moos, R. H., and Hamburg, D. A. 1976. Orgasmic frequency and testosterone levels in normal human males. *Arch. Sexual Behav.*, 5, 125–132.

Loeffler, R. 1977. Penile prostheses do not inhibit partial erectile ability. *Fam. Practice News,* 6, 125–132.

Masters, W. H., and Johnson, V. E. 1970. *Human Sexual Inadequacy.* Boston: Little, Brown.

Newman, G., and Nichols, C. R. 1960. Sexual activities and attitudes of older persons. *J. Amer. Med. Assn.*, 173, 33–35.

Pearl, R. 1930. *The Biology of Population Growth.* New York: Knopf.

Pfeiffer, E., Verwoerdt, A., and Wang, H. S. 1968. Sexual behavior in aged men and women. *Arch. Gen. Psychiat.*, 19, 753–758.

Renshaw, D. 1978. Diabetic impotence — a need for further evaluation. *Med. Aspects Human Sexual.*, 12(4), 18–28.

Small, M. P., and Carrion, H. M. 1975. A new penile prosthesis for treating impotence. *Contemp. Surg.*, 7, 29–33.

Solnick, R. L., and Birren, J. E. 1977. Age and erectile responsiveness. *Arch. Sexual Behav.*, 6, 1–9.

Weiss, H. 1972. The physiology of human penile erection. *Annals of Int. Med.*, 76, 793–799.

Zohar, J., Meiraz, D., Maoz, B., and Durst, N. 1976. Factors affecting sexual activity after prostatectomy. *J. Urol.*, 118, 332–334.

Widowhood: Societal Factors in Life-Span Disruptions and Alternatives

HELENA ZNANIECKI LOPATA

The death of a member of a social unit always disrupts the life-span flow of that unit. The forms, depth, and range of disruptions as well as the process of reorganization can vary considerably. The size of the unit disrupted by death also varies. The importance of the deceased to the functioning of the unit can be determined by the unit's own definition and by the effect upon its life of the presence and the actions of that member and of the interaction of others with him or her. Social units, cognizant of the disruptive possibilities of the death of important members, try to ensure succession without traumatic disorganization. The effectiveness of such succession procedures depends to a great extent on the individualistic quality of the deceased's contribution to the unit; the more charismatic and significant his or her contribution, the more difficult is the solution of the succession problem. Social research on the effects of the death of a member of a social unit can be limited to immediate consequences; the effects of the removal of a unit's member can also be studied over time, longitudinally or cross-sectionally, through the direct and successive waves of change this death produces in a small social unit. This second approach will be followed in this analysis of widowhood as a consequence of the death of a member of a marital dyad in direct and repercussive disruptions of the life-span flow of the survivor.

Widowhood

The disruptive consequences of the death of a member of a marital dyad, seen as a social unit, upon the survivor depends on several factors. One of these is the dependence of the survivor upon that particular person and upon being a member of a team. This dependence can be analyzed in terms of financial, service, social, and emotional support systems involving both the inflow and the outflow of sentiments, actions, and objects. A second factor influencing the disruptive effects of the death of a member of a marital dyad upon the life of the survivor consists of the ways in which the deceased, the team, and the survivor had been immersed in larger social units, be they a family, a community, a work organization, a couple-companionate circle of friends, a society. A third factor, or composite of variables, consists of the resources and limitations for

Source: Abridged from Lopata, H. Z. Widowhood: Societal factors in life-span disruptions and alternatives. In N. Datan & L. H. Ginsberg (eds.), *Life-span developmental psychology: Normative life crises.* New York: Academic Press, 1975, pp. 217–234. Copyright 1975 by Academic Press. Reprinted by permission.

future action and life styles of the survivor individually and as a member of other social units. A fourth factor is the procedure by which the "gap is closed," the affective, behavioral, and integrative steps taken to establish the survivor comfortably in that status role if it is a permanent one, or to convert the survivor into a member of other units or life style if the society does not demand that he or she retain the status of survivor for the rest of the life span.

The death of a spouse disrupts not only this relation but also other relations organized around the marital role, and related social roles sociologically perceived as sets of functionally interdependent social relations (Znaniecki, 1965; Lopata, 1971b). The death of a wife disrupts a man's role of husband, modifying his relations with in-laws, the wife's friends, their mutual couple leisure-time associates, and sometimes even his kin group, since he is now wifeless and particularly if she were the connecting link of interaction. It can also disrupt the many sets of relations involved in his being in other roles: father, church participant, neighbor (Lopata, 1973a). The greater was his dependence upon her as a total human being and as a member of the social circles of the many roles in which he was an active participant, the greater can be the disruptive effect of her death, unless a substitute can be found soon who really replaces the deceased. Some of the secondary effects of these disruptive consequences can make it impossible for the husband to continue functioning in his occupation, or as a "normal" human being in the society. Furthermore, the presence of a widower in a community or any other social unit may have reactive consequences within that unit in that, for example, other husbands may fear for the loyalty of their wives. After all, a widower is not just a survivor of a marriage, but a certain kind of social person, an unattached male, or even a deviant in a social unit composed of married men and women.

Widowhood in the Lives of Women

Most societies of the world have been, and in varying degrees continue to be, patriarchal, with a history of patrilineal and patrilocal structuring (Murdock, 1949). This means that the authority channels follow the male blood line, adjusted for age gradations, and that women are brought into the extended family units to perform specific functions, obtaining their internal and external status from their relation to established members rather than through independent achievement. Since they are strangers and since they enter alone, no matter how close their own families are in proximity and influence, they are almost invariably not assigned positions of great authority over the existing members. This means that their contributions are seen as supplementary to those of the main family members, the males organized by age and the more established older women. Furthermore, since in most historical and many modern societies the reproductive and mothering functions of women have been the most valued of their contributions, being a wife and legitimized mother forms the main source of identity and interaction, particularly in the absence of alternative roles, or their unavailability to any but the exceptional woman.

Because of the preponderance of patriarchal social structures in most of the world and because we have more data on the disruption in the life-span flow of widows than of widowers, the remaining part of this paper will be devoted to the discussion of widows (Lopata, 1971b). Analyses of comparative data indicate that what happens to widows, directly as a result of the death of the husband, indirectly as other aspects of life become disrupted, in consequence of the very status of "widow" and as a result of the restructuring of their life styles, not only varies considerably from society to society but is highly indicative of the social structure and complexity of the social system at large, as well as of the status of women in it.

In the nomadic or agricultural past of most societies, the main functions of women were the bearing of children within specified family systems, that is, to specified men, and the maintenance of a domicile with the help of the spouse. According to Paul Bohannan (1963), men have universally acquired certain rights in women upon marriage, although these vary by the strength of the patriarchal system, proximity of residence to the male consanguine family, and the availability of other than family roles to women. These are the rights to share a domicile managed through a division of labor, to the products of work and any other economic goods deemed by the community as rightfully belonging to the husband, of sexual access, and of *in genetricem* filiation of the children born to the wife with the male family line. These rights were sometimes inherited by the husband's male agnates after his death. Some societies demanded that the widow continue performing the functions she was carrying forth prior to his death. If she were still able to bear children for the family, arrangements were made for a levir or widow inheritor to ''enter her hut'' to ''raise the seed'' of the deceased; or she was remarried, which meant that her new husband became the legal and social father of her future children, sometimes with the rights of adoption of the children previously conceived with the late husband. If the children were filiated to the male line, the widowed mother was expected either to continue socializing them as members of this unit or to leave the unit by herself so that others could perform the socialization function. Which material goods were considered hers in widowhood and the manner by which she was allowed to handle these goods depended upon the culture and the local community variations.

In highly patriarchal societies not only was the wife and consequently the widow under control of the male family line, but women were often not allowed to become involved in social roles outside of the family institution, particularly during the years in which they were preparing for, or being active in, the role of mother. Agricultural and nomadic groups, of course, had few social roles outside of those connected with the family, it being the main economic, political, and recreational unit, while the functions carried on outside of the homestead were usually designated for men. Even more complex societies of the world which had evolved social roles outside of the family unit could forbid or at least discourage their entrance by women. The final consequence of widowhood in such societies also depended upon how important women were as sexual objects, able to conceive children by the wrong man or disrupt other families by enticing their male members. In all but recent Europe and America, and especially in countries influenced by the Muslim religion, women have been encouraged to remain in or near their homes while societal roles in other spheres of life were located in the male province of activity.

The importance assigned to the function of reproduction and the rights of sexual access to wives in an economically more complex society can be exemplified by the differences of social role assignments and the variations in flexibility given women widowed at different stages of their life spans in traditional India. Until forbidden by law during the English control of India, the idealized solution to widowhood among high-caste Hindus was self-immolation upon the funeral pyre of the husband. Suttee was justified religiously, in that the spirit of the husband needed continued service in after-life from the wife as it awaited rebirth. An equally important, though latent, function of self-immolation was the protection of the spirit of the deceased husband from insult by ensuring that his property, especially such important property as a wife with whom he had enjoyed intimate relations, not be made impure by being touched or sexually "violated" by lesser men.

A basic reason for the imposition of strong controls on widows in India was the proscription against remarriage. Widows were defined as dangerous beings, particularly if they were young, and the most restrictive status role (Lopata, 1964) imposed on such women fell upon the child widow, the child bride who had not had her marriage consummated prior to the death of her husband. Since "impure" women were not desired sexual objects, and virgins were, the whole social system imposed elaborate rituals designed to make the child widow as physically unattractive as possible in spite of her sexual purity. Older widows who were no longer sexually dangerous, and especially those who had grown sons to defend and maintain them, were given relative freedom of action and movement not only in India but elsewhere in patriarchal societies (Goode, 1963; Ward, 1963).

As in agricultural and highly structured societies with a strong division of labor along sexual and age lines, most social groups in the world's history have been influenced in their assignment of social roles to widows, or in the roles they leave open for their acquisition, by their view of women in general and wives in particular.

Social Roles of Women in Modern Societies

Although most European societies and their subgroups are anchored in a highly patriarchal family culture, the life styles of women widowed in them are highly divergent from those described earlier and from each other, dependent to a great extent on the structure and culture of society itself and of the community in which they are located, as well as on their personal resources. Numerous social changes of revolutionary strength have modified these two parts of the world con-

siderably, freeing most women, including widows, from total dependence upon roles within the male family unit, although this freedom varies considerably. These social changes include wars of centralization of political states expanding the complexity of societies, the expansion of the size of organizations carrying out segregated institutionalized sets of procedures for conducting their lives, and scientific and commercial revolutions, technological development associated with rapid industrialization, urbanization, mass education, social mobility, ideological democratization, and concentration upon functional more than status components of social roles, etc.

The changes brought about by industrialization, urbanization, and increasing complexity of society in the lives of women have had two major but mutually exclusive and even conflictfull effects. The first has tied them to the home upon marriage and in spite of extensive prior education into societal knowledge; the second has opened up avenues toward involvement in a multiplicity of roles outside of the home.

The very dissolution of the extended patriarchal family as the basic economic and authority unit has increased rather than decreased the importance of the roles of wife and mother, particularly in the absence of societally developed replacements for the larger unit. Although shortened in time, daily and in the life span, the wifehood and motherhood functions of a woman increased in importance because the man and the children become dependent upon a single human being instead of an extended unit for their care. She is needed, by cultural definition, in the home, not outside of it. Simultaneously, however, industrialization and the other social movements changed the home from being the center of social life into being a restricted place to which members active in economic, political, religious, recreational, and educational roles outside of its walls withdraw to rest and restore their energies (Aries, 1965). What is important in life takes place outside of the home, particularly within economic organizations, and the attention of all members has been focused out. Those people who are not actively participating in the economic institution and not drawing visible economic rewards for this participation have been expected to live vicariously through those who do and to adjust their needs to those of the breadwinning member.

As the home lost its significance as a focus of societal life, and as the economic institution acquired focal significance, the role of housewife, of the woman who maintained this home because she was the wife of the breadwinner, decreased in importance. By the twentieth century the traditional functions of women of bearing and caring for children were also foreshortened in their life spans by the decreasing need for many children and an even larger number of pregnancies and by the expansion of the societal claims on the time and education of children. Women's life span itself expanded dramatically with the advance of medical science, which cut into insignificance death from childbirth and communicable disease in areas of the country where its services are available.

Although the functions of women as members of family units, as maintainers of a home, and as bearers and carers of children decreased in the time they took either daily or within their life cycle, modern societies developed no action to solve the economic and social parasitism of women during the remaining parts of their lives. Trained in a manner similar to men in the early years of life, and experienced in social roles away from home, they have still been expected to withdraw from the majority of societal life once they were married or pregnant with their first child, never to return in any but voluntary capacity, although they outlived the presence of children in the home by 30 years and the presence of a husband in the

home by 15–16 years (Glick, 1957; Duvall, 1967). The traditional patriarchal family institution retained sufficient hold until very recent years, with the help of the Protestant and Puritanical (Dulles, 1965) ethics, assisted by the Freudian-based *Feminine Mystique* (Friedan, 1963; LaPierre, 1959), to keep women from being seriously committed to roles outside of the home, even in preparation for widowhood or divorce and in spite of the fact that the role of housewife lost so much of its prestige and complexity (Lopata & Norr, 1974).

The 1960s in American society witnessed a dramatic reentrance of married women into the labor market after the children were grown to an extent judged as reducing the need for a mother at home 24 hours a day (Lopata, 1971a). This action was often accompanied with increased training or education, necessary in order to obtain a paying job after years of economic inactivity. The behavior was initially justified by economic arguments only, as necessary to maintain a desired style of life above the poverty level by lower class women and utilizing some of the products of a society of abundance by women whose husbands earned more than the minimum. Divorce and widowhood added incentives to reentrance into the labor market and other societal roles.

A major recent trend opening up social roles in complex societies to women at various stages of their life cycles has been the women's liberation movement. Its immediate effect has not as yet been in the direction of decreasing prejudice and discrimination with the help of which many societal roles are closed to women, as much as in changing the world view of increasingly large numbers of women and the ideology by which they have voluntarily held back from acquiring the requirements and entering a variety of roles. It has attempted to break through the traditional socialization system, which retained the patriarchal division of the world into ''his'' and ''hers'' and persuaded women not to enter voluntarily and individually into many societal roles. In spite of extensive mass education, this socialization system has prevented women from effective and flexible functioning in the modern, complex, voluntary society throughout their life spans. Many have not learned the skills and personality tendencies needed to analyze societal resources, choose desired ones, plan and carry out steps necessary for social engagement, engage, and then turn to new resources as the definitions of needs are modified by events or changes in the life span. The women's movement is attempting to help women break out of the traditional mold of dependence upon a family and particularly a husband in determining their social role engagement.

Social Roles in the Lives of Widows in Modern Societies

The cultural background of the American society and the changes in the social structure and life patterns touched upon in the preceding section can be expected to have profound effects upon the lives of widows in one of its metropolitan centers. These expectations, framed as basic hypotheses in two studies of widowhood, come from sociological literature dealing with the modern family. One of the assumptions was that the lives of American wives would be highly disorganized through the deaths of their husbands because of the characteristics of marriage and the nuclear family with its division of labor. The next assumption was that the immediate consequences of the death of the husband upon his new widow would be handled through the rituals of mourning and bereavement, which supposedly cover the periods of shock, confusion, disorientation, psychosomatic health attacks, and similar reactions of grief. This expectation ran contrary to the claims of Geoffrey Gorer (1965) that modern Western society has deinstitutionalized these rituals

sufficiently to cause serious problems for the bereaved, accentuated by a "pornography of death" which has made it an obscene event to be ignored. Eric Lindemann (1944) stressed the importance of allowing the bereaved to complete the "grief work" by which they can rework their past and cut ties with the deceased sufficiently to be able to build new relations and a new life. Although Gorer (1965) may be right in showing how mourning has become deritualized, it is still sufficiently active to allow for at least some "grief work"; otherwise there would be higher incidences of traumatic problems following the death of a significant other. . . .

Current literature on grief provided a timetable to this process, and the first study of older widows investigated the extent to which the "stages of grief" and its timing were known to the respondents. Finally, the long-range consequences to a woman's becoming a widow were seen in terms of the degree to which she is expected to remain a widow, as a person whose major focus of life has been removed, or to which she has to or is allowed to change her life. This change can be forced on her if she is expected to take another husband or enter specially designed roles for widows. Since modern urban life does not really contain the social role of widow, there was little expectation of such involvement. On the other hand, we expected the lives of wives and the lives of former wives to be different. In modern society the woman who has performed the function of wife but no longer needs to do so because the husband is dead, particularly if she has already but no longer needs to perform the role of mother as a total commitment, could be expected to be granted freedom to select nonfamilial roles in the broader society. We can expect the most dramatic change in the life of a woman if she had been committed to the role of wife, if the husband dies suddenly, and if she is unable to reproduce this life after the death of the husband. Such change could be predicted as especially strong if she does not have to remain in the role of widow as a former wife but can voluntarily and individually enter new roles. Such engagement can be expected as prevalant in societies in which the patriarchal controls over women by the husband and his family have diminished considerably in strength and in which there is a multiplicity of social roles outside of the home and the family institution which are at least theoretically available to women who no longer need to continually bear children. In other words, the social structure of modern society leads to the expectation that women who become widowed after their children are no longer small shall move into new levels and complexities of social engagement, particularly if they live in American metropolitan centers.

The studies of widows of all ages in metropolitan Chicago indicate the extent to which these expectations are reflective of analyses of broad societal trends rather than the reality of life for women in this historical period of time. The respondents form a very heterogeneous sample, reflecting their own and the society's backgrounds and resources. They vary in the way they were involved in the role of wife and in other social roles prior to the death of the husband; in the form, depth, and range of life-span disruption they experienced immediately after the death and in repercussive waves over time; and in the role clusters in which they are currently engaged. The importance and meaning of the role of wife, as reported in retrospect and apparent from the changes the death of the husband forced on a woman, spans a wide range. At one extreme are the women — and these tend to be more educated and more middle class than the others — who were strongly involved in the role of wife when the husband was still active and built many other roles upon his presence as a person, a father, a partner in leisure-time activities, a member of couple companionate

groups, a coresident in a household in which they were the housewives, a member of two kin groups, and so forth. Even without considering the emotional quality of their relation, which is difficult to obtain retrospectively because of the "sanctification process" that most widows find necessary, these women report strong life disruption after the death of the husband. At the other extreme of involvement in the role of wife are women who lived in a sex-segregated world, but even they varied in the amount of dependence upon the husband in the filling out of the male-designated functions. Some of these wives were relatively independent of their husbands in sex-segregated marriages, solving their problems without their help or having their role engagements clustered around a role in which he was not an important member. The wife immersed in her family relations, in neighboring, in a job, or in voluntary associations may report that she is lonely for her husband or a man in limited ways, but simultaneously that her identities and life style have not changed much (Lopata, 1973b,c,d). Voluntary mate selection does not automatically lead to multileveled involvement with the husband.

The long-range consequences of widowhood are reflected in the life styles of the women interviewed in metropolitan Chicago. Few of them are "liberated women," able to lead truly urban and multidimensional lives as individuals with rounded-out identities. Some are able to lead the lives of "merry widows," involved in a round of social activity, dating and utilizing the resources of the city in pleasurable interaction with friends. The few women who fall into this category vary in their activities and companions depending upon age, financial resources, and other social roles, such as mother of small children or worker. The third type of widow, who tends to utilize at least some of the societal resources, is the working woman who is widowed but who operates on the job, to which she is committed, individualistically. This type of woman is likely to have been trained early in life, or after an educational interruption, into skills guaranteeing an interesting job with satisfactory economic returns, increasing self-confidence. A second subtype of the working woman is, however, more typical. Having withdrawn from the labor market upon marriage or the first pregnancy, and being untrained into the utilization of educational or job-finding societal services, these working women haphazardly take any job that happens to be available, with minimal economic rewards. This does not mean that the woman does not like her job, since there are many aspects of the routine of going to work, of interacting with others, and of being ''out in the world'' and away from an empty house which are reported as sources of satisfaction.

The fourth category of respondent which is sufficiently specific to draw attention is the ''widow's widow,'' who joins the ''society of widows'' found prevalent in Kansas City by Cummings and Henry (1961); she joins in a round of activity out of an independently run home in which she is the only resident. Although some women deeply resent being relegated to such company at social affairs or by the withdrawal of still married friends, and although others sit home wishing for male companionship, there are women in both of the Chicago samples who enjoy other widows, not just during the grieving period (Silverman, 1973) but because of similarities in life style. They often report feelings of independence and an unwillingness to give it up through remarriage or devotion to grandparenting or other helping roles in family groups.

The traditional widow remains immersed in family roles and relations, devoting herself to her children and grandchildren, sometimes also interacting with a sibling group. She tends to live with one of her children, usually a daughter, and to limit her

financial, service, social, and emotional support systems to relatives. No other person or secondary group enters the detailed listing of these support systems and all friends are also relatives. There are other types of women whose life style is sufficiently strong to warrant such generalization, including the ''grieving wife'' who simply cannot enter new social relations or complete her ''grief work'' (Lindemann, 1944). Very frequently such women become socially isolated and bitter, as prior associates withdraw from the asymmetry of the supports demanded from them. There are also isolated widows who wish they could develop new life styles but who do not have the personally developed resources even to know how to start the series of steps needed for social reengagement. They do not know how to train for or enter a job, join a club or even a church, move to a new neighborhood and develop satisfactory levels of interaction, or convert a stranger into a friend because they were socialized according to the traditional ideal of passive femininity, which did not interfere with the needs of the patriarchal family. Even when offered a range of alternative life styles in widowhood, many women are constrained by internalized assumptions about what women in general, and they themselves, are capable of doing. They tend to have always been minimally engaged, and a basic difference between their backgrounds and those of the multi-dimensionally involved women is formal schooling. It is within the formal schooling system that people learn to understand societal complexity, the skills with which to engage in it voluntarily, and the behavioral, attitudinal, and identification tendencies that enable them to mobilize their resources, reach out for new ones, and enter new social relations and social roles. Thus, there are many women who are widows living in metropolitan Chicago who are ''urban villagers'' (Gans, 1962) or at least incompetent to function in the voluntary and individually engagement-demanding society in which they find themselves. Some of them are lucky in that they are surrounded by a protective social unit, be it a family or a neighborhood in which they can exist in spite of a dearth of personal resources.

Others somehow find ways of at least minimal social engagement, but there are many widows who are socially isolated because they have neither socially supplied support systems nor individually achieved ones.

References

Aries, P. *Centuries of childhood.* New York: Vintage Books, 1965.

Bohannon, P. J. *Social anthropology.* New York: Holt, 1963.

Cummins, E., & Henry W. *Growing old.* New York: Basic, 1961.

Dulles, F. R. *A history of recreation,* New York: Appleton, 1965.

Duvall, E. *Family development,* Philadelphia, Pennsylvania: Lippincott, 1967.

Friedan, B. *The feminine mystique.* New York: W. W. Norton, 1963.

Gans, H. *Urban villagers.* New York: Free Press of MacMillan, 1962.

Glick, P. *American families.* New York: Wiley, 1957.

Goode, W. *World revolutions and family patterns.* New York: Free Press, 1963.

Gorer, G. *Death, grief and mourning.* New York: Doubleday, 1965.

LaPierre, R. *The Freudian ethic.* New York: Duell, Sloan and Pierce, 1959.

Lindemann, E. Symptomatology and management of acute grief, *American Journal of Psychiatry,* 1944, CL, 141–148.

Lopata, H. Z. A restatement of the relation between role and status. *American Sociological Review,* 1964, 25, 385–394.

Lopata, H. Z. *Occupation: Housewife.* New York: Oxford Univ. Press, 1971. (a)

Lopata, H. Z. Role changes in widowhood: A world perspective. In D. Cowgill & L. Holmes (Eds.), *Aging and modernization.* New York: Appleton, 1971. (b)

Lopata, H. Z. Loneliness: Forms and Components. *Social Problems,* 1969, 17, (2), 248–262.

Lopata, H. Z. Self-identity in marriage and widowhood. *Sociological Quarterly,* 1973, 14, No. 3, (Summer), 407–418. (a)

Lopata, H. Z. Grief work and identity reconstruction. Paper given at Foundation of Thanatology Symposium on Bereavement, New York, November, 1973. (b)

Lopata, H. Z. *Widowhood in an American city.* Cambridge, Massachusetts: Schenkman, General Learning Press, 1973. (c)

Lopata, H. Z. The effect of schooling on social contacts of urban women, *American Journal of Sociology,* 1973, 79, (3). (d)

Lopata, H. Z., & Norr, K., Changing commitments to work and family among American women and their future consequences for social security. Proposal for future study, 1974.

Murdock, G. *Social structure.* New York: MacMillan, 1949.

Silverman, P. R. Another look at the role of the funeral director, paper given at the Foundation of Thanatology Symposium on Bereavement, New York, November, 1973.

Ward, B. Men, women and change: An essay in understanding social roles in South and Southeast Asia. In B. Ward (Ed), *Women of new Asia.* Paris: UNESCO, 1963. Pp. 25–99.

Znaniecki, F. *Social relations and social roles.* San Francisco, California: Chandler, 1965.

Intellectual Development

CHOOSING WISELY

Intelligence is usually defined as the ability to learn and/or manipulate symbols. Intelligence is an inference from competence demonstrated in several situations, but competence may involve more than simply intelligence; motivation and personal styles may be involved as well. The particular skills and motives necessary to do well on intelligence tests, which were originally designed to predict scholastic performance, may bias such tests in favor of young people.

The early IQ tests typically measure a factor called "general intelligence" or "g." More recent analyses have identified two major dimensions called *crystallized* and *fluid* intelligence, and yet other analyses have identified from six to twelve *primary mental abilities*. And the most complex model of intelligence yet described (that of Guilford) lists as many as 120 identifiable factors.

Early cross-sectional studies of the relation between age and intelligence suggested decline after a peak reached between the ages of twenty and thirty. Tests of information processing skills involved in fluid intelligence seemed to show sharper declines than others; the components of crystallized intelligence such as tests of general information or vocabulary sometimes even increased.

Longitudinal studies, the first of which were published around 1950, showed that cross-sectional findings seriously misinterpreted actual changes in intelligence across age. Individuals traced across their own aging showed wide differences, averaging only little decline, with brighter individuals in challenging professions even increasing. The cross-sectional studies have reflected primarily generational differences in IQ scores, not actual age changes, at least until very advanced age was reached. Longitudinal studies, however, have their own interpretational difficulties. For example, some of the initially selected subjects will drop out or die; these are often those subjects who initially scored somewhat lower.

All these issues are discussed in the selection by *Sherry L. Willis* and *Paul B. Baltes*. They consider questions of research design, the proper assessment of intelligence in older adults, as well as the explanatory role of intervention research in the study of intelligence. This paper also lays the groundwork for the material contained in the next two selections, which deal with one of the recent controversies in the literature on adult intelligence.

Much of the literature on adult intelligence is concerned with quantitative psychometric assessment approaches. An alternate approach to the measurement of intelligence, and one which advocates a stage rather than continuous model of development, is that inspired by the Swiss psychologist Jean Piaget. In the fourth selection *John H. Flavell* discusses a Piagetian approach to cognitive changes in adulthood. He suggests that in contrast to developmental changes in childhood, which occur as a function of irreversible biological-maturational growth processes, adult intelligence is more likely to change as a result of life experiences.

In the final selection, *K. Warner Schaie* carries this theme further by offering a stage theory of adult cognitive development. This theory includes an achieving stage during which temporal monitoring occurs, which involves the planning and periodic assessment of programs designed to achieve major goals in career, family, and life in general. A *responsible* stage involves the application of cognitive abilities to immediate and long-range concerns for family units, coworkers and community groups. A variant called the *executive* stage involves the application of planning and assessment abilities to organizations for which one is at least partly responsible. Finally, a *reintegrative* stage involves simplification by means of relating abilities, interests, and the like to the older person's more egocentric needs.

Additional Suggested Readings

Botwinick, J. Intellectual abilities. In J. E. Birren & K. W. Schaie (eds.), *Handbook of the psychology of aging.* New York: Van Nostrand Reinhold, 1977, pp. 580–605.
> A well-balanced discussion of alternative positions on the issues of maintenance and decline of intelligence over the adult life-span with a good review of the literature on both cross-sectional and longitudinal studies.

Horn, J. L. Human abilities systems. In P. B. Baltes (ed.), *Life-span development and behavior*, (Vol. 1). New York: Academic Press, 1978, pp. 211–256.
> An exposition of the Horn-Cattell theory of fluid and crystallized intelligence, and a review of the evidence of life-span development of intelligence in the light of that theory.

Schaie, K. W. The primary mental abilities in adulthood: An exploration in the development of psychometric intelligence. In P. B. Baltes & O. G. Brim, Jr. (eds.), *Life-span development and behavior.* (Vol. 2). New York: Academic Press, 1979, pp. 67–115.
> An account of the natural history and results of one of the major longitudinal studies of intellectual development in adulthood.

Intelligence in Adulthood and Aging: Contemporary Issues

SHERRY L. WILLIS AND PAUL B. BALTES

Issues in the study of psychometric intelligence are discussed from a life span developmental perspective. A first set of issues involves questions of developmental design aimed at valid identification of ontogenetic life span change; a second set of issues deals with proper assessment of intellectual behavior in older adults; and a third set of issues relates to explanatory-causal work on intellectual aging and the role of intervention paradigms. As a framework of causal-explanatory research, a trifactorial model of influences on life span development is presented which identifies three categories of influences — age-graded, history-graded, and non-normative — assumed to interact in producing regularities and variations in life span development. During the last decade, clarification of these issues has resulted in a major reevaluation of the traditional evidence on intellectual aging. Whereas general decline was traditionally considered the primary characteristic of intellectual aging, it appears that intellectual aging in current cohorts is much more plastic and heterogeneous than past research with limited methodologies would have implied. It is suggested that future research emphasizing the issues outlined will result in a view of intellectual aging that is differential rather than normative and dynamic rather than static.

The area of adult intelligence has received considerable attention in the gerontological literature during the past decade. Contributing to this context of renewed interest, and sometimes controversy (Baltes & Schaie, 1976; Horn & Donaldson, 1976, 1977; Schaie & Baltes, 1977), has been a focus on a series of methodological issues dealing with questions of design and control necessary for valid measurement of developmental change. While such methodological issues may apply to various aspects of developmental aging, it has been in the study of psychometric intelligence that they have been most fully examined. Moreover, findings from data sets employing such methods have suggested the need for possible revisions and extensions in our theories and models of intellectual aging.

This chapter discusses several of these issues that gained considerable attention in the 1970s and that may have important implications for the study of adult intelligence in the coming decade. First, several issues

Source: Willis, S. L., & Baltes, P. B. Intelligence in adulthood and aging: Contemporary issues. In L. W. Poon (Ed.), *Aging in the 1980s.* Washington, D.C.: American Psychological Association, 1980. Copyright 1980 by the American Psychological Association. Reprinted by permission.

dealing with the assessment of change in intellectual behavior are examined. It is suggested here that the methodologies used to assess intellectual aging relate directly to questions regarding the timing, directionality, and pervasiveness of such change and that consideration of intellectual aging within a life span context may provide a broader perspective of such change than has been obtained within a narrow age period approach. Second, two issues related to the definition and measurement of intelligence are explored. The differential patterns of intellectual aging suggested by cohort-sequential research have led some researchers to suggest the need for (a) age/cohort-relevant intelligence measures, and (b) consideration of intraindividual variability (plasticity) as a dimension of intellectual assessment. Finally, the need for an explanatory as well as a descriptive approach to the study of intellectual aging is considered. A multicausal model identifying three possible sets of influences is outlined as a heuristic scheme for interpretation of existing data and the design of future research.

One additional comment is needed. Adult intelligence has been defined in many ways (e.g., Botwinick, 1977; Resnick, 1976; Sternberg & Detterman, 1979). In general, two major approaches to the study of intellectual behavior have been identified. The psychometric approach has been the more dominant of the two, both from a historical perspective and in terms of the volume of theory and research stemming from a given perspective. Psychometric concepts of intelligence have been developed largely in connection with intelligence testing, prediction, and the concept of human abilities (e.g., Cattell, 1971; Guilford, 1967; Horn, 1978; Thurstone, 1938). A second major approach is related to the study of intelligence as cognition, involving processes of perception, learning, memory, and problem solving (Kintsch, 1970; Sternberg & Detterman 1979). . . .

The issues to be discussed in the present chapter have been primarily associated with the psychometric approach to the study of intelligence. Since this chapter focuses on identifying and discussing some of the current salient issues in the field, it does not provide a comprehensive review of the gerontological literature in this area. Several such reviews are available for the interested reader (Baltes & Labouvie, 1973; Botwinick, 1977; Horn, 1978; Labouvie-Vief, 1977; Schaie, 1979).

Developmental Change in Intellectual Aging

Assessment of Change

Longitudinal and cohort-sequential designs   During the past decade considerable attention has been given to clarifying the relation between various forms of age-developmental methods of data collection, such as the cross-sectional and longitudinal methods (Baltes, 1968; Baltes, Reese, & Nesselroade, 1977; Nesselroade & Baltes, 1979; Riley, 1979; Schaie, 1965, 1970; Schaie & Baltes, 1975). It is now recognized that the basic descriptive task of any developmental approach (including the study of aging) consists of the proper identification of two components of variability: (1) intraindividual variability, and (2) interindividual differences in intraindividual variability. Unless designs permit the clear separation of these two components of variability, misidentification of development change and of developmental differences in change will result. In fact, up to a few years ago, much of the literature on intelligence in old age suffered from this methodological flaw.

For a given birth cohort (individuals born at a specified time, say, in 1900), only the longitudinal method can provide for direct information on both intraindividual change and interindividual differences in such change. In a strict sense, the cross-sectional method is never an appropriate substitute for longitudinal (repeated measurement) investigation. However, intellectual aging research is further complicated by possible biocultural changes affecting the course of life span development for individual cohorts. An example of such biocultural changes are cohort effects.

If such biocultural changes exist, single-cohort longitudinal information on change is not sufficient, and developmental designs must consider two additional components of variability: (3) between-cohort differences in intraindividual variability, and (4) between-cohort differences in interindividual differences in intraindividual variability. As a consequence, if biocultural change in intellectual behavior is obtained, findings from single-cohort longitudinal studies cannot tell the entire story about intellectual aging. The reason is that a single-cohort longitudinal study is but a sample from a population of cohort-specific longitudinal studies, and therefore its results cannot be generalized to other cohorts. To what degree the life span development observed in one cohort can be generalized to another is a matter of empirical demonstration.

In psychology, and especially in the area of psychometric intelligence, it has been established that such generalization across cohorts is not possible for current aging cohorts living in the Western world. Cohort-sequential studies, for example, by Schaie and his colleagues (e.g., Nesselroade, Schaie, & Baltes, 1972; Schaie, 1979) in the United States, or by Rudinger (1976) in Germany — the latter based on data from the Bonn Longitudinal Study — represent powerful and persuasive cases. In Schaie's longitudinal sequential study begun in 1956, age changes in intellectual performance on Thurstone's Primary Mental Abilities Test have been examined for

several cohorts of adults over a 14- to 21-year period (Schaie, 1970, 1979). Age changes were measured at 7-year intervals, 1956, 1963, 1970, and 1977. With such a design it is possible to examine age/cohort relations for the five primary abilities. In addition, the inclusion at each 7-year assessment interval of random samples of individuals from the same birth cohorts allows comparison of the selective longitudinal sample with independently drawn random samples from the same population.

Figure 1, which shows 7-year longitudinal age changes (from 1963 to 1970) on the five primary abilities for eight birth cohorts, highlights some of the general trends of age/cohort relations (Schaie & Labouvie-Vief, 1974). With regard to longitudinal age changes (dotted lines), no significant decrement in performance on any ability was noted before the late 60s. Significant increments across the 7-year period were noted at earlier ages (20s, 30s) for Verbal Meaning and Space. Moreover, significant cohort differences favoring younger cohorts are evident for some abilities, notably Verbal Meaning, Reasoning, and Space. The data suggest both cohort effects varying by abilities and the relatively late and limited occurrence of ontogenetic decrement in such healthy, well-educated populations, as represented in longitudinal research.

Control groups Findings from these data must be tempered, however, by consideration of a number of perspectives. First, it is in the nature of cohort effects (and biocultural change in general) that they are not fixed. On the contrary, their direction and magnitude change. As a consequence, the pattern depicted in Figure 1 is specific to the cohorts and historical times studied. In fact, Schaie's (1979) summary presentation of results from additional data points (1956, 1963, 1970, 1977) makes it apparent that cohort change in the mental abilities studied is rarely linear.

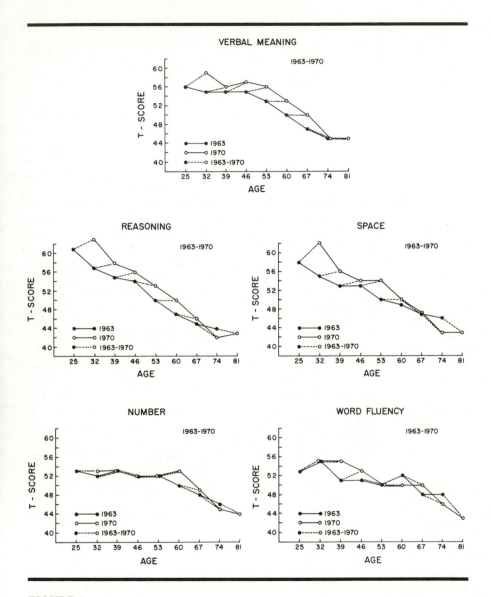

FIGURE 1
Comparison of cross-sectional with longitudinal gradients (dotted lines) in Schaie's cohort-sequential research on adult intelligence. (From "Generational Versus Ontogenetic Components of Change in Adult Cognitive Behavior: A Fourteen-Year Cross-Sequential Study" by K. W. Schaie and G. Labouvie-Vief. *Developmental Psychology,* 1974, 10, 305–320. Copyright 1974 by the American Psychological Association. Reprinted by permission.)

Second, there is the effect of selective attrition on longitudinal samples. Discrepancies between members of the longitudinal sample and independent samples from the parent population tend to increase over time. In Schaie's work, data from the two samples seem to differ primarily in level of function and, for some abilities, in the age range of onset of reliable decrement (Schaie, Labouvie, & Buech, 1973). The attrited longitudinal sample then appears more representative of a stable population of healthy, well-educated, middle-class individuals, whereas the independent sample appears to be more representative of less well-educated, lower-middle-class populations. Differences in data between the two samples may be most important when considering the magnitude of age changes in intelligence. Following Riegel's earlier work, Botwinick (1977) has recently discussed this issue in more detail.

The issue of control groups in longitudinal research is an important one and has received increasing attention in research on psychometric intelligence. Control groups are necessary for at least three sets of possible sources of error in research on aging (see Baltes et al., 1977; Schaie, 1977). A first set deals with changes in the parent population (e.g., birth cohort) itself, from which longitudinal samples are drawn. Biological mortality, if it is correlated with the dependent variable under study, is the classical example. A second set of sources of error that require design control involves changes in experimental samples due to initial selective sampling and selective drop-out. In general, the findings are that biological survivors, longitudinal participants, and longitudinal survivors score higher and show less aging decrement in psychometric intelligence than those who die, fail to participate, or leave a longitudinal study before it is completed.

A third set of control issues relates to questions of measurement validity and measurement equivalence. Examples are the problem of retest effects associated with reactive measures and the possibility of changes in the validities of tests when they are given to different ages and cohorts. In the area of psychometric intelligence, each of these three sets of design problems has been shown to be relevant in empirical work (e.g., Baltes, Schaie, & Nardi, 1971; Blum, Clark, & Jarvik, 1973; Eisdorfer & Wilkie, 1973; Riegel & Riegel, 1972; Rudinger, 1976; Schaie, 1979).

Summary of descriptive evidence and prospects   It is difficult to draw firm conclusions from present evidence on intellectual aging, which has been collected via application of cohort-sequential methodology, given a number of design and measurement limitations.[1] However, in our view there are enough results to suggest the following points about current cohorts:

1. Chronological age per se accounts for a relatively modest amount of the variance observed in intellectual aging during late adulthood up to the 60s or early 70s. Differences between cohorts, up to ages 60–70, equal or exceed in importance chronological age differences (Schaie & Parham, 1977). Chronological age gains in prominence, however, as age reaches the 70s.

2. Interindividual differences (including cohort differences) in intellectual aging are large and suggest differential (heterogeneous) rather than homogeneous patterns of aging.

---

[1] Botwinick's (1977) thoughtful review presents perhaps the best reasoned case for maintaining a position that includes decline in intellectual abilities (small and differential in late adulthood, general and large in old age) as the major feature of intelligence in adulthood and old age. For the data base covered, Botwinick's interpretation has many strengths. However, in our view (see, e.g., Baltes & Willis, 1979), Botwinick does not pay sufficient attention to issues of aging-fair measurement and questions of plasticity. These issues are discussed later in this chapter.

3. There appear to be marked differential changes for various intellectual abilities (e.g., Verbal Meaning Number) with regard not only to age but also to cohort.

The findings from longitudinal and cohort-sequential research suggest that intellectual change be examined from a differential aging perspective. Key features of this approach would be variability, multidirectionality, and multidimensionality (Baltes & Willis, 1979; Labouvie-Vief & Chandler, 1978). Such an approach, emphasizing intra- and interindividual variability in intellectual aging, contrasts somewhat with the more traditional approach to change in intellectual aging that has sought to identify a normative or "classical" pattern of change. Moreover, some evidence is beginning to appear that there may also be differential cohort/ability relationships in terms of level of functioning.

A differential aging perspective, however, is not restricted to *interindividual* variability in development, with cohort differences as one aspect of such interindividual variability. In addition, focusing on differential aging also suggests concern with *intraindividual* variability. The range of intraindividual variability (plasticity), both long-term and short-term, appears not to have received as much attention as interindividual variability and requires further exploration. Recent cognitive intervention studies are one mechanism for examining short-term intraindividual variability and are discussed later in this chapter.

In any case, such an emphasis on variability (both inter- and intraindividual) suggests that intellectual aging must be viewed as a dynamic rather than a static phenomenon. Researchers in the area need to be sensitive to the need for continual reexamination not only of their perspectives on intellectual aging but also of the change in evidence that occurs in conjunction with biocultural variation.

Definition and Measurement of Adult Intelligence

The differential aging perspective suggested by recent cohort-sequential studies also has implications for the definition and measurement of adult intelligence. Such an approach questions the validity of measurement systems developed for younger age groups for assessing age- and cohort-relevant dimensions of adult intelligence. In addition, the wide range of variability shown in intellectual functioning in adulthood suggests consideration of intraindividual plasticity as a further dimension of intellectual assessment.

Age- and Cohort-Relevant Intelligence Measures

When research on adult and gerontological intelligence began, it was common practice to use existing psychometric tools as a framework to define and measure intelligence. However, this strategy is at best a shortcut.

Earlier psychometric research on intelligence with children and young adults was based on careful analyses of the tasks and settings related to intellectual behavior in those age groups. The historical giants of the field of psychometric intelligence, such as Binet and Thurstone, spent considerable time developing appropriate task material and age-appropriate models of intelligence. Researchers interested in late adulthood and old age, however, have a tendency simply to apply the methods of psychometric intelligence that have been developed for younger age populations. Thus we find longitudinal studies into late adulthood based on the Army Alpha tests, developed largely in the context of the military services, or on the Primary Mental Abilities Test, constructed for research with college students. Note that such intelligence tests, in terms of their content and predictive validity, were designed primarily for forecasting successful performance in academic and professional settings characteristic of early adult life.

As a consequence, as suggested earlier by Demming and Pressey (1957) and more recently by Schaie (1978; Schaie & Schaie, 1977), what we know about psychometric intelligence in the older adult is based on instruments and models developed for the young. In other words, we know how to compare the older person with the young in youth-oriented tasks and settings. But we have relatively few instruments that can tell us much about the unique nature of intellectual behavior and its predictive validity in the older adult. Although this critical view of existing measurement instruments was expressed rather persuasively some time ago, the effort invested in counteracting this deficiency has been amazingly meager. Moreover, some of the most aggressive proponents of a trait conception of intellectual aging, which is often associated with positions of marked decline (e.g., Horn, 1978; Horn & Donaldson, 1977), base their own research and interpretation almost exclusively on the use of test instruments developed in the context of young adults, where academic performance served as the major validation criterion.

If a representative assessment of gerontological intelligence is at stake, a youth-oriented approach does not appear defensible, at least not as the primary strategy of assessment. What is imperative in future research on adult and gerontological intelligence is to make the intellectual behavior of older adults and their ecologies the guides for content, predictive, and construct validation. Linking the intellectual behavior of older persons to that of younger ones by using youth-oriented instruments may remain a part of our search for life span knowledge and life span bridges connecting intellectual development. But, in order to produce balance in assessment methods and models of intelligence, future work on gerontological intelligence will need to be life span and old age centered. It will need to consider problems of task analysis and validation that reflect the intellectual demands on the older person and the recognition of multiple-age (or developmental) and multiple-setting criteria as references for validation (Schaie, 1978).

For example, if intelligence is a construct aimed at measuring successful adaptation in particular settings and task situations that are changing as life span development progresses, we need to know what settings and tasks related to intellectual behavior are unique to the older person (Clement, 1977; McClelland, 1973). What are the intellectual tasks of advancing adulthood and how are these tasks related to the task systems of earlier life? To what degree may it be necessary for the older adult to unlearn (rather than passively forget) knowledge and skills acquired in the first part of life? It seems fair to conclude that on this score, research on gerontological intelligence is truly in its infancy, some notable exceptions notwithstanding (e.g., Clayton & Birren, 1981; Gardner & Monge, 1977; Schaie, 1977–78).

Average Performance (Trait) Versus Intraindividual Variability (Plasticity)

A second theme of the dominant approach to the study of psychometric intelligence in late adulthood has been an extraordinary preconception of viewing abilities as largely invariant and fixed, "as attributes that have many of the properties of a trait, as this concept is used in general biology. That is, . . . defined as an enduring characteristic by means of which one person can be distinguished from another" (Horn, 1977, p. 140). This general trait approach is reflected in the usual observational scheme associated with psychometric intelligence, which involves an average performance per individual based on a static, single-occasion measurement of intellectual performance in a variety of tasks. Note that averaging is based on averaging of tasks given on one occasion, rather than on consideration of a developmental (longitudinal) time continuum or the individual's adaptive capacity to different life situations. An additional feature of age-comparative research on psychometric intelligence is that assessment has been conducted under standard fixed conditions, with all persons participating in the same observational procedure, independent of their life (pretest) history.

Obviously, such an average performance- and trait-oriented approach does not lead to information on the *range* (limits) of behavior (Baltes & Baltes, 1980). In the study of psychometric intelligence, the implied premise is that single-occasion observations on a variety of intellectual tasks (with testing conditions held constant) lead to general information about the performance of an individual. This can be true only for the limited case represented by the testing situation. Recognizing this limitation is particularly important if assessment of intelligence is seen as an indicator not only of performance but of capacity or potential. In fact, in the gerontological literature, performance measures in static situations are often taken as measures of what the elderly person is capable of doing in principle (intelligence as capacity or competence). This is a highly questionable inference (see Botwinick, 1977), because it involves generalization from performance in test situations to unobserved settings and to possible treatment benefits and thereby neglects intraindividual variability.[2]

It is rarely recognized that information on intraindividual variability and on the conditions for such variability (e.g., as a function of pretest history or concurrent treatment conditions) is an important ingredient of a comprehensive theory of psychometric intelligence. Historically, the concept of testing the limits had been introduced exactly for the purpose of obtaining information on intraindividual variability or the possible range of performance. The available evidence on gerontological intelligence, however, is thoroughly lacking in knowledge about plasticity or intraindividual variability, whether seen in a short-term (concurrent) or long-term (developmental) framework. Short-term, or concurrent, plasticity refers to the range of performance that a given person can display at any given developmental time, if subjected to different treatment conditions. Long-term, or developmental, plasticity refers to range of performance, not at any given point in time, but in regard to the nature of developmental functions (Wohlwill, 1973) or developmental behavior-change processes as they extend over longer segments of the life course.

Thus we do not know what aged persons could do. All we know is what they do, if they live in the context of the current social ecology, if they are not exposed to varying biological and environmental conditions (whether construed as facilitative or interfering) before assessment begins, and if they are asked to participate in one mode of assessment, one dictated by procedures and models developed in the life context of the young adult. With such evidence, it is not possible to make statements about aspects of intellectual potential but only, to use a statistical analogue, about a "fixed level" of performance delivered in a highly specific setting.

Baltes and his colleagues (Baltes & Danish, 1980; Baltes & Willis, 1977) discuss the importance of intervention research for exploring the possible range of psychological aging in greater detail and in a more general

---

[2] In the literature on abnormal cognition in geriatric medicine, the issue of separating competence from performance deficits has a counterpart problem. A distinction between "true" senility, presumed to be biologically based, and various forms of pseudosenilities is discussed by medical researchers and practitioners (e.g., Libow, 1077). The methodological requirement of testing and studying the limits of performance presented in this chapter applies equally well to that forum of research and diagnosis.

context. There is beginning to be research to counteract the traditional preconception of average performance (trait) in psychometric intelligence (for a review, see Labouvie-Vief, 1976, 1977). The most direct line of inquiry is based on intervention research. Intervention research is aimed at examining the role of various behavioral intervention programs and so-called ability-extrinsic performance factors affecting the intraindividual range of intellectual performance. Such intervention work is aimed not only at assessing what older persons do but what they could do if conditions were different. In general, the relevant data are not yet rich enough to warrant firm conclusions. In our own research, however, the evidence for much more intraindividual plasticity in gerontological intelligence than has been acknowledged by most researchers in the field appears impressive (Hofland, Willis, & Baltes, in press; Plemons, Willis, & Baltes, 1978; Willis, Blieszner, & Baltes, 1981).

In considering the magnitude of such preliminary findings on the responsiveness (plasticity) of older adults to various performance-enhancing treatments, it becomes apparent why research on the conditions for intraindividual variability in intellectual performance is so critical for an understanding of old age. If, for example, the hypothesis (Labouvie, Hoyer, Baltes, & Baltes, 1974) is correct that the majority of older persons generally live (a) in a cognitively deprived environment, and (b) in one which deemphasizes youth-oriented tasks involving academic and occupational achievement, then our current assessment of the intellectual capacity of older persons by means of psychometric instruments is terribly deficient and aging biased. The current assessment focus is on static assessment of intellectual behavior in specific settings, settings that are likely to be unrepresentative or even dysfunctional for the elderly. Appropriate assessment should include examining the range of intellectual behavior and the conditions under which performance variability is obtained.

To prevent a possible misunderstanding, we would like to emphasize here that findings on intraindividual plasticity need not be taken as implying that there is no decline at all in intellectual performance with aging, or that older persons benefit more from cognitive training than younger adults. What the evidence suggests is only that many older persons do benefit from intellectual experiences if (a) they are presented with supportive conditions, and (b) they attend to the tasks involved. The question of whether intellectual "capacity" remains at the same level from adulthood into old age is an open question at this point. In fact, we acknowledge that the basic intellectual capacity may not remain invariant but is likely to show decline, especially in very advanced old age and in the face of brain-related health problems. However, we tend to believe also that intellectual capacity can be "practiced" and, in addition, exhibits a kind of reserve that can be "activated" if necessary (Baltes & Willis, in press). Such a perspective on intelligence is similar to the biological concept of reserve which states that mature organs have a larger capacity than is necessary for regular functioning (Fries, 1980). Intervention research, with its focus on studying the conditions for intraindividual variability (plasticity), is the kind of inquiry that permits further examination of such questions.

Adult and Gerontological Intelligence: Toward Explanation

Thus far our discussion has focused primarily on issues associated with a descriptive approach to intellectual aging. In this section, progression toward an explanatory approach is examined.

What is the current explanatory evidence on the aging of psychometric intelligence? First of all, we now know that the explanatory task is not a simple one, because the picture of descriptive change in psychometric intelligence is not a simple, normative age function. Intelligence is not a unitary construct but involves several dimensions of ability; there is little interindividual homogeneity; there is multidirectionality; and there is emerging evidence for intraindividual plasticity (both in terms of individual life courses and momentary variability). In other words, the descriptive pattern of intellectual aging is one of much complexity and little apparent parsimony.

Such a pluralistic outcome can be taken as evidence that research on psychometric intelligence is not one of the royal roads to understanding processes of aging. Or, if one were to take Comfort's (1964) evolutionary perspective, one could argue that there is little universality and parsimony in aging per se, because the evolutionary process has not led to a specific genetic program for that component of life. According to Comfort, this may be so because aging, as part of the postreproductive phase of life, is only tangentially related to species survival in the evolutionary sense. Such interpretations, while perhaps premature and discouraging, are reasonable alternatives that need consideration (Baltes & Baltes, 1980).

However, there are a few observations that involve constructive implications for explanatory-causal research design. First of all, the key conclusion is that, except for perhaps advanced old age, there is not too much to be gained in explanatory research on psychometric intelligence by focusing on chronological age and age-associated mechanisms alone. For the most part, at least up to the early 70s, chronological age accounts for less variance than such subject variables as cohort, education, social-occupational status, and health (Granick & Friedman, 1973; Green, 1969; Rudinger, 1976; Schaie & Willis, 1978). Second, because of multidimensionality and multidirectionality, there is not much promise in

research using a unitary construct of general intelligence. These observations also imply that for much of late adulthood (but not for advanced old age), age-correlated average biological changes in health are not sufficient either to affect intellectual functioning at the level of group analysis (Eisdorfer, 1977; Eisdorfer & Wilkie, 1973) or to remain uncounteracted by the plasticity of the aging persons, their living environment, or other forms of behavioral and medical intervention.

A Multicausal and Interactive Model of Influences on Aging

One option for future explanatory work is to forcefully expand our conception of causation, to go beyond age-associated determinants and mechanisms, and to include factors that, while affecting intelligence, cannot easily be isolated if one follows a methodological paradigm that is age based. In this spirit, Baltes and his colleagues (Baltes, 1979; Baltes, Cornelius, & Nesselroade, 1979; Baltes & Willis, 1979) have formulated a multicausal and interactive model of influence on life span development. This model is represented in Figure 2. It is not advanced as a theory of development but as a methodological paradigm potentially useful in the search for causal relations and determinants that make for intraindividual and differential development. Explicit recognition of the multiple influences represented may lead to a set of research enterprises that are structurally different from the research themes of the past.

Specifically, Figure 2 identifies three sets of influences that, mediated through the developing individual, act and interact to produce development (aging) and developmental differences. The three sets of influences are age-graded influences, history-graded influences, and non-normative influences or critical life events. Each of these influences can be conceptualized as

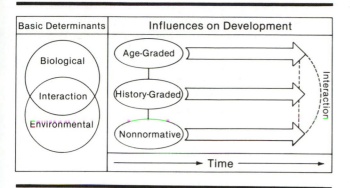

FIGURE 2

Three sources of influence on life-span development that cumulate and interact over time (adapted from Baltes, 1979; Baltes, Cornelius, & Nesselroade, 1979).

having biological and environmental correlates and as reflecting interactive processes.

Age-graded influences are defined as encompassing those biological and environmental determinants that exhibit (in terms of onset and duration) a fairly high correlation with chronological age. For the most part, they are fairly normative (general) and predictable. That is, their occurrence, timing, and duration are fairly similar for all individuals of a given set of aging cohorts. Examples of such age-graded influences are events and processes related to biological maturation and to age-graded socialization, including many aspects of education, the family life cycle, and occupation.

History-graded influences consist of those biological and environmental events that exhibit a fairly high correlation with historical change. Their degree of generality and predictability varies. Some of them, however, are fairly normative, in that they apply to most members of a given set of aging cohorts in similar ways, although the effects do not need to be identical for different age cohorts living at the same time. Examples of history-graded influences would

be effect patterns associated with cohort differences, economic depressions, the impact of wars or major epidemics on the life course of individuals, or the long-term historical processes associated with such events as industrialization and the changing structures of family life.

Non-normative critical life events refer to determinants of development that do not occur in any age-graded or history-graded manner for most individuals, either in terms of their presence or, if they are present, in terms of timing and patterning. Therefore, they are fairly idiosyncratic and less predictable than age- and history-graded influences. Influences on life span development associated with rare opportunities (awards, foreign travel), medical trauma, accidents, temporary unemployment, divorce, or the death of a loved one are examples of such non-normative critical life events (see Schoenfeldt, 1973). In a general context, Hultsch and Plemons (1979) have presented a stimulating discussion of the role of life events in understanding human development. As to cognitive aging, Eisdorfer (1977) has recently explored possible relations between life events and cognitive functioning, using stress as the process by which such a linkage may be specified.

As we approach the explanatory study of intellectual aging from the multicausal framework outlined in Figure 2, it may be possible to be more directed in our search by working from a converging framework of description and explanation (Baltes & Willis, 1979). Convergence between descriptive and explanatory efforts is possible, because the multicausal model outlined makes it possible to coordinate empirical findings on intellectual aging with their explanation. The findings of large interindividual differences and multidirectionality in psychometric intelligence, for example, appear less cumbersome if the assumed determining influences exhibit a corresponding pattern of differential and multiple causation. The definition and operation of history-graded influences, and particularly of non-normative critical life events, are aimed directly at a causal explanation of differences in development. By definition, non-normative life influences, while important in regulating intellectual behavior at the individual level, do not occur in identical ways for groups of individuals. Therefore, they are not expected to produce homogeneous outcomes at the level of interindividual aggregation.

To use a concrete example: If it is correct that much of the evidence on psychometric intelligence suggests little normative age decline prior to the 70s for the majority of healthy older adults, the primary explanation of change occurring in some persons might be found in non-normative life events such as health trauma or other forms of personal crisis. However, research on intellectual aging in advanced old age, which is assumed to exhibit more age-graded normative decline, would appropriately be oriented toward causal schemes that include a search for age-graded influences. Similarly, if one were to follow Botwinick's

(1977) descriptive analysis of differential age-change patterns, for example, in verbal versus performance scores on the Wechsler Adult Intelligence Scale, comparable decisions could be made about the likelihood of success in explanatory work. If age-graded, history-graded, and non-normative influence models and associated search strategies are contrasted as methodological paradigms, diverse models of explanation could be identified and tested to account for the differences in aging patterns observed for distinct classes of intellectual behavior.

In many respects, a focus on age-graded, history-graded, and non-normative critical life events might be seen as posing new conceptual and methodological problems regarding the logical status and further refinement of each of these influences. This would be so if one treated the scheme as the beginnings of a theory rather than as a heuristic device. In that case, problems would arise, for example, because none of the influences would denote an exclusive category of antecedents or a specific process of behavior change. At present, however, the three sets of influences denote search strategies rather than distinct theoretical constructs. As our knowledge about the importance of history-graded and non-normative influences develops, it will be necessary to explore whether it is possible to specify the processes and mechanisms associated with their occurrence and transaction in similar ways, as has been true for the elaboration of age-associated factors. Illustrative examples for such elaboration are the use of stress and adaptation (Eisdorfer, 1977) as the process by which critical life events operate in controlling intellectual behavior, or the use of operant paradigms (Baer, 1973; M. Baltes & Barton, 1977) in specifying the nature of the transaction (or interaction) between aging individuals and age-graded environmental influences.

At this time, it is not clear whether the three sets of influences will lead to distinct process formulations. Alternatively, identical processes (e.g., various types of learning) may be used to account for the operation of each of them, though with perhaps different emphases and different levels of analysis. In any case, however, elevating history-graded influences and non-normative critical life events to a level of explanatory power comparable to that of age-associated factors will mandate new perspectives on research design. For example, one of the methods that appears to be ideally suited for the identification of the processes inherent in the multicausal and interactive model outlined is that of structural equation analysis (Goldberger & Duncan, 1973; James & Singh, 1978; also see chapters by Jöreskog and Rogosa in Nesselroade & Baltes, 1979). This method, developed primarily by researchers in econometrics and sociology, permits the formulation and evaluation of multivariate systems of variables in terms of directional and interactive causality.

Process and Intervention Research Methodology

In an earlier part of this chapter, we emphasized that information on intellectual behavior should include statements about both average performance (trait) and intraindividual range of performance (plasticity). Both types of information are important not only to separate components of capacity (competence) from those of performance in intellectual aging but also to identify the conditions under which stability and change (incremental or decremental) in intellectual aging are obtained.

Process research of the experimental-psychology type is rather standard in work on basic processes such as learning, perception, attention, and cognition. In the area of psychometric intelligence, however, this type of explanatory work is relatively infrequent, although a number of articles have

repeatedly called for it as a methodological paradigm (e.g., Anastasi, 1958, 1970; Baltes & Labouvie, 1973; Buss, 1973; Ferguson, 1954; Tryon, 1935). When does process research on intellectual aging attain particular relevance? There are two features of process research that research aimed at the explanation of aging should exhibit. These features go beyond those usually associated with the design advantages of experimentation per se.

First, for process research to be useful in the study of development (aging), it needs to take an observed developmental or aging phenomenon as the target for explanatory analysis. It is not sufficient to focus on any behavior change or any kind of interindividual variability as a dependent variable. The behavior change under consideration must have meaning in the context provided by a given developmental theory or model.

The requirement of a developmental approach to defining the target for description and explanation has been expressed most forcefully in writings by Birren and Renner (1977), Goulet (1973), Wohlwill (1973), and Baltes et al. (1977). In the context of gerontology, the same perspective applies to the selection of explanatory mechanisms. Not any explanatory effort is likely to be useful. From the viewpoint of developmental theory, those explanatory mechanisms are good candidates that focus on antecedent processes having meaning in the context of a given theory of development or aging. The need for selecting a theoretically meaningful behavior-change process as a target is most apparent when a life span approach to the study of aging is taken (Riley, 1979). This is so because life span developmental research on aging emphasizes aging as a lifelong process. As one attempts to delineate a given behavior-change process, it is important to recognize the limitations of past process research that has largely centered on age functions and age-associated mechanisms. Thus, process research that deals with history-graded and non-normative influences and functions as a guiding framework will benefit if it is oriented explicitly toward a theory-based approach to the definition and explanation of process.

Second, it is important to recognize the dual role of intervention in such process research on aging (Baltes & Danish, 1980; Baltes & Willis, 1977). In any research paradigm involving experimentation to understand process, direct or indirect manipulation of antecedents (and the creation of treatment effects due to such manipulation) is the key rationale. The strategy of experimentation, therefore, is intrinsically linked to some form of intervention. However, interventive work can go beyond the causal control of variability as observed in a given phenomenon prior to the experiment. Intervention can include the planned magnification or reduction of intraindividual and interindividual variability. Such a planned magnification or reduction of a phenomenon is particularly important if the ecology in which a given behavior-change process (the phenomenon) naturally occurs does not present conditions for variability or for certain segments of it, such as those necessary for optimal functioning.[3]

How does this view of intervention apply to the area of psychometric intelligence? Researchers have argued that the naturalistic conditions of behavior (life) of the old person, in general (M. Baltes & Barton, 1977) as well as in intellectual functioning

(Labouvie et al., 1974), are not supportive of efficient behavior in the sense of optimization. If the naturalistic conditions for life with regard to aging are indeed restricted in scope, it is imperative to emphasize process research that incorporates the second role of intervention work, that of planned magnification or reduction of intraindividual and interindividual variability. Information collected on the basis of such intervention paradigms will not only lead to a fuller understanding of the conditions for varying outcomes of life span development, including differential aging in intelligence. It will also provide for the type of information necessary to make recommendations for changes in social policy and health care, where knowledge about the conditions for dysfunctional and optimal aging is a central question (Baltes & Danish, 1980; Baltes & Willis, 1979).

As mentioned before, the recent years have seen a nascent interest in exploring the usefulness of intervention paradigms with the goal of understanding the conditions for diverse and varying forms of intellectual aging. However, the bulk of past research on psychometric intelligence in old age is descriptive and is youth and status quo oriented. Therefore, not having much knowledge about the conditions for and the range of intellectual plasticity is the result of past neglect of appropriate methodology.

The concluding commentary offered on the need for interventive process research in the study of intellectual aging is another example of the critical role that established methodologies and conceptions play as a field evolves. In the area of psychometric intelligence, the conceptual approach to the study of intellectual aging will need to include some radical departures from the mainstream of past practice. Whether the same perspectives are applicable to other areas of psychological research on old age awaits further examination. However, it appears fruitful to venture such a hypothesis.

[3] It is important to recognize that the identification of intervention conditions that produce variability in aging is not identical to the task of identifying the initial conditions responsible for a given phenomenon. The search for the origins of aging in nature requires additional steps aimed at external validation (Baer, 1973; Baltes et al., 1977). The distinction between sufficient and necessary conditions is helpful to understanding the logic of explanatory analysis in the context of developmental research, as is the concept of age or developmental simulation (Baltes & Goulet, 1971).

References

Anastasi, A. Heredity, environment, and the question "How." *Psychological Review*, 1958, 65, 197–208.

Anastasi, A. On the formation of psychological traits. *American Psychologist*, 1970, 25, 899–910.

Baer, D. M. The control of the developmental process: Why wait? In J. R. Nesselroade & H. W. Reese (Eds.), *Life-span developmental psychology: Methodological issues.* New York: Academic Press, 1973.

Baltes, M. M., & Barton, E. M. New approaches toward aging: A case for the operant model. *Educational Gerontology*, 1977, 2, 383–405.

Baltes, P. B. Longitudinal and cross-sectional sequences in the study of age and generation effects. *Human Development*, 1968, 11, 145–171.

Baltes, P. B. Life-span developmental psychology: Some converging observations on history and theory. In P. B. Baltes & O. G. Brim, Jr. (Eds.), *Life-span development and behavior* (Vol. 2). New York: Academic Press, 1979.

Baltes, P. B., & Baltes, M. M. Plasticity and variability in psychological aging: Methodological and theoretical issues. In G. Gurski (Ed.), *Aging and the CNS.* Berlin: Schering, 1980.

Baltes, P. B., Cornelius, S. W., & Nesselroade, J. R. Cohort effects in developmental psychology. In J. R. Nesselroade & P. B. Baltes (Eds.), *Longitudinal research in the study of behavior and development.* New York: Academic Press, 1979.

Baltes, P. B., & Danish, S. J. Intervention in life-span development and aging: Issues and concepts. In R. R. Turner & H. W. Reese (Eds.), *Life-span developmental psychology: Intervention.* New York: Academic Press, 1980.

Baltes, P. B., & Goulet, L. R. Exploration of developmental variables by manipulation and simulation of age differences in behavior. *Human Development*, 1971, 14, 149–170.

Baltes, P. B., & Labouvie, G. V. Adult development of intellectual performance: Description, explanation, and modification. In C. Eisdorfer & M. P. Lawton (Eds.), *The psychology of adult development and aging.* Washington, D.C.: American Psychological Association, 1973.

Baltes, P. B., Reese, H. W., & Nesselroade, J. R. *Life-span developmental psychology: Introduction to research methods.* Monterey, Calif.: Brooks/Cole, 1977.

Baltes, P. B., & Schaie, K. W. On the plasticity of intelligence in adulthood and old age: Where Horn and Donaldson fail. *American Psychologist*, 1976, 31, 720–725.

Baltes, P. B., Schaie, K. W., & Nardi, A. H. Age and experimental mortality in a seven-year longitudinal study of cognitive behavior. *Developmental Psychology*, 1971, 5, 18–26.

Baltes, P. B., & Willis, S. L. Toward psychological theories of aging and development. In J. E. Birren & K. W. Schaie (Eds.), *Handbook of the psychology of aging.* New York: Van Nostrand Reinhold, 1977.

Baltes, P. B., & Willis, S. L. Life-span developmental psychology, cognitive functioning, and social policy. In M. W. Riley (Ed.), *Aging from birth to death.* Boulder, Colo.: Westview Press, 1979.

Baltes, P. B., & Willis, S. L. Enhancement of intellectual functioning in old age: Penn State's Adult Development and Enrichment Project (ADEPT). In F. I. M. Craik & S. E. Trehub (Eds.), *Aging and cognitive processes.* New York: Plenum, in press.

Birren, J. E., & Renner, V. J. Research on the psychology of aging: Principles and experimentation. In J. E. Birren & K. W. Schaie (Eds.), *Handbook of the psychology of aging.* New York: Van Nostrand Reinhold, 1977.

Blum, J. E., Clark, E. T., & Jarvik, L. F. The New York State Psychiatric Institute Study of Aging Twins. In L. F. Jarvik, C. Eisdorfer, & J. E. Blum (Eds.), *Intellectual functioning in adults.* New York: Springer, 1973.

Botwinick, J. Aging and intelligence. In J. E. Birren & K. W. Schaie (Eds.), *Handbook of the psychology of aging.* New York: Van Nostrand Reinhold, 1977.

Buss, A. A conceptual framework for learning affecting the development of ability factors. *Human Development*, 1973, 16, 273–292.

Cattell, R. B. *Abilities: Their structure, growth, and action.* Boston: Houghton Mifflin, 1971.

Clayton, V., & Birren, J. E. Age and wisdom across the life span: Theoretical perspectives.

In P. B. Baltes & O. G. Brim, Jr., (Eds.), *Life-span development and behavior* (Vol. 3). New York: Academic Press, 1981.

Clement, F. *Adaptation au milieu: Méthode et connaissance.* Paper presented at the World Conference on Aging, Vichy, France, April 1977.

Comfort, A. *Aging: The biology of senescence.* New York: Holt, Rinehart & Winston, 1964.

Demming, J. A., & Pressey, S. L. Tests "indigenous" to the adult and older years. *Journal of Counseling Psychology*, 1957, 4, 144–148.

Eisdorfer, C. Stress, disease and cognitive change in the aged. In C. Eisdorfer & R. O. Friedel (Eds.), *Cognitive and emotional disturbance in the elderly.* Chicago: Year Book Medical Publishers, 1977.

Eisdorfer, C., & Wilkie, F. Intellectual changes with advancing age. In L. F. Jarvik, C. Eisdorfer, & J. E. Blum (Eds.), *Intellectual functioning in adults.* New York: Springer, 1973.

Ferguson, G. A. On learning and human ability. *Canadian Journal of Psychology*, 1954, 8, 95–112.

Fries, J. F. *Health and aging in the year 2000.* Paper presented at the NOVA Conference on Behavioral Aging, Fort Lauderdale, Fla., January 1980.

Gardner, E. G., & Monge, R. H. Adult age differences in cognitive abilities and educational background. *Experimental Aging Research*, 1977, 3, 337–383.

Goldberger, A. S., & Duncan, O. D. (Eds.). *Structural equation models in the social sciences.* New York: Seminar Press, 1973.

Goulet, L. The interfaces of acquisition: Models and methods for studying the active, developing organism. In J. R. Nesselroade & H. W. Reese (Eds.), *Life-span developmental psychology: Methodological issues.* New York: Academic Press, 1973.

Granick, S., & Friedman, A. S. Educational experience and the maintenance of intellectual functioning by the aged. In L. F. Jarvik, C. Eisdorfer, & J. E. Blum (Eds.), *Intellectual functioning in adults.* New York: Springer, 1973.

Green, R. F. Age-intelligence relationships between ages sixteen and sixty-four: A rising trend. *Developmental Psychology*, 1969, 1, 618–627.

Guilford, J. P. *The nature of human intelligence.* New York: McGraw-Hill, 1967.

Hofland, B., Willis, S. L., & Baltes, P. B. Fluid intelligence performance in the elderly: Retesting and intraindividual variability. *Journal of Educational Psychology;* in press.

Horn, J. L. Personality and ability theory. In R. B. Cattell & R. M. Dreger (Eds.), *Handbook of modern personality theory.* New York: Halsted Press, 1977.

Horn, J. L. Human ability systems. In P. B. Baltes (Ed.), *Life-span development and behavior* (Vol. 1). New York: Academic Press, 1978.

Horn, J. L., & Donaldson, G. On the myth of intellectual decline in adulthood. *American Psychologist*, 1976, 31, 701–719.

Horn, J. L., & Donaldson, G. Faith is not enough: A response to the Baltes-Schaie claim that intelligence does not wane. *American Psychologist*, 1977, 32, 369–373.

Hultsch, D. F., & Plemons, J. K. Life events and life-span development. In P. B. Baltes & O. G. Brim, Jr. (Eds.), *Life-span development and behavior* (Vol. 2). New York: Academic Press, 1979.

James, L. R., & Singh, B. K. An introduction to the logic, assumptions, and basic analytic procedures of two-stage least squares. *Psychological Bulletin*, 1978, 85, 1104–1122.

Kintsch, W. *Learning, memory, and conceptual processes.* New York: Wiley, 1970.

Labouvie, G. V., Hoyer, W. J., Baltes, P. B., & Baltes, M. M. Operant analysis of intellectual behavior in old age. *Human Development*, 1974, 17, 259–272.

Labouvie-Vief, G. Toward optimizing cognitive competence. *Educational Gerontology*, 1976, 1, 75–92.

Labouvie-Vief, G. Adult cognitive development: In search of alternative interpretations. *Merrill Palmer Quarterly*, 1977, 23, 227–263.

Labouvie-Vief, G., & Chandler, M. Cognitive development and life-span developmental theories: Idealistic vs. contextual perspectives. In P. B. Baltes (Ed.), *Life-span development and behavior* (Vol. 1). New York: Academic Press, 1978.

Libow, L. S. Senile dementia and "pseudosenility'': Clinical diagnosis. In C. Eisdorfer & R. O. Friedel (Eds.), *Cognitive and emotional disturbance in the elderly.* Chicago: Year Book Medical Publishers, 1977.

McClelland, D. C. Testing for competence rather than for ''intelligence.'' *American Psychologist,* 1973, 28, 1–14.

Nesselroade, J. R. & Baltes, P. B. (Eds.), *Longitudinal research in the study of behavior and development.* New York: Academic Press, 1979.

Nesselroade, J. R., Schaie, K. W., & Baltes, P. B. Ontogenetic vs. generational components of structural and quantitative change in adult cognitive behavior. *Journal of Gerontology,* 1972, 27, 222–228.

Plemons, J. K., Willis, S. L., & Baltes, P. B. Modifiability of fluid intelligence in aging: A short-term longitudinal training approach. *Journal of Gerontology,* 1978, 33, 224–231.

Resnick, L. B. (Ed.), *The nature of intelligence.* Hillsdale, N.J.: Lawrence Erlbaum, 1976.

Riegel, K. F., & Riegel, R. M. Development, drop and death. *Developmental Psychology,* 1972, 6, 306–319.

Riley, M. W. (Ed.), *Aging from birth to death.* Washington, D.C.: American Association for the Advancement of Science, 1979.

Rudinger, G. Correlates of changes in cognitive functioning. In H. Thomae (Ed.), *Contributions to human development* (Vol. 3). Basel: Karger, 1976.

Schaie, J. P., & Schaie, K. W. Psychological evaluation of the cognitively impaired elderly. In C. Eisdorfer & R. O. Friedel (Eds.), *Cognitive and emotional disturbance in the elderly.* Chicago: Year Book Medical Publishers, 1977.

Schaie, K. W. A general model for the study of developmental problems. *Psychological Bulletin,* 1965, 64, 92–107.

Schaie, K. W. A reinterpretation of age-related changes in cognitive structure and functioning. In L. R. Goulet & P. B. Baltes (Eds.), *Life-span developmental psychology: Research and theory.* New York: Academic Press, 1970.

Schaie, K. W. Quasi-experimental designs in the psychology of aging. In J. E. Birren & K. W.

Schaie (Eds.), *Handbook of the psychology of aging.* New York: Van Nostrand Reinhold, 1977.

Schaie, K. W. Toward a stage theory of adult cognitive development. *Journal of Aging and Human Development,* 1977–78, 8, 129–138.

Schaie, K. W. External validity in the assessment of intellectual performance in adulthood. *Journal of Gerontology,* 1978, 33, 695–701.

Schaie, K. W. The primary mental abilities in adulthood: An exploration in the development of psychometric intelligence. In P. B. Baltes & O. G. Brim, Jr. (Eds.), *Life-span development and behavior* (Vol. 2). New York: Academic Press, 1979.

Schaie, K. W., & Baltes, P. B. On sequential strategies in developmental research: Description or explanation? *Human Development,* 1975, 18, 384–390.

Schaie, K. W., & Baltes, P. B. Some faith helps to see the forest: A final comment on the Horn and Donaldson myth of the Baltes-Schaie position on adult intelligence. *American Psychologist,* 1977, 32, 1118–1120.

Schaie, K. W., Labouvie, G., & Buech, B. Generational and cohort-specific differences in adult cognitive functioning: A fourteen year study of independent samples. *Developmental Psychology,* 1973, 9, 151–166.

Schaie, K. W., & Labouvie-Vief, G. Generational vs. ontogenetic components of change in adult cognitive behavior: A fourteen-year cross-sequential study. *Developmental Psychology,* 1974, 10, 305–320.

Schaie, K. W., & Parham, I. A. Cohort-sequential analyses of adult intellectual development. *Developmental Psychology,* 1977, 13, 649–653.

Schaie, K. W., & Willis, S. L. Life-span development: Implications for education. In L. S. Shulman (Ed.), *Review of educational research* (Vol. 6). Itasca, Ill.: Peacock, 1978.

Schoenfeldt, L. F. Life history subgroups as moderators in the prediction of intellectual change. In L. F. Jarvik, C. Eisdorfer, & J. E. Blum (Eds.), *Intellectual functioning in adults.* New York: Springer, 1973.

Sternberg, R. J., & Detterman, D. K. (Eds.), *Human intelligence: Perspectives on its theory and measurement.* Norwood, N.J.: Ablex, 1979.

Thurstone, L. L. *Primary mental abilities.* Chicago: University of Chicago Press, 1938.

Tryon, R. C. A theory of psychological components—an alternative to "mathematical factors." *Psychological Review,* 1935, 42, 425–454.

Willis, S. L., Blieszner, R., & Baltes, P. B. Intellectual training research in aging: Modification of intellectual performance on the fluid ability of figure relations. *Journal of Educational Psychology* 1981, 73, 41–50.

Wohlwill, J. F. *The study of behavioral development.* New York: Academic Press, 1973.

Cognitive Changes in Adulthood

JOHN H. FLAVELL

Cognitive changes during childhood have a specific set of formal "morphogenetic" properties that presumably stem from the biological-maturational growth process underlying these changes: Thus, childhood cognitive modifications are largely inevitable, momentous, directional, uniform, and irreversible. No such underlying process constrains and directs adult cognitive changes, and hence their morphogenetic properties should be quite different from those that obtain during childhood. The most important adult cognitive changes are probably the result of life experiences, and would for the most part be expected to lack the across-subject uniformity that characterizes the child's intellectual growth. It is possible that there might be some experience-based adult changes that do meet the uniformity criterion, but the identification of such changes has scarcely begun.

The aim of this paper is to speculate about a topic which unfortunately lies well outside my own field of specialization, namely, the nature of cognitive change, not during childhood, but during the adult years. The anchoring point for these speculations is the cognitive development of the child. We think we have learned something about cognitive changes during this particular portion of the life-span, and it may be that what we have learned can illuminate the state of things in adulthood.

Differences Between Child and Adult Cognitive Changes

In my view, much of what is interesting and distinctive about preadulthood intellectual changes results from their being guaranteed in fact and significantly constrained in form by biological-maturational factors. This is not of course to deny or underplay the role of experience or environmental inputs in the growth process. There are, however, certain characteristic properties of childhood intellectual changes which I believe no theory that considers only environmental inputs could ever satisfactorily explain. One is the very fact that cognitive change is inevitable — guaranteed to occur — in neurologically intact growing children the world over. Another is that the changes we witness between birth and maturity are of immense scope and significance; they are truly *big* changes, both quantitatively and qualitatively. Furthermore, the evidence suggests that at least the major landmarks in the child's cognitive evolution emerge in a fixed order; there is, in other words, considerable intrinsic directionality and interindividual uniformity in the developmental progression. And finally, the changes that occur are

Source: Flavell, J. H. Cognitive changes in adulthood. In L. R. Goulet & P. B. Baltes (eds.), *Life-span developmental psychology: Research and theory.* New York: Academic Press, 1970, pp. 247–253. Copyright 1970 by Academic Press. Reprinted by permission.

221

largely irreversible; that is, the cognitive structures and operations that eventually emerge are essentially permanent, essentially unextinguishable.

This view of the nature of childhood changes is obviously not original to me. For example, Piaget (1967) and Lenneberg (1967) have recently offered similar, strongly biologically oriented accounts of intellectual and linguistic development respectively. Nonetheless, many may disagree with this view on the grounds that it neglects milieu effects, individual variation, and the like. At the risk of accentuating the disagreement, one further speculation will be suggested: As we come to learn more and more about the deeper-lying, essential aspects of childhood cognitive change, this feeling of within-species developmental homogeneity and uniformity will actually increase rather than diminish. This is precisely what appears to be happening already in the psychology of language (Chomsky, 1967), and it will probably also happen in the area of cognitive growth in general.

The picture with respect to adult cognitive changes is at least superficially quite different because it is the underlying presence of a biological growth process that lends to childhood changes their inevitability, magnitude, directionality, within-species uniformity, and irreversibility. It is not immediately obvious, however, that there is any biological process indigenous to the adult portion of the life-span that could impose such definite and strong constraints on intellectual change. This does not imply that there may be no interesting biological changes during the adult years, and the claim is not made that adult cognitive changes cannot and do not occur. What is suggested is that these biological changes are different from their childhood counterparts, and because they are different they would be unlikely, on the face of it, to dictate a set of cognitive changes with the very same "mor-

phogenetic features," so to speak, as the childhood ones have. To put it another way: if we should restrict the meaning of "developmental" to refer to those changes with age that have childhood-type morphogenetic features, then the application of the term to the adult years reflects a hypothesis rather than a statement of established fact. Correspondingly, appellations like "life-span developmental psychology," if meant to be more than metaphors, would need explicit defense.

If one actually looks at reported data on adult cognitive changes (e.g., Botwinick, 1967; H. E. Jones, 1959), one does not find much support for such an extension of the concept "developmental" (it may be revealing that the word does not even appear in the index of Botwinick's book). There seems to be no compelling and consistent evidence that at least the sorts of intellectual changes commonly studied are inevitable, of striking magnitude, or uniform across adulthoods; it could be conceded perhaps that they are irreversible and directional, although the directionality does not seem to manifest itself in a fixed sequence of well-demarcated stages or developmental landmarks. The typical finding seems instead to be a cognitive change with roughly the following sorts of properties: (a) it appears to be more quantitative than qualitative in nature and of considerably less magnitude or moment than the typical infant-to-adulthood change; (b) it does not occur in all adults. My impression, then, is that the physiological changes that occur in normal adulthood do not lead to or support cognitive changes of the consistency, size, and kind that are mediated by the childhood growth process.[1] That a number of findings reported in the literature

---

[1] A recent paper by Kohlberg and Kramer (1969) makes a similar point regarding adult changes in moral thinking, namely, that they are not "developmental" in the above mentioned narrow sense.

on aging (e.g., Botwinick, 1967) are of considerable interest to developmental psychologists of Genevan persuasion probably is true because we are psychologists, rather than because we are developmentalists. If we cannot look to biological processes as a basis for any very interesting (i.e., to a Piagetian) cognitive changes during the adult years, what about the process of experience or environmental stimulation?

The Role of Experience in Adult Cognitive Change

Like the child, the adult may experience an enormous number of important and potentially change-inducing encounters with the world of people and things; moreover, if accorded a normal life-span, he will have a longer period of time in which to experience them. If one could discount the nature of the organisms involved (for instance, that young children might be regarded as intrinsically more environmentally malleable than adults), one could argue that adulthood is the nearest thing we have to a pure experiment-in-nature for assessing the change-making power of experience alone, that is, relatively unconfounded by significant and directional biological changes. The suggestion here is that experience is in fact a far more promising source of interesting adult cognitive changes than are biological events, and that the changes so wrought might also prove to be more similar to the childhood prototypes in their morphogenetic features.

One can imagine some of the major categories of experimental settings which could provide occasions for really significant and enduring changes in an adult's cognition. There are programmed ones, like psychotherapy and adult education, which some adults encounter. There are also unprogrammed ones, such as marriage, child

rearing, occupational activities, grandparenthood, retirement, widowhood, and so on, that many or most adults encounter. The important experiential nutrients for the child's cognitive growth are both human and nonhuman-inanimate in nature, and he accordingly constructs implicit mental models of both the logical-natural world and the social-interpersonal one. Most adult cognitive changes probably concern the latter, that is, they consist of changes in the individual's implicit theories regarding the self, others, and the human condition generally.

Notice that the types of cognitions one would think of here are not of the psychometric or learning task variety, not of the sort so prominently featured in the studies Botwinick (1967) reviews. They have to do with judgments, attitudes, and beliefs rather than skills and you therefore could, if you prefer, categorize them as personality rather than cognitive phenomena. They do, however, most decidedly entail genuine cognitive activity (probably at the developmental level of Piaget's concrete operations, at least for most adults).

Cognitive changes of this ilk, brought about through significant and impactful life experiences, have apparently been little studied by psychologists. There is, however, some interesting recent evidence concerning one of the above mentioned sectors of unprogrammed experience, namely that of rearing one's own children. Stolz and her colleagues (Stolz, 1967) gathered extensive interview data from a group of mothers and fathers on the perceived determinants of their cognitions and behaviors regarding child rearing. It is apparent that tacit conceptual models about the nature and management of children develop and change as a consequence of a wide variety of experiential influences. One such influence is the parent's repeated interactions with the child himself. The following passage provides one illustration of how an adult's experiences can significantly modify and change his thinking in a particular area:

> A parent learns by experience, not only with his spouse, but also with his children. As shown in the previous section, parents are continually responding to children's behavior, and children are responding to their parents'. By this interaction parents gradually build up generalizations concerning children and attitudes concerning specific methods of child-rearing. A mother or father acts in a certain way with his child; if the method used is successful in bringing about what the parent wants, then such behavior is reinforced, and the parent is likely to use this method again, not only with the child with whom it was successful but with other children in the family, especially those born later. If, on the other hand, the parent's method fails, he is less likely to try it on other children in the family. In the process of experience, parents learn not only about the usefulness of their method, but they also gain insight into why it succeeds or fails. It is through interaction with a child that a parent often learns what to expect of a child and what behavior is appropriate for his stage of development . [Stolz, 1967, pp. 196–197].

What sorts of morphogenetic features could such experience-based changes be expected to have, again using childhood development as the yardstick? It was suggested earlier that adult changes of the skill or ability variety are not likely to be either momentous or uniform from adult to adult. In contrast, at least some of the experienced-based changes in attitudes, beliefs, etc., might accurately be characterized as momentous. Although the changes in one's thinking resulting from having lived in a concentration camp, or having raised a family, or having experienced occupational success or failure, etc., are doubtless qualitatively different from the changes defined by say, the child's transition from preoperational to concrete-operational thought, they need not be much less consequential for the individual concerned.

On the other hand, like the above-mentioned skill changes, they ought in general to lack the uniformity feature. While many of the major occasions and settings for change-making experiences are encountered by the vast majority of adults (marriage and parenthood, for example), the actual psychologically defined *experiences* undergone in these "normative" settings must vary widely from individual to individual. Experiential variation could be expected to result in a relative uniformity of change only if operating in concert with a constraining process of biological growth, as suggested to be the case during childhood. In the absence of a maturational "governor," uniformity of changes should be positively correlated with uniformity of experiences — but there simply may not be much uniformity of experiences across adulthoods, even within the same subculture. Parenthetically, a similar state of affairs probably obtains during childhood for those psychological characteristics which are not tied to a direction-giving biological process, that is, which are not "developmental" in the narrow sense. Disregarding initial constitutional differences and other complications in order to make the point, it could be said that some experiences might lead a child to become increasingly aggressive with age, and that others might make him increasingly nonaggressive with age. In both cases there is genuine change over time as a function of experience; however, both the experiences and the ensuing changes differ in the two cases, a fact that need not bother the student of the antecedents of aggressiveness-nonaggressiveness. I think Erikson's (1959) model of life-span changes well illustrates the point I am trying to make. While he does indeed assume a universal sequence of change-inducing problems to be coped with, he definitely does not assume that all people have the same concrete experiences while coping with these problems, nor that they all change in the same way as a result. Likewise, Stolz (1967) never for a moment suggests that the emerging and changing schemas regarding children and their upbringing have the same content from one parent to the next. To be sure, it is at least possible that there might be some uniformity and sequential orderliness for certain very general ego processes. There might, for example, be uniform shifts with age in the distribution of one's identification with, and investment in, the growth and life fortunes of various other egos. The egos in question could include an adult peer who ages with one (one's spouse or intimate friend), an older person whom one sees pass from middle to old age (one's parent), a younger person whose childhood, young adulthood, and perhaps middle adulthood fortunes become objects of concern (one's child, nephew, etc.), a much younger reduplicate of the latter, of whom at least the childhood years may also be available for cathexes (one's grandchild, grandnephew, etc.).[2]

This last point suggests that perhaps we should not be too hasty in giving up the search for universal or near-universal cognitive changes in adulthood, changes presumably based on subtle and hard-to-identify commonalities of adult experience. There might for example, exist common experiences associated simply with the fact that one is now at a particular point in the life stream — with having lived this much of life already and having that much more expected to be lived. Neugarten (1966a, 1966b, 1968, 1969) has nicely elaborated this and other seminal ideas about adult

changes in a recent series of papers. While not all of the interesting changes she discusses could plausibly be regarded as uniform across human adulthoods, some of them might approach universality. For instance, she has evidence from interview data that there is a gradual reversal across adulthood in the way biological time is perceived, namely, from time-since-birth to time-left-to-live. Similarly, as people pass from middle to old age there appears to be a shift from an active-assimilatory to a passive-accommodatory model of how best to cope with the environment. Moreover, the cognitions associated with being of a specific age may only be part of the story. That is, it is possible that one's implicit schema of "the X-aged person" undergoes systematic and possibly uniform changes as age period X is first anticipated in prospect, later lived through and experienced, and finally reviewed in retrospect. In other words, there may be important modifications in a person's image of any adulthood period as a function of his own gradually but inexorably changing relationship to that period, modifications which may, furthermore, be much the same from one aging individual to another. Like the most interesting of childhood cognitive processes, the images in question are probably quite deep lying and hard to articulate — not of the sort that would be readily elicitable by questionnaires and other objective tests. In fact, really extensive, almost psychotherapy-like depth interviewing may be necessary, at least for the preliminary identification of putative universal changes (less time-consuming procedures may suffice later on, once we know exactly what we are trying to measure). If the search for uniform changes, however carried out, should prove successful, we would finally have the adulthood version of something dear to any Piagetian's heart: namely, the Development of Man as contrasted with the developments of men.

---

[2] I am grateful to Harold W. Stevenson and Bernice L. Neugarten for ideas leading to this suggestion. Neugarten nicely captured the essence of the suggestion in saying: "Once a child is born, and perhaps for both men and women, the self concept is never again limited to that which goes on within one's own skin (personal communication)."

References

Botwinick, J. *Cognitive processes in maturity and old age.* New York: Springer, 1967.

Chomsky, N. The formal nature of language. In E. H. Lenneberg (Ed.), *Biological foundations of language.* New York: Wiley, 1967. Pp. 397–442.

Erikson, E. H. Identity and the life cycle: Selected papers. *Psychological Issues,* 1959, 1, 50–100.

Jones, H. E. Intelligence and problem solving. In J. E. Birren (Ed.), *Handbook of aging and the individual.* Chicago: University of Chicago Press, 1959. Pp. 700–738.

Kohlberg, L., & Kramer, R. Continuities and discontinuities in childhood and adult moral development. *Human Development,* 1969, 12, 93–120.

Lenneberg, E. H. *Biological foundations of language.* New York: Wiley, 1967.

Neugarten, B. L. Adult personality: Toward a psychology of the life-cycle. Paper presented at the meeting of the American Psychological Association, New York, September 1966. (a)

Neugarten, B. L. Adult personality: a developmental view. *Human Development,* 1966, 9, 61–73. (b)

Neugarten, B. L. Adaptation and the life cycle. Paper presented at the meeting of the Foundations Fund for Research in Psychiatry, Puerto Rico, June 1968.

Neugarten, B. L. Continuities and discontinuities of psychological issues into adult life. *Human Development,* 1969, 12, 121–130.

Piaget, J. *Biologie et connaissance.* Paris: Gallimard, 1967.

Stolz, L. M. *Influences on parent behavior.* Stanford, Calif.: Stanford University Press, 1967.

Toward a Stage Theory of Adult Cognitive Development

K. WARNER SCHAIE

Specifications are offered for a stage theory of adult cognitive development. It is argued that cognitive processes are differentially organized and expressed during periods labeled as acquisitive, achieving, responsible, executive and reintegrative. Current psychometric technologies may suffice for the description of cognitive behavior during the acquisitive and achieving periods. Such techniques are inadequate, however, to describe and understand cognitive function beyond young adulthood, and the development of novel technologies is suggested for the study of cognitive development in mid-life and old age.

Introduction

Throughout my scientific career, perhaps with the exception of a very minor transgression (1), I have taken a strictly empiricist position and have devoted myself to the description of cognitive change over the adult life span, utilizing what seemed to be the best available techniques for such description. Having become older, and if not wiser, at least less defensive about admitting to the possible utility of arm-chair speculation, I am now ready to confess agreement with the dialectic position, that taking no position, takes a position as well, albeit not an explicated position. Indeed, in my previous theoretical exposition I took a regression view of aging (1), while in my more recent integrative writing (Baltes & Schaie, 1974; Schaie, 1973, 1974; Schaie & Gribbin, 1975) I have opted in essence for a stability model of cognitive development (2–5).

Further, positions such as mine, or those of writers such as Bayley, Horn or Comalli imply a continuity position for age changes in adult cognitive development regardless of the empirical findings as to decrement or stability of cognitive function (6–8). That is, no matter what we say, when we assess cognitive function by means of procedures found valid for young adults, we assume quantitative change in cognitive structures which remain qualitatively uniform throughout life.

In my own work, I have assiduously tried to show that most apparent differences in cognitive function between young and old are not ontogenetic in nature. Instead, such differences are often found because individuals are compared who belong to generations differing in the asymptotic level of acculturated materials acquired by them in young adulthood (4). But even if there is little change over age within individuals on measures validated for the young, this does

Source: Schaie, K. W. Toward a stage theory of adult cognitive development. *Journal of Aging and Human Development,* 1977–78, 8, 129–138. Copyright 1977 by Baywood Publishing Co., Inc. Reprinted by permission.

not tell us that the young and the old are cognitively alike. Indeed, simple observation requires the admission, if only in terms of simple face validity, that there ought to be some qualitative age differences. And, what I may have done over the past decades is to show, first, that old people do not necessarily show intellectual decrement on certain tasks developed for the young; second, that the old are obsolete rather than decrepit; but, also unfortunately that this does not help us much to understand fully intellectual functioning in old age.

My first clues regarding the problems posed by continuity models of cognitive development in adulthood came with my more appreciative digestion of reviews of changes in factor structure of intelligence across age. Some of this material is certainly not new, since Cohen (1957) almost two decades ago reported changes both in the number and composition of factors derived from the Wechsler tests. But more recent discussions have made it quite clear that it may be overly simplistic to interpret developmental change in adulthood to be straightforward quantitative change (9–11).

A further persuasive argument was presented to me by an interesting study by Alpaugh who investigated creativity in a group of school teachers sampled over the adult age range but equated for education and performance on the WAIS vocabulary test (12). In this group, creativity decreased with age, even though vocabulary performance did not. This finding would be explained by a continuity model of cognitive function only if there were cohort differences in creativity which are independent from those found for intelligence. But the latter possibility is of a low order of probability and I would rather believe that once again qualities are measured in ways appropriate for the young but not necessarily for the old.

I feel compelled, then, to argue now that the processes which have been documented for the acquisition of cognitive structures and functions in childhood and during the early adult phase may not be relevant to the maintenance of functions and reorganization of structures required to meet the demands of later life. But if I adopt this position, I feel I must go a step further and begin to articulate an alternative model for adult cognitive development which might provide a blueprint for the development of new descriptive strategies. This is what I shall now propose to do.

Are There Adult Cognitive Stages?

It seems to me that all previous models for intellectual development are narrowly confined to what we might denote as the acquisition of problem solving skills. In a sense Piaget merely describes successive modes of increased efficiency in the solution of problems which involve the acquisition of new information (13). Within such a sequence of increasingly efficient acquisitional processes it is quite possible to describe the extent to which different classes of problem solving have been mastered by a structure of intellect model (14). But what happens when the young adult has reached some kind of asymptote in this acquisitional process?

Flavell claims that childhood cognitive modifications involve formal "morphological" properties that result from the biological-maturational growth process underlying these changes (15). In contrast, he argues that "no such underlying process constrains and directs adult cognitive changes . . . the most important adult cognitive changes are probably the result of life experiences, and would for the most part be expected to lack the across-subjects uniformity that characterizes the child's intellectual growth."

I think Flavell is wrong on the first count; that is, the morphological basis of children's cognitive development has never been fully documented, at least not to my satisfaction.

Children's cognitive growth then, is likely to reflect experiential factors as well, but is experience relevant to the acquisition of both process and substance. The adult experience, on the contrary, is likely to be relevant to quite different goals.

If we conceptualize cognitive growth as the stage of acquisition and postulate an asymptote for such growth in young adulthood, I believe, we have then by definition set forth a requirement for further adult stages. For if it be the purpose of the first part of life to acquire the intellectual tools needed to fully participate in the human experience, it then becomes necessary to postulate, if only on teleological grounds, that such preparation must have some further goals.

Now, it may be argued that survival into adulthood may be solely determined by the need for species reproduction. Even if this be so, in a species endowed with a prolonged period of immaturity, adult cognitive skills would as a minimum have evolutionary significance in their contribution to the survival, protection and acculturation of the next generation.

I would like to suggest then, that the period of acquisition described, for example, by Piagetian models, whether mediated primarily by biological or experiential events, in the main ends in young adulthood, and is replaced by other life stages, requiring different models.

What Is the Nature of Adult Stages?

If we accept the notion that adult development stages occur in response to experiential phenomena, we must next consider the attributes of such phenomena. Let me suggest that our search should lead us to an analysis of changes in cognitive requirements posed by environmental press. Here the work of social psychologists and anthropologists (and most noteworthy, that of the Langley Porter group under the leadership of

Marjorie Lowenthal and her associates) concerned with the analysis of adult life transitions gives us important cues (16).

A tentative scheme involving five possible adult cognitive stages is sketched in Figure 1. These sequential stages are denoted as *acquisitive, achieving, responsible, executive and reintegrative.*

Throughout the period characterized by us as *acquisitive,* the young organism has typically functioned in a protected environment. We believe that an important qualitative change in the environmental press occurs when the young adult is required to establish his own independence. For one thing, his problem-solving behavior no longer can be an isolated phenomenon, the consequences of which can be blunted by societal and/or parental protection. From now on, the adult will be held responsible fully and individually, and he must therefore embed his cognitive structures in a broader network, whose goal is no longer mere acquisition, but is now concerned with the achievement of competence.

I would like to suggest that the *achieving stage* (which age-wise may occur anywhere from the late teens to the early twenties) requires further progress beyond the processes associated with the level of formal operations described by Piaget and his disciples as occuring in adolescence. That is, we are now concerned with much more goal-directed formal operations; task resolution is embedded in the consequences of the solution for achieving independent social function of the organism. As a consequence, we would predict more efficient and effective cognitive function with respect to tasks which have role-related achievement potential, while the peak may indeed have passed for problem solving activities which are task-limited. Adolescence may see peak function in behaviors which are task-specific, respectively where the task, no matter how trivial, is important for the organism in the sense of the acquisition of skills regardless of their social

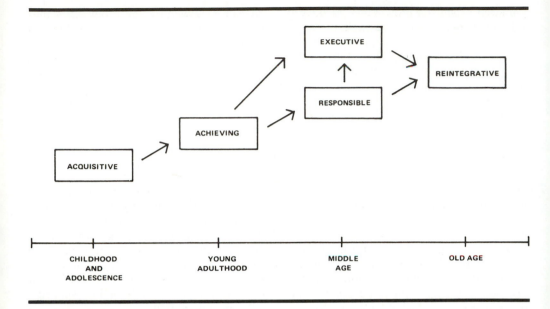

FIGURE 1

implications. Young adulthood, in contrast requires goal orientation. Different peak ages found on the Primary Mental Abilities would fit this contention (17).

The next postulated stage of adult cognitive development occurs when the individual has mastered cognitive competence to the point of implementing his role independence, and is now about to assume responsibility for other individuals (mate and/or offspring) at the inception of a new family unit. In western culture this transition would typically occur from the early twenties to the early thirties.

Transition to the *responsible* stage which extends in most individuals from the late thirties to the early sixties should again require qualitative changes in cognitive function. That is the free-wheeling style of the acquisitive period and the goal-directed entrepreneurial style of the achieving stage will be replaced by a pattern which facilitates integrating long-range goals as well as consequences for one's family unit in the solution

of real life problems. In laboratory situations, this should imply increased skills in relevant problem solving tasks, shifts in cognitive style to greater flexibility and lessened field dependence, gain in what has been described as the crystallized, but loss in the fluid abilities, the latter being of lowered relevance to the experiential demands upon the individual.

For some individuals, in the thirties and into the early forties, another stage may be reached which has been described by Neugarten in terms of the *executive* abilities of the middle-aged (18). The elicitative experiential press here would seem to be the assumption of responsibility for societal systems, instead of simple units, with the corresponding need to develop cognitive strategies which are efficient at integrating complex and high level hierarchical relationships. Here we should expect further gains on laboratory tasks such as pattern recognition, inductive thinking, and complex problem solving tasks, with corresponding lowering of skills in task specific situations as well as possibly some increase in difficulty in dealing with new bits of information as contrasted to the retrieval of past data.

For both the "responsible" and the "executive" stages, common psychometric tests of intelligence are likely to prove quite inadequate. The "building blocks" of intelligence are, of course, most important during the "acquisitive" and "achieving" stages, but they fail to tell us the whole story, when the emphasis of cognitive function changes to organizational, integrative and interpretive roles. Now it may be possible that a variety of task measuring problem solving skills and cognitive styles may be suitable vehicles for measuring intellectual competence at these stages of cognitive development (19–21). I fear, however, that it will be necessary to develop new measurement technologies which will borrow heavily on the information processing and systems analysis literature.

We have now described levels of cognitive development whose common mode is the need for the integration of acculturated intellectual skills at increasing levels of role complexity. It remains to consider a further stage or stages which will account for cognitive behavior during that part of life when the extent of societal involvement and responsibility relaxes and when biological changes may indeed once again impose constraints upon cognitive function.

I believe that the final phase of cognitive development, which I have elected to denote as the *reintegrative* stage, completes the transition from the "what should I know," through the "how should I use what I know," to the "why should I know" phase of life. Adaptive cognitive processes, at this level of development may well operate in an orthogonal fashion to a young adult structure of intellect model. Cognitive processes here are most certainly moderated by motivational and attitudinal variables to a much larger degree than would be true at any other life stage, an intuitive recognition,

which up to now has received only limited attention (and that only with respect to the attribute of cautiousness) (22, 23).

The transition of the "reintegrative" stage occurs at a time when the complexity of the adult cognitive structure has reached an over-load stage, and consequently demands simplification, and where environmentally programmed role requirements are reduced due to occupational retirement, relinquishment of responsibilities for children and family, and other role restrictions previously described as "disengagement" phenomena. But the cognitive response is not that of disengagement at all, it is one of achieving more selective attention to cognitive demands which remain meaningful or attain new meaning. Thus problem solving now no longer occurs as a simple response to a competence-motivation linked stimulus situation, but requires meaning and purpose within the immediate life situation of the individual, or within the more cosmic interests of selected older individuals who exemplify what folk myth describes as the "wisdom of old age" (also see Kohlberg's [24] description of his Stage 7).

Completely new strategies for the measurement of intellectual competence of the elderly will obviously be required. Such strategies, will first of all require an analysis of criterion variables relevant to the life experience and life roles of both the recently retired (or young) old and the very aged. Some of the pioneering work of Deming and Pressey may be illustrative, but the network of item content will have to be wide and the processes to be investigated need yet to be identified (25). The task will be no less than that faced by Binet in initially measuring the intelligence of school children.

Some Unfinished Business

I have now sketched some very gross outlines of my thinking on the characteristics of adult stages of cognitive development and the kind of operations that might be suitable for the differential investigation of such stages. I am quite aware of the fact that I have not addressed myself to the question of how my scheme related to models of adult development such as those suggested by Erikson (26) or by Kohlberg (23), some of whose stages may sound quite similar to mine. More importantly I have not addressed other implicit issues in the construction of developmental paradigms (27). For example attention will have to be given to the question of what might be necessary and sufficient conditions for transition from one adult state to the next, or whether such transitions imply substitutive or superimposed behavior patterns. Some progress has been made in analyzing the specific nature of Piaget's formal operations and the role of his concept of equilibration in adulthood (28).

Significant progress in the study of intellectual competence in adulthood and old age will not be made until we turn to ecologically valid criteria and develop a technology predicated upon the life context of the population under study rather than populations at other life stages. Hopefully, specifications such as those offered here will encourage movement towards the new models and operations required in this direction.

Other issues yet to be dealt with concern the manner in which the increasing complexity of environmental press interacts with the individual's cognitive structure such that a change in shifting from one stage to the next is required. And, finally we need to specify just how a hierarchical model of cognitive complexity can be related to the motivational parameters which I have suggested may become predominant in moderating cognitive behavior in old age.

References

1. K. W. Schaie, A Field-Theory Approach to Age Changes in Cognitive Behavior, *Vita Humana*, 5, pp. 129–141, 1962.

2. P. B. Baltes and K. W. Schaie, Aging and IQ: The Myth of the Twilight Years, *Psychology Today*, 7: 10, pp. 35–40, 1974.

3. K. W. Schaie, Reflections on Papers by Looft, Peterson and Sparks: Towards an Ageless Society?, *Gerontologist*, 13, pp. 31–35, 1973.

4. ——, Translations in Gerontology–From Lab to Life: Intellectual Functioning, *American Psychologist*, 29, pp. 802–807, 1974.

5. K. W. Schaie and K. Gribbin, Adult Development and Aging, *Annual Review of Psychology*, 26, pp. 65–96, 1975.

6. N. Bayley, Cognition and Aging, *Theory and Methods of Research on Aging*, K. W. Schaie, (ed.), West Virginia University Library, Morgantown, West Virginia, 1968.

7. J. L. Horn, Intelligence: Why It Grows, Why It Declines, *Human Intelligence*, J. M. Hunt, (ed.), Transaction Books, Brunswick, New Jersey, 1972.

8. P. E. Comalli, Jr., Life-Span Changes in Visual Perception, *Life-Span Developmental Psychology: Research and Theory*, L. R. Goulet and P. B. Baltes, (eds.), Academic Press, New York, 1970.

9. P. M. Bentler, Assessment of Developmental Factor Change at the Individual and Group Level, *Life-Span Developmental Psychology: Methodological Issues*, J. R. Nesselroade and H. W. Reese, (eds.), Academic Press, New York, 1973.

10. J. R. Nesselroade, Application of Multivariate Strategies to Problems of Measuring and Structuring Long-Term Change, *Life-Span Developmental Psychology: Research and Theory*, L. R. Goulet and P. B. Baltes, (eds.), Academic Press, New York, 1970.

11. G. Reinert, Comparative Factor Analytic Studies of Intelligence Throughout the Human Life-Span, *Life-Span Developmental Psychology: Research and Theory*, L. R. Goulet and B. P. Baltes, (eds.), Academic Press, New York, 1970.

12. P. K. Alpaugh, Variables Affecting Creativity in Adulthood: A Descriptive Study, un-

published M. A. thesis, University of Southern California, 1975.

13. J. H. Flavell, *The Developmental Psychology of Jean Piaget,* Van Nostrand, Princeton, New Jersey, 1963.

14. J. P. Guilford, *The Nature of Human Intelligence,* McGraw-Hill, New York, 1967.

15. J. H. Flavell, Cognitive Changes in Adulthood, *Life-Span Developmental Psychology: Research and Theory,* L. R. Goulet and P. B. Baltes, (eds.), Academic Press, New York, 1970.

16. M. F. Lowenthal, M. Thurnher, D. Chiriboga, et al., *Four Stages of Life,* Jossey-Bass, San Francisco, 1975.

17. K. W. Schaie, A Reinterpretation of Age-Related Changes in Cognitive Structure and Functioning, *Life-Span Developmental Psychology: Research and Theory,* L. R. Goulet and P. B. Baltes, (eds.), Academic Press, New York, 1970.

18. B. L. Neugarten, Continuities and Discontinuities of Psychological Issues Into Adult Life, *Human Development,* 12, pp. 121–130, 1969.

19. H. Rimoldi, et al., Problem Solving in High School and College Students, Cooperative Research Project No. 2199, Loyola University, Chicago, 1964.

20. K. W. Schaie and I. A. Parham, *Examiner Manual for the Test of Behavioral Rigidity,* 2nd revised edition, Consulting Psychologists Press, Palo Alto, California, 1975.

21. H. A. Witkin, D. R. Goodenough and S. A. Karp, Stability of Cognitive Style from Childhood to Young Adulthood, *Journal of Personality and Social Psychology,* 7, pp. 291–300, 1967.

22. J. Botwinick, Disinclination to Venture Response Versus Cautiousness in Responding: Age Differences, *Journal of Genetic Psychology,* 119, pp. 241–249, 1969.

23. W. R. Birkhill and K. W. Schaie, The Effect of Differential Reinforcement of Cautiousness in the Intellectual Performance of the Elderly, *Journal of Gerontology,* 30, pp. 578–583, 1975.

24. L. Kohlberg, Continuities in Childhood and Adult Moral Development, *Life-Span Developmental Psychology: Personality and Socialization,* P. B. Baltes and K. W. Schaie, (eds.), Academic Press, New York, 1973.

25. J. A. Demming and S. L. Pressey, Tests Indigenous to the Adult and Older Years, *Journal of Counseling Psychology,* 4, pp. 144–148, 1957.

26. E. H. Erikson, *Childhood and Society,* Norton, New York, 1963.

27. P. B. Baltes and K. W. Schaie, On Life-Span Developmental Research Paradigms: Retrospects and Prospects, *Life-Span Developmental Psychology: Personality and Socialization,* P. B. Baltes and K. W. Schaie, (eds.), Academic Press, New York, 1973.

28. K. W. Schaie and B. W. Marquette, Stages in Transition: A Bio-Social Analysis, paper presented at the ISSBD satellite symposium to the 10th International Congress of Gerontology, Kiryat Anavim, Israel, 1975.

8

Motivation

THE WHYS AND THE WHEREFORES

Motivational theories try to answer the question "Why?" by describing the determinants of behavioral choice, intensity, and persistence. Very little is known about age changes in basic biological drives such as hunger and thirst. There does seem to be a decrease with age in the ability to arouse oneself and, once aroused, to maintain one's arousal within the most desirable range for nonflustered and maximally competent behavior.

Although lack of success in mastering stress typically produces anxiety, and multiple stresses increase with age, it seems that anxiety is less of a problem for older adults than for younger adults. This may be partly due to biological reasons, such as the just mentioned decreases in arousability, but it may also be due in part because of better coping strategies. Even when primitive emotions like fear and anxiety are involved, thought plays a powerful role in human motivation, permitting cognitive control of anxiety.

The intimate relationship between cognition and motivation is illustrated by the concept of *locus of control*. Locus of control can be either external (exercised by other people or an impersonal fate) or internal (assumption of personal responsibility for one's successes and failures). Older adults are more likely than young adults to view control as external, perhaps realistically. But such views, unfortunately, may lead to passive acceptance of one's fate and to depression over the inability to control one's destiny. When the locus of control of unpleasant events is clearly external this may lead to *learned helplessness*. This concept was developed in studies where animals stopped trying to control their environment through their own actions; they "learned" to be "helpless." In humans, a lengthy learning phase seems to be unnecessary; simply placing humans in an environment in which they *perceive* the locus of control to be external is sufficient. It is possible, however, to reduce this learned helplessness by means of therapeutic intervention.

Our first selection, by *Ellen J. Langer* and *Judith Rodin,* describes a field experiment in a nursing home in which patients were encouraged to assume greater responsibility for themselves and for something outside themselves (taking care of a plant). This intervention resulted in substantial improvement in alertness, active participation, and general sense of well-being.

As people grow older, moral principles and religious values frequently assume a greater role in their lives. *Lawrence Kohlberg* has intensively studied this progression and has offered a theoretical framework of how moral principles develop from childhood into adulthood. According to Kohlberg's theory of moral development, adults generally hold a *law-and-order* view of morality or a *social-contract* view. But a few people reach a stage based on *universal ethical principles*. Development of moral thought in childhood is concerned with the learning and comprehension of social norms and social ideals, and thus develops through trying out roles and engaging in symbolic social interactions. By contrast, adult principles seem to require personal experiences of moral choice and responsibility, following a period of questioning and moral "moratorium" in adolescence and young adulthood.

Participation in religious activities, such as attending church, declines with age, but personal interest in religious questions increases. *David O. Moberg* provides a thoughtful analysis of the role of religious thought and behavior in the last portion of life and reviews the fairly sparse research literature. Although written some years ago, it still is the most authoritative summary we could find, and surprisingly little empirical work has been done in the interim. Moberg's conclusions suggest that for those people who have an intrinsic interest in religion — those who are drawn to its philosophic values — religion often provides solace, during life as well as at the time of death.

Additional Suggested Readings

Marsh, G. R., & Thompson, L. W. Psychophysiology of aging. In J. E. Birren & K. W. Schaie (eds.), *Handbook of the psychology of aging*. New York: Van Nostrand Reinhold, 1977, pp. 219–248.
> Comprehensive review of the literature on autonomic and central nervous system correlates of behavior important for understanding age changes in the physiological mechanisms that mediate motivated behavior.

Seligman, M. E. P. *Helplessness*. San Francisco: Freeman, 1975.
> The concept of learned helplessness is traced from animal behavior to human response in different social and interpersonal settings. Research findings are discussed which distinguish responses by those who are self-contained from those by persons who depend primarily on external input.

The Effects of Choice and Enhanced Personal Responsibility for the Aged: A Field Experiment in an Institutional Setting

ELLEN J. LANGER AND JUDITH RODIN

A field experiment was conducted to assess the effects of enhanced personal responsibility and choice on a group of nursing home residents. It was expected that the debilitated condition of many of the aged residing in institutional settings is, at least in part, a result of living in a virtually decision-free environment and consequently is potentially reversible. Residents who were in the experimental group were given a communication emphasizing their responsibility for themselves, whereas the communication given to a second group stressed the staff's responsibility for them. In addition, to bolster the communication, the former group was given the freedom to make choices and the responsibility of caring for a plant rather than having decisions made and the plant taken care of for them by the staff, as was the case for the latter group. Questionnaire ratings and behavioral measures showed a significant improvement for the experimental group over the comparison group on alertness, active participation, and a general sense of well-being.

The transition from adulthood to old age is often perceived as a process of loss, physiologically and psychologically (Birren, 1958; Gould, 1972). However, it is as yet unclear just how much of this change is biologically determined and how much is a function of the environment. The ability to sustain a sense of personal control in old age may be greatly influenced by societal factors, and this in turn may affect one's physical well-being.

Typically the life situation does change in old age. There is some loss of roles, norms, and reference groups, events that negatively influence one's perceived competence and feeling of responsibility (Bengtson, 1973). Perception of these changes in addition to actual physical decrements may enhance a sense of aging and lower self-esteem (Lehr & Puschner, Note 1). In response to internal developmental changes, the aging individual may come to see himself in a position of lessened mastery relative to the rest of the world, as a passive object manipulated by the environment (Neugarten & Gutmann, 1958). Questioning whether these factors can be counteracted, some studies have suggested that more successful aging — mea-

Source: Langer, E. J., & Rodin, J. The effects of choice and enhanced personal responsibility for the aged: A field experiment in an institutional setting. *Journal of Personality and Social Psychology*, 1976, 34, 191–198. Copyright 1976 by the American Psychological Association. Reprinted by permission.

sured by decreased mortality, morbidity, and psychological disability — occurs when an individual feels a sense of usefulness and purpose (Bengtson, 1973; Butler, 1967; Leaf, 1973; Lieberman, 1965).

The notion of competence is indeed central to much of human behavior. Adler (1930) has described the need to control one's personal environment as "an intrinsic necessity of life itself" (p. 398). deCharms (1968) has stated that "man's primary motivation propensity is to be effective in producing changes in his environment. Man strives to be a causal agent, to be the primary locus of, causation for, or the origin of, his behavior; he strives for personal causation" (p. 269).

Several laboratory studies have demonstrated that reduced control over aversive outcomes increases physiological distress and anxiety (Geer, Davison, & Gatchel, 1970; Pervin, 1963) and even a nonveridical perception of control over an impending event reduces the aversiveness of that event (Bowers, 1968; Glass & Singer, 1972; Kanfer & Seidner, 1973). Langer, Janis, and Wolfer (1975) found that by inducing the perception of control over stress in hospital patients by means of a communication that emphasized potential cognitive control, subjects requested fewer pain relievers and sedatives and were seen by nurses as evidencing less anxiety.

Choice is also a crucial variable in enhancing an induced sense of control. Stotland and Blumenthal (1964) studied the effects of choice on anxiety reduction. They told subjects that they were going to take a number of important ability tests. Half of the subjects were allowed to choose the order in which they wanted to take the tests, and half were told that the order was fixed. All subjects were informed that the order of the tests would have no bearing on their scores. They found that subjects not given the choice were more anxious, as measured by palmar

sweating. In another study of the effects of choice, Corah and Boffa (1970) told their subjects that there were two conditions in the experiment, each of which would be signaled by a different light. In one condition they were given the choice of whether or not to press a button to escape from an aversive noise, and in the other one they were not given the option of escaping. They found that the choice instructions decreased the aversiveness of the threatening stimulus, apparently by increasing perceived control. Although using a very different paradigm, Langer (1975) also demonstrated the importance of choice. In that study it was found that the exercise of choice in a chance situation, where choice was objectively inconsequential, nevertheless had psychological consequences manifested in increased confidence and risk taking.

Lefcourt (1973) best summed up the essence of this research in a brief review article dealing with the perception of control in man and animals when he concluded that "the sense of control, the illusion that one can exercise personal choice, has a definite and a positive role in sustaining life" (p. 424). It is not surprising, then, that these important psychological factors should be linked to health and survival. In a series of retrospective studies, Schmale and his associates (Adamson & Schmale, 1965; Schmale, 1958; Schmale & Iker, 1966) found that ulcerative colitis, leukemia, cervical cancer, and heart disease were linked with a feeling of helplessness and loss of hope experienced by the patient prior to the onset of the disease. Seligman and his co-workers have systematically investigated the learning of helplessness and related it to the clinical syndrome of depression (see Seligman, 1975). Even death is apparently related to control-relevant variables. McMahon and Rhudick (1964) found a relationship between depression or hopelessness and death. The most graphic description of this association comes from Bettelheim (1943), who in his analysis of the "Muselmanner," the walking corpses in the concentration camps, described them as:

> Prisoners who came to believe the repeated statements of the guards — that there was no hope for them, that they would never leave the camp except as a corpse — who came to feel that their environment was one over which they could exercise no influence whatsoever. ... Once his own life and the environment were viewed as totally beyond his ability to influence them, the only logical conclusion was to pay no attention to them whatsoever. Only then, all conscious awareness of stimuli coming from the outside was blocked out, and with it all response to anything but inner stimuli.

Death swiftly followed and, according to Bettelheim,

> [survival] depended on one's ability to arrange to preserve some areas of independent action, to keep control of some important aspects of one's life despite an environment that seemed overwhelming and total.

Bettelheim's description reminds us of Richter's (1957) rats, who also "gave up hope" of controlling their environment and subsequently died.

The implications of these studies for research in the area of aging are clear. Objective helplessness as well as feelings of helplessness and hopelessness — both enhanced by the environment and by intrinsic changes that occur with increasing old age — may contribute to psychological withdrawal, physical disease, and death. In contrast, objective control and feelings of mastery may very well contribute to physical health and personal efficacy.

In a study conceived to explore the effects of dissonance, Ferrare (1962; cited in Seligman, 1975; Zimbardo & Ruch, 1975) presented data concerning the effects of the ability of geriatric patients to control their place of residence. Of 17 subjects who answered that they did not have any other alternative but to move to a specific old age home, 8 died after 4 weeks of residence and 16 after 10 weeks of residence. By comparison, among the residents who died during the initial period, only one person had answered that she had the freedom to choose other alternatives. All of these deaths were classified as unexpected because "not even insignificant disturbances had actually given warning of the impending disaster."

As Zimbardo (Zimbardo & Ruch, 1975) suggested, the implications of Ferrare's data are striking and merit further study of old age home settings. There is already evidence that perceived personal control in one's residential environment is important for younger and noninstitutional populations. Rodin (in press), using children as subjects, demonstrated that diminished feelings of control produced by chronic crowding at home led to fewer attempts to control self-reinforcement in the laboratory and to greater likelihood of giving up in the face of failure.

The present study attempted to assess directly the effects of enhanced personal responsibility and choice in a group of nursing home patients. In addition to examining previous results from the control-helplessness literature in a field setting, the present study extended the domain of this conception by considering new response variables. Specifically, if increased control has generalized beneficial effects, then physical and mental alertness, activity, general level of satisfaction, and sociability should all be affected. Also, the manipulation of the independent variables, assigning greater responsibility and decision freedom for relevant behavior, allowed subjects real choices that were not directed toward a single behavior or stimulus condition. This manipulation tested the ability of the subjects to generalize from specific choices enumerated for them to other aspects of their lives, and thus tested the generalizability of feelings of control over certain elements of the situation to more broadly based behavior and attitudes.

Method

Subjects

The study was conducted in a nursing home, which was rated by the state of Connecticut as being among the finest care units and offering quality medical, recreational, and residential facilities. The home was large and modern in design, appearing cheerful and comfortable as well as clean and efficient. Of the four floors in the home, two were selected for study because of similarity in the residents' physical and psychological health and prior socioeconomic status, as determined from evaluations made by the home's director, head nurses, and social worker. Residents were assigned to a particular floor and room simply on the basis of availability, and on the average, residents on the two floors had been at the home about the same length of time. Rather than randomly assigning subjects to experimental treatment, a different floor was randomly selected for each treatment. Since there was not a great deal of communication between floors, this procedure was followed in order to decrease the likelihood that the treatment effects would be contaminated. There were 8 males and 39 females in the responsibility-induced condition (all fourth-floor residents) and 9 males and 35 females in the comparison group (all second-floor residents). Residents who were either completely bedridden or judged by the nursing home staff to be completely noncommunicative (11 on the experimental floor and 9 on the comparison floor) were omitted from the sample. Also omitted was one woman on each floor, one 40 years old and the other 26 years old, due to their age. Thus, 91 ambulatory adults, ranging in age from 65 to 90, served as subjects.

Procedure

To introduce the experimental treatment, the nursing home administrator, an outgoing and friendly 33-year-old male who interacts with the residents daily, called a meeting in the lounge of each floor. He delivered one of the following two communications at that time:

[*Responsibility-induced group*] I brought you together today to give you some information about Arden House. I was surprised to learn that many of you don't know about the things that are available to you and more important, that many of you don't realize the influence you have over your own lives here. Take a minute to think of the decisions you can and should be making. For example, you have the responsibility of caring for yourselves, of deciding whether or not you want to make this a home you can be proud of and happy in. You should be deciding how you want your rooms to be arranged — whether you want it to be as it is or whether you want the staff to help you rearrange the furniture. You should be deciding how you want to spend your time, for example, whether you want to be visiting your friends who live on this floor or on other floors, whether you want to visit in your room or your friends' room, in the lounge, the dining room, etc., or whether you want to be watching television, listening to the radio, writing, reading, or planning social events. In other words, it's your life and you can make of it whatever you want.

This brings me to another point. If you are unsatisfied with anything here, you have the influence to change it. It's your responsibility to make your complaints known, to tell us what you would like to change, to tell us what you would like. These are just a few of the things you could and should be deciding and thinking about now and from time to time everyday. You made these decisions before you came here and you can and should be making them now.

We're thinking of instituting some way for airing complaints, suggestions, etc. Let [nurse's name] know if you think this is a good idea and how you think we should go about doing it. In any case let her know what your complaints or suggestions are.

Also, I wanted to take this opportunity to give you each a present from the Arden House. [A box of small plants was passed around, and patients were given two decisions to make: first, whether or not they wanted a plant at all, and second, to choose which one they wanted. All residents did select a plant.] The plants are yours to keep and take care of as you'd like.

One last thing, I wanted to tell you that we're showing a movie two nights next week, Thursday and Friday. You should decide which night you'd like to go, if you choose to see it at all.

[*Comparison group*] I brought you together today to give you some information about the Arden House. I was surprised to learn that many of you don't know about the things that are available to you; that many of you don't realize all you're allowed to do here. Take a minute to think of all the options that we've provided for you in order for your life to be fuller and more interesting. For example, you're permitted to visit people on the other floors and to use the lounge on this floor for visiting as well as the dining room or your own rooms. We want your rooms to be as nice as they can be, and we've tried to make them that way for you. We want you to be happy here. We feel that it's our responsibility to make this a home you can be proud of and happy in, and we want to do all we can to help you.

This brings me to another point. If you have any complaints or suggestions about anything, let [nurse's name] know what they are. Let us know how we can best help you. You should feel that you have free access to anyone on the staff, and we will do the best we can to provide individualized attention and time for you.

Also, I wanted to take this opportunity to give you each a present from the Arden House. [The nurse walked around with a box of plants and each patient was handed one.] The plants

are yours to keep. The nurses will water and care for them for you.

One last thing, I wanted to tell you that we're showing a movie next week on Thursday and Friday. We'll let you know later which day you're scheduled to see it.

The major difference between the two communications was that on one floor, the emphasis was on the residents' responsibility for themselves, whereas on the other floor, the communication stressed the staff's responsibility for them. In addition, several other differences bolstered this treatment: Residents in the responsibility-induced group were asked to give their opinion of the means by which complaints were handled rather than just being told that any complaints would be handled by staff members; they were given the opportunity to select their own plant and to care for it themselves, rather than being given a plant to be taken care of by someone else; and they were given their choice of a movie night, rather than being assigned a particular night, as was typically the case in the old age home. However, there was no difference in the amount of attention paid to the two groups.

Three days after these communications had been delivered, the director visited all of the residents in their rooms or in the corridor and reiterated part of the previous message. To those in the responsibility-induced group he said, "Remember what I said last Thursday. We want you to be happy. Treat this like your own home and make all the decisions you used to make. How's your plant coming along?" To the residents of the comparison floor, he said the same thing, omitting the statement about decision making.

Dependent Variables

Questionnaires   Two types of questionnaires were designed to assess the effects of induced responsibility. Each was administered 1 week prior to and 3 weeks after the communication. The first was administered directly to the residents by a female research assistant who was unaware of the experimental hypotheses or of the specific experimental treatment. The questions dealt with how much control they felt over general events in their lives and how happy and active they felt. Questions were responded to along 8-point scales ranging from 0 (none) to 8 (total). After completing each interview, the research assistant rated the resident on an 8-point scale for alertness.

The second questionnaire was responded to by the nurses, who staffed the experimental and comparison floors and who were unaware of the experimental treatments. Nurses on two different shifts completed the questionnaires in order to obtain two ratings for each subject. There were nine 10-point scales that asked for ratings of how happy, alert, dependent, sociable, and active the residents were as well as questions about their eating and sleeping habits. There were also questions evaluating the proportion of weekly time the patient spent engaged in a variety of activities. These included reading, watching television, visiting other patients, visiting outside guests, watching the staff, talking to the staff, sitting alone doing nothing, and others.

Behavioral measures   Since perceived personal control is enhanced by a sense of choice over relevant behaviors, the option to choose which night the experimental group wished to see the movie was expected to have measurable effects on active participation. Attendance records were kept by the occupational therapist, who was unaware that an experiment was being conducted.

Another measure of involvement was obtained by holding a competition in which all participants had to guess the number of jelly beans in a large jar. Each patient wishing to enter the contest simply wrote his or her name and estimate on a piece of paper and

deposited it in a box that was next to the jar.[1]

Finally, an unobtrusive measure of activity was taken. The tenth night after the experimental treatment, the right wheels of the wheelchairs belonging to a randomly selected subsample of each patient group were covered with 2 inches (.05 m) of white adhesive tape. The following night, the tape was removed from the chairs and placed on index cards for later evaluation of amount of activity, as indicated by the amount of discoloration.

Results

Questionnaires   Before examining whether or not the experimental treatment was effective, the pretest ratings made by the subjects, the nurses, and the interviewer were compared for both groups. None of the differences approached significance, which indicates comparability between groups prior to the start of the investigation.

The means for responses to the various questionnaires are summarized in Table 1. Statistical tests compared the posttest minus pretest scores of the experimental and comparison groups.

In response to direct questions about how happy they currently were, residents in the responsibility-induced group reported significantly greater increases in happiness after the experimental treatment than did the comparison group, $t(43) = 1.96$, $p < .05$.[2] Although the comparison group heard

---

[1] We also intended to measure the number of complaints that patients voiced. Since one often does not complain after becoming psychologically helpless, complaints in this context were expected to be a positive indication of perceived personal control. This measure was discarded, however, since the nurses failed to keep a systematic written record.

[2] All the statistics for the self-report data and the interviewers' ratings are based on 45 subjects (25 in the responsibility-induced group and 20 in the comparison group), since these were the only subjects available at the time of the interview.

TABLE 1

Mean Scores for Self-report, Interviewer Ratings, and Nurses' Ratings for Experimental and Comparison Groups

Questionnaire responses	Responsibility induced (n = 24)			Comparison (n = 28)			Comparison of change scores (p <)
	Pre	Post	Change: Post–Pre	Pre	Post	Change: Post–Pre	
Self-report							
Happy	5.16	5.44	.28	4.90	4.78	− .12	.05
Active	4.07	4.27	.20	3.90	2.62	− 1.28	.01
Perceived Control							
Have	3.26	3.42	.16	3.62	4.03	.41	—
Want	3.85	3.80	− .05	4.40	4.57	.17	—
Interviewer rating							
Alertness	5.02	5.31	.29	5.75	5.38	− .37	.025
Nurses' ratings							
General improvement	41.67	45.64	3.97	42.69	40.32	− 2.39	.005
Time spent							
Visiting patients	13.03	19.81	6.78	7.94	4.65	− 3.30	.005
Visiting others	11.50	13.75	2.14	12.38	8.21	− 4.16	.05
Talking to staff	8.21	16.43	8.21	9.11	10.71	1.61	.01
Watching staff	6.78	4.64	− 2.14	6.96	11.60	4.64	.05

a communication that had specifically stressed the home's commitment to making them happy, only 25% of them reported feeling happier by the time of the second interview, whereas 48% of the experimental group did so.

The responsibility-induced group reported themselves to be significantly more active on the second interview than the comparison group, $t(43) = 2.67$, $p < .01$. The interviewer's ratings of alertness also showed significantly greater increase for the experimental group, $t(43) = 2.40$, $p < .025$. However, the questions that were relevant to perceived control showed no significant changes for the experimental group. Since over 20% of the patients indicated that they were unable to understand what we meant by control, these questions were obviously not adequate to discriminate between groups.

The second questionnaire measured nurses' ratings of each patient. The correlation between the two nurses' ratings of the same patient was .68 and .61 ($ps < .005$) on the comparison and responsibility-induced floors, respectively.[3] For each patient, a score was calculated by averaging the two nurses' ratings for each question, summing across questions, and subtracting the total pretreatment score from the total posttreatment score.[4] This yielded a positive average

[3] There was also significant agreement between the interviewer's and nurses' ratings of alertness ($r = .65$).

[4] Since one nurse on the day shift and one nurse on the night shift gave the ratings, responses to the questions regarding sleeping and eating habits were not included in the total score. Also, in order to reduce rater bias, patients for whom there were ratings by a nurse on only one shift were excluded from this calculation. This left 24 residents from the experimental group and 28 from the comparison group.

total change score of 3.97 for the responsibility-induced group as compared with an average negative total change of -2.37 for the comparison group. The difference between these means is highly significant, $t(50) = 5.18$, $p < .005$. If one looks at the percentage of people who were judged improved rather than at the amount of judged improvement, the same pattern emerges: 93% of the experimental group (all but one subject) were considered improved, whereas only 21% (six subjects) of the comparison group showed this positive change ($\chi^2 = 19.23$, $p < .005$).

The nurses' evaluation of the proportion of time subjects spent engaged in various interactive and noninteractive activities was analyzed by comparing the average change scores (post-precommunication) for all the nurses for both groups of subjects on each activity. Several significant differences were found. The experimental group showed increases in the proportion of time spent visiting with other patients (for the experimental group, $\overline{X} = 12.86$ vs. -6.61 for the comparison group), $t(50) = 3.83$, $p < .005$; visiting people from outside of the nursing home (for the experimental group, $\overline{X} = 4.28$ vs. -7.61 for the comparison group, $t(50) = 2.30$, $p < .05$; and talking to the staff (for the experimental group, $\overline{X} = 8.21$ vs. 1.61 for the comparison group), $t(50) = 2.98$, $p < .05$. [5] In addition, they spent less time passively watching the staff (for the experimental group, $\overline{X} = -4.28$ vs. 9.68 for the comparison group), $t(50) = 2.60$, $p < .05$. Thus, it appears that the treatment increased active, interpersonal activity but not passive activity such as watching television or reading.

Behavioral measures   As in the case of the questionnaires, the behavioral measures showed a pattern of differences between groups that was generally consistent with the predicted effects of increased responsibility. The movie attendance was significantly higher in the responsibility-induced group than in the control group after the experimental treatment ($z = 1.71$, $p < .05$, one-tailed), although a similar attendance check taken one month before the communications revealed no group differences. [6]

In the jelly-bean-guessing contest, 10 subjects (21%) in the responsibility-induced group and only 1 subject (2%) from the comparison group participated ($\chi^2 = 7.72$, $p < .01$). Finally, very little dirt was found on the tape taken from any of the patients' wheelchairs, and there was no significant difference between the two groups.

Discussion

It appears that inducing a greater sense of personal responsibility in people who may have virtually relinquished decision making, either by choice or necessity, produces improvement. In the present investigation, patients in the comparison group were given a communication stressing the staff's desire to make them happy and were otherwise treated in the sympathetic manner characteristic of this high-quality nursing home. Despite the care provided for these people, 71% were rated as having become more debilitated over a period of time as short as 3 weeks. In contrast with this group, 93% of the people who were encouraged to make decisions for themselves, given decisions to make, and given responsibility for something outside of themselves, actually showed overall improvement. Based on their own judgments and by the judgments of the nurses with whom they interacted on a daily

---

[5] This statistic is based only on the responses of nurse on duty in the evening.

[6] Frequencies were transformed into arc sines and analyzed using the method that is essentially the same as that described by Langer and Abelson (1972).

basis, they became more active and felt happier. Perhaps more important was the judged improvement in their mental alertness and increased behavioral involvement in many different kinds of activities.

The behavioral measures showed greater active participation and involvement for the experimental group. Whether this directly resulted from an increase in perceived choice and decision-making responsibility or from the increase in general activity and happiness occurring after the treatment cannot be assessed from the present results. It should also be clearly noted that although there were significant differences in active involvement, the overall level of participation in the activities that comprised the behavioral measures was low. Perhaps a much more powerful treatment would be one that is individually administered and

repeated on several occasions. That so weak a manipulation had any effect suggests how important increased control is for these people, for whom decision making is virtually nonexistent.

The practical implications of this experimental demonstration are straightforward. Mechanisms can and should be established for changing situational factors that reduce real or perceived responsibility in the elderly. Furthermore, this study adds to the body of literature (Bengtson, 1973; Butler, 1967; Leaf, 1973; Lieberman, 1965) suggesting that senility and diminished alertness are not an almost inevitable result of aging. In fact, it suggests that some of the negative consequences of aging may be retarded, reversed, or possibly prevented by returning to the aged the right to make decisions and a feeling of competence.

Reference Note

1. Lehr, K., & Puschner, I. *Studies in the awareness of aging.* Paper presented at the 6th International Congress on Gerontology, Copenhagen, 1963.

References

Adamson, J., & Schmale, A. Object loss, giving up, and the onset of psychiatric disease. *Psychosomatic Medicine,* 1965, 27, 557–576.

Adler, A. Individual psychology. In C. Murchinson (Ed.), *Psychologies of 1930.* Worcester, Mass.: Clark University Press, 1930.

Bengtson, V. L. Self determination: A social and psychological perspective on helping the aged. *Geriatrics,* 1973.

Bettelheim, B. Individual and mass behavior in extreme situations. *Journal of Abnormal and Social Psychology,* 1943, 38, 417–452.

Birren, J. Aging and psychological adjustment. *Review of Educational Research,* 1958, 28, 475–490.

Bowers, K. Pain, anxiety, and perceived control. *Journal of Consulting and Clinical Psychology,* 1968, 32, 596–602.

Butler, R. Aspects of survival and adaptation in human aging. *American Journal of Psychiatry,* 1967, 123, 1233–1243.

Corah, N., & Boffa, J. Perceived control, self-observation, and response to aversive stimulation. *Journal of Personality and Social Psychology,* 1970, 16, 1–4.

deCharms, R. *Personal causation.* New York: Academic Press, 1968.

Geer, J., Davison, G., & Gatchel, R. Reduction of stress in humans through nonveridical perceived control of aversive stimulation. *Journal of Personality and Social Psychology,* 1970, 16, 731–738.

Glass, D., & Singer, J. *Urban stress.* New York: Academic Press, 1972.

Gould, R. The phases of adult life: A study in developmental psychology. *American Journal of Psychiatry,* 1972, 129, 521–531.

Kanfer, R., & Seidner, M. Self-Control: Factors enhancing tolerance of noxious stimulation. *Journal of Personality and Social Psychology,* 1973, 25, 381–389.

Langer, E. J. The illusion of control. *Journal of*

Personality and Social Psychology, 1975, 32, 311–328.

Langer, E. J., & Abelson, R. P. The semantics of asking a favor: How to succeed in getting help without really dying. *Journal of Personality and Social Psychology,* 1972, 24, 26–32.

Langer, E. J., Janis, I. L., & Wolfer, J. A. Reduction of psychological stress in surgical patients. *Journal of Experimental Social Psychology,* 1975, 11, 155–165.

Leaf, A. Threescore and forty. *Hospital Practice,* 1973, 34, 70–71.

Lefcourt, H. The function of the illusion of control and freedom. *American Psychologist,* 1973, 28, 417–425.

Lieberman, M. Psychological correlates of impending death: Some preliminary observations. *Journal of Gerontology,* 1965, 20, 181–190.

McMahon, A., & Rhudick, P. Reminiscing, adaptational significance in the aged. *Archives of General Psychiatry,* 1964, 10, 292–298.

Neugarten, B., & Gutmann, D. Age-sex roles and personality in middle age: A thematic apperception study. *Psychological Monographs,* 1958, 72 (17, Whole No. 470).

Pervin, L. The need to predict and control under conditions of threat. *Journal of Personality,* 1963, 31, 570–585.

Richter, C. On the phenomenon of sudden death in animals and man. *Psychosomatic Medicine,* 1957, 19, 191–198.

Rodin, J. Crowding, perceived choice, and response to controllable and uncontrollable outcomes. *Journal of Experimental Social Psychology,* in press.

Schmale, A. Relationships of separation and depression to disease. I.: A report on a hospitalized medical population. *Psychosomatic Medicine,* 1958, 20, 259–277.

Schmale, A., & Iker, H. The psychological setting of uterine cervical cancer. *Annals of the New York Academy of Sciences,* 1966, 125, 807–813.

Seligman, M. E. P. *Helplessness.* San Francisco: Freeman, 1975.

Stotland, E., & Blumenthal, A. The reduction of anxiety as a result of the expectation of making a choice. *Canadian Review of Psychology,* 1964, 18, 139–145.

Zimbardo, P. G., & Ruch, F. L. *Psychology and life* (9th ed.). Glenview, Ill.: Scott, Foresman, 1975.

Continuities in Childhood and Adult Moral Development Revisited

LAWRENCE KOHLBERG

This chapter is addressed to the question of existence of adulthood stages and stage change in moral development. *Stage change* is defined as directed, sequential, qualitative transformations in psychological structure. The existence of adulthood psychological stage change is theoretically important since such change must be the result of experiential interaction with the environment, rather than being linked to biological maturation.

Evidence of Piagetian cognitive stages indicates continuing development of formal thought past adolescence but no new postadolescent cognitive stage. In contrast, this chapter indicates that there are moral stages that first appear in young adulthood (over 21) in a longitudinal sample. These are the stages of principled moral reasoning (Stage 5, social contract utilitarian orientation and Stage 6, universal principles of justice orientation). An earlier study by Kohlberg and Kramer (1969) reported attainment of principled moral reasoning in high school followed by "retrogression" to a skeptical egocentric relativism. A scoring system which better differentiates structure from content indicates that this skeptical relativism is a transitional state between conventional and principled morality rather than a retrogression. It also indicates that the high school reasoning scored as principled was only an advanced form of conventional reasoning (Stage 4, member of society orientation). It was suggested that the nature of the experiences leading to adulthood development, e.g., to principled moral thought, were somewhat different than those involved in childhood and adolescent movement to the conventional stages of moral reasoning. Development of moral thought in childhood is an increasingly adequate comprehension of existing social norms and social ideals. Accordingly, it develops through the usual experiences of social symbolic interaction and role taking. In contrast, construction of principles seems to require experiences of personal moral choice and responsibility usually supervening upon a questioning period of "moratorium."

This view of adulthood moral stages linked to experience of personal choice suggests a rapprochement between Erikson's stage theory of adult development and a more cognitive–structural stage theory. This, in turn, invites speculation as to a more ontological or religious seventh stage which might correspond to Erikson's stage of integrity–despair.

Source: Abridged from Kohlberg, L. Continuities in childhood and adult moral development revisited. In P. B. Baltes & K. W. Schaie (eds.), *Life-span developmental psychology: Personality and socialization.* New York: Academic Press, 1973, pp. 179–204. Copyright 1973 by Academic Press, Inc. Reprinted by permission.

Introduction

Probably the most important problem for life-span psychology is that of the existence of developmental stages in adulthood. This paper will survey the scanty evidence on the existence of adulthood cognitive and moral stages, and consider the way experience in adulthood could lead to stage change. . . .

Concepts of Stage in Relation to Adulthood

Before reviewing the evidence, it might be pointed out that the existence of adulthood stages has not yet been the subject of any serious direct systematic study other than my own. In saying this, a rigid and precise notion of the stage concept is used. This notion comes from the structural tradition of Piaget and other cognitive–developmental child psychologists. The notion of stage used in most discussions of adult change is not structural; it is, rather, the notion of socio-cultural or social role-defined *developmental tasks*. In this conception, a culture (responding, in part, to maturational events) outlines a rough sequence of roles or tasks from birth to death, and adaptation to this task sequence leads to age-typical personality changes. Such *stages* are defined primarily by new socio-cultural environments or roles as they impact upon already established maturational capacities and acquired response patterns. To research such adult stages involves all the complexities of sampling and design elaborated by Schaie (1973). The relation of the stage to age must be defined independent of cohort, and it must be defined across a representative sample for the culture or subcultures for which the stage is postulated.

Often opposed to such socio-environmentally defined stages are biological-maturational stages. In the psychological realm, an example would be the stages of classical psychoanalytic theory, psychosexual stages,

defined by the biological activation of a new organ. This may be called the embryological stage model. Oral, anal, and phallic psychosexual stages correspond to the neurological sensitization or libidinalization of new organs. Such a direct biological model of stages is unlikely to postulate adult stages. After early adulthood, biological notions of development are notions of either stabilization or decrement in biological functioning, rather than of new biological activation of a structure or qualitative biological change in a structure.

The cognitive–developmental or structural model of stages involves both different theoretical postulates and a different research strategy than do socio-cultural and maturational concepts of stages. The cognitive–structural model starts with the distinction between quality and quantity in age-related change. Most age-related changes are changes in quantitative rather than qualitative (structural–organizational) aspects of responses. A related distinction to quantity–quality is competence–performance. Structural theories treat most quantitative changes as changes in performance rather than changes in structural competence. As an example, there are decrements in speed and efficiency of immediate memory and information processing with age, but such changes do not imply a regression in the logical structure of the aging individual's reasoning process. In general, structural theory does not treat any change as a change in structural competence unless the change is evident in a qualitatively new pattern of response. Qualitative novelty involves the distinction between form and content. A really new kind of experience, a really new mode of response, is one that is different in its form or organization, not simply in the element or the information it contains.

In summary, the kinds of age change relevant to a stage model are restricted to those implied by the distinctions between quality and quantity, competence and performance, and form and content. In addition to focusing upon quality, competence, and form, a cognitive–developmental stage concept has the following additional general characteristics (Piaget, 1960):

1. Stages imply distinct or qualitative differences in structures (modes of thinking) which still serve the same basic function (e.g., intelligence) at various points in development.
2. These different structures form an invariant sequence, order, or succession in individual development. While cultural factors may speed up, slow down, or stop development, they do not change its sequence.
3. Each of these different and sequential modes of thought forms a structured whole. A given stage-response on a task does not just represent a specific response determined by knowledge and familiarity with that task or tasks similar to it; rather, it represents an underlying thought-organization. The implication is that various aspects of stage structures should appear as a consistent cluster of responses in development.
4. Stages are hierarchical integrations. As noted, stages form an order of increasingly differentiated and integrated *structures* to fulfill a common function. Accordingly, higher stages displace (or, rather, reintegrate) the structures found at lower stages.

In addition to the formal characteristics of stages and the kind of data relevant to their verification, there is need to note briefly the theory of the role of experience in development which lies behind structural stages. Stages are viewed neither as the direct reflection of maturation, nor as the direct reflection of learning in the sense of specific environmental stimulus exposures, reinforcements, etc. Stages represent, rather, the equilibrated pattern of interaction between the organism and the environment. If the child's responses indicate a different structure or organization than the adult's, rather than a less complex one, and if this structure is similar in all children, it is extremely difficult to view the child's mental structure as a direct learning of the external structure. If stages cannot be accounted for by direct learning of the structure of the outer world, neither can they be explained as the result of innate patterning. If children have their own logic, adult logic or mental structure cannot be derived from innate neurological patterning because such patterning should hold also in childhood. It is hardly plausible to view a whole succession of logics as an evolutionary and functional program of innate wiring, particularly in light of the fact that the most mature logical structures are reached only by some adults. . . .

The importance of adult stages in this regard springs from the fact that childhood *interactional* or *structural* stages cannot be completely distinguished from maturational stages. As an example, while Piaget asserts that his cognitive stages are "interactional" and not maturational, they are closely tied to the maturation of the nervous system. If one combines a knowledge of the child's chronological age with a knowledge of his long-term IQ, with its hereditary component, one can predict quite well a child's Piagetian stage (Kohlberg & Mayer, 1973). Presumably, chronological age and the hereditary component of IQ generate an index of maturation with which Piaget stages are correlated. Until maturation is completed, presumably in adolescence, then, it is impossible to disentangle roles of maturation and experience in generating stages or stage change.

Accordingly, it falls upon the student of adult development to determine whether there are structural stages that arise through experience. Furthermore, it is primarily the student of adult development who may be able to distinguish the roles of personal experience and of generalized-symbolic experience in development, a distinction centrally dividing "emotional" and "cognitive" theories of personality development.

Cognitive Stage Development in Adulthood

In raising the issue of adult cognitive stages, it is necessary to discriminate between the existence of adult stages and the existence of continuing stage development in adulthood. Piaget, himself, does not postulate adult cognitive stages, but he does postulate continuing cognitive development through early adulthood (Piaget, 1972). Piaget's highest stage, formal operations, is defined by him as appearing in the era of early adolescence, ages 12 to 15. While Piaget views the onset of the highest stage as occur-

ring in adolescence under typical or favorable conditions, he sees continuing development of formal operational thought as occurring in early adulthood.

This continuing development is of the following sort:

1. Adolescents who have been slow in cognitive development because of biological and cultural conditions and who are still concrete-operational at 15 may develop formal operational thought in early adulthood.

2. There is continuing *horizontal decalage* of formal-operational thought in early adulthood so that it is applied to more spheres or activities.

3. Related to this decalage, there may be *stabilization* of formal thought, i.e., increased subordination of, or rejection of, lower

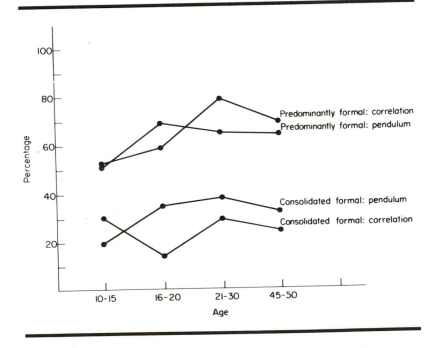

FIGURE 1
Proportion of subjects exhibiting predominantly formal operations (III, II, and above) and consolidated formal operations (IIIA/B or IIIB), by age group.

forms of thought for formal–operational thought in adulthood.

The available evidence is of exactly this sort. Age trends in the development of formal operational thinking in two tasks, the pendulum and correlation problems, in 265 California subjects between the ages of 10 and 50 were studied by Kuhn, Langer, Kohlberg, and Haan (1974). The results are presented in Figure 1. As Figure 1 indicates, the correlation problem was a more difficult problem to solve at the formal-operational level than was the pendulum problem; it represents a form of *horizontal decalage* in formal thought. On this task there was continuing development to formal-operational thought after ages 16–20, but on the pendulum problem there was not. In addition to horizontal decalage of formal thought, there was also development in this period in the form of *stabilization* in the pendulum task.

This is indicated in Figure 2. The mixture of concrete and formal operational thought present in 10–15% of adolescents, disappears in the 20–30 age group.

Three types of cognitive development in adulthood have been discussed: (1) continued development among the "slow"; (2) developers' horizontal decalage; and (3) stabilization. The critical question, however, is whether any new cognitive stage may be found in adulthood. The three forms of continuing development discussed could all exist without the existence of any new cognitive stage in adulthood. If these forms of development exist without a new adult stage, it would follow that formation of a stage demands experience as well as neurological maturation, i.e., that neurological maturation in early adolescence is a structural condition necessary for a new cognitive stage. The actual appearance of the cognitive stage may lag way behind the

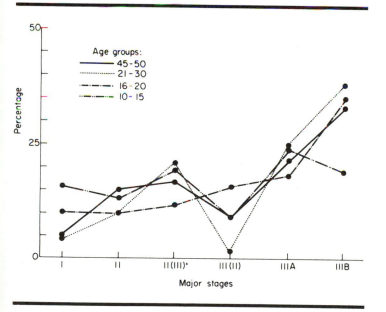

FIGURE 2
Pendulum problem: percentages of each group at major stage.

maturational change, or may never occur because of experiential factors. However, in that case, the maturational change is still a necessary, if not sufficient, condition for the existence of the stage. This conclusion is consistent with Piaget's view. Piaget does not rule out the possibility of a stage beyond formal operations, citing Godel's proof that the impossibility of another form of logic cannot be proved by formal–operational logic. However, he does seem inclined to believe that there is no later cognitive stage.

Now, if there is some new adulthood stage, it is not likely to appear in logical-cognitive tasks as such. This may be concluded for two reasons: First, as noted, Piagetian cognitive growth is correlated to both the hereditary and the age-maturational factors found in general intelligence. Secondly, logical stages are by definition relatively experience-free. If anything, experience appears to represent something of a hindrance to pure formal-logical thought as evidenced by the fact that the greatest work in mathematical and pure physical theory has been commenced in late adolescence.

The Existence of Adult Moral Stages—The Kohlberg and Kramer Conclusions

While the existence of adult moral stages seems plausible, the conclusions drawn 4 years ago were that no new structural moral

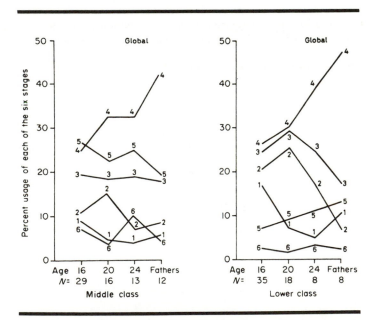

FIGURE 3
Moral judgment profiles (percentage usage of each stage by global rating method) for middle- and lower-class males at four ages. [From Richard Kramer, "Changes in Moral Judgment Response Pattern During Late Adolescence and Young Adulthood," Ph.D. Dissertation, University of Chicago, 1968; reprinted in Kohlberg & Kramer, 1969.]

stage could be found in adulthood (Kohlberg & Kramer, 1969). Instead, forms of development with regard to logical stages were reported. It was found that some subjects at lower stages of moral judgment (Stages 1–3) continued to develop toward Stage 4 from age 16 to 24. This result parallels the tendency for subjects not yet formal-operational to become formal–operational in the period 16 to 25–30. These trends from Kohlberg and Kramer (1969) are presented in Figure 3.

Other findings suggested stabilization among the higher-stage subjects with age. Higher-stage subjects (Stages 4, 5, and 6) increasingly dropped out lower-stage thinking with age and became more consistently high-stage. This stabilization of moral thought is not only reflected in the trends of stage usage for the group as a whole, but it is also reflected in the trends of variability of stage usage within individuals.

Figure 4 presents the trends in decreased variability with age found by Kohlberg and Kramer (1969). Although the major moral change past high school was noted to be stabilization of higher stages rather than the formation of a new stage, it was reported that this stabilization was often a dramatic developmental process. Prior to stabilization at a higher or principled stage, *retrogression* was found on an increased usage of preconventional Stage 2 thinking. Under ordinary conditions, individuals are capable of using all stages below their own, but prefer to use the highest stage they understand

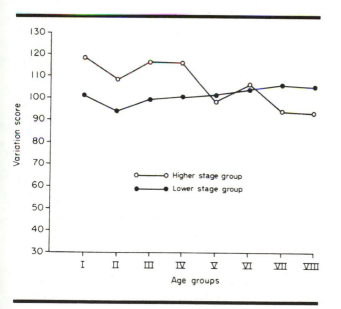

FIGURE 4
Mean variation scores for higher-stage and lower-stage subjects in the Kramer group at the following eight age ranges: 14.0–15.11 (I); 18.0–18.11 (II); 17.0–17.11 (III); 16.0–18.11 (IV); 19.0–20.11 (V); 21.0–22.11 (VI); 23.0–23.11 (VII); and 24.0–26.11 (VIII). [From Kohlberg & Kramer, 1969.]

and are capable of using (Rest, 1973). However, at around the college sophomore age, individuals often did not seem to use the highest moral stages of which they were capable, but instead made use of preconventional thought previously abandoned.

The findings on retrogression and return to the social contract were interpreted in terms of Erikson's concepts of moratorium, identity crisis, and renewed commitment. It was suggested that after an individual had formed the capacity for morally principled thought, he still had to commit himself to do so. This commitment often was part of the resolution of an identity crisis or moratorium in which the individual displayed retrogression in moral thought.

An interpretation of retrogression and return in terms of Eriksonian ego development may be juxtaposed with the interpretation of the same phenomena as structural stabilization. Thus, a Piaget–Kohlberg structural stage theory could interpret the phenomena only as stabilization, not as adulthood structural stage change. What could be seen by structural theory only as stabilization could be seen from another theoretical perspective, the Eriksonian, as adult development. Accordingly, it was suggested that if there were adult stages and development in adulthood, such stages would have to be defined in terms of Erikson's *functional* stages, rather than in terms of structural stages or of qualitatively new patterns of thought and judgment.

For a variety of reasons, the conclusions of Kramer and Kohlberg just summarized, need revision. These revisions arise from:

1. a more careful analysis of the sense in which moral stage theory can tolerate regression, provided by Turiel (1973);
2. a thorough revision of the stage-scoring system to reflect more directly the structure rather than the content of moral thought;
3. a further wave of longitudinal interviews on the subjects.

Once these revisions are made, a new conclusion arises; the conclusion is that there are indeed adult stages. Fully-principled or Stage 5 and especially Stage 6 thinking is an adult development, typically not reached until the late twenties or later. Structural development and stabilization are not two different things. The fact that the apparently Stage 5 thinking of high school students was vulnerable to retrogression or was not yet stabilized was, in fact, evidence for the fact that such thinking was not really principled.

Each of the three points that lead to this revision will now be considered. With regard to the first point, the theoretical status of regression, the apparent resurgence of Stage 2 reasoning in college sophomores had been interpreted as a *structural retrogression,* i.e., a return to a lower structural stage, but a *functional advance.* It was a functional advance in flowing from a questioning of previous commitments and standards necessary before these standards could be stabilized as "one's own identity." This question, in turn, reflected a new awareness of the relativity of value and choice which was a developmental advance, though the response to it appeared to be a regression to Stage 2 instrumental egoism.

It was suggested, then, that one could regress in the service of development. In the breakup of one stage and the movement to a higher stage, one could recycle to an earlier position. This view, of course, is held by Gesell, Werner, and other developmental theorists. Turiel holds that the apparent regression involved in stage development is a disequilibrium of transition very different than the disorganization or dedifferentiation involved in regression. According to Turiel, relativistic regressions to Stage 2 are in a disequilibrated transitional stage in which the breakup of conventional morality is easy to confuse with the resurgence of preconventional morality.

In summary, longitudinal data now suggest that Stage 5 is a stage reached in adulthood, not in adolescence. With regard to Stage 6, something similar is to be said. Thinking which had been labeled Stage 6 in high school was misclassified. No longitudinal subject in high school had been predominantly Stage 6, nor has any become predominantly Stage 6 by the age of 30 (although we will not predict that none will reach Stage 6). Essentially, the material that was scored as Stage 6 was another form of sophisticated Stage 4 thought, one which appealed to "conscience" and "moral law" instead of to "the will of the majority" and "the welfare of the greatest number."

Adult Experiences Involved in Moral Stage Development

If new moral stages do form as a result of adult experience, it would be well to understand how this happens. In particular, Piaget's cognitive–structural model of experience leading to development needs to be integrated with a model of adult personal experience. The bulk of moral stage development occurs in childhood and adolescence and does not require the extensive personal experience of moral choice and responsibility found in adult life. Elsewhere an account has been presented of the role of experience in leading to moral development that does not stress personal experience of moral choice and responsibility. Instead, following Piaget, it stresses the role of cognitive conflict between and within contradictory judgmental structures as leading to development (Turiel, 1973). Following this theory, a one-stage-up movement has been induced for the moral judgment of a majority of preadolescents and adolescents with the logical capacity for reasoning at the next stage (Blatt, 1973; Hickey, 1973).

These findings support the notion that the experience necessary for moral stage development in childhood and adolescence is largely cognitive and symbolic and does not require large amounts of personal experience. In using the term "cognitive," as opposed to "personal," it is not intended to oppose cognition to the emotional, the social, or the behavioral. The moral structures of judgment studied as stages can be hotly emotional, are manifestly social, and determine choice and action. But in calling moral stages cognitive, it should be implied that they are centrally forms of *thinking;* they are *generalized* and *symbolic.* Accordingly, the experiences which generate stage movement have a strong general and symbolic component; they are experiences involving thinking.

It has been noted that the experiences involving thinking leading to moral development are not simply logical experiences. Moral stage development is not merely the horizontal decalage of logical thought to social situations. In order for a formal operational adolescent to attain morally principled reasoning, he must undergo social and moral experiences that cannot be conceptualized as experiences that aid him in transferring logical principles to social situations. They are experiences, rather, that lead him to transform his modes of judgment of the morally right and the fair. Often, the experiences that promote such change have a fairly strong emotional component. As emotion enters into experiences leading to change, it is, however, the emotion that triggers and accompanies rethinking. . . .

Because structural moral stages represent general forms of thinking, both the capacity for higher stages and the preference for higher stages can develop relatively speedily in a cognitively and socially rich environment. A great deal of experience of personal moral decision and choice is not necessary for movement from one stage to the next in childhood and adolescence. The tentative finding, however, that principled thinking does not appear until adulthood suggests that perhaps a different kind of experience is required for attainment of principled moral judgment than is required for attainment of the prior stages. While our cognitive developmental theory stresses that the child constructs each new stage "for himself," the sense in which the individual constructs the stage of principled moral reasoning for himself is somewhat different than the sense in which he constructs earlier stages for himself. Through Stage 4, each new stage represents a wider and more adequate process of role taking, of perception of the social system. Principled thinking, however, is not a more adequate perception of what the social system *is;* rather, it is a postulation of principles to which the society and the self *ought to be committed.* To be principled in moral judgment is not just to cognitively "see" principles. It is: (1) to see their ideal adequacy in spite of the fact that they are not a social reality to conform to; (2) to see a basis for commitment to these ideals; and (3) at the same time, to see a commitment to a real society in which one acts consistently with these ideals. This seems to require more than the vicarious experiences of role taking sufficient for movement through the stages to Stage 4, which represents a fairly adequate cognition of the social system.

While the evidence is limited, there appear to be two different sorts of "personal" as opposed to vicarious-symbolic experiences important in movement to principled thought. Both share common features and both occur, at least typically, only after high school. The first experience is the experience of leaving home and entering a college community with conflicting values in the context of moratorium, identity questioning, and the need for commitment. As indicated earlier, this experience precipitates the relativistic crisis of Stage 4 ½. In the earlier interpretation (Kohlberg & Kramer, 1969), it was thought that the sophomore "identity-crisis" questioning of moral values was a retrogression from Stage 5 principled thinking, and that the mid-twenties commitment to moral values through a social contract was a stabilization of moral thought. With the revised definition of the stages, it may now be said that the sophomore questioning and the young-adult

commitment to the social contract are part of the process of movement to Stage 5, rather than a process of questioning of and commitment to morality, separable from moral stage development itself.

The importance of the college moratorium experience is suggested by the following findings:

1. None of the longitudinal subjects who did not attend college, but went directly into the army and/or to adult occupations developed principled thinking.

2. As noted, none of the high school longitudinal subjects showed principled thinking.

3. Working with classroom moral discussion, Blatt succeeded in moving high school Stage 3 students to Stage 4 (and Stage 2 students to Stage 3). But he failed to move any Stage 4's to Stage 5 (Blatt, 1973).

4. In contrast, a moral discussion program led 40% of the Stage 4 freshmen and sophomore participants in the program to move to a Stage 5 orientation (Boyd, 1973).

These findings suggest an interaction between cognitive experience components of moral development and experience in a particular life phase. One study even suggests that high school cognitive experience has a sleeper effect, manifest only after the college moratorium–independence experience. Beck, Sullivan, and Porter (1972) found that a high school moral discussion class showed no upward moral change on posttest in high school, compared to controls. On college follow-up, however, the class showed considerably more Stage 5 thought compared to the control group.

In stressing an interaction between cognitive stimulation and moratorium experience components of college experience, it should be emphasized that questioning one's identity and resolving it by commitment is far from sufficient to lead to principled moral thought. . . . A study by Podd

(1969) suggests that college students can go through the questioning and commitment process with regard to identity without moving to principled moral thought. When identity questioning, however, is combined with explicit cognitive-moral stimulation as in the Boyd (1973) college moral discussion programs, movement to principled thought is more likely.

In addition to the moral-stimulation component often missing in the college period of identity-questioning and commitment, there are personal experience components also frequently lacking in a student-moratorium period. This moratorium period is one of new responsibility only for the self; it is primarily an experience of attained freedom to make one's own choices for oneself. Until college, the adolescent usually lives within a world he did not make and in which the choices he must make are circumscribed. Insofar as there is movement to principled thought in the college period, it is in relation to anticipated commitment. Now free, the student seeks the moral terms or contract which he should accept in terms of future commitments. Only later, however, does the student typically have the experience of *sustained responsibility for the welfare of others* and the experience of irreversible moral choice which are the marks of adult personal moral experience, and which Erikson makes central to the development of the ethical sense in the state of generativity.

It is obvious that, in themselves, experiences of responsibility do not lead to movement to a stage of moral principle. Most adults have such experiences; most never become principled. For some young adults, however, experiences of moral responsibility are the sources of moral reflection leading to principles, just as for some young adults, experiences of freedom or moratorium are the sources of reflection leading to principles. This occurs particularly when responsibility, accepted on a conventional basis, leads to some conflict with

the universally human. For example, in war, as opposed to American young men in vociferous moratorium, one thinks of Israeli young men in full commitment to a group code. When these men encountered, in the six-day war, a real crisis of moral choice born out of responsibility, many seemed to engage in the kind of reflection leading to principle.

In summary, personal experiences of choice involving questioning and commitment, in some sort of integration with stimulation to cognitive-moral reflection, seem required for movement from conventional to principled (Stage 5) thought. It is probably for this reason that principled thought is not attained in adolescence. The conditions for movement to fully-principled or Stage-6 thought are probably even more of this order, though no real data exist on movement to this highest moral stage.

Notes Toward a Seventh Stage

Erikson's ideal man passes through his seventh stage of generativity and becomes an ethical man, an ideal corresponding to the Kohlberg Stage 6. There remains for Erikson's man a task that is partly ethical, but more basically religious (in the broadest sense of the term religious), a task defining an eighth stage whose outcomes are a sense of integrity versus a sense of despair. The problem of integrity is not the problem of moral integrity, but the problem of the integration and integrity of meaning of the individual's life and its negative side, despair, which hovers around the awareness of death. This problem is also psychological. The concept of the self's integrity is psychological, but the concept of the integrity of the meaning of the self's life is philosophical or religious. As Santayana (1954) says:

> This struggling and changing force of religion seems to make for an ultimate harmony within

the soul and for an ultimate harmony between the soul and all that the soul depends upon. So that Religion, in its intent, is a more conscious and direct pursuit of the Life of Reason than is society, science or art. For these approach the ideal life tentatively and piecemeal, hardly regarding the goal or caring for the ultimate justification of their instinctive aims. Religion also has an instinctive and blind side, but it soon feels its way toward the heart of things and veers in the direction of the ultimate [p. 181].

A discussion of a Stage 7 in our own series, a discussion purely hypothetical and based on no data, is primarily an effort to make Erikson's concept more explicitly philosophical. It is related to Fowler's (1972) efforts to define religious stages which parallel both this author's moral stages and Erikson's ego stages. A first basic notion is that there is a postconventional religious orientation, as there is a postconventional ethical orientation. A second basic notion of a Stage 7 is that an adequate postconventional religious orientation is both dependent upon, and demanded by a Stage 6 orientation to universal human ethical principles.

After attainment of a clear awareness of universal ethical principles valid against the usual skeptical doubts, there remains the loudest skeptical doubt of all: the doubt of "Why be moral?" "Why be just, in a universe that is largely unjust?" This is, of course, one of the problems thought to be unanswerable at the stage of transitional relativism and skepticism. The Stage 5 answer, the social contract, is essentially a compromise answer, the answer that one's own happiness is pursued socially or with due regard to the rights and welfare of others. While Stage 6 ethical principles offer a more complete solution to the problem of relativity of values than Stage 5, it has an even less complete solution for the problem "Why be moral?" There is a sharper contrast between ethical principle and egoistic

or hedonistic concerns than there is between the social contract and hedonism.

The answer to the question "Why be moral?" at this level entails the question "Why live?" (and the parallel question, "How face death?") so that ultimate moral maturity requires a mature solution to the question of the meaning of life. This, in turn, is hardly a moral question per se; it is an ontological or a religious one. Not only is the question not a moral one but it is not a question resolvable on purely logical or rational grounds as moral questions are. Nevertheless, a purely metaphorical notion of a Stage 7 may be used as pointing to some meaningful solutions to this question which are compatible with rational science and rational ethics (Kohlberg, 1971). The characteristics of all these Stage 7 solutions are that they involve contemplative experience of nonegoistic or nondualistic variety. The logic of such experience is sometimes expressed in theistic terms, but it need not be. Its essential is the sense of being a part of the whole of life and the adoption of a cosmic, as opposed to a universal humanistic (Stage 6) perspective.

The concept of such a Stage 7 is familiar, of course, both in religious writing and in the classical metaphysical tradition from Plato to Spinoza. In most accounts the movement starts with despair. Such despair involves the beginning of a cosmic perspective. It is when we begin to see our lives as finite from some more infinite perspective that we feel despair. The meaninglessness of our lives in the face of death is the meaninglessness of the finite from the perspective of the infinite. The resolution of the despair which we call Stage 7 represents a continuation of the process of taking a more cosmic perspective whose first phase is despair. It represents, in a sense, a shift from figure to ground. In despair we are the self seen from the distance of the cosmic or infinite. In the state of mind metaphorically termed Stage 7, we identify ourselves with the cosmic or infinite perspective, itself, and value life from its standpoint. . . .

Because the logical structure of Stage 7 is vague and its philosophic adequacy hard to justify, our concept of it must rest more on the psychological testimony of lives than upon structural analysis. In this testimony, it appears that the men from Socrates to Martin Luther King, who are most easily pointed to as having lived and died for their ethical principles, have had something like a strong Stage 7 orientation in addition to a commitment to rational principles of justice.

Turning from world history to our longitudinal study it is found that the concerns and ideas necessary for anything like a Stage 7 seem absent in all our longitudinal subjects in their twenties, even those at the highest moral stage in the sample, Stage 5.

Of the longitudinal subjects, even those who have reached postconventional Stage 5 morality, none has gone far toward development of a postconventional religious orientation. This appears to be at least negative evidence for Stage 7, indicating an area in which later adult morally-relevant development may occur. Although this area will probably not be amenable to a structural approach, with its philosophic notion of adequacy, the chief value of studying this area is philosophical, and requires a philosophic approach. One of the major aims of a lifespan psychology may be to aid in communicating from generation to generation such wisdom as humans accumulate. Our experimental studies demonstrate that higher structural stages are not understood by lower stages, and that stage psychology is an aid to such understanding.

As an example, one of the chief values of the study of moral stages is the tentative isolation of a Stage 6 trend of moral thought. The number of adults who reach Stage 6 makes the study of this advanced moral stage meaningless for the description and explanation of most lives. It helps very much, however, for making understandable and viable a more adequate and difficult mode of moral thought. Our experimental college course suggests that the isolation and formulation of this stage helps Stage 5 students to transform the academic study of moral philosophers into a reformulation of their own thoughts to a more adequate level. In suggesting a more diffuse, but still philosophically articulated stage in the development of the sense of the meaning of life corresponding loosely to Erikson's seventh stage, it may be suggested that the study of lives may someday aid in the comprehension and communication of more adequate life meanings.

In conclusion, then, the questions to be asked in the study of lives are not simply those brought from psychology or sociology as disciplines. In the end, lives are studied so humans will learn how to live better. To ask questions of life-span psychology from this point of view is to engage in philosophy.

References

Beck, C., Sullivan, E., & Porter, N. Effects of a moral discussion program on moral judgment. Unpublished manuscript. Ontario Institute for the Study of education, Toronto, Canada, 1972.

Blatt, M. Change in moral judgment through the classroom discussion process. In L. Kohlberg & E. Turiel (Eds.), *Recent research in moral development.* New York: Holt, Rinehart & Winston, 1973.

Boyd, D. A developmental approach to undergraduate ethics. Unpublished doctoral dissertation. Graduate School of Education, Harvard University, 1973.

Fowler, J. Toward a developmental perspective

on religious faith. Unpublished manuscript. Harvard University Divinity School, 1972.

Hickey, J. Changes in moral judgment through a prison intervention. In L. Kohlberg & E. Turiel (Eds.), *Recent research in moral development.* New York: Holt Rinehart & Winston, 1973.

Kohlberg, L. The ethical life, the contemplative life and ultimate religion — notes toward Stage 7. Unpublished manuscript. Harvard University, 1971.

Kohlberg, L., & Kramer, R. Continuities and discontinuities in childhood and adult moral development. *Human Development,* 1969, 12, 93–120.

Kohlberg, L., & Mayer, R. Early education: A cognitive developmental view. II. The developmental-philosophic strategy for defining educational aims. In L. Kohlberg & E. Turiel (Eds.), *Recent research in moral development.* New York: Holt, Rinehart & Winston, 1973.

Kuhn, D., Langer, J., Kohlberg, L., & Haan, N. The development of formal operations and moral judgment. *Genetic Psychology Monographs,* 1974.

Piaget, J. The general problem of the psychobiological development of the child. In J. M. Tanner & B. Inhelder (Eds.), *Discussions on child development.* Vol. 4. New York: International University Press, 1960.

Piaget, J. Intellectual evolution from adolescence to adulthood. *Human Development,* 1972, 15, 1–12.

Podd, M. H. Ego identity status and morality: An empirical investigation of two developmental concepts. Unpublished Doctoral Dissertation, University of Chicago, 1969.

Rest, J. The hierarchical nature of moral judgment: Patterns of comprehension and preference of moral stages. In L. Kohlberg & E. Turiel (Eds.), *Recent research in moral development.* New York: Holt, Rinehart & Winston, 1973.

Santayana, G. *Life of reason.* New York: Scribner, 1954.

Schaie, K. W. Methodological problems in descriptive developmental research on adulthood and aging. In J. R. Nesselroade & H. W. Reese (Eds.), *Life-span developmental psychology: Methodological issues.* New York: Academic Press, 1973.

Turiel, E. The effects on cognitive conflict on moral judgment development. In L. Kohlberg & E. Turiel (Eds.), *Recent research in moral development.* New York: Holt, Rinehart & Winston, 1973.

Religiosity in Old Age

DAVID O. MOBERG

Geriatricians and gerontologists hold divergent opinions about the importance of religion in the later years of life. The differences reflect a combination of facts and personal biases. Religious persons tend to praise the influence of religious faith and practice and to believe that people become more religious as they approach death, while secularists are prone to believe religiosity declines and to condemn the ''ill effects'' of both personal and organized religion.

There is no question about the relative importance of the church among voluntary association memberships of the aged. Study after study in various parts of the nation and in different types of communities have found that the aged (like most younger people) are more apt to be church members than members of any other one type of voluntary organization and, indeed, than of all other associations together. Disagreements arise, however, on several topics: What are the trends of personal religion over the life cycle? (Are the aged more likely to be church members than middle-aged and young adults? What is their comparative rate of participation in the church?) What are the effects of church participation? (Does it promote personal adjustment or does it reflect a search for security by maladjusted persons?) What are the characteristics of religious faith among the elderly? (Do they revert to the religion of their childhood? Are they progressively emancipated from traditional religion?)

Contradictory answers to questions of these kinds are based not only upon the personal opinions of experts but also upon empirical data from research surveys of behavioral scientists. The confusion that results leads to both traditionalistic attempts to perpetuate past practices and radical proposals that religion be drastically changed or else ignored entirely in geriatric programs.

The confusion of gerontologists about the role of religion is readily transferred to geriatricians, for scientific generalizations eventually influence practical action.

After considerable study and research, I have concluded that the confusion and contradictions about religion in old age are a product of more than a simple lack of research on the subject. The concept of ''religion'' is very broad, and it is defined in the research operations of social scientists in a variety of ways. The ''religiosity'' of scientist A is so greatly different from the ''religiosity'' studied by scientist B that they are not dealing with the same subject even though the same words may be used in their reports. Examination of the ''operational definitions'' (questions asked and other techniques used to describe and classify people's religious behavior) of relevant research projects reveals several types of ''religiosity.''

The best analysis of this conceptual problem is the five-fold classification of ''dimensions of religiosity'' developed by Professor Glock of the Survey Research Center at the

Source: Moberg, D. O. Religiosity in old age. *Gerontologist,* 1965, 5, 78–87. Copyright by the Gerontological Society. Reprinted by permission.

University of California (Berkeley). I shall briefly describe each of his five modes or types of religious expression and then summarize some findings on each dimension from studies about religion in old age.

Dimensions of Religiosity

Glock's (1962) analysis of the "core dimensions of religiosity" within which "all of the many and diverse manifestations of religiosity prescribed by the different religions of the world can be ordered" provides the most satisfactory extant frame of reference for studying and assessing religion scientifically.

1. The *experiential* dimension reflects the expectation that religious persons "will achieve direct knowledge of ultimate reality or will experience religious emotion," although the emotions deemed proper or experienced may vary widely from one religion or one person to another. Subjective religious experience or feeling is difficult to study but may be expressed chiefly in terms of "concern or need to have a transcendentally based ideology," cognition or awareness of the divine, trust or faith, and fear.

2. The *ideological* dimension concerns beliefs that the followers of a religion are expected to hold (official doctrine), the beliefs they actually hold, the importance or saliency of beliefs, and their functions for individuals.

3. The *ritualistic* dimension has to do with the religious practices of adherents to a religion. It includes public and private worship, prayer, fasting, feasting, tithing, participation in sacraments, and the like.

4. The *intellectual* dimension deals with personal information and knowledge about the basic tenets and sacred writings of one's faith. Again official expectations and the actual achievements of constituents tend to diverge considerably and need to be clearly distinguished from each other. Misconceptions, intellectual sophistication, and attitudes toward both secular and religious knowledge are important aspects.

5. The *consequential* dimension "includes all the secular effects of religious belief, practice, experience, and knowledge on the individual." It includes all specifications of what people ought to do and to believe as a result of their religion. In Christianity it emphasizes the theological concept of "works" and especially Christian perspectives of man's relationships to other men, in contrast to his relationships to God. Rewards and punishments, expectations and obligations, commandments and promises are all aspects of this measure of religiosity.

Obviously, there are distinctions both in kind and in degree within each of the five dimensions. Just as religiosity itself is not a unilateral concept, each of its major dimensions may also be complex and multidimensional. The areas of religious commitment are all inextricably bound up with each other in real life; none can be studied effectively without recognition of and consideration for the others.

The attempt to clarify the present status of knowledge about religion in old age through use of Glock's dimensions is not simple, as we shall see in the following summary. A wide variety of techniques has been used. Measuring instruments and operational definitions of concepts have not been the same; therefore the actual phenomena studied are not identical even when presented under the same terms. The studies have had divergent objectives and in many additional ways have not been directly comparable. Can order be introduced into such a conglomeration of findings and interpretations?

Religious Feelings

On the basis of her 25 years of medical practice, Dr. Nila Kirkpatrick Covalt (1960),

Director of the Kirkpatrick Memorial Institute of Physical Medicine and Rehabilitation in Winter Park, Florida, stated that she found no evidence to support the common assumption that people turn to religion as they grow older. Patients do not talk with their physicians about religion. The religious attitudes of most old people are those they grew up with. Patients' thoughts, visions, and dreams when regaining consciousness are often given a spiritual significance, Dr. Covalt stated, but

> I recall no person who called out to God or audibly prayed when he knew he was dying. Usually these persons are exerting every bit of energy in a struggle to keep alive.

At least the overt manifestations of their feelings do not indicate a high degree of experiential religiosity.

Contrary evidence is also available, however. The panel of persons in the Terman Gifted Group apparently had greater interest in religion in 1960 (at their median age of 56) than they had in 1940 and 1950 (Marshall & Oden, 1962). Over half (54.1%) of 210 people past age 65 in a Chicago working-class area said religion had become more helpful over the preceding decade; 30.1% said that it had not become more helpful, and 6.2% said that there had been no change (9.6% gave no answer) (O'Reilly & Pembroke, n.d.).

Jeffers and Nichols (1961) found in their study of 251 persons in North Carolina past age 60 that religion means more to most Ss as the years go by and the end of life approaches and that this is especially true of disabled persons for whom the end is more imminent. Similarly, 57% of 140 retired Negroes in South Carolina reported that religion and the church held more meaning since retirement than they did before; 42% reported that they held the same meaning, and only two persons said they held less meaning (Lloyd, 1955).

A large study of 1700 elderly Minnesotans found that only from 7 to 19% of the subcategories of men and from 2 to 5% of the women reported that religion does not mean much to them. In contrast, 52 to 55% of the men and 66 to 71% of the women reported religion was the most important thing in their lives (Taves & Hansen, 1963). Among the 143 older people in a rural New York community, the church and clergy were much more important than formerly to 34 persons, somewhat more important to 28, about the same to 56, somewhat less important to 10, and much less important to only 7. Corresponding answers about the meaning of God and religion ranged from 46 who said they held much more meaning than formerly, through 25, 59, and 3 in the respective intermediate categories, to only 1 who said they held much less meaning (9 gave no response). Yet only 13 mentioned religion as one of the things that provided them the greatest satisfaction (Warren, 1952).

Wolff's (1961) summary of psychological aspects of aging includes the statement that geriatric patients have ambivalent feelings toward life and death and may turn toward religion, which "gives them emotional support and tends to relieve them from the fear that everything soon will come to an end."

The contrasting results of studies which refer to religious feelings of the aged may result from a basic difficulty in scientific research on religious feelings. American societal expectations hold that religion is helpful in any time of trouble. Anyone who expresses a perspective contrary to the position that religion helps the aged may feel that he is in danger of being socially rejected for his seemingly heretical views. With the fear of such reprisals, biased responses to questions about religious feelings may distort the results of questionnaire as well as interview studies. A type of self-fulfilling prophecy mechanism also may be at work: the expectation that religion will help may lead the person to receive genuine help through religious channels or at least to feel as if he had.

While the bulk of the evidence available to date indicates that religious feelings increase for more people than those for whom they decrease, we must retain an open mind on this subject while awaiting additional research.

Religious Beliefs

There is some evidence from public opinion survey data that belief in life after death may increase with age; at least a higher proportion of old people than of younger generations believe that there is a life after death. Older people also are more certain that there is a God and apparently are more inclined to hold to traditional and conservative beliefs of their religion (Gray & Moberg, 1962).

A study of 496 persons in New York City, 325 of whom were Jewish, found that the proportion who believed in a life after death (heaven) increased from 30.1 to 40.5% from ages 30–35 to ages 60–65. Non-belief for the same age categories diminished from 36.1 to 25.1, with the remainder uncertain (Barron, 1961). The nationwide *Catholic Digest* (Anon., 1952) survey revealed that 81% of the respondents aged 65 and over compared to 79% of all and 76% of those aged 45–54 thought of God as a loving Father. Belief in God was held the most certainly by persons aged 65 and over, and a somewhat higher proportion of the aged (56%) than of the total sample (51%) believed one should prepare for life after death rather than be concerned with living comfortably. This lends some support to the opinion of Starbuck (1911), the pioneer in the psychology of religion, that religious faith and belief in God grow in importance as the years advance. His research data were skimpy and his highest age category was "40 or over," but his conclusion has been adopted so widely that Maves (1960) has called it a "part of the folklore of the psychology of religion."

Surveys have revealed that older people as a whole tend to have more conservative religious perspectives than younger adults. Indirect evidence of this also comes from St. Cloud, Florida, where more than half the population in the mid-1950s was aged 60 and over. Its churches were generally more fundamentalistic than was usual in peninsular Florida, and over one-third were evangelical and sectarian (Aldridge, 1956).

Whether the differences in religious beliefs between the generations are a result of the aging process or of divergent experiences during the formative years of childhood and youth, which are linked with different social and historical circumstances, is unknown. Longitudinal research might reveal considerably different conclusions from the cross-sectional studies which provide the foundation for current generalizations about age variations in the ideological dimension of religion.

Religious Practices

The ritualistic dimension has received considerable attention from social scientists, perhaps because the observation of more religious practices is relatively simple. The findings are not wholly consistent, however.

All American studies which have come to my attention indicate that more of the formal social participation of the elderly, as well as of other age groups, is in the church than in all other voluntary community organizations together. This holds true whether measured by membership, attendance, or other indicators. For example, 87% of 1,236 persons aged 60 and older in two Kentucky communities participated in the church, 35% in Sunday school, and 8% in other church activities. The next highest participation was 6% in "service and welfare organizations." As also is consistently true, women participated in the church to a somewhat greater extent than men, 94% compared with 85% of the men in a Lexington sample and 93 and 73%, respectively, in a Casey County sample (Youmans, 1963).

The highest Chapin social participation scores for religious participation among the heads of households in four rural New York communities studied in 1947–1948 were found among men aged 75–79, followed closely by those aged 45–54. Among homemakers in the same study, the highest scores were found among those aged 70–74 and 75–79, with women aged 60–64 in third place and 45–54 fourth. Female participation in religious organizations exceeded that of the males at every age, but male participation exceeded that of the females in nonreligious organizations (Taietz & Larson, 1956). (Chapin scores are based upon a combination of membership, attendance, financial contributions, committee positions, and offices held.)

The peak of intensity of social participation, based on Chapin's scale among 1,397 persons aged 10 and over in two North Carolina localities, came at ages 55 to 59 with a sharp drop thereafter. Four-fifths of this participation was in religious activities, and six-tenths of the persons participated only in churches and their auxiliary organizations (Mayo, 1951).

Some studies have revealed increases in religious practices in old age. Public opinion poll data indicate consistently higher figures for church attendance, Bible reading, and prayer among persons aged 50 and over than among younger groups (Toch, 1953). Age among 597 institutionalized women aged 65 or older living in Protestant homes for the aged was positively correlated with increased religious activities as well as with increased dependence upon religion (Pan, 1954). Contrasting evidence from other samples of older people suggests that the relative youthfulness of the "over 50" group compared to samples with a higher mini-

mum age and the unusual environmental circumstance of residents in Protestant church homes, which facilitate participation in organized religious activities, may account for the variation between these two studies and others reported below.

A survey of 100 first admissions of persons aged 60 and over to a county hospital found evidence which was interpreted tentatively as contrary to the common assumption that people become more interested in religion as they grow older. Several were found to attend church less frequently than at age 50, and few attended more often than before (Fiske, 1961). (The report sensibly qualifies the finding by suggesting that a change in behavior does not necessarily imply less concern with spiritual matters. It refers to a University of Chicago study which found that the decrease in church attendance among aging persons is accompanied by increased listening to religious programs on radio and television.)

In the "Back of the Yards" Chicago study (O'Reilly & Pembroke, n.d.) approximately equal proportions of men attended church more (34%) and less (32%) than they did before the age of 65, but among women the respective figures of 27 and 46% indicate a decrease in attendance. Increasing age among Catholics in Fort Wayne, Indiana, was associated with decreasing church attendance, chiefly because of poor health (Theisen, 1962). Fichter's (1954) study of 8,363 active white Catholic parishioners found that the percentage who received monthly Communion diminished fairly consistently in each 10-year category from age 10 to 60-and-over. However, a higher percentage of the eldest category (86.6) made their Easter duties (confession and Holy Communion) than any other age except the youngest (ages 10–19, 92.1%), and only the youngest exceeded the elderly in the percentage attending Mass every Sunday (92.8 versus 90.9%). Physical disabilities may account for differences. Although variations over the total life span cannot be accounted for solely on the basis of age, both the young and the old were significantly more religious as measured by these practices than persons aged 30–39, who had the lowest record for both sexes (63.4% made their Easter duties, 69.3% attended Mass every Sunday, and 31.6% received monthly Communion).

Only 4% of a representative stratified sample of people aged 65 and over studied in 1948–1949 in a small midwestern city rejected religion and the church, but an additional 18% had no church affiliation and no attendance, and 15% had only a passive interest. The other 63% participated in religious activities frequently and actively. Most people evidently continued to carry on the religious habits of their middle years, but they also customarily dropped gradually out of church leadership positions after the age of 60 (Havighurst and Albrecht, 1953). In a metropolitan Kansas City study (Cumming & Henry, 1961) the proportion of persons aged 50 and over who seldom attended church was lowest at age 60–64 in both sexes and reached its highest figure among those aged 75 and over (64.3% of the men and 75.0% of the women).

Senior citizens surveys of a cross-section of the population aged 65 and over in Long Beach, California (McCann, 1955), and Grand Rapids, Michigan (Hunter & Maurice, 1953) indicated a definite tendency of the aged to attend church less often than they did ten years earlier, and increasing nonattendance accompanied increasing age. Problems of physical mobility and finances were among the most significant factors related to declining attendance. Listening to religious services on radio or television and "lost interest" followed health or physical condition in importance among the reasons respondents gave for attending church less often than they had a decade earlier; where the former is a major reason for decreased attendance (17.1% of the Long Beach and 33.9% of the Grand Rapids sample), nonattendance can hardly be accepted as an indicator of a loss of religiosity.

Fifty-five per cent of 131 aged members of two urban Baptist churches in Minnesota attended church every Sunday. The percentages ranged from 71.4 among the 14 persons aged 80–84 to 20 among the 5 aged 85–89. Nearly half (45.6%) of the persons aged 75 and over attended church every Sunday, compared with 64.5% of those aged 65–69 and 60.5% of those aged 70–74. The evidence pertinent to attendance at other church activities clearly supported the hypothesis that participation declines in old age. This decline was even more pronounced in regard to holding lay leadership positions, which reached its peak in both churches at the age of 25–44. Only 4.6% said that they were more active in the church now than they were in their fifties, but 72.5% said that they were less active than in their fifties (Moberg, 1965).

The survey (Barron, 1961) of 496 residents of New York City (325 of whom were Jewish, 98 Roman Catholic, 65 Protestant, and 8 of other or no faiths) found only insignificant differences between the age categories 30–35, 40–45, 50–55, and 60–65 in the proportion that attended church or synagogue "often" in contrast to "sometimes" and "hardly ever" or "never."

The strongest criticism of the "contemporary folklore that 'older' people are more religious than others . . . , and that there is a turning to religion in old age" comes from Orbach's (1961) interpretations and research. In support of his position, Orbach appealed to sociological interpretations of the functions of religion in our "youth-centered society," evidence of the significance of religious beliefs, feelings, and conversion among the young rather than the aged, and empirical findings from studies like those mentioned above which indicate that participation in religious activities decreases in old age.

Since other studies are weak on the levels of both sampling and the analysis of relevant sociological variables other than sex, Orbach made a careful analysis of five probability samples of 6,911 adults aged 21 and over who resided in the mid-1950's in the Detroit Metropolitan Area. Church attendance on a five-point scale from once a week to never was related to age in five-year intervals with sex controlled. Age *per se* was found to be unrelated to changes in church attendance; there was no indication of an increase in attendance in the later years, although the data suggest that there is a polarizing effect in which intermediary categories of "casual" and "cursory" churchgoers tend to shift into a dichotomous distribution of regular church attenders and non-attenders.

When the data were grouped into four age categories (21–39, 40–59, 60–74, 75 and over), the most striking finding was the constancy of attendance in all age groupings, with the one exception of significantly increased non-attendance among the oldest group, which can be attributed at least partly to the effect of age on physical health. Multivariate analysis of church attendance in relationship to age with religious preference, sex, and race as control variables found only Protestant Negro males and Jewish males and females to show increased attendance with age. The small number of cases of Negro males in the oldest age category and the historical decline of Jewish orthodoxy, which is directly reflected in the age groupings, may account for these exceptions to the general pattern of declining attendance as age increases. When other sociological variables were controlled, the relationships between age and attendance were mixed and inconsistent and lent no support to the hypothesis that religiosity increases with age.

The bulk of reliable evidence thus indicates that church attendance of people generally remains fairly constant but tends to decline in the later years compared with younger ages. It is hazardous, however, to assume that church attendance is anything more than a crude indicator of religiosity; it is only one subdimension of religious practices, which themselves comprise but one of Glock's five major dimensions of religious commitment.

Orbach (1961) states that "participation in religious bodies through attendance and involvement in ceremonial worship is perhaps the most crucial and sensitive indicator of overt religiosity." This may apply satisfactorily to the most sacramentally oriented religions — those which believe that the religious institution is the channel of God's grace and that salvation is bestowed upon the individual only through institutionalized participation in church rituals. It probably does not apply to non-sacramental Protestants and to Jews. Orbach (1961) also wisely reminds us that "objective criteria such as attendance cannot replace study of the area of religious beliefs and attitudinal changes or approximate the subjective aspect of inner religious feelings." Attendance is easier to study, but it should be used as a measure of religiosity only provisionally and with a clear recognition of attendant dangers.

Although church attendance tends at most to remain constant with increasing age in cross-sectional studies of the population and more often to decline, regular listening to church services and other religious broadcasts on the radio and reading from the Bible at least weekly have been found to increase among the elderly with advancing age (Cavan, Burgess, Havighurst, & Goldhamer, 1949). Evidently religious practices outside the home diminish while those within the home increase. Physical condition may be the chief intervening variable responsible for such trends. Comparative studies reveal that participation in other social organizations declines at a much more rapid rate than participation in the church.

Religious Knowledge

Relatively little research has been done on age differences in the intellectual dimension of religiosity among older adults. I have been unable to locate any published research which bears directly upon this topic.

Effects of Religion

Although many of the other dimensions of religiosity have been only crudely defined, they have been used as independent variables in research designed to discover the effects of religion upon other aspects of personal and social life. Examples of some of these explorations of the consequential dimension of religion will be presented here.

A number of studies have demonstrated that church members hold a larger number of memberships in voluntary community associations and other organizations than those who are not members and that lay leaders in the church are more active in nonchurch organizations than are other church members (Moberg, 1962), but relatively little attention has been given to age variations in this pattern.

A national survey of adults (Lazerwitz, 1962) in the spring of 1957 related the age of persons with Protestant and Catholic religious preference to the number of voluntary association memberships they held. It was found that the lowest membership levels prevailed among Protestants in the youngest (21–24) and oldest (60–64 and 65 and over) categories and the highest membership rates at ages 30–59. Among Catholics the highest percentage of persons with no organizational memberships was at ages 65 and over and 45–49, with the greatest number of memberships at ages 35–44. Most of the Protestants and Catholics who seldom or never attended church also lacked membership in voluntary associations, while most of those who attended faithfully had one or more such memberships.

Other studies support the conclusion that there is a positive correlation between church participation and other formal social participation at all ages. It is not unreasonable to think that associating with people in church-related activities and organizations contributes to knowledge of other voluntary organizations; friendships in the church with persons who are members of other groups may lead to social participation in them. The lower organizational membership levels of Catholics hence could result from their lesser stress upon "fellowship" in the church as compared to Protestants, as well as from their somewhat lower position in the social class structure of American society.

Barron's (1961) New York City study included a question about the respondent's self-image, "Would you say you are a religious person, or doesn't religion mean very much to you?" Of all the respondents, 44.7% responded affirmatively and 25.2% expressed an irreligious self-image. Among the 116 persons aged 60–65, however, the respective percentages were 55.1 and 19.9 (25.0% were undecided compared with 30.1% in the total sample).

The most significant aspect of the chronological age distribution in answer to this question was the steadily increasing proportions of the religious self-image and the steadily declining proportions of indecision regarding the self-image of the ascension of chronological age.

The relationship of religion to personality problems has been observed and commented upon by a number of behavioral scientists. Religion was the preferred topic of discussion in group therapy sessions with geriatric patients at a state hospital. Religious beliefs and faith in God helped disorganized members to overcome their grief when unhappy, lonesome, and despondent. They were eager to discuss a better life after death; other members sensed the support religion gave them because they themselves also received greater "Ego strength" from religion. Delusions and hallucinations involving religious symptoms were, however, not accepted by other members of the group as true and correct; when they occurred the possibility of a mistake or incorrect interpretation was discussed (Wolff, 1959a).

Elderly patients who have ambivalent feelings toward life and death often want to die, since they believe they have nothing for which to live. Yet as they sense death is approaching, they may become disturbed and insecure, want others near at all times, and fear the dark. They may attend church more often than previously, confess, and ask that their sins be forgiven. They thus turn toward religion, which gives them emotional support and relief from the fear that everything soon will end (Wolff, 1959b).

Fear of death was one topic probed in a study of 260 community volunteers aged 60 and over in North Carolina. Such fear was found to be significantly related (at the 1% level of confidence) to less belief in life after death and less frequent Bible reading (Jeffers, Nichols, & Eisdorfer, 1961). Swenson's (1961) psychological study of 210 Minnesota residents aged 60 and over similarly found a significant relationship between death attitudes and religiosity as measured by both religious activity and the MMPI religiosity scale, a measure of devotion to religion. "Persons with more fundamental religious convictions and habits look forward to death more than do those with less fundamental convictions and less activity. Fearful attitudes toward death tend to be found in those persons with little religious activity. . . . It seems logical to infer that the eschatologically oriented person contemplates death in a positive manner."

These findings support the conclusion that a sense of serenity and decreased fear of death tend to accompany conservative religious beliefs. This does not necessarily prove, however, that religious faith removes the fear of death. It is conceivable that attitudes toward death of the religiously faithful differ from those of nonreligious people because of differences in their social integration (Treanton, 1961); the religious have a reference group that gives them support and security and the nonreligious are more likely to lack such social support. Swenson's finding that fear of death is related to solitude supports this hypothesis; social isolation may be an intervening variable explaining the observed relationships.

The traditional cultural definition of death complicates research on this subject among people of Christian convictions. The faithful believer is expected so to rest upon the promise of his salvation that he has no fear of death; he is expected to see death as a portal to immortality. His affirmation that he does not fear the advent of death could be an expression of a neurotic personality which disguises death and pretends that it is not a basic condition of all life (Fulton, 1961). Feifel (1956) has hypothesized that "certain older persons perceive death as the beginning of a new existence for the purpose of controlling strong anxieties concerning death." While this hypothesis may be perceived by some religious people as an impudent attack upon the genuineness of religious faith, it may also be viewed as a compliment to it. If the hypothesis is verified, one of the social-psychological functions commonly attributed to religion by even the most faithful when they seek comfort in biblical teachings about the resurrection will have received scientific support.

Happiness was significantly related to frequency of church attendance among both Catholics and non-Catholics in the Chicago

"Back of the Yards" study. The "very happy" attended church the most frequently, the "moderately happy" the next most frequently, and the "less happy" persons attended the least of all. Lonely Catholics tended to be less active in the practice of their religion, but the relationship was not statistically significant (O'Reilly & Pembroke, n.d.).

Feelings of satisfaction and security were provided older persons by religion and church participation in a small midwestern community studied by McCrary (1956). Yet in her general medical practice in Muncie, Indiana, Dr. Covalt (1958) observed little or no relationship between religion and good adjustment to illness. The patient who brought a Bible to the hospital with him thereby gave the physicians a sign of anticipated trouble, for the stable, secure person did not bring a Bible. These insecure individuals often were members of fringe-type religious sects. They were uncooperative, did not carry out instructions, fought the nurses, complained about even the most minor matters, and unpleasantly hindered their own recovery.

Contradictory evidence thus emerges on the matter of whether religion performs such functions as promoting happiness, increasing personal security, combatting loneliness, and removing the fear of death. Several of these concepts are reflected in studies of personal adjustment or morale in old age. To discuss the techniques and findings of these in any detail is impossible in the short space available here, but a brief summary of some of the major studies will help to illuminate this aspect of the consequential dimension of religion. More thorough surveys are found in Gray and Moberg (1962) and Maves (1960).

These studies generally have found that there is a direct relationship between good personal adjustment and such indicators of religiosity as church membership, church attendance, Bible reading, regular listening to radio church services, belief in an after life, and religious faith. Yet a carefully planned experimental design to explore this relationship further, with the use of the Burgess-Cavan-Havighurst Attitudes Inventory as the measure of personal adjustment, revealed that controlling other factors which also are linked with good adjustment removed the correlation between adjustment and church membership (Moberg, 1953a). The relationship observed in cruder studies must be a result of linking with church membership certain other factors which contribute to adjustment rather than a result of church membership in and of itself.

Further analysis (Moberg, 1956) through additional experimental designs demonstrated that religious activities (church attendance in the past and present, lay leadership in the church, grace at meals, reading from the Bible and other religious books, family prayers, etc.) were significantly correlated with high adjustment scores. It was concluded that either those who are well-adjusted engage in many religious activities or else engaging in many religious activities contributes to good adjustment in old age.

Similarly, an experimental design (Moberg, 1953b) to analyze the relationships between adjustment and leadership in the church, as indicated by office-holding and committee work in the past and present, revealed that personal adjustment was positively related to lay leadership. An investigation (Moberg, 1958) of Christian beliefs about sin, prayer, the future, the Bible, and Jesus in relationship to personal adjustment also revealed a positive relationship between holding conventional Christian beliefs and good adjustment in old age when other factors were controlled. The evidence from these experimental designs, based upon institutionalized persons in homes for the aged, a county home, and a soldiers' home, supports the conclusion that religious beliefs and activities, in contrast to church affiliation *per se,* contribute to good personal adjustment in old age.

This conclusion is supported by additional studies of elderly people. The most significant of these (Moberg & Taves, 1965) involves over 5,000 persons aged 60 years and over interviewed in five surveys in four midwestern states. It was found that the adjustment scores of church "leaders" (church officers and committeemen), other church members, and non-church members were significantly different, with the leaders consistently highest and non-members lowest. Cross-tabulations of the data for 1,340 urban respondents in one of the states demonstrated that these differences remained

> statistically significant at the .001 level when analyzed within categories of sex, age, education, marital status, home ownership and type of residence, participation in civic, social, and professional organizations, organizational activity levels compared to those during the respondents' fifties, self-rating of health, and self-identification of age. Only in the area of employment were the variations non-significant, but even these were in the anticipated direction,

so the hypothesis that church participation is related to good personal adjustment in old age was overwhelmingly supported by the evidence.

A study (Oles, 1949) of Orthodox Jews aged 65 and over also found that adjustment was related to religious adherence. No non-religious persons were in the well-adjusted category; all were intensely or fairly religious. Three-fourths of the fairly adjusted group were intensely or fairly religious, but only 35% of the poorly and very poorly adjusted group were.

Religious beliefs and activities seem, on the basis of these and other studies, to be positively related to good personal-social adjustment in old age. Contrary evidence, but on a somewhat different basis, comes from Barron's (1961) New York City study. Only 39% mentioned that religion and the church gave them the most satisfaction and comfort in their lives today. This was exceeded by being home with the family, keeping house, "doing things I like to do by myself at home," having relatives visit, and spending time with close friends. Worry about getting older was significantly less among these who found religion comforting only for the age group 40–45; the comparative figures for all ages indicate that 37% of those who derive comfort from religion worry about aging compared with 40.6% of those who do not find religion comforting. Both of these measures of religiosity are very limited, but this finding suggests the need for further research before making sweeping generalizations about the impact of religion upon personal adjustment.

Another consequential aspect of religion is the large number of retirement homes and communities, nursing care facilities, social clubs, literary projects, counseling centers, volunteer services programs, educational activities, and other programs by and for the aged which are under church sponsorship (Culver, 1961). While these, like all human behavior, are based upon a wide range of economic, social, political, psychological, and humanitarian interests, the very fact that religiously based institutions are their sponsors demonstrates this to be a consequence of organized religion. Religious beliefs, feelings, knowledge, and practices undoubtedly are an underlying factor in much of the humanitarian work that is done through other institutional structures as well. The educational and inspirational work of the church often is directly oriented toward such goals; to whatever extent it is effective, it serves as an enlightening and motivating influence in society, and more often produces change through its constituents than through formal institutional action. This aspect of the consequential dimension of religious commitment is obviously very difficult to study empirically because it is so intricately woven into the total fabric of society.

Interrelations of the Dimensions

Some studies have shown both the interconnectedness and the relative independence of various dimensions of religious commitment. The bi-serial correlation coefficient between the religious activity and religious attitude scores in the Chicago Activities and Attitudes Inventories by Burgess, Cavan, and Havighurst, for example, was significant at the .001 level of confidence in a North Carolina study (Jeffers & Nichols, 1961). The correlation co-efficient between attitudes toward religion and frequency of attendance at religious services in the original Chicago study was .55 among 1,024 males and .37 among 1,894 females (Cavan et al., 1949). In a study (Moberg, 1951) of 219 institutionalized aged persons, the product-moment correlation of a religious activities score and a religious belief score was .660 with a standard error of .038.

Such relationships are the kind one would expect; if a person has religious faith, he is more apt to participate in the personal and social activities which simultaneously nourish that faith and are consequences of it. Belief in life after death thus is significantly associated with more frequent church attendance, more frequent Bible reading, a greater number of other religious activities, a feeling that religion is the most important thing in life, less fear of death, and stronger religious attitudes than are found among those who lack such a belief (Jeffers et al., 1961).

Nevertheless, it is a fallacy to assume that *all* dimensions of religiosity are highly inter-correlated. Hospitalized old people, we know, are somewhat more likely than the elderly in the community to identify with a religious group, but they also are con-

siderably less likely to attend religious services than nonhospitalized old people (Fiske, 1960). To judge the totality of the religiosity of a person on the basis of one of the five major dimensions of religious commitment or, as is a common practice, of but one subdimension thereof, can lead to serious errors. Religious preference, church attendance, religious self-identification, and other simple indicators of religiosity must be used with great caution of interpretation. Religious commitment is a complex phenomenon with many ramifications. Until research has demonstrated the ways in which and the extent to which the experiential, ideological, ritualistic, intellectual, and consequential dimensions of religious commitment are inter-correlated, it is wise to refrain from jumping to conclusions about any of them on the basis of evidence only from another.

Summary and Conclusions

Research to date seems to indicate fairly conclusively that ritualistic behavior outside the home tends to diminish with increasing age, while religious attitudes and feelings apparently increase among people who have an acknowledged religion. To use Kuhlen's (1962) words in his summary of research findings on adult religion,

. . . in all studies examined, with the exception of those relating to church attendance, trends indicate an increased interest in and concern about religion as age increases, even into extreme old age.

In other words, religion as a set of external extradomiciliary rituals apparently decreases in old age, while the internal personal responses linked with man's relationships to God apparently increase among religious people. Thus both disengagement from and re-engagement with religion are typical in old age!

We have seen that some religious practices decline in the later years, but religious feelings and beliefs apparently increase. These contrasting tendencies account for most of the apparently contradictory statements about the place of religion in old age. The use of non-comparable "indicators" or "measures" of religiosity has led to confusion. More research is needed on the major dimensions of religiosity; it will have implications for the specialist in geriatrics as well as for churchmen and gerontologists.

This distinction is related to the age-old contrast between faith and works. Most of the objective practices ("works") of religion become increasingly difficult to perform in old age as the body and mind gradually show the effects of the aging process. Yet in his "spirit" the religious person may remain devout; his religious beliefs and feelings can become more intense even though his institutionally-oriented religious practices diminish.

Recognition of these distinct dimensions of religiosity thus helps to resolve differences of opinion about the role of religion among the elderly. Research can clarify the subject further; it also can lead to more realistic and wholesome relationships between clergymen and psychologists, social workers, and medical personnel and to keener awareness of the religious implications of geriatric practice.

References

Aldridge, G. J.: The role of older people in a Florida retirement community. *Geriatrics,* 11: 223–226, 1956.

Anon.: Do Americans believe in God? *Cath. Digest,* 17: 1–5, Nov., 1952.

Barron, M. L.: *The aging American: an introduction to social gerontology and geriatrics.* Thomas Y. Crowell, New York, 1961, pp. 164–183.

Cavan, R. S., E. W. Burgess, R. J. Havighurst, and H. Goldhamer: *Personal adjustment in old age.* Sci. Res. Assoc., Chicago, 1949, pp. 58, 198.

Covalt, N. K.: The meaning of religion to older people—the medical perspective. *In:* D. L. Scudder (Editor), *Organized Religion and the Older Person.* Univ. Florida Press, Gainesville, 1958, pp. 78–90.

Covalt, N. K.: The meaning of religion to older people. *Geriatrics,* 15: 658–664, 1960.

Culver, E. T.: *New church programs with the aging.* Association Press, New York, 1961.

Cumming, E., and W. E. Henry: *Growing old: the process of disengagement.* Basic Books, New York, 1961, pp. 91–94.

Feifel, H.: Older persons look at death. *Geriatrics,* 11: 127–130, 1956.

Fichter, J. H.: *Social relations in the urban parish.* Univ. Chicago Press, Chicago, 1954, pp. 83–93.

Fiske, M.: *Some social dimensions of psychiatric disorders in old age.* Langley Porter Neuropsychiat. Inst., San Francisco, 1960, p. 13 (mimeo.).

Fiske, M.: Geriatric mental illness: methodologic and social aspects. *Geriatrics,* 16: 306–310, 1961.

Fulton, R. L.: Symposium: death attitudes. Comments. *J. Geront.,* 16: 63–65, 1961.

Glock, C. Y.: On the study of religious commitment. *Relig. Educ.,* 57: S-98–S-110, 1962.

Gray, R. M., and D. O. Moberg: *The church and the older person.* Wm. B. Eerdmans, Grand Rapids, 1962, pp. 41–43, 153.

Havighurst, R. J., and R. Albrecht: *Older people.* Longmans, Green, New York, 1953, pp. 201–203.

Hunter, W. W., and H. Maurice: *Older people tell their story.* Univ. Mich., Ann Arbor, 1953, pp. 62–63.

Jeffers, F. C., and C. R. Nichols: The relationship of activities and attitudes to physical well-being in older people. *J. Geront.,* 16: 67–70, 1961.

Jeffers, F. C., C. R. Nichols, and C. Eisdorfer: Attitudes of older persons toward death: a preliminary study. *J. Geront.*, 16: 53–56, 1961.

Kuhlen, R. G.: Trends in religious behavior during the adult years. *In:* L. C. Little (Editor), *Wider Horizons in Christian Adult Education.* Univ. Pittsburgh Press, Pittsburgh, 1962, p. 23.

Lazerwitz, B.: Membership in voluntary associations and frequency of church attendance. *J. Scient. Study Religion,* 2: 74–84, 1962.

Lloyd, R. G.: Social and personal adjustment of retired persons. *Sociol. soc. Res.,* 39: 312–316, 1955.

Marshall, H., and M. H. Oden: The status of the mature gifted individual as a basis for evaluation of the aging process. *Gerontologist,* 2: 201–206, 1962.

Maves, P. B.: Aging, religion and the church. *In:* C. Tibbitts (Editor), *Handbook of Social Gerontology.* Univ. Chicago Press, Chicago, 1960, pp. 698–749.

Mayo, S. C.: Social participation among the older population in rural areas of Wake County, North Carolina. *Soc. Forces,* 30: 53–59, 1951.

McCann, C. W.: *Long Beach senior citizens' survey.* Community Welfare Counc., Long Beach, 1955, pp. 50–52.

McCrary, J. S.: *The role, status, and participation of the aged in a small community.* Ph.D. thesis, Washington Univ., St. Louis, 1956.

Moberg, D. O.: *Religion and personal adjustment in old age.* Ph.D. thesis, Univ. Minnesota, Minneapolis, 1951, p. 105.

Moberg, D. O.: Church membership and personal adjustment in old age. *J. Geront.,* 8: 207–211, 1953 (a).

Moberg, D. O.: Leadership in the church and personal adjustment in old age. *Sociol. soc. Res.,* 37: 312–316, 1953 (b).

Moberg, D. O.: Religious activities and personal adjustment in old age. *J. soc. Psychol.,* 43: 261–267, 1956.

Moberg, D. O.: Christian beliefs and personal adjustment in old age. *J. Amer. Sci. Affil.,* 10: 8–12, 1958.

Moberg, D. O.: *The Church as a social institution.* Prentice-Hall, Englewood Cliffs, N.J., 1962, pp. 393–395, 414–418.

Moberg, D. O.: The integration of older members in the church congregation. *In:* A. M. Rose and W. A. Peterson (Editors), *Older People and Their Social World.* F. A. Davis, Philadelphia, 1965.

Moberg, D. O., and M. J. Taves: Church participation and adjustment in old age. *In:* A. M. Rose and W. A. Peterson (Editors), *Older People and Their Social World.* F. A. Davis, Philadelphia, 1965.

Oles, E. S.: *Religion and old age, a study of the possible influence of religious adherence on adjustment.* Thesis, Bucknell Univ., Lewisburg, Pa., 1949. Reviewed in *J. Geront.,* 5: 187, 1950.

Orbach, H. L.: Aging and religion: church attendance in the Detroit metropolitan area. *Geriatrics,* 16: 530–540, 1961.

O'Reilly, C. T., and M. M. Pembroke: *Older people in a Chicago community.* Loyola University, Chicago, n.d. (survey made in 1956).

Pan, J. S.: Institutional and personal adjustment in old age. *J. gen. Psychol.,* 85: 155–158, 1954.

Starbuck, E. D.: The psychology of religion (3rd ed.). Walter Scott, New York, 1911, p. 320.

Swenson, W. M.: Attitudes toward death in an aged population. *J. Geront.,* 16: 49–52, 1961.

Taietz, P., and O. F. Larson: Social participation and old age. *Rur. Sociol.,* 21: 229–238, 1956.

Taves, M. J., and G. D. Hansen: Seventeen hundred elderly citizens. *In:* A. M. Rose (Editor), Aging in Minnesota. Univ. Minnesota Press, Minneapolis, 1963, p. 172.

Theisen, S. P.: *A social survey of aged Catholics in the deanery of Fort Wayne, Indiana.* Ph.D. thesis, Univ. Notre Dame, Ind., 1962.

Toch, H.: Attitudes of the "fifty plus" age group: preliminary considerations toward a longitudinal study. *Publ. Opin. Quart.,* 17: 391–394, 1953.

Treanton, J. R.: Symposium: death attitudes. Comments. *J. Geront.,* 16: 63, 1961.

Warren, R. L.: Old age in a rural township. *In:* *Old Age Is No Barrier.* N.Y. State Jt. Legis.

Com. on Problems Aging, Albany, 1952, pp. 155–166.

Wolff, K.: Group psychotherapy with geriatric patients in a state hospital setting: results of a three year study. *Group Psychotherapy,* 12: 218–222, 1959 (a).

Wolff, K.: *The biological, sociological and psychological aspects of aging.* Charles C. Thomas, Springfield, Ill., 1959, p. 75 (b).

Wolff, K.: A co-ordinated approach to the geriatric problem. *J. Amer. ger. Soc.,* 9: 573–580, 1961.

Youmans, E. G.: Aging patterns in a rural and an urban area of Kentucky. *Univ. Ky. Agric. Exp. Sta. Bull.* 681, 1963, p. 45.

9

The Middle Years

RESPONSIBILITY OR FAILURE

The period of life called "middle age" begins around the age of thirty-five and ends around the age of sixty or sixty-five. It is a period that, in Erikson's terms, involves the issue of *generativity* — creativity and productivity in family life (children) and in one's career. *Stagnation* is the opposite, the basis for *midlife crisis.*

Middle-aged people are in the "sandwiched" generation, with responsibilities for their adolescent or young-adult children *and* their aging parents. Middle age is also a time of leadership. Middle-aged persons fill most of the positions of power in government, business, labor, and education.

One of the primary midlife developmental tasks of women in our culture is to deal effectively with the launching of their children and the biological end to childbearing capacity known as menopause. Although many women experience "hot flashes" and some dryness of the vagina during menopause, the frequency and intensity of symptoms has been greatly exaggerated. Women commonly fear menopause for a variety of reasons, but they usually find the actual experience much less unpleasant than they had imagined — and not without unexpected benefits.

Many men and women experience the kind of "psychological menopause" — fear of aging — that we now call the midlife crisis. In our culture, men most often experience midlife crisis in regard to their career, which often does not seem to be going as well as had been hoped for. *Douglas W. Bray* and *Ann Howard* have done a twenty-year followup of a group of managers who were recruited by the Bell system in the 1950s. Our selection describes some of the variables that seem to make for success as well as some of the personality changes which have occurred along the way and which may lead to success or failure by the time midlife is reached. After twenty years, the most successful men are those who are more aggressive, less friendly, but also still turned on by their career prospects.

A broader treatment of midlife crises for both men and women is presented in an essay by *Nancy Datan,* who, in a literate manner, shows that the theme of the midlife crisis is an ancient one, and tries to draw meaning for today's problems out of an analysis of ancient myths concerned with adult life crises. She relates the story of Adam and Eve to the price of maturity, that of Prometheus to the price of technology, King Midas to the achievement crisis, and the story of the fisherman's wife to the suburban housewife's concern about life's emptiness. The stories of Oedipus, Hansel and Gretel, and Snow White, finally, are related to problems of merciless parents, empty cupboards, and grown children.

Additional Suggested Readings

Erikson, E. *Insight and responsibility.* New York: Norton, 1964.
  A classic, applying psychoanalytic theory to the problems of resolving the conflict between the needs of the individual and his or her responsibility to society.

Harragan, B. L. *Games mother never taught you.* New York: Warener, 1977.
  A readable discussion of the problems of modern women in succeeding in a masculine-dominated world of work, while maintaining their feminine identity and self-respect.

Keeping in Touch with Success

DOUGLAS W. BRAY and ANN HOWARD

Over 20 years ago, the Bell System launched what is perhaps the most exhaustive study of executive lives and careers ever undertaken. This research project, called "The Management Progress Study," is still in full operation today and has recently begun examining the characteristics of a group of managers who are now middle-aged and in mid-career.

The people originally recruited for the study in the 1950's were new managers, on the bottom rung of their Bell System careers. All were considered potential candidates for middle management. The 422 young men originally participating in the Management Progress Study included both college graduates who entered management directly and high school graduates who had been promoted into first-line management after several years of service in vocational jobs. (Because these candidates were selected in the 1950's, they all were, alas, white males; a similar group recruited today would contain women and members of minorities.) So far, only a portion of the *college graduates* in the study have reached the 20-year mark. This report is based on the lives and careers of 80 of them.

As the two decades went by, the men in the study experienced varying degrees of career success. For someone who is not a technical specialist in the Bell System, "success" is typically measured in terms of the management level attained. The manage-

ment hierarchy in a telephone company has seven levels. Only the President is at level seven and new management recruits are at level one.

About half of the men in the study had reached the third or "district" level of management after 20 years; this denotes entry into middle management and success in reaching the goal set for them when they were recruited into the company. At this level they typically have functional responsibility for one aspect of telephone service in a given geographical district. For example, a District Plant manager in a major city might be responsible for the installation and maintenance of communications equipment for 152,000 business and residential customers, with a force of around 400. A District Traffic Manager, responsible for operator services, might have a force of about 750, while a District Commercial Manager might be in charge of a group of about 130 employees handling collections of accounts and customer questions regarding billing and service. About 24 percent of the men in the Management Progress Study have not reached this goal of district manager, however, and are still at levels one and two.

The remaining 28 percent have actually exceeded the minimum goal and are at the fourth and fifth levels of management. Some no doubt are on their way to vice presidencies, or level six. But even without further

Source: Bray, D. W., & Howard, A. Keeping in touch with success: A mid-career portrait at AT&T. *The Wharton Magazine*, Vol. 3. No. 2. pp. 28–33. Copyright 1979 by the Wharton School of the University of Pennsylvania. Reprinted by permission.

promotions, the men at levels four and five would have to be counted as highly "successful." They have been promoted higher than the majority of their peers and their annual salaries range from about $40,000 to $70,000.

As they made their way through the Bell System management hierarchy, the participants in the Management Progress Study were studied both thoroughly and regularly. At the beginning they went through an elaborate three-day management assessment center. Here they participated in a variety of individual and group exercises, including simulations, interviews, leaderless group discussions, projective tests and various paper-and-pencil measures of aptitudes, interests, personality and attitudes. They repeated that experience eight years later.

After 20 years, they underwent a quite different assessment that focused on mid-career issues and the problems and·challenges of middle life. In between these assessments, the men were interviewed intensively by psychologists on 11 different occasions. In addition, other company personnel, particularly their bosses, have been frequently interviewed about them.

What Are They Like?

One salient thing that can be said about the successful manager is that he is usually middle-aged. This may not be the case in small or self-owned businesses, but it is likely to be true in large hierarchical organizations. Future middle and upper managers typically enter such organizations at the lowest rung of management or even in non-management assignments. Then, no matter what one's ability, time must be served in moving up the hierarchy level by level. The participants in the Management Progress Study, for example, had 20 years of service in the Bell System; they averaged 44 years of age and none was less than 40.

But middle age, as more and more researchers and writers are emphasizing, connotes more than just the passage of time. People change. The 45-year-old is no longer seen as merely a slightly less vigorous 25-year-old. If those 20 years involve developmental changes in ability, motivation, and personality, then the fact that successful, upwardly mobile middle managers are middle-aged may have great implications for their commitment and performance.

Another characteristic of successful managers is that they have greater intellectual ability than do less successful ones. This doesn't apply, of course, in every case; all comparisons here refer to the average or typical case. Primary evidence comes from the administration of a standardized mental ability test (the School and College Ability Test), which measures capacity for learning. The more successful managers score higher on this test today, just as they did 12 years ago and 20 years ago.

In the Management Progress Study, two key ingredients of managerial performance stand out: *administrative skills,* including planning and organizing ability and decision-making: and *interpersonal skills,* particularly those having to do with leadership. Successful managers, not unexpectedly, have considerably more of these skills. In addition, their job performance is less likely to suffer under conditions of stress and uncertainty.

Not only are successful managers more capable, they are more motivated to use the capabilities they have. They are highly involved in their jobs and rate their careers as one of the most important things in life. When asked to rank the relative importance of career development and advancement with such things as social activities, self development, family activities, hobbies, rest and relaxation, the more successful managers consistently give higher rankings to career factors than do the less successful managers.

Several personality/motivational needs also distinguish highly successful managers from the typical Bell System recruit. On the Edwards Personal Preference Schedule, a paper-and-pencil measure of such needs, the fourth and fifth level managers scored particularly high on needs for *achievement* (to do a difficult job well, irrespective of advancement), for *dominance* (to lead and direct others), for *autonomy* (to be independent and avoid being controlled), and for *aggression* (to express hostility). They were low in motivation for *deference* and *affiliation,* meaning they are not eager to conform to authority or regulations nor are they keen on making friends or enjoying friendship for its own sake. (See Table 1.)

Although the material available on the "successful" managers is voluminous and detailed, they are still a rather small group. Fortunately, however, just as the 20-year data were being analyzed, the opportunity arose to study a comparable group of 35 managers attending the Bell System Advanced Management Program at the University of Illinois. These managers were also at the fourth or fifth level of management and were generally considered to have still higher potential. At these high levels, 33 of the 35 were white males. Nearly half were 40 years of age or older and only one was less than 35.

The mid-life assessment center was too time-consuming to be included in the University of Illinois program, but it was possible to administer many of the same biographical and personality questionnaires originally used in the Management Progress Study. The results for both groups were highly similar, which enhanced our confidence in the original conclusions about successful managers.

In summary, the intensive research on the participants in the Management Progress Study (and corroborating data from those in the Bell Advanced Management Program) yield a clear and consistent picture of the successful manager — at least the successful white male manager. He possesses important managerial abilities and is highly motivated to use them. He is deeply involved in his work and career. His personality emphasizes achievement and leadership with a corresponding desire for independence and freedom from the demands of others. Perhaps the only surprise is that he is rather indifferent to friendships (though casual observation often reveals outward sociability) and is aggressively hostile, in spite of having achieved career success.

How Do They Get That Way?

If this is what successful managers are like, how do they get that way? One possible explanation is that they were like this when

TABLE 1

Differences in Motivation Between Young and Older Managers Are Due to Age, Not to Social Changes of the Last 20 Years. (From Edwards Personal Preference Schedule.)

	New Managers		Middle-Aged Managers		
Needs For:	1956–60	1977	Levels 1–3 1976–77	Levels 4–5 1976–77	Levels 4–5 1978
Achievement	63%	67%	78%	89%	84%
Aggression	55%	55%	69%	71%	76%
Autonomy	57%	66%	82%	85%	82%
Affiliation	56%	58%	36%	29%	24%

they entered the Bell System as new college recruits. Another is that general life developmental changes have taken place between youth and middle age for the more successful and less successful alike. A third is that the successful manager has changed over the years in a way different from the less successful, perhaps because he has experienced greater job challenges and career success. The longitudinal data of the Management Progress Study permitted us to examine each of these possibilities.

Predictions of career progress which were made at the assessment center 20 years ago have turned out to be excellent indicators of which new managers would reach the fourth level of management or higher. About half of the new college recruits did notably well in the original management assessment while the remainder did less well. Some 16 years later, 46 percent of those who assessed well were at the fourth or fifth level or higher. Only 19 percent of those who assessed poorly had progressed that far. The fact that such long-range prediction was possible implies that important managerial characteristics were apparent at the time of employment.

Many of the managerial qualities that differentiated the potentially more successful candidates from the very start of their careers have persisted over time. The successful managers had greater intellectual ability from the start, and they were also stronger in planning and organizing ability. For example, when given a simulation of a middle manager's in-basket at the original assessment center, the potentially successful managers were better able to differentiate the most important items and maximize use of the available time. They had higher inner work standards or desire to do a job well for its own sake, and they initially had more urgent needs for advancement (although these needs declined over time). On the Edwards Personal Preference Schedule, the potentially successful tended to show more motivation to dominate and lead and less

motivation to defer to higher authority. Thus to a large extent, the die had already been cast when these recruits first appeared at the doors of the telephone company.

What part, then, does general adult development play in the characteristics of successful managers? Even though changes over time were evident among the Management Progress Study participants, there is a danger in interpreting these as developmental changes. An equally tenable explanation might be cultural changes, or changes in society over time. For example, an increase in the need for autonomy over time may be due to a growing independence and antagonism toward constraints that generally accompanies age and experience—or it may be due to a societal change in the direction of "doing your own thing."

The most appropriate method for disentangling these two types of explanations is to take a look at another group of managers in what we call a "cohort analysis." Fortunately such a group was at hand: the first wave of the Bell System's new Management Continuity Study had just begun.

The Management Continuity Study is intended to be a longitudinal study of *today's* young management recruits. Its major purpose is to determine the abilities and motivations of these newcomers. An important byproduct is to add perspective to the findings of the older Management Progress Study. Only 47 participants have so far been assessed in the new study, with white males in the minority. Nevertheless, results so far have provided valuable comparisons, and no race or sex differences show up in the data reported here.

The first column of the accompanying table shows the average percentile for the managers in the Management Progress Study when they were tested on their motivations (needs) as new college recruits in the years 1956–60. The second column shows the results for the college recruits of today, those in the Management Continuity

Study, tested in 1977. It is apparent that the percentile scores for these two groups of new managers differ very little from each other. Young people today score about the same as young people did 20 years ago.

The remaining three columns in the table are made up of middle-aged managers: the men in the Management Progress Study who had gone no further than the lowest three levels of management in 1976–77; those in the same study who had arrived at levels four and five; and the selected fourth and fifth level managers in the Bell System Advanced Management program, tested in 1978. Scores of these three groups are quite similar to each other but significantly different from those of the new recruit groups in the first two columns. This means that the considerable differences in scores are probably *not* due to general societal changes, but more likely due to age differences.

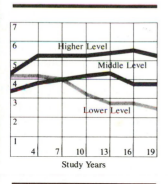

Study Years

There is another factor that points to the influence of age differences in this change. Just as successful managers had changed in these traits over time, so had the less successful. This leads to the conclusion that the successful middle manager is achievement-oriented, hostile, independent, and unaffiliative not because he is a successful manager, but because he is a middle-aged manager.

If the changes just discussed are char-

acteristic of managers regardless of the level they have reached in the organization, there still remains the matter of changes that might accompany success itself. One of the most dramatic of these changes concerns the importance that work assumes. Illustrating this is a major assessment dimension rated 20 years ago, 12 years ago, and again this year is called "Primacy of Work": "to what extent does this individual find satisfactions from work more important than those from other areas of life?"

The ratings on this dimension were almost identical 20 years ago for men who later wound up at the first and second level of management, men who achieved the third level, and men who achieved the fourth level or higher. In sharp contrast, the ratings today show a highly significant difference between these groups—those who have reached higher levels are much more likely to give work a top place in their lives.

This finding is strongly supported by an analysis of the interviews conducted over the years with the same three groups of managers. The accompanying graph shows the dramatic differences that have taken place.

When the initial interviews of 20 years ago were scored (on a seven-point scale) by a clinical psychologist who was rating involvement with "occupational life theme," there was little difference between the three groups. By the time of the most recent interviews, the differences were wide indeed. There is no doubt that success in management involves rewards, including not only pay, recognition and power, but the satisfaction of achievement on more challenging assignments. It is highly likely that such rewards themselves intensify one's involvement in work (which in turn leads to even greater rewards).

Given this increased work involvement, some people have asked, "Isn't success in management achieved at the expense of the rest of life, such as family and recreation and service to the community?" The interview data in the Management Progress Study provide some answers to such questions.

Higher level managers showed almost no change in their involvement with their wives and marital families over the two decades of the study, and they showed only a small decline in involvement in recreational activities, such as hobbies, sports and partying. Although the least successful managers were at a comparable level at the start of the study, they showed a substantial increase on both of these non-work themes with time, perhaps because they did not find as many rewards in the world of work. Thus the impression that successful managers are sacrificing other important parts of life may be only in contrast to people who haven't risen as far in the business hierarchy and are investing more in family and recreational pursuits.

Using the Knowledge

What implications do all these findings have for management staffing? For one thing, the importance of initial selection is once again underlined. Among the factors to be emphasized in such selection are general mental ability, planning and organizing skill, high work standards, and the motivation to advance and lead without instruction from others.

The importance of initial selection is strongly enhanced by two additional findings from the Management Progress Study. First, attrition does not improve the average quality of managers on the payroll. Among those who left the company within the first eight years, about the same proportion of men had been originally assessed as promotable to middle management as among those who stayed. Secondly, over time the great majority of people added to the payroll will reach at least the lowest rung of middle management. In the Management Progress Study, 76 percent of those who remained

with the business had reached middle management 20 years later. Hence, if you don't want lower quality managers in middle management, it is better not to hire them in the first place rather than counting on them to remain in lower level positions.

Another implication of the findings is that general life developmental changes do take place. The average person doesn't stay the same as he gets older. The developmental changes are not, however, what we might have expected based on popular literature. The changes may be seen as favorable for business management in that people become more independent and achievement-oriented. On the other hand, they also tend to become more hostile and less affiliative. The notion that the maturing manager, at least up to age 45, becomes kinder, more nurturant, and willing to happily fade into the background as he hands the mantle of responsibility to those he has trained appears to be a sentimental fantasy.

Finally, we can expect that the rich will get richer and the poor, poorer. Those who are more capable and more motivated will tend to be given advancement and increased responsibility (although mistakes are not rare). In turn, this will result in their becoming even more job-involved and motivated. It is important to note, however, that even those who haven't done so well have shown a rise over the years in their motivation for achievement. One difficult challenge for management is to provide assignments and situations that can lead to achievement satisfactions when opportunities for advancement may not be available, or in fact appropriate, for certain managers.

The Management Progress Study will continue after the mid-career, midlife assessment center in order to examine developments in the pre- and post-retirement years. It is only the cooperative group of men — who have given their time and revealed their innermost thoughts and feelings with very few personal rewards in return — that makes this valuable program possible. For their patience and forbearance to date, we are immeasurably grateful.

What Is an Assessment Center?

The management assessment center is a method of evaluating managerial ability and motivation in an *off-the-job* situation. Candidates for employment, advancement, or development are put through a variety of standardized situational exercises which elicit behavior crucial to managerial performance. Exercises commonly used include short business games, leaderless group discussions. In-baskets (simulations of a manager's incoming mail), fact-finding problems, and analysis-presentation assignments (requiring diagnosis of problems and oral presentation of solutions).

Behavior in the exercises is observed by a trained staff (usually higher level managers in the same organization) and reported at an "integration" session where the observations of the assessors are pooled. Candidates are then rated on dimensions such as leadership skills, planning and organizing, oral communication skills, career motivation and independence. Finally, overall ratings are made as to whether the candidate is capable of advancement to the next level of management.

The management assessment center was devised and first used in the Bell System's Management Progress Study in the mid-1950's. It is now utilized by hundreds of businesses and governmental organizations and is also applied to non-supervisory work such as sales and engineering. A recent development has been its application to the measurement of professional competence in diverse fields such as pharmacy and clinical psychology.

The assessment center is also a powerful tool in the study of human personality and development. The method was first used at the Harvard Psychological Clinic in the 1930's under Dr. Henry A. Murray. Current utilization in research into personality and motivation in midlife recalls its origins four decades ago.

Suggested Reading

Douglas W. Bray, Richard J. Campbell, and Donald L. Grant, *Formative Years in Business,* John Wiley and Sons, 1974. Describes and interprets the initial findings for the college sample of the Management Progress Study (274 men) for the first eight years of the study.

Ann Howard, *"An Assessment of Assessment Centers." Academy of Management Journal, Vol. 17, No. 1, 1974.*

Midas and Other Mid-Life Crises

NANCY DATAN

Mid-life crises are in fashion today: We all know someone who is having one, or treating one, or writing a paper on the subject. Analyses of the mid-life crisis are nearly as numerous as cases of crisis, but, despite a diversity of theories, certain common themes emerge (Brim, 1974; Gould, 1978; Levinson, Darrow, Klien, Levinson and McKee, 1978). Like other transitions in the life cycle, the mid-life crisis is a product of multiple determinants. It has been traced to factors such as possible stagnation in marriage and career, declining opportunities with advancing age, and biological deficits: in brief, intrinsic and extrinsic causes, maturational, social, and existential.

It is often suggested that the crisis of meaning in middle age is, at least in part, a consequence of recent social changes and concomitant changes in the life cycle, such as increased longevity, fewer children born closer together, leaving the family nest sooner and consequently leaving the middle-aged parents with nothing to do. Children no longer fill the home and the daily routine, while affluence has removed the taste of struggle from life and simultaneously increased the availability and visibility of options, leading not only to freedom of choice but also to discontent.

These views of middle age sound like a Schoolroom Theory of Mid-Life Crisis. Teachers know that if a roomful of children are left to their own devices, they will soon be making trouble. Life span developmental theory seems to suggest that the same is true of middle-aged adults: Left to themselves, they will soon find trouble. Their maturity is demonstrated by the relocation of trouble from the interpersonal to the intrapsychic. In the rooms where the middle-aged live, quarrels are not between people but deep within the self, and the aggression of youth is turned inward, to become the depression of middle age.

I am prepared to accept the pessimistic view of human nature suggested by developmental psychology, but I am unwilling to agree that the problems of middle age are new. A dynamic perspective on the life cycle, I believe, permits us to anticipate trouble, because the dynamic perspective suggests the ubiquity of conflict, and the brevity of resolution. An abundance of clichés testifies to the conflict in the life cycle: "We get too soon old and too late smart"; "Little children, little problems — big children, big problems"; and the ultimate threat — "Wait until you grow up and have children of your own." Gould (1978) suggests that the discovery of truth in cultural clichés is one of the tasks of middle adulthood. It is my purpose to demonstrate that this discovery reaches back into antiquity, and to suggest that a recognition of the truth in cultural clichés is more than trivially interesting.

The themes of our Western myths of knowledge contain recognition of conscious self-determination, responsibility for the self and an attendant sense of loneliness, the un-

Source: Datan, N. Midas and other mid-life crises. In W. H. Norman & T. J. Scaramella (eds.), *Mid-life: Developmental and clinical issues.* New York: Brunner/Mazel, 1980, pp. 3–19. Reprinted by permission.

easy appetite for knowledge, recognition of the necessity of work, desire for the fruits of one's own labor, and, finally, ambivalence about one's relationship to the next generation. I shall suggest that the prominent themes of our cultural heritage are also the prominent themes of the developmental transition to adulthood — from dependency to autonomy, and finally to responsibility for others — and thus, of the developmental dynamics of middle age. . . .

I shall demonstrate the antiquity of crisis through an application of the dynamic perspective to myth, folklore, and fairy tales. A series of surprises initiated my inquiries, and, since I believe that the distinction between investigator and investigation is by no means as sharp as we like to suppose, I shall share my surprises — all the better to share my theories.

Several years ago, I was preparing a lecture on Freud's paper, "The Development of the Libido," in which his model of the Oedipus complex is derived from a sensitive analysis of Sophocles' tragedy of *Oedipus Rex* (1966). All psychologists and psychiatrists are familiar with Oedipal dynamics — the small boy who desires his mother to the exclusion of his father. I would venture to say, however, that not many have gone from Freud's lectures back to Sophocles' original drama, or they would have been as startled as I was to realize that Oedipus Rex is a play for and about adults. Sexual passion and murderous rage abound, but it is adults who are moved by these forces, beginning with the father of Oedipus, who is the only person in this tragedy to attempt premeditated murder.

King Laius, hearing the prophecy that he will be killed by his son, instructed a shepherd to take the baby out to the mountains to die. This attempted murder failed not through any weakening of the father's murderous intention, but because the shepherd was moved by compassion to save the baby, and gave him into the hands of a neighboring king. In Greek tragedy, as in dynamic psychology, one cannot escape one's doom, and so Oedipus, fleeing his foster parents' home to avert the prophecy of patricide and incest, met a stranger at the place where three roads intersect, murdered him and married his widow, and so, of course, fulfilled the prophecy in seeking to escape it.

Reading the drama with dynamic psychology in mind, I judged that we have been looking too long at little boys, and too little at their fathers and mothers. I saw the Oedipus complex as only one-half of a dynamic interaction between child and parents, in which the second half, the sexual and aggressive passions of the parents, seemed curiously neglected. For example, Erikson asserted in 1970 that "parricide remains a much more plausible explanation of the world's ills than does filicide" — a highly improbable statement in light of current statistics on child abuse, which make it all too easy to establish the ubiquity of rage and lust among adults (Justice and Justice, 1976).

Just as I had taken my first steps toward formulating a model of ongoing conflict between parent and child, it was my privilege to hear Bruno Bettelheim lecture on "The Hidden Message of the Fairy Tale" (in Jerusalem, 1972), later to become part of his book, *The Uses of Enchantment* (1976). I was captivated by his analyses, which demonstrated the ego-appropriate solutions to the dynamic dilemmas of childhood, conveyed through the medium of the fairy tale. I felt it was possible to study adult developmental dynamics as well, through attention to the adults who inhabit fairy tales — the neglected villains as well as the occasional good fairies.

In this chapter, I shall explore two dimensions of development which may find expression in mid-life crises: the individual's course of development, and the development seen in the family life cycle. I shall argue that the components of the mid-life crisis are not new: On the contrary, I will suggest that myths, folk and fairy tales carry abundant warnings about the dynamics of middle life, and describe the developmental dilemmas of adulthood in the twentieth century with an accuracy which might be called embarrassing — or eternal.

Individual Development: Forbidden Fruits and Sorrow

"The love of learning is a dangerous thing, and whoever increases knowledge increases sorrow," Ecclesiastes warns the generations to come, anticipating the ambivalence which accompanies each new stage of growth and development in the individual life cycle, with its mixed blessings of autonomy, mastery, and power — and the attendant loss of dependency. The testimony for this claim is written across human history, from prehistoric myths to contemporary accounts of riots on university campuses.

I believe that the story of the Garden of Eden and the record of student riots share significant elements, reflecting aspects of a major transition in adult personality development: the transition from dependency to an awareness of self-determination and reliance upon the self. Two aspects of this transition can be seen in the ancient story of the Garden of Eden and the recent history of student riots: an irresistible desire for knowledge, and pain as the price of this knowledge — the price of self-consciousness and responsibility. These are two major components of the dialectical dynamics of the transition into adulthood.

I propose that this transition into adulthood is best seen in the context of a developmental model of personality. I see this transition as a passage from dependency to responsibility, and from innocence to knowledge. This passage can be seen on three dimensions: in the transition to self-

sufficiency represented by the story of the Garden of Eden; in the search for mastery over nature represented by the story of Prometheus; and in the price of power, represented by the legend of Midas and the tale of the Fisherman's Wife.

While the self and its solitude are major themes in existential psychology, the developmental model of the transition to adulthood has focused on the fit between self and society. Erikson's discussions of identity and youth (1963; 1964; 1965; 1970) deal with commitment to or alienation from society, and this is the perspective taken by subsequent writers such as Keniston (1970). The problem of young adulthood, in developmental theory, is often conceived in sociological terms. It would be unkind but not at all untrue to say that a brief overview of Erikson's (1963) description of the core problem in ego development, identity versus role confusion, might lead the reader to conclude that the problem of ego identity can be resolved by competent career counseling.

It is not my intention to deny or even to diminish the importance of fit between self and society, but I shall argue that the external process of role commitment is a manifestation of an internal process in which the individual moves from the dependency of infancy and childhood toward the independence of adolescence and young adulthood, and finally to the point of responsibility for the new and dependent generation to come. This maturationally-determined series of transformations can be discerned in the life cycle of all animal species not wholly governed by instinct, and it takes on increasing complexity as we ascend the phylogenetic scale.

"It is human to have a long childhood," Erikson remarks (1963); the uniquely prolonged childhood of human beings is mandated by our slow growth. This is the time when parents teach their children, since instincts do not; it is easy to see the evolutionary advantage of a prolonged childhood for our behaviorally plastic species. Parents may, if necessary, impose their instructions by force on the small child. This advantage is illustrated if we consider the alternative: an angry child who wants the cookie jar, and who, like the horse, has reached adult size at two years of age.

If the long dependency of childhood is shaped by biological imperatives, the child's transition to adulthood is arbitrarily determined by cultural patterns within the very broad context bounded by biology. While betrothal may occur at or before birth in some cultures, cohabitation, even in primitive societies, comes with sexual maturity. Prolonged adolescence and youth can be seen in societies such as our own, where physical maturity comes in the teens, legal adulthood is set by political decree at eighteen years, and economic and social maturity may not come until several additional years of dependency and apprenticeship have passed. This long, ambiguous transition, it is often suggested, creates ambivalence and insecurity in young adulthood.

I am not convinced that the ambiguity of transition in contemporary society engenders ambivalence in young adulthood, nor do I hold the related belief that this particular set of growing pains is part of the malaise of modernity. It is my contention that both desire and doubt concerning the independence which comes with biological maturity can be seen in our best-known myths, and that ambivalence has marked the transition to maturity since the beginning of Western culture. While twentieth-century technology facilitates expressions of doubt, and our comparative affluence and its attendant options may cause conflicts to become more salient, the crises of adult life so prominent in current developmental psychology are foreshadowed in ancient myths.

The sense of the self and its solitude as a normative developmental phenomenon is a common theme in descriptions of middle age, such as the increased interiority of personality (Neugarten et al., 1964), the personalization of death (Neugarten, 1968), and the awareness of oneself as the head of the line (Jacques, 1965). I propose that these themes first emerge in young adulthood, and that the developmental tensions between individual growth and the needs of the next generation which may create a crisis in middle life are best understood as integral components of the transition to maturity.

Adam and Eve: The Price of Maturity

I have never been comfortable with Erikson's (1963) notion that we bite into the apple of Eden with our baby teeth, and forfeit paradise before we can stand upright. My daughters fueled my doubts when they brought home their own versions of the story of Adam and Eve from their Israeli kindergarten and first grade. The Hebrew verb פתה encompasses persuasion and seduction: hence, my second-born daughter, at five, asked: "The woman persuaded/seduced her husband, right?" and added, with evident pride, "Then she was the *first* to eat" — rewriting, with one bold stroke, two thousand years' interpretation of Woman as Sinner.

Not long afterward, my firstborn daughter came home from first grade with the *chutzpah* of latency: "I want to eat from the fruit of the Tree of Knowledge." Against mythic desires, motherhood pales: I asked her, "Don't you think that's what happens when you go to school?" "But I want my eyes to be opened *all* the way."

Mothers and daughters are unrepresented in the ranks of the Talmudic scholars. I offer this narrative not as a revision of Biblical interpretation but as the context in which I first became aware of the sexual and intellectual passions in the story of the Garden of Eden. I pursued the questions my children had raised by asking my students in developmental psychology to tell me the story of the Garden of Eden. Over the years, not one student has been unable to tell me the story — but not one has told it accurately yet. The story my students tell is this: There was a tree in the center of the Garden of Eden whose fruit gave knowledge of good and evil. This tree was forbidden to Adam and Eve, but the serpent tempted Eve and she took the fruit, ate of it, and persuaded Adam to eat. For their transgressions, Eve was punished with the pain of childbirth and Adam condemned to labor for his bread, and both were expelled from the Garden of Eden.

This retelling includes every element of the tale but one, and I think the omission is not insignificant. In all my years of teaching, I have not yet heard a student spontaneously recall — though all remember it when reminded — that Adam and Eve were expelled from the Garden of Eden so as to prevent their obtaining the fruit of the second forbidden tree, the Tree of Life. I am prepared to conclude that if we were given a second chance in the Garden of Eden — as each of us is, in every generation — we would make straight for the Tree of the Knowledge of Good and Evil once again: for knowledge, however dangerous, is evidently a more potent temptation than immortality.

I reject, therefore, Erikson's reading of this story (1963). He suggests that the oral stage of development may be the ontogenetic contribution to the story of Adam and Eve, who in biting the apple lost paradise — as does the infant, Erikson proposes, when his teeth come through. I doubt that paradise is lost so swiftly, and I suggest that the prominent theme in the story of Adam and Eve is the forced transition from dependency, where all is provided, into the wider world of love and work — the tasks of the healthy adult. Despite the centuries of technological progress since the story of Adam and Eve first found expression — centuries which have seen the mitigation of women's woe in childbirth through modern medicine,

and the conquest of sweat by Madison Avenue — this tale continues to tell us about the one-way, bitter, but tempting road into adulthood.

Prometheus: The Price of Technology

Nietzsche has argued in *The Birth of Tragedy* that the story of Adam and Eve, with its dependency, seduction, and deceit, represents the feminine element in humanity. He contrasts this femininity unfavorably with the "higher" masculinity of Prometheus — an active defiance of the gods, not the passive disobedience in response to persuasion. Prometheus deceived Zeus and stole fire from the gods, bringing its light and the light of astronomy, mathematics, and early agriculture to humanity. For his sins the punishment was correspondingly more grave: not expulsion from paradise, but an eternity of torment. He was chained to a rock, his entrails devoured each day; and each night the devoured flesh grew back so that the torture could continue; his only hope lay in the prophecy that one day his chains would fall away of themselves.

Current concerns over destructive technology and its threats to our environment bear out the message of the myth of Prometheus, rather than the hopes of the mythical Prometheus himself or the judgment of Nietzsche. Indeed, the history of technology indicates that controversy almost always accompanies a major scientific advance. Resistance often takes the form of concern over damage to nature, and sooner or later, it seems, this concern is often justified.

Furthermore, the advances of civilized technology fail to deliver their promise of spiritual reward. Freud remarked in 1930 that man with all his devices had the splendor of a prosthetic god, and yet it seemed to bring him no happiness (1962). While Freud predicted continuing dramatic advances in technology, he also warned that present-day man was ill at ease with his magnificence. Almost half a century has passed since Freud issued this warning, and it would seem that humanity has come no closer to happiness, while Freud is no farther from truth.

Like Adam and Eve, however, Prometheus is impelled by irresistible forces which appear to be universal, for, like the myth of the Fall from a natural environment where all is provided, the myth of stolen knowledge is found in all civilizations (Campbell, 1970). We have no myths at all, however, in which there is a voluntary restoration of the *status quo,* a return of stolen knowledge in exchange for lost innocence and dependency. Nor have we heard a majority yet declare its willingness to renounce mastery over nature in exchange for the ecological balance of an earlier age. Like knowledge, mastery over nature is a theme with many variations in our mythologies, including our current developmental mythologies of middle age. Through all its variations, a common theme is found: conquest and consequences, the first irresistible, the second inevitable.

Midas and the Mid-Life Crisis of Achievement

The tale of the Garden of Eden records the most primitive of truths: the transition from dependency to toil and autonomy. The legend of Prometheus reflects a measure of progress, for the knowledge obtained by Prometheus is meant to lead to mastery over nature and a mitigation of the curse of Adam and Eve. The dynamics of the mid-life crisis are anticipated in these cultural messages which describe individual growth toward autonomy and achievement. Ambivalence about knowledge and mastery runs through these stories, and it is this ambivalence — a combination of greed and anticipated despair — which is captured by the myth of Midas, a myth about wealth and its consequences.

In Midas we see a man who has gone beyond the struggle for subsistence to accumulate an effortless surplus. Midas was born of a union between a nameless satyr —

the species which gave its name to the state of surplus sexual passion — and the Great Goddess of Ida. While he was still an infant in the cradle, an omen foretold a future of wealth. The prophecy was fulfilled when Midas grew into adulthood: He extended hospitality to the debauched satyr Silenus, and thus found favor with Dionysus, whom the Greeks credit with discovering wine and divine madness. Dionysus asked Midas how he would like to be rewarded, and Midas requested that all he touch turn to gold. His wish was granted, and before long, he had touched his lunch and deprived himself of the sustenance of food, and touched his beloved daughter and deprived himself of the sustenance of love. Like so many other folk heroes, Midas begged to be released from his wish; Dionysus, much amused, granted his request.

Midas, in going beyond subsistence, achieved wealth — and with it complete impoverishment, a perversion of excess. And yet the excess of Midas was simply an excess of mastery, a complete instead of a partial victory in the struggle to win subsistence. Nevertheless, the parallels between Midas and those whom we describe today as workaholics, whose dedication to work and its rewards at the expense of the inner self and its needs, are sufficiently close to persuade me that the mid-life crisis of affluence and achievement is not new. Current developmental and clinical portraits of the impoverished inner self in middle life (Gould, 1978) are foreshadowed in the myth of Midas and others like him, who carry their wishes just a little too far, and come to grief — a grief as old as human legends, and not a product of our times.

The Fisherman's Wife

King Midas knew when to stop, but other folk tales record the fate of men and women who did not. Of these, one is the fisherman's wife, who was able to move from her hovel of poverty, through the powers of a magical fish her husband had caught and mercifully returned to the sea. But her cottage gave her no pleasure; she sent her husband back to the seashore to ask for a palace. Next she asked to be emperor, then Pope, and finally she told her husband to command the fish to make her God. With this last wish the skies clouded over, and the fisherman's wife found herself once again in her poor hovel by the sea.

If the greed of Midas is the forerunner of the empty inner life of the middle-aged workaholic, then the poverty of the fisherman's wife, whose demands on her husband have no bounds, is a forewarning to the housewives of the suburbs, who sometimes discover their palaces to be empty, impoverished shells. Jessie Bernard's provocative comments on the future of marriage (1973) suggest that the bargain struck in the traditional marriage is less than equitable: The enhanced psychological well-being of the married man, when compared to the single man, is achieved at the expense of the mental health of the married woman, who is disadvantaged compared to the single woman. This bargain, which is under critical scrutiny by contemporary feminists, suggests that a woman surrenders independence for comfort and protection. The message of the tale of the fisherman's wife, as well as of contemporary family sociology, is that this exchange may carry its own seeds of doom.

While the flaws in women's myths of dependency and security are becoming evident, the complementary myths of men are not yet being explored. The woman who hopes to find complete happiness in a comfortable home is matched by the man whose workday is spent in the belief that he provides it. The fisherman, sent to the seashore again and again by his wife's insatiable dreams of power, is fortunate to discover himself a victim of nothing worse than his original poverty, when his drama of marital greed has been played out. The fate of con-

temporary partners in similar dramas can be less kind. Young executives on the rise, suddenly dead of early heart attacks or other stress-related illnesses, testify to the unexamined price paid by men in a marital exchange which brings losses to both partners.

The Family at Mid-Life: A Bird-Watcher's Guide to the Empty Nest

Conventional wisdom in developmental psychology suggests that the trials of the earlier stages in the family life cycle culminate in the tribulations of the empty nest. This choice of idiom invites our critical scrutiny: Birdwatchers know that fledglings are pushed from the nest by their parents. Myth, folk, and fairy tales, from Oedipus Rex to Snow White, provide familiar cultural idioms suggesting that human parents may do the same, a suggestion which finds support in anthropological observations of infanticide (Harris, 1977), as well as the growing problem of child abuse in this country (Bakan, 1971). The dark side of parental passions, no secret to police and social workers, is insufficiently appreciated in developmental psychology; and it is to this dimension of the parent-child relationship that I wish to turn, looking for lessons about adult developmental needs in myth and fairy tales.

Merciless Parents

A child enters the world at the mercy of its parents — a phrase underscored if we remember one of history's most merciless and misunderstood fathers, the celebrated father of the inadvertent patricide, Oedipus Rex. It is a curious commentary on our personal mythologies that, with a little initial squeamishness, we have absorbed Oedipal murder into the developmental sequence of childhood while censoring Laius out of our image of fatherhood. It might be argued that in the drama itself Oedipus' accidental murder of his father despite his efforts to escape the dreadful prophecy overshadows Laius' deliberate plan to murder his infant son. But no such defense can be offered to Medea, whose murder of her children is the climax of a play of which she is the central figure — the heroine, according to audiences who, we might surmise, have been agreeing for 2500 years that if pushed too far they would kill their children too.

The adversary relationship between parent and child expressed by these myths reflects an underlying biological conflict between individual survival and species survival. The bearing and rearing of children serve the species whether or not they serve the individual. And indeed personal desire for children is no protection against risk: Loving mothers can die in childbirth too. If biological reproduction is accompanied by a measure of personal danger, it is hardly surprising to find this conflict manifest at the intrapsychic level as well, where the needs of the adult may clash with the needs of the offspring.

Empty Cupboards

The story of Hansel and Gretel is an example of the conflict between parents and children as it might find expression early in the family life cycle. Bettelheim (1976) sees this as a tale of children who regress to primitive oral needs, seeking limitless satiation in the gingerbread house in the woods — which proves to be inhabited by a wicked witch. They overcome her and their own infantile needs, and are then able to return home triumphant.

I find the parents' motives of interest. Hansel and Gretel are sent out of their home and into the woods by their father and stepmother because there is not enough food at home — a scarcity not confined to fairy tales or to the pantry. Faced with the boundless neediness of the very young child, what parent has not sometimes feared a scarcity — whether of money, time, energy, or in the cupboards of the heart? The ubiquity of this fear finds expression in a curious social readiness to condemn couples who elect to remain childless. Such couples are often condemned as "selfish," and the cure — curiouser and curiouser — is seen as having children. This hazardous treatment is a kind of folk testimony that children take and take, and thus deplete reserves, whether or not they successfully cure adult selfishness. And yet the childless couple is guilty of nothing more serious than accuracy at arithmetic; any finite quantity, divided by two, yields more than when it is divided by three — and the demands of children may expose the parents' resources as inadequate.

Grown Children

Dependency diminishes as childhood ends; but conflict, rather than ceasing, takes a new form. My own moment of personal discovery came when my firstborn daughter reached adolescence and the family went, as we had so often done before, to see Walt Disney's *Snow White*. Some may be surprised, and others share my surprise, to discover that my sympathies had suddenly transferred themselves to the witch.

Where the small child threatens finite resources, the maturing child threatens to take over. And indeed, in time, the normative course of the individual life cycle ends in death, with surviving children; the parent bereaved of children is a tragic figure. Nevertheless, the orderly succession of generations is not necessarily seen by the older generation as a happy ending. The adolescent, we might surmise, threatens the parent on a more primitive level than does the small infant, for the infant's needs require an omnipotent parent, while the adolescent's vigor threatens to underscore the parent's finitude and mortality. Faced by her own vanishing youth in the person of her blossoming step-daughter, Snow White's stepmother acts on the ambivalent rage that may stir in many mothers, and finally succeeds in halting her daughter's transition to adulthood with the long sleep of the poisoned apple.

Bettelheim (1976), sees Snow White as the expression of the Oedipal conflicts which revive in adolescence, and must be mastered for the transition into sexual maturity and adulthood: Snow White is wakened by a kiss into a happy ending. It is not only the child, however, who must renounce the magic Oedipal ties to the parent; the parent too must renounce the child. And the child's renunciation is facilitated by the presence of alternate objects of love. The parent's renunciation, by contrast, is not facilitated but is mandated by the fact that the small child, once loved so tenderly and so completely, is no longer there. The small child's place has been taken by a large, vigorous youth — a possible object of sexual desire, as incest taboos and incidents testify, but no longer a possible object of parental tenderness and nurturant care, and slipping swiftly out of the reach of parental control. This period, when the children are grown but not yet out of the home, might well be called the period of the *crowded nest*—a period fully as interesting as the widely studied period of the empty nest.

Regret over departing children is not a theme in our folk inheritance. Indeed, quite the opposite is true: Children of all ages are turned out of the home. They are too hungry, too beautiful, too dangerous; if they threaten parental resources, they are sent away or killed. If the hidden message of the fairy tale for the listening child is that soon he must make his own way in the world (Bettelheim, 1976), the message adults have been sharing is no less clear: Parenthood ends when the children are grown. The period of the empty nest, interpreted by demographers of the family (Glick, 1955) as a consequence of recent changes in family spacing and concomitant changes in longev-

ity — children born sooner and departing earlier, parents surviving longer — can thus be seen to have developmental meaning as well, which reaches further back into human history. Like the mid-life crisis of achievement, the empty nest of middle life is not a phenomenon of modernity but a theme echoing through Western culture for centuries.

Conclusion: Beyond the Twentieth Century

I have suggested that of the multiple determinants of the mid-life crisis, many are not new. A brief overview of our common myths, folk and fairy tales has suggested developmental themes in the struggle for autonomy, intimacy, achievement, and generativity which are entirely consonant with current clinical and developmental models of the mid-life crisis. It is my belief that a life-span developmental psychology exclusive of historical and social change is sterile; at the same time, a developmental model dependent largely on historical and social change is transient. It has been my concern to trace the origins of certain common developmental themes in the mid-life crisis, and to suggest that our cultural heritage is fully as rich with insights as our current psychologies of middle age.

It is certainly true that the study of contemporary social change can contribute to an understanding of crisis in middle age. Consider, for example, a woman now in her 40s who chose 20 years ago to give up her career for the sake of her husband and children. She currently faces the statistical possibility of divorce and the developmental certainty of departing children — and with these two primary roles gone, a climate of opinion which is likely to add insult to injury with the suggestion that it was all a mistake in the first place to sacrifice anything for personal development. Our understanding of such an individual is surely enhanced by a knowledge of recent social changes, which have rendered once-reasonable decisions now obsolete. At the same time, I would argue that it is equally essential to recognize that the conflict between the personal needs of a woman and the contextual needs of marriage and children is at least as old as the legend of Medea.

Similarly, the executive at the peak of his career who faces a sudden crisis of meaning is surely a part of the context of the contemporary affluence, along with the "one-life, one-career imperative" (Sarason, 1977). Nevertheless, our understanding of his dilemma is incomplete without an awareness of its ubiquity and antiquity: A coupling of knowledge and doom, of power and doom, of wealth and doom, of greed and doom, is as old as Adam, as old as Prometheus, as old as Midas, as old as the Fisherman's Wife. A recognition of the developmental context of the crises of middle age must begin with an acknowledgment of ancient case histories.

References

Aeschylus: *Prometheus Bound.*

Bakan, D.: *Slaughter of the Innocents.* San Francisco: Jossey-Bass, 1971.

Bernard J.: *The Future of Marriage.* New York: World (Bantam), 1973.

Bettelheim, B.: *The Uses of Enchantment.* New York: Alfred A. Knopf, 1976.

Brim, O. G.: Selected theories of the male mid-life crisis: A comparative overview. Invited address to Division 20, American Psychological Association, New Orleans, September 1974.

Campbell, J.: *The Masks of God: Primitive Mythology.* New York: Viking, 1970.

Ecclesiastes 1:18; 9:16.

Erikson, E. H.: *Childhood and Society,* (2nd ed.). New York: W. W. Norton, 1963.

Erikson, E. H.: *Insight and Responsibility.* New York: W. W. Norton, 1964.

Erikson, E. H.: Youth: Fidelity and diversity. In E. H. Erikson (Ed.), *The Challenge of Youth.* New York: Anchor Books, 1965.

Erikson, E. H.: Reflections on the dissent of contemporary youth. *International Journal of Psychoanalysis,* 1970, 51, 11–22.

Euripides: *Medea.*

Freud, S.: *Civilization and Its Discontents.* New York: W. W. Norton, 1962.

Freud, S.: Lecture xxi: The development of the libido and the sexual organizations. *The Complete Introductory Lectures on Psychoanalysis.* New York: W. W. Norton, 1966.

Genesis 2:8–3:24.

Glick, P. C.: Life cycle of the family. *Marriage and Family Relations,* 1955, 17:3–9.

Gould, R.: *Transformations: Growth and Change in Adult Life.* New York: Simon & Schuster, 1978.

Harris, M.: *Cannibals and Kings.* New York: Random House, 1977.

Jacques, E.: Death and the mid-life crisis. *International Journal of Psychoanalysis,* 1965, 46: 502–514.

Justice, B. & Justice, R.: *The Abusing Family.* New York: Human Sciences Press, 1976.

Keniston, K.: Youth as a stage of life. *American Scholar,* 1970, 39:631–654.

Levinson, D. J., with Darrow, C. N., Klein, E. B., Levinson, M. H., & McKee, B.: *The Seasons of a Man's Life.* New York: Alfred A. Knopf, 1978.

Neugarten, B. L. & Associates: *Personality in Middle and Late Life.* New York: Atherton Press, 1964.

Neugarten, B. L.: The awareness of middle age. In B. L. Neugarten (Ed.), *Middle Age and Aging.* Chicago: University of Chicago Press, 1968.

Nietzsche, F. W.: *The Birth of Tragedy.* (trans. F. Golfing). New York: Doubleday, 1956.

Sarason, S. B.: *Work, Aging, and Social Change: Professionals and the One Life-One Career Imperative.* New York: The Free Press, 1977.

Sophocles: *Oedipus Rex.*

Learning and Memory

OLD DOGS, NEW TRICKS!

Human memory is commonly viewed as a three-stage process, involving the *acquisition, storage,* and *retrieval* of information. Human learning, although traditionally viewed in stimulus-response terms as "behavior modification," can also be considered as the acquisition or encoding phase of memory. The research literature suggests that very few significant age changes in learning occur until the sixties. Late life changes may be due to distracting or debilitating disease, changes in motivation, or factors concerned with learning strategies; that is, the observed changes may not necessarily reflect "normal" decline in the nervous system's capability for processing information.

Three storage systems of memory have been hypothesized. Older persons are thought to be particularly deficient in the *sensory store,* a very short-term system that appears to have little effect on memory as a whole, although it may affect retention of material presented rapidly, as in speech. There appear to be few, if any, age differences in the *short-term store,* which typically holds a few items for a few seconds. But it is the encoding processes that result in the transfer of information from the short-term store to the nearly permanent, high-capacity *long-term store* that are less effective in older individuals.

Another variable known to affect old learners more than the young is the *pace of learning.* Old learners seem to prefer a slower pace, especially in the time needed to make a response. These data suggest retrieval difficulties for the older person. Motivational factors such as anxiety and arousal (more disruptive for older persons), cautiousness (leading to more "omission" error in the elderly), or disinterest (material in the lists presented by psychologists is often perceived to be silly) have all been suggested as causes of age differences in learning performance.

In our first selection, *Carl Eisdorfer, John Nowlin,* and *Frances Wilkie* discuss the role of arousal in the learning performance of older men. These authors report results of a study that bears upon the reasons why older persons have more omission errors in rapidly paced learning situations. They suggest that this is due to disruptive overarousal, and to test their contention administered a drug that partially blocks end-organ responses to the autonomic nervous system. Their findings showed improvement of performance under the drug condition, supporting their hypothesis that learning difficulties in old age may indeed be related to inadequate control of autonomic arousal.

It was noted that one reason older persons do less well than younger individuals is that the material to be learned does not get encoded as well. Organizing the material to be remembered is one way to encode information effectively. For whatever reason, older subjects do not typically organize information as efficiently as do the young. But as a result they profit more than younger persons from instructions on how to organize material. Similarly, older persons do not seem to use mediational techniques — "mnemonic devices" — as effectively as younger individuals.

The selection by *Elizabeth A. Robertson-Tchabo, Carol P. Hausman,* and *David Arenberg* uses a classic mnemonic described originally by Cicero, the Roman sage, to improve free recall in men and women over sixty years of age. In this procedure they take a mental trip through their residences stopping in a number of places, into each of which upon learning a list of words they mentally place a word. This procedure did indeed improve memory performance, even though there was some question whether it would continue to be applied to real-life circumstances.

Taken as a whole, the research evidence shows little decline in the ability to learn and remember until very late in life. Adult education, as a result, is a thriving industry, as adults struggle to keep up with the times or change careers in mid-life. It is quite a step, though, from the simple laboratory tasks studied by laboratory psychologists to more complex behavior. An intermediate step is to examine whether older persons' performance can be improved on complex cognitive tasks, particularly those abilities that are involved in new learning (sometimes called fluid abilities). The last selection in this chapter, by *Sherry L. Willis, Rosemary Blieszner,* and *Paul B. Baltes,* reports on a study in which persons in their sixties and seventies were trained to improve their performance on the fluid ability of figural relations (working with series of figures, classifying figures, identifying missing parts of matrices, and other topological tasks).

In comparison to a control group, the experimental subjects showed significant training gains — of about the magnitude of the reported age decline on this ability. Training effects were maintained over a six-month period, suggesting the continued modifiability of performance on intellectual abilities into advanced age. It seems then that old dogs rarely have real difficulty *learning* new tricks; they more often have difficulty convincing themselves that it is worth the effort.

Additional Suggested Readings

Klatzky, R. L. *Human memory: Structure and process.* 2nd ed. New York: Freeman, 1980.
  This volume provides up-to-date background material on the complex characteristics of the human memory process.

Hartley, J. T., Harker, J. O., & Walsh, D. A. Contemporary issues and new directions in adult development of learning and memory. In L. W. Poon (ed.), *Aging in the 1980s.* Washington: American Psychological Association, 1980, pp. 239–252.
  Summarizes three basic lines of research: information and retrieval processes, organizational processes, and depth of processing. Ecological validity of past research is discussed and new directions are proposed.

Schaie, K. W., & Willis, S. L. Life-span development: Implications for education. *Review of Research in Education,* 1978, 6, 120–156.
  Discusses problems faced by the older learner, needs of adult education, and implications for programming in postsecondary education.

Improvement of Learning in the Aged by Modification of Autonomic Nervous System Activity

CARL EISDORFER, JOHN NOWLIN, and FRANCES WILKIE

Partial blockade of beta-adrenergic end-organ response to the autonomic nervous system was effected in a group of older men by administration of propranolol. The result was improved performance in a learning task. The data support the hypothesis that the learning decrement found among older men is not simply a manifestation of structural change in the central nervous system but is, at least in part, associated with the heightened arousal of the autonomic nervous system that accompanies the learning task.

Studies of verbal learning in older men have consistently demonstrated a prominent decrement in performance with advancing age, presumably indicative of a decline in a higher order cognitive functioning. Increasing evidence indicates, however, that such a decline cannot be attributed solely to the structural changes in the central nervous system that are known to accompany aging (1). Instead, differences in learning performance appear related, in part, to the failure of older persons to respond where rapid response is required. In situations where the pace of a learning task is slowed, the older person improves in performance significantly and responds relatively rapidly (2–6). Another age-related difference found in the learning situation is the more pronounced extent and persistence of plasma free fatty acid (FFA) mobilization among older subjects than among younger controls (7). It has

been demonstrated that this age-related physiologic response is not simply a difference in ability to metabolize plasma FFA or to respond to infused catecholamine (8). Further, with plasma FFA mobilization again used as an indicator of autonomic arousal, evidence of a curvilinear relationship between autonomic activation and learning task performance was found (4). Therefore, it has been suggested that the heightened and prolonged autonomic arousal found during learning task performance in the older person is directly implicated in the tendency of older persons to commit more errors of omission, indicative of response suppression, in the rapidly paced learning situation (9).

Although the autonomic arousal found in conjunction with the learning task might merely reflect activation of the central nervous system associated with cognitive func-

Source: Eisdorfer, C., Nowlin, J., & Wilkie, F. Improvement of learning in the aged by modification of autonomic nervous system activity. *Science*, 1970, 170, 1327–1329. Copyright 1970 by the American Association for the Advancement of Science. Reprinted by permission.

tioning, feedback from the peripheral manifestations of this arousal might, in itself, actively contribute to performance decrement. If this were the case in older persons, the masking of such autonomic effects should result in improvement in learning scores.

Propranolol (Inderal), by producing partial blockade of autonomic beta-adrenergic receptor sites in peripheral end organs, largely mitigates most physiologic concomitants of central nervous system arousal. Although small amounts of the drug might cross the "blood-brain barrier" (10), there is no evidence of resulting central nervous system activation or deactivation. With the use of this drug, it is therefore possible to test our hypothesis about the influence of autonomic arousal on learning in older persons. The impact of propranolol on learning performance could be interpreted as the effect of partial blockade of autonomic end-organ response. As a monitor of the drug effect, all subjects could be assessed for autonomic reactivity, with heart rate, plasma FFA level, and galvanic skin response serving as indices of physiologic arousal.

For this study the subjects were 28 paid male volunteers, 60 years of age or older (mean age, 68.6 years; range, 60 to 78 years). Prospective subjects were told that the investigators were evaluating the effect of a drug on "blood chemistry" while they performed a "learning test"; they were also told to anticipate no subjective drug effect. Several days before the actual drug study, each subject was interviewed, received a physical examination, and was given a set of psychologic screening tests. Persons on long-term medication were excluded from the study group, as were individuals with a medical history or findings of emphysema, diabetes, or arteriosclerotic cardiovascular disease. At the time of the pretest interview, they were familiarized with the laboratory and its staff members. The physician who performed the physical examination during the screening visit also administered the drug in the subsequent experimental situation. Psychological screening at this time included the Vocabulary and Digit Symbol subscales of the Wechsler Adult Intelligence Scale [WAIS (11)], the Taylor Manifest Anxiety Scale [an indicator of "state anxiety" (12)], and the Figure Embedment Scale [a test sensitive to change in cognition accompanying organic brain syndromes (13)]. Only individuals who attained a raw score in the range of 7 to 12 on the WAIS Vocabulary subscales were included as subjects. Subjects took no food from the midnight preceding the study to ensure maximum plasma FFA response. They reported to the laboratory at 8:30 A.M. and were seated in a comfortable chair within a sound-attenuated, air-conditioned chamber. Chest wall electrodes were affixed for continuous electrocardiographic recording and an indwelling venous catheter was placed in the right arm, under local anesthesia, for blood sampling and drug administration. Silver–silver chloride electrodes were placed on the palmar surface of the left index finger and over the triceps muscle mass of the left upper arm.

The experimental design called for the collection of two blood samples 15 minutes apart for baseline plasma FFA determination; then, on a random basis, subjects were given either an intravenous solution of 10.0 mg of intravenous propranolol hydrochloride or an equivalent amount of isotonic saline. Except for the foreknowledge of the physician injecting the solutions, the drug or saline was given in double blind fashion; the technical staff responsible for conducting the learning task were unaware of the nature of the injection. The learning task, described in detail elsewhere (3), requires the serial rote learning of a list of eight high association words. In this study, the words were projected in order on a screen for a 4-second exposure interval with a 1-second interval between words; there was a 45-second interval between each list of eight words. The first word was preceded by an asterisk. The subject was instructed to repeat the word immediately succeeding the one being projected. Each subject performed 15 of the eight-word trials. A third blood sample for FFA determination was collected immediately before the learning task began, and additional samples were taken after the 5th, 10th, and 15th learning trials. The final blood samples were collected 10 and 20 minutes after conclusion of the learning.

The drug and placebo groups each included 15 subjects. However, a subject preselection error was detected, with the resulting exclusion of two members of the drug group from the statistical analysis.

Heart rate was averaged for the 4th, 8th, and 12th minute after each blood sample was collected; these values afforded two sets of baseline heart rate levels, before intravenous infusion of propranolol or placebo. During the learning task, heart rate was determined over each of the eight-word trials and then averaged for each block of five trials. Change in galvanic skin response was evaluated by extent of deviation from basal level at the time heart rate was being monitored. Plasma FFA determinations were by the method of Dole (14) modified by Trout, Estes, and Friedberg (15).

Performance on the learning task was evaluated by the number of errors made during the testing. Total errors were further analyzed as either commission errors (inappropriate or incorrect responses) or omission errors (failures to respond). The learning data are depicted graphically in Figure 1. The between-group difference for total errors was significant at the 0.05 level of confidence (t test for independent groups = 2.3, d.f. = 26). Fewer omission errors were committed among the drug group than among the control group, but the group difference was not significant (t = 1.7, d.f. = 26). Finally, the drug group also

made fewer commission errors than did the placebo group; again the between-group difference was not statistically significant (t = 1.6, d.f. = 26).

Plasma FFA response during the learning task is presented in Figure 2. After intravenous infusion, the drug group showed a decrease in FFA level, with only minimal rise during the learning task itself. Conversely, the control group FFA levels remained at a comparatively higher level and responded to the learning situation with an increased plasma FFA mobilization. This divergent response, evaluated by the group-by-trial interaction term in a repeated measures analysis of variance design [2-by-9 Lindquist model (16)], was highly significant (F = 31.6, d.f. = 8/208, P < .01). Heart rate presents a similar response pattern. After the intravenous infusion, the heart rate of the drug group was consistently lower than that of the control group. The same statistical analysis that was applied to plasma FFA level showed the interaction term assessing the group difference in patterning of heart rate response to be highly significant (F = 12.0, d.f. = 7/175, P < .01). The difference in galvanic skin response between drug and placebo groups did not present overall statistical significance in the analysis of variance format; however, there was a consistent trend for galvanic skin response to be lower among subjects receiving propranolol. Finally, there was no between-group difference found in age or in the pretesting results of intellectual function; nor was there evidence of impaired cognitive function secondary to central nervous system structural change, or of "state anxiety." Therefore, the contrast in learning performance between the drug and control groups is not likely to stem from any obvious differences between the two groups. The data show that propranolol was effective in establishing at least a partial blockade of the beta-adrenergic receptors as measured by heart rate, plasma FFA mobilization, and

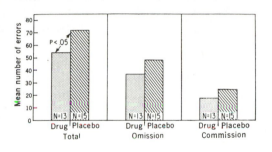

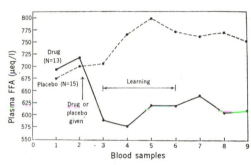

FIGURE 1
The mean number of errors on a verbal learning task among aged men while under the influence of either 10.0 mg intravenous propranolol hydrochloride (drug) or an equivalent amount of intravenous isotonic saline (placebo).

FIGURE 2
Plasma free fatty acid (FFA) level among aged men exposed to a verbal learning task after having been given either 10.0 mg intravenous propranolol hydrochloride (drug) or an equivalent amount of intravenous isotonic saline (placebo).

galvanic skin response. In this situation, the effect upon learning in older men was significant. Subjects receiving the drug performed better than those receiving the placebo. Moreover, the autonomic response patterns within the placebo group are similar to those reported in an earlier study (7), which employed the identical learning task but without intravenous infusion. This similarity of response would indicate that the impact on the subjects of receiving an intravenous infusion did not bias patterns of autonomic arousal in the learning task situation. However, the learning performance of both the drug and placebo groups in this study was markedly superior to that found in

previous studies (2–4, 7, 9), where the same technique was used but without drug or placebo. The importance of placebo effect on this learning task, particularly in relation to the instructions given, is worthy of note.

The findings from this study are significant in two respects: first, they confirm the contention that learning in older persons can be improved by pharmacologic modification of autonomic nervous system state. Second, and perhaps more important, these findings support the hypothesis that a state of heightened rather than depressed autonomic end-organ arousal is responsible for the decrement of learning performance found in older age groups.

References

1. C. Eisdorfer, *Gerontologist* 10, 5 (1970).

2. ———, S. Axelrod, F. Wilkie, *J. Abnorm. Soc. Psychol.* 67, 594 (1963).

3. C. Eisdorfer, *J. Genet. Psychol.* 107, 15 (1965).

4. W. Troyer, C. Eisdorfer, F. Wilkie, M. Bogdonoff, *J. Gerontol.* 21, 415 (1966).

5. R. Canestrari, *ibid.* 18, 165 (1963).

6. D. Arenberg, *J. Abnorm. Psychol.* 70, 419 (1965).

7. A. Powell, C. Eisdorfer, M. Bogdonoff, *Arch. Gen. Psychiat.* 10, 192 (1964).

8. C. Eisdorfer, A. Powell, Jr., G. Silverman, M. Bogdonoff, *J. Gerontol.* 20, 511 (1965).

9. C. Eisdorfer, in *Human Aging and Behavior,* G. Talland, Ed. (Academic Press, New York, 1968), pp. 189–216.

10. J. Black, W. Duncan, R. Shanks, *Brit. J. Pharmacol. Chemother.* 25, 577 (1965).

11. D. Wechsler, *The Measurement and Appraisal of Adult Intelligence* (Williams & Wilkins, Baltimore, ed. 4, 1958).

12. J. Taylor, *J. Abnorm. Soc. Psychol.* 48, 285 (1953).

13. L. L. Thurstone, *A Factorial Study of Perception* (Univ. of Chicago Press, Chicago, 1944).

14. V. Dole, *J. Clin. Invest.* 35, 150 (1956).

15. D. Trout, E. Estes, S. Friedberg, *J. Lipid Res.* 1, 199 (1960).

16. E. Lindquist, *Design and Analysis of Experiments in Psychology and Education* (Houghton Mifflin, Boston, 1953).

A Classical Mnemonic for Older Learners: A Trip That Works!

ELIZABETH A. ROBERTSON-TCHABO, CAROL P. HAUSMAN, and DAVID ARENBERG

A mnemonic procedure, a method of loci, was used with men and women over 60 years old in two studies of free recall. In this procedure, the learners take a mental trip through their residences stopping in order at 16 places. When they learn a list of words, they retrace the trip visualizing one of the items in association with each stopping place. This method was selected because it capitalizes on the familiarity of the stopping places and their natural order; these attributes provide strong retrieval cues that can be applied without adding to the information overload typically experienced by older learners. In the first study ($N = 5$), all subjects acquired the mnemonic readily and used it effectively during the training trials. An unexpected result was that the subjects did not use the mnemonic in a·posttraining trial when no explicit instruction was given to use it. In the second study ($N = 30$), two experimental groups (with different instructional sets in a posttest trial) and a control group were included. Again all experimental subjects were able to master the mnemonic and apply it effectively during training. Furthermore, each experimental group ($N = 10$) improved more (from pretest to posttest) than did the control group. The two experimental groups did not differ in performance during training or in the posttest trial.

Introduction

Individuals transform or encode verbal material as they process information; that is, subjects do not store a literal copy of the nominal stimulus. Furthermore, the information retained by an individual is related to the degree of organization of the material at the time of input (Bower, 1970). Atkinson and Shiffrin (1968) identified two dimensions of central processing: structural features and control processes. The former refer to permanent features of the system while the latter refer to features that can be modified by an individual and that may vary substantially from one situation to another. This distinction between permanent and modifiable aspects of learning has important ramifications for research in aging since the evidence indicates that age-related differences in verbal processes are due largely to age differences in the use and effectiveness

Source: Robertson-Tchabo, E. A., Hausman, C. P., & Arenberg, D. A classical mnemonic for older learners: A trip that works! *Educational Gerontology,* 1976, 1. 215–226. Copyright 1976 by Hemisphere Publishing Corporation. Reprinted by permission.

of control processes (see Arenberg & Robertson, 1974). Such control processes not only include the organization of information into temporal groups, semantic clusters, or hierarchies, but also include the use of mnemonic devices as a means of facilitating information organization. Infrequent or ineffective use of organizational strategies limits the amount of information stored. Any age-related decrease in the amount of information encoded about an item, whether due to the pacing of the input or to an inability to devise an encoding strategy, will limit the variety of retrieval cues available to direct the search process at the time of recall.

Older people tend not to use mnemonics in a variety of memory tasks (e.g., Hulicka & Rust, 1964; Hulicka & Weiss, 1965; Rowe & Schnore, 1971). However, when they have been instructed to use a specific encoding procedure they do improve their performance; sometimes they improve more than the young (Hulicka & Grossman, 1967). While elaboration encoding, for example, adding a visual image or a verbal association to the item information, does make material more memorable, initially the additional information can increase the storage load and may even overload the older individual's information-processing system. Until older individuals have extensively practiced using an unfamiliar mnemonic technique, there is more information to remember, and they are unable to make optimal use of additional cues to direct a subsequent search. Thus, while mnemonic techniques benefit all learners, older learners have more difficulty using them because the devices typically used in laboratory experiments necessitate acquiring new information. Thus, an appropriate mnemonic for an older subject probably is one in which the components are overlearned already.

The purpose of this study was to identify a mnemonic that would be effective for older individuals in terms of the ease with which it could be learned and applied. The type of mnemonic studied, a variant of the method of loci, was recognized by the ancient Greeks and was described by Cicero in *De Oratore*.

Study 1

Method

Subjects   The subjects were five elderly volunteers, one man and four women, aged 60–76($\overline{X}$ = 69.3 yr) who were neighbors of Ms. Hausman in metropolitan Washington, D.C. The mean raw score for the WAIS vocabulary subtest was 62.8 (range 38–78). The subjects were paid for their participation in the study.

Materials   The stimuli were 96 high-imagery nouns drawn from the Paivio, Yuille, and Madigan norms (1968). Each of the 6 lists consisted of 16 items. The order of presentation of the lists to a subject was randomized.

Procedure   Each subject was tested individually in five sessions on five consecutive days. The first testing session required approximately 40 min and each subsequent session required about 20 min. On the first day, the vocabulary subtest of the WAIS was administered. Next, a preliminary practice trial was used to familiarize the participant with the testing procedure. Subjects were given a deck of six 3 × 5 cards face down, each printed with a common adjective, and they were instructed to turn over one card at a time and to read the word aloud. Subjects were informed that they could take as much time as they wanted to study each word, and that they should hand each card to the experimenter before turning over the next card for inspection. Furthermore, subjects were instructed to remember in any order as many words as possible since they would be asked to write the words after studying the list.

Following the short practice trial, subjects were given a deck of 16 cards with a common noun written on each card. Again, they were instructed to turn over one card at a time, to read each word aloud, to study it, and to hand the card to the experimenter before turning over the next card. Subjects were told to go as slowly as they wished and to remember as many words as possible in any order. After all the words in the list had been inspected, they were asked to write as many words as they could recall in any order. The number of words correctly recalled was the dependent variable. The free-recall score for Day 1 was the pretest measure for each subject.

Following the free-recall task, subjects were asked to picture in their minds the interior of their apartments or houses and to take an imaginary walk through their residences, stopping at 16 places. The places could be pieces of furniture, rooms, or anything in the rooms, but the places must be sites that would be reached in succession on an imaginary walk through their homes. Each subject generated a list of 16 "stopping places," and the experimenter wrote each of the loci on an index card and put a number in the upper right-hand corner of the card to indicate the ordinal position of the locus, for example, "entrance hall [1]." After subjects had listed the 16 loci, the experimenter rehearsed the "trip" with them. They were asked to begin their walks and to "stop" at each of the 16 locations. As they stated each locus, an index card was turned over to confirm the correct response. Each subject was required to make the trip without error.

On the second day, subjects were again asked to take their imaginary walks around their homes and to stop at each of the 16 locations in order. After stating each stopping place, subjects turned over the next cue card for verification. Again, subjects were required to make a trip without an error. Then, they were told that there were 16 other cards with a common word written on

each card. The experimenter simultaneously turned over the cue card with the first locus and a card with a word. Subjects were asked to picture in their minds the word and the stopping place, for example, an "alligator" in the "entrance hall." Each person was told that a word could be connected to the stopping place in any way that it could be visualized — "on top, in a silly position, hanging there, or any other way you want to imagine it that will help to remember the word." The subjects were required to describe the picture of, for example, the "alligator in the entrance hall," and of each of the other pairs of words and stopping places. Following the study trial, subjects were shown stopping-place cue cards and were asked to write the word that had been associated with each place.

On the third day, the locations were rehearsed. Individuals were given their particular stopping-place cue cards and another list of 16 words and were requested to visualize the object in association with the locus and to describe the picture. Each subject was asked to remember the words without having the stopping-place cards for cues at the time of recall. Each participant was instructed to be sure to picture the words and stopping places in order on the imaginary walk.

On the fourth day, the locations were rehearsed again. Each person was given another deck of cards with 16 words but the stopping-place cue cards were not presented. Each subject was requested to state the stopping place that would be associated with the to-be-remembered item and to describe the picture. Following the study trial, subjects were instructed to write the words, picturing each one as they took the imaginary walks around their homes.

The posttreatment test trial was given on the fifth day. Unlike the training sessions on Days 2, 3, and 4, on Day 5 neither the locations nor the "trip" was mentioned. The subjects were given another deck of cards and asked to turn over one card at a time, to read the word, to study it, and then to hand the card to the experimenter before turning over the next card. They were told to take as much time as they wished and to remember as many words as possible.

Results

Table 1 reports the number of words recalled by each of the five subjects for each of the five sessions. It should be mentioned that on Day 1, Subject 1 was the only person to use a method-of-loci mnemonic (a technique that she had used successfully for many years), and that her performance was superior to that of the other subjects. Table 1 shows that using the mnemonic was effective in improving recall performance; all five of the subjects recalled more words on Days 2, 3, and 4 than they had on the pretest on Day 1. The t tests of gain from Day 1 for Days 2, 3, or 4 indicated that the change was statistically significant for each of the training sessions (Day 2, $t = 3.73$, $df = 4$, $p < .05$; Day 3, $t = 3.52$, $df = 4$, $p < .05$; Day 4, $t = 3.01$, $df = 4$, $p < .05$). However, the gain of the posttest (Day 5) over the pretest (Day 1) measure was not statistically significant ($t = 1.22$, $df = 4$). Table 1 shows that each of the five subjects performed more poorly on Day 5 than on Day 4. Moreover, the dif-

ference between the gain score on Day 4 compared to that on Day 5 was statistically significant ($t = 2.51$, $df = 4$, $p < .05$).

Discussion

The results show that our attempt to identify a mnemonic that would be effective for older individuals was successful. The superior recall on Days 2, 3, and 4 for each of the subjects demonstrated that the mnemonic was readily acquired.

The lack of transfer of the technique to the performance on the posttest was unexpected. It seems particularly surprising in view of the marked improvement in recall performance and of the subjects' recognition of the efficacy of the "imaginary walk." Clearly, most of the subjects did not apply the mnemonic on the posttest, free-recall trial. Goulet (1972) has pointed out the importance of distinguishing between specific and nonspecific transfer effects in gerontological studies. Apparently, without a specific instructional set to use the mnemonic, the subjects did not perceive that its application was appropriate on the free-recall posttest. Therefore, a second study was carried out to determine the effect of the degree of specificity of instructions on the application of the mnemonic.

TABLE 1
Number of Words Recalled for Each Session

Subject	Age	Vocabulary	Pretest Day 1	Training Day 2	Day 3	Day 4	Posttest Day 5
1	62.8	68	15	16	16	16	15
2	76.8	38	9	14	13	12	7
3	74.2	58	3	15	15	14	9
4	72.4	78	5	15	14	16	5
5	60.2	72	8	16	16	13	12
Mean	69.3	62.8	8.0	15.2	14.8	14.2	9.6

Study 2

Method

Subjects Thirty volunteer elderly subjects were recruited from senior citizens centers in the Washington, D.C., metropolitan area. All subjects were paid for their participation in the study. The subjects were randomly assigned to one of two experimental groups or to the control group so that there were 10 subjects in each group. In Group I, there were two men and eight women aged 62–84 ($\overline{X}$ = 70.63 yr), in Group II there were four men and six women aged 60–80 ($\overline{X}$ = 71.74 yr), and in the control group there were three men and seven women aged 60–82 ($\overline{X}$ = 70.70 yr). Mean raw scores for the vocabulary subtest of the WAIS were 60.00 (range 46–69), 61.00 (range 35–76), and 55.60 (range 40–68) for Group I, Group II, and the control group respectively. An analysis of variance showed that there were no statistically significant group differences in the vocabulary measure (F = 0.84, df = 2,27).

Materials

The stimuli were those used in Study 1.

Procedure Table 2 summarizes the procedures in Study 2 for each of the three groups, indicating the specific cues that were provided on each of the five days. For experimental Groups I and II, Days 2, 3, and 4

were identical to the first four days described in Study 1. The procedures for Groups I and II differed only with respect to the instructions on Day 5. For Group I, the direction to use the mnemonic was weak. These subjects were told to remember as many words as possible "using the method we've been using all week." Subjects in Group II were given stronger directions to use the mnemonic. They were instructed to picture the to-be-remembered words with the locations and to describe the images. For neither group did the experimenter rehearse the locations with the subjects before they were given the deck of 16 cards.

In the control group, subjects were given the same instructions as those in Groups I and II for Day 1. The control group subjects were also required to generate 16 locations on an imaginary walk through their homes and to rehearse the order of the stopping places. Similarly on Days 2, 3, and 4, subjects in the control group also rehearsed the 16 locations on their trip. However, control subjects were not instructed to associate one of the to-be-remembered words with a particular stopping place, and of course control subjects were not asked to describe the item-locus "picture." For the control subjects, Days 2, 3, and 4 were similar to Day 1. After rehearsing the locations, subjects were given a deck of cards with the 16 to-be-remembered words and requested to turn over the first card, to read the word aloud, to study it, taking as much time as they wished, and to hand the card to the experimenter before

TABLE 2
Summary of the Procedure

Procedural components	Group I	Group II	Control
Rehearsal of loci	Days 2, 3, 4	Days 2, 3, 4	Days 2, 3, 4
Loci cues at input	Days 2, 3	Days 2, 3	—
Verbal description of image	Days 2, 3, 4	Days 2, 3, 4, 5	—
Loci cues at recall	Day 2	Day 2	—

turning over the next card. They were then asked to write as many words as they could recall. On Day 5, control subjects also did not rehearse the locations, and the free-recall trial procedure was as described above for Days 2, 3, and 4.

Results

Table 3 reports the mean number of words recalled for each of the five sessions for each of the groups. An analysis of variance showed that there was no statistically significant difference among the three groups in the number of words recalled on the pretest ($F = 2.96$, $df = 2,27$).

As in Study 1, the subjects in the two experimental groups recalled more words on Days 2, 3, and 4 than they had on the pretest on Day 1. Once again the t tests of gain from Day 1 for Days 2, 3, and 4 showed the change to be statistically significant for each of the training sessions for both of the experimental groups ($t = > 6.0$, $df = 9$, $p < .01$, for every test). Moreover, an analysis of variance of the gain scores on Days 2, 3, and 4 for both of the experimental groups found no statistically significant difference between the gain scores of the two groups

($F = 0.57$, $df = 1,18$), no effect for days ($F = 0.01$, $df = 2, 36$), and no interaction effect ($F = 0.56$, $df = 2,36$). Therefore, the training method was equally effective for both experimental groups.

To determine the relative effectiveness of the training method over practice in free recall, the gain scores on Days 2, 3, and 4 for the combined treatment group (Groups I and II together) and for the control group were compared in an analysis of variance. The results showed that there was a statistically significant difference between the experimental and control groups ($F = 19.26$, $df = 1,28$, $p < .01$), the improvement from pretest in the recall performance of the combined treatment groups being superior to that of the control group on Days 2, 3, and 4.

The mean gain from pretest (Day 1) to posttest (Day 5) was statistically significant for each of the treatment groups (Group I, $t = 3.39$, $df = 9$, $p < .01$; Group II, $t = 4.07$, $df = 9$, $p < .01$), and the difference between the mean gain scores of the two groups was not statistically significant ($t = 0.46$, $df = 18$). The difference in the mean gain from Day 1 to Day 5 between the combined experimental groups and the control group

TABLE 3
Mean Number of Words Recalled for Each Session

Group	Age	Vocabulary	1	2	3	4	5
I							
$\overline{X}$	70.63	60.00	7.40	13.00	13.50	13.50	11.10
SD	7.06	8.29	2.46	2.45	3.03	3.03	3.98
II							
$\overline{X}$	71.74	61.00	6.70	12.20	11.80	11.80	11.10
SD	5.88	12.30	2.26	4.05	3.85	2.57	3.90
Control							
$\overline{X}$	70.70	55.60	5.30	7.30	7.60	7.40	7.00
SD	7.73	8.66	0.67	1.49	2.27	2.37	2.94

was statistically significant ($t = 1.83$, $df = 28, p < .05$). Means declined from Day 4 to Day 5 for both training groups, although this decline was statistically significant only for Group I ($t = 2.47$, $df = 9, p < .05$). The difference in mean declines between the two groups was not statistically significant. Nevertheless, the recall performance of six of the ten subjects in Group I and five of the ten subjects in Group II declined from Day 4 to Day 5.

Discussion

As in Study 1, each of the subjects in the two experimental groups was able to acquire the mnemonic readily. Recall of 16 stopping places (loci) was nearly perfect in a single trial. Moreover, subjects were successful in using the "trip" at the time of recall to "visit" each locus and to retrieve the associated item as evidenced by the statistically significant gain scores on Days 2, 3, and 4 for both Groups I and II. Furthermore, the recall performance of the experimental groups on the training trials was superior to that of the control group, which indicates that the improvement in recall performance when the method of loci was applied was greater than that attributable to practice. Therefore, a method of loci in which older individuals mentally associate to-be-remembered information with a well-known, familiar set of spatial locations is extremely effective in improving the recall performance of older individuals.

How does the mnemonic aid recall? The method of loci facilitates recall performance by improving organization at the time of encoding and subsequently the loci provide effective retrieval cues to direct the search at the time of recall. Tulving and Thomson (1973) have presented evidence for an encoding specificity principle which states that "specific encoding operations performed on what is perceived determine what is stored,

and what is stored determines what retrieval cues are effective in providing access to what is stored" (p. 369).

Furthermore, this particular method of loci has additional attributes that, by reducing interference at the time of input as well as at the time of recall, can be especially beneficial for older individuals. It is critical that older individuals generate their own spatial locations to avoid conditions of information overload resulting from attempts to process two new sets of information at the same time. Using familiar spatial locations reduces the interference from having to divide their attention between input and storage. Moreover, if subjects lose their way on their "trips," the search need not fail as they know where to resume the trip or, failing that, they may begin the walk again. The familiarity of the loci has been reported to affect search time. With young college students, Lea (1975) showed that the mean search time for overlearned loci (600 msec) was considerably shorter than for less familiar locations (1000 msec). Furthermore, it has been demonstrated that search time in both primary and secondary memory is longer for old than for young subjects (Anders & Fozard, 1973). Therefore, to reduce the opportunity for interference at the time of recall it is important for older individuals to direct their search with strong, familiar retrieval cues to minimize the search time.

In both Studies 1 and 2, it was shown that older individuals improved their performance after receiving specific training and instructions to apply the mnemonic at the time of recall. The subjects in Study 1 did not apply the technique unless given specific instructions to do so; that is, they failed to transfer the training to another learning task. In Study 2, an attempt was made to improve the transfer of training to performance on the posttest. The minimal direction to Group I on Day 5 to "use the method we've been using all week" was sufficient instruction for some of the subjects to continue to use the mnemonic. Nevertheless, the recall performance of six of the ten subjects in Group I and five of the ten subjects in Group II declined from Day 4 to Day 5, which indicates that the transfer of training could be improved. It should be noted that the experimenter did not review the locations with the subjects before beginning the posttest, free-recall trial. To the extent that the subjects did not rehearse the loci list before commencing to study the to-be-remembered items, there may have been some division of attention at the time of encoding between recalling a particular locus and making the locus-item association. Perhaps the training procedure should include an instruction to

review quickly the loci list before attempting to make new associations.

Small declines from Day 4 to Day 5 are attributable to slightly less effective use of the mnemonic without the experimenter's direction. For subjects with small declines, additional practice with the mnemonic would likely maximize recall performance. However, marked declines from Day 4 to Day 5 were found for a few subjects who had acquired the mnemonic easily but did not recognize a situation where the technique could be applied. For the benefit of these subjects, it seems that during the training session explicit information concerning the application of the mnemonic in specific real-world contexts would be appropriate.

References

Anders, T. R., & Fozard, J. L. Effects of age upon retrieval from primary and secondary memory. *Developmental Psychology*, 1973, 9, 411–415.

Arenberg, D., & Robertson, E. A. The older individual as a learner. In S. M. Grabowski & W. D. Mason (Eds.), *Education for the aging*. Washington: Capital Publications, 1974.

Atkinson, R. C., & Shiffrin, R. M. Human memory: A proposed system and its control processes. In K. W. Spence & J. T. Spence (Eds.), *Advances in the psychology of learning and motivation* (Vol. 2). New York: Academic, 1968.

Bower, G. H. Organizational factors in memory. *Cognitive Psychology*, 1970, 1, 18–46.

Goulet, L. R. New directions for research on aging and retention. *Journal of Gerontology*, 1972, 27, 52–60.

Hulicka, I. M., & Grossman, J. L. Age-group comparisons for the use of mediators in paired-associate learning. *Journal of Gerontology*, 1967, 22, 46–51.

Hulicka, I. M., & Rust, L. D. Age-related retention deficit as a function of learning. *Journal of the American Geriatrics Society*, 1964, 11, 1061–1065.

Hulicka, I. M., & Weiss, R. L. Age differences in retention as a function of learning. *Journal of Consulting Psychology*, 1965, 29, 125–129.

Lea, G. Chronometric analysis of the method of loci. *Journal of Experimental Psychology: Human Perception and Performance*, 1975, 104, 95–104.

Paivio, A., Yuille, J. C., & Madigan, S. Concreteness, imagery, and meaningfulness values for 925 nouns. *Journal of Experimental Psychology Monograph Supplement*, 1968, 76(1, Pt. 2).

Rowe, E. J., & Schnore, M. M. Item concreteness and reported strategies in paired-associate learning as a function of age. *Journal of Gerontology*, 1971, 26, 470–475.

Tulving, E., & Thomson, D. M. Encoding specificity and retrieval processes in episodic memory. *Psychological Review*, 1973, 80, 352–373.

Intellectual Training Research in Aging: Modification of Performance on the Fluid Ability of Figural Relations

SHERRY L. WILLIS, ROSEMARY BLIESZNER, and PAUL B. BALTES

The effectiveness of cognitive training on older adults' performance on the fluid ability of figural relations was examined. Posttraining performance of 58 older adults (M age = 69.8 years) was assessed on a battery of fluid and crystallized ability measures. A pattern of differential transfer was found with greater training effects to near fluid transfer measures (figural relations). This pattern of training effects was maintained across three posttest occasions, spanning a 6-month period. Significant practice (retest) effects were also obtained for both training and control groups. Retest effects, however, did not follow the pattern of differential training transfer. These findings suggest the continued modifiability of intellectual performance through cognitive intervention across the adult life span.

Although considerable cognitive training research has focused on the age periods of childhood and young adulthood (Glaser, 1978; Levin & Allen, 1976; Wittrock, 1966), comparable research in middle and later adulthood has been meager. This discrepancy reflects not only our society's concentration of formal educational efforts in the first part of the life span but it also reflects early research findings regarding adult intelligence.

Much of the research on adult intelligence has been cross-sectional in design and has typically reported a peak in intellectual functioning in young adulthood, with a normative pattern of decline for some reasoning and perceptual–motor abilities beginning in early middle age (see Botwinick, 1977; Matarazzo, 1972, for reviews). Verbal ability, in contrast, has typically shown a pattern of stability or increment into late adulthood. However, recent longitudinal research suggests more variability in adult intellectual development than traditionally assumed. As shown primarily by the work of Schaie (1979), a peak in intellectual performance for many abilities appears to occur later for current adult cohorts than indicated by cross-sectional research. Moreover, ability decrement begins later and appears less pervasive in current adult cohorts (Botwinick, 1977; Schaie, 1979). In addition, significant cohort differences in intellectual performance have been noted. When cohort-se-

Source: Willis, S. L., Blieszner, R., & Baltes, P. B. Intellectual training research in aging: Modification of performance on the fluid ability of figural relations. *Journal of Educational Psychology,* 1981, 73, 41–50. Copyright 1981 by the American Psychological Association. Reprinted by permission.

quential methodologies were applied to longitudinal samples to compare the intellectual performance of adults of different cohorts at the same chronological age, earlier cohorts of adults were found to function at a lower performance level on many abilities than did later cohorts at the same age (Baltes & Schaie, 1976; Schaie & Parham, 1977). Thus, what was interpreted as age-related decrement in prior cross-sectional research may be partially attributable to cohort differences in intellectual functioning. Such cohort differences may indicate the impact of rapid and pervasive sociocultural change occurring during this century on current older adults' intellectual functioning; the elderly may suffer from considerable cohort-related obsolescence as a function of societal change.

In concert, these recent findings call for an altered perspective of adult intelligence, with emphasis on continued developmental change across adulthood and on the potential impact of environmental factors. Educational policy and practice would appear directly relevant to understanding the role of environmental factors in adult intellectual functioning and the possible cohort-related obsolescence experienced by the current older adult generation (Baltes & Willis, 1979; Havighurst, 1976; Schaie & Willis, 1978). Such factors suggest a rationale for examining the modifiability of intellectual performance in the aged through educational training. Research in this area should contribute information toward the development of life-span educational programming.

Several earlier gerontological training studies have offered support for the modifiability of intellectual performance on a variety of cognitive abilities (e.g., Hornblum & Overton, 1976; Labouvie-Vief & Gonda, 1976; Plemons, Willis, & Baltes, 1978; Schultz & Hoyer, 1976). Most of these studies, however, did not provide a systematic framework for conceptualizing and assessing training effects, particularly with

regard to the criteria of training transfer and temporal maintenance of training effects.

The present study examined training effectiveness within a theoretical framework provided by a structural model of intelligence. Several aspects of the study were guided by the particular model of intelligence selected: the target ability for training, conceptual design of the training program, and specification of the pattern of training and transfer effects. Specifically, the theory of fluid and crystallized intelligence provided the conceptual framework for this study. Fluid–crystallized theory is a hierarchical, structural model of psychometric intelligence postulating two broad, second-order dimensions of fluid and crystallized intelligence (Cattell, 1971; Horn, 1970, 1978). These two dimensions are said to show differential, normative patterns of development in adulthood, with fluid intelligence exhibiting gradual decline beginning in early adulthood while crystallized intelligence increases or remains stable across much of adulthood (Horn & Cattell, 1967). The present study examined to what degree short-term educational training could modify the assumed normative deficit in older adults' performance on figural relations, a component of fluid intelligence. Training effectiveness was assessed for a transfer-of-training paradigm and for maintenance of training effects across a 6-month period.

Method

Subjects

Subjects were older adults from several rural communities in central Pennsylvania, who were recruited from community organizations and paid ($2/hour) for participation either individually or by a contribution to their organizations. For all subjects, self-reported health status was good, with no substantial hearing or visual impairment noted.

Of the 69 subjects pretested, 58 (84%: 15 males, 43 females) completed all three posttests. Mean age of these 58 subjects was 69.8 years ($SD = 5.7$, range = 61–84 years), with no significant sex differences in age. An equal number of training and control subjects completed the study. Comparison of dropouts and subjects completing the study on pretest scores, age, and educational level indicated only significant educational differences, $F(1, 67) = 5.67, p < .05$, with dropouts having a higher educational level ($M = 13.2$ years, $SD = 4.4$) than the remaining subjects ($M = 10.3$ years, $SD = 3.49$).[1]

Design and Procedure

Following a pretest session, subjects were randomly assigned to one of two conditions: figural relations training, and no-contact control. Training began within 1 week of the pretest and involved five 1-hour sessions extending over approximately 2 weeks. Subjects were trained in groups of 4–8 by a middle-aged female trainer. The no-contact control group received the pretests and posttests but no training. Three posttests were administered, approximately 1 week, 1 month, and 6 months after training. Training and control subjects were pretested and posttested together in groups of no more than 12 persons. The pretest session (1.5 hours) involved two tests: the Adult Development and Enrichment Project (ADEPT) Figural Relations Test (Form A; Plemons et al., 1978) and the ADEPT Induction Test (Form A; Blieszner, Willis, & Baltes, in press). A battery of fluid and crystallized intelligence measures (to be described below) was administered at each of the three posttests. Pretests and posttests were conducted by two graduate assistants.

Training Program

The training program focused on the fluid ability of figural relations. Figural relations is characterized as one of the more "pure" primary abilities representing fluid intelligence (Cattell, 1971; Horn, 1970) and is defined by tasks involving the education of relations within figural patterns.

The content of the training program was based on a task analysis of the Culture Fair Test (Scale 2; Cattell & Cattell, 1957), previously shown to be a strong marker of figural relations (Cattell, 1971). The Culture Fair Test has four subtests (Figure Series, Figure Classify, Matrices, Topology), each involving a different type of figural relations problem. The task analysis identified relational rules (e.g., size, shape, position) utilized in solving items in each subtest. Training problems were then developed for the most frequently occurring relational rules associated with each subtest. None of the new items were identical to those on the Culture Fair Test.

Each of the first four training sessions was focused on one of the four types of figural relations problems (Figure Series, Figure Classify, Matrices, Topology). These sessions included a review of content from the previous session, the trainer's modeling relational rules associated with the problems trained during that session, individual practice with pencil-and-paper training materials, feedback, and group discussion. A fifth training session involved a review of all four types of problems. An adaptation of verbal rule learning, shown to be effective in prior problem solving (Wittrock, 1966) and Piagetian (Beilin, 1976) training research, was the primary instructional strategy utilized.

[1] Subject attrition tended to occur early in the study and to be evenly distributed for experimental ($n = 6$) and control groups ($n = 5$). The number of dropouts at each test occasion was 7 (Posttest 1), 1 (Posttest 2), and 3 (Posttest 3).

Assessment of Training Effects

Two major criteria were used in assessment of training effects. The first criterion focused on training and transfer effects within a theory-based measurement paradigm; the second focused on maintenance of training and transfer effects across three posttest occasions (1 week, 1 month, 6 months).

Training transfer   Training and transfer effects were assessed at each posttest occasion with a broad battery of fluid and crystallized measures (see Table 1). A hierarchical, theory-based pattern of transfer was predicted across these measures. The predicted transfer pattern follows both from the Cattell-Horn theory of intelligence (i.e., empirical factor-loading patterns) and the level of similarity of the transfer measures to the training program content.

Near and far levels of training transfer were assessed. Near transfer was examined across three measures of figural relations. Two levels of far transfer (far fluid, far nonfluid) were assessed. The most direct measure of near transfer, the ADEPT Figural Relations Test (Form B), was developed in earlier pilot research (Plemons et al., 1978) and involved test items based on the relational rules identified in the task analysis described for the training program. The two other tests of figural relations were the Culture Fair Test (Scale 2, and Power Matrices, Scale 3; Cattell & Cattell, 1957, 1961, 1963), and the Raven's Advanced Progressive Matrices (Raven, 1962).[2] The Culture Fair Test was the next-nearest transfer measure, involving both the trained relational rules and additional rules not included in training. The Raven matrices represented a more difficult level of the figural relations ability, involving distractors as

_____
[2] Due to the length of the posttest battery, only the odd-numbered items of Raven's Advanced Progressive Matrices (Set II) were administered.

well as more complex rules. Inclusion of three tests marking figural relations permitted examination of a broad continuum of within-ability (figural relations) transfer.

The first level of far transfer was to the fluid intelligence dimension of induction, another "pure" fluid ability, factorially distinct from figural relations at the primary ability level (Horn, 1970). Two measures of induction were included. The Induction Composite measure involved three published tests: Letter Series and Number Series (Thurstone, 1962), and Letter Sets (Ekstrom, French, Harman, & Derman, 1976). The ADEPT Induction measure included three tests patterned after those in the Induction Composite measure (Blieszner et al., in press).

The second level of far transfer was to two nonfluid dimensions, Crystallized Intelligence and Perceptual Speed. Within the fluid-crystallized theory, Crystallized Intelligence and Perceptual Speed were considered to have different developmental antecedents and to be factorially distinct from fluid intelligence. Crystallized intelligence was represented by a marker test of Vocabulary (V–2; Ekstrom et al., 1976), and Perceptual Speed was represented by the Identical Pictures test (Ekstrom et al., 1976).

Maintenance of training effects   The second major assessment criterion examined the maintenance of training and transfer effects across the three posttest occasions (1 week, 1 month, 6 months). Temporal maintenance of training effects was critical if training was interpreted to represent modification of the level of functioning on the target ability. The immediate posttest included in many training studies was considered insufficient to assess the stability of training effects; thus, the assessment design involved three posttests across a 6-month period.

However, the repeated posttesting in-

TABLE 1
Transfer Assessment Battery: Figural Relations Training Study

General intelligence dimension	Primary mental ability	Predicted transfer pattern and marker measures	Source
Fluid	Figural relations	Near-near transfer	
		ADEPT Figural Relations Test (Form B)[a]	Plemons et al., 1978
		Near transfer	
		Culture Fair Test (Scale 2, Form A)	Cattell & Cattell, 1957
		& Power Matrices (Scale 3, Form A, 1963 ed.; and Form B, 1961 ed.)	Cattell & Cattell, 1961, 1963
		Near transfer	
		Raven's Advanced Progressive Matrices (Set II)	Raven, 1962
	Induction	Far fluid transfer	
		ADEPT Induction Test (Form B)[a]. Letter Sets, Number Series, Letter Series	Blieszner et al., in press
		Induction Composite Test:	
		Letter Sets, Number Series, Letter Series	Ekstrom et al., 1976; Thurstone, 1962
Speed	Perceptual speed	Far nonfluid transfer	
		Identical Pictures	Ekstrom et al., 1976
Crystallized	Verbal comprehension	Far nonfluid transfer	
		Vocabulary (V-2)	Ekstrom et al., 1976

Note. ADEPT = Adult Development and Enrichment Project. The terms *Fluid, Speed,* and *Crystallized* refer to general intelligence dimensions. All measures were included at Posttests 1, 2, and 3. More complete information on tests and their factorial structure is contained in Baltes, Cornelius, Spiro, Nesselroade, and Willis (1980).
[a] ADEPT Figural Relations and Induction Tests (Form A) were administered at pretest.

volved in assessment of training maintenance was predicted to result in strong practice (retest) effects for a test-naive population such as the elderly. Such practice effects have been demonstrated both in prior training research with the elderly (Plemons et al., 1978) and in current research on practice (Hofland, Willis, & Baltes, in press). Retest effects resulting from practice in test taking per se must be distinguished from transfer effects attributed to training. In contrast to training effects, retest effects were predicted to be general in that they would be exhibited by both experimental and control subjects and would occur for all or most transfer measures but would not show the differential transfer pattern predicted for training. The differentiation between training and practice effects is important for an ability-specific interpretation of training.

Results

No significant difference existed between training and control groups on the two pretest scores: ADEPT Figural Relations

Test, $F(1, 56) = .018$, $p > .05$; ADEPT Induction Test, $F(1, 56) = .255$, $p > .05$.

Results of the study are presented with regard to training and transfer effects, temporal maintenance of training effects, and practice effects. The entire data matrix (across treatments and occasions) for each of the seven posttest measures was standardized, using the control group's score on that measure at Posttest 1 as the standardization base ($M = 50$, $SD = 10$). This procedure was employed for two reasons: (a) It pro-

vided a common baseline of performance on each measure to which all other data points for the measure were compared and (b) it eliminated scale-level differences between measures and thus facilitated comparison of transfer effects across measures.

Transfer of Training

Table 2 shows the training and control groups' mean standardized scores and standard deviations for the seven transfer

TABLE 2

Mean Standardized Scores and Standard Deviations on Seven Transfer Measures for Training and Control Groups for Three Posttest Occasions

	Occasion					
	Posttest 1		Posttest 2		Posttest 3	
Measure	Training	Control	Training	Control	Training	Control
ADEPT Figural Relations						
M	59.0	50.0	61.1	51.4	59.1	52.5
SD	10.4	10.0	11.7	11.1	12.6	10.7
Culture Fair						
M	55.9	50.0	57.4	51.2	55.2	51.9
SD	10.4	10.0	10.6	12.0	10.6	10.5
Raven						
M	54.3	50.0	54.2	50.6	55.6	50.0
SD	9.9	10.0	11.4	12.3	10.4	10.6
ADEPT Induction						
M	52.6	50.0	54.2	51.9	56.0	52.7
SD	10.8	10.0	10.2	11.2	11.2	10.0
Induction Composite						
M	53.0	50.0	56.3	53.8	55.5	53.0
SD	10.2	10.0	12.5	11.0	11.1	11.7
Identical Pictures						
M	52.5	50.0	53.9	51.9	55.0	50.6
SD	9.5	10.0	11.3	9.2	10.2	8.7
Vocabulary						
M	52.8	50.0	53.0	50.1	52.9	50.1
SD	9.1	10.0	9.4	9.8	9.0	10.2

Note. ADEPT = Adult Development and Enrichment Project. All data points for each measure were standardized with the control group's Posttest 1 scores as base ($M = 50$, $SD = 10$). For the training and control group, $n = 29$ each.

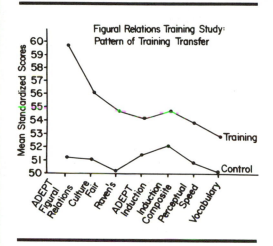

FIGURE 1

Mean standardized scores on seven transfer measures for training and control groups averaged across three posttest occasions.

measures for each posttest. A summary of the training and control groups' mean standardized scores averaged across posttests is shown in Figure 1. The pattern of training transfer is represented by the relative difference between the mean standardized scores for the training and control groups for each measure. Note that the difference between mean scores for training and control groups is larger for the three near (figural relations) transfer measures than for the four far (fluid and nonfluid) transfer measures.

To obtain an initial assessment of training effects, an overall 2 (treatment: training, control) × 3 (occasion: Posttests 1, 2, 3) × 7 (measure) analysis of covariance (AN-COVA) with repeated measures was conducted (Table 3). The ANCOVA was used to reduce the large individual differences within training and control groups often found in aging research. The covariate was the pretest score for the nearest transfer measure (ADEPT Figural Relations Test). This overall analysis resulted in a significant

treatment main effect for training. In addition, the significant Treatment × Measure interaction indicated differential treatment effects across the seven transfer measures. The significant occasion main effect was interpreted as primarily reflecting practice effects, common to both training and control groups. A significant measure main effect involved the summation of differential training and retest effects, given the standardization procedure used in which all data points were standardized with reference to the control group's scores at Posttest 1.

Following this overall analysis, training and transfer effects were examined more specifically at two levels. First, the pattern of differential training transfer across the seven measures was assessed by a series of orthogonal planned comparisons. Second, transfer effects at the individual test level were examined. In Table 4 a summary of the orthogonal planned comparisons is shown. For the Treatment × Measure and Treatment × Occasion × Measure comparisons, differential weights were assigned to each measure. The three levels of near (figural relations) transfer were weighted according to their conceptual relatedness to the training program.

In Table 3 a summary of the results for these planned comparisons is presented within the context of the 2 × 3 × 7 ANCOVA. Two planned comparisons (ψ_3, ψ_4) of the Treatment × Measure interaction were conducted. Comparison ψ_3 indicated that the predicted pattern of greater training transfer to near than to far transfer measures was significant ($p < .001$). Follow-up contrasts conducted separately for the training and control groups indicated a significant effect, $F(1, 292) = 22.05, p < .001$, for the training but not for the control group. To examine whether a pattern of further differential transfer also existed within the four far transfer measures, Comparison ψ_4 was conducted, contrasting the two far fluid transfer measures with the two far nonfluid transfer

TABLE 3
Summary of Analysis of Covariance and Orthogonal Planned Comparisons

Source	SS	df	F
Pretest	49,998.104	1	
Treatment (T)	5,652.278	1	11.81[b]
Occasion (O)	576.175	2	12.00[b]
ψ_1	574.705	1	23.94[b]
ψ_2	1.468	1	.06
T × O	1.951	2	.04
Error	2,688.288	112	
Measure (M)	1,754.846	6	3.43[a]
T × M	1,152.432	6	2.25[a]
ψ_3	1,013.324	1	11.87[b]
ψ_4	1.477	1	.02
T × M residual	137.632	4	.40
Error	28,694.170	336	
O × M	361.660	12	1.39
T × O × M	244.579	12	.94
ψ_5	11.790	1	.54
ψ_6	2.190	1	.10
T × O × M residual	230.599	10	1.06
Error	14,609.660	672	

[a] $p < .05.$
[b] $p < .001.$

TABLE 4
Summary of Orthogonal Planned Comparisons

	Measure (M)							Occasion (O)			Treatment (T)	
Comparison	ADEPT FR	CF	R	ADEPT I	IC	IP	V	1	2	3	Training	Control
O												
ψ_1								2	−1	−1		
ψ_2								0	1	−1		
T × M												
ψ_3	3	2	1	−1.5	−1.5	−1.5	−1.5				1	−1
ψ_4	0	0	0	1	1	−1	−1				1	−1
T × O × M												
ψ_5	3	2	1	−1.5	−1.5	−1.5	−1.5	2	−1	−1	1	−1
ψ_6	3	2	1	−1.5	−1.5	−1.5	−1.5	0	1	−1	1	−1

Note. ADEPT = Adult Development and Enrichment Project; FR = ADEPT Figural Relations; CF = Culture Fair; R = Raven; I = ADEPT Induction; IC = Induction Composite; IP = Identical Pictures; V = Vocabulary.

measures; this comparison was not significant.

Examination of training effects separately by measure was conducted via the Tukey WSD Method. Training and control groups differed significantly on each of the three near transfer (figural relations) measures, across posttests: ADEPT Figural Relations Test (p = .001), Culture Fair Test (p = .008), Raven's matrices (p = .018). No significant differences between training and control were found for the four far transfer measures separately: ADEPT Induction (p = .151), Induction Composite (p = .16), Perceptual Speed (p = .122), Vocabulary (p = .138). However, increasing the statistical power by using a repeated-measured ANCOVA conducted on just the four far transfer measures resulted in a significant treatment main effect, $F(1, 54)$ = 4.15, p = .047, for the four far transfer measures as well.

Maintenance of Training Transfer

To examine whether the pattern of differential training transfer indicated by Comparison ψ_3 was maintained at each posttest occasion, two comparisons (ψ_5, ψ_6) of the Treatment × Occasion × Measure interaction were conducted. Neither comparison was significant, indicating that the predicted pattern of training transfer did not vary between occasions but was maintained across posttest occasions over 6 months.

Practice Effects

Due to the test naivete of elderly subjects, strong practice effects were predicted across posttest occasions. Such retest effects would be common to both training and control groups and would be reflected in an occasion main effect. Two comparisons (ψ_1, ψ_2) of the occasion main effect were conducted. Only Comparison ψ_1 was significant (p = .001), suggesting strong retest effects across treat-

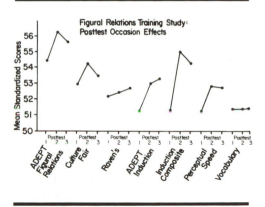

FIGURE 2
Mean standardized scores for seven transfer measures at three posttest occasions.

ment and measure levels from Posttest 1 to the average of Posttests 2 and 3. Comparison ψ_2 indicated the absence of significant retest effects between Posttests 2 and 3. Although the Occasion × Measure interaction was not significant, there appeared to be a trend toward differential practice effects by measure. Figure 2 presents a summary of the occasion effects separately by measure. Note, however, that the occasion effects do not follow the same differential pattern as predicted for training transfer.

Discussion

Training and Practice Effects

A theory-based cognitive training study with older adults was conducted, with emphasis on a differential pattern of training transfer and maintenance of training effects across multiple posttests. The predicted pattern of differential training transfer was established and maintained, with significant effects for the three near transfer measures (ADEPT Figural Relations Test, Culture Fair Tests, and the Raven's matrices). Such training effects represent a broad continuum of training transfer within the target ability (figural relations). The significant effects obtained to near transfer measures are in agreement with prior training research for children and young adults (Levin & Allen, 1976; Wittrock, 1963). Moreover, training effects were maintained over a 6-month period. The literature on long-term maintenance of training effects is limited, and thus the extent to which such a finding is corroborative of past research with younger subjects needs further exploration.

The data also suggest that transfer, to a lesser degree, occurred beyond the figural relations ability. Two levels of far transfer assessed in the study involved far fluid transfer to another fluid ability (Induction) and far nonfluid transfer to perceptual speed and crystallized intelligence abilities. The training group's scores on all four far transfer measures at all posttest occasions were higher than those for the control group. Second, although training effects were not significant for the far transfer measures separately, an ANCOVA on the combined four measures indicated a significant treatment main effect ($p < .05$). In our view, such an effect may reflect generalized, non-ability-specific transfer attributable to situational or ability-extraneous factors (e.g., increased test wiseness, response speed, and anxiety reduction). Such effects could have accrued as a function of the training program but were not intrinsic to performance on the target ability (figural relations) per se. The literature on non-ability-specific transfer effects is limited, since most training transfer paradigms have focused on ability-specific transfer (Royer, 1979). However, the likelihood of non-ability-specific transfer occurring may be greater with educationally and/or test-disadvantaged populations, such as young children, the retarded, and the elderly (Baltes & Willis, 1981; Baltes & Willis, in press).

The considerable practice effects occur-ring across posttest occasions and represented in the analyses as occasion effects are of further interest. Practice effects were differentiated from ability-specific training effects in that they occurred for both experimental and control groups and did not follow the predicted differential pattern of training transfer. The magnitude of such practice effects has been noted in prior training research with both young and older-adult populations (Hofland et al., in press; Sarnacki, 1979; Wing, in press; Wittrock, 1963). Practice effects provide additional support for the modifiability of intellectual performance, since they occur as a function of a very limited, no-feedback retest condition. Moreover, the magnitude of such retest effects and their occurrence over a wide variety of ability measures suggests that considerable caution is required in interpreting single-occasion assessment of test-naive populations, such as the elderly.

Aging and Training Research

The findings of this study, in conjunction with prior gerontological training research (see Willis & Schaie, 1981, for review), offer support for the effectiveness of educational training programs in modifying the intellectual performance of older-adult populations. Such training research, therefore, has significant implications both for theories of adult intelligence and for educational policy.

First, current models of adult intelligence focus on the normative or average pattern of intellectual aging and do not address the potential for modifiability in intellectual functioning in middle and later adulthood (Willis & Baltes, 1980). Although intelligence models in childhood and young adulthood have also typically focused on normative (average) patterns of intellectual development, cognitive training research has examined the range of modifiability of intellectual performance during these age periods. This training research has contributed to a more comprehensive theory of intellectual development early in the life span, involving both potential and normative ranges of intellectual development (Brown & French, 1979). Examination of the range of modifiability in intellectual aging is similarly needed to supplement current theories of normative adult intellectual development. Comprehensive theories of intelligence, including both potential and normative (average) dimensions, may be particularly important in adulthood given recent cohort research regarding the potential impact of sociocultural change on adult intelligence. Moreover, training research may provide insight into the determining factors or mechanisms of intellectual aging. Evidence from educational training research supports the interpretation that the cohort-related obsolescence experienced by current generations of older adults may indeed be a major factor in the lower level of functioning of some of today's older adults.

Second, with regard to educational policy, the effectiveness of cognitive training research in later adulthood provides empirical support for the growing emphasis on a life-long learning approach to education (Dave, 1976; Knox, 1977; Schaie & Willis, 1978). A wide range of social issues, including our society's changing age structure, mandatory retirement, and the threat of rapid technological obsolescence, argue persuasively that educational efforts cannot continue to be concentrated in the first quarter of the life span. A life-long approach to learning is required. However, such an approach requires the assumption that learning capacity extends across the life course. Training studies, such as this one, provide support for the modifiability of intellectual performance across the life span. However, much more research, examining training effects with regard to a variety of cognitive abilities and instructional strategies, is required to provide a satisfactory theoretical and empirical base for a life-long approach to education.

References

Baltes, P. B., & Baltes, M. M. Plasticity and variability in psychological aging: Methodological and theoretical issues. In G. Gurski (Ed.), *Effects of aging on the CNS*. Berlin, Germany: Schering, 1980.

Baltes, P. B., Cornelius, S. W., Spiro, A., III, Nesselroade, J. R., & Willis, S. L. Integration vs. differentiation of fluid-crystallized intelligence in old age. *Developmental Psychology,* 1980, 16, 625–635.

Baltes, P. B., & Schaie, K. W. On the plasticity of intelligence in adulthood and old age: Where Horn and Donaldson fail. *American Psychologist,* 1976, 31, 720–725.

Baltes, P. B., & Willis, S. L. Life-span developmental psychology, cognition, and social policy. In M. W. Riley (Ed.), *Aging from birth to death*. Boulder, Colo.: Westview Press, 1979.

Baltes, P. B., & Willis, S. L. Enhancement of intellectual functioning in old age: Penn State's Adult Development and Enrichment Project (ADEPT). In F. I. M. Craik & S. E. Trehub (Eds.), *Aging and cognitive processes*. New York: Plenum Press, in press.

Beilin, H. Constructing cognitive operations linguistically. In H. W. Reese (Ed.), *Advances in child development and behavior* (Vol. 2). New York: Academic Press, 1976.

Blieszner, R., Willis, S. L., & Baltes, P. B. *Training research on induction in aging: A short-term longitudinal study. Journal of Applied Developmental Psychology,* in press.

Botwinick, J. Aging and intelligence. In J. E. Birren & K. W. Schaie (Eds.), *Handbook of the psychology of aging*. New York: Van Nostrand Reinhold, 1977.

Brown, A., & French, L. The zone of potential development: Implication for intelligence testing in the year 2000. *Intelligence,* 1979, 3, 255–277.

Cattell, R. B. *Abilities: Structure, growth, and action.* New York: Houghton-Mifflin, 1971.

Cattell, R. B., & Cattell, A. K. S. *Test of "g": Culture Fair* (Scale 2, Form A). Champaign, Ill.: Institute for Personality and Ability Testing, 1957.

Cattell, R. B., & Cattell, A. K. S. *Test of "g": Culture Fair* (Scale 3, Form B, 2nd ed.). Champaign, Ill.: Institute for Personality and Ability Testing, 1961.

Cattell, R. B., & Cattell, A. K. S. *Test of "g": Culture Fair* (Scale 3, Form A). Champaign, Ill.: Institute for Personality and Ability Testing, 1963.

Dave, R. H. (Ed.). *Foundations of lifelong education.* Oxford, England: Pergamon Press, 1976.

Ekstrom, R. B., French, J. W., Harman, H., & Derman, D. *Kit of factor-referenced cognitive tests, 1976 revision.* Princeton, N.J.: Educational Testing Service, 1976.

Glaser, R. (Ed.), *Advances in instructional psychology.* Hillsdale, N.J.: Erlbaum, 1978.

Havighurst, R. J. Education through the adult life span. *Educational Gerontology,* 1976, 1, 41–51.

Hofland, B. F., Willis, S. L., & Baltes, P. B. Fluid intelligence performance in the elderly: Retesting and intraindividual variability. *Journal of Educational Psychology,* in press.

Horn, J. L. Organization of data on life-span development of human abilities. In L. R. Goulet & P. B. Baltes (Eds.), *Life-span developmental psychology: Research and theory.* New York: Academic Press, 1970.

Horn, J. L. Human ability systems. In P. B. Baltes (Ed.), *Life-span development and behavior* (Vol. 1). New York: Academic Press, 1978.

Horn, J. L., & Cattell, R. B. Age differences in fluid and crystallized intelligence. *Acta Psychologia,* 1967, 26, 107–129.

Hornblum, J. N., & Overton, W. F. Area and volume conservation among the elderly: Assessment and training. *Developmental Psychology,* 1976, 12, 68–74.

Knox, A. *Adult development and learning.* San Francisco: Jossey-Bass, 1977.

Labouvie-Vief, G., & Gonda, J. Cognitive strategy training and intellectual performance in the elderly. *Journal of Gerontology,* 1976, 31, 327–332.

Levin, J. R., & Allen, V. L. (Eds.). *Cognitive learning in children: Theories and strategies.* New York: Academic Press, 1976.

Matarazzo, J. D. *Wechsler's measurement and appraisal of adult intelligence* (5th ed.). Baltimore, Md.: Williams & Wilkins, 1972.

Plemons, J. K., Willis, S. L., & Baltes, P. B. Modifiability of fluid intelligence in aging: A short-term longitudinal training approach. *Journal of Gerontology,* 1978, 33, 224–231.

Raven, J. C. *Advanced progressive matrices, Set II, 1962 revision.* London: Lewis, 1962.

Royer, J. M. Theories of transfer of learning. *Educational Psychologist,* 1979, 14, 53–69.

Sarnacki, R. E. An examination of test-wiseness in the cognitive test domain. *Review of Educational Research,* 1979, 49, 252–279.

Schaie, K. W. The primary mental abilities in adulthood: An exploration in the development of psychometric intelligence. In P. B. Baltes & O. G. Brim, Jr. (Eds.), *Life-span development and behavior* (Vol. 2), New York: Academic Press, 1979.

Schaie, K. W., & Parham, I. A. Cohort-sequential analyses of adult intellectual development. *Developmental Psychology,* 1977, 13, 649–653.

Schaie, K. W., & Willis, S. L. Life-span development: Implications for education. In L. S. Shulman (Ed.), *Review of research in education* (Vol. 6). Itasca, Ill.: Peacock, 1978.

Schultz, N. R., & Hoyer, W. J. Feedback effects on spatial egocentrism in old age. *Journal of Gerontology,* 1976, 31, 72–75.

Thurstone, T. G. *Primary mental abilities, Grades 9–12, 1962 revision.* Chicago: Science Research Associates, 1962.

Willis, S. L., & Baltes, P. B. Intelligence and cognitive ability. In L. Poon & A. Smith (Eds.), *Contemporary issues in the psychology of aging.* Washington, D.C.: American Psychological Association, 1980.

Willis, S. L., & Schaie, K. W. Maintenance and

decline of adult mental abilities: II. Susceptibility to experimental modification. In F. Grote (Ed.), *Ninth symposium on learning: Adult learning and development.* Bellingham: Western Washington University, 1981.

Wing, H. Practice effects with traditional mental test items. *Applied Psychological Measurement,* in press.

Wittrock, M. C. Verbal stimuli in concept formation: Learning by discovery. *Journal of Educational Psychology,* 1963, 54, 183–190.

Wittrock, M. C. The learning by discovery hypothesis. In L. S. Schulman & E. R. Keisler (Eds.), *Learning by discovering: A critical appraisal.* Chicago: Rand McNally, 1966.

Biological Development

Life expectancies have increased dramatically in the United States, from forty-seven in 1900 to nearly seventy-five today. Women live an average seven to eight years longer than men, perhaps because they have a second X chromosome or some other source of biological superiority. The increase in life expectancy is thought to be due to improved nutrition, sanitation, and medical cures for diseases that formerly cut short the life span; there is no evidence of any increase in the maximum potential span of life. A longer-than-average life is predicted for people whose ancestors were long-lived, who avoid cigarettes, who keep their weight under control, and who face life with a temperate and flexible attitude. Reports of exceptionally long-lived people in the Caucasus mountains of Russia, in Pakistan, and in South America, however, are generally believed to be without substance.

Theories about the genetic causes of biological aging include the notions of "aging genes"; the absence of genetic controls in an organism that is "winding down"; and more or less inevitable damage to genetic molecules, possibly caused by *cross-linking*, which impairs the body's ability to replace and repair cells. Physiological theories of aging implicate the body's endocrine system and, specifically, the thymus gland, which controls immune reactions. Defective immune reactions make cancerous growth and other diseases more likely. On the other hand, "wear and tear" do not appear to be major factors in aging.

All these matters are discussed in a masterful essay by *Leonard Hayflick,* who considers the biological aspects of the question "Why grow old?" He addresses the question of what would happen if cancer, heart disease, and stroke were to be eliminated, disposes of the controversial reports on long-lived persons, considers the possibility of tampering with our biological clocks, and discusses his own seminal work on cellular aging. He reviews some of the current hypotheses about the nature of biological aging and suggests the directions research might take if we wish to control the human aging process.

The probability of disease increases dramatically as the sixties are reached. However, only 5 percent of those over sixty-five are so disabled that they require institutional care, and only 9 percent rate their personal health as poor. Disease has many effects on the elderly; draining their financial resources, limiting their activity and mobility, and in general threatening to place them in the much feared position of being dependent on others. A major question, one not easily answered, is whether there can be disease-free aging. It appears that even ''normal'' aging produces changes in the body that make disease more likely, so that a disease-free person of eighty or ninety is a rare individual. However, disease is at least an exaggeration of normal aging, and it is often preventable (through proper nutrition and exercise, for example) or reversible (through medical treatment).

The selection by *Isadore Rossman* provides a thorough review of bodily changes occurring from middle adulthood into old age. The version provided in this reader was considerably abridged to delete technical material of interest only to geriatric physicians and other professional clinicians. Topics covered include changes in stature and posture; other contour changes; changes in muscle, bones, joints, and skin tissues; declines in organ function within the cardiovascular, pulmonary, renal excretory, reproductive, and digestive systems. It is concluded that although shrinking organ and muscle size and decline in function reduce the ability of individuals to cope with stress, sufficient capacity remains that most people can cope in normal circumstances and under mild stress. Sufficient success has been attained with medical treatment of even the very old, that the major limiting factors for adequate function now seem more likely to be psychiatric than somatic.

It is a reasonable estimate that the average person loses only 5 to 10 percent of his cortical neurons by the age of seventy-five, if he or she remains free of diseases that can destroy brain tissues in larger quantities (e.g., cardiovascular disease or alcoholism). Some psychologists have used reaction-time tasks to study what they consider to be age-related increases in the ''sluggishness'' of the *central nervous system* (the brain plus the spinal cord). Reaction time typically increases with age, especially in complex tasks that require ''preparation'' for the impending stimulus. But hypotheses proposing that this ''sluggishness'' is caused by irreversible neural deterioration are troubled by studies showing that there are few age differences on simple reaction-time tasks; that reaction times improve after practice or experience with the task; and that they are lower for persons, young or old, who tend to exercise frequently. Reversible deficiencies in blood-oxygen supplies to the brain and in the ability to prepare for an impending stimulus (perhaps because of faulty arousal processes) are alternative hypotheses to explain the general slowing of reactions with age.

In his essay on psychophysiology and speed of response *James E. Birren* asks how the study of slowing of behavior with age might be relevant to the circumstances of older people. He consequently examines the role of time as a variable in behavior and relates it to performance in diverse functions of interest to psychologists, including perception, memory and learning, motor skills, intelligence, and neural activity. Illness, particularly in the cardiovascular area, is seen as contributing to behavioral slowing with age. The fact remains, however, that although response times of young adults may be slow or quick depending on the demands of the environment, older adults tend to be slow as a general feature of their behavior. The urban environment, paced as it seems to be for the young, poses hazards for the old, but much further research may be needed before we can reasonably recommend changes that will facilitate the slower pace of the old without creating new hazards for the young.

Additional Suggested Readings

Busse, E. W., & Blazer, D. G. Disorders related to biological functioning. In E. W. Busse & D. G. Blazer (eds.), *Handbook of geriatric psychiatry.* New York: Van Nostrand Reinhold, 1980, pp. 390–414.

   Describes conditions and treatment of disturbances in physiological functioning affecting behavior, such as sleep disturbances, psychosexual disturbances, psychosomatic reactions, and effects of drug use.

Fozard, J. L., Wolf, E., Bell, B., McFarland, R. A., & Podolsky, S. Visual perception and communication. In J. E. Birren & K. W. Schaie (eds.), *Handbook of the psychology of aging.* New York: Van Nostrand Reinhold, 1977, pp. 497–534.

   Comprehensive review of structural changes in the eye, basic visual functioning, visual information processing, context effects in perceptual judgments, and the practical implication of age changes in these processes.

Why Grow Old?

LEONARD HAYFLICK

The processes of aging are responsible for the only affliction to which all of us are destined to succumb. Yet the fundamental causes of biological aging are almost as much a mystery today as they have ever been. How remarkable it is that despite the universality of the problem, it has occupied, and still does occupy, the attention of very few biologists.

Although many life scientists are engaged in studies of biological development — or events preceding age changes — comparatively few biologists identify themselves as gerontologists. This may reflect the view that developmental changes and age changes are inseparable. An extreme position is that aging begins at the moment of conception. Others argue that true age changes begin only after animals, including humans, reach maximum adult size and ability to procreate. The latter view seems more tenable and I believe a distinction can be made between the processes of ripening and rotting.

The Problem

For the first time in man's history significant numbers of people alive today are already aged by usual standards but can still anticipate at least another decade or more of life. Through advancements in medical care and hygiene, industrial societies have produced a large new group of aged individuals,

yet the same culture which created them has not yet learned how to incorporate them effectively into the social structure.

Since 1900 the percentage of the population in this country aged 65 and over has more than doubled (from 4.1 percent in 1900 to 9.9 percent in 1970), while the actual number has increased more than six-fold (from 3 million to 20 million). The 65-and-over population constitutes the fastest growing age group in the country. A child born in 1900 could expect to live an average of about 48 years. A child born in 1974 could expect to live an average of 22 years longer — or 70 years — primarily because of reduced death rates for children and young adults. While the entire population 65 years old and over will rise 43 percent (to 29 million) between 1970 and 2000, persons 75 to 84 will increase by 65 percent, and those 85 and over, 52 percent.

These impressive figures have often been erroneously interpreted to mean that the human life span is increasing. As far as can be determined, however, the human life span has not changed since recorded history. What has changed is *life expectancy,* that is, the number of people able to reach what appears to be the fixed, immutable endpoint (Figure 1). With improvements in medical care and hygienic conditions more of the younger members of our population are living longer, but the endpoint (life span) has remained fixed. From data similar to those expressed in Figure 2, we have learned that,

Source: Hayflick, L. Why grow old? *The Stanford Magazine.* 1975, 3 (1), 36–43. Reprinted by permission.

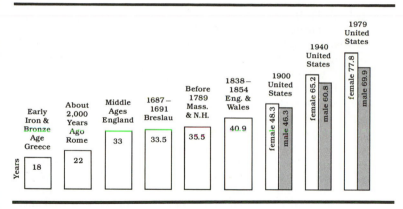

FIGURE 1
Average length of life from ancient to modern times.

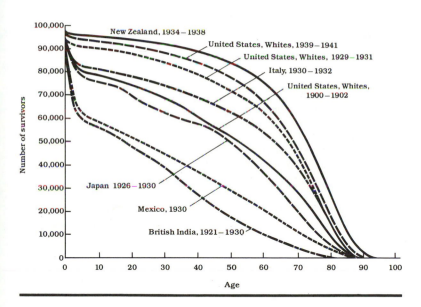

FIGURE 2
Number of survivors at various ages.

as various diseases come under control, the survival curves become more rectangular, but all terminate at the same point. The human life span, therefore, will not be significantly changed until the underlying, non-disease-related biological causes of aging are either slowed or stopped.

What Will Happen If Cancer, Heart Disease, and Stroke Are Eliminated?

If the two leading causes of death in this country — heart disease and stroke — were eliminated, approximately 18 years of additional life could be expected (Table 1). If the third greatest cause of death — cancer — were eliminated, about two years of additional life expectancy would result. To cynical observers, 20 years may not seem worth the prodigious efforts now being made to eliminate these causes of death. In fact, eliminating heart disease, stroke, and cancer as causes of death will only reduce the possible ways in which the inevitability of our death will occur, and will allow accidents then to become the leading killer. Because the causes of accidents are statistically determined, the likelihood of completely controlling them is virtually impossible.

These concepts have forced gerontologists to conclude that the disease-oriented approach to medical research will do very little to increase the human life span. If such an increase is desirable then we must first separate the disease-related causes of death from the age-dependent physiological decrements which give rise to the manifestations of old age. The fundamental causes of death are not diseases but the age-associated physiological decrements that make their occurrence more likely. In short, only research into this area can lead us to materially influence the human life span. The present order of priorities in biomedical research support in this country is not likely to achieve this goal, since we are currently spending $3 per person per year on cancer research, $2 per person per year on heart disease and stroke research, and less than $.03 per person per year on the fundamental causes of aging.

TABLE 1

Gain in Expectation of Life at Birth and at Age 65 due to Elimination of Various Causes of Death

Cause of Death	Gain in Years in Expectation of Life if Cause was Eliminated	
	At birth	At age 65
Major Cardiovascular-Renal Diseases	10.9	10.0
Heart Diseases	5.9	4.9
Vascular Diseases affecting the central nervous system	1.3	1.2
Malignant Neoplasms	2.3	1.2
Accidents excluding those caused by motor vehicles	0.6	0.1
Motor Vehicle Accidents	0.6	0.1
Influenza and Pneumonia	0.5	0.2
Infectious Diseases (excluding Tuberculosis)	0.2	0.1
Diabetes Mellitus	0.2	0.2
Tuberculosis	0.1	0.0

Source: Life tables published by the National Center of Health Statistics, USPHS and U.S. Bureau of the Census, "Some Demographic Aspects of Aging in the United States," February 1973.

Aging Russian Style

No discussion of human longevity would be complete without considering the claims of super-longevity attributed to three geographically disparate peoples: the Vilcabambans in Ecuador, the Hunzukuts in the Karakuram Range of the Pakistani region of Kashmir, and the Russians in the Abkhazia and Osetia regions in the Caucasus of the Georgian Republic of the U.S.S.R.

In other parts of the world, the number of centenarians in the population is normally about two or three per 100,000. Only one person in a million reaches the age of 105, and only one in 40 million will live to be 110. Yet in these three regions, not only are there claims of much higher proportions of centenarians but many individuals report ages of 120, 130, and even 150 and 160 years. If these claims were true, one might reasonably conclude that one or more factors exist that lead to increased human longevity, and that if these factors were known they could be manipulated to apply equally to other groups of people.

Unhappily, however, none of these claims, which have enjoyed widespread popularity in the news media, can be authenticated.

Very little statistical data is available about the Hunzukuts who, with no written language, cannot even point to falsified birth records. The Vilcabambans are very isolated and their birth records are either nonexistent or totally unreliable. One gerontologist, who recently revisited the Vilcabambans after a lapse of five years, was told by several super-centenarians that they were seven to ten years older than they had reported on his previous visit.

Because of the availability of more written records, the regions of the Soviet Caucasus are far more amenable to study and provide some interesting insights into the notion of super-longevity.

Foremost is the complete lack of valid documentation for reports of super-longevity, since all census information is based on verbal replies unsubstantiated by documentation. Internal identity cards came into use in the U.S.S.R. in 1932 for urban areas only, and dates of birth were recorded from oral information. Furthermore, in the Moslem areas of the Caucasus, where the centenarian claims are most exaggerated, there is no birth registration at all. Not one of 500 super-centenarians questioned in the Caucasus could produce a valid document in support of his claim.

In most industrialized countries tendencies to exaggerate age do occur more frequently in the very young and very old age groups, whereas persons in their middle years are more apt to reduce their real ages. General census statistics in the U.S.S.R. clearly show that there are three times as many females as males 90 to 99 years of age, yet the male Georgian super-centenarians clearly outnumber the females. Is it more likely for super-centenarian men than women to exaggerate their age?

Dr. Zhores Medvedev, a Russian gerontologist now living in London, offers some interesting notions about why these claims persist. Very old people in these regions enjoy the highest levels of social authority— the older a person is, the more respect and honor he receives: "The most elderly people are almost regarded as saints." These traditions stimulate age exaggeration especially when documentation does not exist, and there are no living witnesses to contradict the claims. Furthermore, the national and international publicity surrounding the super-longevous — images on postage stamps, frequent news media photographs and stories, the establishment of centenarian bands and chorale and dance groups — have made these regions profitable tourist attractions. The Novosti Press Agency itself derives income from the sale of stories and photographs of the super-centenarians to the news media in other countries.

Associated with these claims of super-longevity and providing further fuel for exaggeration is the political propaganda which unabashedly refers to these people as a special social achievement of the Soviet Union. Articles in central newspapers and magazines with such titles as "The U.S.S.R. — State of Longevity" promote this legend. Dr. Medvedev cites statements from purported "scholarly" academic publications, for example: "The Soviet Union is the country with the record longevity of human beings. The number of centenarians is increasing parallel with our approach to the creation of a communist society."

That Joseph Stalin was a Georgian is also significant to the legend of the Soviet centenarians. Stalin was very much interested in the phenomenon of super-longevity and because of this interest, local Georgian authorities were anxious to provide more and more cases of longevous people. But perhaps the most reasonable explanation for the genesis of this phenomenon in the Soviet Union is the likelihood that hundreds of thousands of known deserters and draft dodgers of the First World War and the Russian Revolution (most of whom were from the Caucasus) used their fathers' documents (most with the same forename) to falsify their own ages. In order to maintain the fiction, they have had to continue the masquerade and have exaggerated their ages even further when the several benefits cited were likely to accrue.

Tampering with Our Biological Clocks

If the control of aging is dependent upon an understanding of the basic biological processes, one profoundly important question arises: How desirable is it to be able to manipulate our biological clocks? The answer to this question is not simple. Who would ask: What are the goals of cancer research, or of cardiovascular or stroke research? The answers are so obvious as to preclude asking the question. But the goals of gerontological research are quite a different matter because we are not certain whether "resolution" of age changes will indeed benefit the individual and/or society as a whole. Many different biological resolutions can be suggested but each has an important potential side effect. Take, for example, the possibility that we might be able to eliminate totally all diseases. If we could, and no control were had on the age-related physiological decrements produced by the biological clock itself, we would create a society whose members would live full, physically vigorous, youthful lives until the stroke of midnight on (say) their ninetieth birthday — at which time they would drop dead!

If, on the other hand, we were to learn how to tamper with our biological clocks, at what "time" would one choose to reset his own clock? Surely one wouldn't choose to spend an additional ten years suffering from the infirmities of old age — yet that might, initially, be the only way to intervene. We are presently hard put to deal with a mean maximum life span of 80 years, to say nothing of the further social, economic, and political dislocations that might occur if we added a decade to this figure. A third consideration of clock tampering is the prospect of spending more years at a particular stage of our lives. Your clock might be made to stall for ten years at a chronological age of 20. Is this desirable? Each of us, after pondering this provocative question, would likely agree that the time at which we would like our biological clocks arrested should correspond to those years in which maximum life-satisfaction and productivity occurred. Yet this is a decision one can only make retrospectively.

A more complex question is: When in the human life span are individuals most productive? An interesting and exhaustive study of this question was made by Dr.

Harvey C. Lehman in 1953; some of the results appear in Table 2. The conclusion from this data is that, depending upon the particular area of human endeavor, the period of maximum productivity can occur at any time during the human life span. Clock tampering is a game that very few of us can play intelligently.

Current Research in Aging

Biological research in aging can be divided into two broad categories: descriptive and hypothesis-testing. Most investigators believe that the era of descriptive research in gerontology is ending. For many species, including man, a voluminous literature now exists describing age-related changes at the cell, tissue, organ, and whole animal level. The likelihood that these descriptive studies, if continued, will yield any meaningful clues as to the mechanism of aging is remote. Rather, attention now is being focused on the formulation and testing of hypotheses.

Excluding those hypotheses rooted in genetic mechanisms, several theories of aging currently under study involve events occurring at an organizational level higher than the gene or other information-containing molecules. These theories include immunological mechanisms, the age-accelerating effect of radiation energy, the effect of free radicals, and changes in collagen chemistry. (Free radicals are highly reactive chemical entities produced during biological reactions which can combine with and impair the function of important molecules. Collagen is the most abundant protein in most vertebrates and is susceptible to structural changes with time that many gerontologists believe can produce the characteristic age changes seen in skin, tendon, bone, cartilage, and connective tissue.)

Yet all of these theories involve either events occurring at levels of biological complexity that do not apply to all animals that age or secondary or tertiary changes mani-

TABLE 2

Human Creativity, Leadership and Income as a Function of Age

Discipline or area	Age range
Sciences	
Chemistry	26–30
Mathematics, Physics	30–34
Geology, Astronomy	35–39
Botany	30–34
Genetics, Entomology, Psychology	30–39
Bacteriology, Physiology, Pathology	35–39
Philosophy	
Logic, Ethics, Aesthetics, Philosophy	35–39
Metaphysics	40–44
Contributions to Economics and Political Science	30–39
The Arts	
Oil Paintings	32–36
American Sculpture	35–39
Modern Architecture	40–44
Oil Paintings by Contemporary Artists	40–44
Instrumental Selections	25–29
Vocal Solos, Symphonies	30–34
Pastoral Poetry, Narrative Poetry	25–29
Short Stories	30–34
"Most Influential Books"	35–39
Novels, "Best Books," Best Sellers	40–44
Athletes	
Professional Football Players	22–26
Professional Prizefighters	25–26
Professional Baseball Players	27–28
Professional Tennis Players	25–29
Automobile Racers	26–30
Leading Contestants at Chess	29–33
Professional Golfers	31–36
Winners of Bowling Championships	31–36
Income	
Receivers of "Earned" Annual Incomes of $50,000 or More	60–64
Outstanding Commercial and Industrial Leaders	65–69
Receivers of Annual Incomes of $1,000,000 or More	80–89
Leaders	
College Presidents	50–54
U.S. Presidents Prior to Truman	55–59
Popes	82–92

fested by fundamental events occurring at the gene level. It is more likely that the fundamental causes of age changes are the result of gene actions which in turn produce changes at higher orders of complexity.

Aging of Cultured Human Cells

Of those observations made in the past ten years that bear on our understanding of the biology of aging, technological developments allowing for the growth of cells in a culture medium outside of an animal's body appear to have contributed significant new knowledge. Just as cell culture revolutionized virology in the 1950s and cytogenetics in the 1960s, many scientists believe that gerontology will be the benefactor in the 1970s. More than 50 years ago an inverse relationship was found between the growth rate of embryonic chick fibroblasts (structural cells) cultured in plasma clots and the age of the chicken supplying the plasma. A few years later it was found that the latent period preceding the first appearance of cells migrating from tissue scraps grown *in vitro* (in laboratory glassware) increased as a function of donor age. The last observation made prior to the renaissance of cell culture techniques in 1950 was Alexis Carrel's purported finding that fibroblasts grown from a chicken's heart could proliferate indefinitely in culture, in other words, were immortal. Since 1950 the first two observations have been confirmed, but the last, and by far the most important to gerontologists, has not.

We now know that it is a *rare* event when human or animal cells spontaneously acquire the property of unlimited capability for division *in vitro*. Furthermore, such cells are inevitably abnormal in one or more properties, often resembling cancer cells. Since aging is a property of normal cells in the animal *(in vivo)*, it follows that we should be studying similar cells in bottle culture *(in*

vitro). It cannot be emphasized too strongly that immortality *in vitro* is a property of abnormal, not normal, cells.

Fourteen years ago our laboratory experiments demonstrated that normal human cells do have a limited ability to multiply *in vitro*. We interpreted this to be an expression of human aging at the single-cell level. We further suggested that manifestations of aging might very well have an intracellular basis and, in particular, might involve the genetic apparatus of the cell.

In our earlier work with normal human embryonic diploid (having the correct number and form of chromosomes) cell strains, we observed that after a period of active multiplication (generally less than one year) these cells demonstrated an increased doubling time (normally 24 hours), gradual cessation of cell division, accumulation of cellular debris, and ultimately total degeneration of the culture. These phenomena, called *Phase III*, are now commonly observed by cell culturists when growing normal cells from many types of human and animal tissues. Cultured fibroblast populations derived from normal human fetal tissue undergo about 50 population doublings over a period of about ten months. We view this limit as an innate characteristic of all normal cells grown *in vitro*. The so-called immortal chick heart cell population described by Alexis Carrel is now known to have been contaminated with fresh chicken cells which were inadvertently added to the culture at each weekly feeding.

Because of the limited doubling potential of cultured normal cells, studies on any single strain would be severely curtailed were it not possible to preserve these cells at sub-zero temperatures for apparently indefinite periods of time. The reconstitution of frozen cells has revealed that, regardless of the doubling level reached by the population at the time it was preserved, the cells "remember" at what doubling level they were arrested in the cold and proliferate from that point to a total of about 50 after they are reconstituted.

Since 1962 we have reconstituted one vial of the same cell strain approximately each month and all have yielded cell populations that have undergone 50 ± 10 cumulative population doublings.

In 1965 all 13 human *embryo* lung fibroblast populations we studied reached senescence after undergoing about 50 population doublings. When human *adult* fibroblast populations were tested an average of 20 population doublings occurred. Although we were unable to find a precise correlation between the specific donor age and the number of cell population doublings, it was clearly evident that cultures derived from embryo donors as a group underwent significantly more population doublings (40 to 60) than those derived from adults as a group (10 to 30). More recently, however, it has been shown that there is an inverse proportionality between the number of population doublings that occurs in cultured normal human fibroblasts and the age of the donor.

Aging of Normal Cells Derived from Different Animal Species

A phenomenon that is fundamental to our understanding of the biology of aging is that interspecies differences in life spans are far greater than individual intraspecies differences. A fruitfly is ancient in 40 days, a mouse at 3 years, a horse at 30, a man at 100, and some tortoise species not until about 150 years. Although for man we are preoccupied with the variability within a species and would like to know how far it can be stretched, I believe that our understanding would be furthered best by inquiring into the mechanism that sets the life span of each species in a relatively narrow range and on a scale that embraces several centuries. Only recently have sufficient laboratory studies

TABLE 3
The Finite Lifetime of Cultured Normal Embryonic Human and Animal Fibroblasts

Species	Range of population doublings for cultured normal embryo fibroblasts	Mean maximum life span in years
Galapagos tortoise	90–125	175(?)
Man	40–60	110
Mink[a]	30–34	10
Chicken	15–35	30(?)
Mouse	14–28	3.5

[a] Data from 20 embryos.

been done with the cells of several different animal species to provide us with a clue to this intriguing question. A summary of the available data appears in Table 3.

The Finite Lifetime of Normal Cells in Vivo

If the concept of the finite lifetime of cells grown *in vitro* is related to aging in the whole animal, then it will be most important to know whether normal cells, given the opportunity, will reproduce indefinitely *in vivo*. If all of the multitude of animal cell types were continually renewed, without loss of function or capacity for self-renewal, we would expect the organs composed of such cells to function normally indefinitely and their host to live on forever. Unhappily, however, renewal cell populations do not occur in most tissues, and when they do, a reproductive limit is often manifest.

Most animal species obviously have a specific life span. When the animal dies, the normal cells composing its tissues die as well. The important question then becomes: Is it possible to circumvent the death of normal animal cells that results from the death of the "host" by serial transplantation of marked normal cells to a new, young, inbred host each time the current host approaches old age? Under these conditions do transplanted normal cells proliferate indefinitely?

Data from four different laboratories, in which mammary tissue, skin, and blood-forming cells were employed, indicate that (1) normal cells, serially transplanted to inbred hosts, do not survive indefinitely; (2) the trauma of transplantation does not appear to influence the results; and (3) survival time is related to the age of the grafted tissue. Under similar conditions of tissue transplantation, cancer cell populations can be serially passed indefinitely. This leads to the conclusion that in order for mammalian somatic (non-germ) cells to become biologically "immortal" they must first be induced to the cancerous state in the organism or in culture, whereupon they can then be subcultivated or transplanted indefinitely.

Aging Due to Loss of Function

To be sure, the several classes of cells that are incapable of division in mature animals (e.g., neurons, muscle cells) may play a greater role in the expression of age changes than the cell classes in which division commonly occurs. It is therefore important to indicate that the cessation of division activity is only one functional decrement whose genetic basis may be similar to that which causes functional losses in non-dividing cells. Age changes orchestrated by gene action may not result from loss of cell division capacity but simply from loss of function — function which might be measured as reduced division capacity or as a decrement in any other cell property.

Is it possible that a limit on cell proliferation or function in some strategic organ could orchestrate the entire phenomenon of aging? Sir MacFarlane Burnet, a noted Australian immunologist, has speculated that, if this is so, the most likely organ is the thymus and its dependent tissues. Burnet reasons that aging is largely mediated by autoimmune processes that are influenced by progressive weakening of the function of immunological surveillance. He further argues that weakening of immunological surveillance may be related to weakness of the thymus-dependent immune system. He concludes that the thymus and its dependent tissues are subject to a reproductive limit similar to the Phase III phenomenon or aging evidenced by human cells in culture. Whether the role played by the thymus and its dependent tissues as the pacemaker in the aging process is important or not still remains to be established.

Can Cell Death Be Normal?

The death of cells and the destruction of certain tissues and organs is, indeed, a normal part of morphogenic or developmental sequences in animals. It is the common method of eliminating those organs and tissues that are useful only in the larval, embryonic, or early developmental stages of many animals, for example, the gills of the tadpole, primitive kidney tissue, and the thymus in man. During the development of vertebrate limbs, cell death and cell resorption model not only digits but also thigh and upper arm contours. In the limbs of vertebrates the "death clocks" function on schedule even when tissue grafts are made. Thus cell death, heralded by functional loss, is an intrinsic part of normal development and its causes may be similar to those producing similar cell changes as animals age.

In my view, it is very unlikely that animals age because one or more important cell populations lose their capacity to proliferate. As we have shown, normal cells have a finite capacity for replication, and this finite limit is rarely, if ever, reached by cells within the organism but is, of course, demonstrable in tissue culture. I would suggest that functional losses that occur in some cells prior to their loss of division capacity (and which can be observed *in vitro*) produce age changes in animals much before their normal cells have reached their maximum division limit. The subtler biochemical changes now known to herald the approaching loss of division capacity are likely to play a greater role in the expression of aging and result in death of the individual animal well before his cells fail to divide. As previously mentioned, the *in vitro* endpoint measured by us as loss of capacity for division is simply a very convenient and reproducible system but may have little to do with the actual cause of aging.

If the finite lifetime of normal human cells is about 50 population doublings, can that number account for all of the cells produced during our lifetime? Fifty population doublings is equivalent to about 20 million tons of cells — considerably more than what is produced by anyone during a lifetime.

Hypotheses

Probably no other area of scientific inquiry abounds with as many untested or untestable theories as does the biology of aging. Three of the most tenable hypotheses on which most other theories ultimately rest, are based on scientific advancements that have resulted in a better understanding of the molecular biology of the genetic apparatus. Several considerations, not the least of which is the constancy of the life span within each animal species, lead to the conclusion that the probable cause of aging is somehow contained in the genetic code.

The first hypothesis suggests that the manifestations of aging are the result of the playing out of the genetic program, which contains specific information or "aging genes" that code for the senile changes presaging death of the organism. All developmental changes that take place can be considered to result from a pre-existing genetic program that plays out as a function of time. Consider the occurrence of menopause or

graying of the hair, two examples of biological events whose expression generally occurs late in life, is predictable, and is probably genetically based. Advocates of the pre-written genetic program theory argue further that the survival of a species depends on the ability of its members to reach the age of procreation — and that what occurs after is essentially irrelevant. The biological changes that do occur during this irrelevant period we recognize as aging.

This reasoning has been extended further to argue that profound clinical manifestations of aging occur only in man and in his domestic or zoo animals. If the human life span, for example, extends along a scale of ten units and if age changes resulting from physiological losses begin to occur at point five, then 50 percent of the human life span is spent in a period of physiological decline. Unprotected wild animals, by analogy, also reveal physiological losses at point five, but may spend only 10 percent of their potential remaining life span in that decline because they quickly succumb to disease and predators. Thus, the profound senile changes seen in man may actually be artifacts of civilization, inadvertently unmasked because of man's success in controlling his environment.

A second hypothesis involving the genetic apparatus has many of the features of the preceding argument, except that specific "aging genes" do not exist; the organism simply runs out of genetic information, which results in those biological changes that we call aging.

The third hypothesis, now embraced by a large community of gerontologists, maintains that the genetic apparatus, although admittedly programmed for sequential biological events, does not include a program for senescent changes per se, but that molecules simply accumulate inaccurate information or misspecified proteins. The loss of accurate or reliable information is seen to occur from an accumulation of random events which damage the essential information-containing molecules. When a threshold of "hits," "damage," "insults," or "errors" is reached, normal biological activities cease and the manifestation of age-related changes becomes evident.

The precise nature of damage to such essential molecules is not clearly understood, but that it does occur is known. Furthermore, systems for repairing some of these misspecified macromolecules are known, and one might account for the broad range of life spans in animal species as equivalent to the degree of perfection evolved by their respective repair systems. Medvedev has conjectured that the great duplication of identical message units in human DNA, for example, is simply due to the vulnerability to errors inherent in this system, and that the presence of highly redundant information serves to lengthen the time before "hits" accumulate and completely confound the message bit.

Whether any of the aforementioned hypotheses, alone or in combination, will ultimately explain the biology of aging cannot now be determined. Nevertheless, most gerontologists would argue that the fundamental events which orchestrate age-related changes are likely to be found in our genetic machinery.

The Control of Human Aging

Biological gerontology has long been regarded as an impractical pseudoscience dealt with only by eccentrics and charlatans. Philosophers, theologians, and scientists themselves have helped perpetuate this attitude with their long history of apologism — the belief that the prolongation of life is neither possible nor desirable. Neglect of research on aging by qualified biologists can also be traced to the field's historic lack of scientific respectability — for no area of biology has been more deceptive to the gullible nor more profitable to the unscrupulous.

Merely consider the four major age-decelerating hoaxes perpetrated in this century: first, the fermented milk (yogurt) craze of the early 1900s; second, the transplantation of animal gonads to man attempted in the 1920s; third, the cytotoxic serum advocates of the 1940s; and finally, the current fads described as "cell therapy," "cryogenic preservation," and the highly touted but unproven nostrum Gerovital H_3.

None of these approaches to the control of aging is supported by genuine scientific data. The likelihood of proving the efficacy of any treatment producing significant life-extension is, for our generation, very remote. Scientific common sense dictates that in order to prove the worth of any such procedure a treated and untreated group of a significantly large number of individuals must be studied either throughout their life span or for a specific number of years subsequent to treatment. Only when statistically significant differences in longevity are found between treated and untreated groups can any claim for efficacy be made. None of the previously or currently in vogue nostrums have been subjected to this essential test.

Most authoritative suggestions for controlling human aging propose to slow down the process rather than entirely circumvent its inevitability. Studies which reduced body temperature a few degrees have resulted in a significant increase in longevity of fruitflies, rotifers, and fish. In man, it is thought that a reduction in body temperature of two to three degrees centigrade would result in an extension of the life span by about 20 years. If the presence of free radicals accelerates aging, then it is conjectured that the use of antioxidants (inhibitors of free radicals) will ameliorate the phenomenon. Work with mice to which antioxidants have been fed has been interpreted to show a 30 to 40 percent increase in mean life span.

Perhaps the most practical approach to increasing longevity in man will be based on the experiments of Dr. Clive McCay of Cornell University, in which he showed that underfeeding rats by providing a very low calorie intake (but all essential nutrients) resulted in a 50 percent increase in longevity. Similar results have been obtained in rotifers, silkworms, fruitflies, bees, chickens, and other animals. The effect, however, is most pronounced when low-calorie diets are started while the animals are still very young; this results in a stretching out of the entire genetic program over a longer period of time. Infancy, puberty, maturity, adulthood, and aging simply occur later than usual, with no particular period seemingly lengthened more than others. If this low-caloric approach is practical for extending the human life span, the question then becomes: Which is more important, the quantity of life, or the quality?

Goals for the Old

In this discussion of research on aging, I have purposely avoided the notion of biological immortality, for one principal reason — to attain immortality is so far beyond any practical realization that any discussion of it would be more science fiction than likely science fact. Furthermore, among the most serious effects of an even modest success in increasing human life expectancy are the societal consequences. Most gerontological sociologists believe that even as little as a five-year increase in life expectancy would be so profound as to probably rupture our present economic, medical, and welfare institutions.

In spite of the apparent dilemma in establishing goals for aging research, I believe there is one wholly desirable — and even attainable — short-range objective: to reduce the physiological losses associated with biological aging so that vigorous, productive, non-dependent lives could be led up until the mean maximum life span of, say, 90 years.

Gerontological research attempts to understand the biological basis of aging in order to extend the number of vigorous and productive years and to reduce the time spent in senility and the infirmities of old age. If tampering with our biological clocks ever comes a reality, I believe that it would be tragic in the extreme if such clock-tampering resulted only in the extension of those years spent in declining physical and mental health.

Having stated this objective, I feel the prospects of achieving it are beginning to brighten. One important development was the establishment in 1974 of the National Institute on Aging at the National Institutes of Health in Bethesda, Maryland. For the first time, the discipline of gerontology has been given a degree of national recognition to ensure that significant research efforts will be devoted to understanding the biology of aging. The field now has a level of national visibility that is almost commensurate with the magnitude of the problem. But more important is the long-awaited recognition that something can and should be done about biological aging.

Bodily Changes with Aging

ISADORE ROSSMAN

The clinician who is objective in his evaluation of aging changes should be as impressed by individuality and variability as he is by their universality. Time of onset, rate of progression, and clinical import of aging processes are strikingly variable and should be kept in mind lest the patient fall victim to inaccurate generalization and symbolic reactivity by the practitioner. This is despite the fact that true aging processes have been defined as possessing the characteristics of universality, progressiveness, irreversibility, and being essentially detrimental. Evaluation problems are compounded because age changes can be classified as (a) anatomical, which includes alterations such as loss of stature or that loss of cells from any tissues somewhat pejoratively referred to as "senile atrophy"; (b) functional, such as declines in cardiac output, vital capacity, renal excretion, nerve conduction velocity, etc.; (c) pathological, of which common examples would be arthritic changes in many joints, sclerotic changes in arteries, cataract formation, and the like. Some of these alterations, for example the arcus senilis, are so common as to elicit little or no comment on many records of physical examinations. In Western society, at least, such also would be the case for mild to moderate degrees of atherosclerosis even with diminutions in blood flow to some important organs.

Though expected and accepted, there are hopeful implications in the fact that most of the pathologic or other changes observed in older patients are not universal and thus may not be true aging changes (1). Therefore, therapeutic programs and prophylactic regimes may serve to diminish and perhaps prevent many of them. Better understanding of the impact of such factors as diet (salt, fats, fiber, total calories, calcium intakes) may make great inroads on hypertensive cardiovascular disease, several serious colonic diseases, atherosclerosis, and osteoporosis, all common in old age. The effect of smoking and the other variables elicited in the Framingham longitudinal study marked a historical milestone in our approach to the atherosclerosis of the elderly (2). Consideration of another group of common aging changes such as osteoarthritis further exemplifies the problems of classification and orientation. Narrowing of intervertebral discs and osteoarthritic changes of the vertebrae have a linear relationship both to age and, quite clearly, to use (3,4). The major osteoarthritic changes in the vertebral spine occur in the regions of greatest mobility, at the cervical and lumbar levels. These use-related changes are universal and have sometimes been referred to as "wear and tear changes."

Aging human beings typically present a variable mix of morphologic and functional modifications, not all of which are "true"

Source: Considerably abridged from Rossman, I. Bodily changes with aging. In E. W. Busse & D. G. Blazer (eds.), *Handbook of geriatric psychiatry.* New York: Van Nostrand Reinhold, 1980, pp. 125–146. Copyright 1980 by Van Nostrand Reinhold. Reprinted by permission.

aging changes. Classification systems which dwell on inevitability, progressiveness, and irreversibility can be taken with a grain of salt, and may have less validity than anticipated in an ongoing clinical setting.

Changes in Stature and Posture

Old people tend to be short, and even the seasoned geriatrician may be surprised when a patient initially encountered bedridden, becomes ambulatory and turns out to be well under 5 feet in height. A number of factors contribute to this. Older patients were born at a time when average heights were less by several inches than is currently the case. Increase in height during the 20th century is regarded by physical anthropologists as a secular trend ascribable to better environments, which now seems to be plateauing, at least in better nourished populations. An example would be the intergenerational jump of over 2 inches in Italo-Americans noted by Damon (5). Thus shortness in our elderly is in part due to shortness at maturity. However, a lifetime loss of 1 to 2 inches has been demonstrated in longitudinal studies. The decrement in height appears to start in the fifth decade and is progressive thereafter (6,7). Initial losses are ascribed to shrinkage in the intervertebral discs followed by declines in height of vertebrae. Thus loss of height with aging is primarily due to shrinkage in trunk length, and indeed the length of the long bones in general is unaltered.

In females, the loss of height is commonly aggravated by osteoporosis, with a bone loss which is particularly manifest in vertebrae. As osteoporotic vertebrae narrow, particularly in the thoracic spin, characteristic bowing with marked loss of stature results. Shrinkage in height and deformity, needless to say, has an impact on the self-image. Women complain of getting smaller, of "dowager's hump," and of the ugliness of the round back deformity.

Other Contour Changes

Redistribution in the fat and subcutaneous tissue possesses a life history of its own. Its shifting about accounts for many of the contour changes seen in the progression from youth to old age. In general, one might characterize the shift by contrasting the firm and fully packed roundness of youth to the sagging asymmetry and deepening hollows seen in the aged. This is not to disregard the importance of constitutional factors such as degrees of endomorphy and mesomorphy and weight fluctuations due to calorie intake. In most individuals a loss of fat from depots in the extremities and the face becomes apparent past age 50. This loss of fat can be obvious despite a gain in weight in preferred depots such as the upper arm, scapular area and abdomen. Differences between the sexes are also apparent. For example, the upper arm in women possesses a thicker skinfold which is preserved longer than in males. In males with aging, the triceps skinfold may begin to shrink while the subscapular skinfold concurrently shows increased deposition (Figure 1). Deposition of periumbilical and buttock fat in both the sexes becomes increasingly manifest past the sixth decade. This, too, is more marked in the female, sometimes standing in marked contrast to the loss of fat in the hands and forearms. Attenuation of fat in the subcutaneous tissue of the face is cosmetically important. With its loss increased wrinkling and the more haggard "older" appearance ensues. Ethnic differences partly attributable to pigment protection play some part in this, as it is a matter of everyday observation that shrinkage and wrinkling of the face occurs at a lesser rate in blacks and Asians than in lighter skinned whites. Decrements in facial fat may act as an inhibition (or excuse) against weight reduction programs, since the fat loss component increases the aged look.

Despite the apparent loss of fat in sub-

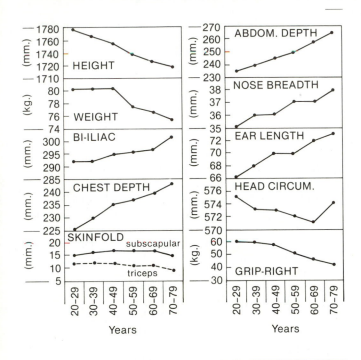

FIGURE 1
Age-related anthropometric findings in Boston veterans. Though
derived from cross-sectional data, they are in agreement
with longitudinal measurements.

cutaneous fatty depots it often comes as a surprise to learn that the fat content of the human body reaches a maximum in the older years, higher than in infancy, childhood or middle age (8,9). The rising fat content is notable in several sites: in muscle, increasing numbers of fat cells appear between muscle fibers and larger muscle groupings. The transformation can perhaps be grossly likened to that which occurs from veal to beef. In addition, "internalized fat," fat in the viscera, between the organs, including also the constituent parts of the organs, also rises. As a result of absolute rise in fat content, the specific gravity of the ag-

ing human body decreases (Figure 2), since fat is the only constituent with a specific gravity of less than 1.

Muscle

A bodily decline in muscle mass, and, therefore, in strength, seems to be characteristic of the aging process. It is not, as is sometimes thought, a disuse atrophy. Smaller upper extremity muscles are noted in older working longshoremen, and shrinkage occurs in the eye and laryngeal muscles, muscles used continually into old age. Involuntary changes result in disappearance

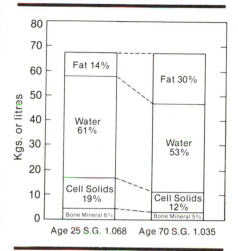

FIGURE 2

Aging changes in major body components contrasting "reference males" ages 25 and 70. Due to rising fat content, specific gravity falls. Diminished water and cell solids reflects loss in lean body mass (From Fryer, J. H. pp. 59–78 in N. W. Shock (Ed.) *Biological Aspects of Aging*, 1962. N. Y. Columbia University Press.)

of some muscle fibers with shrinkage and fragmentation of other muscle fibers along with the above mentioned fat infiltration. Sex differences related to the larger muscle mass of the male are obvious. Of interest also is the earlier onset of this decline in the male. This decline is evidenced by the thirties and parallels the decrement in muscle strength that also begins at this time. The regression continues in the ensuing decades and accelerates late in life. In contrast, the female with a lesser initial muscle mass has a steady state through the fourth and fifth decades; the decline in the muscle mass of the female thus appears later. The rate of decline is steeper in both the sexes past 60. Though an exercise program in a sedentary middle-aged individual with involuted muscles may produce a measurable rise in his radioactive

potassium, remeasurements of these individuals as the years go by still shows the inevitable nature of this phenomenon. There is thus a clear anatomical basis for the complaints of older people of increasing weakness in carrying out their usual tasks. Why muscle cells degenerate and muscle mass declines with aging remains a mystery.

Bone and Joint Changes

Change in the bony skeleton is complicated by the existence of hypertrophic and anabolic processes simultaneously with catabolic ones. The bone is a unique tissue in simultaneously being an arena in which mineral deposition by osteoblasts and resorption by osteoclasts are concurrent. With age, overall bone loss triumphs. However, it is now well established that bony growth can and does go on in the middle and late years. Increments in growth of the bone, such as rib, metacarpal, and the femoral cortex have been demonstrated by various investigators (10,11,12). Finding of an approximately 3.5% increase in the width of the pelvis in both sexes that goes on into old age has modified earlier thoughts that dimensions of the bony pelvis were fixed after maturity. The skull thickens into advanced old age, with some sutures such as the masto-occipital and parietomastoid not closing over until ages 70 to 80 (13). In many long bones deposition on the surface may be occurring simultaneously with resorption from the endosteum. In the case of the femur this leads to a slightly wider bone with a wider marrow cavity and, therefore, structurally weaker (14).

Of more significance in the bony weakening is the usually slow progressive loss of osteoid tissue generally. This is the phenomenon of osteoporosis, already noted in relationship to statural shortening due to vertebral osteoporosis. The gradual demineralization of bone is the background to that most important fracture in old age, that of the femur. The risk factors for osteoporosis are being female, having a low calcium intake for many years, and being white of northern European extraction with a delicate build to start with. Clinical osteoporosis and femoral fractures are both less marked in blacks (15).

Changes in joints are generally ascribed to use and stress of weight bearing, multiplied by a time factor. But here too, other variables are involved. Obvious thickening appears as early as the thirties with gross distortions taking place over the next decade or two. There is no evidence that use or abuse plays a significant role, and such osteoarthritic changes in the fingers are not correlated to changes elsewhere.

Though seldom more than a cosmetic disorder, some pain may be complained of. The thickening and distortion of the fingers may also serve as a daily early warning signal to the person of the uncontrollable nature of age-related changes. Among the most common and predictable joint changes are those that occur in the spine. Such vertebral changes are sufficiently time-related as to be of value to the physical anthropologist in estimating age. In addition to narrowing of discs, the characteristic changes are the bony proliferations known as osteophytes. These occur on both the anterior and posterior aspects of vertebrae.

Studies of the knees have documented the early onset and age-related progression of change (16). Microscopic changes in the knee cartilages are visible during the second decade of life. The originally smooth glistening cartilage progressively thereafter shows fibrillar degeneration, fragmentation and irregularity. As this proceeds through the middle years, hypertrophic changes may take place and the end result may be a more or less complete loss of cartilage with eburnation of the bony surfaces and variable degrees of osteophyte formation. Osteoarthritic changes in the knees, like those of

vertebrae, thus seem inevitable. Often, there is no significant disability and even where the disorder is well established, evidence of effusion and pain may be episodic and respond to appropriate therapies. Earlier onset seems to be characteristic of overweight middle-aged women. What has been said of the knee seems to be true also for the hip. Severe change in this joint may lead to such profound disability as to warrant hip replacement. Oddly, the ankle more or less escapes osteoarthritic change, despite its location and weight-bearing function.

Anthropometric changes with aging have long been an area of interest to the physical anthropologist. Some of this literature is discussed elsewhere, and illustrated in Figure 1. As can be seen, in the male veterans lengthening and broadening of the nose, lengthening of the ears, decline in grip strength as an index to muscle regression, increasing bi-iliac and antero-posterior chest measures are some of the characteristic age-related changes. Over all, similar changes occur in females, the greatest sex-related variable perhaps being differences in redistribution of fat in the skin folds. Shrinking muscle mass is relatively greater in the male, and in the aging male the decline in hemoglobin is also relatively more marked. This is attributed to decline in androgens, so that the male-female difference in red blood cell mass diminishes. By this and other parameters (e.g. muscle, body hair) the two sexes become more alike in old age.

Ectodermal Changes

On inspection of the aged individual, it is obvious that most of what one sees are ectodermal changes. One observes wrinkling, decrease in hair with graying, atrophy of subcutaneous tissue, or the arcus senilis and these chiefly contribute to our estimate of age and our reaction. Hair loss with aging is universal although subject to a great deal of variability and having an important sex-related component. Patterns of baldness in the male have important genetic determinants, being transmitted from mother to son and unfolding under the influence of androgens. Ensuing patterns of baldness are a matter of every day observation: when severe in the male, almost all of the head hair may be lost except at the periphery. Such peripheral hairs when transplanted into the formerly bald areas continued to thrive, thus pointing up some of the unknowns in the hair loss process. Even in the absence of this hereditary component, thinning of scalp hair does occur in progressive fashion in middle-aged and older males and at a lesser rate in most females. Many women note a distressing amount of hair loss post menopausally, and it is unclear as to why this affects some women earlier and to a greater degree than others. In addition to hair loss, hairs that remain tend to be finer, so that the thinning is both quantitative and qualitative. Also, body hair tends to be lost especially past age 50. Very old men and women have very little body hair (17). In part, this seems to be an atrophy much like the atrophy of other components of the subcutaneous tissue. Striking degrees of hair loss in the axilla may occur in women. Here the loss is from the periphery to the center and thus occurs in the reverse manner to that seen during puberty. Japanese women have virtually no axillary hair 10 years post menopause and aging Caucasian women exhibit fewer and fewer axillary hairs. Pubic hairs also become sparse. Graying of the hair has traditionally and symbolically been recognized as an aging parameter. It begins in the twenties, tends to progress thereafter, but does show considerable variability. Damon et al. (18) found that of many parameters, the one that best correlated with biologic aging was the extent of graying.

Wrinkling of the skin of the face is well known to be worsened by solar exposure. However, even in the most sun-protected individuals, use lines proceed linearly with aging. These are the predictable indentations of the skin produced by the action of the muscles of facial expression. They result in the familiar parallel wrinkles of the forehead, the fan-shaped groups at the corners of the eyes, the radial wrinkles around the mouth, all of which are more marked in older persons.

Despite computer generated correlates such as those linking graying and age, there is considerable question as to whether we have any quantitative ectodermal change that is a simple parameter to the aging process. There is no reason to doubt that the many changes in the skin described above may have some positive correlate with age-related changes in deeper tissues and even the brain. On the basis of present knowledge, it would be difficult to assess the clinical value or validity of the correlations in a great body of aging data. Gray hairs may be more a sign of experiential wisdom, as has often been thought in some societies, than an indicator of aging decline, as has been implied by some investigators.

Arterial Changes

Elongation, sometimes associated with increasing tortuosity, occurs in many of the larger arteries with aging. In part, it is thought to reflect the loss of the elastic tissue and increased stiffness of connective tissue in the arterial wall, changes which are characteristic of collagen in other parts of the body. The process is certainly abetted by hypertension. On chest x-ray, widening of the aorta and elongation are commonly observed in the older patient especially if blood pressures are elevated. Below the diaphragm, a similar elongation and bowing in the abdominal aorta may simulate early abdominal aneurysm. A serpentine tortuosity of the brachial artery in the subcutaneous tissue of the arm is easily seen in some older persons. Variable degrees of coiling and kinking are found in carotid angiography and initially were also thought related to aging changes. However, some kinking has been found in cerebral angiograms in every decade from the 1st to the 8th, and Weibel and Fields (19) in reviewing the carotid angiograms of almost 1500 patients concluded that tortuosity and coiling of the internal carotid artery was a congenital condition which could worsen with aging of the artery but that kinking was an acquired condition which occurred later in life.

Declines in Organ Function

Since morphologic changes are often the visible base for functional change, it comes as no surprise that decremental functioning is characteristic of aging. Despite this, homeostasis is generally preserved although adaptive capacity to stress does diminish. As an example, body temperature will still be pegged at the normal level, though it may rise and fall excessively in different environments, hence an increased incidence of heat stroke and hypothermia (20). The somatic picture is quite variable: some primitive systems such as the gastrointestinal tract show comparatively little impairment through the life cycle, in contrast to the renal-excretory system which shows marked diminution in reserve. Similarly, cerebral cortical function is impaired far more than brain stem function. The endocrine system continues to function surprisingly well for a complex set of regulatory glands linked through the feedback of chemical messages. Some of the highlights and contrast from system to system are considered in the following:

Cardiovascular System

Contrary to previous statements, it is now thought that the heart normally undergoes a physiological hypertrophy with aging in the absence of hypertension. Despite this, the resting cardiac output decreases almost linearly with aging past maturity, the decrement being on the order of 30–40% between ages 25 and 65 (21). This exceeds the decline in lean body mass, but doubtless reflects diminished physiological need. In addition, when stressed, the cardiac output cannot be pushed to the same heights as in younger years, and the exercise-induced tachycardia achieves a lower peak level. In addition to these declines in physiological capacity, there is much impairment because of the widespread silent or overt existence of coronary atherosclerosis. Coronary artery disease progresses through the decades past 60 so that an increasing percentage of older individuals may quite slowly rather than dramatically develop congestive heart failure. In some homes for the elderly even in the ambulatory group, as many as half the group may need to be digitalized. Needless to say, most elderly persons pace themselves almost unconsciously in making appropriate adjustment to cardiac limitation. There is some reason to believe that continued vigorous exercise can favorably modify the normal rate of decline in cardiac capacitance.

The connective tissue of the arteries, as is true of connective tissue elsewhere, tends to stiffen with aging. This loss of elasticity contributes to the tendency of the arteries to elongate, to diminution in elastic recoil in the aorta and increased propagation of pulse wave, and to the widening of the pulse pressure. In addition, vascular sclerosis is well nigh universal, certainly in Western society, and is regarded by some as a normal aging change, up to some levels at least. Although most prominent clinically in the coronary arteries, atherosclerosis once manifest is always generalized to some degree.

Pulmonary Function

The vital capacity decreases with aging although total lung capacity remains more or less unchanged. The residual capacity doubles over the life span. Anthropometric studies suggest that some deepening of the chest is a normal aging change found in non-smokers and in various groups studied. In contrast, the maximum voluntary ventilation may decrease by up to 50% between 20 and 80, as do other pulmonary functional parameters such as the forced expiratory volume (22). Some of the anatomical changes have been likened to emphysema, but it is probable that the so-called ''senile emphysema'' represents dilatation of alveoli without breakdown of alveolar septa or the usual chronic bronchitis and out flow obstruction seen in the typical emphysema patient. With aging there is a lowered resting arterial oxygen tension ascribed to ventilation-perfusion defects which do not, however, affect the CO_2. Decreased ventilatory capacity is generally ascribed to stiffening of the tissues of the chest wall including its musculature, to calcification of the costal cartilages with decreased rib motion and other changes that alter lung compliance. Probably the shortness of breath complained of by elderly persons as they climb stairs represents a combination of both cardiac and pulmonary factors in an interaction which will diminish the capacity for exercise or other efforts. Also, chronic bronchitis and emphysema do rise with age and in varying degrees contribute to declining pulmonary function. It has been noted that a marked drop in vital capacity precedes a steep rise in mortality in the elderly. It has been ascribed to weakness superimposed on pulmonary aging changes.

Renal Excretory System

There is a sharp decline in the renal mass with aging. This anatomically reflects chiefly a continuing subtraction from the approximately 1 million nephrons present at birth. Both renal weight and number of nephrons decrease by approximately 30–40% over the life span. As a consequence the glomeruler filtration rate decreases 45% from age 20 to age 90. The renal plasma flow decreases slightly more over the same span. These declines in renal excretory capacity do not ordinarily impair the capacity to excrete such metabolites as urea or creatinine.

However, the aged kidney responds less well to the stresses that may be caused by infusions of large amounts of fluid or salt solutions. The diminished renal capacity is also the background to prolongation of the half life of some important drugs. Because of its diminished renal excretion, their daily maintenance dose may frequently be half that required by a younger person. Vascular diseases produced by hypertension and pyelonephritis are further frequent contributors to diminished renal function. For this and other reasons the elderly are far more likely to experience adverse drug reactions. For drugs whose route of excretion is mainly by way of the kidneys, cuts in the usual dosage in the very old may be mandated.

The Bladder

The reservoir function of the bladder also undergoes change with aging. As has been emphasized by the British geriatrician, J. C. Brocklehurst, the characteristics of the geriatric bladder are: (1) A diminished capacity; (2) a higher residual volume; thus a 100 cc. residual volume is not uncommon in many older women; (3) an earlier onset of tetanic bladder contractions. The compounded effects of all these changes in both sexes is to produce increased frequency, an increased sense of urgency, and increasing nocturia (23). Prostatic hypertrophy may further compound these findings, but these changes in bladder behavior hold for females and for males without prostate enlargement. However, the common development of prostatic hypertrophy may superimpose an often stealthy disease which has been known to result in uremia without the patient's consulting a physician. Even with the best of bladders, significant prostatic hypertrophy will generally make its presence known by marked increase in frequency day and night and weakness of the urinary stream, especially with dribbling and hesitancy on arising in the morning. Provided all these symptoms do not interfere markedly with rest and do not produce bladder infection or obstructive uropathy, it is possible to nurse many elderly men with various grades of prostatic hypertrophy through the remainder of their life span.

Urinary incontinence is the bane of patient, family, and geriatrician alike. As a single symptom, it may tip the scale in favor of institutionalization. Overflow incontinence results from obstructive or neurogenic interference with bladder emptying. An atonic bladder fills up (it may reach the umbilicus), and empties in small dribbling amounts as it attempts to decompress itself. Diabetes is one common cause of neurogenic bladder which is potentially reversible. Rather more common is the incontinence associated with organic brain changes. In the life history of the individual, the cerebral cortex assumes a dominant, chiefly inhibiting, role in control of bladder function in the early childhood years. Brain damage, whether due to stroke or neuronal degeneration, and rarely, other causes such as tumor, is the usual cause for uninhibited neurogenic bladder with incontinence. Incontinence can be transient or short-lived, as in association with surgical operations and anesthesia, in early phases of a stroke, a debilitating illness, or toxic delirium. With improvement, the urinary incontinence is reversed.

Changes in the Reproductive System

Aging changes in the female are ushered in more or less abruptly with the onset of the menopause, with cessation of usual ovarian activity and loss of menses. It may or may not be accompanied by such vasomotor changes as flushes and sweats. Some of the disability is explainable by the annoyance of nocturnal sweats with awakening, perhaps with depressive reactions to the realization of one of life's passages. ''Nervousness'' and irritability seem to be frequent. There is a striking decrease in estrogens particularly the ''true'' ovarian hormone, estradiol. The drop in estrogen alters the feedback circuit to the pituitary, and as a consequence there are marked rises in pituitary gonadotropins. The ovary is by no means reduced to a state of nonsecretion, however. Direct analyses of ovarian blood samples in postmenopausal women indicate a goodly output of androgens such as testosterone and androstenedione, with estrogen barely higher in concentration there than in the peripheral blood. The androstenedione is known to be converted by the peripheral tissues, probably the fat, to estrone. This may be the chief source of estrogen in the postmenopausal female but is not sufficient to prevent various atrophic phenomena in the reproductive tract and breasts. These progress with the passage of the years and include atrophic changes in the vagina, shrinkage of the body and cervix of the uterus, and involutionary changes in the vulva, labia, and loss of pubic hair (24).

As atrophy continues, there is a progressive narrowing and shrinkage of the vagina readily recognizable by loss of rugae, thinning of the epithelium, and fragility. This often leads to complaints of dyspareunia. On sexual stimulation, lubrication occurs more slowly and may be considerably less abundant than in the younger female. The total amount of lubrication may be inadequate, and supplementation by the usual lubricants may be necessary. Many of these changes are reversible by the administration of estrogen. Since other involutionary changes such as osteoporosis seem synchronous with the menopause, estrogens were widely prescribed throughout the 1950s and 1960s. There seems little doubt about the value of estrogen replacement, but this widespread use declined precipitously with the demonstration that the risk of endometrial carcinoma increased in estrogen-treated females, the risk being proportionate to dose and duration of estrogenic treatment. Many geriatricians do not hesitate to prescribe them in women who have had hysterectomies. It is also possible that the addition of progesterone to the estrogenic treatment, which may reproduce the normal cycle, may lessen if not abolish, the threat of endometrial cancer. This area is under active investigation currently.

In the male reproductive system, aging changes proceed much more slowly without the sudden decline in sex hormone production seen with the menopause. Though histologic and involutionary changes may be seen in the testes past the age of 50, adequate sperm production may continue for decades thereafter, and feisty old men in their 70s can certainly become fathers. There is no significant decline in blood testosterone levels up until age 60 at least and considerable individual variability thereafter. Thus, there is no hormonal background or explanation for the declining capacity to have intercourse which occurs in most males past 30. The normal range of this capacity is certainly subject to great individual variability in older men. Probably with males past 60–65 once a week to once a month might be considered to be a median range. This is to be contrasted with the far greater sexual frequency of earlier decades.

Older men take longer to reach erection and have a longer latent period following ejaculation before further erection is possible (25). The intensity of the muscle contractions associated with orgasm is diminished, and seminal spurts are considerably lessened. Some of the data on the decrement in frequency of sexual intercourse and the rising rate of impotence are noted in Tables 1 and 2.

What is most difficult to evaluate are the complaints of diminished potency or outright impotency in aging men (26). Diabetes, depression, thyroid disorders, falls in testosterone titers may all be coexistent, and are sometimes regarded as causal. There is even some loose talk about the "male menopause," with the possibility raised that with low testosterone titers, testosterone replacement therapy may be the key to successful treatment. Psychological factors are often easy to note, but depression may be secondary to the realization of other losses than that of potency. The data for males suggest an age-related concurrent rising incidence of outright impotence with the lessened capacity for sexual intercourse. It is, therefore, difficult to judge whether impotence in aging males always has a pathological base, or may fall under the bell-shaped curve describing a deterioration in any biological function. Granting that chronic illness, fatigue, depression, and other influences frequently associated with aging are clearly operative with many individuals does not gainsay the fact that overall the capacity to have intercourse as revealed in the surveys cited in Table 1 undergoes a more marked decrement with aging than almost any other physiological function.

Digestive System

There is a gradual loss of taste with age. This may be due to age-related atrophy of the taste buds or to repeated trauma to these

TABLE 1
Incidence of Impotence Cited by Various Authors.

Age	% Impotence	Age	% Impotence
Kinsey		Bowers	
40	1.9	60–64	28.0
45	2.6	65–69	50.0
50	6.7	70–74	61.0
55	6.7		
60	18.4	Newman	
65	25.0		
70	27.0	60–64	40.0
75	55.0	65–69	37.0
80	75.0	70–74	42.0
		75 +	75.0
Finkle		Perlman, Kobashi	
55–59	31.0		
60–64	37.0	40–49	5.0
65–69	37.0	50–59	11.3
70–74	61.0	60–69	36.6
75–79	76.0	70–79	59.0
80 +	60.0	80 +	85.0

From "Frequency of Intercourse in Males at Different Ages" by C.K. Perlman. Reprinted from *Medical Aspects of Human Sexuality.* November 1972. Hospital Publications, Inc. 1972 All rights reserved.

TABLE 2
Prevalence of Intercourse in Males by Age Group.

Age group	25	40	55–65	65–75
Median age	25	40	59.9	68.5
Number	85	85	49	45
Median frequency of intercourse per month	27.6 ± 3.1	17.2 ± 1.8	3.9 ± 0.7	1.8 ± 0.3
Extreme values	1–180	1–135	0–24	0–8

From "The Effects of Age on Male Sexual Activity" by H. Cendron and J. Vallery-Masson, *La Presse Médicale,* 1970, 78, 1975. MASSON, S.A. Paris.

structures (27). Results of such changes may include loss of appetite and subsequent weight loss. These symptoms may be mistaken for mental illness (such as depressive illness) or may complicate such conditions. Significant changes occur in the stomach with aging, leading to a decrease in mucosal thickness.

Colonic dysfunction in the aged is typically manifested by constipation and diverticulosis. Though the evidence remains unclear, constipation in late life is likely to be caused more by lack of bulk in the diet, decreased fluid intake and the chronic abuse of laxatives than by the chronic colonic morbidity. Diverticular disease of the colon increases with age, especially in females. Again, dietary changes to low residue food are considered important etiological factors.

There appears to be an increase in connective tissue in the liver of older persons along with a progressively diminishing liver weight, yet the evidence is conflicting. Some reduction in hepatic enzyme concentrates and response to stimuli also occurs, though the liver has a large reserve capacity (28). The only known relationship between the gallbladder and aging is the common presence of calculi with increasing age.

Temperature Regulation and Control

At resting or basal conditions, the body temperature of an elderly person is maintained within the same limits as that of the young (29), yet response to high or low environmental temperatures is less effective. Exposure to a cold environment may lead to the development of hypothermia, a significant cause of death in the geriatric population. All older persons may not be at risk for the development of hypothermia, however. A group of individuals who are at risk may show a fall in core body temperature when exposed to cold for more than one hour (30). The older person living alone, who becomes depressed and therefore pays little attention to the external environment may be particularly at risk for the development of hypothermia.

Conclusion

As we have seen in the above, irreversible, decremental processes occur with aging. These are manifested by shrinking organ and muscle size and declining functional capacity in many organs such that the ability

of the aging organism to cope with stresses diminishes. In normal circumstances and mild stress states, the aging human organism can cope adequately. In major stressful circumstances, as for example the events that might be associated with gastrointestinal bleeding and the need for surgery, the diminished functional capacity of the heart, lungs, and kidneys may be quickly manifested by a disproportionate degree of shock, organic mental syndrome, increased incidence of pneumonia, congestive heart failure and/or impairments in the excretory capacity for intravenous fluids. These declines, brought out by stress, need not produce therapeutic catastrophes but make successes more difficult to attain. The increasing success rate of major surgery, including coronary bypass operations on the very old (e.g. over 70), are indicative of the triumph over age. Indeed, our ability to compensate for the declines of the aging organism have increased to a point where the major limiting factor may not be somatic but psychiatric. Thus organic mental syndromes are often the chief obstacle in the ability to deal with stress and are a prognostic factor in limiting the life span. Older patients with severe organic mental syndrome do have shortened life spans compared to individuals of the same age with reasonable degrees of psychological functioning. A patient with organic mental syndrome may have difficulty in following directions, in carrying out therapeutic programs such as those associated with successful surgery for hip fracture, have a greater tendency to aspirate foods and to develop bronchopneumonia. Such a patient may lack ability to recognize bodily changes of pathological import and call them to the attention of the doctor. For these and other obvious reasons, the organic mental syndromes associated with aging have become a major problem of the geriatrician, the psychiatrist, and society as a whole.

References

1. Rossman, I. 1977. Anatomic and body composition changes with aging, pp. 189–221. In C. E. Finch and L. Hayflick (eds.) *Handbook of the Biology of Aging,* New York: Van Nostrand Reinhold.

2. Kannel, W. B. 1976. Some lessons in cardiovascular epidemiology from Framingham. *Am. J. Cardiol.* 37: 269.

3. Nathan, H. 1962. Osteophytes of the vertebral column. *J. Bone Joint Surg.* 44: 243–268.

4. Howells, W. W. 1965. Age and individuality in vertebral lipping: Notes on Stewart's data. *Homenaje a Juan Comas* 2: 169–178. Mexico.

5. Damon, A. 1965b. Stature increase among Italian-Americans: Environmental, genetic, or both? *Am. J. Phys. Anthropol.* 23: 401–408.

6. Büchi, E. C. 1950. Änderung der körperform beim erwachsenen menschen, eine untersuchung nach der Individual-Methode. *Anthrop. Forsch., Heft 1.* Anthrop, Gesel., Wien.

7. Hooton, E. A. and Dupertuis, C. W. 1951. Age changes and selective survival in Irish males. Studies in Physical Anthropology (American Association of Physical Anthropologists and Wenner-Gren Foundation). 2: 1–130.

8. Brozek, J. and Keys, A. 1953. Relative body weight, age and fatness. *Geriatrics.* 8: 70–75.

9. Fryer, J. H. 1962. Studies of body composition in men aged 60 and over. In N. W. Shock (ed.) *Biological Aspects of Aging,* New York: Columbia University Press, pp. 59–78.

10. Garn, S. M., Rohmann, C. G., Wagner, B. and Ascoli, W. 1967. Continuing bone growth throughout life: A general phenomenon. *Am. J. Phys. Anthropol.* 26: 313–318.

11. Epker, B. N. and Frost, H. M. 1966. Periosteal appositional bone growth from age two to age seventy in man. A tetracycline evaluation. *Anat. Record.* 154: 573–578.

12. Israel, H. 1973b. Age factor and the pattern of change in craniofacial structures. *Am. J. Phys. Anthropol.* 30: 11–128.

13. Todd, T. W. and Lyons, D. W., Jr. 1924. Endocranial suture closure. Its progress and age relationship. Part 1. Adult males of white stock. *Am. J. Phys. Anthropol.* 7: 325–384.

14. Smith, R. W., Jr. and Walker, R. R. 1964. Femoral expansion in aging women: Implications for osteoporosis and fractures. Science. 145: 156–157.

15. Moldawer, M., Zimmerman, S. J. and Collins, L. C. 1965. Incidence of osteoporosis in elderly whites and elderly negroes. J. Am. Med. Assoc. 194: 859–862.

16. Bennett, G. A., Waine, H. and Bauer, W. 1942. Changes in the Knee Joint at Various Ages. With Particular Reference to the Nature and Development of Degenerative Joint Disease. New York: The Commonwealth Fund.

17. Melick, R. and Taft, H. P. 1959. Observations on body hair in old people. *J. Clin. Endocrinol.* 19: 1597–1607.

18. Damon, A., Seltzer, C. C., Stoudt, H. W. and Bell, B. 1972. Age and physique in healthy white veterans at Boston. *Aging and Human Development.* 3: 202–208.

19. Weibel, J. and Fields, W. S. 1965. Tortuosity, coiling and kinking of the internal carotid artery. I. Etiology and radiographic anatomy. *Neurol.,* 15, (11): 7–18.

20. Agate, J. 1979. Special hazards of illness in later life. Ch. 7. In I. Rossman (ed.) *Clinical Geriatrics.* Phila.: J. B. Lippincott.

21. Brandfonbrener, M., Landowne, M. and Shock, N. W. 1955. Changes in Cardiac Output With Age. Circ. 12, p. 577.

22. Muiesan, G., Sorbini, C. A. and Grassi, V. 1971. Respiratory function in the aged. *Bull. PhysioPathol. Respir.* 7: 973–1007.

23. Brocklehurst, J. C. 1973. The bladder. In J. C. Brocklehurst (ed.) *Textbook of Geriatric Medicine and Gerontology.* Edinburgh & London-Churchill Livingstone, pp. 298–320.

24. Goldfarb, A. F. 1979. Geriatric Gynecology. Ch. 17. In I. Rossman (ed.) *Clinical Geriatrics.* Philadelphia: J. B. Lippincott.

25. Masters, W. H. and Johnson, V. E. 1966. The aging male. Ch. 16. In *Human Sexual Response.* Boston: Little Brown, pp. 248–270.

26. Rossman, I. 1978. Sexuality and aging: An internist's perspective, In *Sexuality and Aging* (Rev. Ed. 1978) Robert L. Solnick (ed.) Andrus Gerontol. Center, Los Angeles, California University S. Calif. Press. pp. 66–77.

27. Arey, L. B., Tremain, M. J., Manzingo, F. L. 1935. The numerical and topographical relation of taste buds to circumvallate papillae throughout the life span. *Anat. Record.* 64: 9.

28. Bhanthumnavin, K., Shuster, M. M. 1977. Aging and gastrointestinal function. In C. E. Finch, L. Hayflick (eds.), *Handbook of the Biology of Aging.* New York: Van Nostrand Reinhold, p. 709.

29. Shock, N. W. 1952. Aging of homeostatic mechanisms. In A. I. Lansing (ed.) *Cowdry's Problems of Aging.* Baltimore: Williams and Wilkins, p. 415.

30. MacMillan, A. L., Corbett, J. L., Johnson, R. H., et al. 1967. Temperature regulation in survivors of accidental hypothermia of the elderly. *Lancet,* 2: 165.

Translations in Gerontology — From Lab to Life: Psychophysiology and Speed of Response

JAMES E. BIRREN

This article states some principles and gives a perspective on research findings on aging that lie behind some of the daily life circumstances of growing old. Usually a science and real-life dialogue such as this is caught in a division between a humanistic orientation and the empirical scientific traditions or what one might call the mechanistic traditions. My proposition is simply that laboratory research on the psychology of aging is a potential friend of the aging adult and that we ought to utilize the findings of the laboratory for the benefit of an aging population.

Much of my own research and that of several of my colleagues has been devoted to the study of the differences that occur with advancing age in speed of response (Birren, 1963, 1965). The issue is, How is such research relevant to the circumstances of older persons? I believe it has several points of relevance. For one thing, older people are strikingly affected by accidents. Accidents occur to older people whether they are pedestrians, drivers of cars, or in their own homes utilizing the normal appliances in everyday life. In particular, older people hurt themselves through falls, often fatally.

Sometimes it would appear that the older person lacks the speed and agility to execute an evasive action in the face of an impending accident. Sometimes the accident-avoiding action has a limiting physical quality about it; that is, the younger person would or could move or jump out of the way more quickly and thus avoid an impact. Sometimes the action also has to do with time taken to scan one's environment and make a decision rapidly enough to take appropriate action. Observation of an older adult can suggest that attention may become sluggish and shifting from task to task occurs more slowly than for the teenager whose mind appears to dart rapidly.

I think you might agree that following an older adult driver suggests that aged behavior on the road has some different qualities than the behavior of a younger driver. In their favor it must be said that older drivers rarely drive too quickly. Offsetting this is a tendency to unpredictable behavior and making errors of judgment as to when a turn is appropriate. My fundamental proposition here is that some of these qualities of behavior shown with advancing age are intimately involved with the speed of processing information by the nervous system.

Time as a Variable in Behavior

Usually one builds up to a principle by a review of the literature; however, in view of the nature of this article I wish to state my basic proposition at the beginning, then trace its development and implications. My basic proposition is that with advancing age individuals on an average show a tendency to a slowness in response which reflects a basic change in the speed with which the central nervous system processes information. For some reason this principle seems difficult for psychologists to accept, and indeed I note my own students after spending several years in study with me sometimes miss the main point as well as its implications. The main point is that with age any event processed by the nervous system takes longer. Whereas in the young adult speed of response is usually related to such things as familiarity, uncertainty, and motivation, a limiting factor emerges in the older adult, that of processing time. I would like to introduce an analogy to make my principle clear.

If in this period of energy shortages one has an electrical brown-out, one will discover that many of the electrical appliances used in the home will run more slowly. The voltage drop results in a slowness of motor-driven activities. If one considers a calculator that is running with a slower motor during a voltage drop, any process the calculator was used for, such as addition, multiplication, subtraction, or division, would be slower than usual. Large computers are often characterized in terms of their unit processing time; the faster the time the larger the capacity.

I want to go a step further to extend my analogy with respect to an aging human organism, with the expectations that I am probably right but I may be wrong. General observations suggest that the aging individual can do most if not all of the things he did when he was younger but not do them as quickly. Often there is a tendency to want to regard the quickness of behavior as not an intrinsic property. The technical sense that I am suggesting is simply that speed of behavior in the young adult is commonly regarded as a dependent variable; it depends on other circumstances surrounding the performance. In the case of the aging individual I believe that speed itself becomes the independent variable with which we must interpret and explain other kinds of behavior. This has to do with the proposition that if there is a central slowing of processing or mediation then all phenomena we regard as important in behavior will slow down. Perception and memory will become less efficient, as will retrieval from the long-term store of previously learned material. Furthermore, the likelihood of novel associations will decrease.

Young adults appear to be quick or slow in their behavior in accord with the needs of the situation in which they find themselves. On the other hand, older adults seem to have a characteristic or general slowness of behavior, an expression of a primary process of aging in the nervous system. While the precise location or the physiological basis of this slowness is not known, its consequence of behavior is becoming more apparent. Although I appear to be saying that there is a generalized brown-out in behavior with advancing age such that speed of intrinsic events of the nervous system is a limiting function, it should not be assumed from this that it had to be inevitable. As some of my colleagues are pointing out (Schaie, 1974; Schonfield, 1974), the range of individual differences is considerable, and one might make the obvious statement that the speed of an event is not necessarily the determiner of the pleasure we derive from it.

Historical Position of Time in Relation to Behavior

Early psychologists and physiologists differed in their approach to timing of behavior with advancing age. In the second edition of Cowdry's *Problems of Aging,* Malcolm Critchley, a neurologist, reviewed the nature of the changes in the nervous system with advancing age. He noted that there was a change in reflexes, a kind of sluggishness in response. Also he noted that with regard to motor activity ''a slight generalized poverty of movement, is characteristic and is usually associated with slowness of movement, an attitude affliction in a mild state of hypertonus or — better perhaps — difficulty in relaxation'' (Critchley, 1942, p. 523).

In the same volume, Walter Miles pointed out that speed of movement did appear slower in his older subjects. He tended, however, to keep separate the data on speed of motor movements and perception from the information about intelligence and age. In discussing intelligence he said,

> Speed of response is . . . dependent to no small extent on the physiological equipment available for psychological perception and response and it is with interest but without surprise that we learn that when the speed factor is eliminated the coefficient of age-score correlation for intelligence during the life span of adult maturity drops from an average of .4 or .5 in various more or less homogeneous groups to .3 or less for a single somewhat heterogeneous population [Miles, 1942, p. 769].

Miles, I believe, was hoping that in partialing out speed it would leave intelligence uncorrelated with age. In fact, by so partialing time out one may be throwing out one of the most intrinsic factors of intellectual activity, speed of association. Miles, as well as other psychologists, had been embarrassed by the data on speed and aging which seemed to suggest that the older organism was not efficient when data on verbal skills showed no decline or perhaps an increase.

Somewhat earlier than Miles and Critchley, Pavlov had observed that it was more difficult to establish conditioned responses in older dogs; he generalized his observations to suggest that with advancing age the neural processes were less lively. This somewhat metaphorical way of expressing the relationship does, however, imply that the nervous system was slowing down. An earlier psychologist, Thorndike (1928), had maintained that speed was a different property of mind along with power and attitude in the consideration of effective intelligence. Both he and his students, however, tended to neglect speed as though it were a peripheral matter. In Thorndike's day, age 45 was old, and one of his interests may have been to assure that people in their 30s and early 40s could still learn effectively. Presumably we would now move up this age considerably. Following Thorndike, his students argued that timed psychological tests were particularly embarrassing to older persons. Given a certain slowness in responding, older people will not answer as many questions on an intelligence test within a fixed time limit. By removing the time limits, performance becomes higher and presumably better reflects the true intellectual power of the individuals. Herein lies the fallacy, however. One did not know 30 years ago whether an intelligence test taken with or without time limits was a more valid indicator of that elusive quality we call intelligence. One had a tendency if one were a psychologist a generation ago to regard this speed as somehow peripheral or distant from the important qualities of the mind. In the parlance of the learning investigators, speed was regarded as a ''performance factor'' somehow not intrinsic to the process itself. What a strange kind of nervous system was implicitly being postulated as though the vital neural junctions leading up to the response or indeed the operation of the motor neurons in the spinal cord as well as the descending tracts from the cortex which carry the neural activity necessary in voluntary movement were uninvolved. It seems most unparsimonious to regard the operation of the peripheral neural elements as independent of the higher processes in the aging nervous system.

Magladery (1959) pointed out the effect that the higher centers of the nervous system have on simple reflexes:

> The results emphasize, rather, potential prolongation of relatively low level responses when potentiation from higher centers may be diminished. In the case of monosynaptic reflex discharge, and the processes subserved by such, this increased delay can not be of great functional significance in terms of any one motorneuron pool. When cumulative, however, and particularly when processes such as these are operative over complex spinal reflex arcs which are more dependent for excitation than single synapses on influences from higher centers, these increased central delays may be very important indeed. They may well be sufficient to account for good proportions of the slowed motor response times in the elderly [Magladery, 1959, p. 181].

Thus, we have a rather unique situation in which the neurologist and the neurophysiologist suggest that slowness of responses becomes increasingly important as the responses involve higher centers and the psychologist wants that slowness to be restricted to the periphery and limited to such things as movement and not to involve processes of thinking. This indeed, I believe, was wishful thinking on the part of the early psychologists, when they hoped that older persons would simply be slow in their behavior but that the processes of mind remained unchanged, that is, such processes as thinking, reasoning, perception, and recall from memory. However embarrassing it may be to us as individuals, it seems that we have an obligation as objective observers to tell ourselves and our fellowmen how it really is as we grow old and indeed how the nervous system itself changes and influences behavior.

From a physiological standpoint it would appear that the more complex the behavior and the higher the level of the nervous system involved, the greater the slowness in the response with age. It is possible that a central process associated with the ascending reticular activating system might lead to the observed slowness, but it would seem to be an unrealistic position to hold that the reduction in activation and alerting would affect only the voluntary or pyramidal motor system. I would counter this line of reasoning with the observation that given a rapid decay system in memory, a sluggishness in processing information would preclude the opportunity of using decaying information in combination with other stimuli. In brief, I suggest that man is not simply a calculator that is slowing down because of an electrical brown-out, but man is a calculator that has some components that decay with time such that if the events are not completed within a time limit the possibility of the task being completed successfully is diminished. This leads us now to consider the role of diminished speed in the various adaptive capacities of the organism's perception, memory, learning, intelligence, and perhaps personality.

Perception

A variety of past as well as recent studies have shown differences with age in perceptual functions, particularly vision. For example, it has been known for quite some time that the flicker fusion threshold increases with age. That is, a flickering light is regarded as a continuous light at a lower frequency by older subjects than by younger subjects. This suggests that the neural events may not be quick enough to allow discrimination of the series of events (Weiss, 1959). More recently this has been shown elegantly in a perceptual masking experiment by Donald Kline (1972). In his study of monoptic visual masking, a second stimulus defined as visual noise followed the first stimulus by a variable interval. The effect of the blocking or masking stimulus occurs at longer intervals for the older individual. It was also shown that in order to be perceived, the minimum exposure time of the initial or target stimulus was longer for the older subjects. One is left with dual phenomena in which the excitation corresponding to the initial stimulus takes a longer time to reach its maximum effectiveness as well as to decay, as shown by a longer masking interval. Both of these findings suggest some loss either in Pavlov's terms of neural liveliness or speed of neural events with age.

If one begins with the notion that neural events are slower with age and uses this as the explanatory independent variable, then the perceptual phenomena would be subsumed as part of a slowness in general processing time.

Memory

Not only are perceptual processes likely influenced by a slowness in central nervous systems processing, but memory also. In 1965 I reported some limited data on the relationships of tests of memory to measures of speed of writing digits. An important result in the present context was that the correlations between the Wechsler Memory Scale and speed in young subjects was not significantly different than zero. In fact, it was − .01. In elderly subjects, that is, those over 60 years, the correlation between the Wechsler Memory Scale and speed of copying digits was .52. While the content of the Memory Scale may be difficult to define in the context of laboratory learning studies, it does indicate that with older adults the

intercorrelations between speed measures and such tests of memory increase.

More recent studies of memory in the context of verbal learning (Johnson, 1973; Robertson, 1972; Schonfield & Robertson, 1966) indicate that the largest difference with age in memory functions is not in the storage of information but in retrieving it from store. It is shown that recovery of information from long-term storage is best done by recognition rather than by total recall. Furthermore, Johnson's experiments showed that cued recall benefits disproportionately the older person. While it is premature to directly implicate an effect of slower central processing time, it is not premature to speculate about its role.

One possibility is that if neural events are indeed slow, the scanning of currently presented information and information from long-term store may be slow. Under these circumstances the individual may show a decreasing probability of eliciting the appropriate material from long-term store and the high probability of distraction. The set or search criterion may decay during a protracted process of retrieval. Robertson (1972) in her studies indicated that older subjects do retain material but frequently will allow this material to intrude as inappropriate associations; that is, memory itself is less affected than its retrieval at an appropriate time. An alternative interpretation is that older subjects do not employ mediating processes to the same extent as young persons. Under this circumstance the aged are disproportionately aided when cues are supplied to them because they do not themselves tend to use cues in both the original learning and perhaps in the recovery from the memory store. Further research in this area is needed to either refute or substantiate the role of speed of central nervous system processing in both primary and secondary memory processes and in scanning and retrieving. The proposition being favored here is that the primary change is in speed of neural events which influences memory. Put in other terms, we do not remember because our associations are slow, not that we are slow because we cannot remember.

Learning

Presumably, if perceptual and memory processes are influenced by changing central information processing, then learning itself must be influenced. Considerable research has been devoted to the issues of pacing in learning. Results indicate that older subjects should be given longer intervals between stimuli to elicit a response. If crowded by short intervals, they failed to respond, and one notes a rise with age in omission errors rather than commission errors. This recently has been brought into question by Robertson's work which indicates that both errors of commission and omission occur. Apparently whether one commits more or less errors of commission is a function of the particular experimental context.

In learning experiments the issue may be discerned as to whether older subjects want more time or need more time. Given the interpretation that they are cautious and seek more certitude before they respond, they want more time. Taking the interpretation that the central processing time is limited, then they need more time. In the case of perceptual and memory processes it would appear to the writer at least that the older individual needs more time rather than wants more. In the case of learning the situation is not so clear-cut. One of the uncertain areas is how to interpret the evidence that the older individual is relatively better in incidental learning than in directed learning (Johnson, 1973; Wimer, 1960). The fact that older subjects have a more difficult time in intentional or directed learning would suggest some difficulty in controlling attention or

set. Thus, in the learning situation the older adult is taking in too much information and therefore cannot concentrate on crucial information most relevant to the task. Here one can point out that some very illuminating experiments could be carried out at the present time on relationships between attention processes and speed of information processing in relation to learning and age. Given a change with age in the central nervous system such that information processing is slower in all aspects, then attention itself should not be spared. Indeed, the establishment and maintenance of a set should be more difficult in the older individual. There is in fact some evidence for this in the reaction time studies of Botwinick (1957). He found that for expected stimuli, set is more difficult to establish and maintain in the older individual. Future research should be directed at the relations of slowness in CNS function with age and attention.

Motor Skills

Considerable research from the Cambridge Laboratory established the fact that the greatest difference between young and old adults in slowing of motor skills occurred at decision points. That is, movement itself was not so much changed with age as was the redirecting of movement in response to new information (Welford, 1959). This of course fits the earlier expressed idea that the higher one goes in the centers of the nervous system the more the slowing becomes evident. While repetitious movements such as tapping are slower with age, it is in the redirection of movements that the additional time is taken (Rabbitt & Birren, 1967). Thus sequential tasks that require intervening decisions are disproportionately lengthened with age in contrast to simple repetitious movements. This of course fits the thesis that the change in central processing time is the critical one with advancing age.

Intelligence

Much of the newer research findings on intelligence with age are showing significant cohort differences or differences between the generations in intelligence. Indeed the review by Schaie (1974, pp. 802–807) amply documents this. Nevertheless, despite the large differences in cohorts there is still a difference between verbal tests and those involving perceptual speed, the latter still showing decrements in an older population. The study of healthy older men at the National Institute of Mental Health reported differences in both speed measurements and on nonverbal intelligence measures such as the Raven Progressive Matrices, in contrast with vocabulary and information tests (Foulds & Raven, 1948). Horn and Catell (1966) commented about the fact that crystalized intelligence representing the store of information acquired over time continues to rise with age whereas fluid intelligence, a more dynamic catalytic cognitive property, declines. Schumacher (1970) emphasized these points and drew inferences about altered physiology of the nervous system that may account for this. It would of course fit the hypothesis advanced here that fluid intelligence should decline because it would represent a decline in the rapidity with which one can scan stored information and recombine it with current input for a needed and perhaps novel response.

Earlier research by Chown (1961) in which she correlated tests of rigidity with age and with intelligence indicated that with advancing age there was a tendency to show greater rigidity. It was difficult to interpret the rigidity outside of the context of cognitive functioning itself; that is, the central change may lead to cognitive deficit and to the apparent changes in rigidity. In this sense, then, rigidity may be less a personality predisposition or a reversible set but

rather a required difference in behavior due to the changes occurring within the nervous system itself. That is, many older individuals do not want to be rigid but are rigid because of a necessary consequence of the way the older nervous system functions.

Timing and Its Relation to Neural Activity

One of the current dilemmas is how to interpret the tendency for older subjects to show a lowered alpha frequency with advancing age (Obrist, 1965; Thompson & Marsh, 1973). Surwillo (1963) interpreted this as reflecting a change in the basic timing in the nervous system and, in fact, regarded the alpha frequency as a pacemaker of behavioral processes. Subsequently, the biofeedback conditioning experiments of Woodruff (1972) indicated that to some extent one could reverse the drift toward lower frequencies of alpha in the older subject by appropriate biofeedback conditioning and this would be correlated with the faster timing of responses. While the correlation between response speed and alpha was significant, the data suggest that most of the variance attributable to the relation between age and reaction time is unexplained by the change in alpha per se. Nevertheless it does show a linking in speed of response with neural activity.

Eisdorfer (1968), in his experiments with learning and autonomic nervous system activity, has emphasized that with advancing age there tends to be an overarousal of the sympathetic nervous system or, more particularly, increased activity of the peripheral autonomic end organs. This would seem to lie in contrast with the hypothesis that the central nervous system was showing a quality of underarousal. The unpublished evidence of Jeffrey shows that older subjects will improve their speed of response given amphetamines or stimulating adrenergic-like drugs. There remains considerable uncertainty as to the relative contributions of central versus peripheral sympathetic effects on age changes in behavior. Earlier, Birren (1963) reported data which indicated that elevated blood pressure was associated with slowness in response; thus a balance of central nervous system activity and peripheral autonomic activity was implicated. Increased sympathetic activity may reflect a relative inhibition or underarousal of the central nervous system with regard to facilitation of perceptual and motor responses. Thus the issue that older subjects on the average may show increased sympathetic activity may not in itself deny the possibility that there is a concomitant slowness in central information processing.

Implications of Data on Timing, Behavior, and Aging

For a considerable period of time behavioral data on aging appeared to be very compartmentalized, and very little thought was given to the possibility that there were any major common underlying processes. More recently, however, there seems to be recognition of the fact that with age there may be some general changes in behavior due to common processes. An important study was carried out in the Netherlands using 150 psychological and physiological variables (Dirken, 1972). The measurements were obtained on 316 male workers in Dutch industry. Of interest was the fact that the cluster analysis of the main variables included psychological as well as physical variables. Investigators concluded, "This can be considered as an indication that the somatic and mental aspects of aging are highly interdependent; it even confirms that aging is controlled by a general process, influencing all subsystems simultaneously" (Dirken, 1972, p. 209). With this encouragement one may regard the changes with age in central processing time as the major independent variable in explaining much of the behavioral changes with age. However, the timing itself becomes dependent on other

physiological phenomena, particularly its relationship to somatic disease. As mentioned earlier there is a correlation between slowness of response and blood pressure such that the higher the blood pressure the slower the response. Also, subjects with cardiovascular disease show a disproportionate slowing in information processing relative to others their age. One of the more recent developments in this area is linking slowness of response to predisposition to cardiovascular disease.

Rosenman has established the association of a personality style with the likelihood of developing cardiovascular disease, specifically coronary artery disease (Rosenman, Friedman, Jenkins, & Bortner, 1968). Subjects who show a constellation of time pressure, restlessness, responsibility, and many diffuse goals have a much higher likelihood of developing coronary disease than individuals who are not so time pressured. Taking this evidence as a point of departure, Abrahams (1972) studied a group of young adults and classified them according to their predisposition or nonpredisposition to cardiovascular disease. Reasoning that later in life slowness of behavioral functions is related to cardiovascular disease, he thought that individuals early in life that were so predisposed would show slowing. Indeed, his results do bear this out. The fact that the reaction time of subjects in their early years who are predisposed to coronary heart disease is significantly slower than their nonpredisposed peers would indicate that there is a common basis for the predisposition to cardiovascular disease and the timing in the central nervous system itself. Slowness of information processing with age is an issue directly involved in questions about the basis of somatic changes with advancing age.

The data on slowness of reaction time with age have direct implications for how older adults can manage themselves in their environment. While response times of young adults may be slow or quick depending on the demands of the environment, older adults are slow as a general feature of their behavior. Furthermore, since disease is intimately related to the slowness shown by older adults, the view is advanced that while age appears to be accompanied by normal psychophysiological slowing it is exacerbated by the presence of disease, particularly those diseases of a stress character and involving the sympathetic nervous system.

Summary

One application of available information is that we may begin to attempt to identify individuals early in life who are predisposed to coronary heart disease by behavioral assessment. Subsequently, by suitable conditioning it may be possible to minimize the coronary risk that these individuals are to incur. Psychology would appear to have an important contribution to make to the early detection and management of somatic disease.

Research results to date have clear implications for the design of the environment to maximize the potentials of the older adult. One of the largest areas of potential contribution of psychologists is likely to be in the management of accidents, which are so disastrously high in frequency for older adults. Evidence suggests that it is not so much the motor response or muscular strength itself which leads to accident-prone behavior in the aged but rather slowness of decision times and the inability of the older person to rapidly discriminate relevant information from irrelevant information. Automobile accidents and pedestrian accidents often imply failure of judgment. One may speculate that the time taken to scan traffic flow, traffic lights, and other information and to arrive at relevant decisions at an appropriate time is often not possible given the timing characteristics of the older nervous system. A pacing of environmental events which is appropriate for the 25-year-old is not appropriate for the average 75-year-old to permit effective behavior. Time and pacing of the environment, particularly an urban environment, are commonly hostile to optimum adaptive behavior of the older person. While the environmental principles that are sound for older adults may also be sound for young people, such as minimizing irrelevant information and maximizing relevant information by important judgments, the basic issue of time itself is not readily resolved. That is, safe street crossing by an older pedestrian may require twice the length of time that it will for a young adult. Given the impatience of motorists, the young drivers' timing and the timing of young pedestrians dominate the present scene. The urban microenvironmental situation is harried for the older adult, and time itself is a key element.

As a point of departure for further research on the older nervous system I can think of no greater vantage point than studying speed and timing. Such information has prospects for considerable scientific gain in understanding the organization of behavior and for the design of an environment that will be supportive of older adults.

References

Abrahams, J. P. Psychomotor performance and change in cardiac rate in subjects behaviorally predisposed to coronary heart disease. Unpublished doctoral dissertation, University of Southern California, 1972.

Birren, J. E. Psychophysiological relations. In J. E. Birren (Ed.), *Human aging.* (USPHS Publ. 986) Washington, D.C.: U. S. Public Health Service, 1963.

Birren, J. E. Age changes in speed of behavior: Its central nature and physiological correlates. In A. T. Welford & J. E. Birren (Eds.), *Behavior, aging and the nervous system.* Springfield, Ill.: Charles C. Thomas, 1965.

Botwinick, J., Brinley, J. F., & Birren J. E. Set in relation to age. *Journal of Gerontology,* 1957, 12, 300–305.

Chown, S. M. Age and the rigidities. *Journal of Gerontology,* 1961, 16, 353–362.

Critchley, M. Aging of the nervous system. In E. W. Cowdry (Ed.), *Problems of aging.* Baltimore, Md.: Williams & Wilkins, 1942.

Dirken, J. M. (Ed.), *Functional age of industrial workers.* Groningen, The Netherlands: Wolters-Noordhoff, 1972.

Eisdorfer, C. Arousal and performance experiments in verbal learning and a tentative theory. In G. A. Talland (Ed.), *Human aging and behavior.* New York: Academic Press, 1968.

Foulds, G. A., & Raven, J. C. Normal changes in the mental abilities of adults as age advances. *Journal of Mental Science,* 1948, 94, 133–142.

Horn, J. L., & Cattell, R. B. Age differences in primary mental ability factors. *Journal of Gerontology,* 1966, 21, 210–220.

Johnson, L. K. Memory loss with age: A storage or retrieval problem? Unpublished doctoral dissertation, University of Southern California, 1973.

Kline, D. W. Signal processing time and aging: Age differences in backward dichoptic masking. Unpublished doctoral dissertation, University of Southern California, 1972.

Magladery, J. W. Neurophysiology of aging. In J. E. Birren (Ed.), *Handbook of aging and the individual.* Chicago: University of Chicago Press, 1959.

Miles, W. R. Psychological aspects of ageing. In E. W. Cowdry (Ed.), *Problems of ageing.* Baltimore, Md.: Williams & Wilkins, 1942.

Obrist, W. D., & Busse, E. W. The electroencephalogram in old age. In W. P. Wilson (Ed.), *Applications of electroencephalography in psychiatry: A symposium.* Durham, N. C.: Duke University Press, 1965.

Rabbitt, P. M., & Birren, J. E. Age and responses to sequences of repetitive and interruptive signals. *Journal of Gerontology,* 1967, 22, 143–150.

Robertson, E. A. Age differences in primary and secondary memory processes. Unpublished doctoral dissertation, University of Southern California, 1972.

Rosenman, R. H., Friedman, M., Jenkins, C. D., & Bortner, R. W. Is there a coronary-prone personality? *International Journal of Psychiatrics,* 1968, 5, 427–429.

Schaie, K. W. Translations in gerontology — from lab to life: Intellectual functioning. *American Psychologist,* 1974, 29, 802–807.

Schonfield, A. E. D. Translations in gerontology — from lab to life: Utilizing information. *American Psychologist,* 1974, 29, 796–801.

Schonfield, A. E. D., & Robertson, E. A. Memory storage and aging. *Canadian Journal of Psychology,* 1966, 20, 228–236.

Schumacher, S. S. Psychological evidence for primary aging in the brain. In H. T. Blumenthal (Ed.), *The regulatory role of the nervous system in aging.* Vol. 7. Basel, Switzerland: S. Karger, 1970.

Surwillo, W. W. The relation of simple response time to brain-wave frequency and the effects of age. *Electroencephalography and Clinical Neurophysiology,* 1963, 15, 105–114.

Thompson, L. W., & Marsh, G. R. Psychophysiological studies of aging. In C. Eisdorfer & M. P. Lawton (Eds.), *Psychology of adult development and aging.* Washington, D.C.: American Psychological Association, 1973.

Thorndike, E. L., Bregman, E. O., Tilton, J. W., & Woodyard, E. *Adult learning.* New York: Macmillan, 1928.

Weiss, A. D. Sensory functions. In J. E. Birren (Ed.), *Handbook of aging and the individual.* Chicago: University of Chicago Press, 1959.

Welford, A. T. Psychomotor performance. In J. E. Birren (Ed.), *Handbook of aging and the individual.* Chicago: University of Chicago Press, 1959.

Wimer, R. E. Age differences in incidental and intentional learning. *Journal of Gerontology,* 1960, 15, 79–82.

Woodruff, D. A. Biofeedback control of the EEG alpha rhythm and its effect on reaction time in the young and old. Unpublished doctoral dissertation, University of Southern California, 1972.

12

Mental Disorders

Groups of people with relatively less power in our society tend to have higher rates of mental disorders: women, lower social classes, minority groups, and the elderly. Feelings of helplessness and an external locus of control, often somewhat realistic in these relatively powerless groups, appear to be related to anxiety or depression or both. Especially among the elderly, depression is sometimes masked by physical complaints and is often mistaken for irreversible brain disorder.

Schizophrenia, the neuroses, and mental retardation are more likely to be diagnosed among young adults than among older people. Alcoholism is a problem in disproportionate numbers for middle-aged adults, while depression and organic brain disorder are more frequently found among elderly mental patients. Age and sex biases exist in certain diagnostic categories such as "involutional melancholia," which until recently was used only for post-menopausal women. Women, especially housewives, are more likely than men to be diagnosed as mentally disordered. Beginning with the late sixties, however, it is men who are more likely to be so diagnosed.

Suicide, which often results as a consequence of severe depression, may claim as many as 50,000 to 100,000 victims a year. The ratio of unsuccessful suicide attempts is higher among women than men, and higher among young adults than old people, which may reflect a greater tendency of women and young adults to use suicide attempts as a "cry for help." White males have the highest suicide rate, especially late in life; white females' suicide rate peaks in midlife, while that for blacks (both male and female) peaks in young adulthood.

Asser Stenback provides the most recent review of the literature on suicidal behavior in old age. He defines the terms needed to understand the problem, gives some cross-cultural data on suicide rates in many parts of the world, and defines different types of suicides. He then considers factors leading to suicide including mental illness, physical illness, social factors such as marital status and loneliness, and cultural factors. He also reflects on the meaning of suicide in old age and suggests methods of suicide prevention and reacting to suicide attempts.

Goals of psychotherapy, as a treatment of mental disturbances, change with the age of the client or patient. Young adults have identity and intimacy crises, middle-aged clients have midlife crises, and elderly adults need help integrating their lives, which may be aided by life review techniques. The selection by *Myrna I. Lewis* and *Robert N. Butler* shows how therapists can help older persons evaluate the meaning of their life by actively encouraging recall of the past. They describe a number of life review techniques encouraged as part of individual psychotherapy. These include written or taped autobiographies, pilgrimages to important places in a person's past (in person or by correspondence), reunions, genealogy, scrapbooks and other memorabilia, summation of life work, and preservation of ethnic identity. Extensions to group psychotherapy are also considered.

Older people do not always get the psychotherapy they need because of the expense, beliefs that psychotherapy marks an individual as "mentally ill," and the unwillingness of many therapists to treat elderly clients. Times are changing, however, and the future relationships between providers of mental-health care and their elderly clients promise to be more rewarding for everyone concerned. *Robert L. Kahn* analyzes the contributions of the mental health system to serving the elderly and examines what must be done to provide adequate service to the future aged. He points out that as mental health ideologies have changed, the system actually serves a smaller proportion of older persons today than it did at earlier times. However, changes in the characteristics of future elderly will reverse this trend and the mental health system must begin to accommodate to this new trend.

Additional Suggested Readings

Butler, R. N., & Lewis, M. I. *Aging and mental health,* 2nd ed. New York: Mosby, 1977.

> A popular treatment of the mental health problems of older people and their families. The senior author is a well-known psychiatrist who has done much research on old age, and most recently has been director of the National Institute of Aging.

Sloane, R. B. Organic brain syndrome. In J. E. Birren & R. B. Sloane (eds.), *Handbook of mental health and aging.* Englewood Cliffs, N.J.: Prentice Hall, 1980, pp. 554–590.

> A discussion of the problems of organic brain disease, their classification, and assessment.

Sparacino, J. Individual psychotherapy with the aged: A selective review. *International Journal of Aging and Human Development,* 1978/79, 9, 197–220.

> Although mental health professionals in the past have been reluctant to conduct psychotherapy with the elderly, there is now a growing experience base, which is reviewed in this article.

Suicidal Behavior in Old Age

ASSER STENBACK

From time immemorial the study of suicide (from Latin, *sui,* of oneself, *-cide,* from *caedere,* to cut, kill, killing) has exerted uncanny attraction. During the last few decades the scope of behaviors related to suicide has largely expanded. Inspired by Freud's theory of a death-instinct, Karl Menninger (1938) wrote his highly influential treatise *Man Against Himself.* Viewing suicide as direct self-destruction, he described a vast array of behaviors as forms of indirect self-destruction: asceticism, martyrdom, neurotic invalidism, alcohol addiction, antisocial behavior, psychosis, self-mutilations, malingering, polysurgery, purposive accidents, impotence, frigidity, and physical disease. These citations from the list of contents in *Man Against Himself* indicate the vast scope of indirect self-destruction, a much discussed subject in current suicidology. All unhealthy and harmful behaviors can be included in "indirect self-destruction." This in many respects fruitful concept is, however, diffuse and will not be dealt with in this presentation.

Erwin Stengel (1973) has made a major contribution to the present generally accepted differences in the psychodynamics of suicide and attempted suicide. A purpose of self-destruction is not always inherent in the suicidal act. Instead the suicidal attempt serves as an alarm signal and has the effect of an appeal for help. The persons who attempt suicide and those who commit suicide represent essentially two different, although overlapping, populations (Stengel and Cook, 1958).

Stengel (1973) put forward the definition: "A suicidal act is any deliberate act of self-damage which the person committing the act could not be sure to survive." Attempted suicide and suicidal attempt are used as synonyms although the terms have different connotations: suicide may really be attempted but in many cases the attempt may only have a suicidal character.

Frequency

In the literature on suicide of the elderly it is often stated that the frequency of suicide rises with age. Although true in many countries, as a general statement, it is, however, not correct.

In a study of suicides during the period 1950–1971, Ruzicka (1976) discerned three types of typical age-related suicide rates for both males and females. For males, the first type (A) is represented by continuously increasing suicide rates with age. The majority of countries (e.g., Austria, Czechoslovakia, France, Hungary, Japan, Mexico, and United States) belong to this type. The second type (B) has suicide rates gradually or steeply increasing to a peak, generally at ages around 50 to 60 years, and declining thereafter. Canada, Finland, Norway, and Poland belong to this group. The third type

(C) is a modification of type B: the rates around 50 and 60 years are followed by a decline but subsequently turn up again at the age 75 and over. This type is represented by Denmark, Scotland, Sweden, and Switzerland. Japan makes up a type of its own: very high rate at the youngest age group (15–24), rapidly declining to middle age (35–45), and steeply rising thereafter.

Suicide rates for females in the 30 countries studied also exhibited three well-discernible age patterns. The first one is identical with the male type (A), that is, gradual growth of suicide rates with increasing age. Interestingly, rather few countries belong to this type, which holds the majority of male suicides. Instead, the second type (B), similar to the one identified for males, with decline in old age, was most frequently found. Austria, Czechoslovakia, France, Hungary, Italy, Netherlands, Portugal and West Germany represent the type A, whereas Australia, Belgium, Canada, Denmark, England and Wales, Finland, Israel, New Zealand, Norway, Poland, Sweden, Switzerland and United States belong to the type B. The third female type C differs from the male type C: suicide rates are high at the younger ages, descend to a trough of various lengths, and thereafter resume an upward trend progressively rising with age. This type of suicide rate is found in Bulgaria, Greece, Japan, Singapore, and Yugoslavia.

If the rates per 100,000 are compared in the age groups 65–74 and 45–54 in the 41 countries which have reported to the World Health Organization on deaths due to "suicide and self-inflicted injury" in 1974 (WHO 1977), the following observations can be made. The rates for males age 65 and over increased in 26 countries and were about the same or decreased in 15 countries. For females in this category, the rates increased in 22 countries and decreased or remained the same in 19. The increases in rates were marked in 12 countries for males and in 11 countries for females. These rates

for one year corroborate the overall picture of no regular relationship between higher rates and higher age.

The suicide statistics in the United States provide interesting evidence for the absence of a connection between suicide and age. Analyzing the US suicide rates for the period 1933–1968, Diggory (1976) found that among white males, the highest suicide rates were in the age group 75 and older, whereas the US white female suicide rate was at a maximum in the 50–54 year age group with a tendency to become increasingly lower at higher ages. During 1933–1968, the maximum suicide rates of nonwhite males occurred in the 60–64 year age group. For nonwhite females this age group had rates similar to the 30–34 year age group. Diggory remarked that sex and race have greater bearing upon suicide rates than does age.

The US has seen a decrease in suicide rates of the aged during the last decades (Diggory, 1976). Rates in the 65–69 age group have fallen from about 45 per 100,000 in 1933 to about 20 per 100,000 in 1968. A similar decrease has been observed in England (Sainsbury, 1973). For Swedish males, the rates for this age group in 1921 remained about 55 per 100,000 from 1921 to 1960, and then fell to 48 per 100,000 in the decade 1961 to 1969. A gradual rise took place for females from 11 in 1921–1930 to 16 in 1961–1968 (Bolander, 1972).

From the practical point of view, rates are not the only way to visualize the scope of the problem of suicide among the aged. The proportion of suicides to the total deaths in an age group indicates the significance of suicide among the aged. In 1974 in the US in the 45–54 year age group there was one suicide out of 34.5 deaths, whereas in the age groups 65–74 and 75 and over the corresponding figures were one in 176.7 and one in 471.3 respectively (WHO, 1977).

The absolute number of suicides also reflects the quantitative aspect of suicides. It can be calculated that if the distribution of suicides and age groups were geographically even (which is not the case) in a US city of 500,000 inhabitants the total annual number of suicides would be about 60, out of which 10 would occur in those aged 65 or older. In West Berlin (pop. 2.1 million) the percentage of males and females over 60 years of age is 22.2 and 35.7 percent respectively, and the absolute numbers of suicides for the years 1973 and 1974 were 264 males and 353 females; this results in an annual rate of 308.5 suicides per year, or 73.5 suicides per 500,000 population, obviously the highest suicide frequency for the aged in the world (WHO, 1977). Although Finland has a markedly higher suicide rate than the US, in the years 1970 and 1971 no more than 33 suicides (10.5 per year) occurred among persons aged 65 and over in the city of Helsinki (pop. 500,000) (Lönnqvist, 1977).

The frequency of *attempted suicide* is difficult to estimate because many unsuccessful attempts do not reach the attention of the recording authorities. There is reason to assume that only the more dramatic or almost successful attempts will be reported and recorded, such as the "aborted successful suicidal attempts" described by Weiss, Nunez, and Schaie (1961).

Shneidman and Farberow (1961) traced 5906 attempted suicides in Los Angeles county in 1957, whereas the number of committed suicides was 768, according to the official records of the coroner's office. This yields a ratio of 7.69 attempted suicides to one committed suicide. Twenty-seven percent of the committed suicides and 6 percent of the attempted suicides occurred in the age group 60 and over, whereas 64 percent of the attempted suicides and 30 percent of the committed suicides occurred before age 40. Parkin and Stengel (1965) made a two-year survey covering the hospitals and general practitioners in Sheffield, an English industrial town, and found four attempts to one suicide in the age group 60 and over, and 20 attempts to one suicide in the population

aged under 40. The ratio of nonfatal to fatal suicidal acts doubled between 1960 and 1970 (Smith, 1972). In 1970, the rates for attempted suicide in the 20–24 age group in Edinburgh were about 400 per 100,000 for males, and about 450 per 100,000 for females. The corresponding rate for both males and females aged 65 and over was about 80 per 100,000 (Kreitman, 1972). In a random sample of attempted suicides admitted to an emergency clinic in West Berlin, Grüneberg (1977) found that the rate for attempts was eight times higher in males and females aged 26 to 30 than in the age group 66 to 75.

Two Types of Suicide

Without explicit reference to Durkheim's (1951) classification of four types of suicides (egoistic, anomic, altruistic and fatalistic), Ovenstone and Kreitman (1974) presented evidence for two types of suicide which correspond to a high degree to Durkheim's egoistic and anomic types. In a series of 106 consecutive suicides they were able to differentiate two subgroups according to absence or presence of previously attempted suicides. One subgroup, the "non-parasuicide group," comprised individuals who had led stable if precariously adjusted lives until dislocation occurred; they then reacted with a relatively brief depressive episode, sometimes associated with excessive drinking, and soon after killed themselves. The second group, the "para-suicide group," consisted of individuals with long-standing and severe personality problems, commonly with chronic alcoholism, who had a history of at least one attempted suicide, and who eventually committed suicide in a setting of interpersonal chaos frequently associated with events and problems that were dependent on their own behavior.

There are a number of studies pointing to the validity of these two subgroups. Studying 134 successful suicides, Robins, Murphy, Wilkinson, Gassner, and Kayes (1959) found that most cases were suffering either from manic depressive depression or chronic alcoholism. Prior to the study of Ovenstone and Kreitman, Seager and Flood (1965) and McCulloch, Philip and Carstairs (1967) also brought forward evidence for two subgroups to which most suicides could be allocated.

There is a dearth of information concerning the personality structure of the aged suicides. The few pertinent studies indicate that most aged suicides belong to the group with stable personalities. This may be due to selective factors: most people surviving to old age are more or less free from manifest character disorder. Barraclough (1971) found only one case of chronic alcoholism among 30 elderly suicides. Patel (1972) found that for those without a previous history of attempted suicide, suicide occurred most commonly in the sixth decade. In detailed descriptions of characteristics of suicide in old age, Ringel (1969) and Seidel (1969) made no reference to asocial personalities and alcoholism.

This evidence indicates that the suicides of the aged belong to Ovenstone and Kreitman's "non-parasuicide group," or are egoistic rather than anomic according to the terminology of Durkheim.

Mental Illness

In the studies of suicides, the percentages of suicides suffering from mental illness vary from 20 to 94 (WHO, 1968). There are only a few systematic studies aimed at establishing a psychiatric diagnosis of the deceased subjects. Robins *et al.* (1959) found that nine out of 134 suicides were "apparently clinically well," whereas the numbers of manic-depressives and chronic alcoholics were 42 and 27 respectively. In his study of suicides in London, Sainsbury (1955) concluded that mental disorders were the principal factor in 37 percent and a contributory factor in a fur-

ther 10 percent. Referring to later studies, Sainsbury (1973) stated that nearly all suicides are psychiatrically ill. According to diagnoses made independently by three consultant psychiatrists, over two-thirds had a depressive illness, 13 percent were alcoholics, and eight percent suffered from other mental illness. Analyzing the 30 elderly suicides in this study group Barraclough (1971) found 26 persons with depression, one chronic alcoholic, one possible confusional state, and four who were deemed not mentally ill. In a study of the 31 suicides committed by persons aged 65 and over in Helsinki in 1970 and 1971, Lönnqvist (1977) found that 14 were severely mentally ill, 13 had mild mental symptoms, and no mental symptoms were discovered in four.

The role of organic brain factors in the etiology of suicides in elderly is of particular interest. Sainsbury (1955) reported that between 15 and 20 percent of suicides over 60 had signs of intellectual deterioration before death.

The observed frequencies of mental illness in suicides of old age are related to diagnosis of depression. If the diagnosis of depression is considered justified only when there are severe symptoms (deeply depressive mood associated with retardation or agitation), the incidence of depression in suicides will remain at around 20 percent (WHO, 1968). But if a wider diagnosis of depression is employed, the percentage of depression preceding suicide will rise almost to 100, as stated by Sainsbury (1973). In many cases chronic alcoholism may lead to depression. The core of depression is the hopelessness subsequent to repeated failures at restitution. Suicide can be viewed as an act carried out to relieve this state of hopelessness.

In the consideration of mental illness and attempted suicide, the preponderant role of depressions also comes to the fore. Batchelor and Napier (1953) diagnosed depressive illness in 80 percent and organic syndrome in

10 percent of attempted suicides. The corresponding figures reported by O'Neal, Robins, and Schmidt (1956) were 47 percent and 42 percent, by Kreitman (1976) 58 percent and 8 percent, and by Feuerlein (1977) 50 percent and 14 percent.

Neither acute confusional states nor late paraphrenia seems to play a conspicuous role in attempted suicide in old age. In a study of 34 attempted suicides in persons aged 60 years or over, Sendbuehler and Goldstein (1973) found organic brain syndrome in 18 cases, or 53 percent compared with an incidence of 5 to 10 percent in the normal population. In most cases the organic brain syndrome coexisted with other mental diseases, mostly depression (with only one case of character disorder). In many cases a diagnosis of "life crisis" or acute depression seems most appropriate, seen not infrequently in association with psychopathic or hysterical traits.

There is slight evidence for a higher incidence of chronic alcoholism among aged people who attempt suicide, compared to aged people who complete the act. In studies of attempted suicides, Batchelor and Napier (1953) reported 10 percent chronic alcoholism, O'Neal *et al.* (1956) 11 percent, Böcker (1975) 15 percent, Kreitman (1976) 12 percent or 26 percent if only men were considered, Feuerlein (1977) 15 percent among men, and Grüneberg (1977) 23.5 percent among men and 6 percent among women. The frequency of chronic alcoholism among the elderly who attempt suicide is clearly less than in persons under 65 years of age who do so (Feuerlein 1977; Kreitman 1976).

Physical Illness

Because of the high frequency of chronic physical diseases in old age, the mere finding of physical ill-health in suicides and attempted suicides is of no import without a simultaneous estimation of the personal significance allocated to the illness. Sains-

bury (1955) estimated that physical illness contributed to the suicide in 35 percent of the elderly cases, compared with 27 percent in the middle-aged and 10 percent in young people. Analyzing 80 cases of suicides committed by persons over 65 years, Hedri (1967) found the most common factor was the attitude to somatic illness. Making a comparison between 30 suicides over 65 and 30 accidental deaths of the same age, Barraclough (1971) found 17 important physical disorders in the suicides compared to nine in the accidental deaths. Studying suicidal notes Kulawik and Decke (1973) found physical illness most frequently mentioned, particularly by elderly female suicides. In his study of 31 completed suicides aged 65 and over, Lönnqvist (1979) found severe physical illness in 16 cases.

Comparing attempted and committed suicides Shneidman and Farberow (1961) found that physical illness played a lesser role in attempted suicide than in committed suicide. In fair agreement with this finding, Böcker (1975), Feuerlein (1977), and Grüneberg (1977) established a heavy preponderance of interpersonal problems compared to illness problems among elderly who had attempted suicide. Dorpat, Anderson, and Ripley (1968) found physical illness to be the most common precipitating factor in completed suicide, whereas no statistically significant relationship between age and prevalence of physical illness could be established in the attempted suicides.

Hypochondria

Hypochondria is part of man's attitude to his body. Man views his body and physical illness in many ways: adequately, with "high bodily concern" (Busse, 1970), with denial of illness, with an unfounded fear of suffering from a disease (hypochondriac fear), or with a conviction to the same effect (hypochondriac delusion). It stands to reason that fear of being ill fights against illness and death, including suicide. Accordingly, no hypochondriac fear was discovered in a randomly selected series of suicides committed by mental hospital patients (Stenback, Achté and Rimón, 1965). In a randomly selected series of 80 alcohol addicts, hypochondria was found in only three subjects, none of whom belonged to 12 subjects who had attempted suicide (Stenback and Blumenthal, 1964). This incompatibility of suicide and hypochondriac fear is not found in cases with hypochondriac delusions. In these cases the risk of suicide is high, because a hypochondriac delusion acts psychologically like a physical disease. The finding of De Alarcón (1964) of more attempted suicides among aged depressive patients with hypochondria points to the seriousness of depressive delusions with hypochondriac content.

Social Factors

Social Isolation and Loneliness

Along with social disintegration and social disorganization, social isolation and loneliness are frequently mentioned in the analysis of causes of suicidal behavior in the aged (Böcker, 1975; Gardner, Bahn, and Mack, 1964; Sainsbury, 1962; Stengel, 1965). Social isolation and loneliness are treated as corollaries of living alone. Frequently many aspects of isolation and loneliness do not get the attention they deserve.

In a study of isolation, loneliness, and suicidal ideation, Bungard (1977) differentiated three dimensions of isolation: objective quantitative isolation, subjective quantitative isolation, and qualitative isolation. Objective quantitative isolation indicates frequency of weekly social contacts. Subjective quantitative isolation is the subject's self-estimation of the frequency of his social contacts. Based on the concept of intimacy put forward by Lowenthal and Haven

(1968), qualitative isolation is a measure of intimacy experienced in the social contacts. According to responses given by 134 subjects aged 65 and over who live alone, 15.7 percent were highly isolated, 11.9 percent regarded themselves as isolated, and 18.7 percent were "qualitatively isolated" (Bungard, 1977). When asked about feelings of loneliness, only half of the quantitatively isolated reported that they suffered from loneliness. This loneliness correlated clearly with loss of intimacy and not with the other measures of isolation. The percentage of suicidal ideation was no higher in these 134 subjects than in 271 subjects who were not living alone. The highest correlation was found between qualitative isolation and suicidal ideation. An unsatisfactory marriage and poor relationship to children proved to be the most crucial factors in qualitative isolation with suicidal ideation. This study of Bungard has been reported in some length in order to illustrate the intricate interplay between social and psychological factors.

Marital Status

The suicide rates for single men are double that for married men (Monk, 1975). In a study of 2,064 suicides comprising all suicides in the adult population 25 years of age and older in Finland during 1969-1971, Lönnqvist, Koskenvuo, Sarna, and Kaprio (1979) found that the rates for single women in the 25-44 age group were almost three times higher than the rates for married women, but in the age group 65 and over the rates of single and married women were almost the same. The rates for widows and divorcees in the age group 65 and over were higher than those for the married women, but were less than the rates for the age group 45-64. Thus living alone, widowhood, or marital separation contribute to suicides among the elderly but to a lesser degree than among the young and middle-aged.

Bereavement

As reported above, the rates of suicide are higher among the widowed than among the married. A reasonable supposition is that the event of bereavement may predispose to suicide. MacMahon and Pugh (1965) compared 320 widowed suicides with the same number of widowed persons having died of other causes. Deaths from suicide clustered in the first four years of widowhood, particularly in the first year. This was more marked in the older age groups, especially among males. For example, there were 12 suicides within one year of widowhood among males 70 years and over, where only two would have been expected on the basis of the comparison deaths. In a study of all suicides aged 65 and over in Helsinki during 1970–1971, Lönnqvist (1977) found that out of 11 widowers and widows, three men and one woman had lost their spouse within six months prior to suicide.

Bunch, Barraclough, Nelson and Sainsbury (1971) found a high proportion of bereavements of mothers among suicidal single males aged 50 and over. In addition to marital break-up, the death or admission to hospital of a friend or relative was the reason for living alone on the day of suicide in 34 percent of 30 aged suicides studied by Barraclough (1971). Moss and Hamilton (1956) found that among the aged, the loss or death of close relatives occurred twice as often for a group of attempted suicides as for a control group. Finding simultaneous mental illness, particularly depression, in the bereaved suicides, Barraclough (1971) referred to the obvious fact that bereavement acts through the mental illness, mostly through the depression that it elicits.

Living Alone

In his study of suicide in London, Sainsbury (1955) found that the percentage of suicides living alone was as high as 29.7 percent. The percentage of suicides 60 years and over living alone was even higher, 39.0 percent. In 10 percent of cases the loneliness was considered as a contributory factor. In an ecological study of suicide in England and Wales, Whitlock (1973a, 1973b) showed that unfavorable social factors had considerably less impact upon suicides aged 65 and over except for loneliness in men. Whitlock (1973b) concluded:

> There is good reason to regard suicide in old age as a distinct phenomenon, compared with suicide by younger persons. When one examines the intercorrelations between the suicide rates for men and women in the three age samples (15–44, 45–64, and 65 +), there are no significant correlations between suicides of those aged 65 and over with the younger age groups, whereas both the younger age groups correlate highly significantly with each other and with the general suicide rate for all ages. Hence, one might conclude that social environmental circumstances have greater impact on younger suicides than they do on the oldest age group.

When emphasizing the high percentage among the elderly of suicides living alone, the high percentage of persons living alone aged 65 and over is frequently overlooked. In the study of Lönnqvist (1977) six men (33 percent) and four women (31 percent) were living alone, the corresponding percentages in the normal population being 19 percent and 50 percent respectively. In a less urbanized sample, Barraclough (1971) found that nearly half of the elderly suicides were permanently living alone whereas only 20 percent of the old population lived in one-person households.

Moving House

In his analysis of precedents to suicide, Sainsbury (1973) took considerable interest in the bearing of moving house. He found that suicides had moved more often than controls. Analyses by age indicated that elderly men and middle-aged women are the groups most vulnerable to the effects of moving house. Most frequently the suicides took place within two years after the move.

Retirement

The impact of retirement on suicidal behavior is difficult to estimate because an event taking place after the age of 65 is not necessarily due to the retirement at 65. There is no evidence indicating that the "retirement shock" is a common cause of suicide. According to the "status integration theory" (Gibbs and Martin, 1964), suicide is associated with moving from one occupational status to another. Retirement implies moving from the status of a gainfully employed worker to a nonworker status void of meaningful roles. It seems plausible to assume that such a change, which may have only a minor immediate effect, can in the long run have weighty consequences, particularly when retirement involves less income and less prestige in addition to loss of work and workmates. Having observed that the rates of suicides had decreased in the retirees belonging to higher classes and increased in the lower status groups, Sainsbury (1962) hypothesized that the capacity to retire to opportunities for more varied interests and outlets may protect the higher class aged against suicide. However, Lönnqvist et al. (1979) found a decrease in suicide rates of the age group 65 and over in all social classes.

Social Class

According to a highly extant opinion, suicide is more common among the higher social classes. However, the only evidence found for this idea is the higher suicide rates of males aged 20–64 in social classes I and II in England and Wales (Sainsbury, 1963). Sainsbury's own study of suicide in London

(Sainsbury, 1955) did not provide an answer to this question. It is important to make the distinction between ecological and individual correlation with social class. By ecological correlation is meant that suicide rates correlate with the proportion of the upper social classes in the population. There is evidence of such correlation in England (Bagley, Jacobson, and Palmer, 1973; Whitlock, 1973a, 1973b) but not in Buffalo, N.Y. (Lester, 1970). Ecological correlations with social classes I and II (i.e., more suicides were committed in regions with higher proportion of people in these social classes) were found for males and females in the age groups 15–44 and 45–64 but not in the age group 65 and over (Whitlock, 1973a, 1973b). In studies of individuals, a strong correlation between suicide and lowest social class was found (Achté, 1962; Breed, 1963; Lalli and Turner, 1968; Maris, 1967; Yap, 1958). Studying suicide in New Haven, Connecticut, Weiss (1954) found that after the age of 65, the rates for lower-class males were considerably higher than those for upper-class males. Differentiating the suicides according to marital status (single, married, widowhood and divorce), age (25 to 44, 45 to 64, and 65 and over), and social class (I to IV), Lönnqvist et al. (1979) found the highest rate for men aged 65 and over in social class IV. For women, the highest rate was in social class I but the result was not statistically significant. In general, the figures for males 65 and over showed an overall small decrease from the rates for the 45–64 age group in almost all social classes and marital status groups. The rates for women 65 and over were mostly lower than in the 45–64 age group in all social classes and marital status groups.

Poverty is related to social class, because social class is primarily constructed on the basis of occupation and associated income. Sainsbury (1962) very strongly emphasized that "wealth, not poverty, is associated with suicide.'' However, he recognized the significance of secondary poverty, the condition of becoming poor after having been well-to-do. The low rate of suicide in the Southern blacks points to the minor role of poverty as such. The role of economic misery however is stressed by the finding that 40 percent of black suicides in New Orleans had worried about debts (Swanson and Breed, 1976).

Sainsbury (1963) argued that old-age pension systems have not reduced suicide frequency in the elderly. He based this statement upon the equal rise in frequency both in countries with the most comprehensive old-age pension schemes and in countries with the least. Kruijt (1960), basing his conclusions on the WHO statistics, pointed out that the old-age regression in suicide rates was most apparent in Great Britain and Scandinavia and in the white populations of the commonwealth countries, where the health and social status of old people were better than in countries not showing such a decline in the suicide rates.

As mentioned previously, the decrease of suicide rates in the population 65 years and over in the U.S. went from 45 per 100,000 in 1933 to about 20 per 100,000 in 1968, whereas the decrease for all ages was only from 15.9 to 10.7 per 100,000 (Diggory, 1976). This relatively greater decrease for the aged can be related to the Social Security developed just during this time period.

Social Disorganization

Suicides are more frequent in urban than in rural areas, and in central city than in suburban areas. To a high degree this is due to selective migration. A community can be considered as having an optimal social organization when its population is a balanced cross-section of the national population. Conversely, a community can be regarded as disorganized when its share of children, persons living alone, old people, men, and women is uneven. An additional dimension in social disorganization is the proportion of old dilapidated buildings lacking continuous repair and new buildings considered by the residents as good residences. Social disorganization as a structural term has to be differentiated from social integration or social functioning. In his ecological study of suicide in London, Sainsbury (1955) emphasized that districts with a high proportion of lodging-houses, hotels, and flatlets had high suicide rates. In his study of high- and low-risk areas within a city, Lönnqvist (1977) found that the areas characterized by absence of slum formation and with a high proportion of retired old women had low suicide rates, i.e., there were only few suicides in districts where old people lived quietly by themselves.

Cultural Factors

The impact of culture, including religion, upon suicide is two-fold. Culture has a direct impact through the creation of concepts on life and death, life after death, old age, suicide, personal responsibility, and other values. An indirect effect is seen in the influencing of society and other modes of social life, resulting in social integration or disintegration.

Durkheim (1951) strongly emphasized that religion has a prophylactic effect upon suicide and that this effect is related to the social integration religion brings about:

If religion protects man against the desire for self-destruction, it is not that it preaches the respect for his own person to him with arguments sui generis; but because it is a society. What constitutes this society is the existence of a certain number of beliefs and practices common to all the faithful, traditional and thus obligatory. The more numerous and strong these collective states of mind are, the stronger the integration of the religious community, and also the greater its preservative value. The details of dogmas and rites are secondary. The essential thing is that they be capable of supporting a sufficiently intense collective life.

However, "details of dogmas" are part of the cognitive structure of culture. The impact of culture upon suicidal behavior has to be estimated according to the role allocated to cognitive factors in human behavior. Thomae (1976) views human personality as highly influenced by cognitive processes, and according to Beck (1967) cognitive factors are more crucial in the development of depression, the mental state preceding suicide, than is generally believed. Obviously, the obstacles related to the study of cognitive factors in suicide hinder the acquisition of adequate knowledge about the cognitive aspects of culture, including religion.

In the interaction between social factors proper and cultural factors, the adverse social situation may override the prophylactic effect of culture. In his report on suicide in Hong Kong, Yap (1958) presented the figures for suicides in Peking in 1917. In contrast to the increased suicide rates for old Chinese in Hong Kong in the early 1950s, the rates for the aged in Peking in 1917 were about the same as for the younger adult population. Yap interpreted these findings in the light of the traditional culture with its great emphasis on filial piety and respect for the aged. This culture could not, however, protect the old in the social upheaval characteristic of Hong Kong in the fifties. In their explanation of the high suicide rates in Japan, Iga and Tatai (1975) also allocated more weight to social defects than to cultural attitudes accepting or even idealizing suicide.

Cultures disapproving suicide overtly or covertly take a more permissive stand concerning suicide in old age than suicide committed in young or middle age. An old person is regarded entitled to relieve himself — and his relatives — from the burden of chronic illness, loneliness, and feelings of uselessness. The present discussion of euthanasia exemplifies this. Nevertheless, a negative attitude to suicide in old age is still prevalent in most cultures.

In his overview on suicide, Sainsbury (1973) formulated four "strands" in his explanation of suicide: psychological predisposition, social predisposition, personal crisis, and the attitudes to death and self-destruction prevailing within a society and its institutions, particularly its religious ones. He believes that if a church anathematizes suicide, its practicing members will be protected simply on this account. In addition, following Durkheim's line of thought, Sainsbury allocates great significance to religion's capacity to strengthen the social cohesiveness of its members. In his study he found that nearly half of the controls but only 25 percent of the suicides were somewhat religiously active.

Some General Aspects

Suicide as an Act, Not a Symptom

Only in extreme cases can suicide be viewed as a pure symptom of a psychiatric disturbance characterized by confusion and auto-aggressiveness. Dementia and confusion generally weaken the ability to act with the sufficient intentionality required to commit a suicide. According to the degree of psychological intent, Weiss (1974) divided the suicidal acts into serious acts, gestures, or gambling with death. The proportion of completed suicides to attempted suicides is higher in old age. This is taken to indicate that the use of suicidal acts for appeal (Stengel, 1973) is not common in old age. Evidence to the effect that suicidal attempts are, nevertheless, not rare in the elderly population was provided by Grüneberg (1977), who found that two-thirds of the attempted suicides in persons aged 60 and over in West Berlin could be classified as gestures or gamblings. Although suicide is an act and not a symptom in the proper sense, it is not an act of free will. Weiss (1974) has clearly stated this point: "The evidence indicates that suicidal behavior is most often a symptom (or a terminating act) of biologically, psychologically and culturally determined psychiatric disorder, not a free moral choice."

Aggression

According to psychoanalytical thought, suicide is caused by aggression directed toward the self (Menninger, 1938; Ringel, 1952). Autoaggression can be implicated in the cases when depression and suicidal thoughts are linked with guilt feelings, indicating that the subject views himself as the source and cause of his failure and emotional distress. But, as dealt with elsewhere, depressions in old age are mostly not distinctly guilt depressions. Judging from the low rate of aggressive delinquency in old age (Riley and Foner, 1968), the aggressive potential of old people is markedly low.

If aggression inappropriately loses its connotation of hostile, emotionally forceful activity and becomes a verbal expression for any form of forceful activity, aggression can be said to play a role in every suicide. The higher rates of male suicides can be attributed not to aggression as such but to men's particular position in culture and society and to the biologically and culturally stronger disposition in men to settle difficulties by action.

Impulse and Purpose

Man's behavior can in a general sense be classified as impulse behavior and purpose behavior. The bulk of studies provide evidence indicating that the proportion of impulse suicides — almost identical with anomic, psychopathic and hysteric suicides — decreases with age. The typical suicide of old age is a suicide seriously

planned and carried out. Nevertheless, the very execution of the frequently long-harbored purpose often has the psychological features of impulse behavior. A tiny incident may put the suicidal idea into execution. Nevertheless, this impulse behavior in the last crucial phase does not contradict the premeditated, deliberate character of the suicide in the aged.

Old Age Suicide Is "Egoistic"

In many ways, evidence indicates that the suicide of the aged is of the type Durkheim (1951) called "egoistic." Egoism or excessive individualism, as Durkheim also put it, involves deficient commitment to the cultural, ethical or religious values of the society in which the individual lives. In addition, egoism in Durkheim's sense implies that emotional bonds tying the individual to other people are few, frequently resulting in social isolation. The individualistic withdrawal makes it difficult for the supporting social networks, if they exist at all, to build up the reality and feelings of social integration badly needed in the times of losses and failures.

Five Main Factors

Although aging in many cases is associated with factors conducive to suicide, it is not plausible to consider, as was done by Seidel (1969), the general biological and psychosocial characteristics of aging as the crucial causes of suicide. The main factors contributing to the suicidal behavior can be condensed as follows: first, general and age-specific losses and failures which cause depression with hopelessness and despair; second, an "egoistic" or excessively individualistic personality, emotionally shallow or cold; third, a society unable to create social integration by means of family bonds, community interest groups, or supporting social services; fourth, a personality trait of resolving problems by action and not by passive adaptation; fifth, a suicide-promoting environment, either personal (e.g., suicides in the family) or cultural (e.g., acceptance and idealization of suicide).

Treatment

Shneidman (1969) introduced the concepts of prevention, intervention, and postvention of suicide. Prevention is roughly synonymous with the concept of prevention in public health and preventive medicine. Intervention and postvention equal the old notion of treatment, including followup treatment. The aim of treatment is early identification of prospective cases of suicide and attempted suicide, and prevention.

As discussed earlier, physical and mental illness have a great impact upon suicidal behavior in old age. This fact indicates that the doctor who treats the elderly for the physical illness (usually a general practitioner) is the key person in the treatment of mental illness, including the suicidal intent. The presence of depression, particularly if hopelessness is a pronounced symptom (Minkoff, Bergman, Beck, and Beck, 1973), should alert the doctor to the possibility of suicide. The treatment of a presumptive suicide is basically the same as the treatment given to a person suffering from depression. This includes drug treatment, psychotherapy, and sociotherapy. In a psychologically appropriate way, although not too cautiously, the therapist has to search for suicidal ideation and explicitly discuss the nature of suicide and its consequences. Because a truly significant personal relationship, a "confidant" (Lowenthal and Haven, 1968), may be the crucial life-saving thing, the treating person (doctor, social worker, psychologist, or minister) has the moral obligation to see to it that the help-seeking person finds such a helper or friend. Although the general practitioner has to first deal with the physical ailments, he also is obliged to treat the presuicidal state. He

should try to get family members, friends, and social welfare personnel to help the patients. In addition to the humane obligation to relieve elderly persons from loneliness, the concrete provision of continuing medical services and home care is of crucial significance. The old person will almost always take recourse to suicide only when he feels himself abandoned. Particular attention should be paid to acute crises during which the elderly person, who has long harbored a suicide intent, may put intent into execution.

In addition to the emergency telephone service, The Samaritans in Great Britain have established a "befriending" service within which ordinary people befriend lonely people (Fox, 1976). In towns where the Samaritans had been in operation for at least two years, Bagley (1968, 1971) found a decrease of 58 percent in the suicide rate compared with a rise of 19.8 percent in matched control towns. However, the proportion of old people making use of "suicide prevention centers" was low. The Samaritan Organization had fewer old clients of both sexes than expected, amounting to 6 percent of the total against an average of 13 percent in the general population. "It seems universally the experience of helping agencies that the elderly are likelier to suffer, stoically, in silence" (Fox, 1976).

It seems obvious that treatment of the suicidal aged must take place primarily in hospitals, outpatient clinics, social welfare agencies, and other places where the aged seek help for their diverse needs, rather than in community suicide services, although they are also highly necessary for the older age groups.

Prevention

In connection with suicide, prevention describes the measures to be taken for preventing an individual from committing suicide. This is in contrast to public health and preventive medicine, where prevention is mainly "primary prevention," group-directed activity aimed at reducing morbidity. Because of the central role physical and mental disorders have in the etiology of suicide in old age, an important preventive measure is provision of good medical care, including good mental health services. Studying the effect of introduction of community-oriented mental health services, Walk (1967) found evidence indicating that the community care may have protected some elderly patients from suicide. A similar project in a more rural area failed to repeat these results (Nielsen and Videbeck, 1973).

Health services are intimately interwoven with the social services and good personal relationships. Prevention of suicide in old age can succeed only by a combination of macrosocial measures (pension, housing, transport, etc.) and microsocial action (family, friend, social case work, group work, leisure activities, etc.). As an overall aspect, "community organization" can describe the whole spectrum of community activities which must be put to bear on the situation of the aged.

Information on the suicide problem has to be given to all professional groups dealing with old people. In addition, the general public should be informed about the risks involved in letting old people with chronic disorders live in isolation. The organizations for aged people could have a considerable preventive role. Of particular significance is a culture that allocates general esteem to the elderly and creates meaning and optimism for the last decades of life.

In his essay on self-destruction, Menninger (1938) pointed to the close relationship between alcohol addiction and suicide. As was discussed earlier, one of the two types of suicide put forward by Ovenstone and Kreitman (1974) was characterized by a chronic alcoholism. In a study of committed suicides among clients at the Los Angeles Suicide Prevention Center, Litman and Wold (1976) found that the cases who did not respond to the center's "crisis intervention" suffered from chronic alcoholism to a high degree. Suicide prevention has to face the challenge of a culture favoring self-destruction by means of alcohol. Nevertheless, the basic problem is not alcohol but a hedonistic life-style which does not view bodily integrity as a basic value and as a means for using life for self-fulfillment and for service of fellow men and cultural goals.

Durkheim's comprehensive view of suicide as caused by disturbances in structure and function of society still has relevance. Prevention of suicide in old age has to make possible the integration of the old into society on all levels, not least on the personal level. In the words of Litman and Wold (1976), "extended personal relationships are the most potent of anti-suicide remedies." Failures and losses are burdens easier to bear when a friend is at hand.

References

Achté, K. 1962. Sosiaalinen tutkimus Helsingissä 1958–1960 tehdyistä itsemurhista. *Duodecim,* 78, 677–682.

Bagley, C. 1968. The evaluation of a suicide prevention scheme by an ecological method. *Soc. Sci. Med.,* 2, 1–14.

Bagley, C. 1971. An evaluation of suicide prevention agencies. *Life-Threatening Behavior,* 1, 245–259.

Bagley, C., Jacobson, S., and Palmer, C. 1973. Social structure and the ecological distribution of mental illness, suicide, and delinquency. *Psychol. Med.,* 3, 177–187.

Barraclough, B. M. 1971. Suicide in the elderly. In D. W. K. Kay and A. Walk (eds.), *Recent Developments in Psychogeriatrics,* pp. 87–97. Brit. J. Psychiat. Special Publication No. 6. Ashford, Kent: Hedley Bros. Ltd.

Barraclough, B. M., Nelson, B., Bunch, J., and Sainsbury, P. 1970. The diagnostic classification and psychiatric treatment of 100 suicides. In R. Fox (ed.), *Proceedings of Fifth International Conference for Suicide Prevention.* Vienna: I.A.S.P.

Batchelor, I. R. C., and Napier, M. B. 1953. Attempted suicide in old age. *Brit. Med. J.,* 2, 1186-1190.

Böcker, F. 1975. Suizidhandlungen alter Menschen, *Münch. med. Wschr.* 117, 201-204.

Bolander, A-M. 1972. Nordic suicide statistics. In J. Waldenström, T. Larsson, and N. Ljungstedt (eds.). *Suicide and Attempted Suicide,* pp. 57-88. Stockholm: Nordiska Bokhandelns Förlag.

Bunch, J., Barraclough, B., Nelson, B., and Sainsbury, P. 1971. Suicide following bereavement of parents. *Soc. Psychiat.,* 6, 193-199.

Bungard, W. 1977. Isolation, Einsamkeit und Selbstmordgedanken im Alter. *Aktuelle Gerontologie,* 7, 81-89.

Busse, E. W. 1970. Psychoneurotic reactions and defense mechanisms in the aged. In E. Palmore (ed.), *Normal Aging,* pp. 84-90. Durham N.C.: Duke University Press.

De Alarcón, R. 1964. Hypochondriasis and depression in the aged. *Geront. Clin.,* 6, 266-277.

Diggory, J. C. 1976. United States suicide rates 1933-1968: An analysis of some trends. In E. S. Shneidman (ed.), *Suicidology: Contemporary Developments,* pp. 25-69. New York: Grune & Stratton.

Dorpat, T. L., Anderson, W. F., and Ripley, H. S. 1968. The relationship of physical illness to suicide. In H. L. P. Resnik (ed.), *Suicidal Behaviors,* pp. 209-219. Boston: Little, Brown and Company.

Durkheim, E. 1951. *Suicide.* New York: The Free Press.

Feuerlein, W. 1977. Ursachen, Motivationen und Tendenzen von Selbstmordhandlungen im Alter. *Aktuelle Gerontologie,* 7, 67-74.

Fox, R. 1976. The recent decline of suicide in Britain: The role of the Samaritan suicide prevention movement. In E. S. Shneidman (ed.), *Suicidology: Contemporary Developments,* pp. 499-524. New York: Grune & Stratton.

Gardner, E. A., Bahn, A. K., and Mack, M. 1964. Suicide and psychiatric care in aging. *Arch. Gen. Psychiat.,* 10, 547-553.

Gibbs, J., and Martin, W. T. 1964. *Status Integration and Suicide.* Eugene, Ore.: The University of Oregon Press.

Grüneberg, F. 1977. Suizidalität bei Patienten einer geriatrischen Abteilung. *Aktuelle Gerontologie,* 7, 91-100.

Hedri, A. 1967. Selbstmord im höheren Alter. *Schweiz. Arch. Neurol. Neurochir. Psychiat.,* 100, 179-202.

Iga, M. and Tatai, K. 1975. Characteristics of suicides and attitudes toward suicide in Japan. In N. L. Farberow (ed.), *Suicide in Different Cultures,* pp. 255-280. Baltimore: University Park Press.

Kreitman, N. 1972. Aspects of the epidemiology of suicide and "attempted suicide" (parasuicide). In J. Waldeström, T. Larsson, and N. Ljungstedt (eds), *Suicide and Attempted Suicide,* pp. 45-52. Stockholm: Nordiska Bokhandelns Förlag.

Kreitman, N. 1976. Age and parasuicide ("attempted suicide"). *Psychological Medicine,* 6, 113-121.

Kruijt, C. S. 1960. *Zelfmoord.* Utrecht: van Gorum.

Kulawik, H., and Decke, D. 1973. Letzte Aufzeichnungen — eine Analyse von 223 nach vollendeten Suiziden hinterlassenen Briefen und Mitteilungen. *Psychiat. Clin.,* 6, 193-210.

Lalli, M., and Turner, S. H. 1968. Suicide and homicide: a comparative analysis by race and occupational levels. *J. Criminal Law, Criminol. and Police Sci.,* 59, 191-200.

Lester, D. 1970. Social disorganization and completed suicide. *Soc. Psychiat.,* 5, 175-176.

Litman, R. E., and Wold, C. I. 1976. Beyond crisis intervention. In E. S. Shneidman (ed.), *Suicidology: Contemporary Developments,* pp. 525-546. New York: Grune & Stratton.

Lönnqvist, J. 1977. *Suicide in Helsinki.* Helsinki: Psychiatria Fennica.

Lönnqvist, J. 1979. Personal communication.

Lönnqvist, J., Koskenvuo, M., Sarna, S., and Kaprio, J. 1979. Social status and suicide. In manuscript.

Lowenthal, M. F., and Haven, C. 1968. Interaction and adaptation: intimacy as a critical variable. *Amer. Sociol. Rev.,* 33, 414–420.

MacMahon, B., and Pugh, T. F. 1965. Suicide in the widowed. *Am. J. Epidemiol.,* 81, 23–31.

Maris, R. 1967. Suicide, status and mobility in Chicago. *Social Forces,* 46, 246–256.

McCulloch, J. W., Philip, A. E., and Carstairs, G. M. 1967. The ecology of suicidal behavior. *Brit. J. Psychiat.,* 113, 313–319.

Menninger, K. 1938. *Man Against Himself.* New York: Harcourt, Brace and Company.

Minkoff, K., Bergman, E., Beck, A. T., and Beck, R. 1973. Hopelessness, depression and attempted suicide. *Amer. J. Psychiat.,* 130, 455–459.

Monk, M. 1975. Epidemiology. In S. Perlin (ed.), *A Handbook for the Study of Suicide,* pp. 185–211. New York: Oxford University Press.

Moss, L. M., and Hamilton, D. M. 1956. Psychotherapy of the suicidal patient. *Amer. J. Psychiat.,* 112, 814–820.

Nielsen, J., and Videbeck, T. 1973. Suicide frequency before and after introduction of community psychiatry in a Danish island. *Brit. J. Psychiat.,* 123, 35–39.

O'Neal, P., Robins, E., and Schmidt, E. H. 1956. A psychiatric study of attempted suicide in persons over sixty years of age. *Arch. Neurol. & Psychiat.,* 75, 275–284.

Ovenstone, I. M. K., and Kreitman, N. 1974. Two syndromes of suicide. *Brit. J. Psychiat.,* 124, 336–345.

Parkin, D., and Stengel, E. 1965. Incidence of suicide attempts in an urban community. *Brit. Med. J.,* 2, 133–138.

Patel, N. S. 1972. Life style of the completed suicide. In R. E. Litman (ed.), *Proceedings 6th International Conference for Suicide Prevention,* pp. 158–164. Los Angeles: International Association for Suicide Prevention.

Riley, M. W., and Foner, A. 1968. *Aging and Society. Volume one: An Inventory of Research Findings.* New York: Russell Sage.

Ringel, E. 1952. *Der Selbstmord.* Vienna: Maudrich.

Ringel, E. 1969. Neue Gesichtspunkte zum präsuizidalen Syndrom. In E. Ringel (ed.), *Selbstmordverhütung,* pp. 51–116. Bern: Verlag Hans Huber.

Robins, E., Murphy, G. E., Wilkinson, R. H., Gassner, S., and Kayes, J. 1959. Some clinical considerations in the prevention of suicide based on a study of 134 successful suicides. *Amer. J. Public Health,* 49, 888–899.

Ruzicka, L. T. 1976. Suicide, 1950 to 1971. *World Health Statistics Report,* 29, 396–413.

Sainsbury, P. 1955. *Suicide in London.* London: Chapman and Hall Ltd.

Sainsbury, P. 1962. Suicide in late life. *Geront. Clin.,* 4, 161–170.

Sainsbury, P. 1963. Social and epidemiological aspect of suicide with special reference to the aged. In R. H. Williams, C. Tibbitts, and W. Donahue (eds.), *Processes of Aging. Vol. II,* pp. 153–175. New York: Atherton Press.

Sainsbury, P. 1973. Suicide: opinion and facts. *Proc. Roy. Soc. Med.,* 66, 579–587.

Seager, C. P., and Flood, R. A. 1965. Suicide in Bristol. *Brit. J. Psychiat.,* 111, 919–932.

Seidel, K. 1969. Die eigenständige innere Dynamik des Alters Suizids. *Aktuelle Fragen Psychiat. Neurol. Vol.* 9, pp. 42–62. Basel: S. Karger.

Sendbuehler, J. M., and Goldstein, S. 1977. Attempted suicide among the aged. *J. Amer. Geriat. Soc.,* 25, 245–248.

Shneidman, E. S. 1969. Suicide, lethality, and the psychological autopsy. *Int. Psychiat. Clin.,* 6, 225–250.

Shneidman, E. S., and Farberow, N. L. 1961. Statistical comparisons between attempted and committed suicides. In N. L. Farberow and E. S. Shneidman (eds.), *The Cry for Help,* pp. 19–47. New York: McGraw-Hill.

Stenback, A., Achté, K. A., and Rimón, R. H. 1965. Physical disease, hypochondria, and alcohol addiction in suicides committed by mental hospital patients. *Brit. J. Psychiat.,* 111, 933–937.

Stenback, A., and Blumenthal, M. 1964. Relationship of alcoholism, hypochondria and attempted suicide. *Acta Psychiat. Scand.,* 40, 133–140.

Stengel, E. 1965. The prevention of suicide in old age. *Z. Präventivmed,* 10, 474–481.

Stengel, E. 1973. *Suicide and Attempted Suicide.* Harmondsworth: Penguin Books.

Stengel, E., and Cook, N. G. 1958. *Attempted Suicide.* Maudsley Monographs, No. 4. Oxford: Oxford University Press.

Walk, D. 1967. Suicide and community care. *Brit. J. Psychiat.,* 113, 1381–1391.

Weiss, J. M. A. 1954. Suicide: an epidemiological analysis. *Psychiat. Quart.,* 18, 225–282.

Weiss, J. M. A. 1974. Suicide: In S. Arieti (ed.), *American Handbook of Psychiatry. Vol. III.,* pp. 743–765. New York: Basic Books.

Weiss, J. M. A., Nunez, N., and Schaie, K. W. 1961. Quantification of certain trends in attempted suicide. In *Proceedings of the Third World Congress of Psychiatry,* pp. 1236–1240. Montreal: University of Toronto Press and McGill University Press.

Whitlock, F. A. 1973a. Suicide in England and Wales 1959–63. Part 1: The county boroughs. *Psychol. Med.,* 3, 350–365.

Whitlock, F. A. 1973b. Suicide in England and Wales 1959–63. Part 2: London. *Psychol. Med.,* 3, 411–420.

World Health Organization. 1968. *Prevention of Suicide.* Public Health Papers No. 35. Geneva.

World Health Organization. 1977. *World Health Statistics Annual. Vol. I. Vital Statistics and Causes of Death.* Geneva.

Yap, P. M. 1958. Suicide in Hong Kong. *J. Ment. Sci.,* 104, 266–301.

Life-Review Therapy

MYRNA I. LEWIS and ROBERT N. BUTLER

By actively encouraging recall of the past, the therapist can help older persons evaluate the meaning of their lives.

Consideration of the developmental stages of late life must be part of any psychotherapy with older persons. Yet, surprisingly little theory has been formulated and used for this purpose. What do older people experience as they age? Are there predictable feelings that reflect this last phase of the life cycle? After observing older persons clinically and in research situations, Butler postulated in 1961 the presence of the life review as a prominent developmental occurrence of late life. Since that time, we have been experimenting with the use of the life review in individual and group psychotherapy.

The life review is seen as a universal mental process brought about by the realization of approaching dissolution and death. It marks the lives of all older persons in some manner as their myths of invulnerability or immortality give way and death begins to be viewed as an imminent personal reality. The life review is characterized by the progressive return to consciousness of past experiences and, particularly, the resurgence of unresolved conflicts.

The tendency of older persons to reminisce about the past has often been dismissed derogatorily as living in the past, second childhood, or senility or, somewhat more sympathetically, as an expression of loneliness, absence of new experience, or tenacious clinging to a previous identity. It is regarded as boring, time-consuming, and meaningless. But the predilection toward reminiscence appears to have a much more positive function, a psychotherapeutic one, in which the older person reflects on his life in order to resolve, reorganize, and reintegrate what is troubling or preoccupying him.

In its natural state, the life review is spontaneous, often quite unselective, and occurs in younger persons as well (for example, in adolescence, in middle age, and in the face of death). However, it takes on a striking intensity in early old age. Older persons comment with surprise on their ability to recall previous life events with sudden and remarkable clarity: "It's as though it happened only yesterday," "I felt as though I was there." They may have memories of smell, taste, and feel as well as sight and sound. The capacity for free association seems to be renewed, bringing up memories deeply buried in the unconscious.

Some persons are fully aware of the process and openly state a desire to "put my life in order," while others are only dimly conscious of something compelling them to muse about the past. Still others are totally unaware, perhaps in an unconscious attempt to avoid the pain of unpleasant

Source: Lewis, M. I., & Butler, R. N. Life-review therapy: Putting memories to work in individual and group psychotherapy. *Geriatrics*, 1974, 29, 165–173. Reprinted by permission.

memories or to protect themselves against the stereotype of living in the past.

The emotions accompanying the life review vary, but an element of pain and discomfort often arises as problems surface. The intensity of the experience may range from a mild nostalgia, reminiscing, and storytelling to a feverish preoccupation, sometimes centered on a particular subject. The person may feel compelled to give his entire life story to anyone who will listen. Past happenings may be repeated over and over again. Since repetition and emphasis on the past also are seen in brain-damaged persons, it is important to observe diagnostically whether the compulsion to repeat can be abated by the resolution of underlying issues.

Individual Psychotherapy

Life-review therapy is action-oriented and psychoanalytically influenced. In individual psychotherapy, the life review obviously is not a process initiated by the therapist. Rather, the therapist taps into an already ongoing self-analysis and participates in it with the older person. The outward manifestations of life review are varied. Persons may present themselves as garrulous, agitated, or depressed. They may actively reach out for others or quietly or angrily withdraw. Some appear passive, effectively masking an active life review. Any indication that the person is not viewing something for the first time can be a clue, including such statements as: "Yes, that has been going through my mind," or, "Lately I've been worrying about that."

The purpose of psychotherapeutic intervention into the life review is to enhance it, to make it more conscious, deliberate, and efficient. Therapy begins at the first contact with the gathering of information. History taking or the collecting of facts about an older person can trigger memories of conflict and concern, providing important diagnostic perceptions. The emotional impact of the memories, the emphasis or de-emphasis of crucial areas of memory, and repetitious patterns of remembering can be observed. Some parts of the older person's past may be of little interest to him simply because difficulties have been resolved and the potential benefits of remembering are not worth the effort. Other topics have been buried out of reach of conscious memory because of fear or guilt and should be reviewed and resolved.

We have devised several methods of evoking memory in older persons that are useful and often enjoyable to them.

1. Written or taped autobiographies. We frequently ask older patients to compile an autobiography, which may be as long and as detailed as they wish. This is an interesting and relatively nonthreatening way to open up communication. Again, the therapist searches for clues in the style, detail, and emphasis that a person gives to various aspects of his life. Omissions must be examined. For instance, one man provided an intricate history of his professional and social life, with newspaper clippings, letters from important persons, and pictures of himself and his wife. There was nothing about his two children except for several news items on their graduations and weddings. Upon questioning, the patient revealed that the son, then 45 years old, had not spoken to his parents in 20 years and that the daughter had minimal contact. The focus of therapy became the parents' buried feelings toward these estrangements.

We also have used the autobiography in therapy with younger persons, suggesting that they go to their elders with tape recorder or pencil and pad to talk over family history, personalities in the family, and childhood reminiscences. Younger family members often become intrigued with such efforts and begin to look to their elders as important sources of information. We have seen profound changes in family communications as old and young take a mutual interest in their past.

In addition to aiding memory, the tape recorder is useful for playing back therapy sessions. The older person begins to pick up on his own areas of conflict, to hear what may be boring and repetitious in his manner, and to generally take an outsider's look at himself, sometimes for the first time. Self-confrontation in front of a mirror also is helpful. Many are surprised at what they project to others and, as a result, deliberately begin to alter their behavior or appearance.

2. Pilgrimages (in person or through correspondence). For those persons for whom this is possible, we encourage actual trips back to the location of their birth, childhood, youth, and young adult life. Taking photographs and notes is useful. Even for persons who make such journeys as a matter of course to visit friends and relatives, we emphasize a new use of their time to rediscover the past by recalling and talking over old times with family, neighbors, and friends.

Some people go with a specific purpose. One older woman returned to her childhood home to discover why she was forbidden to go into the attic as a youngster. She discovered that there had never been any stairs, only a hole in the ceiling, thus explaining her parents' "arbitrary" refusal. She recalled many fantasies of what might be in the attic and her anger at her parents for forbidding her to look.

Others make the journey home through correspondence or even through talking with others who have recently been there. These efforts reflect a search both for continuity and for late-life discoveries regarding perceptions of the past.

For example, after talking with persons who had known him in his childhood town, a 69 year old man decided that he had purposefully tried to make himself into a "noble image" as a little boy. "I was orphaned at nine years of age," he recalled. "I was so scared that I decided to be the best boy there

was. To avoid the orphan home secluded behind high brick walls, I vowed to go to church and Sunday school and never to swear, smoke, drink, steal, cheat, or hurt persons or animals. I would work hard to buy presents for everyone, scrub the floors, shovel snow, and split wood. The formula seemed to work, and the philosophy gained a strong hold on me. People tell me I never grieved openly or got angry. Now I'm understanding why I'm still such a damn nice guy all the time."

3. Reunions. Annual reunions (high school and college classes, family, church, etc.) offer a unique opportunity for the intensification of the life review. An individual can look at himself in the context of other meaningful people and take a measure of where he stands in the course of the life cycle as the years pass. Reunions usually are bittersweet experiences. One woman in her 80s met regularly with her college classmates, and only two of them were left when she died. She both mourned the loss of her peers and rejoiced in her own survival. Reunions that occur on a regular basis provide a gradual adjustment to change, but ones that take place irregularly can have a shock effect ("My God, I didn't realize how many years have gone by!").

4. Genealogy. We encourage the interest many older persons begin to take in their own parents and grandparents, as well as distant ancestors, as they strive to find themselves in history and to take comfort in the fact that they are part of a long line of relatives. One of the ways the old seem to resolve fears of death is to gain a sense of other family members having died before them. This reflects the search for universality, a sense of the long chain of birth and death and the basic fairness of each person having a life to live that must eventually be given up.

Some older persons have put ads in newspapers in search of relatives or family information. Others visit cemeteries to look for family names and dates. Local libraries, town and church records, and family bibles also are sources of data.

5. Scrapbooks, photo albums, old letters, and other memorabilia. These are rich sources of information and memory. We frequently ask older persons to bring such items to therapy sessions, where we go through them together. This is an especially pleasant form of interviewing for the older person and quickly establishes positive rapport. Even persons with moderate brain damage can remember many details through pictures and keepsakes. On visits to older persons at home or in nursing homes or hospitals, the therapist can learn a good deal by commenting on pictures, mementos, or other personal items that are likely to have emotional meaning.

Some persons compile scrapbooks and albums in old age. This is helpful in summing up their own lives and handing on a family record to the next generation.

6. Summation of life work. This is a particularly useful technique for persons whose work was important to them and for those who have no children or have had little contact with their children. Persons without families have an especially keen need to feel they have participated meaningfully in the world. We ask people for a verbal or written summation of their work that will reflect what they regard as their contribution and also the history of their particular craft as they experienced it. Some of these summations have grown into full-scale books or published poetry and music.

7. Preserving ethnic identity. Many older persons have an ethnic identity that has been ignored or forgotten. In many instances, first-generation Americans have been so involved in establishing themselves that they have not facilitated the transmission of the ethnic heritage of their immigrant parents to their own children. A resurrection of this identity can have positive personal and social value.

The therapeutic possibilities of the life review are complex. There is the opportunity to reexamine the whole of one's life and to make sense of it, both on its own terms and in comparison with the lives of others. Identity may be reexamined and restructured. There is the chance to resolve old problems, to make amends and restore harmony with friends and relatives. (Family members have been known to decide to talk to one another after 30 or 40 years of angry silence.)

The dreams of youth may be relived through memory. (People seem to regret what they did not do more than what they actually did.) There is the opportunity to understand and accept personal foibles, to take full responsibility for acts that caused true harm but also to differentiate between real and neurotic guilt. The patient may demonstrate a maturing of the ability to tolerate conflict and uncertainty when these exist within himself and in his relationships to others.

Fears of death and dissolution may be mitigated as myths of invulnerability are confronted. People can become ready to die but in no hurry to do so. The future assumes less critical importance as the present is emphasized. "Elementality," the lively capacity to live in the present, may be fostered through the direct enjoyment of people, nature, colors, warmth, love, humor, and beauty in any form. There may be a greater capacity for mutuality, with a comfortable acceptance of the life cycle, the universe, and the generations. Pride in one's life and feelings of serenity often center around having done one's best. Older persons in difficult circumstances may give themselves a diagnosis of "extenuating circumstances," which credits them with surviving against terrible odds.

The elderly often become interested in teaching and in conservation of knowledge and the natural resources of the earth for future generations. They have a need to work out emotional and material legacies. They may revise their wills, give away possessions in advance, and generally simplify their lives. Creativity may be restimulated or emerge for the first time in the form of memoirs, arts, music, handicrafts, teaching, etc. The elderly may put together family records and study their genealogies. They often talk of deciding "how I want to live the rest of my life." For those who are infirm or bedridden, the life review can have the added function of learning how to be "responsibly dependent" in the appropriate acceptance of help.

The success of the life review depends on the outcome of the struggle to resolve old issues of resentment, guilt, bitterness, mistrust, dependence, and nihilism. All the truly significant emotional options remain available until the moment of death — love, hate, reconciliation, self-assertion, and self-esteem.

A reason used for not offering life-review therapy (and psychotherapy in general) to older persons is the fear that they are psychologically fragile. This is especially true if they look physically frail. What we fail to remember is that older persons are master survivors compared with the young. They can hardly be seen as inexperienced in defending themselves from the painful forces of life. As in all good therapy, the therapist begins where the older person is and proceeds sensitively and respectfully. Inappropriate interpretations or poor timing will be met with a variety of defenses perfected over a lifetime (withdrawal, denial, open hostility) as well as new ones that capitalize on the possibilities of old age (pretended senility, pseudofrailty, or even deafness that conveniently comes and goes).

However, the life review, by its very nature, evokes a sense of regret and sadness at the brevity of life, the missed opportunities, the mistakes, the wrongs done to others, the chosen paths that turned out badly. The therapist sees anxiety, guilt, despair, and depression. In extreme cases, persons may become terror-stricken, panicked, and even suicidal, particularly if they have irrevocably decided that life was a total waste. However, in our experience, this is more likely to happen when the person makes judgments on his own, without testing or sharing them. Most people have the capacity to reconcile their lives, to confront real guilt, and to find meaning, especially in the presence of acceptance and support from others.

Life-review therapy need not be ruled out because of brain damage. The Goldstein catastrophic reaction, resulting from overwhelming stimuli, can be minimized or avoided if the therapist proceeds carefully and observantly. Brain damage, of course, cannot be reversed, but overlying depression may be alleviated and adaptation may be encouraged.

Some therapists fear that encouragement of the life review will lead to egocentricity and "getting stuck" in the past, with neglect of the present. A certain self-centeredness occurs naturally during the life review. This may appear to become fixed if problems are not resolved. "Enshrinement" of certain ideas and possessions may occur as the person goes back to think about them again and again. This problem may be spontaneously resolved in time by the patient himself, or it may respond to attentive listening by others or to active psychotherapy.

Psychiatrists, psychologists, social workers, psychiatric nurses, and other professionals trained in the art of psychotherapy can be helpful to the older person. But beyond that, the life review is greatly enhanced by listeners, that is, persons who personally bear witness to the older person's struggles. We have seen high school students successfully aid the elderly in nursing homes, for example, by listening attentively by their beds as they talk. Family members and friends can partake in an older person's life review, adding their own memories and commenting with insights and support. The therapist must realize that some older persons prefer to work alone, with a tape recorder or pencil and paper. One of the interesting fringe benefits for therapists and listeners is in obtaining a rich supply of information and models for their own eventual old age.

The most introspective part of the life review seems to occur in the 60s and then begins to abate in the 70s and 80s. Gorney noted that the very old may enter a further developmental stage involving ego integration and serenity in the face of death.

Group Psychotherapy

In our opinion, the life review as it occurs in age-integrated group psychotherapy can be a rich, active reexperiencing of the past through the lives of others. All the generations participate in clarifying problems and working at solutions for the older person. There is a kind of recapitulation of the family.

We began experimenting with age-integrated group psychotherapy in 1970. Five groups of 8 to 10 members each were formed. Each group contained elderly persons over age 65, adults, young adults, and teenagers. The oldest member was 75 years of age; the youngest was 15. Criteria for inclusion were the absence of active psychoses and the presence of a major life crisis. Under study were reactions, ranging from essentially normative to pathologic, to the usual changes that occur in the life cycle (adolescence, marriage and divorce, parenthood, retirement, widowhood, and impending death). Groups met weekly with both of us as cotherapists.

Initially the older members tended to treat the young as mascots, not to be taken too seriously, while deferring leadership to the middle-aged. Some elderly persons assumed a rigid pedant role; others withdrew in silence. As therapy progressed, the elderly dropped some of their more rigid defenses and began to openly demonstrate their feelings about themselves, particularly with regard to aging. One woman spoke with indignation, "I don't like old age. I'm damn angry at the fact that I'm getting old and that I'm going to die."

Some displayed an unwillingness to grow up and accept their age, exhibiting a kind of Peter Pan wistfulness about youth. Certain individuals separated themselves from their peers as if to say, "I'm unique, not like the rest of those old fogies." Others overplayed aging through a pseudosenility that involved feigned forgetfulness and other pretenses aimed at fulfilling popular misconceptions about senility. In a similar ploy, of pseudofragility, persons declared themselves too emotionally fragile to deal with certain subjects in order both to avoid difficult issues and to make the younger generations feel guilty.

Closely related to this was the "old man" or "old woman" act, wherein persons in their 60s acted as though they were decrepit and about to die. They were determined that life was over, there was no hope, and group members might as well give up on them. Yet, they became resentful if ignored. Some older persons worked hard at projecting an image of sweetness and tranquility when they were in fact boiling over with rage. Others cast dire threats to the younger generation: "You'll see what it's like when *you* are old," or, "Wait until you reach my age. You won't talk so smart."

Reminiscence was occasionally used as a defense and even as a weapon to irritate others. Especially striking was the stubbornness of certain defenses that had been practiced over a lifetime but proved even more tempting to use in old age, for example, manipulation. Older persons who have been stripped of social status easily turn to manipulating others emotionally to achieve a sense of power.

Some persons will cling to old-fashioned theories and beliefs for psychologic purposes. A college-educated and thoroughly informed woman nonetheless insisted on believing in a totally hereditary basis for mental illness so that she could punish herself for her son's troubles. In doing so, she managed to avoid the guilt she felt about her own sexual activities after the death of her husband.

There is a danger that certain older men will commit "social suicide" on entering a new group. They show themselves as severely judgmental, especially of the young, and they rigidly refuse to accept anyone's point of view but their own. They will not tolerate negative reactions to themselves and usually insist that they could handle their own problems if everyone simply would listen and cooperate. These have been hard-driving, highly successful, often professional men who are used to a leadership role and have forgotten how to interact in any other manner. Therapists must intervene quickly before irreparable damage is done and the person flees the group as it becomes rejecting. Several individual sessions with the person may help.

Initially, young and middle-aged members are prone to see the old members in stereotyped terms. One young man openly stated, "My first reaction in coming to this group was to ask myself what I had in common with that old fart." The young are influenced by powerful cultural patterns of age prejudice and discrimination. The old in turn show prejudice toward the young through active dislike or more subtle avoidance. They may be embarrassed at the concept of sharing and learning with the young and have fears of losing status and self-respect. Some feel that they should arbitrarily be in a position of authority and teaching, while others feel they have nothing relevant to teach, that their knowledge is obsolete. There also is the fear of measuring their own education and intelligence against that of the young, whom they see as smarter and much better educated. The frequent

envy of youth is based on a view that younger people have the prerogatives and priorities, which, of course, is partly grounded in reality. Many especially envy the young their experiences in a more open sexual climate. Others covet their educational opportunities, financial security, medical advantages (nasal plastic surgery, orthodontia), and lack of experience with catastrophe (the Great Depression).

These issues are dealt with overtly and covertly as groups progress. The elderly often assume an active learning role as well as a teaching role. They may go through a period of saying outrageous things to those who are younger and thus slowly defuse anger and envy toward youth and middle age. Members of all ages comment on becoming less conscious of age and are surprised if a new member, on entering an already long-functioning group, begins reacting to someone in a stereotyped way as "old" or "young."

Groups are especially useful in decreasing the sense of isolation and uselessness felt by many elderly persons. One man commented, "My life is so 'daily.' I love to share the adventures of others." In a well-functioning group, the generations unite against the vicissitudes of the life cycle rather than warring against each other. There is a sense of solidarity in facing grief, anger, intimacy, fear, aging, and death. (An interim step often is an alliance between the young and the old against the middle-aged.) The old also see these groups as a way to "catch up with the times." For example, sex is a favorite topic of discussion as the elderly test their views.

A common experience for the old is to "hear echoes of my own life" as they listen to those who are younger. In many instances, the old become skilled at how and when to use their accumulated life experience to instruct and serve as a model for others. Rather than forcing their views and feeling hurt when they are rejected, they learn to listen for the appropriate time when a younger person is open to this kind of learning. Their unique contributions to younger members include a personal sense of life's flow from birth through death, per-sonal solutions for encountering grief and loss regarding old age and death, and models for growing older and for creating meaningful lives.

References

1. Butler, R. N.: Re-awakening interest. *Nursing Homes* 10:8–19, 1961.
2. Butler, R. N.: The life review: An interpretation of reminiscence in the aged. *Psychiatry* 26:65–76, 1963.
3. Butler, R. N., Lewis, M. I.: *Aging and Mental Health.* St. Louis, The C. V. Mosby Company, 1973.
4. Falk, J. M.: The Organization of Remembered Life Experience in Old Age: Its Relation to Subsequent Adaptive Capacity and to Age. Thesis, Committee on Human Development, University of Chicago, 1969.
5. Gorney, J. E.: Experience and Age: Patterns of Reminiscence Among the Elderly. Thesis, Committee on Human Development, University of Chicago, 1968.
6. Havighurst, R. J., Glasser, R.: An exploratory study of reminiscence. *J Gerontol* 27:245–253, 1972.
7. Liton, J., Olstein, S. C.: The specific aspects of reminiscence. *Social Casework* 50:263–268, 1969.
8. McMahon, A. W., Rhudick, P. J.: Reminiscing: Adaptational significance in the aged. *Arch Gen Psychiatry* 10: 294, 1964.
9. Pincus, A.: Reminiscence in aging and its implications for social work practice. *Social Work* 15:47, 1970.
10. Tobin S. S., Etigson, E.: Effect of stress on earliest memory. *Arch Gen Psychiatry* 19: 435–444, 1968.

The Mental Health System and the Future Aged

ROBERT L. KAHN

As mental health ideologies have changed, the system serves a smaller proportion of older persons than in earlier decades. This paper discusses likely future changes in the characteristics of older persons and of mental health professionals and makes recommendations for changes in the system.

Prediction of the future, in considering the mental health needs of the aged, requires an understanding of the past. Accordingly, we will first consider the patterns of mental health care of the aged in the first half of this century and then contrast it with more recent changes. It is our contention that such an analysis discloses a clear-cut pattern of negative age bias, that some of the factors underlying this bias will remain, while others will have altered significantly by the year 2000, and, finally, that it is then possible to make predictions both about what *will* happen and what *should* happen.

The early 1900s were characterized by the great buildup of mental hospitals, particularly those operated by states and counties. In 1904 there were 150,151 persons resident in mental hospitals in the United States, while the total was 633,504 in the peak year of 1955 (Willner, 1974). During this period there was a systematic age bias, with older persons being disproportionately hospitalized.

Figure 1 shows first admission rates per 100,000 persons of each age group in the state of New York from 1909–1911 to 1949–1951. At every decade there was a con-

sistent age gradient; the older the age, the higher the rate of admission. Although the rates for other age groups remained fairly constant over this 40-year period, remaining between 50 and 150 per 100,000, the aged not only had an initially much higher rate, but the rate continued to rise, more than doubling the 1909–1911 rate by 1949–1951, and going from around 200 to approximately 435 per 100,000.

After World War II there was a dramatic alteration in our conceptions and patterns of mental health care. With such milestones as the establishment of the National Institute of Mental Health in 1948, the organization of the Joint Commission on Mental Illness and Health in 1955, and the passage of the Community Mental Health Centers Act of 1963, there was a more active and optimistic attitude toward mental illness, characterized by radically reducing the resident mental hospital population and developing such other services as psychiatric units in general hospitals, outpatient services of all kinds, and the vaunted community mental health centers.

These developments did result in drastically changed patterns of use of

Source: Kahn, R. L. The mental health system and the future aged. *Gerontologist,* 1975, 15, 24–31. Copyright 1975 by the Gerontological Society. Reprinted by permission.

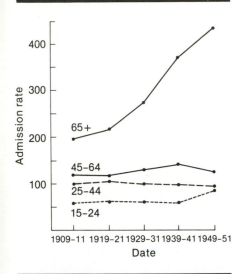

FIGURE 1
First admissions to all hospitals for mental disease in New York State, 1910–1950: Rates per 100,000 population in each age group (derived from Malzberg, 1967).

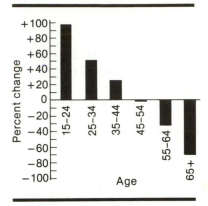

FIGURE 2
Percentage of change between 1946 and 1972 for each age group in rate of first admissions per 100,000 population to state and county mental hospitals (USA) (derived from Kramer, 1973a).

psychiatric facilities, but patterns which varied strikingly according to age. In Figure 2 the percentage of change for each age group is shown in the first admission rates to all state and county mental hospitals in the United States between 1946 and 1972. Once more there is an age gradient but now it is diametrically opposite to that shown for the earlier years of this century. In the past 25 years there has been an enormous increase in the first admission rate for the very young, 97%, with the amount of change progressively decreasing with age, being unchanged for the 45–54 year group, and then showing a great *decrease* for the older patients, going down over 71% for those aged 65 and over.

These figures are based on first admissions to mental hospitals, but a similar trend is found when examining patient care episodes in all psychiatric services. Patient care episodes are defined as the number of residents or enrolled patients in all types of psychiatric facilities at the beginning of the year plus the total additions to these facilities during the year. Comparing the years 1966 and 1971, with all the new facilities and services available, there was an increase of 37% in patient care episodes for the total population (Redick, 1973). Again, as shown in Figure 3, there is an enormous age differential, and a consistent gradient, with younger persons showing the largest increases (as much as 67.5% for those 18–24 years of age), with lesser increases for successively older age groups, and with those aged 65 and over showing an actual *decrease* of almost 22%.

Rather than helping older persons, the great mental health revolution has only led to their dropping out of the psychiatric system. Certainly the new programs have not helped the aged. If we look, for example, at psychiatric units in general hospitals, from 1966 to 1971 there was a 45% reduc-

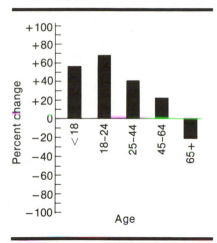

FIGURE 3

Percentage of change between 1966 and 1971 for each age group in rate of patient care episodes per 100,000 population for all psychiatric services (USA) (derived from Redick, 1973).

tion in the number of patient care episodes for the aged. In Community Mental Health Centers, in 1971 the aged represented only 7% of inpatient service, and only 3% of their outpatient cases. Of all other outpatient services, the aged were only 2% (Kramer, 1973a).

To the question of what has happened to the aged mental health dropouts, obviously much of the answer can be found in the data on nursing homes. In an analysis by Redick (1974) of changes in the utilization of psychiatric services by the aged mentally ill during the decade 1960–1970, he concludes that there is an "emerging custodialism" in which the aged are now being displaced to nursing homes. Showing an incredible increase from 554,000 residents in 1963 to 1,098,500 10 years later, and with a current bed capacity of over 1,200,000, the nursing homes have replaced the state and county hospitals as the custodial warehouses. This has led to an increase in the total proportions

of persons aged 65 + who are institutionalized, with the proportion rising from 4% to 5% from 1960 to 1970.

In 1963 almost two-fifths of the aged who were diagnosed as mentally ill and who were in long-term care institutions were to be found in state and county mental hospitals, while 53% were in nursing homes and personal care homes. These proportions changed drastically in 1969, when 75% of the aged mentally ill were in nursing homes.

It is obvious that the elderly are being neglected by the mental health establishment. The explanation for this unfortunate state of affairs is undoubtedly complex. It is a common stereotype among clinical gerontologists that other mental health professionals avoid the aged because of psychological problems such as ". . . unresolved conflict with parental images and the need to deny our own mortality . . ." (Lawton & Gottesman, 1974). Although there may well be some degree of psychological selectivity in determining which professionals become gerontologists, there is no *a priori* basis for presuming that this group are more mentally healthy than other professionals, or that they have fewer unresolved conflicts over growing old. It could just as well be hypothesized that those who work with the elderly may have *excessive* unresolved parental conflicts, or excessive problems in confronting their own mortality. In any case, such simplistic psychological explanations would damn the aged to continued neglect so long as human beings have parents and so long as human beings die.

Nor can the data be interpreted mechanically in terms of administrative considerations or idiosyncratic financial status of the aged, although these are obviously contributory factors. It is not a situation of the aged against the world. There is a consistent age gradient over the entire life-span which must be accounted for, in which the aged, defined here as those who are 65 and over, are simply the extreme of a continuum.

In contrast to the views just mentioned, the patterns of psychiatric care of the aged can be better explained on the basis of a reciprocal aversiveness between the mental health establishment and older persons, based on the interaction of such factors as mental health ideology, social class characteristics, and considerations of age appropriateness.

Ideological Factors

Over the past two centuries in this country, there have been several clear ideological movements and patterns with regard to mental health. Originally the mental hospitals were established as part of a great humanitarian movement to provide treatment for the mentally ill instead of merely depositing them in prisons or poorhouses. In the 19th century the advocates of "moral treatment" endeavored to improve the quality of care in the mental hospitals; but with the increasing flow of lower class immigrants as patients, the hospitals became very custodial in their orientation, relying heavily on the use of restraints (Grob, 1966). In the 20th century the mental hospital continued to deteriorate until our World War II experiences and some new developments in England (e.g., Carse, Panton, & Watt, 1958; Macmillan, 1958) contributed to a reconceptualization of our mental health ideology.

The prevailing practices in hospital treatment were so bad that even politicians could make the obvious criticisms, as evident in President Kennedy's message to Congress on "Mental Illness and Mental Retardation" in 1963:

> . . . [these new programs] have rendered obsolete the traditional methods of treatment which imposed upon the mentally ill a social quarantine, a prolonged or permanent confinement in huge, unhappy mental hospitals where they were out of sight and forgotten.

The mental health ideology that had led to these conditions, often implicit in the actions of society and of professionals, can be summed up in the concept of "custodialism" (Greenblatt, Levinson, & Williams, 1957; Greenblatt, York, & Brown, 1955; Stanton & Schwartz, 1954). Gilbert and Levinson (1956) actually developed a Custodial Mental Illness Ideology Scale to measure the extent of this ideology which they contrasted with "humanism." The components of an ideology can be found in attitudes toward the nature, causes, and treatment of mental illness, including hospital aims and policies. The principal components of custodialism are a basically negative or therapeutically pessimistic approach to the mentally ill; patients are perceived as being categorically different from normal people; patients are perceived as unpredictable and dangerous, requiring care in a highly controlled setting; the setting is concerned mainly with detention and safekeeping; and the institution is conceived as a rigid status hierarchy with lines of communication following the chain of authority, and with the patient occupying the lowest status position in the hierarchy.

Opposition to custodialism took many forms, both inside and outside the institution, with some who challenged the role of the institution itself. Much of the change within the institution was embodied in the concept of the "therapeutic community" which originated in Britain (Jones, 1953; Main, 1946). Taking a more optimistic view of mental illness, the proponents of the therapeutic community believed that much pathology was induced by the institution itself which compelled the patient to learn and act the "sick role." To prevent such a development they advocated democratizing the hospital, flattening the hierarchy, opening up two-way communication channels, and utilizing the skills of the total personnel of the institution, with special emphasis on the expanded role of the patient.

The new philosophy was indeed accompanied by many changes,[1] with meetings of staff and patients on psychiatric wards, by establishing "open" hospitals by unlocking the doors, by increasing personnel, and by accelerating patient turnover. But the application of the ideological shifts were uneven in their effect on different age groups. There seems to be a consistent relationship between custodialism and age. Prior to World War II, with mental illness regarded as a stigma, with custodialism as the dominant philosophy, and with the mental hospital serving primarily to extrude the mentally ill from society, older persons were more frequently hospitalized than younger persons. With the change in orientation after the war, the age gradient was reversed. For the young, the changed ideology represented new possibilities for treatment. For the aged, custodialism continued to prevail but with one difference — earlier the aged were treated custodially in mental hospitals (despite the presence of psychiatrically-trained personnel); now they are treated custodially in nursing homes (without any pretense of psychiatric service).

Part of the great displacement of the mentally ill aged from the state hospitals to nursing homes has resulted from a mechanical adherence to slogans, such as "alternatives to hospitalization." Based on the principle that state hospitals are unsuitable settings for the elderly, programs have been developed to find alternatives; but this usually means the use of nursing homes, without the realization that nursing homes are even more custodial in their care than the

hospitals they are meant to replace (Epstein & Simon, 1968). The confusion of slogan and substance is, of course, common in contemporary mental health trends. The shift from the hospital to the community, for example, may simply represent a changed location but the same old philosophy (Polak & Jones, 1973).

Custodialism as a Self-Fulfilling Prophecy

In part, the age biases in mental health treatment demonstrated above are a direct consequence of the policy of custodialism. The negative attitudes associated with custodialism resulted in the accumulation of chronic patients, predominantly schizophrenics, who were hospitalized at an early age and then remained institutionalized, commonly for life. Such persons thus constituted an aging resident population for whom custodialism had been a self-fulfilling prophecy, teaching them the "sick role," isolating them from their families and from normal community activities, and making them incapable of living without extensive protective care. Custodialism applied to the young eventually created a cohort of older persons who required it or could be moved out of the mental hospital only by heroic efforts. These patients were galling to the hospital staffs, taking up so much time, space, and money and with such little benefit. On reaching age 65 these patients were routinely shifted to the "geriatric" ward, and their evident need for custodial care was now attributed to their age rather than to their chronic schizophrenia and long-term custodial history. The myth about these patients has been augmented by life-cycle professionals who endeavor to set up programs in mental hospitals for geriatric patients, but who fail to distinguish between those aged who developed mental disorder in their early life, such as schizophrenics,

---

[1] Sometimes the effects of the ideological shift are not properly appreciated because of the temporal proximity of the use of chemotherapy. The large-scale use of drugs, which began in the middle 1950s, coincided with the start of the reduction in the resident patient population in mental hospitals. But the changes in ideology and practice antedated the drugs. Macmillan (1958), for example, started opening his hospital in 1945 and completed the changeover in 1952.

and persons who developed mental disorder in old age (Kahn & Zarit, 1974). Since the management of older patients in mental hospitals did not fit the new treatment philosophy, it was considered preferable to shift them to other institutions, still complacently custodial.

The philosophy of custodialism is so entrenched that benevolent gerontological planners talk about the need to provide custodial care as part of any new comprehensive care system. Since there are persons who manifestly fit the custodial operation, it is easy to overlook the fact that the need for custodial care is highly exaggerated and that its very application is self-perpetuating. Studies of aged persons in custodial settings have demonstrated the phenomena of "excess disability" (Kahn, 1971) in which the level of function is poorer than the patient's physiological capability (Brody, Kleban, Lawton, & Silverman, 1971; Kellman, 1962). Excess disability is characteristic of both self-care and cognitive functioning. A person may have all the necessary physiological capacities yet be unable to feed or bathe himself. Cognitively, the old person may show "unorientation" (Kahn, 1971), a state in which the impairment demonstrated in areas where the patient has personal and emotional involvement is greater than the impairment shown in more neutral areas. Thus, he may know the date or the name of the President of the United States, but be unable to state where he is, even after having been in residence for months or years. In a large-scale institutional study it was found that the level of mental status of aged patients was related to certain characteristics of the institutions, being better when the institution was less custodial (Kahn, 1971). It has been demonstrated that breaking down the custodial pattern of a mental hospital ward by mixing young and old patients on the same ward will result in improved cognitive function in the older patient (Kahana & Kahana, 1970).

Although there is much difference of opinion among gerontologists on the use of institutions, assaults are now appearing from new directions, and some of the basic assumptions and practices of custodialism are being challenged. Notable among these are new research findings (Schaie, 1974) which question the generality of cognitive decline with age, findings which, by undercutting one of the stereotypes about "senility," are also undercutting one of the stereotypes about the need for custodial care.

Effects of Social Class

The relationship between age and custodialism can be explained further on the basis of cohort differences in social class. It is a well-established research finding that mental health treatment varies according to the social status of the patient, with upper-class persons receiving psychological treatment such as psychotherapy and psychoanalysis, while lower-class patients receive somatic therapy and custodial care (Hollingshead & Redlich, 1958). Since, compared to the young, a higher proportion of the old have been poorly educated, and a higher proportion of old mental patients are working class rather than middle class, differences in treatment reflect these social class differences, thus compounding the age difference.

The effects of social class are complex and do not necessarily reflect discriminating prejudice. The new treatment philosophies, whether represented by the "therapeutic communities" or some form of psychotherapy, emphasize verbal interaction and the patient's recognition of psychological causation of mental disorder. Since these are the very characteristics that distinguish social classes, the aged may be treated custodially not only because they are aged, but because, with their lesser education and other cultural differences, they are less receptive to verbal psychological treatments (Hollingshead & Redlich, 1958; Kahn, Pollack, & Fink, 1957).

Thus there is mutual avoidance; the mental health professionals prefer the young, educated patients, and the aged reject the psychological treatments of psychotherapy and psychoanalysis so highly valued by the professional.

Age Appropriateness

In addition to the social class factors, there may be an intrinsic life cycle phenomenon of age appropriateness for types of psychiatric treatment. Comparable to attitudes toward other life events, there is apparently a sense that psychiatric treatment is appropriate or optimum at a given time of life. Certainly the professionals, starting with Freud himself, have encouraged the notion that psychological treatment is best undertaken early in life. Among the present-day young it may be almost a status symbol to be in treatment, but for the present-day old it is a disgrace.

A Look at the Future

From this analysis insights can be derived regarding critical theoretical issues regarding mental illness and treatment in the aged and how these will be affected by changing social factors by the year 2000.

Effects of Changes in the Aged

Perhaps the major changes in the relationship of custodialism and the aged in the year 2000 will come about because of predictable changes in the aged themselves. We know that they will have characteristics of higher social status: much better education — the median education will be high school graduation, far fewer foreign-born, and more social and political awareness. These people will have much less tolerance for custodialism in all its aspects, including the use of custodial institutions such as nursing homes.

The aged are also likely to be much better off because of better economic resources through improved pensions and social security, better comprehensive medical care, and better preparation for, and participation in, retirement. Because of all these changes the aged may actually manifest fewer extreme cases of disordered behavior for which custodial care might be considered.

Effects of Changes in the Professionals

The mental health professionals can also be expected to change significantly. Responding partly to the improved social status of the aged, no longer contaminated in their thinking by large numbers of chronically institutionalized schizophrenics who will have died off, and with a greater awareness of the etiology and modifiability of acute organic brain syndromes, the professional will also eschew custodialism and will become increasingly concerned with prevention in all its aspects. Although primary prevention through such measures as good nutrition will be major efforts, secondary and tertiary prevention will also receive greater attention than today. These will stress mitigating or terminating a disorder once it is manifest by using such methods as early detection and crisis intervention, and reducing the disabilities consequent upon disorder by using such techniques as the therapeutic community and rehabilitation. At the very least, there will be a recognition that the negative consequences of mental dysfunction can be minimized by exposing old persons to more demanding and stimulating environments, in contrast to the isolation and dependency effects of the custodial institution. There will be less infantilization and greater opportunities for the old person to maintain control of his own situation.

Needed New Developments

New developments within the mental health system must also be undertaken directly. For one thing, the very fact of increasing numbers of the aged require new approaches.[2]

Concepts for new programs that should be developed, as well as the operational examples, already exist, although decisive evaluative studies remain to be done. Allowing for many variations depending on the resources of specific settings, the following are suggested as guiding principles:

(1) Mental health and illness are not categorically different, and the same individual will have both healthy and pathological components of personality. As much as possible we should respond to the healthy aspects rather than reinforce the "sick role."

(2) Psychopathology is not fixed or inevitable within the organism, even with altered central nervous system dysfunction.

___

[2] From a conventional viewpoint, the problem would be almost insoluble if we reckoned the fantastic costs or professional needs as described by Kraner (1973b). For example, reckoning on a 20% psychiatric need in the total population in the year 1980, and providing a total of 10 hours of care per year per patient per discipline, he indicates that over 300,000 professionals will be required in each of the disciplines of psychiatry, psychology, and nursing, with an additional 609,000 social workers needed to provide minimal service.

Different environments produce different consequences on function, contributing to enhancement or to deterioration.

(3) "Senility" is a psycho-social-biological phenomenon. Although we may have limited means for changing the biological component, the psychological and social factors are modifiable.

(4) If an old person is under protective care, his functional level should correspond to his physiological capacity.

(5) Intervention can be harmful as well as helpful. Although resources for intervention should be available when needed, it is best to follow a policy of *minimal intervention;* that is, intervention that is least disruptive of usual functioning in the usual setting. Thus, it would be more sensible to provide care in the home or day-care center than in the hospital; in the storefront rather than in the clinic; in the neighborhood rather than downtown; for brief rather than for long periods; with neighborhood personnel rather than with explicit medical or social agency professionals.

Minimal intervention as a positive concept must be differentiated from neglect. It must also be differentiated from "maximal-minimal" intervention, in which the person is removed from his community, then placed in an institution that provides no psychological or social compensatory measures.

(6) Effective care is quite different from the *number* of services. The structural dynamics may be far more important than the component parts. In particular, *continuity of care* is essential, in which personnel, agencies, and institutions are integrated. The same personnel should be able to deal with the person in a variety of settings, whether in or out of the institution. Institutions will not be as effective if they are encapsulated units, even with high staff/patient ratios, as if they are part of a coordinated comprehensive system.

(7) Both the needs of the old person and

his family must be considered. More good may be done for both by providing supportive help to the family, for example, than by dealing directly with the patient's psychosis. One of the most useful techniques is to provide "holiday relief," in which the old person may be hospitalized for a week or two to enable the family to take a vacation. This limited support may often be sufficient to prevent permanent institutionalization of the old person.

There may also be a legitimate conflict of interests. It may relieve emotional pressures on a family to place an old person in an institution permanently, but the effects of the move may be deleterious to the old person. In those cases, ethical as well as clinical judgment is required.

(8) Expectations may be decisive in achieving mental health goals. In using an institution, for example, setting a time limit at the point of entry may help the old person, his family, and the institution to act in ways more likely to lead to his return home.

(9) *Decentralization* and *"de-medicalization"* of services are desirable. Outreach workers, nonprofessionals preferably coming from the same background, same neighborhood, and same general age group as the prospective clients, would be the first line of contact, serving at least in a confidante role, providing the liaison to professionals. The latter would serve as indirect consultants to nonprofessionals, providing brief *direct* service only to a small number of persons, but providing *indirect* consultation to "firing line professionals such as police, clergymen, general physicians, and to others such as bank tellers, bus drivers, and storekeepers." Most persons could be helped without ever becoming an administratively official "patient" or "client."

(10) Instead of being the passive recipient of services which the professional decides are good for him, the old person's sense of control should be maintained. The very act of being helped can have the paradoxical effect of increasing the impairment because of the infantilization and sense of loss of control that results.

(11) Those principles can be carried further by realizing that *"potential service"* may be as useful as any form of *actual* help. The basis of this concept is to guarantee that service will be available when needed. If a community were assured of the validity of the commitment of service it would be increasingly possible to cope with many problems, either autonomously or with minimum help, that might otherwise have involved more extensive use of resources. Thus, guaranteeing that brief hospitalization will always be available when needed should not only reduce the amount of long hospitalization, but the amount of brief hospitalization as well.

(12) The most effective mental health programs for the aged have been achieved in the context of the public health technique of a geographically-defined catchment area (e.g., Macmillan, 1958; Perlin & Kahn, 1967). By explicitly defining the responsibility and commitment for a given target population and physical locale, there has been the greatest opportunity for facilitating such necessary components as comprehensiveness and continuity of care, guaranteed service, and maximum use of community resources. In practice the application of the catchment area concept has resulted in providing for the mental health needs of the entire population. (Without such a definition, programs follow the conventional criteria for selecting patients, resulting in the characteristic biases toward the aged, so that their needs are overlooked or evaded by "dumping" old people into an external institution or resource.)

These concepts and changed practices have considerable promise in meeting the mental health needs of the aged by the year

2000. They will have an impact on both the established mental health system and the innovative community services. The new approaches may have the multiple virtues of not only being more effective than many conventional practices but also far more economical and efficient in the use of our resources.

References

Brody, E. M., Kleban, M. M., Lawton, M. P., & Silverman, H. A. Excess disabilities of mental impaired aged: Impact of individualized treatment. *Gerontologist,* 1971, 11, 124–132.

Carse, J., Panton, N. E., & Watt, A. A district mental health service: the Worthing experiment. *Lancet,* 1958, 1, 39–42.

Epstein, L. J., & Simon, A. Alternatives to state hospitalization for the geriatric mentally ill. *American Journal of Psychiatry,* 1968, 124, 955–961.

Gilbert, D. C., & Levinson, D. J. Ideology, personality and institutional policy in the mental hospital. *Journal of Abnormal & Social Psychology,* 1956, 53, 263–271.

Greenblatt, M., Levinson, D. J., & Williams, R. *The patient and the mental hospital.* Free Press, Glencoe, IL, 1957.

Greenblatt, M., York, R., & Brown, E. L. *From custodial to therapeutic care in mental hospitals.* Russell Sage Foundation, New York, 1955.

Grob, G.N. *The state and the mentally ill.* Univ. of North Carolina Press, Chapel Hill, 1966.

Hollingshead, A. B., & Redlich, F. C. *Social class and mental illness.* John Wiley, New York, 1958.

Jones, M. *The therapeutic community.* Basic Books, New York, 1953.

Kahana, E., & Kahana, B. Therapeutic potential of age integration: Effects of age integrated hospital environments on elderly psychiatric patients. *Archives of General Psychiatry,* 1970, 23, 20–29.

Kahn, R. L. Psychological aspects of aging. In I. Rossman (Ed.), *Clinical geriatrics.* J. B. Lippincott, Philadelphia, 1971.

Kahn, R. L., Pollack, M., & Fink, M. Social factors in the selection of therapy in a voluntary mental hospital. *Journal of Hillside Hospital,* 1957, 6, 216–228.

Kahn, R. L., Pollack, M., & Goldfarb, A. I. Factors related to individual differences in mental status of institutionalized aged. In P. Hoch & J. Zubin (Eds.), *Psychopathology of aging.* Grune & Stratton, New York, 1961.

Kahn, R. L., & Zarit, S. H. Evaluation of mental health programs for the aged. In P. O. Davidson, F. W. Clark, & L. A. Hamerlynck (Eds.), *Evaluation of behavioral programs.* Research Press, Champaign, IL, 1974.

Kellman, H. R. An experiment in the rehabilitation of nursing home patients. *Public Health Reports.* PHS, DHEW, 1962, 77, 356–366.

Kramer, M. Historical tables in changes in patterns of the use of psychiatric facilities 1946–1971. Biometry Branch, NIMH, Rockville, MD, 1973. (a)

Kramer, M. Implications of expected changes in composition of the U. S. population for the delivery of mental health services during the period 1971–1985. Paper presented at the Southeastern Divisional Meeting of the American Psychiatric Assn., Williamsburg, VA, Oct., 1973. (b)

Lawton, M. P., & Gottesman, L. E. Psychological services to the elderly. *American Psychologist,* 1974, 29, 689–693.

Macmillan, D. Hospital-community relationships. In *An approach to the prevention of disability from chronic psychoses: The open mental hospital within the community.* Milbank Memorial Fund. New York, 1958.

Main, T. The hospital as a therapeutic institution. *Bulletin of the Menninger Clinic,* 1946, 10, 66–70.

Malzberg, B. *Mental disease in New York State 1910–1960: A study of incidence.* Research Foundation for Mental Hygiene, Albany, 1967.

Perlin, S., & Kahn, R. L. The development of a community mental health center model. In

Psychiatric Research Report 22, American Psychiatric Assn., Washington, 1967.

Polak, P., & Jones, M. The psychiatric non-hospital: A model for change. *Community Mental Health Journal,* 1973, 9, 123–132.

Redick, R. W. Patient care episodes in psychiatric services, United States 1971. *Statistical Note 92.* Biometry Branch, NIMH, Rockville, MD, 1973.

Redick, R. W. Patterns in use of nursing homes by the aged mentally ill. *Statistical Note 107.* Biometry Branch, Rockville, MD, 1974.

Schaie, K. W. Translations in gerontology — from lab to life: Intellectual functioning. *American Psychologist,* 1974, 29, 802–807.

Stanton, A., & Schwartz, M. *The mental hospital.* Basic Books, New York, 1954.

Willner, S. G. Patients resident in mental hospitals by type of hospitals, United States, 1904–1970. Biometry Branch, NIMH, Rockville, MD, 1974.

Late Life

REINTEGRATION OR DESPAIR

Old age is often viewed as a single stage of life. But the "young-old" in the late sixties and seventies are in many respects more like middle-aged adults than the "old-old" in their eighties and above. Poor health, for example, is a threat in late life, but most young-old people think of their health as good. It is the old-old adult who is more likely to suffer serious afflictions.

In Erik Erikson's view, the basic developmental issue of late life is *integrity* versus *despair*. One of the chief impediments to personal integrity is the fear or the reality of financial, physical, or emotional dependency. Many old people, however, are financially secure and in reasonably good health, with friends and family helping them to combat loneliness. In addition, senior centers and other publicly sponsored programs have done much to alleviate the problems of dependency in late life.

In healthy old people, creativity flourishes in a degree not significantly reduced from the levels exhibited by younger adults. The creative productions of old scholars, scientists, and artists benefit from their experience and wisdom. Often their works represent an intellectual integration of the observations of a lifetime, and many of these works have to do with old age itself.

Our first selection comes from the Pultizer-prize-winning book *Why Survive? Being Old in America* by *Robert N. Butler.* It bears directly on the issues of quality of life that make it worthwhile to continue on into the last part of life. Butler presents a manifesto on what public policy changes may be needed to deal with the fact that most of us will reach old age. He discusses issues related to the prevention of illness and the development of sensible life styles, and reviews studies of healthy old age. He also deals with the right to die and the handling of death itself.

One of the prominent writers on the topic of death, Elizabeth Kübler-Ross, has described the process of dying to consist of five stages: denial, anger, bargaining, depression, and acceptance. Denial or avoidance of the topic of death in the presence of dying is common and understandable, although it can prevent the dying person from carrying out important last-minute duties. Anger results from frustration and imminent loss. Bargaining may take the form of changes in behavior that the individual hopes will allow a few more days or weeks of life, perhaps until some important event, like a birthday. Depression, as might be imagined, is the most common emotion among the dying. Kübler-Ross's stage theory of dying has not received much empirical support, although it has done much to stimulate interest in the emotional life of the dying.

An alternate approach to the issue is presented by *Robert Kastenbaum*. He examines the role of death as a life crisis, and considers the confrontation with death in both theory and practice. In a detailed analysis, death is examined in its role as a variable, an event, a state, an analogy, and a mystery. In this context Kastenbaum cautions against the premature acceptance of stages of dying, or of the characterization of death as a major crisis for the dying or their survivors.

Additional Suggested Readings

Schulz, J. H. Income distribution and the aging. In R. H. Binstock & E. Shanas (eds.), *Handbook of aging and the social sciences.* New York: Van Nostrand Reinhold, 1976, pp. 561–591.

> Facts and fictions regarding the actual economic status of the elderly, including a review of the adequacy of the money income of the elderly and the status of major pension and welfare programs.

Peterson, J. A. Death and dying and mental health. In J. E. Birren & R. B. Sloane (eds.), *Handbook of aging and mental health.* Englewood Cliffs, N.J.: 1980, pp. 922–942.

> Provides a theoretical basis for analyzing death and dying, and discusses the personal and social support for the dying and those left behind during bereavement.

The Gift of Life

ROBERT N. BUTLER

Vanity is to wish a long life and take but little pains about a good life.

THOMAS À KEMPIS, *Imitation of Christ*

Wish not so much to live long as to live well.

BENJAMIN FRANKLIN, *Poor Richard's Almanac*

By the year 2000 — the magic year that commentators and planners so often refer to — there will be some 33 million retired persons. Actually, between now and that year some 65 million Americans will attain the age of 65, not all of them, of course, surviving to the year 2000. Should our nation maintain zero population growth, some 15 percent of the population will be 65 and above. If heart disease, cancer and some of the other major killers are conquered, these figures will be much larger.

Major social changes are taking place, reflecting the impact of enhanced survival (1). But they are occurring slowly, tentatively and in piecemeal fashion. We are ill prepared for the increased survival of large numbers of older people. We have been unable to provide adequately even for the elderly alive today. To extend the quantity of life but not its quality is a macabre joke. It is not enough to have more and more people simply surviving; they have to be a vigorous, involved, contributory, self-respecting group of people who are still a vital part of their society.

If in the past scientists have been reluctant to spend their careers in the field of growth and aging because of insufficient theoretical and technical knowledge, today some scientists may be equally reluctant because of the awesome social consequences of major breakthroughs in aging. Given significant research developments in biochemistry, in molecular biology and in genetics, the possibilities of understanding such diverse phenomena as "wild" growth (cancer) and aging have been enhanced. But how can we handle the enormous impact and the long-term consequences of such accomplishments?

One alternative would be to adopt an antiscientific attitude right now — to call off all medical and gerontological research, to regulate death and birth rates in order to restrain population growth. This radical view has been proposed to buy the time we need to deal with the many other factors that now contribute to the worsening quality of life around us, our sulfurized cities, contaminated waters and depleted energy. Some, like the retired chairman of the

Atomic Energy Commission, Glenn Seaborg, hold that "knowledge is born without moral properties." But others, including Professor Jerome Wiesner of the Massachusetts Institute of Technology, believe that the scientist is responsible for the knowledge he gains because he decides what kind of knowledge to seek. Perhaps governments, consciously or unconsciously, do not provide generous support for medical and gerontological investigations for fear that success will create burdensome numbers of older persons.

Actually, in the Western nations where the risk of infectious disease has become negligible, we have begun to see mortality rates reach an irreducible minimum.[1] Only major medical breakthroughs could reduce it further in any significant way. Mankind has progressively eliminated the causes of premature death but has done little as yet to add to basic longevity. Thus the greatest result of medical advances has been to allow many more people to reach old age rather than to extend old age itself. We are seeing more physically "younger" older persons, while at the same time we are also accumulating a greater number of severely sick and disabled elderly. It is here that an appropriate research aim should be focused —not simply on the extension of life but on the creation of a healthy, vigorous, self-productive old age, with a much briefer and shorter period of disability prior to death. This would help reduce the present crushing burden on the middle-aged to support and care for the sick elderly.

In this chapter I shall discuss public policy in relation to increased survival, along with the improvement of the quality of survival itself through a broadened conception of preventive medicine. I shall also consider the point in time when life is no longer a gift,

when it is a burden to oneself and to others, when it is time to consider the right to die.

Public Policy on the Gift of Life

What kinds of public-policy proposals need to be considered as part of an appropriate national response to the challenge of increased survival?

First we need to know how major breakthroughs in medical science and technology will affect our lives. An orderly, scientific investigation into the consequences on human living has yet to be undertaken. To meet the need, a flexible pool of federal and foundation research funds should be established and tailored to specific medical development. For example, perhaps 5 percent of the medical research grant for heart transplants, or tracking down an aging deterrent, should be removed from the research itself and set aside for the study of probable demographic, ecological, economic and personal results of the particular development. An additional percentage (perhaps also 5 percent) should be set aside for educating the public about the development and its consequences.

In this manner a social form of preventive medicine may be brought to bear on many potentially disruptive changes. It will be more economical and humane to plan for the consequences of change than to have to make a tardy diagnosis and offer emergency treatment in a crisis atmosphere. We must make major commitments to the social and behavioral sciences if we are to react appropriately to the effects of major medical and health progress on the social and economic aspects of the life cycle. At present only 3 percent of the funds spent for science in America is devoted to these human sciences.

Second, comprehensive multidisciplinary research on the process of aging ought to be fostered through the National Institute on

---

[1] Seventy percent of all deaths in the United States occurred after 65 in 1970, compared to 15 percent in 1900.

Aging, and regional institutions. Such research should aim toward the enhancement of late life and not just its extension.

Third, . . . education, work and leisure ought to be distributed throughout the life span rather than concentrated at the three distinct periods of childhood, middle life and later life. If through inadequacies of education we fail to make people productive, thus isolating specific groups (for example, racial minorities), or if we automatically retire older people and make them unproductive, we make them parasitical, they feel parasitical, and they are seen as parasitical. Clearly such social policies are abhorrent.

Fourth, we should be building a new kind of education, one that will prepare people for survival and leisure. To be able to live alone, to experience human solidarity beyond the family, to learn to live fully and joyfully and not lose the free play of imagination—these should be considered critically important educational goals. . . . Enrichment of life and self-education should be stressed. Students of all ages should not only be "taught" but should be encouraged to extract from within themselves what they have already learned from life.

Fifth, it is not enough to give consideration only to a person's direct participation in the present. We need a sense of national commitment to the future. Values change in the course of life, and subjective interest in the future becomes most pronounced in later life. How much do we guide public policy on the basis of this concern? There is no major government agency for the long-range, coordinated planning that would demonstrate our commitment to future generations. We operate on annual budgets and tend not to project beyond the year 2000. Yet the pollution of the environment, the poor utilization of our resources are symbols of our mindless failure to consider those who follow us. There should be a major agency or department considering what the world will be like several generations from now and determining what we ought to be doing now to prepare for it.

Preventive Medicine

Prevention of Illness

In spite of advances in the field of medicine and increases in the numbers of persons living to old age, life expectancy in the United States is still less than in many other nations. In 1971 Americans were fortieth in life expectancy from birth for men and tenth for women. Overall health, especially in old age, is far from what it could be. This is a function of inadequate health care, an unsupportive socioeconomic system, and poor health and dietary education. Prevention of illness and early treatment to prevent exacerbation of existing illnesses are underemphasized. For example, patients may be untrained in responding to the warning signals of serious illness. One study found that as many as half of the persons who die of heart attacks outside of hospitals do so because they have waited at least five and one-half hours before seeking medical care. That would mean that at least 250,000 of the 400,000 Americans who die annually from heart attacks do not have the advantage of any kind of medical effort (2). Intensive coronary-care units that provide constant electrical and personal monitoring in hospitals are proving useful if heart attacks are treated early enough. Deaths which used to be caused by bradycardia (slow heartbeat) and paroxysmal tachycardia (fast heartbeat) can now be prevented.

Emergency medical care for all types of illnesses "is one of the weakest links in the delivery of health care in our nation" according to the National Academy of Sciences in 1972. A Health, Education, and Welfare Department study in 1972 reported that some 60,000 persons of all ages who died from accidents, heart attacks and other sudden illnesses could have been saved through proper emergency care. Poor ambulances, slow service, untrained attendants and inadequate equipment were all part of the problem.

Of the ten leading causes of death, the diseases of the heart, malignancies and cerebrovascular disease (mostly stroke) account for about 70 percent of annual deaths for older people. These causes of death — along with accidents, ranking fourth; cirrhosis, fifth; suicide, ninth; and homicide, tenth — all present some potential for control and prevention. The generalization that to be long-lived one must have long-lived ancestors is increasingly less valid as we learn how to prevent and control disease. (Indeed, there is some evidence that the effect of heredity upon life expectancy has been exaggerated.)

A 1971 governmental Task Force on Arteriosclerosis called for a major national effort against the "natural epidemic" of heart diseases, mainly due to arteriosclerosis. More than one million die annually from arteriosclerosis or its effects, and many more are disabled. Successful efforts against this disease would alter the picture of old age as we know it today — alleviating some of the wrinkling, slowing and other physical features associated with old age that are undoubtedly due to reduced blood supply following "hardening of the arteries."

Arteriosclerosis begins early, progresses slowly, is chronic and more common and devastating as the years go by. Blood vessels have three layers. In arteriosclerosis proper, the vessel hardens as a result of fibrous and mineral deposits in the middle layer of the vessel wall. The more critical associated condition is atherosclerosis. Fatty substances collect on the inside vessel wall, forming atheromas (pulpy, fat-laden deposits), narrowing the passage and impeding the blood flow. The heart, brain, kidneys and other organs are impaired by the diminished supply of food and oxygen that reaches them because of the impaired blood circulation.

Heart attacks and strokes result from the impairment and clots that form. Arteriosclerosis and atheromata are not distributed uniformly throughout the circulatory system of the body. Consequently there may be discrete, local lesions, causing damage in specific organs in the absence of ill effects elsewhere.

Because the development of arteriosclerosis begins in childhood, prevention must begin early. Dr. Sidney Blumenthal, University of Miami professor of pediatric cardiology, has offered guidelines for the early recognition of the high-risk child. He looks for primary hyperlipemia, hypertension, diabetes and obesity. He urges taking careful, complete family histories. In the absence of family history of physical indications, the disease may develop silently. Prevention and treatment are still controversial since much remains to be learned, but diet is an important factor.

The Task Force on Arteriosclerosis sharply criticized current federal efforts in arteriosclerosis research as "totally inadequate" because of "sparse and discontinuous funding, a dearth of long-range planning, and uncoordinated programming." The group proposed a permanent national commission to monitor progress against heart disease and to help direct future efforts to combat it.

At present, despite the lack of a complete answer to the diet-disease controversy surrounding arteriosclerosis, the Task Force recommended dietary changes for the general public as a preventive measure. "Pending confirmation by appropriate diet or drug trials, it . . . would appear prudent for the American people to follow a diet aimed at lowering serum lipid concentrations. For most individuals, this can be achieved by lowering intake of calories, cholesterol, and saturated fats." This is the first time that the National Heart and Lung Institute has ever endorsed a recommendation for changing the United States diet.

Hypertension, or high blood pressure, afflicts an estimated 23 million Americans, playing a direct role in the deaths of at least 60,000 men and women yearly, the majority in their fifties. Black people are more frequently affected than white. Government figures show that one in seven blacks has high blood pressure. Former HEW Secretary Elliot Richardson reported, "hypertension kills more than 13,000 blacks every year compared with sickle cell's toll of 340.[2] The death rate points up the racial disparity even more sharply; the nonwhite death rate for hypertension is 58.4 per 100,000, more than twice the 27.1 per 100,000 rate for whites." There are data showing that those blacks who live in the highest urban stress areas have the highest blood pressure of all. Stress and inhibition in the freedom to express anger seem clearly related to rising blood pressure. Here we see social conditions that affect both life style and bodily adjustments.

Atherosclerosis is aggravated and accelerated by hypertension, but there is no established evidence that reducing blood pressure reduces the incidence of myocardial infarctions (the medical name for heart attacks). A Veterans Administration Cooperative Study has indicated that antihypertensive drugs do prevent hemorrhagic stroke, congestive heart decompensation, renal failure and accelerated hypertension. The National Heart and Lung Institute began a nationwide campaign against hypertension in 1972, aimed at educating both the medical profession and the general public. Since antihypertensive medication is effective, it is all the more irresponsible to allow people to go untreated.

Alcoholism is the fourth leading killer in the United States, producing more than 85,000 deaths annually through liver diseases, highway and other accidents, and crime. Is drinking a disease, or is it much

more than that? Acculturation has persuaded many people that drinking is manly or daring, sexually useful, fun, relaxing, sophisticated or helpful in solving problems (3). Actually, alcohol is a depressant, rather than a stimulant, of the central nervous system. In some measure drinking is within societal and individual control. The conspicuous public use of alcohol in governmental, entertainment, fashion, industry and professional circles reinforces the public feeling that drinking is harmless and acceptable.

More patients with histories of alcoholism survive into old age than in the past, as a result of more effective treatments (nutrition, antibiotics). In addition, late-life alcoholism can develop for the first time in a person's life in the wake of grief and the presence of loneliness. I am of the opinion that alcoholism and concomitant malnutrition are causes of significant portions of the memory impairment in old age erroneously attributed to "hardening of the arteries." There are also dangers in the casual prescription of alcohol for older people to help them sleep, improve their appetite and add to their sociability. Alcohol blunts reaction time, impairs coordination and fuzzes mental abilities, especially memory. Serious falls and misjudgments can result.

We badly need continued research on alcoholism. In 1972 the American Hospital Association reported the astounding fact that 25–30 percent of all adult medical-surgical patients in metropolitan hospitals, regardless of diagnosis, had alcoholism. As many as nine million Americans may be alcoholics. It ranks very high among the country's major health and social problems.

Sensible Life Styles

Seneca, the Roman philosopher, said, "Man does not die, he kills himself." There is no question but that much of our behavior over which we can exercise some degree of control is influential both in the quality and

---

[2] Sickle-cell anemia is a hereditary anemia found among black people, characterized by oxygen-deficient sickle-shaped red blood cells, episodic pain and leg ulcers.

length of our lives. Yet we do not take personal responsibility either for ourselves individually or collectively as a society by shaping our lives into the kind of regimen that would enhance both the character and length of life.

With due respect to Seneca, the rights of human beings over their own lives must be preserved — including the rights to gourmandize, to smoke, to drink, to be physically indolent. These are defensible individual rights as long as they do not impinge on others, but they should be freely chosen. Advertising on behalf of tobacco and alcohol exerts undue influence on people from childhood on. The excessive emphasis of the American diet upon meat and dairy products remains basically unchallenged in the public eye. There is little serious public discussion, education and encouragement regarding the merits of physical exercise, prevention of illness and recognition of health danger signals.

Poor diets, overeating, smoking, physical inactivity, excessive drinking, the overuse and misuse of drugs, accidents, stress and life-endangering life styles[3] are all targets of preventive medicine. One can see interrelations between these elements and many physical conditions. A graphic example is found in the work being done on the influence of personality and life styles on heart attacks. The great physician Sir William Osler was among the first to suspect that emotional factors contribute to coronary heart disease. In 1955 a San Francisco cardiologist at the Mount Zion Hospital and Medical Center, Dr. Meyer Friedman (5), described a behavioral pattern he called the Type A personality, characterized by "an overwhelming sense of time urgency and competitive drive." The Type A personality "usually

confidently advances to grapple with his challenges; the subject with a true anxiety neurosis despondently retreats before his." As important as diet, inactivity, smoking, and other factors may be in the genesis of heart attacks, Friedman believes the Type A behavioral pattern may be more significant.

A Type A man insists upon being on time, eats rapidly, "wastes" no time with hobbies, does several things simultaneously, like reading while eating or listening to the radio while shaving, and is materialistic, quantitative, punctilious and impatient. He even tends not to take a vacation unless he can organize it around a business trip. While the Type A may link his drive with his creativity, the truth is that he is no more creative than the less frantic Type B personality which Friedman also describes.

Friedman recommends the establishment of counter habits, a new regimen and behavior pattern. He suggests that people discontinue their simultaneous thinking and working, and begin to listen without interrupting, read books that demand concentration, learn to enjoy good food and relaxation, find a way of retreating at home, take trips and vacations unrelated to business, and *plan to waste time*. There should be joy, the fulfillment of personal qualities and the lowering of daily stress.

In contrast to Friedman's results and theory, Jules B. Quint and Bianca R. Cody (6) noted that "their findings contradict the beliefs in some quarters that the mercilessness by which men drive themselves during their forties to outstanding careers was reflected in broken health during their fifties." They reported a twelve-year study of men listed in the 1951–52 edition of *Who's Who in America*. All men of high achievement, they live longer than the average citizen. The situation is complex indeed and obviously more study is indicated.

Nutrition is a vital element in preventive medicine. One's food habits may serve one well or badly in old age. Quite apart from

[3] For example, contrary to popular belief some studies have shown that when there is less organization and complexity in the daily activities of life, mortality is more likely(4).

malnutrition due to limited incomes, one sees nutritional inadequacy in the diets of older people resulting from poor habits, misinformation, grief and loneliness.

Older persons need help in planning diets which promote vigor and well-being. Many, of course, need financial assistance in obtaining such diets. Food packaging for one- or two-person families, menus for persons on special diets and help in preparing meals should be available. Meals on wheels and group dining are essential for some. Perhaps more than any other life-style element, good nutrition is critical for well-being in later life.

Just as with nutrition, accident prevention and safety training should begin early in life. Many of the injuries and disabilities of middle and later life could thereby be avoided. In old age, people especially need training in avoidance of home accidents and pedestrian travel mishaps. Special precautions may be necessary to compensate for physical and mental changes.

"Exercise is the closest thing to an anti-aging pill now available. It acts like a miracle drug, and it's free for the doing," writes researcher Josef P. Hrachovec (7). Yet about 45 percent of adult Americans — 49 million of 109 million men and women — are sedentary, not engaging in physical exercise (8).

Substantial evidence supports the value of exercise in maintaining health, improved circulation and respiration, better sleep and diminished stress. Exercise reduces the risk of heart attack and enhances survival following an attack. Swimming, walking, running and bicycling are especially good and inexpensive forms of exercise, since they actively strengthen the circulatory and respiratory systems.

Age need not be an impediment to bicycling and other forms of exercise. Tolstoy learned to ride a bike at age sixty-seven. Paul Dudley White, President Eisenhower's physician, urged bicycling as a preventive and curative exercise. Nineteen seventy-two saw

the sale of 13 million bicycles in the United States, exceeding the sale of American and foreign automobiles by some 2.4 million. It is estimated that about 18 million Americans now ride bicycles, both as recreation and as a form of transportation. By 1973 there were at least five bills before Congress to appropriate money or land or both to provide safe and separate bicycle paths, special lanes in traffic, shelters, parking facilities and traffic control devices. Bicycles with side wheels can be used by older people who worry about balancing but want the exercise. A basket on the back makes it easy to carry packages, and the bicycle can be used for going distances too long to walk.

Exercise must be planned on a routine daily basis. One simply must make time for it. In addition, advantage must be taken of spontaneous opportunities for physical activity. Emptying the trash, mowing the lawn and walking upstairs instead of taking the elevator should follow a redefinition of what is called drudgery and what is exercise. So-called labor- and time-saving devices may reduce physical fitness. Gardening is a fine hobby as well as an attraction that gives pleasure to others. It saves money to garden, cut the grass, pull weeds, do household chores. Purchase of a handyman guide for work around the house can lead to exercise and save repair costs too.

Dancing is an activity that combines social, interpersonal and physical pleasure. Folk dancing, square dancing and ballroom dancing should be part of the available repertoire. The rugged outdoor life — hiking and trail blazing — is also valuable for older people.

Medical monitoring of exercise is important in later life. Regular physical exams and discussions of appropriate exercise with a doctor can lessen the chance of overdoing or miscalculating one's abilities. Treadmill electrocardiac surveillance (including testing under stress) is very valuable. Education around common dangers is another imperative. For example, in 1970 the Federal Trade Commission warned the elderly and infirm to be careful about sauna and steam baths because of adverse effects of rising body temperature, blood pressure and pulse rates. There is evidence also to suggest that isometric, static or overly sustained exercises may elevate blood pressure to the point of provoking a heart attack.

Sexual activity is a useful form of exercise for the relief of tension, mild tuning-up of circulation and muscles and for emotional well-being. Massage is another very helpful technique, especially crucial for the bedridden, but relaxing and stimulating for all.

Studies of Healthy Old Age

If the child was "discovered" in the seventeenth century (before that, children were not thought of as a separate category with special capacities and needs), old age has been "discovered" in the twentieth. But the discovery is new and much remains to be learned about health in old age.

In the study of things, our attention seems always to turn first to disorder before it is directed to order, to disease before health, to problems before successes. Yet we need to study order, health and successes for several reasons — not the least of which is to prevent problems to whatever degree possible.

Though the over-75 age group is the fastest growing of American population groups (between 1960 and 1970 it increased 37.1 percent compared to 13 percent for the group between 65 and 75), studies of people this age are still rare and this is even truer of women and of minority groups. . . .

In order to gain a realistic picture of aging and of the elderly some investigators in the late 1950s and the early 1960s began to study healthy, community-resident, socially autonomous old people by a wide spectrum of research procedures. Some of the first studies began at the University of Colorado under the auspices of Dr. Ewald W. Busse.

These studies of community-resident old people were carried on at the Duke University Medical Center after Busse moved there. This continuing work has been recently summarized by Busse in a 1967 monograph. The many articles of the Duke group have been collected in a 1970 volume *Normal Aging.*

To look anew at some of the prevailing ideas and previously reported findings concerning both the processes of human aging and the nature of aging persons, some of us at the National Institute of Mental Health, representing a number of separate academic disciplines and medical specialties, undertook a series of collaborative studies in 1955 (9).

We selected medically healthy, community-dwelling aged so that we might maximize the opportunity of studying the effects of time, of chronological aging itself, and minimize the effects of sickness, institutionalization and social adversity. To our general surprise we found that psychological flexibility, resourcefulness and optimism characterized the group we studied rather than the stereotype of rigidity. Many of the manifestations heretofore attributed to aging *per se* clearly reflected medical illness, personality factors and social-cultural effects. Not confirmed was the previous belief that cerebral (brain) blood flow and oxygen consumption necessarily decrease as a result of chronological aging. It was found rather that when such changes did occur they were the probable result of vascular disease, which the public calls "hardening of the arteries." The nearly 50 elderly men in our sample who were over 65 (who had an average age of 71) were found to have brain physiological and intellectual functions that compared favorably with those of a young control group. Intellectual abilities did not decline as a consequence of the mysterious process of aging but as the result of specific diseases. Therefore "senility" is not an inevitable outcome of aging. Studies at Duke and elsewhere point in the same direction. All the usual psychiatric disorders found among the elderly seemed to be similar in their genesis and structure to those affecting the young.

There was evidence of slowing of speed and response which was found to be a function of aging. However, such slowing — which on the surface appears so characteristic of old age— was also found to relate statistically to environmental deprivation and depression as well as to decreasing health.

The importance of the immediate environment for adaptation was repeatedly observed. For example, education, occupation and other lifelong social factors were not as decisive to adaptation as was the degree of current environmental deprivation.

Over the eleven years from 1955 to 1966 the original NIH sample was followed (10). The group was readmitted and re-evaluated at the end of five years. Much of the report of the five-year follow-up centered upon aspects of survival and adaptation. Nonsurvivors, compared to the survivors, showed statistically significant differences in the following: greater incidence of arteriosclerosis (i.e., hardening of the arteries) and a greater percentage of chronic cigarette smoking. Nonsurvivors also tended toward other statistically significant differences: they had not adapted as well psychologically, had suffered widowhood and were more dissatisfied with their current living situations. They also had less clearly defined goals. Thus survival was associated with the individual's self-view and a sense of continued usefulness, in addition to good physical health. At the end of eleven years, as at the end of five years, good physical status and absence of cigarette smoking were related to survival. Structured, planned, varied new contacts and self-initiated activities and involvement (referred to as "organization of behavior") were found associated with survival. The fact that

organization of behavior was so strongly a statistical predictor of survival runs counter to the disengagement theory.

Much more work of this kind needs to be done. In addition, specific areas demand research attention because they represent such an integral part of aging as we know it today. For example, the sex differential in mortality between men and women has been widening and is mainly a function of heart disease, chronic respiratory diseases and lung cancer. Studies of death are important too and cross-cultural studies could be useful in clarifying the elements of life which enhance survival for the old. . . .

A word of caution needs to be added to the general call for more research on aging and the elderly. Any human experimentation must be strictly monitored. This is especially true in studies of those who are ill or incapacitated. Old people in institutions who are without living or involved relatives are especially vulnerable. One of the twelve points in the Patient's Bill of Rights the American Hospital Association announced in 1973 reads: "The patient has the right to obtain from his physician complete information concerning his diagnosis [and] . . . any proposal to engage in or perform new experiments on the patient affecting his care or treatment." Federal legislation to tighten the rules for clinical research theoretically affected some 85 percent of biomedical research conducted in the United States. But enforcement is not simple. Many older people want the opportunity to contribute to others through participation in research studies. But they should have the choice and not be misled or abused.

The Right to Die

"Passive" euthanasia[4] refers to permitting a patient to die naturally, rather than exercising heroic means to keep him "alive"

---
[4] Literally meaning "a good death."

when such life leads to a vegetative existence or unmitigated suffering. "Active" euthanasia is the active killing of those presumed to be hopelessly sick or disabled. Both lend themselves to abuses of all kinds, including the possible use by the state to rid itself of expensive helpless victims (not to mention political "undesirables"). But passive euthanasia is beginning to be cautiously considered as a viable social and medical practice under carefully controlled circumstances. This is because we have begun to take seriously the individual's right to die.

As a result of medical advances, persons with previously fatal illness can be maintained at minimal functioning even though they can no longer experience life in any meaningful way. Others are kept alive to suffer interminably through long, costly, painful illnesses. Heart-lung machines, intravenous feedings, organ transplants, artificial kidneys, auxiliary heart defibrillators, pacemakers, respirators, life-sustaining drugs can sustain people indefinitely with minimal-to-no conscious activity. These are the living dead, the extreme examples in the passive euthanasia controversy. They breathe, their hearts beat, but they are incapable of any of the functioning we call "human."

The modern definition of death itself is gradually being revised to mean the irreversible destruction of the brain. Two states, Kansas and Maryland, have adopted laws allowing medical efforts to cease when the brain is declared dead. However, it is not an easy matter emotionally, morally or even scientifically. Present clinical criteria are unacceptable and the electroencephalogram is not infallible. With the increased use of organ transplants, a more acceptable and reliable definition of death has become even more urgent.

In the absence of arrangements for passive euthanasia, do we force some suffering people to commit suicide, or their loved ones to consider killing the sufferers? How far can we go in giving individuals the right to decide when they no longer wish to live? It would all be so much easier if loss of the will to live and the natural time of death would coincide nicely. It is essential, of course, that we consider the right to die from the ethical perspective. It is healthy that it should always be a lively, open and controversial subject.

The medical profession is increasingly criticized for maintaining life irresponsibly. Doctors are seen as espousing "the vitalistic urge of the medical profession, which makes biological continuance the absolute good even when the price is the loss of dignity of the individual" (11). Yet doctors should not be given the sole power to end life. I strongly feel that the medical profession should be primarily concerned with the prolongation of life, and must share with others any decisions concerning dying. Indeed, as a physician I would not trust doctors any more than any other persons acting on their own with the power to make decisions about death. In 1967 in a London hospital the initials N.T.B.R. (Not to Be Resuscitated) were found marked on the treatment cards of over sixty-five patients with chronic chest or kidney diseases or malignancies. An English physician, Dr. Kenneth A. O. Vickery, also suggested that a specific age, 80, be the limit after which there would be no resuscitation. Arbitrariness based on specific diseases or ages leaves totally out of account the unique qualities and characteristics of an individual, his family and their needs. Today, in point of fact, it is all too often left to doctors to make decisions about death. They decide out of their own personal biases, incomplete information concerning the wishes and needs of the patient and his family, and as a result of cultural attitudes. Self-appointed "skillful neglect" is an illustrative attitude of some doctors. From hearsay and observation it is known that the majority of doctors probably do practice passive euthanasia. They should not be left to their own devices.

How can the individual's right to die be clarified and provided for satisfactorily with maximum safeguards? The right to obtain a full explanation of one's medical condition in clear, concise terms and to choose death by rejecting medical therapy were affirmed in the "Bill of Rights" issued by the American Hospital Association in 1973. For some time numbers of people have been signing living wills — documents which state that if there is "no reasonable expectation of my recovering from physical or mental disability I . . . request that I be allowed to die. I do not want to be kept alive by 'artificial means or heroic measures.' " It asks that one's wish be honored if one is not in a position to make such a decision in the future. It is addressed to a patient's family, physician, clergyman and lawyer. This document is not legally binding. As of 1972 some fifty thousand copies had been distributed through the Euthanasia Education Fund.

Old people — all people — fear and dislike pain, dependency, deterioration, indignity. Physician-legislator Walter W. Sackett of Florida has tried unsuccessfully each year since 1967 to gain approval for a proposal to allow every person to "have the right to die with dignity; that his life shall not be prolonged beyond the point of meaningful existence."

If we are to have legislation to provide for the "right to die," I suggest there be a panel in each case composed of the patient, family members (if any), two independent doctors (and the doctor in charge of the case), an attorney, a social worker, a clergyman (if desired) and a representative of the state. The panel would participate in the decision as to whether to honor the patient's expressed wish to die, made in the present or in the past through a living will. The panel, for instance, would consider the contemporary activity level of research into the patient's particular disease; how imminent is an advance or a cure? The entire family's emotional and financial health would be evaluated. A dying younger father, for example, needs all the meaningful time he can have with his sons and daughters.

Older persons may want to effect reconciliations or finish other uncompleted work. Individual wishes and needs must be respected (12).

Laws allowing passive euthanasia must be cautiously worded, fastidiously applied and subject to continuing review. Once the patient is not able to signify his wishes and is helpless — as in coma — there should be a third party involved, whose interests must also be evaluated. I agree with Dr. Angelo D'Agostino, both a Jesuit priest and a psychiatrist, who said, "Laws have to be very carefully written, otherwise you end up with human guinea pigs. Remember Nazi Germany."

In 1957 Pope Pius XII said that a doctor is not required to employ "extraordinary means" to keep alive a patient in a coma and beyond recovery. Death — in the abstract — is the enemy of medicine; it must never be regarded as casual. On the other hand, dying persons are not abstractions and should never be treated in dehumanized fashion.

The Handling of Death

And is not the awareness of death the chief distinction between animals and ourselves: Has not the awareness of death and timor mortis been the chief preoccupation of fully self-conscious mankind, and the fountain spring of most of its thinking and planning, from the first endeavors to preserve the corpse, to Christian Scientists who deny death? How few face it even now? (13)

Dying

Death is a powerful psychological fact of life, helping motivate people to action for both positive and negative change. The idea of death can also be paralyzing. Clinical experience leads me to share the impression of other observers that some of what is so casually termed ''senility'' is a defense against death: certain older people simply regress in the face of eternity (14). But this, obviously, is not a theory susceptible of experimental corroboration.

On the other hand, older persons tend to fear death less than the young, and many can accept the idea of personal death with equanimity. At times it represents a welcome relief from the pain of a terminal illness. In other situations older persons feel they are ready, they have lived out their lives and are able to let go. Strong religious or philosophical convictions can be of immense comfort in the process of dying. Attitudes toward death give clues as to the life that has been lived, reflecting the problems, resolutions, fears and hopes faced by each person during the course of his life.

Historical circumstances, too, influence personal attitudes toward death. As the plague stalked Europe and Asia in the fourteenth century, death was a pre-eminent literary, musical and artistic theme, preoccupying entire nations of people. In this era of the atomic bomb, children have discovered the fear of death in a new way at an early age. Yet, with most people dying in hospitals rather than in their homes, there is little personal experience with the death process. One seldom sees the last moments of death. Everything is taken care of swiftly and silently with no opportunity for the experience to sink in visually or tactilely. At the very least, children (and adults for that matter) should visit their dying relatives in institutions, attend funerals and discuss openly what dying means to them and to others.

A survey by *Geriatrics* magazine, reported in July, 1970, found that fewer than one in five physicians voluntarily tells a patient that he is going to die. Researchers on death have urged more open disclosure regarding death, thereby giving people an opportunity to work through the process of their dying. Dr. Elizabeth Kubler-Ross vividly describes dying. She finds there are five stages through which people pass: denial and isolation, anger, bargaining, depression and finally acceptance. If persons have sufficient time and support they can reach a peaceful resolution of the fight against inevitable death.

When death becomes imminent it must be handled openly. Every person has the right to know when he is dying. It gives him some control over his own life, if not his death. He can make arrangements for any bequests and order his relationships with friends and loved ones as well as prepare himself psychologically and spiritually. Perhaps most important, death should be shared with people close to the dying person. The fear of dying alone is an unnecessary and cruel fear to add to the burden of death. The living have the capacity to comfort the dying and to learn more about life in the process. Dr. Cicely Saunders' work at St. Christopher's Hospice in London is concerned with affirmation of life until its termination.

Legacy

Human beings tend to feel a sense of completion and accomplishment if they can arrange to leave a legacy behind after their death. These legacies can be personal possessions or money to children, friends, relatives, churches and charities. Children and grandchildren are themselves gifts to the ''future.'' Some persons create lasting works of art or perform acts that will be remembered afterwards. The donation of one's body or parts of the body to science or a medical school is a further example of legacy. Since 1968 the Uniform Anatomical Gift Act, adopted by fifty states and the District of Columbia, has made it possible for people to donate their body parts for transplantation or their body for anatomical study. One may carry the Uniform Donor Card as a "pocket will."

Of course not everyone feels the urge to leave legacies. Man's relation to the future and to posterity has been emphasized throughout time, but a variety of responses are called forth. Consider the following four illustrative attitudes toward death and personal legacy.

1. Nihilism — "Let the world end with me!"

2. Cynical indifference — exemplified by Mark Twain, who said, "The future does not worry about us, so why should we worry about the future?"

3. Leaving a trace — concern with a legacy to the future and to the later generations, the wish to teach or support the young or the culture, to write a memoir, or to influence grandchildren.

4. Preservation — efforts to conserve what is valuable in the present for the future, but in some necessarily new form. An example would be an art collector who arranges to have his collection housed in modern, climatically controlled surroundings for the future.

These several attitudes delineate different ways of handling one's grief over the loss of oneself. All have their individual adaptive value. The last two have social adaptive value as well because they make contributions to others.

Memorial and Funeral Services

The high cost of dying can be a serious financial burden to families at a time when they are most vulnerable and least able to judge what would be appropriate. . . . Expenses can go much higher as arrangements become more elaborate. Consequently, the funeral business has been under attack, and nonprofit memorial societies have evolved to provide less ostentatious, more economical funerals. "In a funeral the center of attention is the dead body; the emphasis is on death. In a memorial service the center of concern is the personality of the individual who has died."

Memorial societies enable persons to "obtain simplicity, dignity and economy in funeral arrangements through advance planning (15). These 120 societies are organized as nonprofit organizations that are democratically controlled by their 600,000 members.

In addition to educating the public about alternative services, the tendency toward elaborate showy funerals can be minimized by encouraging the open expression of grief, guilt and remorse toward the dead — thus eliminating some of the psychological motivation for compensatory, lavish funerals. Finally, in a society which has become increasingly secular, there may be a need to establish social rituals around death to replace religious ones.

Mourning   Geoffrey Gorer observed that the majority of people today are "without adequate guidance as to how to treat death and bereavement, without social help in coming to terms with grief and mourning." He describes three distinct stages of mourning. The first is a short period of shock lasting a few days; the second, a time of intense grief during which the mourner suffers psychological changes, such as listlessness, disturbed sleep, failure of appetite and loss of weight; and third, a gradual reawakening of interest in life. Gorer emphasizes that during the second phase, lasting six to eight weeks, "the mourner is more in need of social support and assistance than at any time since infancy and early childhood." Open grieving, alone and in the presence of others, is a crucial outlet. If grief is denied expression, depression is a possible reaction.

Another is an insulation against feeling that may border on callousness. Denial of grief is not the sole cause of depression, of course; ambivalence toward the deceased, anger and conflict can complicate the usual course of grief. It is the task of therapy to help open up the grief process. It is the goal of prevention to see that grief is not bottled up to begin with.

Simultaneous lengthening and invigoration of life may make it possible to create a strikingly different kind of old age, freed from most of the present physical incapacity and suffering. Death, when it does come, may eventually be preceded by a gentle, predictable decline. Sensitivity to the psychological meaning of death will contribute toward making the last crisis of the life cycle a time for potential meaning and summation. We actually have within our grasp the chance to live the gift of life fully and completely up to the moment of death itself.

References

1. Robert N. Butler, "The Effect of Medical and Health Progress on the Social and Economic Aspects of the Life Cycle," *Industrial Gerontology*, 1 (1969), pp. 1–9.

2. Manning Feinleib and Michael J. Davidson, "Coronary Disease Mortality. A Community Perspective," *The Journal of the American Medical Association*, 222 (1972), pp. 1129–34.

3. Don Calahan, *Problem Drinkers: A National Survey* (San Francisco: Jossey-Bass, 1971).

4. Robert D. Patterson, Lee Freeman and Robert N. Butler, "Psychiatric Aspects of Adaptation, Survival and Death," in S. Granick and R. D. Patterson (eds.), *Human Aging II* (Washington, D.C.: U.S. Government Printing Office, 1971). See also John Bartko, Robert D. Patterson, and Robert N. Butler, "Biomedical and Behavioral Predictors of Life Span Among Normal Aged Men," in E. Palmore (ed.), *Prediction of Life Span* (Lexington, Mass.: D.C. Heath, 1971).

5. Meyer Friedman and R. H. Rosenman, "Type A Behavior Pattern: Its Association with Coronary Heart Disease," *Annals of Clinical Research*, 3 (1971), pp. 300–12. See also *Type A Behavior and Your Heart* (New York: Alfred A. Knopf, 1974).

6. Jules V. Quint and Bianca R. Cody, "Preeminence and Mortality: Longevity of Prominent Men." Paper presented before the American Public Health Association, November 13, 1968. Summary published in *Statistical Bulletin* of the Metropolitan Life Insurance Company, January, 1968, pp. 2–5.

7. J. Hrachovec, *Keeping Young and Living Longer* (Los Angeles: Sherbourne Press, 1973).

8. Report, President's Council on Physical Fitness and Sports, 1973.

9. James E. Birren, Robert N. Butler, Samuel W. Greenhouse, Louis Sokoloff, and Marian R. Yarrow, *Human Aging: A Biological and Behavioral Study*, Public Health Service Publication (Washington, D.C.: U.S. Government Printing Office, 1963). Reprinted in 1971, 1974.

10. Samuel Granick and Robert D. Patterson, *Human Aging II: An Eleven-year Follow-up Biomedical and Behavioral Study*, Public Health Service Publication (Washington, D.C.: U.S. Government Printing Office, 1971).

11. T. Reich Warren, senior researcher, the Kennedy Center for Bioethics, testimony, U.S. Senate Special Committee on Aging, 1972.

12. Kurt W. Back and Kenneth J. Gergen, "Individual Orientation and Morale of the Aged," Chapter 19 in Ida H. Simpson and J. C. McKinney (eds.), *Social Aspects of Aging* (Durham, N.C.: Duke University Press, 1966).

13. Bernard Berenson, *Sunset and Twilight: From the Diaries of 1947–1958* (New York: Harcourt, Brace and World, 1963).

14. W. H. Gillespie, "Some Regressive Phenomena in Old Age," *British Journal of Medical Psychology*, 56 (1962), pp. 303–309.

15. Ernest Morgan, *A Manual of Death Education and Simple Burial* (Chicago: The Celo Press, 1973).

Is Death a Life Crisis?
On the Confrontation with Death in Theory and Practice

ROBERT KASTENBAUM

Life and death are not strangers to each other. However, life-span developmental theory as such has taken little notice of death and dying. This exploration of possible relationships between the two realms offers a discussion of death as variable, event, state, analogy, and mystery. Detailed consideration is given to a well-known stage theory of dying, and selected problems in theory and practice are then identified. Caution is advised against the premature enshrinement of death as one more "normative life crisis."

Purpose and Scope

Intergenerational dynamics in life-span developmental theory cannot be fully comprehended without careful attention to the ways in which we mind each other's deaths. And, if a personal response is acceptable here, there can be value in the simple act of permitting thoughts and feelings to rise up within ourselves as in the little thought experiment sketched earlier. Appreciation for the people who are important in our lives, while they are still alive, is one of the ways in which focus upon death can enrich their lives and ours.

Yet much theory has been promulgated in the social and behavioral sciences that assumes the nonexistence or nonrelevance of death. Theories that guide or rationalize clinical practice and administrative policy also, in general, take little account of death. Developmental psychology is no exception. As this subject area is usually conceived,

taught, researched, and packaged, death is thrown a footnote here and a dated reference there. It is not part of the basic structure of the field. One can move from student to expert without thinking about (let alone thinking through) the mutual implications of life and death. Perhaps, however, there is some point in exploring the interface between life and death within the emerging realm of life-span development. It is a realm in which we might expect both range and perspective, and in which theoretical positions have not yet become fixed and "official." . . .

It would be fashionable to propose death as one more "normative life crisis" among others already acknowledged by the field. But this would be premature. Further, it would deprive us of the opportunity to explore new modes of understanding. Let us neither enshrine nor reject death as a normative life crisis, at least for a while. Instead, let us first examine some of the most relevant meanings of death as a term of discourse.

Source: Abridged from Kastenbaum, R. Is death a life crisis? On the confrontation with death in theory and practice. In N. Datan & L. Ginsburg (eds.), *Life-span developmental psychology: Normative life crises.* New York: Academic Press, 1975, pp. 19–50. Copyright 1975 by Academic Press, Inc. Reprinted by permission.

Next, we shall select one major test case of possible relationships between death and life-span developmental theory. The paper will then conclude with a broader sampling of observations concerning death in theory and practice.

Death:
Some Definitions and
Interpretations

There is little chance of thinking and communicating clearly about death unless we share some definitions in common. What follows here is simply one person's way of differentiating and organizing the multitudinous ways in which death has taken shape in our minds. The treatment is brief, not exhaustive, and intended to be especially germane to life-span issues.

Death as a Variable

Begin with the familiar. We all know something about variables. Consider some of the ways in which death presents itself to us as a variable.

Death: the stimulus   A corpse is a stimulus. So is a cemetery. And so is the word "death" itself, as well as such related terms as "fatal," "lethal," "dying," "passed away," and so on. Death words spring out at us from both expected and unexpected sources, from print and from tongue. Certain visual configurations serve as death stimuli through the meanings they have accumulated in our society (e.g., the black border around a card).

Some stimuli convey aspects of "deathness" to almost anybody; other stimuli take on death meanings only to certain individuals or groups who have been sensitized by their experiences. An X-ray plate or laboratory report might register as death stimulus to a physician. From morning through night, from infancy through advanced old age, we are all exposed to a variety of death-pertinent stimuli. It would be interesting to learn what developmental sequence, if any, obtains in the perception of death stimuli.

Death can be a most subtle stimulus. We tend to recoil from the person we believe, correctly or incorrectly, to be touched by death. It is not necessary that he "look different." We are told: He is a funeral director . . . has fatal illness . . . is a survivor of the H-bomb, and we sense ourselves to be in death's presence although there is nothing deathly to see and hear. Silence when we expect sound, emptiness when we expect content, absence when we expect presence, coldness when we expect warmth, immobility when we expect response — these are among the ways in which a sense of "deathness" may be conveyed to us. Under some circumstances, the very fact that there is "no stimulus" represents death to us. "Nothing" can be the most terrifying and convincing of death stimuli (Kastenbaum, in preparation). Perception of our own inner states can yield death stimuli, as in the psychophysiological state we have characterized elsewhere as "deathly fear" (Kastenbaum & Aisenberg, 1972).

As a stimulus, then, or more properly, as a set of stimuli, death comes to us on occasion in palpable physical dimensions, but also in culturally shaped verbal and nonverbal representations, and in subtle personal encounters. Clearly, in discussing death as stimulus we are not in the realm of rare phenomena.

Death: the response   Death can be response as well as stimulus. A trauma or toxic substance may be the stimulus that elicits the response of death. The stimulus to which death is response can be evident ("Nobody could have walked away from that accident") or problematic ("We just found him like that in his room"). Death may be salient on both the stimulus and response sides, as when a person suffers a fatal heart attack upon hearing of a loved one's sudden demise (Engel, 1971). Death is a possible response to a large number of stimuli and a probable response to others. One cannot be completely certain either as to when a death stimulus might be encountered or when death might prove to be the response to even the most familiar and innocuous-seeming of stimuli.

Organismic death is not the only form of death response. A person may respond to stimulation with death-tinged words and thoughts. Deprivation and stress may lead to "lifeless" behavior, and the individual himself may feel that "something inside me has died." Many of the specific senses in which deathness is conveyed can be expressed either as stimulus or as response. And it often depends upon our own timing and perspective as observers whether we perceive the deathness in a situation as stimulus or response.

Death: the statistical abstraction   As a psychologist I am accustomed to thinking about real people in real situations. Yet we must acknowledge a more abstracted level in which death figures as a prominent variable. The statistical behavior of death, or death translated into statistical behavior, is of concern to every insurance broker in the nation, as well as morticians, economists, ecologists, demographers, and their varied kith and kin. How many people of what age, sex and socioeconomic echelon will die of what causes, when? Our knowledge of the statistical behavior of death, in answer to such questions, has become more precise and sophisticated over the years (Preston, Keyfitz, & Schoen, 1972). And the answers help the manufacturer decide whether to emphasize diapers or shrouds, the political adviser whether to advocate or oppose birth control, the employer whether to offer the union concessions on holidays and work breaks rather than health insurance, etc.

Every human detail of death has been lost at this level of abstraction; nevertheless, the uses to which this information is put might have profound effect upon both quality and duration of life. An influential book such as *World Dynamics* (Forrester, 1971) exemplifies the seriousness with which some planners take death as social statistic. The "population loop" (birth in/death out) is one of the major sets of variables in conceptualizing, projecting, and perhaps influencing the future of societies. Fraction-of-mineral-resources-remaining-in-the-earth, a pollution quotient, and a crowding index can be juggled in the same formula with projected mortality rate. Decontextualized and abstracted death is a major variable in the description, prediction, and control of congregate human existence.

Death as an Event

Death functions as stimulus or response, as independent or dependent variable. But death can also be regarded as an event. It is a happening. We may conceive of it as an active and externally engendered event ("Death strikes!") or as a more passive and internal event ("He has slipped away to his final rest"). In either case, something has happened, and it has happened in a particular place at a particular time. All death certificates are intended to specify the temporal–spatial markings of the event, and at least go through the motions of indicating "cause." Death, when defined as "the act of cessation," can be further understood in terms of two major perspectives that will be briefly delineated in the next section.

As a social-symbolic event   Each death takes on a set of significations as a social-symbolic event. These significations vary from culture to culture, but also vary within a culture depending upon who it is that has died under what circumstances. The noninvolved observer might insist that death is death, no matter who, how, and when. In practice, however, the sudden and violent death of a person who is eminent in his culture elicits a response quite different from the expected and "natural" demise of a relatively "inconsequential" person. How important the actual or presumed circumstances of death are in shaping the social-symbolic significations also varies. Some detail of the death event can dominate the signification. In other instances, the death becomes of general interest only because of a function it serves, not because a particular human life has come to an end.

As a social-symbolic event, death often challenges our assumptions and beliefs about life in general. The death of a young child may precipitate a religious crisis in the parents: "Are you there, God? I hate you!" The death of a powerful and seemingly invulnerable individual may leave others feeling helpless and exposed: "If death can take even him, what chance do I have?" The death event often is associated with punishment or failure in our culture. It may also be taken to signify the futility of life, or the prelude to eternal bliss. The physician, nurse, hospital administrator and funeral director all have their own significations to bestow upon the death event, involving a configuration of personal, cultural, and occupational responses.

As an immediate event   It is only when we have become well aware of the social-symbolic responses to and uses of death that we can focus clearly upon the actual particulars of the death event itself. Even so, it is not safe to assume that we ever witness or analyze death except through the filters of our own preconceptions. What we notice about the death event and when we judge that the event itself has occurred depends much upon our own background, needs, and relationship with the deceased.

Our usual expectations regarding the death event include the establishment of one or more "causes" for an occurrence that can be fixed precisely into our system of temporal–spatial coordinates. We may also be concerned with what the person is experiencing up to and at the "moment of death." Recently there has also been an upsurge of concern for what everybody else should be doing as the death event approaches.

It is worth keeping in mind that these are expectations rather than facts. Each of the expectations deserves to be challenged. Arguments might center around issues such as the following:

(a) Some, perhaps all, deaths do not have "causes" in a simplistic or classical sense of the term. What we choose to call death is itself part of an extraordinarily complex multilevel process that requires an alternative mode of conceptualization to the usual cause–effect model. Sophisticated coroners and pathologists, as well as practitioners of the "psychological autopsy" method, regularly deplore the inadequacy of conventional cause-of-death categories, and some question the basic adequacy of our causal thinking with respect to death.

(b) The death event seldom if ever occurs at a precisely specifiable moment. Similar pressures to specify "time" and "cause" do result in statements being made. But there are both methodological and judgmental problems involved in determining the time (and therefore, also, the place) of death which maintain a large potential error range. A more radical challenge comes from the view that, method aside, the death event has an extended temporal trajectory both before and after any arbitrarily selected "moment."

(c) There is a market for transcendental "last words" and for a general romanticization of death that goes far beyond the actual experiences and utterances of most people who are at point of exitus. It may be that people do not experience anything at the mo-

ment of death, or that what they experience must remain forever beyond the knowledge of the survivors. Further, as more people receive heavy medication and are maintained in a marginal zone between life and death, we might expect even fewer significant experiential states on the death bed. Most unfortunately perhaps, attention too often is devoted to the awaited last words or last breath, when the attention would have been more valuable for everybody concerned if it had been given consistently during the total course of the dying process.

(d) Those who habituate the hospital environment know that the death event often arouses the need to be doing something or, failing that, to watch somebody else doing something. ''Going away,'' physically or mentally, is a kind of doing something about the death event for those who can devise no other activity. The *need* to do something in the face of the death event should not coerce us into assuming that there really are many things that should be done at the hypothetical moment of death, or that these activities can be governed by a standard administrative ritual.

The emerging conception of the death event in our own society emphasizes technical description and control. Most people who find themselves in frequent contact with the death event would feel more comfortable if death could be classified, predicted, and explained in a simple and systematic manner. An authoritative scientific model of death, bolstered by new legislation to cover most contingencies, would relieve anxiety. But this preference for the technical and the systematic does not of itself demonstrate that the death event is best regarded in such terms. It just implies that there will be continuing pressure to arrive at consensus, to agree upon what should be done in the death situation — and probably diminished tolerance for those who view the death event differently.

Death as a State

The death event can be regarded as an act of separation or rite of passage. Whether or not death in fact has its special moment, it suits many of us to think of a sudden and decisive event that evicts one from the world of the living. But how are we then to understand what follows the death event? We court confusion by using the same term to refer to both an event and a state. Does death (the event) make us dead (the state)? In practice as well as theory we can create difficulties for each other by failing to distinguish between these two uses of the term. Of two people who are equally afraid of death, for example, one might have his apprehensions focused upon a possible specific mode of dying, while the other is fixed in terror upon the prospect of eternal damnation. To remind ourselves that death as a state can be conceptualized in more than one way, we shall briefly characterize some of the approaches that have been taken by individual thinkers or cultural traditions.

More of the same After the death event, ''life'' might continue much the same as before. The deceased passes from one realm to another. However, personality, motives and challenges remain little affected by the transition. This view, held by a number of tribal societies (Hertz, 1960), makes it clear that *continuation* after the death event is not identical with immortality. Life after the death event is imagined to follow the same general outlines as the life that is familiar to the community, with allowances made for encounters with menacing or kindly gods. . . .

Perpetual development Today's life-span developmental theorist has yet to match the broad conceptualizations offered by some philosophers and scientists of previous generations. Inspired by various inputs, such as the excitement of evolution theory, the crumbling of the block universe, a whiff of oriental cosmology, imaginative thinkers described a universe in which the primary principle is development. A bare temporal–spatial manifold is in process of "flowering into deity," in Samuel Alexander's poetic phrase (Alexander, 1920), and human growth is part of this process. Both Gustav Fechner . . . and the American philosopher William Ernest Hocking specified individual and conditional trajectories of development. At any particular point in the life span, an individual might be more or less advanced in his own progress toward fulfillment. The same holds true at the point of the death event. Accordingly, death as a state varies from person to person, contingent upon the kind of development that has already been achieved (Fechner, 1960; Hocking, 1957). "Awareness," "enlightenment," "higher consciousness" — any of these terms would be suggestive of the basic dimensions of development. The opportunity for perpetual development both before and after the death event exists for all of us. But there are no guarantees. One can flunk developmental tasks on both sides of the grave. Death, then, is not a fixed state. The death state can vary from a complete depletion of awareness to an experiential heightening beyond our powers of imagination. . . .

Less of the same   More common than either the continuity or perpetual development models of the death state is the decremental model. The death event is not simply a transition to either a postmortem replica of previous life or a new realm for conditional development. Instead, we are plunged into a dark pit from which there is no escape, only a gradual submergence. This is the "underworld" of miserable shades whose individual characteristics erode with time until all differentiation has disappeared. . . .

Perhaps, then, the death state is to life as

aging is to development. Both involve decrement that cannot be escaped. Yet our ancestors revered many of their aged and attempted to bring comfort to them. A person might still have significant psychosocial value, though very old or very sick. The death event, however, tended to repel those who had cared faithfully for the aged and the sick. Who would want to touch a body that was now beyond the pale of life and, by so doing, dip one's own hand into the dark and dismal stream of *Sheol?*

Waiting   Many people today and in centuries past have conceived of the death state as an exercise in waiting. It would be more precise, perhaps, to speak of it as a state of restful waiting. After the death event, the deceased (or some component thereof) reposes until the Day of Judgement. One then moves to the final destination or state. This is a triphasic conception. The first phase of the death state resembles sleep or suspended animation. The middle phase is that dramatic moment when disposition is made of the soul. Finally, the deceased takes his or her "place" for "eternity" or for "all time" (fundamentally different concepts but, for most people, functionally equivalent).

I have characterized this conception of the death state as *waiting* to emphasize its temporal characteristics. A certain tension is established between the death event itself (usually regarded here as a sudden and decisive happening) and the end state. The death event does not tell the entire story; there is more to come. The idea that the dead are in some sense waiting deserves consideration within the broader context of our culture's relationship to time. . . . The notion of a "do-nothing eternity" seems repugnant to many who retain belief in an afterlife death state. Perhaps we have become so accustomed to change and striving that the idea of any final state (before or after the death event) is alien to us.

Recycling   One of the most radical conceptions of the death state is also one of the most traditional and popular. In our own as well as in ancient times there have been many who regard the death state as but a temporary and alternating condition. The individual seems to pass from life to death. But, in some essential sense, the dead return to the world in one form or another. This general view has many variants, but its common theme is the conservation of identity and/or energy. The core of one's being (however this may be conceived) cannot be destroyed (or only under very special circumstances). Each of us is obliged, privileged, fated, or doomed to put up with ourselves through round after round of recycling. There are abundant anthropological observations on beliefs and practices associated with the recycling of identity through birth–death–rebirth loops (e.g., Ellis, 1968; Frazer, 1966; Henderson & Oakes, 1971).

The death state can be seen as one position on the constantly revolving great wheel of life and death (e.g., Kapleau, 1970). It can be conceptualized in cosmological and theological terms, or as an extension of scientific principles (e.g., matter–energy interchange and indestructibility). But recycling also can be regarded as a transposition of the child's view of reality. Cyclical experiences are much in evidence in infancy and early childhood, and probably exercise considerable influence upon the development of cognitive structures (Kastenbaum & Aisenberg, 1972). It is not difficult for our bodies to believe that every ending has its new beginning, and every sleep its awakening. . . .

End point of biological process   In recent years the medical, legal, and scientific communities have taken renewed interest in another traditional interpretation of the death state: as the end point of a biological process. Under precisely what conditions can we act with the secure knowledge that the death event is no longer in progress, but that the death state itself has been reached? This question is of concern to people involved with organ transplants, cryonic suspension, and the euthanasia–death-with-dignity issues. Others are finding the problem fascinating for basic research purposes apart from practical implications, and still others believe that a more accurate and "modern" view of the death state should be established and then incorporated into our legal, educational, legislative, and social institutions. *Updating Life and Death* (Cutler, 1969) is the title of one book, but represents the task that many have set for themselves.

There are methodological, philosophical, and even political problems to contend with in establishing either the general or specific case of biological death. The definition of "irreversible damage," for example, has been changing for at least 200 years. There is no reason to believe it has achieved a fixed form today. Social, political, and economic values influence decisions reflecting our judgments on who is dead and who worth keeping alive. In short, there is both scientific and humanistic hazard in the rigid and premature establishment of a final death state. The aura of objective medical science might persuade the easily persuaded that we now really do know what, when and how death is. A more appropriate interpretation would be that we are merely continuing exercises in the "pragmatics of death" (Kastenbaum & Aisenberg, 1972) that were begun for us long ago by thoughtful and attentive observers that history has chosen to neglect. . . .

Death Concepts and Developmental Theory and Research

Presumably death concepts will appear with increasing frequency in developmental theory and research: These concepts could hardly appear with less frequency than they have in the past. We will be performing a service to ourselves and to each other if we exercise care in matching word to concept, and communicating precisely what type of death we have in mind in a given context. There is little point in generating elaborate theory and research if we are confused about the central terms involved.

Awareness that death has multiple meanings and usages should also make us more useful to individuals whose lives intersect with our own. We should be less likely to assume that somebody else thinks of death as we do (or as we think we think we do). And quick generalizations about the development of death thoughts and orientations throughout the life span might give way to alert and patient observation.

There are more potential points of contact between death and developmental theory than can be sketched here. What we can do, however, is to examine one problem area that is of substantial interest for both human well-being and systematic understanding—the process of dying. Even more specifically, attention will focus upon the proposition that we die in stages.

Death in Theory and Practice: Selected Problems

Steady State or Change?

Developmental theorists find their various ways of coming to terms with two sets of dynamics that might appear to be independent or oppositional. One can emphasize the forces that hold the individual together, enable him to retain "homeostasis," "steady state," or "equilibration" (these terms being used uncritically in the present discussion). But one might emphasize instead the dynamics of "change," "maturation," or "development." Major theories usually incorporate both dynamics, but seldom achieve "equilibration" of the steady state versus change components. . . .

The relationship between steady state and change dynamics, for example, is not necessarily the same when we are concerned with the (seemingly) slower tempo of affairs in midlife. The constricting, slowing, entroping, energy-conserving phenomena of later life comprise a different context for steady state/change dynamics than the growth spurts of the early years. . . .

The prospect of death may set into motion other dynamics, or hasten some of the changes already in process. One may organize himself around the family name, his bank account, or a very personal, idiosyncratic identity core known only to himself. It is this symbol of himself that he most wishes to protect against the onslaught of aging and/or terminal illness. The sensitive friend, the professional care-giver, and the life-span researcher all have reason to be concerned about the individual's priorities of self-constants as stress increases, threat mounts, and resources fail. We need, in other words, a life-span developmental approach that can bear the full length and weight of human experience.

Death as Life Crisis

Let us finally touch upon the title question: *Is* death a life crisis? If magnitude of consequence is the criterion, then death would come highly recommended as a life crisis. But we have already seen that death is a term with many meanings, and rare is the person who is consistently clear about his own meanings, let alone those of others. The fact that perspectives on death differ within as well as among individuals suggests that a simple answer to our question is unlikely.

Consider first that death is not a crisis from the statistical standpoint. A death for every birth is a certainty. The "death system" (Kastenbaum & Aisenberg, 1972) of our culture and most others has built-in provisions for death. The suspension of death, as imagined in several works of fiction, might constitute more of a social crisis than the orderly, predictable demise of thee and me. A particular death may shock, confound, or disorganize. This cannot be said of all deaths. Note how many deaths daily pass through us with scarcely a blink. A crisis atmosphere may develop when we are confronted with the wrong death, death in the wrong way, or too many deaths at once. Viewed in this light, death is just one of many phenomena that have variable social consequences, ranging from piddling to profound, from immediate to delayed, from debilitating to strengthening the social order — for instance, the fine state funeral that reinforces national unity and pride when the death itself is of a long-used-up public figure.

Death is not invariably a crisis from the individual standpoint, either. There are people among us who seldom give thought to death. Some of these people come to death before death has come to mind — accidents, foul play, sudden traumata of various kinds. A crisis was neither anticipated nor experienced in such instances.

Others among us do think of death, but minus the doomsday visions. There are people who seem to view personal annihilation with equanimity, and others who are serene because, for them, death does not represent annihilation. Still others feel sorely troubled with the life they are experiencing, and death is seen as the solution rather than the problem. Concepts of death are closely linked to our ideas of time, both structurally (e.g., how extended our projections and retrospections, how many events an-

ticipated, etc.) and through the affective–thematic coloration (e.g., a future for ambitions to be achieved, or deserved pleasures to be relished). As one future prospect among others, the phenomenological status of death is influenced by our total relationship to time. Some temporal orientations may lend themselves more readily to crisis perception than others.

The dying process itself can be a time of crisis — but this, too, is contingent upon many factors. Our clinical and research experience accords with an underlying if unstated premise of Kubler-Ross's theory: Most people do not just fall apart as death approaches. A chaotic state that persists through terminal illness strongly suggests that treatment has been mismanaged, badly. Something important has been done wrong, or left undone. The dying person is also a living person. General laws of personality and behavior and those specific rules that have developed for a particular individual are not suddenly suspended because death is in prospect. Although in my judgment it is premature to declare that people die according to certain stages, it is also incorrect to suppose that we are entirely defenseless or random in our response. We are not obliged to accept the premise that it is normal for dying to be a crisis. We are, however, well advised to hone our own sensitivities to the situation of the dying person and those who stand by him, without imposing a ready-made theoretical orientation.

References

Alexander, S. *Time, space, and deity.* London: Macmillan, 1920.

Cutler, D. R. (Ed.). *Updating life and death.* Boston, Massachusetts: Beacon Press, 1969.

Ellis, H. R. *The road to Hel.* Westport, Connecticut: Greenwood Press, 1968.

Engel, G. L. Sudden and rapid death during psychological stress. *Annals of internal medicine* 1971, 74, 771–782.

Fechner, G. *The little book of life after death.* Chicago, 1960.

Forrester, J. W. *World dynamics.* Cambridge, Massachusetts: Wright-Allen Press, 1971.

Frazer, J. G. *The fear of the dead in primitive religion.* (1933). Edition consulted: New York: Biblo & Tannen, 1966.

Henderson, J. L., & Oakes, M. *The wisdom of the serpent.* New York: Colliers Books, 1971.

Hertz, R. *Death and the right hand* (1907). Edition consulted: Glencoe, Illinois: Free Press, 1960.

Hocking, W. E. *The meaning of immortality in human experience.* New York: Harper, 1957.

Kapleau, P. *The wheel of death.* New York: Harper, 1970.

Kastenbaum, R., & Aisenberg, R. B. *The psychology of death.* New York: Springer, 1972.

Preston, S. H., Keyfitz, N., & Schoen, R. *Causes of death.* New York: Seminar Press, 1972.

General Resources for Students of Adult Development and Aging

Handbooks

Binstock, R. H., & Shanas, E. *Handbook of aging and the social sciences.* New York: Van Nostrand Reinhold, 1976.

Birren, J. E., & Schaie, K. W. (eds.). *Handbook of the psychology of aging.* New York: Van Nostrand Reinhold, 1977.

Birren, J. E., & Sloane, R. B. (eds.). *Handbook of mental health and aging.* Englewood Cliffs, N.J.: Prentice-Hall, 1980.

Busse, E. W., & Blazer, D. G. (eds.). *Handbook of geriatric psychiatry.* New York: Van Nostrand Reinhold, 1980.

Finch, C. E., & Hayflick, L. W. (eds.). *Handbook of the biology of aging.* New York: Van Nostrand Reinhold, 1977.

Poon, L. W. (ed.). *Aging in the 1980s.* Washington: American Psychological Association, 180.

Serials

Baltes, P. B., & Brim, O. G. (eds.). *Life-span development and behavior.* New York: Academic Press, 1978, 1979, 1980, 1981. (Vols. 1–4 now available)

Eisdorfer, C. (ed.). *Annual Review of Gerontology and Geriatrics.* New York: Springer, 1980, 1981, 1982. (Vols. 1–3 now available)

Volumes with Broad Coverage of Topics

Atchley, R. C. *The social forces in later life.* 3rd ed. Belmont, Cal.: Wadsworth, 1980.

Baltes, P. B., Reese, H. W., & Nesselroade, J. R. *Life-span developmental psychology: Introduction to research methods.* Belmont, Cal.: Wadsworth, 1977.

Baltes, P. B., & Schaie, K. W. (eds.). *Life-span developmental psychology: Personality and socialization.* New York: Academic Press, 1970.

Brim, O. G., Jr, & Kagan, J. (eds.). *Constancy and change in human development.* Cambridge, Mass.: Harvard University Press, 1980.

Datan, N., & Ginsberg, L. H. (eds.). *Life-span developmental psychology: Normative life crises.* New York: Academic Press, 1975.

Datan, N., & Reese, H. W. (eds.). *Life-span developmental psychology: Dialectical perspectives on experimental research.* New York: Academic Press, 1977.

Decker, D. L. *Social gerontology.* Boston: Little, Brown, 1980.

Goulet, L. R., & Baltes, P. B. (eds.). *Life-span developmental psychology: Research and theory.* New York: Academic Press, 1970.

Hendricks, J., & Hendricks, C. D. *Aging in mass society: Myth and realities.* 2nd ed. Cambridge, Mass.: Winthrop Publishers, 1981.

Knox, A. B. *Adult development and learning.* San Francisco: Jossey-Bass, 1977.

Nesselroade, J. R., & Reese, H. W. (eds.). *Life-span developmental psychology: Methodological issues.* New York: Academic Press, 1973.

Nesselroade, J. R., & Baltes, P. B. (eds.). *Longitudinal research in the study of behavior and development.* New York: Academic Press, 1979.

Schaie, K. W. (ed.). *Longitudinal studies of adult psychological development.* New York: Guilford, 1982.

Storandt, M., Siegler, I. E., & Elias, M. P. (eds.). *The clinical psychology of aging.* New York: Plenum, 1978.

Journals

Developmental Psychology
Educational Gerontology
Experimental Aging Research
The Gerontologist
Geriatrics
Journal of Gerontology
Human Development
International Journal of Behavioral Development
International Journal of Aging and Human Development
OMEGA, The International Journal of Death and Dying